P9-DNG-335

Pit Master's Hymn

Great barbecue,

like a wonderful dream,

is best left undisturbed.

Please don't open the pit.

Memories in progress.

Ethan Hileman,
Pit master at The Greenbrier resort,
White Sulphur Springs, West Virginia

Steven Raichlen's

BBQ USA

425 FIERY RECIPES from all across AMERICA

"George Washington loved it, Elvis devoured it, and barbecue-hungry Americans fire up their grills 3 billion times a year"

WORKMAN PUBLISHING · NEW YORK

To Barbara, a.k.a. Mrs. Raichlen,
who lights my fire, bastes my briskets,
tickles my ribs, and keeps me honest.

Copyright © 2003 by Steven Raichlen

Front cover photographs: Ribs, clam pot, and Drunken Steak © Greg Schneider; author by Fernando Diez; Hog Island © Rory McNamara; Brisket © Stan Schier; Possum Trot courtesy trueart.net; BBQ Queens Jim Barcus/Kansas City Star; Alder-Grilled Salmon © Scott Eastman Photography; S'Mores © Tom Stewart/CORBIS. Back cover photographs: Donna Myers © Daryl Stone/Asbury Park Press; Pizza © Greg Schneider; Thelma Williams © Derron Neblet/Houston Press; author by Fernando Diez. Interior grill illustration © Ron Tanovitz.

All rights reserved.
No portion of this book may be reproduced—mechanically, electronically, or by any other means, including photocopying—without written permission of the publisher. Published simultaneously in Canada by Thomas Allen & Son Limited.

Library of Congress Cataloging-in-Publication Data
Raichlen, Steven.
BBQ USA/by Steven Raichlen.
p. cm
ISBN 0-7611-2015-7 (alk. paper) — ISBN 0-7611-3133-7
1. Barbecue cookery. I. Title
TX840.B3R3552 2003
641.5'784—dc21   2003042287

Cover design by Paul Hanson
Book design by Lisa Hollander with Lori Malkin and Sophia Stavropoulos

Workman books are available at special discounts when purchased in bulk for premiums and sales promotions as well as for fund-raising or educational use. Special editions or book excerpts can be created to specification. For details, contact the Special Sales Director at the address below.

Workman Publishing Company, Inc.
708 Broadway
New York, NY 10003-9555
www.workman.com

Printed in the U.S.A.
First printing April 2003
10 9 8 7 6 5 4 3 2 1

"f I have seen further [than other men] it is by standing upon the shoulders of Giants," observed Isaac Newton. It's a sentiment I feel whenever I write a book, and now especially at the end of the five years I've been working on this one. Perhaps the best place to start is with the long list of people who helped make this book possible—starting with the man whose name appears on its spine. Yes, there is a Peter Workman, and his genius and vision are matched only by his generosity and commitment to quality. We always knew barbecue was a religion. Who knew it could become a whole library?

Peter's efforts are seconded by my sensitive and sensible editor and friend, Suzanne Rafer, indefatigable copy editor Barbara "Hawkeye" Mateer, masterful art director Paul Hanson, visionary designer Lisa Hollander, and publicity director Jim Eber and publicist Kate Tyler, who actually managed to convince me that a thirty-city bus tour was a good idea. Thanks to Kit Warren for the terrific job she did of assembling the photos and to Leora Kahn for filling in the extras; to Karen Lee and Robyn Schwartz for checking on my factual accuracy and Cathy Dorsey for her comprehensive index; to Katherine Adzima

for managing all the pieces; to Barbara Peragine, Jarrod Dyer, Lorraine Lerner, and Patrick Borelli for their typesetting prowess; and to Elizabeth Gaynor for taking care of production. Licensing and sales mavens Pat Upton, Jenny Mandel, James Wehrle, Jeanne Emanuel, Page Edmonds, Jodi Weiss, Heather Carroll, Claudia Boutote, and of course publisher Bruce Harris have my thanks. Carolan Workman and Peggy Boulos keep the barbecue fires burning abroad. A warm thanks to Angela Miller of The Miller Agency, and to a major new player in my barbecue world, Charlie Pinsky, producer of my Barbecue University TV show on public television.

The next big thanks goes to the heroes of barbecue themselves—some famous, some working in relative obscurity, but all extraordinarily generous in sharing their expertise. Dr. Rich Davis, creator of KC Masterpiece Barbecue Sauce turned over to me a lifetime of research on the history of American barbecue— the basis of the piece beginning on page 5. Equally generous in sharing their knowledge were many legendary pit masters

Acknowledgments

and mistresses and barbecue enthusiasts, including: Terry Black, Skip Steele, and Ron Skinner of Super Smokers in St. Louis; Jim Budros and Rick Malir of City Barbecue in Columbus, Ohio; "Oklahoma" Joe Davidson and Danny Edwards of Danny Edwards' Famous Kansas City Barbecue; Ethan Hileman and Riki Senn of The Greenbrier resort in West Virginia; Mark Hewitt of Tillicum Village in Seattle; Don McLemore and Chris Lilly of Big Bob Gibson's in Decatur, Alabama; Mike Mills of the 17th Street Bar and Grill in Murphysboro, Illinois; Danny Meyers, Michael Romano, and David Swinghamer of Blue Smoke in New York City; Chris Schlesinger of the East Coast Grill in Cambridge, Massachusetts; John and Nick Vergos of the Rendezvous in Memphis; and Carolyn Wells and Paul Kirk of the Kansas City Barbecue Society.

I also benefited from the knowledge of barbecue and food industry experts, including Donna Myers of the Barbecue Industry Association; Rebecca Juretic of the Santa Maria Valley Chamber of Commerce and Visitor & Convention Bureau; Mike Kempster Sr. and Mike Kempster Jr., Christina Schroeder, Betty Hughes, and Sherry Bale of the Weber-Stephens Company; Floyd Benson and Diane Hampton at Memphis in May World Barbecue Cooking Contests; Karen Adler of Pig Out Productions; Mary Engle and Ceci Snyder of the National Pork Board; Mary Jo Plutt at the National Cattlemen's Beef Association; Brenda McDowell and Jessie Vicha at McDowell & Piasecki Food Communications, Inc.

A huge thanks to my indefatigable recipe tester Elida Proenza.

Finally, and most important, I'd like to thank my family—stepson, chef Jake, stepdaughter nutritionist, Betsy, and my extraordinarily generous and supportive wife, Barbara. "Mrs. Raichlen" put up with four years of recipe testing at home, months on end of research on the road, and sixty hour work weeks as I wrote this book. If there's a true Barbecue Goddess, it is she, and I thank her.

It takes a village to produce a barbecue book.

LIVE-FIRE SALADS 108

Grilling brings out the best in a salad. Wait until you try the Grilled Caesar Salad or the Tomato and Hearts of Palm. Plus Calamari Salad with White Beans and Bitter Lettuce, and four kinds of slaw.

BREADS AND PIZZAS 132

The grill makes the perfect toaster. There's plenty of room for that Little Italy favorite, garlic bread. Or A New Corn Stick from the West Indies. Or pizzas the way they grill them in Rhode Island and New York. Bread takes to fire like smoke to the grill.

GLORIOUSLY GRILLED BEEF 162

North America's love affair with beef is celebrated in a luscious round-up of steaks from Tucson, San Antonio, New York, Miami, Dallas, Toronto, L.A., Indianapolis, and of course, Philadelphia (sizzling with cheese). Plus briskets from North Dakota, Oklahoma, and Ohio, and everything else big and beefy.

A short course in choosing a grill, setting it up, getting it lit, and knowing when the food is cooked.

Begin the meal with pizzazz. Flame cook Prosciutto-Wrapped Peaches like they do in Virginia, chicken wings the Louisville way, Mojo-Marinated Pork Florida style, and Tiki Beef Kebabs with California flare. Dozens of choices, plus some drinks to serve alongside, including a Chimayo Cocktail.

Table of Contents

There's nothing like live fire to bring out a vegetable's sweetness. Not to be missed are Louisiana's Cajun Grilled Asparagus or Midwestern Grilled Corn with Maytag Blue Cheese. Or how about Hawaii's Grilled Plantains, or Vermont's Madeira Grilled Acorn Squash.

Grill up a New England "baked apple." Prepare brown beans the West Virginia way. Serve spaghetti with a smoky sauce like they do in Tennessee or grilled macaroni and cheese New Mexico style. These side dishes are stand-out sensational.

Dozens of sauces to choose from, covering all the great barbecue regions.

Soft-shell crabs grilled the Delaware way. A Canadian dill-grilled lobster. Five West Coast ways to grill oysters. Shellfish is more than shrimp on the barbie, but they're here, too, grilled both Louisiana and Indiana style.

Portobello "Cheese steaks" from Pennsylvania, Hickory-Smoked Baked Bean Squash from Maine, and three different quesadillas from across the country are barbecued dishes so good, no one will beef!

Try St. Louis Red and Nashville Sweet, Central Texas Barbecue Sauce, or a trio of sauces from Kentucky. There are also Liquid Fire from Florida and The Doctor's Medicine from Tennessee. Plus slathers, salsas, and chutneys.

HERE'S THE RUB

Make great barbecue even better with the pit master's secret weapons—the rubs, marinades, mop sauces, and glazes used to add flavor and sheen to meat or fish. Try Tennessee's versatile sweet-hot Cold Mountain Rub—it's good on just about everything. If you're looking for something more tongue-torturing, Missouri's K.C. Pepper Rub fills the bill. No barbecue should leave the grill without a little something from this chapter.

GREAT GRILLED DESSERTS

Don't let the fire die down until you've flame seared dessert: Smoke-Roasted Apple Crisp, Cinnamon Grilled Peaches, Smoked Alaska, and Grilled S'Mores are all worth keeping the coals aglow.

WHAT IS BARBECUE?

What is barbecue? I pose this question at the many cooking classes I teach each summer and at lectures, seminars, and book signings across the country. I ask it to take the pulse of my audience and to widen my knowledge. The answers I get are always fascinating and always different.

For some people, a barbecue is a piece of equipment—the barbecue grill. That, depending on who you are talking to and where he or she lives, will be charcoal fired or gas. The identification of barbecue with the grill goes back to the original meaning of *barbecue,* defined by the *Oxford English Dictionary* as "a rude wooden framework, used in America . . . for supporting above a fire meat that is to be smoked or dried."

For others, a barbecue is a cookout and, by extension, a festive or communal meal prepared and served outdoors. For still others, barbecue describes one of several ways of cooking using live fire. On the East and West Coasts barbecue is a catchall term for grilling—the process of quickly cooking thin pieces of food directly over a hot fire. In the South, Midwest, and Texas, to barbecue means to roast or smoke in a pit. The cuts of meat being cooked tend to be larger and tougher, the heat is usually lower, and the cooking time is measured in hours or half days, not minutes.

Elsewhere, descriptions of barbecue refer not to a cooking method but to the traditional condiment—barbecue sauce. For people who think of barbecue this way, the soul of barbecue is the sauce, much to the chagrin of the pit master.

Then there's the question of what you are barbecuing. Ask someone from the Carolinas, and it will be pulled or chopped pork. Just which cut it's made with (a pork shoulder or a whole hog), how it's cooked (over a pit or in a smoker), and how it's served (with the thin, fiery, vinegar-based

Jack "Dr. McQue" Davidson and his son Jason grill a whole hog.

sauce favored in eastern North Carolina; with the tomato-based vinegar sauce preferred in the western part of the state; or with the mustard barbecue sauce popular in South Carolina) depends on the location.

If you are in Memphis, ask for barbecue and you'll get a plateful of ribs—either with a crust of dry spices in the style of the Rendezvous restaurant, or wet, in the style of Corky's Bar-B-Q. That is, if you're not offered some barbecued pork shoulder (either sliced or chopped), most likely served on a hamburger bun with a big mound of mustardy coleslaw. Then there are the mahogany-hued barbecued game hens served at Memphis's beloved Cozy Corner and the three other inimitable local delicacies: barbecued baloney, barbecue pizza, and barbecue spaghetti.

A LONG AND WINDING TRAIL

The answer is not any more straightforward in Kansas City, where barbecue may refer to beef, pork, or chicken. The beef will most likely be brisket or "burnt edges" (brisket trimmings); the pork could be shoulder or ribs; and everything will probably come with the thick, sweet red sauce typified by KC Masterpiece—unless you're eating at the landmark

Texas—a major stop on the American barbecue trail.

"grease house," Arthur Bryant's, where the sauce is a peppery amalgam of spice and vinegar that's not in the least bit sweet.

You'd think Texans at least could agree on the definition of barbecue. In the Lone Star State it's synonymous with beef, and that means a brisket, right? Well, maybe when you're at Sonny Bryan's Smokehouse in Dallas, but what about the clod (crusty smoke-roasted beef shoulder) at the Kreuz Market in Lockhart or the "hot guts" (spicy smoked beef sausage) at the Southside Market and BBQ in Elgin? If you think that barbecue in Texas begins and ends with beef, you haven't tried the *cabrito* (roast goat) at Cooper's Old Time Pit Bar-B-Que in Llano or the barbecued duck at Houston's Goode Co. Texas Bar-B-Q.

And in California? The sign "Barbecue Today" prompted me to stop at a restaurant in a farmhouse in the town of Olema, a couple hours north of San Francisco.

The waitress there brought me a plate of grilled oysters bubbling with butter, wine, and garlic. Another time, I was driving in the San Fernando Valley when I saw a similar sign. This time, I was rewarded with a heaping plate of tri-tip—spit-roasted bottom sirloin, crusty on the outside, rare and juicy inside, thinly sliced and dished up with garlic bread, pinquito beans, and a Mexican-style salsa by way of a sauce. In the last twenty years, tri-tips have become the meat of choice for barbecue throughout southern California.

NO SINGLE ANSWER

Or has it? My travels on the barbecue trail have also taken me to Walt's Wharf in Seal Harbor, California, where the house specialty is grilled artichokes with a Worcestershire-flavored cream sauce. In Los Angeles's Koreatown, restaurants have charcoal-burning

braziers built right into the tables for grilling *bool kogi* (sweet soy and sesame marinated shell steaks).

In Connecticut, barbecue means planked shad (fillets nailed to a board and roasted in front of a campfire), while in Washington State and British Columbia, the ultimate outdoor cooking experience is a salmon bake or, more precisely, split whole fish roasted on cedar stakes in front of a blazing alder fire. Rhode Island's contribution to the world of barbecue is grilled pizza, which got its start at a restaurant called Al Forno.

There's nothing offbeat about barbecued chicken—except in upstate New York, where Cornell chicken is grilled with a mixture of eggs, oil, cider vinegar, and poultry seasoning. Down in my neck of the woods, Miami, the sauce of choice for grilled chicken (not to mention such popular Cuban American barbecue fare as *palomilla,* cumin-scented top round steak, and *lechon asado,* pit-roasted pork) is *mojo,* a thin, pungent condiment

Owensboro, Kentucky's Main Street during the annual barbecue festival.

made with garlic, cumin, and sour orange juice.

Every autumn, the streets of Santa Fe, New Mexico, fill with the perfume of green chiles roasting over flaming heavy metal drums. For almost two centuries, once a year the streets of Owensboro, Kentucky, have been lined with barbecue pits cooking the local specialty, barbecued mutton.

Markets in Vancouver sell ready-to-grill Filipino *tocino*, pork marinated in a pungent blend of paprika, pepper, garlic, and sugar.

FREEDOM OF CHOICE

So what *is* barbecue? Well, it's all these things and then some. My personal definition of barbecue is expansive enough to include a grill, a pit, a meal, a party, and every possible food I can imagine being cooked by live fire. I don't discriminate, and you can't accuse me of favoritism. This book is about American barbecue in all its magnificent variations—from Memphis ribs to California's grilled oysters to the reindeer sausage of Alaska. The book was written to reveal the mysterious ways of smoke and fire—and to celebrate America's most distinctive culinary tradition.

Steven Raichlen
March 11 (my birthday!)
Miami, Florida

A Brief History of
BARBECUE IN AMERICA

On April 11, 1514, a young adventurer named Gonzalo Fernández de Oviedo y Valdes left Spain with a twenty-ship armada bound for the city of Santa María del Antigua, in what is now Columbia. His mission was to supervise the smelting of local gold into ingots to enrich the Spanish treasury. En route the fleet stopped at the island of Dominica, in the Caribbean. Unlike some of the more avaricious of his compatriots, Oviedo was a curious, passionate observer of his surroundings, an equitable administrator, and a writer of no small talent (he even wrote a popular novel).

Oviedo was also what today we'd call a foodie, fascinated by the cuisine of Spain's new Caribbean territories. His writings provide some of the first records of how people ate in the New World in the sixteenth century. He chronicled many native foods and how they were prepared, including such popular tubers as yucca and boniato ("roasted in the hot embers of the fire"), avocados ("the juice and flesh taste much like butter"), and pineapples (which he pronounced "one of the best fruits in the world"). He noted with keen interest how bread was made from ground corn and cassava, wrapped

A communal hunt preceded the barbecues of Caribbean Indians.

in leaves, and roasted in the coals of a campfire.

But the reason we remember this author and adventurer today is that he was the first European to report on a method of cooking unique to the New World—barbecue.

They trap deer and pigs with branches and traps made of nets, into which the animals fall. At times they hunt and beat them out, and with a great number of people they attack them and take those that they can kill with arrows and spears. After they have killed the animals, since they do not have knives with which to skin them, they quarter them and cut them into pieces with stones and flints. They roast the flesh on sticks which they place in the ground, like a grating or trivet, over a pit. They call these *barbacoas*, and place fire beneath, and in this manner they roast fish also. Since this land is naturally hot, even though it is tempered by Divine Providence, fish and meat soon spoil if they are not roasted on the same day that they are killed or caught.

The passage comes from Oviedo's *Natural History of the West Indies,* published in Toledo, Spain, in 1526, and it's the first written account of barbecue. It tells us a lot about the origins of this New World style of cooking. For starters, even back then barbecue was a social activity, involving "a great number of people." And the preparation involved considerable meat-cutting skills (as anyone who has tried to trim a rack of spareribs will appreciate), especially when the "knife" was a shard of flint.

The Taino Indian word for a piece of equipment—a framework of sticks—gives us the word *barbecue.* (It's clear the Tainos knew how to live well. They also gave us the words *canoe, hammock,* and *tobacco.*) Curiously, the high wooden frames could also be used as a sleeping platform: You reposed on a *barbacoa* while waiting for your meat to cook. The practice of smoke grilling meats on wooden sticks survives in Jamaica, where jerk is made by cooking spiced pork on a grate made of allspice wood sticks laid over blazing allspice embers.

Spice and smoke were essential to early barbecue, we learn from Captain John Gabriel Stedman, who explored the Surinam coast in the 1770s: " . . . every thing they eat, is so highly Seasoned with Cayenne Pepper, that only the tasting of their victuals excoriates the mouth of an European, they use little or no Salt, but barbacue [sic] their Game and fish in the Smoak [sic], which equally preserves it from Putrefaction." We'll never know exactly how the early Caribbean barbecue tasted, but with its fiery seasoning and intense smoke flavor, I bet it resembled Jamaican jerk.

Thomas Hariot's *A Brief and True Report of the New Found Land of Virginia,* published in London in 1588, has an engraving showing a

Barbecue takes its name from the barbacoa, *a wooden grate upon which Taino Indians smoke grilled fish and meat.*

Native American fish barbecue. Two fish cook on a wooden frame that is several feet above the fire, an example of what I call modified direct grilling—grilling directly over the fire but at a distance so the food doesn't burn (the same setup is used today at the popular Rendezvous restaurant in Memphis). Two more fish grill in an upright position on stakes next to the fire.

That second grilling technique is not unique to Virginia. The Indians of the Pacific Northwest smoke-roasted salmon next to blazing alder, splitting the fish through the belly, securing it to cedar stakes, and grilling it by the fire. Lewis and Clark encountered this in the Clatsop and Chinook Indian villages on their journey down the Columbia River. Two centuries later, you can feast on the delicious result at Tillicum Village in Puget Sound (see page 454 for a fuller description). The process is a forerunner of what has become the Connecticut shad bake (see page 518).

So did barbecue really originate in the Americas? Well, yes and no. Humans have made use of fire for at least 400,000 years and cooked over it for at least 250,000 years. The practice of roasting meat or fish on a stick or stone in front of a flame is so elemental, it came into use wherever human beings congregated. Europeans have spit roasted beef and lamb since the time of Homer.

But early American barbecue had several unique aspects. One was the deliberate and controlled use of smoke (in addition to spice) as a flavoring. Equally characteristic was the use of a pit and raised grill grate.

BARBECUE AND THE BIRTH OF A NATION

Even though as early as the 1600s, Virginia had laws banning the discharge of firearms at barbecues, we know from numerous accounts that the Old Dominion remained

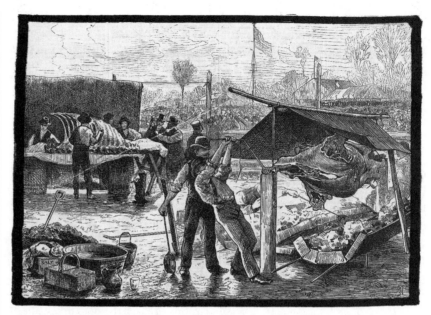

American barbecue assumed heroic proportions during the nineteenth century. It took real muscle to spit roast a whole ox.

the epicenter of American cookouts. "The ladies of Virginia . . . are immoderately fond of dancing, . . . and now and then [venture] into the woods to partake of a barbacue [sic]," decried the Reverend Andrew Burnaby when he visited from England in 1759. In 1784, Lawrence Butler would write to friends there, "I am continually at Balls & Barbecues."

The Englishman Isaac Weld observed at the end of the eighteenth century:

The people in this part of the country, bordering upon James River, are extremely fond of an entertainment which they call a barbacue [sic]. It consists in a large party meeting together, either under some trees, or in a house, to partake of a sturgeon or pig roasted in the open air, on a sort of hurdle over a slow fire; this, however, is an entertainment chiefly confined to the lower ranks, and, like most others of the same nature, it generally ends in intoxication.

Weld's observations were only partially correct, for like the fledgling nation, barbecue was democratic in nature, enjoyed by high-born and low, rich and poor, freemen and slaves alike. Nor were all barbecues drunken affairs, although then, as now, most would be thought incomplete without some sort of alcoholic beverage.

George Washington loved "barbicue," and attended as many as he could. His diary records one particularly festive cookout in Alexandria, Virginia, that lasted three full days. One biographer speculates that Washington lost the first election in which he ran—for a seat in the House of Burgesses—because he neglected to stage a barbecue for potential voters, refusing "to provide the customary refreshments at the polls."

Years later, when a triumphant Washington accepted the surrender of the British General Charles Cornwallis in 1781, spontaneous barbecues sprung up all over the country to celebrate the United States' independence. Here's how one such event was described in Philip Henry Smith's *General History of Duchess County, from 1609 to 1876, Inclusive.*

When a herald passed through the country announcing the surrender . . . the tidings met with a hearty response from every patriot. Bonfires, illuminations, and the thunder of artillery everywhere demonstrated the joy that was felt throughout the land. The people of Pawling Precinct instituted a barbecue in commemoration of the event. A hole was dug in the bank near the site of the residence of Richard Chapman, Esq., a fire was built therein, and a fine, full-grown bullock was spitted before it. The cooking was not a pronounced success, but Pawling charged upon it with all her chivalry. Patriotic speeches were made, patriotic songs sung, and patriotic toasts drank in profusion; and nothing prevented the thundering of cannon, but the want of cannon and powder.

Independence Day and other civic occasions were celebrated with barbecues. The laying of the cornerstone of the Capitol in 1793 was the occasion for a particularly splendid ceremony. Following an impressive parade, President Washington placed the cornerstone. Then the assembled company feasted on a barbecued five-hundred-pound ox.

Even matrimony was an excuse for a barbecue, as Abraham Lincoln undoubtedly knew: His parents, Thomas Lincoln and Nancy Hanks, feted their vows at a barbecue. Here's how Christopher Graham, one of the guests, recalled the event, as quoted by Doug Worgul in *The Grand Barbecue:* "We had bear meat, venison, wild turkey and ducks, eggs wild and tame, maple sugar lumps tied on a string to bite off for coffee or whisky, syrup in big gourds, peach and honey, a sheep barbecued whole over coals of wood burned in a pit, and covered with green boughs to keep the juices in; and a race for the whisky bottle."

It can't have hurt that William Henry Harrison staged enormous barbecues during his successful 1840 campaign for the presidency. One such event took place in Wheeling, West Virginia. Thirty thousand voters were wooed with 20 calves, 25 sheep, 360 hams, 1,500 pounds of beef, 8,000 pounds of bread, and 4,500 pies for dessert.

Charles Lanman wrote the best description of an early-nineteenth-century American barbecue in *Adventures in the Wilds of the United States and British American Provinces,* which was published in 1856.

They first dig a pit, four feet wide, two or three deep, and as long as they require, into which they throw a quantity of wood, for the purpose of obtaining there-from a bed of burning coals. This done, the more expert kitchen [help] proceed to roast (by laying them upon sticks across the fires) the various animals prepared for the occasion. In the meantime, all the other arrangements are progressing, such as spreading the white cloths upon the temporary board tables, and clearing a place for dancing.

One of the first recipes for barbecue appeared in a book published in 1732.

Frontiersman and war hero William Henry Harrison staged elaborate barbecues during his 1840 election campaign.

THE FLAVOR OF THE FLAME

What did the barbecue of early Virginia taste like? Numerous recipes have survived in eighteenth-century American and British cookbooks. One of the first, published in London in 1732, is found in R. Bradley's *The Country Housewife and Lady's Director in the Management of a House, and the Delights and Profits of a Farm*. Here it is with its original punctuation and spelling:

Take an Hog of five or six Months old, kill it, and take out the Inwards . . . Then stretch out the Ribs, and open the Belly, as wide as may be; then strew into it what Pepper and Salt you please.

After this, take a large Grid-Iron, and set it upon a stand of Iron, about three Foot and a half high, and upon that, lay your Hog, open'd as above, with the Belly-side downwards, and with a good clear Fire of Charcoal under. Broil [grill] that side till it is enough, flouring the Back at the same time often. *Memorandum*, This should be done in a Yard, or Garden, with a Covering like a Tent over it.

When the Belly-part of the Hog is enough, and turn'd upwards, and well fix'd, to be steady upon the Grid-Iron, or Barbacue, pour into the Belly of the Hog, three or four Quarts of Water, and half as much White-Wine, and as much Salt as you will, with some Sage cut small; adding the Peels of six or eight Lemons, and an Ounce of fresh Cloves whole.

Then let it broil [grill] till it is enough, which will be, from the beginning to the end, about seven or eight Hours; and when you serve it, pour out the Sauce, and lay it in a Dish, with the Back upwards. *Memorandum*, The Skin must not be cut before you lay it on the Gridiron, to keep in the Gravey.

MOPPING AND SAUCING

As any self-respecting pit master knows today, you can't make barbecue without a mop sauce (the liquid brushed on meat to keep it moist as it cooks). Mop sauces have been around for a couple centuries—at least if we're to believe Mr. Butler of Westmoreland Country, Virginia, who wrote the following to friends in England in 1784: "Then they lay the Meat over that [a wooden grate] within about six inches of the Coals, & then they Keep basting it with Butter & Salt & Water & turning it every now and then, until its done." (On page 382 you'll find a spit-roasted, butterflied leg of lamb basted in this manner. I think you'll be impressed.)

By the 1820s, the first barbecue sauces began to appear— rich gravies made with butter, wine, and ketchup. This was not the red tomato ketchup we associate with modern barbecue sauce; tomatoes were considered poisonous in those days. (Legend has it that in 1820 a daredevil named Robert Johnson ate tomatoes on the steps of the Salem, New Jersey, courthouse; the crowd expected him to keel over in front of them.)

Pit masters could choose from mushroom, walnut, and other exotic ketchups (most of which tasted like what we'd call chutney). Consider this early sauce recipe, which appeared in

Mary Randolph's *The Virginia Housewife* in 1824: "Put it [the pork] in a pan with a pint of water, two cloves of garlic, pepper, salt, two gills of red wine, and two of mushroom catsup, bake it, and thicken the gravy with butter and brown flour . . . if it be not sufficiently brown, add a little burnt sugar to the gravy."

THE RISE OF THE BARBECUE JOINT

When the Civil War liberated African Americans, many became pit masters.

The end of the Civil War changed barbecue profoundly. Many emancipated slaves who had formerly worked in plantation kitchens turned to barbecue as a means of earning a livelihood. In the decades that followed, seeking better economic opportunities, tens of thousands of African Americans moved north. Soon black neighborhoods in Kansas City, Detroit, and Chicago became hotbeds of great barbecue.

The turn of the century marked the appearance of the first commercial barbecue eateries—establishments where you could buy enough barbecue for your family or just lunch for yourself. Well, *establishment* is a pretty fancy word for these country shacks, roadside stands, and street-corner carryouts—like the one founded by Henry Perry in Kansas City in 1907.

Kansas City had all the ingredients for great barbecue: a booming meatpacking industry to supply the raw ingredients, lush hickory and oak forests nearby to furnish the wood, and a longstanding love of barbecue. (The opening of the Hannibal Bridge in 1869—the first bridge to span the Missouri River—was celebrated with a huge public barbecue.) The city also had a growing black community schooled in the art of Southern-style barbecue.

Born in Shelby County, Tennessee, in 1875, Perry was a steamboat cook and a kitchen hand. After decades of plying the Mississippi River, he settled in Kansas City to cook barbecue. His operation was decidedly no frills; he grilled directly over wood in a hole in the ground and served his barbecue wrapped in newspaper. His peppery sauce brought tears to people's eyes. Perry also established the Kansas City pit master's reputation for brusqueness.

A sign at the eatery reminded patrons: "My business is to serve you, not entertain you."

As Perry's business grew, he moved his operation several times, at one point working out of an old streetcar barn. He inspired a new generation of pit masters. One was Charlie Bryant, who came to work for Perry in the 1920s. When Perry died in 1940, Charlie took over, and when Charlie retired a few years later, his brother, Arthur, became the pit master. Arthur changed the name of the business to Arthur Bryant's, and a Kansas City legend was born.

Meanwhile, barbecue places were springing up all over the country. In the 1890s, German and Czech immigrants began settling in the central Texas Hill Country. Many of these meat-loving Europeans opened butcher shops and grocery stores. Charles Kreuz (rhymes with brights), who founded the now legendary Kreuz Market in Lockhart, Texas, in 1900, is a case in point. At the end of each day, Kreuz would cook any unsold meat over a pit fueled with blazing post oak and sell it at bargain prices.

By 1924 his barbecue had become so popular he installed a massive brick pit with a thirty five-foot brick chimney and a chopping block the size of a large table. The barbecued clod (beef shoulder), brisket, prime rib, and smoked sausage were so tasty Kreuz didn't even bother to serve barbecue sauce.

The restaurant has survived Prohibition, the Depression, a family feud, and a relocation. The meat's as good as ever, and you still won't find a drop of barbecue sauce on the premises (you'll find more about Kreuz Market on page 166).

Today we take for granted restaurants where you can order a single serving of barbecue at just about any hour or day of the week. But it's thanks to barbecue pioneers like Henry Perry or Charles Kreuz, like Harry Green (who opened a barbecue restaurant in Owensboro, Kentucky, in 1890) or Adam Scott (a janitor from Goldsboro, North Carolina, who dished up barbecue from his back porch in the 1920s), that this is possible.

Automobile pioneer Henry Ford manufactured the first commercial charcoal briquettes.

BARBECUE COMES TO YOUR HOME

You wouldn't think the transportation industry had much of anything to contribute to barbecue, yet it was instrumental in moving grilling from communal cookouts and restaurants to the American backyard. Charcoal had been used for hundreds of thousands of years (traces of it turn up at Neanderthal archeological sites and in the paintings of the Lascaux caves). The modern charcoal briquette, however, we owe to Henry Ford. The auto manufacturing genius operated a sawmill in the forest near Iron Mountain to make wooden parts for the Model T. As wood scraps piled up, the thrifty Ford took advantage of a new charcoal-making process patented by Orin F. Stafford. Wood scraps were chipped into small pieces, burned to charcoal, ground into powder, mixed with a binder, and compressed into pillow-shaped briquettes. By 1921 Ford's charcoal-making plant was operating at full steam. The first customers were blacksmiths, institutional kitchens, and hotels.

Ford placed a distant relative, a former lumberman and one of the first automobile dealers, E. G. Kingsford, in charge of his charcoal factory. Recognize the name? It was the Kingsford Company that went on to become synonymous with charcoal briquettes.

WHAT A GOOD IDEA

Still, the ready source of charcoal was of little use without a convenient device in which to burn it.

One of the first Weber salesmen shows off the kettle grill, which would start a revolution in backyard barbecue.

Enter George Stephen, a metal worker from Palatine, Illinois, just outside of Chicago. Like many Midwesterners, Stephen loved to barbecue in his backyard, but he was frustrated with the flat, brazier-type grills popular in the 1950s. He disliked the way they performed in windy or rainy weather and the fact that they could only be used to grill using the direct method.

At the time, Stephen worked for the Weber Brothers Metal Works, a manufacturer of nautical buoys. His brainstorm was to turn one of the spun metal buoy bowls into a barbecue grill. He mounted the bowl on legs and placed a metal grate over it to hold the food. A second metal bowl, fitted with vents to control the air flow, and thus the temperature, became a lid. He began marketing the Weber kettle grill in 1952. Eventually he bought the Weber Company and manufactured grills full-time.

The genius of the Weber kettle lay in the dome of its lid, as well as the vent system. The lid was high enough to accommodate whole pork shoulders, turkeys, and rib roasts. The vent system allowed you to bank coals at the edges of the grill and cook the meat in the center, using an indirect cooking method similar to the old-fashioned barbecue pits of the South. Moreover, by tossing wood chips or chunks on the coals, you could turn a grill into a smoker. Today, the company manufactures both charcoal and gas grills, and the name Weber has become virtually synonymous with barbecue grills.

Thanks to the advent of the Weber kettle grill and to the introduction of easy-to-use gas grills (the first models—manufactured by gas utility companies—began appearing in 1960), barbecue has become a national pastime. The boom was helped by America's massive migration to the suburbs, where for the first time in our history, everyone had a backyard. Today 85 percent of American families own some sort of grill, and more than 40 percent own two or more. (A few of us have more than twenty!) In much of the country grilling has become a year-round activity: According to the Barbecue Hearth & Patio Association, the barbecue trade organization, 54 percent of Americans use their grills twelve months of the year.

THE HEAT IS ON

The 1980s witnessed two additional trends in barbecue—the proliferation of the first barbecue restaurant chains and the advent of competition barbecue. The chains are a mixed blessing. "Barbecue" is now available everywhere, but a lot of what's passing itself off as the real McCoy is actually meat flavored with liquid smoke and baked in the oven.

In the same vein, it's now possible to find "North Carolina" pulled pork in Texas and "Texas" brisket in the Deep South. On the plus side, this certainly broadens barbecue's recognition and acceptance. On the minus side, the regional character of barbecue (and barbecue is one of the last bastions of regional culture in America) suffers from such homogenization.

Fortunately, authentic regional barbecue is enjoying a resurgence—a process that began in

1974, when journalist Calvin Trillin proclaimed Arthur Bryant's in Kansas City the best restaurant in the world in no less than *The New Yorker*. Trillin's article and subsequent book, *Alice, Let's Eat,* not only popularized barbecue but gave it cachet.

Competition barbecue—a uniquely American phenomenon that reaches its apotheosis at the great cooking contests in Memphis and Kansas City—also attests to the strength of regional barbecue. Each year, thousands of barbecue buffs, cooking on rigs towed from fairground to fairground and state to state, compete in hundreds of regional barbecue cooking contests, from the Big Pig Jig in Vienna, Georgia, to the Pioneer Days BBQ Cookoff in Fort Worth, Texas. The winners are invited to strut their stuff at the barbecue "Super Bowls"—mega cook-offs like the American Royal in Kansas City, the Jack Daniel's Invitational in Lynchburg, Tennessee, and Memphis in May in, where else? Memphis. Contestants compete for tens of thousands of dollars in prize money before crowds that can swell into the tens of thousands. The first Memphis in May took place in 1978; at a recent competition, there

were close to 300 teams and 80,000 spectators. (For more about competition barbecue, see page 560.)

LOOKING AHEAD

And the future of barbecue? Well, technological advances in grills, like superhot infrared heating systems, now make it possible for ordinary folks to prepare chophouse-quality steaks, seared over a blast furnace heat once available only to restaurants. Thanks to the advent of portable barrel and water smokers, smoke buffs can turn out competition-quality ribs and briskets in their

backyards. Barbecue sauces crowd the shelves of supermarkets and gourmet shops. (A recent sauce contest at the American Royal in Kansas City logged in close to 400 different bottled sauces.) Stainless steel supergrills have become the sort of status symbols that Porsche sports cars once were.

True barbecue is alive and well, and for every new fast food chain taking a shortcut, there's a dedicated smoke jockey out there who nurses a beer as he or she fusses and frets over a brisket in a cooking process that can take fourteen hours. If you worry about the future of barbecue, just look into the bloodshot eyes of a pit master who has stayed awake all night lovingly basting a hog at Memphis in May or the Jack Daniel's. What you'll see is dedication, and dedication is the very soul of barbecue.

In the five centuries since its "discovery" in the West Indies, barbecue has become an inextricable part of American culture. To paraphrase Mark Twain, reports of its demise are greatly exaggerated. One thing we share as Americans is barbecue, and as long as there's an America, barbecue will be what we eat.

Competition barbecue festivals—
a uniquely American phenomenon.

1492 Columbus attempts a western passage to Asia, discovering the Americas in the process. His voyage will introduce a bold new world of ingredients, flavors, and cooking techniques to Europe.

A Taino Indian barbacoa, precursor of barbecue.

1526 Barbecue (*barbacoa*) is mentioned in print for the first time by the Spanish explorer Gonzalo Fernández de Oviedo y Valdes. The term describes the Taino Indian method of smoke roasting.

1600 Spanish farmers and shepherds settle in southern Texas, introducing a technique of spit roasting lamb called *al pastor* (shepherd style). Today *tacos al pastor* (spiced spit-roasted pork and pineapple tacos) are popular in Mexican American communities across the United States.

1830 Skilton Dennis opens what is possibly the first commercial barbecue business in the United States, barbecuing pigs to serve at large church camp meetings in Ayden, North Carolina. He also sells barbecue from the back of a chuck wagon. Skilton's great-great-grandson Pete Jones is still in the barbecue business, as the proprietor of the Skylight Inn in Ayden.

1831 Johann Friedrich Ernst, the first German to settle in Texas, gets a land grant for more than 4,000 acres in Austin County. Over the next seventy years, German and Czech immigrants will settle in the area, opening butcher shops and grocery stores that will become the first Texas barbecue restaurants.

James Willis has been a pit master at Leonard's Barbecue in Memphis for more than 60 years.

1834 The first recorded mutton barbecue is held in Owensboro, Kentucky, on the banks of the Ohio River on July 4th, to celebrate Independence Day.

1865 Slaves are emancipated, following the end of the Civil War. For the first time African American pit

Beef barbecue, no bum steer in Texas.

masters are free to stage barbecues for their own profit.

1867 The first cattle drive up the Chisholm Trail from Fort Worth to Abilene, Kansas takes place. Texas quickly becomes a cattle-raising state, and beef becomes its preferred barbecue.

1869 Kansas City stages a grand barbecue to celebrate the completion of the Hannibal Bridge, the first permanent bridge to span the Missouri River.

1882 The Southside Market and BBQ opens in Elgin, Texas—home of the famous Elgin hot guts.

A Look at American

1900 The Kreuz Market opens in Lockhart, Texas. Clod and brisket will become classic Texas barbecue cuts.

1907 Henry Perry, former porter and steamboat cook, opens a barbecue stand in the Banks Street alley, the first commercial barbecue operation in Kansas` City. Such twentieth-century legends of Kansas City barbecue as Arthur Bryant and George Gates train with Perry and keep his legacy alive.

1915 Adam Scott, a black janitor and elevator operator, cooks his first public barbecue in Goldsboro, North Carolina. Within a decade, he's selling barbecue from a pit in his backyard. By 1933, Scott's is a full-fledged restaurant.

1918 Charles "Pappy" Foreman opens an eatery specializing in barbecued mutton in Owensboro, Kentucky. The restaurant, Old Hickory Bar-B-Q Pit, is now run by the fourth generation of the family.

1921 Henry Ford starts America's first commercial charcoal briquette manufacturing facility. He puts a relative, E. G. Kingsford, in charge of the facility. Kingsford Charcoal will become a household name.

1948 A German American butcher founds Louie Mueller's in Taylor, Texas.

Brisket has been sliced to order by hand at Louis Mueller's in Luling, Texas, for half a century.

1950s Americans flock to the suburbs, creating the first boom in backyard barbecues.

1952 Metal worker George Stephen puts legs on half of a nautical buoy to create the first Weber charcoal kettle grill.

1958 Sonny Bryan opens a barbecue joint on Inwood near Love Field airport in Dallas. Sonny Bryan's Smokehouse becomes one of the most famous barbecue restaurants in Texas.

1970s The first commercially manufactured portable smoking rigs become available for amateur use.

1974 *New Yorker* writer Calvin Trillin proclaims Arthur Bryant's "The single best restaurant in the world," giving barbecue a cachet it had never had before.

1978 Memphis in May is founded. It will eventually become the world's largest barbecue contest.

1984 Child psychiatrist Dr. Rich Davis gives up medicine to develop KC Masterpiece barbecue sauce. This is destined to become America's best-selling premium barbecue sauce, redefining our very notion of barbecue.

The sauce doctor, Rich Davis, gives new meaning to the words mop sauce.

1985 The Kansas City Barbecue Society is founded.

1995 Bobby Flay and Jack McDavid launch "Grilling and Chilling" on the Food Network, bringing barbecue to American TV.

1998 Workman publishes *The Barbecue! Bible* and Raichlen has a new calling.

Barbecue

Getting Started

A CONCISE PRIMER ON GRILLING & BARBECUING

Grilling is America's oldest, simplest, and most widespread cooking method, requiring little more than food and fire. So why has it become so complicated? Gas versus charcoal? Direct versus indirect grilling? Charcoal kettle or high-tech gas grill? And, of course, grilling versus smoking? These are a few of the decisions facing the would-be griller—and that's *before* you contemplate what to cook for dinner.

Well, part of the complication lies in the fact that grilling has traditionally been a man's domain (and as everyone knows, we men like to complicate our hobbies). In addition, our growing connoisseurship of regional and ethnic barbecue, our willingness to grill everything from starters to dessert, and the advent of home smokers and stainless steel supergrills that aren't just cooking devices but veritable high-tech outdoor kitchens have led us to take on greater grilling challenges.

It's time to demystify the arts of grilling and smoking. Let's start with the grill.

THE GREAT GAS VS. CHARCOAL DEBATE

A great deal of ink, beer, and maybe even blood have been spilled over the great debate: charcoal or gas. Guys in my line of work generally voice a preference for charcoal—touting a superior flavor and delighting in charcoal's general messiness and unpredictability. I, too, have espoused this party line at various points, but the reality is almost 70 percent of Americans own gas grills. They (or, I should say we, since I do own several gas grills and use them often) love the convenience of push-button ignition and an even, consistent heat. The chief drawback of gas grills is that they don't work particularly well for producing wood smoke.

If I could use only one grill for the rest of my life (or take it to a deserted island), it would be my trusty charcoal kettle. Why? For starters, charcoal burns hotter than gas, so it sears better (better searing makes for bolder flavors). It's also easier to smoke on a charcoal grill—more on that later (see page 23). Charcoal imparts a distinct flavor all its own, one less pronounced than that from grilling over a wood fire (which, by the way, is easy to build in a charcoal grill), but definitely more discernable than what you get from gas. And of course, charcoal gives you the thrill of playing with fire.

In a way the question of whether to buy a charcoal or gas grill boils down to temperament as much as technique: Do you enjoy building a fire, waiting for it to reach the right temperature, and waltzing the food from hot to cool spots? Or are you less concerned with the sport of grilling than the results on your plate? Perhaps the best solution is to follow the example of a growing number of Americans: Own at least one of each (you'll find profiles of the various grill types in the chart on page 30).

HOW TO LIGHT A GRILL

Once you have selected your grill, you need to light the fire. If it's a gas grill, all you need to do is push a button or turn a knob. It's slightly more complicated with charcoal, but no big deal once you know how to do it. In the old days, you dumped in briquettes, doused them with lighter fluid, stood back, and tossed on a lit match. A lot of scorn gets heaped on the lighter fluid method these days—after all,

Spotlight on pit masters: the late Raymond Robinson of the Cozy Corner in Memphis.

who wants petroleum products near their food?

The truth is that if you use lighter fluid correctly (letting the coals burn down to glowing embers, which burns off any petroleum residue in the process), there will be no petroleum aftertaste. In fact, this is how the big boys start their fires at the Kansas City Royal or Memphis in May barbecue competitions, and I never heard a judge complain about the taste of lighter fluid.

However, today the politically correct method is to light the charcoal in a chimney starter, an upright metal tube with a heat-proof handle and a wire partition in the center. The chimney starter eliminates the need for a petroleum-based lighter fluid and, more important, it ignites coals evenly.

How do you get the charcoal burning in a chimney starter? You

can either use a burning sheet of newspaper or ignite a paraffin starter. Paraffin starters look like white ice cubes and are an alternative to petroleum-based lighter fluids—I highly recommend them. To use a chimney starter follow these simple steps:

1. Fill the top of the chimney starter with charcoal. If you are using newspaper to light the charcoal, place a crumpled sheet in the bottom compartment. A double sheet of newspaper is enough; more will clog the starter.

2. Remove the top grate of the grill. If you are using a paraffin starter, place it on the bottom grate or in the fire box. Light the paraffin starter with a match or lighter, then place the chimney starter on top of it.

If you are using newspaper, place the chimney starter on the

WHAT TO LOOK FOR WHEN BUYING A GRILL

All grills have two parts: the firebox (which holds the fire) and the grate (the metal gridiron where you do the actual grilling). Many grills have lids, which enable you to use the indirect grilling method and to smoke. Here are the features that are essential no matter what type of grill you purchase and those you'll want to look for in charcoal and gas grills.

All Grills:

- Sturdy construction and stable legs

- Thick metal grill grate, preferably with cast-iron or ¼-inch stainless steel bars (I'm not crazy about enameled or porcelainized grill grates; these can be harder to clean and create less pronounced grill marks, but they certainly have their partisans)

- Built-in thermometer so you can monitor the heat

- Side tables; you can never have enough workspace

- Multiyear warrantee for parts and labor

Charcoal Grills:

- A tight-fitting lid for indirect grilling

- Adjustable vent holes in the firebox and lid, so you can control the heat

- Side baskets for indirect grilling

- Hinged grill grates (with side panels you can lift to add coals or wood) when grilling indirectly

- An ash catcher (a saucepan-shaped device that attaches to the bottom of the grill to collect the ashes from the fire)

Gas Grills:

- An easy-to-use drip pan for collecting grease; one you can empty without spilling

- A gas gauge—you'd think this would be standard equipment, but you'd be amazed how many high-end grills don't have them

- A separate smoker box (a metal tray where you can put wood chips or chunks for smoking) with a dedicated burner

- A rotisserie with its own burner

- Side burners for heating sauces and keeping food warm

bottom grate or in the fire box, tip it to one side, then light the newspaper with a match or lighter. After the first burst of flame, it may look like nothing is happening (that's why I prefer a paraffin starter). After about five minutes have passed, hold your hand over the chimney starter. If you feel any warmth whatsoever, the coals in the bottom of the chimney are lit. Just wait patiently until all the rest catch fire. If it's not warm, try again by lighting another sheet of newspaper.

3. Let the charcoal burn until the coals glow bright orange. This will take twenty to thirty minutes. A billowing cloud of smoke may pour out of the chimney in the beginning, this is normal.

4. Carefully invert the chimney starter over the bottom of your grill (it's a good idea to wear a leather grill glove when you do this) and rake out the coals—a garden hoe is great for doing this. When the orange coals are just beginning to ash over, they're ready for you to cook.

You'll get forty to sixty minutes of grilling time from a large chimney starter full of charcoal. But remember, a charcoal fire will lose as much as 75°F over the course of an hour. If you plan to grill for longer than that, you'll need to replenish the coals.

I much prefer natural lump charcoal to briquettes. Lump charcoal, recognizable by its jagged edges, is made from trees;

Spotlight on pit masters: Chuck Primus of Chuck's Smokehouse BBQ in Hope, Arkansas.

gas in the middle of cooking.

TIP: Recent federal safety regulations mandate that all propane tanks come with an overfill protection device (OPD), an internal mechanism that keeps you from adding too much gas to the tank. If the valve handle (the part you turn to start the flow of gas) has 3 points, your tank is a newer model with an OPD. If the valve has 5 points, you have an older model and the gas service may refuse to fill it. Trade it in for a new tank.

GRILLING OVER A WOOD FIRE

A wood fire gives you a taste that is quite distinct from, and I think superior to, the one charcoal imparts. It's a delicate smoke flavor that may remind you of a California wine country cookout. It's certainly not as pronounced as the heavy smoke flavor of traditional Southern-style American barbecue. Wood grilling is exquisite for steaks, veal and lamb chops, fish, and even vegetables.

Until recently, wood grilling was the province of restaurants—most home cooks simply didn't have grills heavy-duty enough to handle entire oak or mesquite logs. That's changed, thanks to the burgeoning availability of packaged hardwood chunks, which you can buy at hardware stores or grill shops. If you place these chunks in a chimney starter and light them exactly as you would charcoal, after fifteen minutes or so, you'll

briquettes are fabricated from furniture scraps, coal dust, borax, and petroleum binders. Lump charcoal lights quickly and burns cleanly, without imparting the acrid smoke you sometimes get with briquettes. Lump charcoal burns faster than briquettes, so you may need to replenish the coals sooner. Look for lump charcoal at grill shops and natural foods stores, or see the Mail-Order Sources on page 742.

TIP: When buying a chimney starter, get the largest one you can find.

Now, as I've said, most gas grills light with the push or turn of a button. But you *do* need to remember to open the lid before you light the grill. Failure to do so may result in an explosion if too much gas accumulates underneath. And don't forget to open

the valve on the top of the tank to start the gas flowing.

In the past, gas grills didn't burn as hot as charcoal. As a result they weren't as good for searing. Most new models have corrected this problem. When grilling over a gas fire, I preheat the grill on high for the ten to fifteen minutes recommended by the manufacturer, then continue the preheating for about ten minutes longer. In most cases this makes the grate as hot as that of any charcoal grill.

The amount of grilling time you'll get from a standard tank of propane varies considerably, depending on the size of the grill, the number of burners, and even the outdoor temperature. In general, figure on sixteen to twenty hours per tank. I always keep one or two full tanks in reserve—there's nothing worse than running out of

THE MISSISSIPPI TEST

So how do you gauge the temperature of a fire? Hold your hand three to four inches above the grill grate and start counting: "One Mississippi, two Mississippi," and so on. Over a hot fire, you'll get to two or three Mississippi before the heat forces you to pull your hand away. When the fire is medium-high, you can hold your hand over it for a count of about four Mississippi. With a cool fire, you can count as high as nine to twelve Mississippi. For a full breakdown of grill temperatures and their Mississippi counts, see page 24.

have fragrant, blazing wood embers that are ideal for grilling. Just remember, wood burns faster than charcoal, so you'll need to replenish the chunks every twenty minutes or so.

If you have a large front-loading charcoal grill or wood-burning grill, you can fuel it with logs. Start your fire with kindling or charcoal, then pile on the logs and let them burn down to embers.

THE FIVE METHODS OF GRILLING

If you ask most people to define grilling, they'll say cooking food directly over a fire. But there are actually five distinct grilling methods: direct, indirect, modified direct, smoking, and spit roasting (a.k.a. rotisserie grilling). Here's an overview of each.

Spotlight on pit masters: The late Charlie Vergos of the Rendezvous in Memphis.

Direct Grilling

As the name suggests, direct grilling involves cooking food directly over a fire, usually three to six inches above the flame. This method is used to cook relatively small, thin, tender pieces of food —steaks, chops, chicken breasts, fish fillets, vegetables, tofu, sliced pineapple—foods that cook quickly, benefiting from the searing heat of the fire. To grill using the direct method, all you do is place the food on the grate over your heat source. The challenge of direct grilling—especially when using charcoal—is to control the heat. One way to do this is to build a three-zone fire.

A Three-Zone Charcoal Fire

To build a three-zone fire in a charcoal grill, rake half of the lit coals into a double layer on one side of the grill, so that they cover about a third of the bottom grate (you can use a garden hoe to rake out the coals). The rest of the coals go in a single layer in the center of the bottom grate. Leave the remaining third bare. This gives you three heat zones—a hot zone for searing, a medium zone for cooking, and a cool or safety zone where you can move what you are grilling if it starts to burn or keep cooked food warm.

Spotlight on pit masters: Charlie Riddle of Sonny Bryan's in Dallas.

A Three-Zone Gas Fire

To control the heat on a gas grill, you could adjust the burner controls, but I prefer to set up a three-zone fire here, too. Turn one burner on to high heat, then turn one or two burners on to medium. Leave the remaining burner turned off. If your grill has only two burners, use the warming rack as your safety zone.

A Two-Zone Fire (Charcoal and Gas)

When you are grilling only a couple of steaks or chicken breasts, you can use a two-zone fire. Depending upon what you are cooking, if you are using a charcoal grill, spread the coals out in an even layer, leaving a quarter of the grill bare, or make a double layer of coals in half of the grill and a single layer in the other half. If you are using a gas grill, preheat half or two out of three of the burners to the desired temperature; leave the rest turned off. This gives you a hot zone for grilling and a cooler zone for dodging the flames or resting the meat.

When should you cover the grill? When grilling thin pieces of food, like shrimp, fish fillets, asparagus, or small boneless, skinless chicken breasts using the direct method, it's not necessary to cover the grill. In fact, it's a good idea to leave the grill open, so you can watch these quick-cooking foods.

However, when grilling thicker foods, like steaks, chicken pieces, and portobello mushrooms, I like to cover the grill. This captures more of the fire and smoke flavors and it definitely speeds up the cooking time. I use the "rule of palm": If what you plan to cook is thicker than the palm of your hand (viewed from the side), grill it with the lid on. Open grills like table grills or hibachis don't have covers, of course, and when grilling thicker cuts on these, you may need to increase the cooking time slightly or place a metal pie pan on top.

Indirect Grilling

Direct grilling is great for steaks and burgers, but how do you grill spareribs, a whole chicken, or a pork shoulder? Indirect grilling allows you to cook large or tough cuts of meat so that they are cooked through without burning the exterior. To grill using the indirect method, you place the food next to, not directly over, the fire, and cover the grill to hold in the heat. This turns the grill into a sort of outdoor oven or barbecue pit.

To grill with charcoal using the indirect method, rake the coals into two piles on opposite sides of the bottom of the grill. Place an aluminum foil drip pan in the center. The food goes on the grate over the drip pan, away from the fire. When using the indirect method to grill a really large piece of food on a standard-size kettle grill, you may need to rake the coals into a single pile on one side of the grill and place the drip pan and the food on the grate on the opposite side.

To control the heat on a charcoal grill when grilling indirectly, adjust the top and bottom vents to obtain the desired temperature (closing the vents cuts off the oxygen, which makes the fire burn cooler).

If you grill or smoke large or tough pieces of food that require more than an hour to cook, you'll need to replenish the coals. Uncover the grill, add eight to twelve chunks of lump charcoal to the coals on each side, leave the grill uncovered for five to ten minutes until the new charcoal lights, then put the lid back on. Leaving the grill uncovered oxygenates the fire, helping the charcoal catch fire more quickly. You also avoid the acrid smoke taste that newly lit briquettes sometimes emit. Another option, and one I prefer, is to light fresh charcoal in a chimney starter and transfer the hot coals to the grill.

To grill with gas using the indirect method, with a two-burner grill, light the gas on one side and place the food over the other. With a three- or four-burner gas grill, light the outside or front and rear burners and place the food in the center to cook. You control the heat on a gas grill by turning the knobs to obtain the desired temperature (most indirect grilling is done using a moderate heat, 325° to 350°F). Many gas grills have built-in drip pans or grease catchers, so you won't need to place a separate aluminum foil drip pan under the grate. Just be sure you start with an empty drip pan—a duck or prime rib puts out a lot of fat.

TIP: If your gas grill does not have a drip pan or grease catcher (believe it or not, some gas models don't), or if there's a smoker box with a dedicated burner (see Smoking on a gas grill, at right) in the center of the grill, you'll need something to catch the fat when you grill using the indirect method. Just place whatever you are grilling—pork shoulder, ribs, or a turkey—in an aluminum foil drip pan and put this on top of the grate. Trust me on

this: I once had a beer-can chicken catch on fire when I was using a grill with the smoker box burner in the center—exactly under where the bird was grilling "indirectly."

Modified Direct Grilling

This is my name for a technique used primarily at barbecue restaurants—especially in the Southern barbecue belt. In modified direct grilling, as in direct grilling, the food is cooked above a bed of glowing embers, but the grill grate is positioned so high above the coals (typically two to six feet) that the gentle heat that results is more typical of indirect grilling. Unless you own a front-loading charcoal grill or wood-burning grill with an adjustable grate (see page 30), you probably won't be able to try this method at home. Instead, use the indirect grilling method and then move the food directly over the fire for the last few minutes it cooks in order to sizzle and sear the outside.

Smoking

Smoking, what many people think of as true barbecuing, is a particular kind of indirect grilling done slowly over a low heat in the presence of a lot of wood smoke. The traditional device used to cook this way is a pit or smoker— a large metal cylinder or box with a separate firebox on the side or at the bottom. Smoking typically

takes a long time; Texas pit masters, for example, spend up to sixteen hours cooking their briskets. A number of companies make smokers and pits for home use, but you can smoke on a charcoal grill, and to a lesser extent on a gas one, and still achieve that authentic barbecue flavor. All you'll need are some hardwood chips or chunks, such as hickory, oak, apple, or cherry, which are readily available at hardware stores and grill shops.

To smoke on a grill, the first step is to soak the wood chips or chunks in water to cover, for about an hour; soaking slows the combustion rate of the wood, allowing the chips to smolder, not ignite.

To smoke on a charcoal grill: First, set up the grill for indirect grilling. Toss a handful of chips ($\frac{1}{2}$ to $\frac{3}{4}$ cup) on each mound of charcoal, then cover the grill. Adjust the vent holes on the top and bottom to obtain the desired temperature (325° to 350°F for indirect grilling; 250° to 275°F for true smoking). With foods that cook a long time (a brisket or turkey, for example), you'll need to add $\frac{1}{2}$ to $\frac{3}{4}$ cup of fresh wood chips or chunks to each side every hour, along with fresh charcoal.

Smoking on a gas grill is a little trickier, especially if you are using an inexpensive one. Most high-end gas grills have a separate smoker box—a metal tray or box that holds wood chips or chunks directly over a dedicated burner.

If your grill is equipped this way, all you need to do is add the wood and run the smoker box burner on high until you see smoke, then reduce the grill heat to the desired temperature.

A smoker pouch is easy to make if you don't have a smoker box. Just wrap one or two cups of soaked wood chips or chunks in a piece of heavy-duty aluminum foil. Poke a few holes in the top of the pouch with a pencil to allow the smoke to escape. Place the smoker pouch under the grate directly over one of the burners and, again, run your grill on high until you see smoke, then reduce the heat to the desired temperature.

Compressed wood pellets, such as those made by BBQr's Delight (see Mail-Order Sources, page 742), are particularly effective for smoking on gas grills. Still, your average gas grill rarely produces the intense smoke flavor you get from a charcoal grill or smoker. If you really want to get smoking, buy a charcoal grill as an auxiliary to your gas one.

TIP: The hottest area of many gas grills is the junction of one of the gas burner tubes with the pilot light or pilot burner. Place the smoker pouch there, if you can.

Spit Roasting

When I was growing up in the 1960s every grill had a rotisserie. After decades of being out of favor, spit roasting has returned

GAUGING GRILLING TEMPERATURES

The recipes throughout this book specify the level of heat to use when grilling— high, medium-high, medium, and so on. The chart below indicates what specific temperatures these levels of heat are equivalent to and how to tell, using the Mississippi test (see page 21), when a charcoal grill has reached that temperature. If your grill has a built-in thermometer, of course you can use it to gauge the heat. However, the readings of these thermometers can be somewhat approximate. Depending on where it's positioned and which burners are turned on, the grill thermometer may show a temperature that is higher or lower than the one at the actual level of the grill. To double check, you can always use the Mississippi count.

HEAT	TEMPERATURE	MISSISSIPPI COUNT
High	450° to 650°F	2 to 3 Mississippis
Medium-high	400°F	4 Mississippis
Medium	325° to 350°F	5 to 6 Mississippis
Medium-low	300°F	7 to 8 Mississippis
Low	250° to 275°F	9 to 12 Mississippis

with a vengeance—now often done next to special ceramic or infrared burners positioned behind the turnspit. The slow, gentle rotation of the spit produces chickens, roasts, and even ribs (thread the spit between the bones) of incomparable succulence, thanks to the internal and external basting that occurs as they turn. Each rotisserie works differently, so follow the grill manufacturer's instructions. Be sure to place an aluminum foil pan under the rotating bird or roast to catch the dripping fat.

PUTTING IT ALL TOGETHER

There are a few final things to keep in mind before you start grilling. Be organized: Have everything you need—the food, marinade, basting sauce, seasonings, and equipment—on hand and at grill side before you start grilling. Then there are Raichlen's three rules for great grilling:

- Keep it hot.
- Keep it clean.
- Keep it lubricated.

You want to start with a hot grill grate, especially when grilling steaks, chops, and other relatively thin foods using the direct method. A hot grate gives you better searing (hence flavor) and more attractive grill marks. And foods are less likely to stick to a hot grate.

To clean a grill grate, preheat it to high, then brush it with a long-handled, stiff wire grill brush. If you don't have a grill brush, use a crumpled ball of aluminum foil held in tongs. Always clean a grate when it's hot—it's a lot easier to do then than when it's cold.

To oil a grill grate, fold a paper towel into a small wad, dip it in a bowl of oil, and holding it with tongs, rub it over the bars before grilling (this not only lubricates the grill, it gets the grate even cleaner). Or you can do what the pros do and make a cloth grate oiler: Roll up a clean white cotton washcloth or towel into an egg roll shape, tie it with butcher's string, and dip this in the oil. Or, depending upon what you are grilling, you can use a chunk of bacon or steak fat to grease the grate; hold it in a pair of tongs and rub it over the bars of the grate.

Cleaning and oiling the grate reduces the likelihood of food sticking and gives you better grill marks. Brush and oil your grill grate again after you're finished cooking. It's easier to clean a grate while it's hot, and the oil will help prevent rusting. As for the firebox and the outside of a grill, don't worry too much about cleaning these, although obviously, you'll want to wipe off or scrape off any large pieces of debris.

SOME THOUGHTS ON GRILL SAFETY

Grilling is about the best way I know to cook anything, and it's fun and theatrical to boot. But you're also working with live fire and highly flammable materials. Follow these simple steps and you'll never lose control.

- Place the grill on a stable surface away from porches, overhangs, walls, and trees and shrubbery.

- Keep small children and pets away from lit grills.

- Store lighter fluid and combustibles well away from the fire.

- Have a fire extinguisher and a large quantity of salt or a box of baking soda on hand, just in case you have a major flare-up.

- When grilling, don't wear gauzy clothing or loose sleeves and tie back long hair. Do wear sunscreen if you're grilling in the daytime.

- Use a flashlight or grill light to help you see what you're doing at night.

Spotlight on pit masters: Amazing Grace Hams of the Grand Emporium in Kansas City.

- Never desert your post. Grilling is easy, but it demands constant attention. Once you put something on the grate (especially when using the direct method), stay with it until it's done

HOW TO CONTROL FLARE-UPS

Flare-ups are inevitable. While they lend excitement, dare I say even a touch of drama, to the grilling process, you *do* need to know how to control them. The best way is to reduce the chances of flare-ups occurring in the first place. You can do this by working over a three-zone fire (see page 21) and leaving plenty of open space on the grate. If a flare-up happens, you can simply move the food from the hot to the medium zone of the grill, or even to the cool safety zone, until the flames die down. And to give you room to move food around, it's important not to crowd the grill—I always try to leave at least 30 percent of the grate free of food.

Another pregrilling precaution you can take to control flare-ups is to trim excess fat off steaks and chops and drain off oil-based marinades before placing the food on the grill. Likewise, make sure the drip pan of a gas grill is empty before you light the grill.

Covering the grill will help stop flare-ups once they've started. If you're cooking on a charcoal grill, be sure to close both the top and bottom vents when you cover it. This will deprive the fire of oxygen, and extinguish the flames. The down side to using this method is that it often gives the food a sooty taste, since as the flare-up dies down, the smoke is trapped inside the grill.

A few squirts from a spray bottle or water pistol can also help control the offending flames. Use this technique sparingly: The steam from the water may stir up the ashes, scattering them onto the grilling food. If you use too much water, it can extinguish the fire. Over time the water could crack the enamel coating of the grill.

A way-cool variation on this water technique is favored by Tex-Mex grill jockeys: Hold your thumb over the hole of an open long-neck bottle of beer. Shake the bottle gently, point the bottleneck toward the fire, and partially remove your thumb from the hole. This will release a thin spray of beer that you can use like a fire extinguisher. Not only does this quell the flames and look very dashing, it will add an unexpected flavor to your food. Again, don't go overboard.

In the event that a flare-up turns into a raging conflagration, transfer the food from the grill to a platter. Dump salt or baking soda over the fire to extinguish it. Use this technique only as a last resort.

HOW DO YOU KNOW WHEN IT'S DONE?

One of the hallmarks of master grillsmanship is the ability to cook food to just the desired

HOW DONE IS IT?

The following temperatures indicate these degrees of doneness for beef:

Rare:	125°F
Medium-rare:	145°F
Medium:	160°F
Well-done:	180° to 195°F

When cooking brisket and pork shoulders, you'll get maximum tenderness at 190° to 195°F. Food safety experts recommend cooking pork roasts and beef hamburgers to at least 160°F. Chicken and turkey should be cooked to at least 170°F.

degree of doneness. Grill masters use a variety of tests, both low- and high-tech, to recognize a rare steak or well-done brisket.

The poke test is the low-tech method—you poke the meat with your forefinger. Depending on its resilience, you will know that the meat is rare, well-done (heaven forbid), or somewhere in between.

If the poked meat feels:

- Downright squishy: It's still raw in the center.

- Soft and yielding (a bit like the flesh between your thumb and forefinger): It's rare.

- Gently yielding (like the flesh at the base of your thumb): It's medium-rare.

- Firmly-yielding (like the flesh on the base of your thumb when you loosely close your fingers): It's medium.

- Firm and springy (like the flesh on the base of your thumb when you make a fist): It's well done.

Another low-tech doneness test: Make a small cut in a steak or chop with tip of a paring knife and examine the interior. Use this technique as a last resort, as you are marring the look of a handsome steak when you cut into it (place the meat cut side down when you serve it). Even more important, each cut allows some meat juices to escape.

Use an instant-read meat thermometer for a more scientific verification of doneness. These thermometers are readily available at cookware shops. No grill jockey should be without one. To check for doneness you insert the needle end of the thermometer into the center of the meat, but do not let it touch a bone, if there are any; leave it there for fifteen seconds. To test a thick steak, flank steak, or brisket, insert the thermometer in the side (the sensor is located about an inch in from the end, so you won't get a proper reading if you insert it in the top). Thin steaks and chicken breasts are best tested for doneness using the poke method.

To check the doneness of fish, gently press the top with your finger. It will break into clean flakes when cooked through. Another way to see if fish is fully cooked is to insert a metal skewer into the thickest part of the fish and leave it there for twenty seconds. It should come out very hot to the touch if the fish is done.

Let it rest peacefully. Don't forget to let meat sit a bit before serving. Steaks, chops, roasts, even chicken breasts will be juicier if you let them rest for a few minutes (longer than that for larger cuts) before carving and/or serving.

TIP: Remember that all foods continue cooking even after they come off the grill. You may want to remove a steak or roast when it's 5 to 10 degrees less than the temperature you ultimately desire.

A NOTE ABOUT INGREDIENTS

Your food can be only as good as your raw materials.

Here are my thoughts about some ingredients you'll find used frequently in this book.

Salt: I like a coarse salt, either kosher or sea. I like the way it feels when I take a pinch, and coarse salt crystals dissolve more slowly than fine salt, giving you a bolder flavor. Kosher salt is prized for its

FIVE GRILL UTENSILS YOU CAN'T LIVE WITHOUT

1 A long-handled, stiff wire grill brush. Essential for cleaning grates. Look for a sturdy handle. I'm partial to the jumbo grill brushes you find at restaurant supply houses, but the home-size variety are available just about everywhere.

2 A pair of long-handled tongs with a spring-loaded hinge. Use these for turning food, adding wood chips, and generally poking the fire. The handles should not only be long, to keep you away from the heat, but they should also be stiff enough that you can pick up a whole chicken without their buckling. The spring-loaded kind gives you an extra-firm grip; you'll find these at restaurant supply houses.

3 A grill spatula. Good for turning tofu and prying fish fillets off the grill if they start to stick.

4 A long-handled basting brush. Essential for basting meats to keep them moist. Choose a brush with natural bristles, not synthetic ones, which can melt.

5 An instant-read meat thermometer. Essential for gauging the doneness of briskets, pork shoulders, and turkeys, among other things (for more about testing for doneness, see the opposite page). These thermometers are available in any cookware shop.

purity; sea salt for the trace elements from seawater.

Pepper: Most pit masters use commercially ground black pepper. When a recipe calls simply for black pepper, this is what to use. In many dishes, however, I prefer freshly ground black pepper. This does not necessarily mean having to wrap your sticky hands around a peppercorn grinder every time a recipe calls for freshly ground black pepper. What I do is grind a handful of black peppercorns in a spice mill or coffee grinder once a week and store the resulting powder in a sealed jar. This gives you the fresh-ground flavor with take-a-pinch convenience.

Brown sugar: Brown sugar comes both light and dark—dark contains more molasses than light does. It has a richer, earthier flavor. Nonetheless, the difference is not so pronounced that if you have light brown sugar on hand and you only need one to three tablespoons, you should run out and buy dark brown sugar. However, when large quantities are called for, use the kind that is specified.

Molasses: You'll find molasses comes in both sulfured and unsulfured versions. The sulfered has a slightly stronger flavor, but they can be used interchangeably.

Fresh herbs: I call for fresh herbs throughout the book. In general, if you don't have the one the recipe specifies, you're better off substituting one fresh herb for another

SEVEN GRILLING ACCESSORIES THAT DEFINITELY IMPROVE PERFORMANCE

1 A grill mop. Use it for applying cider, bourbon, beer, and mop sauces.

2 A rib rack. This is a stiff wire rack designed to hold baby back ribs and spareribs vertically, so you can grill four to six racks in the space that would normally hold only two.

3 A vegetable grate. A flat wire or perforated metal plate you place on top of the grill grate to cook fish fillets, shrimp, sliced or diced vegetables, and other delicate or small foods that might stick to or fall through the grate.

4 A fish basket. This is a hinged wire basket designed for holding whole fish or fish fillets while they grill. The beauty of the fish basket is that you turn the basket over with the fish inside it, so the fish never sticks to the grate. You can also buy square or rectangular baskets for grilling burgers and vegetables.

5 A mister or spray bottle. Useful for two things: You can use a mister or spray bottle filled with water to control flare-ups (you can also use a water pistol for this; for more about flare-up control, see page 26). Filled with vinegar or apple cider, misters and spray bottles are good for basting pork shoulders and ribs.

6 A "pig tail." A metal rod with a curled hook at one end and a wooden handle at the other, a "pig tail" is for lifting pork shoulders, ribs, and other foods that are hard to grab with tongs. It will also make you look (and feel) like a Texas pit master.

7 A beer-can chicken roaster. Grilled chicken on top of a beer can is one of the hottest dishes on the barbecue circuit (for a recipe see page 369). Several companies manufacture devices that facilitate the cooking process by holding a can upright so it doesn't tip.

rather than the dried herb for the fresh.

Tomatoes: Tomatoes should be red, fragrant, and so ripe they go splat if you drop them on the floor. Never buy a refrigerated tomato, if you can help it, and never refrigerate tomatoes—you'll kill the flavor and juicy texture.

Liquid smoke: Yes, liquid smoke is a natural product. It's made by dissolving real wood smoke in water.

SEASONING MEAT

You've chosen your grill, you know how to set it up, and you've decided on the most appropriate method for the meat you plan to cook. Before you put anything on to cook, let's talk a bit about seasonings. Grilling is inherently a flavor-enhancing cooking method. Add a whiff of wood smoke and the taste increases exponentially. This is why many pit masters use little more in the way of seasoning than salt and pepper, letting wood smoke and time do the work. Nonetheless, most grill jockeys like to use rubs, marinades, bastes, mop sauces, and barbecue sauces to boost the flavor even more.

A rub is a dry mixture of spices and/or herbs that is sprinkled on meat prior to grilling or smoking. The quintessential American barbecue rub contains salt, pepper, paprika, and brown sugar. A rub can be used in two ways: as a seasoning or as a cure. To use one as a seasoning, you sprinkle it over meat, then rub it on with your fingertips (that's why it's called a rub) and grill or smoke the food straightaway. You may want to wear rubber gloves when you do this to keep your hands clean or if you have sensitive skin. To use a rub as a cure, apply it at least four hours ahead so it can flavor the meat more intensely.

Marinades are wet seasonings, and as such, are particularly useful for flavoring foods, such as chicken breasts or fish fillets, that tend to dry out. Most marinades contain some sort of fat (olive oil or coconut milk, for example), an acid element (such as lime juice or vinegar), and a range of aromatic flavorings that can include onions, garlic, ginger, chile peppers, spices, and/or fresh herbs. Larger foods take longer to marinate than

smaller ones—I might marinate a brisket or leg of lamb overnight, but a chicken breast or shrimp will take only one to two hours.

TIP: Never use an uncooked marinade for basting, especially if it was used on raw chicken or pork. If you want to use a marinade to baste, boil it for three minutes first to kill any bacteria.

Bastes and mop sauces are applied while food cooks to keep it moist and add flavor. Bastes are typically based on some sort of fat—olive or vegetable oil, melted butter, or coconut milk—and are applied with a basting brush. Mop sauces are thin liquids and often contain vinegar, wine, beer, or even coffee. These are swabbed on meats. While bastes are mostly used when grilling small cuts of meat or seafood, mop sauces are generally applied to larger, slow-cooking foods, like briskets or ribs.

As for barbecue sauces, these are thick and more complex condiments, frequently containing some kind of sweetener. Barbecue sauces should almost always be applied at the end of grilling or even after the food is done to keep the sugar in the sauce from burning. I personally prefer to serve barbecue sauces on the side, so as not to mask the smoke and fire flavors from the grill.

Spotlight on the pit: where **barbacoas** *(Tex-Mex cow's heads) are roasted underground.*

TYPE	FUEL	DESCRIPTION	BEST SUITED FOR

Charcoal Grills

TYPE	FUEL	DESCRIPTION	BEST SUITED FOR
KETTLE GRILL	**Charcoal or wood chunks**	One of the most perfect grilling devices ever created. Consists of a bowl-shaped metal firebox with a domed lid. Vent holes on the top and bottom allow for heat control.	Everything: direct and indirect grilling; smoking; rotisserie grilling.
FRONT-LOADING GRILL	**Charcoal or wood chunks or logs**	A large metal box on legs, with a door in the front through which you add fuel. The beauty of this grill is that it can burn either charcoal or wood, and since it loads from the front, you can restoke it easily without having to lift the grate.	Direct and indirect grilling; smoking.
WOOD-BURNING GRILL	**Wood or charcoal**	Modeled on the wood-burning grills found in restaurants, this type of grill is typically open in the front, with two shelves or platforms: one to hold the fire; the other a grate for the food.	Great for direct grilling over wood or charcoal.
HIBACHI	**Charcoal**	The traditional grill of Japan, the hibachi consists of a small, deep rectangular or oval box, frequently with grates you can raise or lower. In many models heat is controlled by opening a vent on the bottom.	Grilling small or thin foods, like satés and kebabs, using the direct method. I also like to use hibachis to keep food warm.
CERAMIC OR KAMADO COOKER	**Charcoal**	Looks like a giant, heavy ceramic egg. Once a charcoal fire is built in the bottom, the heavy ceramic firebox and dome absorb and radiate the heat throughout, guaranteeing even, moist cooking—a combination of the best of direct and indirect grilling.	Great for turkeys, chicken, pork shoulders, tandoori, and steaks and chops.
TABLE GRILL	**Charcoal or gas**	Consists of a large flat metal tray or shallow box mounted on legs, with an adjustable grate and optional rotisserie attachment. Mostly available from party supply rental houses.	Use only for direct grilling or spit roasting for large numbers of people.

Grill
and Smoker Types

TYPE	FUEL	DESCRIPTION	BEST SUITED FOR

Gas Grills

TYPE	FUEL	DESCRIPTION	BEST SUITED FOR
BASIC GAS GRILL	**Propane**	Available with one to three burner zones. To grill using the indirect method, you need at least two burners.	Great for just about everything but smoking.
GAS SUPERGRILL	**Propane or natural gas**	Has anywhere from three to eight burners; a rotisserie with its own burner; a smoker box with a dedicated burner; and one or more side burners. Many models are designed for a natural gas hook-up and some even burn charcoal and/or wood in addition to gas.	Great for just about everything.

Smokers

TYPE	FUEL	DESCRIPTION	BEST SUITED FOR
OFFSET BARREL SMOKER	**Charcoal or wood**	Modeled on the rigs used by professional and competition pit masters, it consists of a barrel- or box-shaped smoke chamber that runs either horizontally or vertically, with a separate offset firebox for the fire.	Great for brisket, pork shoulders, ribs, rib roasts, and whole turkeys and hogs.
WATER SMOKER	**Charcoal or electricity**	A vertical cylindrical smoker with a charcoal pan or electric heating unit at the bottom, a water pan in the center, and cooking racks at the top. To use it, you fill the water pan with water, beer, cider, or another liquid, which keeps the food moist as it smokes.	Great for turkey, pork shoulders, briskets, and ribs.
COMPETITION OR COMMERCIAL-SIZE SMOKER	**Charcoal and wood, or sometimes gas**	These are the big rigs you see being towed to barbecue contests behind pickup trucks. The smallest are fashioned from furnace oil tanks; the largest can be the size of a garage. Most rigs are built like oversize offset barrel smokers (see above). Some commercial models have multiple revolving shelves to help meat smoke evenly.	Traditional American barbecue, including large quantities of brisket, pork shoulders, ribs, and of course, whole hogs.

Pseudogrills

TYPE	FUEL	DESCRIPTION	BEST SUITED FOR
ELECTRIC GRILL	**Electricity**	Actually an inverted broiler. No live fire, but electric grills are useful for condominium and apartment dwellers.	Thin or small pieces of food normally grilled using the direct method.
GRILL PAN AND FORMAN-STYLE CONTACT GRILLS	**Gas or electricity**	The ridged cook surface of a grill pan or contact grill produces the attractive grill marks associated with outdoor grills. Again, no live fire cooking, but useful for condominium and apartment dwellers.	Thin or small pieces of food normally grilled using the direct method; also great for toasting sandwiches.

W hen I was growing up, barbecue meant the main course. Today, we grill everything, and I mean everything, from appetizers to desserts. People naturally gravitate around a grill—what better staging area for dishing up appetizers? This chapter focuses on grilled starters, literally from soup to nuts. Soup? How about grilled, chilled, dilled tomato soup? Nuts? Barbecued peanuts coming up! In between you'll find just about every imaginable rumaki, salsa, dip, kebab, saté, and *anticucho*—in short, grilled appetizers of every persuasion, for every appetite, from all across the United States. At the end of the chapter you'll find a tempting assortment of unusual drinks—both alcoholic and non—to slake your thirst. So fire up your grill and let the party begin.

Fiery Start

TIPS

Not sure where to buy shelled uncooked peanuts? A trip to your local natural foods store should do the trick.

Louisville, Ky.

BARBECUED PEANUTS

Any diehard smoke meister aspires to cook every food imaginable on a smoker or grill. Steve Bowles of Louisville, Kentucky, is no exception. A committed pit boss (his wife thinks he should be committed, period), Bowles has figured out how to cook just about everything on his unusual double-barreled smoker—even nuts. He marinates peanuts in a mixture of hot sauce and melted butter and slow smokes them over hickory. If you like your nuts salty, smoky, and spicy, this recipe is for you. I can't think of a better snack to serve with beer.

METHOD:
Indirect grilling

ADVANCE PREPARATION:
30 minutes to 1 hour for marinating the peanuts

INGREDIENTS:
4 cups shelled but uncooked peanuts
⅓ cup salted butter, melted
⅓ cup Tabasco sauce or your favorite hot sauce
1 tablespoon of your favorite barbecue rub (I like the Cold Mountain Rub on page 701)

Coarse salt (kosher or sea) and freshly ground black pepper

YOU'LL ALSO NEED:
1 or 2 large aluminum foil pans; 2 cups wood chips or chunks (preferably hickory), soaked for 1 hour in water to cover, then drained

1 Place the peanuts, butter, hot sauce, and rub in a mixing bowl and toss to mix. Season with salt and pepper to taste. Let the nuts marinate for 30 minutes to 1 hour, stirring them several times so that they marinate evenly.

2 Spread out the peanuts over the bottom of the aluminum foil pan(s). Ideally the nuts will be in a single layer, but it's not the end of the world if they're not.

3 Set up the grill for indirect grilling (see page 23 for gas or page 22 for charcoal) and preheat to medium. If using a gas grill, place all of the wood chips or chunks in the smoker box or in a smoker pouch (see page 24) and run the grill on high until you see smoke, then reduce the heat to medium. If using a charcoal grill, preheat it to medium, then toss all of the wood chips or chunks on the coals.

4 When ready to cook, place the pan(s) with the peanuts in the center of the hot grate, away from the heat, and cover the grill. Cook the peanuts until toasted and golden brown, 20 to 30 minutes, turning them from time to time with a spatula so they roast evenly. Let the grilled nuts cool to room temperature (if you can wait that long), then transfer them to a bowl for serving. In the unlikely case you have any peanuts left over, once cool they can be stored in an airtight container at room temperature for 2 to 3 days.

YIELD:

Makes 4 cups

Memphis, Tenn.

BARBECUE POPCORN

To say that the citizens of Memphis are obsessed with barbecue would be a little like observing that the Mississippi River has water in it. They eat it in every imaginable form, barbecuing anything from ribs to pork shoulders, from game hens to bologna; they stuff it into sandwiches, pile it on pizzas, and put it in spaghetti. Even popcorn comes seasoned with barbecue rub—a specialty at the legendary Rendezvous restaurant in downtown Memphis, where it makes for pleasant munching while you wait for your table

(for more about the Rendezvous see page 36). Serve the popcorn as a snack on Super Bowl Sunday or while your guests wait for more substantial fare to come off the grill.

INGREDIENTS:

About 3 tablespoons vegetable oil

¼ cup popcorn kernels

2 tablespoons unsalted butter

2 tablespoons Memphis Dry Rub (page 298), or your favorite commercial brand, or more to taste

1 Place enough oil in a large deep saucepan to form a ⅛-inch-deep layer and place over medium-high heat. Heat the oil until it ripples, about 2 minutes.

2 Add the popcorn, tightly cover the saucepan, and cook, gently shaking the pan, until you hear the first pop. Increase the heat to high and continue popping the corn until all is popped (the noise will stop), 2 to 4 minutes, gently shaking the saucepan to ensure even popping. Transfer the popcorn to a serving bowl.

3 Add the butter to the hot saucepan to melt it. Drizzle it in a thin stream over the popcorn, stirring it with a wooden spoon. Sprinkle the rub over the popcorn, stirring to mix. Taste for seasoning, adding more rub as necessary. Serve at once.

YIELD:

Makes about 6 cups

TIPS

I call for oil-popped popcorn, but you could certainly pop the corn in a hot air popper. Follow the manufacturer's instructions for popping the corn and then add the melted butter and rub as described in Step 3. You can also make microwave popcorn and sprinkle it with the rub; you probably won't need to add melted butter in this case, as most brands come flavored with butter.

CHARLIE VERGOS RENDEZVOUS

And the Birth of the "Dry" Rib

CHARLIE VERGOS RENDEZVOUS

52 South Second Street
Memphis, Tennessee
(901) 523-2746
www.hogsfly.com

Whenever I go to Memphis I have a little ritual. I check into the Peabody Hotel, then duck down a dumpster-filled back alley, and rush to Charlie Vergos Rendezvous. This rambling basement barbecue joint is almost as hard to locate as it is idiosyncratic in its schedule (it's closed Sunday and Monday, and the restaurant serves lunch only two days a week). But it should certainly be on the National Registry of Historic Places, for the Rendezvous is the birthplace of the Memphis dry rib.

The Vergos family immigrated from Greece in the early 1900s. Charlie's father, John, tried his hand at many trades: bootblacking, running pool halls, even coal mining in West Virginia. Eventually, he moved his family to Memphis, where he opened a hot dog stand on Beale Street. By 1945, Vergos Sr. was famous for his foot long hot dogs, which he served with a pugnacious mustard coleslaw; they cost a nickel. Equally legendary were Vergos's homemade pies.

Charlie Vergos followed in his father's footsteps, eventually opening a sandwich shop in a basement. The menu was standard for the 1940s: sliced sausage and cheese, ham and cheese sandwiches, pickles, peppers, and beer. To distinguish his sandwiches from the stuff served at dozens of other Memphis lunch counters, Charlie smoked his hams and chickens in a pit fitted into a coal chute. Business boomed: Soon Vergos was selling two hundred sandwiches a day.

One day, Charlie's meat salesman brought him a case of ribs. Inspired by an old barbecue joint run by Johnny Mills, a Memphis legend, Charlie seasoned the ribs with the Greek American spices he grew up on—oregano, garlic, salt, and pepper—plus a dose of a uniquely American seasoning, chili powder. "Tastes great, but looks awful," declared the meat salesman. "Barbecue should be red." So Charlie added paprika, and the modern dry rib seasoning was born.

RIBS ON THE RISE

Charlie started cooking a case of ribs every week, then every two or three days. Gradually the ribs sales came to surpass those of the ham and cheese sandwiches.

Charlie Vergos, the man who put the Memphis rib on the map.

Today, the Rendezvous dishes up something on the order of four tons of ribs a week. It still serves the fiery mustard slaw, and in homage to the old days, the house appetizer is a plate of sliced sausage, pickles, and cheddar cheese.

Over the years, the restaurant has grown from seventy seats to seven hundred. Vergos, and his sons John and Nick and daughter Tina Jennings, who now run the business, have spent a lifetime filling the subterranean dining room with every imaginable knickknack and antique—Indian arrowheads, Revolutionary War swords, Civil War muskets, vintage whiskey bottles, smoke-blackened kettles and cowbells, old wooden ship models—some of them priceless, some of them junk, all heaped in a hodgepodge. The floors have worn tiles; the tables sport red-and-white checked tablecloths; and on a typical night, you might wait a half hour or so for a seat.

The focal point of the restaurant is the open kitchen with its smoke-blackened pits. Some of the cooks, like Bobby Ellis, have worked there for more than thirty years, tossing ribs on a grate about eighteen inches above a bed of blazing charcoal and grilling them for about thirty minutes on each side. "Our fuel is Royal Oak one hundred percent hardwood charcoal," explains Nick Vergos. "We start the ribs bone side down to protect the meat." Once cooked, the charred, sizzling ribs are slapped on a cutting board, mopped with a mixture of vinegar, water, salt, and barbecue spices, then thickly sprinkled with Rendezvous seasoning ("We say seasoning, not rub, because it's sprinkled on, not rubbed in," explains John Vergos.) The ribs are served under a thick crust of spice, with nary a slather or dollop of barbecue sauce. The formula for the seasoning is, of course, a closely guarded secret, but you'll find my approximation of the recipe on page 298.

IS IT TRUE 'QUE?

The Rendezvous' dry ribs are the most famous barbecue in Memphis. But are they true barbecue? The ribs are cooked over charcoal, not wood, so there isn't any smoke flavor. The cooking process is direct grilling, not indirect grilling or smoking. Forget about the low pit temperatures of competition pit masters—these ribs cook in a virtual blast furnace. They're not rubbed or seasoned ahead of time, nor mopped during the cooking. "The fact is, we use the fastest method we can simply to be able to cook the eight hundred racks of ribs we serve nightly," Nick says.

But such fine points are not debated by the 3,600 customers who dine here on a typical Saturday night. No, for most people—locals and tourists alike—the Rendezvous' dry ribs are the very essence of Memphis barbecue.

For most people the Rendezvous' dry ribs are the very essence of Memphis barbecue.

Birmingham, Ala.

SMOKY DEVILED EGGS

INGREDIENTS:

12 large eggs (see Notes)

6 ounces smoked chicken or turkey,
cut into ½-inch dice

4 tablespoons mayonnaise,
or more if necessary

2 tablespoons Dijon mustard

1 tablespoon Worcestershire sauce

1 to 3 teaspoons Tabasco sauce

1 drop liquid smoke (optional)

Coarse salt (kosher or sea) and
freshly ground black pepper

Sweet or hot paprika, for serving

12 pitted black olives, cut in half
lengthwise, for serving

YOU'LL ALSO NEED:

Pastry bag with a large (½- to ¾-inch)
open star tip (optional;
see Notes)

WALL OF FLAME

MISS MYRA'S PIT BAR-B-Q

If you've never had northern Alabama smoked chicken with white barbecue sauce, this is a great place to try it. Save room for a slice of made-from-scratch pie. No, save room for two—the chocolate chess and the coconut.

3278 Cahaba Heights Rd. Cahaba Heights, Alabama (205) 967-6004

Barbecue is a guy thing, right? Rennae Wheat would beg to disagree. Wheat is the pit mistress of a smoky down-home barbecue joint called Miss Myra's Pit Bar-B-Q in Birmingham, Alabama. And until you've tasted Miss Myra's smoky pulled pork shoulder (lovingly shredded by hand) or her smoked chicken with white barbecue sauce, you haven't fully lived. That chicken is the inspiration for the appetizer here—deviled eggs stuffed with barbecued chicken. While Rennae doesn't actually put smoked chicken in the deviled eggs served at Miss Myra's, I suspect she'd be amenable to the idea—or at least to the results.

1 HARD COOK THE EGGS: Place the eggs in a large pot and add cold water to cover by 2 inches. Gradually bring to a boil over medium heat. Let the eggs boil for exactly 11 minutes (at sea level; you'll need to cook them longer at high altitudes). Pour off the boiling water and fill the pot with cold water, letting the water run until the

eggs are cool enough to handle. Tap the end of an egg on a work surface to crack the shell, then shell it under cold running water. Repeat with the remaining eggs. Let the eggs cool to room temperature. These may seem like rather involved instructions to make simple hard-cooked eggs, but it's the best way I know to cook an egg through without winding up with an ugly green ring around the yolk.

2 Cut a thin (⅛-inch) slice off the top and bottom of each egg (this will help the egg halves stand upright). Cut each egg in half crosswise. Scoop out the yolks with a spoon.

3 Place the smoked chicken in a food processor and process until finely ground. Add the egg yolks and process until a paste forms. Add the mayonnaise, mustard, Worcestershire and Tabasco sauces, and liquid smoke, if using, and pulse a few times quickly to mix; you want a thick but spreadable paste the consistency of soft ice cream. If the chicken mixture is too dry, which it probably will not be, add a little more mayonnaise. Season with salt and pepper to taste; the mixture should be highly seasoned.

4 Using a spoon or a pastry bag fitted with an open star tip, stuff or pipe the chicken mixture into the upright egg halves. Sprinkle each with paprika and garnish each with an olive half.

YIELD:
Makes 24 egg halves

NOTES:

■ For hard-cooked eggs that are easy to peel, use eggs that are at least a week old.

■ A pastry bag is a device used to pipe decorative swirls of icing or filling. The bag itself is a cone-shaped pouch with a tapered metal decorating tip that fits into the narrow end. An open star decorating tip has a toothed end that forms attractive swirls when you pipe the filling mixture through it into the egg. So *that's* how they get that cool rippled look!

Virginia

PROSCIUTTO-WRAPPED PEACHES
With Balsamic Vinegar Drizzle

Chris Schlesinger is one of the founding fathers of contemporary American grilling. The Virginia-born chef lit our collective fires when he opened the perennially popular East Coast Grill in Cambridge, Massachusetts (for more about the East Coast Grill see page 42). Not long ago, I invited Chris to be

TIPS

■ I'm not saying you need to smoke a chicken from scratch to prepare these deviled eggs (but don't let me stop you if you feel so inclined). Any smoked chicken will do—even one you buy at the supermarket.

■ Deviled eggs are usually sliced lengthwise before stuffing, but I like the ease of eating eggs that have been cut in half crosswise.

Use ripe, fragrant
peaches for this
recipe, but choose
fruit that's still
on the firm side.
Look for freestone
peaches—it's easier
to remove the pits
from these than
from clingstone
peaches.

a guest lecturer at Barbecue
University at The Greenbrier resort in
West Virginia, and he obliged the
class with an unusual appetizer of
peaches wrapped with prosciutto
and grilled. The dish plays to every
taste bud on your tongue with the
brassy sweetness of the peaches,
the salty tang of the prosciutto, the
syrupy tartness of the balsamic drizzle, and the bite of cracked black
peppercorns. Rarely does so little
effort reward you with so much
mouth-filling flavor.

METHOD:
Direct grilling

FOR THE BALSAMIC DRIZZLE:
1 cup balsamic vinegar
1 tablespoon sugar
**1 tablespoon freshly cracked
    black peppercorns**

FOR THE PEACHES:
4 ripe but firm peaches
**12 paper-thin slices prosciutto,
    cut in half lengthwise**
2 to 3 tablespoons extra-virgin olive oil
**Coarse salt (kosher or sea) and
    freshly ground black pepper**

YOU'LL ALSO NEED:
**24 small (6-inch) bamboo skewers
    (see Note); heavy-duty aluminum foil**

*The East
Coast Grill and
Raw Bar
launched a
grilling
revolution.*

1 MAKE THE BALSAMIC DRIZZLE: Place the vinegar and sugar in a small heavy nonreactive saucepan over medium-high heat. Bring to a boil and let boil until reduced by half, stirring occasionally, 15 to 20 minutes. Stir in the peppercorns and remove the pan from the heat. Stored in a sealed jar, the drizzle will keep for several months.

2 PREPARE THE PEACHES: Rinse the peaches under cold running water and blot dry with paper towels. Cut each in half along the crease and twist the halves in opposite directions to separate them. Using a spoon, remove and discard the pit from each. Cut each peach half into 3 wedges. Wrap each wedge with a piece of prosciutto, securing it with a skewer. Lightly brush the wrapped peach wedges with olive oil and season lightly with salt and pepper.

3 Set up the grill for direct grilling (see page 21 for charcoal or gas) and preheat to medium-high.

4 When ready to cook, brush and oil the grill grate. Tear off a piece of heavy-duty aluminum foil that is roughly as long as the grill is wide. Fold the piece of aluminum foil in half lengthwise. Place the folded aluminum foil flat on the grate at the edge closest to you. Arrange the skewered peaches on the grate so that they are over the fire but the exposed ends of the skewers are on top of the foil

Grill master
Chris Schlesinger.

shield to keep them from burning. Depending upon the size of the grill, you may need to cook the peaches in batches. Grill the peaches until sizzling and lightly browned, 2 to 3 minutes per side. Transfer the grilled peaches to a platter and drizzle the balsamic mixture over them. Serve at once.

YIELD:

Makes 24 peach wedges

NOTE: You can also use wooden toothpicks to secure the prosciutto to the peach wedges, in which case you won't need an aluminum foil shield. Remove and discard the toothpicks before serving the peaches or at least warn your guests about them.

EAST COAST GRILL AND RAW BAR

They're lined up on the sidewalk in Inman Square in Cambridge, Massachusetts— girls in black Lycra, guys with goatees—card-carrying members of the Cambridge "hip-oisie," who are waiting for a seat at the perennially packed East Coast Grill and Raw Bar, exactly as they have since the storefront restaurant opened in a former diner in 1985. Some of the outfits may have changed; what hasn't are the big, silly drinks with giraffe swizzle sticks and the belt-loosening portions of tongue-blastingly flavorful food cooked before your eyes amid leaping flames on an oak-burning, open brick grill.

Listen up. There's history here, for the East Coast Grill almost single-handedly launched the modern age of grilling in the United States. Blame it on a bad case of attention deficit disorder or just an excess of plain common sense, but when East Coast Grill founder Chris Schlesinger attended the Culinary Institute of America back in the 1970s, he found lengthily simmered stocks and butter-and-cream sodden sauces much less to his liking than the explosively flavorful grilled fare he ate at beach shacks in Barbados and Hawaii during a

EAST COAST GRILL AND RAW BAR

1271 Cambridge Street
Cambridge, Massachusetts
(617) 491-6568
www.eastcoastgrill.net

tour of the world's best surfing spots. Armed with a knowledge of smoke and fire from growing up in Virginia, he resolved to open a restaurant that would make live fire cooking its raison d'être. Almost two decades later, the East Coast Grill, with its wood-burning grill, is still packing them in. And Chris has gone on to write a half-dozen books on barbecuing, grilling, and big-flavored foods, including the landmark *The Thrill of the Grill*, which won the James Beard cookbook award.

Now, as then, thick slabs of flame-seared, sushi-quality tuna remain a house specialty, as

do smoky Memphis-style ribs, North Carolina pulled pork shoulder, and grilled mahimahi with pineapple salsa. The East Coast Grill has the dubious distinction of having served the world's hottest pasta dish (appropriately dubbed "from hell")—invented to punish an obnoxious customer and sauced with Chris's infamous Scotch bonnet–based "Old Skool Real Inner Beauty Hot Sauce." Chris's wry sense of humor is apparent in the East Coast Grill's Lava Lounge, where you can feast on a New Age *pupu* platter while sitting next to an exploding volcano, complete with light and sound effects.

Coachella Valley, Calif.

BACON-GRILLED DATES

Y ou may think of dates as a Middle Eastern specialty, but about thirty-five million pounds are grown each year in southeast California near the Colorado River. That set me thinking about an almond-stuffed date appetizer you could wrap in bacon and sizzle on the grill. The sweet, salty contrast of fruit, bacon, and nuts is an irresistible combination, especially when the almonds are smoked. You could substitute nut-size pieces of cream cheese, goat cheese, Gorgonzola, or Roquefort for the almonds, or if you're in a hurry, skip the stuffing and just wrap the dates with bacon.

METHOD:
Direct grilling

INGREDIENTS:
24 pitted dates
24 smoked or toasted almonds (page 584)
8 slices bacon, or more as needed

YOU'LL ALSO NEED:
24 small (6-inch) bamboo skewers;
    heavy-duty aluminum foil

1 Stuff each date with an almond. Gently pull on the ends of each strip of bacon to stretch it, then cut it crosswise into thirds (each piece should be just large enough to wrap around a date). Wrap each stuffed date with a piece of bacon, securing it crosswise on the end of a skewer. The recipe can be prepared up to 8 hours ahead to this stage; cover the bacon-wrapped dates with plastic wrap and refrigerate.

2 Set up the grill for direct grilling using a three-zone fire (see page 21 for charcoal or gas) and preheat one zone to high and one zone to medium; leave the third zone unlit.

3 When ready to cook, brush and oil the grill grate. Tear off a piece of heavy-duty aluminum foil that is roughly as long as the grill is wide. Fold the piece of aluminum foil in half lengthwise. Place the folded aluminum foil flat on the grate at the edge closest to you so that it covers part of each heat zone. Arrange the skewered dates on the grate so that they are over the high zone but the exposed ends of the skewers are on top of the foil shield to keep them from burning. Depending upon the size of the grill, you may need to cook the dates in batches. Grill the dates until they are heated through and the bacon is crisp, 2 to 3 minutes per side. Be ready to move the dates to the medium or cool zone of the grill should the dripping bacon fat cause flare-ups. Transfer the grilled dates to a platter and serve immediately.

YIELD:
Makes 24 grilled dates

VARIATION: Prunes wrapped in bacon or prosciutto and grilled make an equally tasty appetizer.

TIPS

You can also use wooden toothpicks to secure the bacon to the dates, in which case you won't need an aluminum foil shield. Remove and discard the toothpicks before serving the dates or at least warn your guests about them.

TIPS

■ Because dripping pancetta fat is so flammable, I suggest grilling over a three-zone fire. Sear the apricots over the hot part of the fire, then move them to the cooler part to finish grilling. If you start to get flare-ups, you can move the apricots to the unlit section of the grill. This is the best way to avoid the sooty taste that often results when you grill bacon.

■ Cabrales (Spanish blue cheese) is available at cheese shops and gourmet markets.

Seattle, Wash.

PANCETTA-GRILLED APRICOTS With Spanish Cheese

The name of Tamara Murphy's restaurant—Brasa—tells you everything. *Brasa* is the Portuguese word for live coals, and Murphy has made a wood-burning oven and grill the focal points of her popular Belltown, Seattle, restaurant. This recipe attests to the love in the Pacific Northwest of locally grown fruits and berries and, in particular, the penchant for pairing fruit with strong, salty flavors.

Murphy contrasts the sweet, brassy flavor of Yakima Valley apricots with the salty tang of pancetta (Italian bacon) and Cabrales (Spanish blue cheese). If you're looking for an hors d'oeuvre or appetizer that roars with flavor and is definitely not run-of-the-mill, these bacon and cheese grilled apricots are your ticket. By the way, the sugar is my own addition to the recipe—I like the transition it provides between the sweetness of the fruit and the salt in the cheese. Try it my way first; if you prefer the dish less sweet, leave the sugar out.

METHOD:
Direct grilling

INGREDIENTS:
6 large ripe apricots (1½ to 2 inches in diameter)
¼ cup firmly packed light brown sugar, spread out in a shallow bowl
3 ounces Cabrales cheese, cut into pieces about ¼ by 2 by 2 inches
Freshly ground black pepper
12 thin slices (7 to 8 ounces total) pancetta (Italian bacon)

YOU'LL ALSO NEED:
12 small (6-inch) bamboo skewers (see Note); heavy-duty aluminum foil

1 Rinse the apricots under cold running water and blot dry with paper towels. Cut each in half along the crease and twist the halves in opposite directions to separate them. Remove and discard the pit from each. Dip the cut side of each apricot half in the brown sugar to lightly coat it. Place a slice of cheese on top of the cut side, then season with pepper. Wrap each apricot half with a slice of pancetta, securing it with a skewer inserted parallel to the cut edge. Trim off any cheese not covered by the pancetta. The recipe can be prepared up to 4 hours ahead to this stage; cover the stuffed apricots with plastic wrap and refrigerate.

2 Set up the grill for direct grilling using a three-zone fire (see page 21 for charcoal or gas) and preheat one zone to high and one zone to medium; leave the third zone unlit.

3 When ready to cook, brush and oil the grill grate. Tear off a piece of heavy-duty aluminum foil that is roughly as long as the grill is wide. Fold the piece of aluminum foil in half lengthwise. Place the folded aluminum foil flat on the grate at the edge closest to you so that it covers part of each heat zone. Place the skewered apricots on the grate so that they are over the high zone but the exposed ends of the skewers are on top of the foil shield. Depending upon the size of the grill, you may need to cook the apricots in batches. Grill the apricots until the pancetta is nicely browned and the cheese is soft and sizzling, 2 to 4 minutes per side. Be ready to move the apricots to the medium or cool zone of the grill should the dripping fat from the pancetta cause flare-ups. Transfer the grilled apricots to a platter and serve at once.

YIELD:
Makes 12 apricot halves

NOTE: You can also use wooden toothpicks to secure the pancetta to the apricot halves, in which case you won't need an aluminum foil shield. Remove and discard the toothpicks before serving the apricots or at least warn your guests about them.

VARIATION: You could substitute Gorgonzola or Roquefort for the Cabrales and bacon for the pancetta. Or replace the apricots with peach or nectarine halves.

Oakland, Calif.

TRADITIONAL RUMAKI
(Bacon, Chicken Liver, and Water Chestnut Kebabs)

Food, like fashion, has fads that come and go. Consider rumaki, a classic of the flamboyant Polynesian restaurant era, which began with Trader Vic's in Oakland, California, in the 1930s. It's probably been a while since you've tasted these crisp, smoky kebabs of chicken livers, water chestnuts, and bacon—indeed, if you were born after 1970, you've probably never tasted them at all. I say it's high time to resurrect a dish that's an American icon. Rumaki is just one more reason to love chicken livers.

METHOD:
Direct grilling

ADVANCE PREPARATION:
1 hour for marinating the chicken livers

an appetizer that roars with flavor...

TIPS

It's always tricky figuring out how many rumaki to serve. Figure on two to three per person with other hors d'oeuvres or four per person on their own.

INGREDIENTS:

1 pound chicken livers
   (about 16 livers)

½ cup soy sauce

½ cup cream sherry or rice wine

¼ cup firmly packed brown sugar

3 cloves garlic, peeled and gently crushed
   with the side of a cleaver

3 slices peeled fresh ginger (each
   ¼ inch thick), gently crushed
   with the side of a cleaver

2 whole star anise

8 drained peeled canned water chestnuts,
   cut in half lengthwise

8 slices bacon, cut in half crosswise

YOU'LL ALSO NEED:

About 16 small (6-inch) bamboo
   skewers (see Note); heavy-duty
   aluminum foil

1 Trim any sinews or bloody or green spots off the chicken livers. Combine the soy sauce, sherry, brown sugar, garlic, ginger, and star anise in a nonreactive mixing bowl and whisk until the sugar dissolves. Add the chicken livers and let them marinate in the refrigerator, covered, for 1 hour.

2 Using a slotted spoon, remove the chicken livers from the marinade and blot them dry with paper towels. Set the marinade aside. Wrap each chicken liver, along with a water chestnut half, in a piece of bacon, securing it with a skewer.

3 Strain the marinade into a nonreactive saucepan over high heat, let it come to a boil, and boil until thick and syrupy, 3 to 5 minutes.

4 Set up the grill for direct grilling using a three-zone fire (see page 21 for charcoal or gas) and preheat one zone to high and one zone to medium; leave the third zone unlit.

5 When ready to cook, brush and oil the grill grate. Tear off a piece of heavy-duty aluminum foil that is roughly as long as the grill is wide. Fold the piece of aluminum foil in half lengthwise. Place the folded aluminum foil flat on the grate at the edge closest to you so that it covers part of each heat zone. Place the rumaki on the grate so that they are over the high zone but the exposed ends of the skewers are on top of the foil shield. Depending upon the size of the grill, you may need to cook the rumaki in batches. Grill the rumaki until the bacon is crisp and the livers are cooked (I like them pink in the center), 2 to 4 minutes per side, basting them with the boiled marinade. To test for doneness, squeeze a rumaki between your thumb and forefinger; it should be gently yielding, not

Trader Vic's, where Polynesian dining on the American mainland began.

soft and squishy. Or, cut into a rumaki with a paring knife; only the center should be pink. Be ready to move the rumaki to the medium or cool zone of the grill should the dripping bacon fat cause flare-ups.

6 Transfer the grilled rumaki to a platter and serve at once, preferably with a flamboyant Polynesian drink.

YIELD:
Makes about 16 rumaki

NOTE: You can also use wooden toothpicks to secure the bacon to the rumaki, in which case you won't need an aluminum foil shield. Remove and discard the toothpicks before serving the rumaki or at least warn your guests about them.

Hawaii

PINEAPPLE RUMAKI

My enthusiasm for grilled fruit extends well beyond dessert. Dates, prunes, and other fruit wrapped in bacon and popped on the grill make delectably different hors d'oeuvres. The charring and smoke flavors seem to intensify a fruit's sweetness. Case in point: If you've never tasted bacon-grilled pineapple, you're in for a revelation.

METHOD:
Direct grilling

ADVANCE PREPARATION:
1 hour for marinating the pineapple

FOR THE MARINADE:
⅓ cup soy sauce
⅓ cup pineapple juice
2 tablespoons brown sugar, or more to taste
1 tablespoon Asian (dark) sesame oil or vegetable oil
1 tablespoon rice vinegar
1 piece (1 inch) fresh ginger, peeled and finely grated

FOR THE RUMAKI:
1 superripe pineapple, peeled
12 slices bacon, cut crosswise into thirds
36 fresh cilantro sprigs, mint leaves, or any other fresh herb you like

YOU'LL ALSO NEED:
36 small (6-inch) bamboo skewers (see Note); heavy-duty aluminum foil

1 MAKE THE MARINADE: Combine the soy sauce, pineapple juice, brown sugar, sesame oil, vinegar, and ginger in a nonreactive bowl and whisk to mix. Taste for sweetness, adding more brown sugar as necessary.

2 MAKE THE RUMAKI: Using a long sharp knife, cut the pineapple in half lengthwise. Working on one half of the pineapple at a time, remove the core by making 2 cuts into the flesh, angling the knife blade down along the core to

■ When buying a pineapple, look for one with a golden rind; it will be sweet and juicy. You can save the rind and trimmings and toss them on the fire to generate smoke.

■ If you're in a hurry, you can omit the marinade and glaze. Even just with bacon, grilled pineapple is amazingly tasty.

cut out a V-shape wedge the length of the fruit. Repeat with the other half. Discard the pieces of core. Cut each pineapple half crosswise into 6 even slices. Cut each slice into 3 wedges; you will have 36 chunks. Place the pineapple in the bowl with the marinade, stir, and let it marinate for 1 hour.

3 Drain the marinade off the pineapple and strain it into a heavy saucepan. Place over high heat, bring to a boil, and let boil until syrupy, about 5 minutes. Set this mixture aside; you'll use it as a glaze.

4 Wrap each pineapple chunk with a cilantro sprig and then with a piece of bacon. Secure the bacon with a skewer. The recipe can be prepared up to this stage several hours ahead.

5 Set up the grill for direct grilling using a three-zone fire (see page 21 for charcoal or gas) and preheat one zone to high and one zone to medium; leave the third zone unlit.

6 When ready to cook, brush and oil the grill grate. Tear off a piece of heavy-duty aluminum foil that is roughly as long as the grill is wide. Fold the piece of aluminum foil in half lengthwise. Place the folded aluminum foil flat on the grate at the edge closest to you so that it covers part of each heat zone. Place the rumaki on the grate so that they are over the high zone but the exposed ends of the skewers are on top of the foil shield. Depending upon the size of the grill, you may need to cook the rumaki in batches. Grill the rumaki

until the bacon is crisp, 2 to 3 minutes per side, basting with some of the glaze. Be ready to move the rumaki to the medium or cool zone of the grill should the dripping bacon fat cause flare-ups. Transfer the grilled pineapple to a platter (or serve directly off the grill). Drizzle any remaining glaze over the fruit before serving.

YIELD:
Makes about 36 rumaki

NOTE: You can also use wooden toothpicks to secure the bacon to the rumaki, in which case you won't need an aluminum foil shield. Remove and discard the toothpicks before serving the rumaki or at least warn your guests about them.

Miami, Fla.

FOIE GRAS RUMAKI

Foie gras (pronounced fwah-grah) is the exquisitely fatty liver of a specially raised duck or goose and it retails in the neighborhood of $50 per pound. That's the bad news. The good news is that nothing on earth rivals foie gras's buttery richness, ethereal texture, and haunting, delicate taste (despite its origins, there's really nothing livery about it). This foie gras recipe comes from my stepson chef, Jake, who created it for a Friends of James Beard dinner in Miami. The fresh foie gras available in the United States comes from ducks, and because it's so rich, Jake sensibly chooses to grill it wrapped in sliced lean prosciutto instead of bacon.

METHOD:
Direct grilling

ADVANCE PREPARATION:
1 hour for chilling the rumaki

INGREDIENTS:
6 ounces fresh foie gras (see Notes)
Coarse salt (kosher or sea) and
**   freshly ground black pepper**
12 large, paper-thin slices prosciutto
**   (ideally without tears or holes)**
8 drained peeled canned water
**   chestnuts, cut into thirds**

YOU'LL ALSO NEED:
24 small (6-inch) bamboo skewers
**   (see Notes); heavy-duty aluminum foil**

1 Cut the foie gras into slender (about ½-inch) strips about 1½ inches long (you'll have roughly 24 strips). Using tweezers or needle-nose pliers, gently pull out any veins or sinews you may see. Season the foie gras strips with salt and pepper. Cut the prosciutto slices in half crosswise.

2 Place a strip of foie gras on top of a piece of prosciutto, positioning it about 1 inch from the rounded end. Place a piece of water chestnut on top of the foie gras. Fold the rounded end of the prosciutto over the foie gras, then fold in the 2 long sides. Starting at the end with the foie gras, roll up the prosciutto to completely enclose the foie gras. Stick the rumaki crosswise on the end of a bamboo skewer, using it to secure the roll. Repeat with the remaining strips of foie gras, water chestnuts, and prosciutto. Refrigerate the rumaki, covered, for at least 1 hour or as long as 12 hours before grilling.

3 Set up the grill for direct grilling using a three-zone fire (see page 21 for charcoal or gas) and preheat one zone to high and one zone to medium; leave the third zone unlit.

4 When ready to cook, brush and oil the grill grate. Tear off a piece of heavy-duty aluminum foil that is roughly as long as the grill is wide. Fold the piece

Chef Jake, grill master and my stepson.

of aluminum foil in half lengthwise. Place the folded aluminum foil flat on the grate at the edge closest to you so that it covers part of each heat zone. Place the rumaki on the grate so that they are over the high zone but the exposed ends of the skewers are on top of the foil shield. Depending upon the size of the grill, you may need to cook the rumaki in batches. Grill the rumaki until the prosciutto is golden brown and the foie gras is just cooked through, 1 to 2 minutes per side. To test for doneness, squeeze a rumaki between your thumb and forefinger; it will feel soft. Or, cut into a rumaki with a paring knife; it should be just starting to melt. Do not overcook, or the foie gras will turn into liquid. Be ready to move the rumaki to the medium or cool zone of the grill should dripping fat cause flare-ups. Transfer the grilled rumaki to a platter and serve at once.

YIELD:

Makes about 24 rumaki

NOTES:

■ Foie gras is available from specialty food shops or some butchers. You can also order it by mail from Hudson Valley Foie Gras or D'Artagnan (see Mail-Order Sources on page 742). A whole one weighs about 1½ pounds; share the largesse with a friend.

■ You can also use wooden toothpicks to secure the prosciutto around the foie gras, in which case you won't need an aluminum foil shield. Remove and discard the toothpicks before serving the rumaki or at least warn your guests about them.

T I P S

The secret to this recipe is to completely enclose the foie gras in the prosciutto, so it doesn't melt into the fire. The way to do this is to roll the liver in the prosciutto, tucking in the sides, rather like you would to make a blintz or an egg roll.

Ferndale, N.Y.

FOIE GRAS With Figs and Port Sauce

While this may be the most expensive appetizer you ever grill, I promise you it's worth it. It used to be that to enjoy foie gras you had to go to France, or at very least to a high-end restaurant in this country, where it would customarily be served chilled as a terrine or flash seared in a sauté pan. But in some parts of the world, foie gras is grilled, a daring feat attempted by a growing number of grill masters in the United States.

Which brings us, in a roundabout way, to Michael Ginor, the co-proprietor of one of the world's largest foie gras producers, Hudson Valley Foie Gras. Chances are, if you've eaten foie gras in the United States, it came from Ginor's state-of-the-art farm in upstate New York.

So what's so daring about grilling duck liver? Well, it's about 90 percent fat, so if you leave it on the grill for even a minute too long, you wind up with a flaming puddle of duck fat. Try the following recipe when you're feeling flush and can be totally focused on the grill.

METHOD:

Direct grilling

ADVANCE PREPARATION:

20 minutes for soaking the foie gras

INGREDIENTS:

**1 whole foie gras (about 1½ pounds;
     see Note)**

8 to 10 large, ripe, fresh purple figs

**1 cup plus 1 tablespoon port,
     or more if necessary**

½ cup balsamic vinegar

6 tablespoons honey

2 tablespoons red currant jelly or apple jelly

1 cinnamon stick (2 inches long)

1 teaspoon grated lemon zest

**2 teaspoons arrowroot or cornstarch,
     or more if necessary**

2 tablespoons unsalted butter

Freshly ground black pepper

2 tablespoons extra-virgin olive oil

**Coarse salt (kosher or sea) and
     freshly ground coarse black pepper
     or cracked black peppercorns**

1 Soak the foie gras in ice water for 20 minutes, then gently separate the liver into two lobes. Holding it with a dish towel to keep it from slipping, use a sharp knife to cut each lobe the short way and on a diagonal into ½-inch-thick slices. Using tweezers or needle-nose pliers, gently pull out any veins or sinews you may see. Lightly score the foie gras slices on both sides by making Xs with the tip of a knife; the cuts should go no deeper than ⅛ inch (the scoring is purely cosmetic and can be omitted if you're pressed for time). Place the foie gras slices on a plate lined with plastic wrap and refrigerate them, covered, until you're ready to grill.

2 Rinse the figs under cold running water and blot them dry with paper towels. Remove the stems and cut each fig in half lengthwise.

3 Place 1 cup of the port and the vinegar, honey, red currant jelly, cinnamon stick, and lemon zest in a heavy nonreactive saucepan and bring to a boil over high heat. Let boil until syrupy, 6 to 10 minutes. Remove and discard the cinnamon stick. Dissolve the arrowroot in the remaining 1 tablespoon of port. Whisk the arrowroot mixture into the sauce and let boil for 30 seconds; the sauce will thicken slightly. If the sauce fails to thicken sufficiently, dissolve a second teaspoon of arrowroot in another tablespoon of port and add this to the sauce. Remove the saucepan from the heat and stir in the butter. Season the sauce with pepper to taste. Keep the sauce warm until ready to serve.

4 Set up the grill for direct grilling (see page 21 for charcoal or gas) and preheat to high. If using a charcoal grill, light a two-zone fire, preheating one zone to high and the other to medium.

5 When ready to cook, lightly brush the figs with the olive oil and season with salt and pepper. Brush and oil the grill grate. Place the oiled figs on the grate over the hot zone and grill until lightly browned, 2 to 3 minutes per side. Transfer the grilled figs to a platter or plates. If using a gas grill, turn it off.

TIPS

Grilling foie gras is only slightly easier than grilling Jell-O. The problem is that foie gras is almost pure fat. The melting fat bursts into flame the moment it hits the fire. This seems to be more likely to happen when using a gas grill than when using a charcoal one, so I've developed an offbeat technique for gas. I preheat the grill to high, then turn it off just prior to putting on the foie gras. The residual heat cooks the foie gras, while the lack of a flame minimizes the chance of flare-ups.

What's so daring about grilling duck liver?

TIPS

A quick bath in ice water firms up the foie gras so you can handle it easily while slicing. Once you're done, keep it cold until you're ready to grill, then work quickly over a hot fire. And of course have your sauce and figs ready before you start grilling. Serve the foie gras the moment it comes off the fire.

6 Generously season the foie gras with salt and pepper. Arrange the foie gras slices on the hot grate, placing them slightly on a diagonal to the bars. If using a charcoal grill, place the foie gras slices over the hot zone, but be ready to move them to the medium zone of the grill if flare-ups occur. If using a gas grill, let it remain unlit; the residual heat will be sufficient to grill the foie gras. Grill the foie gras until sizzling and browned on both sides, 1 to 2 minutes per side, turning with a spatula. Be careful not to overcook the foie gras or it will simply melt into the fire. Place the grilled foie gras on the platter or plates with the figs and spoon the port sauce over both.

YIELD:

Serves 8 to 10

NOTE: You're probably wondering where to find foie gras. Check a gourmet grocer or butcher, or you can order it by mail from Hudson Valley Foie Gras or D'Artagnan (see Mail-Order Sources, page 742).

Seattle, Wash.

GRILLED BREAD, FIGS & GORGONZOLA

Every year four hundred grill buffs gather under the stars in downtown Seattle for a barbecue fundraiser called Grillfest. Grilling authors from all over the country are invited to strut their stuff, aided by students from local culinary schools. The proceeds from the festival go to a local literacy program, and it's hard to say what's more intoxicating—the aromas coming off the grill, the flowing of Washington State wine, or the notion that something so much fun could actually do the world some good.

Michael Ginor (right), the king of foie gras.

Some years ago, one of the top restaurants in the Pacific Northwest, the Herbfarm, served a grilled appetizer of startling simplicity: a slice of grilled bread slathered with Gorgonzola and topped with a fig and thyme-scented honey. The contrast of the salty tang of the cheese and the sweetness of the honey and fruit is beguiling.

METHOD:
Direct grilling

INGREDIENTS:
¼ cup honey
1 sprig fresh thyme
6 tablespoons extra-virgin olive oil
12 to 14 large fresh figs
8 ounces Gorgonzola cheese,
    at room temperature
1 loaf French bread

1 Combine the honey and thyme with 2 tablespoons of the olive oil in a saucepan and bring to a simmer over medium-low heat. Let simmer gently until fragrant, 4 to 6 minutes. Remove and discard the thyme sprig. The recipe can be prepared several hours ahead to this stage; reheat the honey mixture before serving.

2 Rinse the figs under cold running water and blot them dry with paper towels. Remove the stems and cut each fig in half lengthwise. Place the Gorgonzola in a mixing bowl and beat it with a wooden spoon to soften it.

3 Set up the grill for direct grilling (see page 21 for charcoal or gas) and preheat to medium-high.

4 Meanwhile, cut the bread crosswise into 24 to 28 slices each ½ inch thick (you'll need as many slices of bread as you have fig halves). Lightly brush the bread slices with the remaining 4 tablespoons of olive oil. Have all the ingredients on a platter ready to grill and assemble.

5 When ready to cook, brush and oil the grill grate. Place a few fig halves and an equal number of bread slices on the hot grate and grill until the figs are heated and lightly browned, 2 to 3 minutes per side, and the bread is toasted on both sides, 1 to 2 minutes per side. Remove the toasted bread from the grill and spread with the softened Gorgonzola, then place a grilled fig, cut side up, on top. Drizzle a little of the thyme-scented honey over each fig and serve at once. Repeat with the remaining figs, bread slices, Gorgonzola, and honey.

YIELD:
Makes 24 to 28 slices

VARIATION: Feel free to try other cheeses. The last time I made this dish, for example, I used a Spanish Manchego cheese instead of Gorgonzola. (I put a thin slice of cheese on each toast.) Outrageous!

TIPS

■ Because this is such an uncomplicated dish, you need to use first-rate raw materials: a baguette from an artisanal bakery and figs so luscious and ripe, they go splat if you accidentally drop one.

■ You assemble this dish grill-side as the various ingredients come off the fire, so be sure you have everything you need on hand.

TIPS

Cedar planks for grilling can be ordered by mail from Chinook Planks (see Mail-Order Sources on page 742). Or go to your local lumberyard and buy some untreated cedar shingles (never use pressure-treated lumber on a grill). Remember to leave yourself a couple of hours to soak the plank.

Canada

PESTO-GRILLED CAMEMBERT

What could be more American than grilled cheese? Of course, most of what passes for grilled cheese in the United States isn't grilled at all, but cooked on the griddle or panfried. Here's a grilled cheese that's worthy of the name.

I've borrowed a technique from my Canadian grill buddy, Ted Reader: grilling the cheese on a cedar plank. (Ted and Kathleen Sloan wrote *The Sticks & Stones Cookbook,* which is chock-full of offbeat grilling ideas.) The plank helps keep the Camembert from melting through the bars of the grate, and it also imparts a spicy wood flavor that's delicious when combined with pesto. If you're in a hurry, you can use a good store-bought pesto, in which case skip the first step.

METHOD:

Grilling on a plank

Camembert on the grill. Ted also grills the cheese with chutney.

A grilled cheese that's worthy of its name.

INGREDIENTS:

8 cloves garlic, coarsely chopped

½ cup walnuts or pine nuts

1 large bunch fresh basil,
    rinsed, stemmed, and
    spun dry in a salad spinner
    (for about 2 cups)

½ cup freshly grated Romano
    or Parmesan cheese
    (about 2 ounces)

½ teaspoon grated lemon zest

1 tablespoon fresh lemon juice,
    or to taste

⅓ to ½ cup extra-virgin olive oil

Coarse salt (kosher or sea) and
    freshly ground black pepper

2 Camembert cheeses
    (8 ounces each)

Grilled Garlic Bread #5 with Parmesan
    and Chives (page 134) or crackers,
    for serving

YOU'LL ALSO NEED:

1 cedar plank, soaked for 2 hours
    in water to cover, then drained

1 Place the garlic, nuts, basil, and grated cheese in a food processor and process to a coarse paste. Add the lemon zest, lemon juice, and just enough olive oil to create a thick paste (the mixture should be a little thicker than conventional pesto). Season with salt and pepper to taste; the pesto should be highly seasoned.

2 Carefully cut the rind off the top of each cheese (take only a paper-thin layer) and discard it. Spread half of the pesto over the top of each cheese, mounding it in the center.

3 Set up the grill for indirect grilling (see page 22 for charcoal or page 23 for gas) and preheat to medium-high.

4 When ready to cook, place the soaked cedar plank on the hot grate, directly over the fire. Grill until the edges of the plank just begin to smoke, 3 to 5 minutes. Turn the plank over, moving it to the center of the grill, away from the heat. Place the cheeses on top of the plank. Cover the grill and cook the cheeses until the sides are lightly browned, the cheese starts to melt, and the topping is bubbling, 12 to 20 minutes. Transfer the plank to a heatproof platter and serve the grilled cheese at once with grilled bread slices or crackers.

YIELD:

Serves 8 to 10

VARIATION: If you'd like to grill the cheese with chutney instead of pesto, try the Rhubarb Chutney on page 693.

TIPS

A number of American cheese makers, including Westfield Farm in Hubbardston, Massachusetts, make fine artisanal Camemberts. You could also use imported Camembert.

SALSA AND CHIPS
(FIVE GRILLED SALSAS)

Salsa and chips loom so large in the culinary landscape of the United States that it's hard to imagine a time when they weren't two of our favorite snacks. But when I was growing up in the 1950s, neither was a recognized "food category." The Latinization of our diet began in the 1960s, when Mexican restaurants in Texas and California drew their first Anglo clients, and a wave of American college students traveled to and lived in Mexico. The turning point came in 1991, when salsa sales actually surpassed those of ketchup. Now salsa and chips are as American as fried chicken or barbecued ribs. As our understanding of Tex-Mex and authentic regional Mexican cuisine has grown, so has our connoisseurship of salsa. We've recognized that there are dozens—no hundreds—of different kinds of salsas in Mexico and an equal abundance of North American hybrids. Chances are you'll be serving some sort of salsa and chips at your next barbecue. What you may not realize is that by firing up your grill and using the venerable technique of flame roasting, you can turn a commonplace salsa into an unforgettable dip. In the pages that follow you'll find five fire-roasted salsas that will make your guests sit up and take notice.

Salsa and chips are turbocharged by live fire.

DO-IT-YOURSELF TORTILLA CHIPS

Want to make chips from scratch? Here are two options: one using the traditional deep-frying method, the second using a low-fat method called bake-frying, where the chips are crisped in the oven. (If your grill has a side burner, you can fry the tortillas outdoors. It's less messy and keeps the frying odor out of the kitchen.) Homemade chips will keep for several days. Let them cool to room temperature, then store them in an airtight container. Of course, you can always serve good store-bought chips.

INGREDIENTS:

8 tortillas (I like to use a mixture of yellow and blue corn tortillas), each cut into 8 wedges
Vegetable oil, or 1 can of cooking oil spray
Coarse salt (kosher or sea)

DEEP-FRY METHOD: Place about ¾ inch of oil in a frying pan and preheat it to 350°F. Fry the tortilla wedges until crisp and golden brown, 1 to 2 minutes, turning them with a skimmer or slotted spoon and working in several batches so as not to crowd the pan. Transfer the chips to paper towels or a paper bag to drain. Lightly season the chips with salt, arrange them in a basket, and serve.

BAKE-FRY METHOD: Preheat the oven to 350°F. Arrange the tortilla wedges in a single layer on nonstick baking sheets and spray them lightly with oil. Bake the chips until lightly browned and crisp, 8 to 12 minutes. Transfer the chips to a wire rack to cool, then sprinkle with salt and serve.

YIELD:
Makes 64 tortilla chips

San Antonio, Tex.

CHARRED VEGETABLE SALSA

This lively tomato-based salsa is a house specialty of the Zuni Grill on San Antonio's Riverwalk. Its ingredients are commonplace, but charring the vegetables on the grill adds a remarkable depth of flavor, as does an unexpected splash of red wine.

METHOD:
Direct grilling

INGREDIENTS:
8 plum tomatoes
1 medium-size onion, cut lengthwise into quarters (leave the skin and root end on)
2 large jalapeño peppers
5 cloves garlic, skewered on a wooden toothpick or small bamboo skewer (leave the skins on)
¼ cup chopped fresh cilantro
½ teaspoon ground cumin
½ teaspoon dried oregano
2 to 3 tablespoons dry red wine
2 to 3 tablespoons fresh lime juice
Coarse salt (kosher or sea) and freshly ground black pepper

YOU'LL ALSO NEED:
1½ cups wood chips or chunks (optional; preferably mesquite), soaked for 1 hour in water to cover, then drained

1 Set up the grill for direct grilling (see page 21 for gas or charcoal) and preheat to high. If using a gas grill, place all of the wood chips or chunks, if desired, in the smoker box or in a smoker pouch (see page 24) and run the grill on high until you see smoke. If using a charcoal grill, preheat it to high, then toss all of the wood chips or chunks, if desired, on the coals.

2 When ready to cook, brush the grill grate. Place the tomatoes, onion, jalapeños, and garlic on the hot grate and grill until darkly browned on all sides. This will take 2 to 3 minutes per side (8 to 12 minutes in all) for the tomatoes, 3 to 4 minutes per side (9 to 12 minutes in all) for the onion quarters, 3 to 4 minutes per side (6 to 8 minutes in all)

TIPS

■ I like to grill the vegetables for this salsa a day or so ahead of time, when I'm grilling something else (it takes a real diehard to fire up the grill just to make salsa). To increase the smoke flavor, grill them over a mesquite wood fire (see page 23 for instructions on how to do this) or toss some wood chips on the coals.

■ Skewering the garlic cloves on a wooden toothpick will prevent them from falling through the bars of the grill grate.

San Antonio's Zuni Grill.

cumin, and oregano. Pulse once or twice to mix. Add the wine and lime juice and pulse just until you have a coarse salsa (you can also purée the ingredients in a blender, but I like the sort of chunky salsa you get in a food processor). Taste for seasoning, adding more lime juice as necessary, and season with salt and black pepper to taste; the salsa should be highly seasoned. You can make the salsa several hours ahead.

YIELD:
Makes about 2 cups

for the jalapeños, and 2 to 4 minutes per side (4 to 8 minutes in all) for the garlic.

3 Transfer the grilled vegetables to a cutting board and let cool. Remove the toothpick from the garlic and cut the root ends off the onion quarters. Scrape any really burnt skin off the vegetables but leave most of it on; the dark spots will add color and character. For a milder salsa, seed the jalapeños. Cut the vegetables into 1-inch pieces.

4 Place the vegetables in a food processor and add the cilantro,

Texas, Arizona, New Mexico

FIERY SALSA VERDE

Piquant, jade-colored *salsa verde* is one of the Southwest's principal condiments. It's served with chips and it's spooned over poultry and seafood and all manner of tortilla dishes (especially enchiladas). *Salsa verde* owes its distinctive tart-fruity flavor to its main ingredient: tomatillos. Grilling them adds an electrifying dimension.

METHOD:
Direct grilling

INGREDIENTS:

1 pound fresh tomatillos, husked
    and rinsed

1 small onion, cut lengthwise
    into quarters (leave the skin
    and root end on)

3 cloves garlic, skewered on
    a wooden toothpick
    (leave the skins on)

3 to 6 serrano peppers, or
    2 to 4 jalapeño peppers

¼ cup chopped fresh cilantro

½ teaspoon sugar, or more
    to taste

Coarse salt (kosher or sea) and
    freshly ground black pepper

2 tablespoons olive oil or lard

1 cup chicken stock, vegetable stock,
    or water, or more as needed

2 to 3 teaspoons fresh lime juice

YOU'LL ALSO NEED:

1½ cups wood chips or chunks
    (optional; preferably mesquite or
    oak), soaked for 1 hour in water
    to cover, then drained

1 Set up the grill for direct grilling (see page 21 for gas or charcoal) and preheat to high. If using a gas grill, place all of the wood chips or chunks, if desired, in the smoker box or in a smoker pouch (see page 24) and run the grill on high until you see smoke. If using a charcoal grill, preheat it to high, then toss all of the wood chips or chunks, if desired, on the coals.

2 When ready to cook, brush the grill grate. Place the tomatillos, onion, serranos, and garlic on the hot grate and grill until darkly browned on all sides. This will take 6 to 8 minutes for the tomatillos, 3 to 4 minutes per side (9 to 12 minutes in all) for the onion quarters, 3 to 4 minutes per side (6 to 8 minutes in all) for the serranos, and 2 to 4 minutes per side (4 to 8 minutes in all) for the garlic.

3 Transfer the grilled vegetables to a cutting board and let cool. Remove the toothpick from the garlic and cut the root end off the onion quarters. Scrape any really burnt skin off the vegetables, but leave most of it on; the dark spots will add color and character. For a milder salsa, seed the serranos. Cut the vegetables into 1-inch pieces and place in a food processor or blender. Add the cilantro and sugar and process or blend until a coarse purée forms. Season with salt and black pepper to taste.

4 Heat the oil in a deep non-reactive saucepan over high heat. Add the tomatillo mixture and fry it until thick and fragrant, 2 to 4 minutes, stirring with a long-handled wooden spoon to prevent spattering. Add the stock and lime juice and simmer until the salsa is thickened but still pourable, 5 to 8 minutes, stirring with a wooden spoon. If the salsa becomes too thick, add a little more stock. Taste for seasoning, adding more salt and/or sugar as necessary. Let the salsa cool to room temperature before serving. You can make the salsa several hours ahead.

YIELD:

Makes about 2 cups

T I P S

The tomatillo looks like a small green tomato encased in a tan papery husk. Its flavor lies somewhere between that of a green tomato and a very tart apple. There is no substitute. Fortunately, fresh tomatillos are available at Mexican markets, natural foods stores, and most supermarkets. When you husk a tomatillo, the fruit itself will feel sticky. This is normal. Simply rinse it off under cold running water before grilling.

New Mexico

SALSA CHIPOTLE

When the chipotle pepper burst upon the food scene in the United States in the 1970s, we were hooked from our first bite. We continue to relish the tongue-torturing dance of fire and smoke of this pepper (a chipotle is nothing more than a smoked jalapeño). Serve this salsa when major firepower is required.

METHOD:
Direct grilling

INGREDIENTS:
6 tomatillos (about 8 ounces), husked
  and rinsed (see Tips on page 59)
5 plum tomatoes
1 small onion, cut lengthwise into quarters
  (leave the skin and root end on)
5 cloves garlic, skewered on a wooden
  toothpick (leave the skins on)
2 to 4 canned chipotle peppers with
  2 to 4 teaspoons of their juice
3 tablespoons chopped fresh cilantro
1 to 2 tablespoons fresh lime juice
¼ teaspoon sugar
Coarse salt (kosher or sea) and
  freshly ground black pepper

YOU'LL ALSO NEED:
1½ cups wood chips or chunks (optional;
  preferably oak), soaked for 1 hour in
  water to cover, then drained

T I P S

Chipotle peppers come in two forms: dried and canned. I generally avoid canned foods, but chipotles are an exception because the peppers are packed in a spicy vinegar sauce called *adobo*, which gives them extra flavor. Canned chipotles are available at Mexican markets, gourmet shops, and many supermarkets.

1 Set up the grill for direct grilling (see page 21 for gas or charcoal) and preheat to high. If using a gas grill, place all of the wood chips or chunks, if desired, in the smoker box or in a smoker pouch (see page 24) and run the grill on high until you see smoke. If using a charcoal grill, preheat it to high, then toss all of the wood chips or chunks on the coals.

2 When ready to cook, brush the grill grate. Place the tomatillos, tomatoes, onion, and garlic on the hot grate and grill until darkly browned on all sides. This will take 6 to 8 minutes for the tomatillos, 2 to 3 minutes per side (8 to 12 minutes in all) for the tomatoes, 3 to 4 minutes per side (9 to 12 minutes in all) for the onion quarters, and 2 to 4 minutes per side (4 to 8 minutes in all) for the garlic.

3 Transfer the grilled vegetables to a cutting board and let cool. Remove the toothpick from the garlic and cut the root end off the onion quarters. Scrape any really burnt skin off the vegetables, but leave most of it on; the dark spots will add color and character.

4 Cut the vegetables into 1-inch pieces and place in a food processor or blender. Add the chipotles with their juices and the cilantro, lime juice, and sugar. Process or blend to a coarse purée. Season with salt and black pepper to taste. You can make the salsa several hours ahead.

YIELD:
Makes about 2 cups

Texas

SALSA CHILE DE ARBOL

You want hot? We'll talk hot. This salsa from the Mexico-Texas border is a snap to make, but it packs a wallop you won't soon forget. Serve this brute with *carnitas* (spicy shredded pork), *taquitos* (rolled corn tortillas filled with meat), grilled meats, or any dish in need of a decisive blast of heat. Of course, it also goes great with tortilla chips.

METHOD:
Direct grilling

ADVANCE PREPARATION:
1 hour for soaking the chiles

INGREDIENTS:
16 dried chiles de arbol (a little less than 1 ounce), stemmed
1 cup hot water
2 plum tomatoes
1 small onion, cut lengthwise into quarters (leave the skin and root end on)
3 cloves garlic, skewered on a wooden toothpick (leave the skins on)
3 tablespoons chopped fresh cilantro
½ teaspoon coarse salt (kosher or sea), or more to taste

1 Place the *chiles de arbol* in a bowl and add the water. Let the chiles soak until very soft, about 1 hour. For a milder salsa, you could tear open some or all of the pepper pods and remove

■ This salsa owes its heat to a northern Mexican dried pepper called *chile de arbol.* Red as a brick and long and slender like a green bean, the *chile de arbol* is sold at Mexican markets and gourmet shops (for Mail-Order Sources, see page 742).

■ You may be surprised to see I don't call for wood chips in this recipe. The *chiles de arbol* provide so much fire, you wouldn't even be able to taste the smoke.

A barbecuer's battle cry.

the seeds—a procedure disdained by *real* Texas grill jockeys.

2 Set up the grill for direct grilling (see page 21 for charcoal or gas) and preheat to high.

3 When ready to cook, brush the grill grate. Place the tomatoes, onion, and garlic on the hot grate and grill until nicely browned, 2 to 3 minutes per side (8 to 12 minutes in all) for the tomatoes, 3 to 4 minutes per side (9 to 12 minutes in all) for the onion quarters, and 2 to 4 minutes per side (4 to 8 minutes in all) for the garlic.

4 Transfer the grilled vegetables to a cutting board and let cool. Remove the toothpick from the garlic and cut the root end off the onion quarters. Scrape any really burnt skin off the vegetables, but leave most of it on; the dark spots will add color and character. Cut the vegetables into 1-inch pieces.

5 Place the *chiles de arbol* and their soaking liquid in a blender. Add the vegetable pieces and the cilantro and salt. Purée to a smooth paste, scraping down the sides of the blender with a rubber spatula. (If you use a food processor, process the solids first, then stir in the liquids.) Taste for seasoning, adding more salt as necessary. This salsa burns, so use it sparingly.

YIELD:
Makes about 2 cups

Hawaii

GRILLED PINEAPPLE GINGER SALSA

Fruit salsas, inspired by the Mexican condiment, are a uniquely American invention. You'll find many in this book—most designed to be served with simply grilled seafood or poultry. Here grilling transforms luscious Hawaiian pineapple into an unusual salsa you can serve with chips. To keep the tropical theme, why not serve plantain, yucca, or taro root chips? These are available in gourmet shops.

METHOD:
Direct grilling

INGREDIENTS:
1 ripe pineapple
1 red bell pepper
1 bunch scallions
2 to 4 jalapeño peppers,
    Scotch bonnet chiles,
    or other hot peppers
1 tablespoon minced candied
    ginger
¼ cup chopped fresh mint
3 tablespoons fresh lime juice,
    or more to taste
1 tablespoons brown sugar,
    or more to taste

1 Peel the pineapple and cut it crosswise into ¹/₂-inch slices. Remove the core from each slice.

2 Set up the grill for direct grilling (see page 21 for charcoal or gas) and preheat to high.

3 When ready to cook, brush the grill grate. Place the bell pepper, scallions, jalapeños, and the pineapple slices on the hot grate and grill until nicely browned. This will take about 3 to 5 minutes per side (12 to 20 minutes in all) for the bell pepper, 3 to 5 minutes per side (6 to 10 minutes in all) for the scallions, 3 to 4 minutes per side (6 to 8 minutes in all) for the jalapeños, and 3 to 6 minutes per side (6 to 12 minutes in all) for the pineapple slices.

4 Transfer the grilled scallions, jalapeños, and pineapple to a cutting board and let cool. Place the grilled bell pepper in a bowl and cover with plastic wrap. Let the pepper cool to room temperature, about 20 minutes (the steam trapped by the plastic wrap helps loosen the skin from the pepper). Scrape any really burnt skin off the bell pepper, scallions, and jalapeños, but leave most of it on; the dark spots will add color and character. Core and seed the bell pepper. Cut all of the vegetables and the pineapple slices into 1-inch pieces.

5 Place the pieces of bell pepper, scallion, jalapeño, and pineapple in a food processor and add the ginger and mint. Pulse to coarsely chop, running the machine in short bursts. Do not let the salsa become a purée. Add the lime juice and brown sugar and pulse briefly to mix. Taste for seasoning, adding more lime juice and/or brown sugar as necessary; the salsa should be a little sweet, a little sour, and very flavorful. You can make the salsa several hours ahead.

YIELD:
Makes 3 to 4 cups

Toronto, Canada

EGGPLANT DIP With Dill

Grilling neophytes love eggplant, for it not only can, but should, be burnt. Charring the skin imparts an inimitable smoke flavor. Fresh dill gives this dip a distinctly Greek character. It was inspired by one served at Toronto's Ouzeri restaurant.

METHOD:
Direct grilling

TIPS

Variations on this eggplant recipe exist in Greektowns, Little Lebanons, and Little Syrias throughout North America. Purée the eggplant and you get a dip. Chop the eggplant and you get a salad. You can substitute parsley or cilantro for the dill. Whichever way you fix them, choose long, cylindrical-shaped eggplants for grilling: They cook more evenly than the bulbous ones.

INGREDIENTS:

2 long, slender eggplants
    (about 1 pound each)
2 cloves garlic, minced
3 tablespoons tahini
    (optional; see Note)
3 tablespoons extra-virgin olive oil
2 tablespoons fresh lemon juice,
    or more to taste
½ teaspoon coarse salt (kosher or sea),
    or more to taste
½ teaspoon black pepper, or
    more to taste
3 tablespoons chopped fresh dill,
    plus a few sprigs for garnish
1 scallion, both white and green
    parts, trimmed and finely
    chopped
Lemon wedges, for serving
Grilled Pitas with Sesame Seeds
    and Cracked Pepper (page 136),
    or plain pita bread, for serving

1 Set up the grill for direct grilling (see page 21 for charcoal or gas) and preheat to high.

2 When ready to cook, prick the eggplants in a few spots with a fork. Place them on the hot grate and grill until the skins are charred all over and the flesh is very soft, 5 to 8 minutes per side (20 to 32 minutes in all). Transfer the grilled eggplants to a plate to cool.

3 Scrape any really burnt skin off the eggplants, but leave some of it on; the dark spots will add color and character. Coarsely purée the eggplants and garlic in a food processor (or chop them by hand or mash them with a fork). Add the tahini, if using, 2 tablespoons of the olive oil, and the lemon juice, salt, and pepper and pulse just to mix. Add the chopped dill and scallion and process in short bursts, just to mix (overprocessing will turn the dip green). Taste for seasoning, adding more salt, pepper, and/or lemon juice as necessary; the dip should be very flavorful. Transfer the dip to a shallow nonreactive bowl and drizzle the remaining 1 tablespoon of olive oil over it. Garnish with the dill sprigs and serve with the lemon wedges and pita bread.

YIELD:
Makes about 2 cups

NOTE: Tahini is a sesame seed paste. Look for it in cans or jars at your local supermarket or at Greek or Middle Eastern markets.

GREEKTOWN GRILLING

Greeks have been master grillers since the age of Homer (at least that's the first record of Greek grilling that I know of), and whenever I have a hankering for some Aegean-style barbecue, I head for the local Greektown. Chicago has a large Greek community; so does Tarpon Springs, Florida, and Astoria, New York—you can eat well in each of these towns. If you find yourself in Toronto, be sure to visit Ouzeri. The Eggplant Dip with Dill on this page and the Grilled Red Pepper Dip on the facing page were inspired by the mezes (hors d'oeuvres) at this popular restaurant, and they make for explosively flavorful appetizers.

Toronto, Canada

GRILLED RED PEPPER DIP

If you have trouble with flame control, is this the recipe for you! Bell peppers actually benefit from being burned. Charring the skin brings out the natural sweetness of the peppers and imparts an inimitable flavor.

METHOD:
Direct grilling

INGREDIENTS:
3 red bell peppers
1 can (15½ ounces) chickpeas
    (garbanzo beans), rinsed in a
    colander and drained
4 ounces feta cheese, crumbled
    (optional)
2 cloves garlic, coarsely chopped
⅓ cup extra-virgin olive oil
2 tablespoons fresh lemon juice,
    or more to taste
½ teaspoon freshly ground black pepper
Cayenne pepper
Coarse salt (kosher or sea)
Grilled Pitas with Sesame Seeds
    and Cracked Pepper (page 136),
    or plain pita bread, for serving

1 Set up the grill for direct grilling (see page 21 for charcoal or gas) and preheat to high.

2 When ready to cook, place the bell peppers on the hot grate and grill

You'll find great grilling in your local Greektown, even if locally Greektown is limited to one restaurant.

until the skins are black all over, 4 to 6 minutes per side (16 to 24 minutes in all). Don't forget to turn the peppers on end to grill the top and bottom as well. Place the grilled bell peppers in a bowl or baking dish and cover with plastic wrap. Let the bell peppers cool to room temperature, about 20 minutes (the steam trapped by the plastic wrap helps loosen the skin from the peppers).

3 Scrape any really burnt skin off the bell peppers, but leave some of it on; the dark spots will add color and character. Core and seed the bell peppers, then cut them into 1-inch pieces. The bell peppers can be prepared to this stage up to 3 days ahead; refrigerate them, covered, until ready to use.

4 Place the bell pepper pieces, chickpeas, feta, if using, and garlic in a food processor and purée to a smooth paste. With the motor running, add ¼ cup of the olive oil and the

TIPS

I normally make the pepper dip in two stages. I char the peppers a day or so before I plan to use them, when I've got the grill fired up for another meal. Then I throw the dip together a few hours before I want to serve it.

lemon juice through the feed tube. Add the black pepper and ½ teaspoon of cayenne and pulse to mix. Taste for seasoning, adding more lemon juice and/or cayenne as necessary and salt to taste (go easy with the salt, as canned chickpeas are quite salty). Transfer the dip to a shallow nonreactive bowl and drizzle the remaining oil over it. Sprinkle cayenne over the dip and serve with the pita bread.

YIELD:

Makes 2½ to 3 cups

T I P S

When I begin tinkering with a recipe, I never know where it's going to stop. So here is another option: To kick up the heat, you could substitute poblano peppers or horn peppers for the bell peppers.

Miami, Fla.

MOM'S GRILLED PEPPER AND EGGPLANT DIP

My mother-in-law, Miriam Seldin, a Miami Beach resident since the 1940s, has been serving this dip for as long as anyone can remember. To suggest a change in the recipe, as I'm about to do here, is to risk the wrath of three generations. But Miriam has a barbecue fanatic for a son-in-law, and I simply can't resist the temptation to grill the vegetables instead of baking them. This creates an electrifying smoke flavor that makes a family classic taste even better. I hope my mother-in-law forgives me—even if her grandchildren, Betsy and Jake, won't!

METHOD:
Direct grilling

INGREDIENTS:

**2 long, slender eggplants
    (about 1 pound each)**
3 green bell peppers
**3 tablespoons chopped fresh
    flat-leaf parsley**
2 cloves garlic, minced
**1 tablespoon fresh lemon juice,
    or more to taste**
**3 to 4 tablespoons vegetable oil
    or extra-virgin olive oil**
**Coarse salt (kosher or sea) and
    freshly ground black pepper**
**1 small sweet onion, finely chopped,
    for garnish**
**Crackers, matzos, or toast points,
    for serving**

1 Set up the grill for direct grilling (see page 21 for charcoal or gas) and preheat to high.

2 When ready to cook, prick the eggplants in a few spots with a fork and place them and the bell peppers on the hot grate. Grill the vegetables until charred on all sides, 5 to 8 minutes per side (20 to 32 minutes in all) for the eggplants, and 4 to 6 minutes per side (16 to 24 minutes in all) for the peppers. Transfer the grilled eggplants to a plate to cool. Place the grilled bell peppers in a bowl or baking dish and cover with plastic wrap. Let the peppers cool to room temperature, about 20 minutes (the steam trapped by the plastic wrap helps loosen the skin from the peppers).

3 Cut the eggplants in half, scrape the flesh out of the charred skin, and place it in a food processor. Scrape the burnt skin off the bell peppers, then core and seed them. Cut the bell peppers into 1-inch pieces and add these and the parsley and garlic, to the food processor. Finely chop the vegetables, running the machine in short bursts. With the motor running, add the oil and lemon juice, if using, through the feed tube. Taste for seasoning, adding more lemon juice as necessary and salt and pepper to taste; the dip should be highly seasoned.

4 Transfer the dip to a serving bowl. Sprinkle the top with the chopped onion and serve with crackers, matzos, or toast points. The dip will keep for several days in the refrigerator, covered, but bring it to room temperature before serving and sprinkle the onions over it at the last minute if you make it ahead.

YIELD:
Makes about 2 cups

Indianapolis, Ind.

INDY WINGS

The woman in the back of the van said, "I smell fire." My nostrils flared. "It's not fire. It's wood smoke—barbecue," I replied. We were driving to the Indianapolis speedway, where I was staging a barbecue on the eve of the Formula One Grand Prix. Once again, my nose led me to barbecue, and it proved to be a winner. The setup wasn't much: a couple of guys hunched over a furnace oil tank that had been converted into a smoker— streetside grilling at its best. The stop was worth the U-turn—we stumbled onto a smoke fanatic named Carl Bruno. Carl's ribs are awesome (see page 284) and his chicken wings have

Some of these early cars look like they could have doubled as barbecue pits when not used for racing.

the sort of honey-sweet crust and smoked-to-the-bone goodness that make you want to eat a dozen. Here's my rendition.

METHOD:
Indirect grilling

FOR THE WINGS:
4 pounds whole chicken wings
   (about 18)
Garlic salt
Celery salt
Freshly ground black pepper

FOR THE BASTING MIXTURE:
1½ cups Homemade Italian Dressing
   (recipe follows) or your favorite
   commercial brand
¾ cup honey
¾ cup fresh lemon juice
1½ teaspoons liquid smoke
2 teaspoons dried oregano
2 teaspoons hot red pepper flakes
2 teaspoons freshly ground black pepper
Coarse salt (kosher or sea)

YOU'LL ALSO NEED:
1½ cups wood chips or chunks
   (preferably hickory), soaked
   for 1 hour in water to cover,
   then drained

1 PREPARE THE WINGS: Rinse the chicken wings under cold running water and blot them dry with paper towels. Place the wings on a baking sheet and generously sprinkle garlic salt, celery salt, and black pepper over them.

2 MAKE THE BASTING MIXTURE: Place the Italian dressing, honey, lemon juice, liquid smoke, oregano, hot red pepper flakes, and black pepper in a nonreactive bowl and whisk to mix. Season with salt to taste; the basting mixture should be highly seasoned.

3 Set up the grill for indirect grilling (see page 23 for gas or page 22 for charcoal) and preheat to medium. If using a gas grill, place all of the wood chips or chunks in the smoker box or in a smoker pouch (see page 24) and run the grill on high until you see smoke, then reduce the heat to medium. If using a charcoal grill, place a large drip pan in the center, preheat the grill to medium, then toss all of the wood chips or chunks on the coals.

4 When ready to cook, brush and oil the grill grate. Place the chicken wings in the center of the hot grate, over the drip pan and away from the heat, and cover the grill. Cook the wings until golden brown and cooked through, 30 to 40 minutes. Brush the wings with some of the basting mixture after 15 minutes, and every 8 minutes after that, turning the wings to coat both sides.

5 During the last few minutes of cooking, move the wings a few at a time so that they are directly over the heat and, leaving the grill uncovered, cook them until crackling crisp, 1 to 2 minutes per side. Transfer the grilled wings to a platter or plates, pour the remaining basting mixture over them, and serve at once. Provide hot wet towels for sticky fingers.

YIELD:
Makes about 18 wings

TIPS

Carl Bruno uses what I call modified direct grilling. The coals and red oak burn directly under the wings, as in direct grilling. But the grate is positioned high above the coals, resulting in a moderate temperature more characteristic of smoking. To approximate the effect, I smoke roast the wings using the indirect method, then move them directly over the fire for a final sizzle.

Homemade Italian Dressing

Bottled Italian salad dressing is a staple of traditional American barbecue, especially in the Midwest. I find the commercial product to have an unpleasant chemical aftertaste, so I set about creating a similar Italian dressing you can make with natural ingredients from scratch. This recipe has been adapted from my book *Barbecue! Bible Sauces, Rubs, and Marinades.* It makes a little more than you need for Indy Wings; save what's left over for salad.

INGREDIENTS:

2 teaspoons cornstarch

¾ cup distilled white vinegar

1 tablespoon sugar

1 teaspoon coarse salt (kosher or sea)

2 teaspoons dried red bell pepper flakes (optional)

2 teaspoons garlic flakes

2 teaspoons dried oregano

2 teaspoons dried parsley

2 teaspoons dried chives

1 teaspoon onion flakes

1 teaspoon mustard powder

½ teaspoon hot red pepper flakes

½ teaspoon black pepper

1 cup canola oil

1 Combine the cornstarch and 1 tablespoon of water in a small bowl and stir to form a thick paste. Combine the vinegar, sugar, and salt with 7 tablespoons of water in a nonreactive saucepan and bring to a boil over medium-high heat. Stir the cornstarch mixture to recombine and whisk it into the boiling vinegar mixture. Let return to a boil, whisking steadily; the mixture should thicken. Remove the pan from the heat and let cool to room temperature.

2 Transfer the vinegar mixture to a nonreactive bowl and whisk in the remaining dressing ingredients. Or combine the ingredients in a large jar, screw on the lid, and shake to mix. Store the dressing in a sealed jar in the refrigerator. It will keep for several weeks.

YIELD:

Makes about 2 cups

Louisville, Ky.

LOUISVILLE WINGS

Louisville has its sluggers, and I don't just mean baseball bats. I'm thinking barbecued chicken wings of such smoke and spice you'll want to wolf down the whole batch before dinner. Kentucky marks the western limit of mustard country (that is, mustard barbecue sauce country), so it's not surprising that mustard should figure prominently in these Louisville wings. This is my kind of recipe—short on ingredients and quick to throw together, but superlong on flavor.

TIPS

Dried red bell pepper flakes are made from bell peppers that have been freeze-dried. You find them in supermarket spice racks.

TIPS

Lemon pepper is, as the name suggests, lemon-flavored black pepper. One widely sold brand is Lawry's. Or make your own by combining freshly ground black pepper with grated lemon zest.

Tabasco sauce is the jet fuel of barbecue.

METHOD:
Indirect grilling

ADVANCE PREPARATION:
4 to 5 hours for curing and marinating the wings

INGREDIENTS:
4 pounds whole chicken wings (about 18)
2 tablespoons lemon pepper
2 tablespoons sweet paprika
Coarse salt (kosher or sea)
10 tablespoons (1¼ sticks) salted butter
5 cloves garlic, finely chopped
⅔ cup Dijon mustard
⅔ cup Tabasco sauce or your favorite hot sauce
⅔ cup fresh lemon juice
⅔ cup bourbon
3 tablespoons brown sugar
1 teaspoon freshly ground black pepper

YOU'LL ALSO NEED:
1½ cups wood chips or chunks (preferably hickory), soaked for 1 hour in water to cover, then drained

1 Rinse the chicken wings under cold running water and blot them dry with paper towels. Place the wings in a large nonreactive bowl and toss them with the lemon pepper, paprika, and 2 tablespoons of salt. Let the wings cure in the refrigerator, covered, for 1 hour.

2 Melt the butter in a nonreactive saucepan over medium heat. Add the garlic and cook until it is fragrant and sizzling but not brown, about 3 minutes. Stir in the mustard, hot sauce, lemon juice, bourbon, brown sugar, and black pepper. Season with salt to

taste. Bring the bourbon mixture to a boil and let boil for 3 minutes, then let cool to room temperature. You'll use this for the marinade and sauce.

3 Pour half of the bourbon mixture over the wings and toss to mix. Let the wings marinate in the refrigerator, covered, for 3 to 4 hours. Set the remaining sauce aside.

4 Set up the grill for indirect grilling (see page 23 for gas or page 22 for charcoal) and preheat to medium. If using a gas grill, place all of the wood chips or chunks in the smoker box or in a smoker pouch (see page 24) and run the grill on high until you see smoke, then reduce the heat to medium. If using a charcoal grill, place a large drip pan in the center, preheat the grill to medium, then toss all of the wood chips or chunks on the coals.

5 When ready to cook, drain the marinade from the wings and discard the marinade. Brush and oil the grill grate. Place the wings in the center of the hot grate, over the drip pan and away from the heat, and cover the grill. Cook the wings until golden brown and cooked through, 30 to 40 minutes.

6 During the last few minutes of cooking, move the wings a few at a time so that they are directly over the heat and, leaving the grill uncovered, cook them until crackling crisp, 1 to 2 minutes per side. Transfer the grilled wings to a platter or plates and serve at once with the remaining sauce. Provide hot wet towels for sticky fingers.

YIELD:

Makes about 18 wings

VARIATION: You could certainly cook your wings in a smoker, although I prefer indirect grilling. (For starters, it's quicker. And the higher temperature helps crisp the chicken skin.) If you do use a smoker, preheat it to 225° to 250°F, following the manufacturer's instructions. The wings will need 2 to 2½ hours. Consider brushing them with melted butter and grilling them directly over the fire briefly at the end to make the skin crisp.

Nashville, Tenn.

TINDALL'S FAMOUS WINGS

Kurt Tindall is a cameraman from Nashville and a fellow barbecue fanatic. I met him in a TV studio just prior to a taping. Soon our talk turned to his backyard barbecues and to the wings for which he's something of a local legend. Kurt doesn't want to offend any particular part of the country, so he seasons his wings with Cajun spices from Louisiana and a seasoned salt from Puerto Rico. The wings are smoke grilled using the

TIPS

■ *Sazón,* a Puerto Rican seasoned salt, is a mixture of salt, white pepper, garlic powder, cumin, and cilantro. Commercial brands are available. To make your own, combine four tablespoons of salt and one tablespoon each of white pepper, garlic powder, ground cumin, and dried cilantro in a small bowl and stir to mix. Use what's left over from the wings to season grilled chicken, steak, or chops.

■ I like to skewer the wings lengthwise on bamboo skewers (the fat part of the wing should be at the top). This maximizes the surface area exposed to the fire and makes the wings as easy to eat as Popsicles.

indirect method, then spend a few minutes directly over the fire to crisp the skin. This is my version.

METHOD:
Indirect grilling

ADVANCE PREPARATION:
4 to 12 hours for marinating the wings

INGREDIENTS:
4 pounds whole chicken wings
  (about 18)
4 teaspoons Cajun Rub (page 420)
4 teaspoons sazón
4 teaspoons garlic powder
2 teaspoons freshly ground black pepper
⅓ cup Worcestershire sauce
⅓ cup fresh lemon juice
⅓ cup vegetable oil
5 tablespoons (½ stick plus
  1 tablespoon) salted butter,
  melted

YOU'LL ALSO NEED:
About 18 long (12-inch) bamboo skewers
  (optional); 1½ cups wood chips or
  chunks (preferably hickory), soaked
  for 1 hour in water to cover, then
  drained

1 Rinse the chicken wings under cold running water and blot them dry with paper towels. Place the wings in a large nonreactive bowl and toss with the Cajun Rub, *sazón,* garlic powder, and pepper. Let the wings cure in the refrigerator, covered, for 10 minutes. Stir in the Worcestershire sauce, lemon juice, and oil and let the wings marinate in the refrigerator, covered, for as little as 4 hours or as long as overnight.

2 If desired, skewer each wing lengthwise on a bamboo skewer: Stretch a wing out to its full length. Insert a skewer about 1 inch above the wing tip and work the skewer up through the wing so that the wing is extended along the length of the skewer; the thickest part of the wing will be at the top of the skewer. Repeat with the remaining wings and skewers.

3 Set up the grill for indirect grilling (see page 23 for gas or page 22 for charcoal) and preheat to medium. If using a gas grill, place all of the wood chips or chunks in the smoker box or in a smoker pouch (see page 24) and run the grill on high until you see smoke, then reduce the heat to medium. If using a charcoal grill, place a large drip pan in the center, preheat the grill to medium, then toss all of the wood chips or chunks on the coals.

4 When ready to cook, remove the wings from the marinade and discard the marinade. Brush and oil the grill grate. If using bamboo skewers, tear off a piece of heavy-duty aluminum foil that is roughly as long as the grill is wide. Fold the piece of aluminum foil in half lengthwise. Place the folded aluminum foil flat on the grate, then place the skewers on top of it. Place the wings in the center of the hot grate, over the drip pan and away from the heat, and cover the grill. Cook the wings until golden brown and cooked through, 30 to 40 minutes.

5 During the last few minutes of cooking, move the wings a few at

a time so that they are directly over the heat and baste them with the melted butter. Leaving the grill uncovered, cook the wings until crackling crisp, 1 to 2 minutes per side. Transfer the grilled wings to a platter or plates and serve at once.

YIELD:
Makes about 18 wings

Buffalo, N.Y.

BUFFA-QUE WINGS

Buffalo wings were born on October 30, 1964, at the Anchor Bar in Buffalo, New York. The occasion, legend has it, was a happy confluence of a houseful of hungry teenagers and an overshipment of chicken wings. Anchor proprietor Teressa Bellissimo deep-fried said wings, tossed them with melted margarine and hot sauce, and served the house blue cheese salad dressing with them as a dipping sauce. The rest, as they say, is history. Now I'm sure you can guess what my next suggestion is—smoke roasting the wings.

METHOD:
Indirect grilling

ADVANCE PREPARATION:
4 to 12 hours for marinating the wings

FOR THE WINGS AND MARINADE:
16 whole chicken wings
     (about 3½ pounds)
½ cup Tabasco sauce or your
     favorite hot sauce
½ cup fresh lemon juice
¼ cup vegetable oil
2 tablespoons Worcestershire sauce
4 cloves garlic, minced
2 teaspoons coarse salt (kosher or sea)
1 teaspoon freshly ground black pepper

FOR THE MOP SAUCE:
8 tablespoons (1 stick) salted butter
½ cup Tabasco sauce or your
     favorite hot sauce

FOR SERVING:
Maytag Blue Cheese Sauce
     (recipe follows)
4 ribs celery, rinsed and cut into thirds
     lengthwise, then cut crosswise into
     roughly 3-inch sticks

YOU'LL ALSO NEED:
1½ cups wood chips or chunks (preferably
     hickory or oak),
     soaked for 1 hour
     in water to cover,
     then drained

TIPS

In previous books, I called for grilling chicken wings using the direct method. In the recipe here, and several others in this book, they're grilled indirectly, which has three advantages: You don't have to worry about them burning, the wings pick up even more smoke flavor, and the gentle indirect heat crisps the skin without setting the chicken on fire.

Buffalo wings are so popular the Anchor bottles its own sauce.

1 Rinse the chicken wings under cold running water and blot them dry with paper towels. Cut the tips off the wings and discard them (or leave the tips on if you don't mind munching a morsel that's mostly skin and bones). Cut each wing into 2 pieces through the joint.

2 MAKE THE MARINADE: Whisk together the hot sauce, lemon juice, oil, Worcestershire sauce, garlic, salt, and pepper in a large nonreactive mixing bowl. Stir in the wing pieces and let marinate in the refrigerator, covered, for 4 to 6 hours or as long as overnight,

turning the wings several times so that they marinate evenly.

3 MAKE THE MOP SAUCE: Just before setting up the grill, melt the butter in a small saucepan over medium heat and stir in the hot sauce.

4 Set up the grill for indirect grilling (see page 23 for gas or page 22 for charcoal) and preheat to medium. If using a gas grill, place all of the wood chips or chunks in the smoker box or in a smoker pouch (see page 24) and run the grill on high until you see smoke, then reduce the heat to medium. If using a charcoal grill, place a large drip pan in the center, preheat the grill to medium, then toss all of the wood chips or chunks on the coals.

5 When ready to cook, drain the marinade off the wings and discard the marinade. Brush and oil the grill grate. Place the wings in the center of the hot grate, over the drip pan and away from the heat, and cover the grill. Cook the wings until the skin is crisp and golden brown and the meat is cooked through, 30 to 40 minutes. During the last 10 minutes, start basting the wings with some of the mop sauce.

6 Transfer the grilled wings to a shallow bowl or platter and pour the remaining mop sauce over them. Serve with the blue cheese sauce and

The Anchor Bar, spiritual birthplace of the Buffa-que wing.

celery for dipping and of course plenty of paper napkins and cold beer.

YIELD:
Makes 32 pieces

Maytag Blue Cheese Sauce

Salty blue cheese makes a perfect foil for spicy chicken wings. But no bottled blue cheese salad dressing will do for Buffa-que Wings. The recipe here calls for America's most famous blue cheese: Maytag Blue from Iowa.

INGREDIENTS:
4 ounces Maytag Blue cheese
1 cup mayonnaise (preferably Hellmann's)
½ cup sour cream
1 tablespoon distilled white vinegar
¼ cup minced onion
½ teaspoon freshly ground black pepper
Coarse salt (kosher or sea; optional)

Press the blue cheese through a sieve into a nonreactive mixing bowl. Whisk in the mayonnaise, sour cream, vinegar, onion, and pepper. It's unlikely you'll need salt (the cheese is quite salty already) but taste for seasoning and add a little if necessary. The blue cheese sauce will keep in the refrigerator, covered, for several days.

YIELD:
Makes about 3 cups

Virginia Beach, Va.

TINEE'S MARINATED CHICKEN WINGS

Americans are obsessed with chicken wings. There's good reason for this: Properly grilled, no other cut of chicken is quite so crisp or tasty. The best part of the chicken is the skin—an opinion disputed by a few cardiologists but universally acknowledged by everyone else. And wings have the highest ratio of skin to meat.

This brings us in a roundabout way to Tinee Johnston, a Filipino American who lives in Virginia Beach. Tinee comes from Bicol in northern Luzon, where grilling has a decidedly Asian accent. But her marriage to a Navy man from Massachusetts more than a quarter century ago has made her savvy to the ways of American barbecue. She seasons her wings with a Filipino-style marinade of garlic, soy sauce, and vinegar, then lets the fire do the rest.

METHOD:
Direct grilling

ADVANCE PREPARATION:
12 hours for marinating the wings

TIPS

There's an unusual ingredient in Tinee's wings—calamansi, a small, round, sour citrus fruit with a flavor akin to lime. If you live in an area with a good Filipino or Asian market, you may be able to find it. In south Florida or southern California, you can substitute sour orange (*naranja agria*). Otherwise, you can use fresh Persian (regular) lime juice or key lime juice.

INGREDIENTS:

6 cloves garlic, minced

½ cup soy sauce

6 tablespoons distilled white vinegar

¼ cup calamansi juice or fresh lime juice

2 teaspoons grated lime zest (optional; use
     if calamansis are unavailable)

¼ cup olive oil

2 teaspoons freshly ground black pepper

Coarse salt (kosher or sea)

4 pounds whole chicken wings (about 18)

1 Place the garlic, soy sauce, vinegar, calamansi juice, lemon zest, if using, olive oil, and pepper in a large nonreactive mixing bowl and whisk to mix. Add salt to taste; the marinade should be highly seasoned.

2 Rinse the chicken wings under cold running water and blot them dry with paper towels. Prick each wing in 4 or 5 spots with the tip of a metal skewer. Add the wings to the marinade and toss to mix. Let the wings marinate overnight in the refrigerator, covered, turning several times so they marinate evenly.

3 Drain the marinade from the wings into a nonreactive saucepan, bring to a boil over high heat, and let boil for 3 minutes. You'll use this mixture for basting the wings.

4 Set up the grill for direct grilling (see page 21 for charcoal or gas) and preheat to medium-high.

5 When ready to cook, brush and oil the grill grate. Stretch each wing out as long as it will go and then place it on the hot grate. Grill the wings until nicely browned all over and cooked

through, 8 to 12 minutes per side. During the last 5 minutes, baste the wings with the boiled marinade. Transfer the grilled wings to a platter or plates and serve at once.

YIELD:

Makes about 18 wings

VARIATION: Whole or half chickens can be marinated and prepared in a manner similar to Tinee's wings. You'll need to make a double batch of the marinade described in Step 1.

Vancouver, Canada

SOUVLAKI MEATBALLS

Vancouver may be the last place you'd expect to find a die-hard grilling community. But the oceanic climate shelters Vancouver from the low temperatures experienced by the rest of Canada in the winter, and the locals take great pleasure in grilling all year round. Butcher stalls in the Granville Island market sell a staggering variety of meats that are already marinated and skewered, just ready to go on the grill. The following meatballs go by the name of *souvlaki* at the market. The flavorings—garlic, dill, and lemon—may be Greek, but the meatball format, the combination of ground lamb, pork, and veal, and above all, the fact that they're grilled are distinctive to Granville Island.

METHOD:
Direct grilling

ADVANCE PREPARATION:
1 to 2 hours for chilling the meatballs

INGREDIENTS:
½ pound ground lamb or beef
½ pound ground pork
½ pound ground veal
2 cloves garlic, minced
3 tablespoons chopped fresh dill
1½ teaspoons coarse salt (kosher or sea), or more to taste
½ teaspoon freshly ground black pepper, or more to taste
½ teaspoon grated fresh lemon zest
1 tablespoon fresh lemon juice
Pita bread (optional)
Feta and Cucumber Dip (optional; page 143)

YOU'LL ALSO NEED:
About 36 small (6-inch) bamboo skewers

1 Place the lamb, pork, veal, garlic, dill, salt, pepper, and lemon zest and juice in a nonreactive mixing bowl and mix well, using a wooden spoon or your hands (I find fingers work best). To taste for seasoning, form a small meatball and grill or sauté it until cooked through. Add more salt and/or pepper as necessary.

2 Wet your hands with cold water and form 1-inch meatballs with the meat mixture. Lightly flatten the meatballs with your fingertips. Place the meatballs on a plate lined with plastic wrap and refrigerate, covered, for 1 to 2 hours.

3 Set up the grill for direct grilling (see page 21 for charcoal or gas) and preheat to high.

4 When ready to cook, brush and oil the grill grate. Place the meatballs on the hot grate and grill until cooked through, 1 to 2 minutes per side. To test for doneness, break one of the meatballs in half. There should be no remaining traces of pink. Transfer the grilled meatballs to a platter. Stick a bamboo skewer in each and serve at once. Pita bread and yogurt dip would make good accompaniments.

YIELD:
Makes about 3 dozen meatballs

On Granville Island, they mold the ground meat into meatballs to be grilled on bamboo skewers. I find it easier to grill the meat in small patties, then stick these on the bamboo skewers once they're cooked. You could also mold the meat into larger patties and serve these on buns as burgers.

San Francisco, Calif.

TIKI BEEF KEBABS

I acquired my first tiki, a small plaster figurine modeled on one of the long-eared Polynesian statues, in second or third grade. I wore it around

T I P S

There are several possibilities for meat here. If you are feeling flush, you could invest in a couple of New York strip steaks. Sirloin or top round steaks are more affordable. Whichever cut you use, the steaks should be about 1 inch thick.

my neck on a rawhide cord at home, to school, and even to bed; my tiki and I were inseparable. I didn't realize that my beloved tiki had gastronomical ramifications—that it was cultural fallout from the Polynesian restaurants proliferating in the United States in the 1950s and '60s, inspired by San Francisco's Victor "Trader Vic" Bergeron. Well, guess what? The tiki is making a comeback, and modern American bartenders are rediscovering the colorful Polynesian drinks that once beguiled my parents. They were customarily served with cocktail snacks. I suggest tiki beef kebabs, redolent of ginger, garlic, and soy sauce. For a real period touch, pick up some tiny Sterno-fueled braziers and serve the sizzling kebabs on them.

METHOD:
Direct grilling

ADVANCE PREPARATION:
1 to 2 hours for marinating the kebabs

INGREDIENTS:
1 clove garlic, coarsely chopped
1 scallion, trimmed, white part
   coarsely chopped, green part
   finely chopped
1 piece (½ inch) fresh ginger, peeled
   and coarsely chopped
2 strips lemon zest (each about
   1½ by 1½ inches; see Note)
¼ cup soy sauce
3 tablespoons sugar
3 tablespoons Asian (dark) sesame oil
3 tablespoons dry sherry
2 pounds strip, sirloin, or top
   round steaks (each about
   1 inch thick)

YOU'LL ALSO NEED:
About 36 long slender (8- to 12-inch)
   bamboo skewers; heavy-duty
   aluminum foil

1 Place the garlic, scallion white, ginger, lemon zest, soy sauce, sugar, sesame oil, and sherry in a blender and purée until smooth. Or you can make the marinade in a food processor: Place the garlic, scallion white, ginger, lemon zest, and sugar in the processor bowl and process to make a fine paste. Add the soy sauce, sesame oil, and sherry and process to mix.

2 Using a very sharp knife, cut each steak on the diagonal into about 36 thin slices (about ⅛ inch thick). Weave each strip of meat like a ribbon onto a skewer. The meat will bunch up as it goes on the skewer; gently spread it out with your fingers.

3 Arrange 12 of the kebabs in a single layer in a nonreactive baking dish. Pour one third of the marinade over the kebabs in the baking dish. Turn the kebabs to coat both sides with the marinade. Arrange 12 more kebabs on top of the first layer, pour half of the remaining marinade over these, and turn this layer to coat evenly. Arrange the remaining kebabs on top of the second layer, pour the remaining marinade over these, and turn to coat evenly. Cover the kebabs with plastic wrap and let them marinate in the refrigerator for 1 to 2 hours.

4 Set up the grill for direct grilling (see page 21 for charcoal or gas) and preheat to high.

5 When ready to cook, brush and oil the grill grate. Tear off a piece of heavy-duty aluminum foil that is roughly as long as the grill is wide. Fold the piece of aluminum foil in half lengthwise. Place the folded aluminum foil flat on the grate at the edge closest to you. Arrange the kebabs on the grate so that they are over the fire but the exposed ends of the skewers are on the foil shield to keep them from burning. Depending upon the size of the grill, you may need to cook the kebabs in batches. Grill the kebabs until nicely browned, 1 to 2 minutes per side for medium. Transfer the grilled kebabs to a platter and sprinkle the scallion greens over them.

YIELD:

Makes about 36 kebabs

NOTE: You can use a vegetable peeler to remove the oil-rich, yellow outer rind of the lemon in strips of zest. Be careful to leave behind the bitter white pith.

Palm Beach, Fla.

MOJO-MARINATED PORK ON SUGAR CANE

Hubert Des Marais serves as executive chef of the Four Seasons resort in Palm Beach. But don't hold that against him. The classically trained chef knows how to get down and dirty at a barbecue. I know, because we grilled together at a beach party at the Cheeca Lodge in Islamorada in the Florida Keys. The occasion was the Cheeca Lodge Eco-Seafood weekend, a food festival and conference designed to raise consciousness about ecological and earth-friendly cooking practices. The dish Hubert prepared offered

Hubert Des Marais, a classically trained chef and closet pit master.

TIPS

It used to be that to grill on sugar cane, you had to section and slice the cane with a cleaver—a formidable process, take my word for it. Today, the task is no more difficult than locating sugar cane swizzle sticks. Both Frieda's and Melissa's package these, and they are available at many upscale supermarkets and natural foods stores, as well as by mail order (see page 742). Of course, you can always use bamboo skewers instead.

a contemporary Floridian twist on a Cuban favorite: *mojo*-marinated pork grilled on strips of fresh sugar cane. *Mojo* (pronounced MO-ho) is a Cuban table sauce, made with garlic and sour orange juice. Hubert likes to enrich it with a potent dose of cilantro. As for the sugar cane, it releases dulcet juices as you nibble the meat off of it.

METHOD:
Direct grilling

ADVANCE PREPARATION:
4 to 12 hours for marinating the pork

INGREDIENTS:
12 sugar cane swizzle sticks
1½ pounds pork loin or tenderloin,
    cut into 1½-inch cubes
4 cloves garlic, minced
1½ teaspoons coarse salt
    (kosher or sea)
1 teaspoon cracked black
    peppercorns
½ teaspoon ground cumin
¼ cup fresh lime juice
¼ cup fresh orange juice
½ cup chopped fresh cilantro
½ medium-size red onion,
    finely chopped (about ½ cup)
1 cup extra-virgin olive oil
Curried Pineapple Relish
    (recipe follows)

1 Cut each piece of sugar cane in half crosswise sharply on the diagonal.

2 Using a slender chopstick or metal skewer, make a hole in each pork cube, running across the grain. Insert

the sharp end of a piece of sugar cane through each piece of meat to skewer it. Stand the pork kebabs upright, meat end down, in a straight-sided bowl or soufflé dish.

3 Place the garlic, salt, peppercorns, and cumin in a large non-reactive bowl and mash with the back of a spoon. Add the lime juice, orange juice, cilantro, and onion and stir until the salt dissolves. Stir in the olive oil. Transfer ½ cup of the *mojo* to a nonreactive bowl and set aside. Pour the remaining *mojo* over the kebabs, making sure that the meat is completely submerged. Let the pork marinate in the refrigerator, covered, for at least 4 hours or as long as overnight.

4 Set up the grill for direct grilling (see page 21 for charcoal or gas) and preheat to high.

5 When ready to cook, brush and oil the grill grate. Place the kebabs on the hot grate and grill until the meat is nicely browned on the outside and cooked through, 2 to 3 minutes per side (8 to 12 minutes in all). When done, the pork will feel firm to the touch. Depending upon the size of the grill, you may need to cook the kebabs in batches. Transfer the grilled pork to a platter and spoon the reserved *mojo* on top. Serve at once, with the pineapple relish on the side.

YIELD:
Makes about 24 kebabs

Curried Pineapple Relish

Brimming with tropical flavors—tangy fresh mint and cilantro, fiery Scotch bonnet chiles, even fragrant curry powder from the West Indies—this refreshing relish lives and dies by the ripeness of the pineapple. Look for a fruit with a golden rind and perfumed aroma (sniff the bottom). These are the telltale signs of a ripe, sweet pineapple.

By the way, this makes more relish than you need for the pork kebabs. Leftovers go great with grilled poultry and grilled seafood, like spiny lobster and mahi mahi.

INGREDIENTS:

1 ripe pineapple (for about 8 cups diced)
**⅓ cup fresh lime juice, or more
   to taste**
⅓ cup honey, or more to taste
**½ teaspoon West Indian curry powder
   (see Note), or more to taste**
**1 red bell pepper, cored, seeded,
   and cut into ¼-inch dice**
**½ to 2 Scotch bonnet chiles, seeded
   and minced (for a hotter relish,
   leave the seeds in)**
¼ medium-size red onion, finely chopped
¼ cup chopped fresh cilantro
¼ cup chopped fresh mint

1 Lay the pineapple on its side with the leafy crown away from you. Using a long, sharp knife, cut the pineapple in half lengthwise, starting at the base of the fruit and cutting through the leaves as well. Remove the core from one half by making 2 cuts into the flesh, angling the knife blade down along the core to cut out a V-shape wedge the length of the fruit. Repeat with the second half. Discard the core, then remove the flesh from the pineapple, cutting within ½ inch of the rind and following its contours (a grapefruit knife works well for this). It is easier to cut out the flesh if you make a few cuts that run the length of the fruit but be careful not to pierce the rind. Cut the flesh into ½-inch dice. Set the pineapple shells aside. The pineapple can be diced several hours before you make the relish.

2 Not more than 20 minutes before serving, combine the lime juice, honey, and curry powder in a large nonreactive mixing bowl and stir until well mixed. Gently stir in the diced pineapple and the bell pepper, Scotch bonnet(s), onion, cilantro, and mint. Taste for seasoning, adding more lime juice, honey, and/or curry powder as necessary; the mixture should be sweet, sour, and highly flavored. Spoon the relish into the pineapple shells and serve.

YIELD:

Makes about 9 cups

NOTE: West Indian curry powder is available at specialty food stores and West Indian markets. You can substitute an equal amount of East Indian curry powder.

There are many strategies for keeping slender bamboo skewers from burning on the grill. I recommend placing an aluminum foil shield under them.

Seattle, Wash.

LEMONGRASS PORK SATES

Seattle may be the birthplace of designer coffee, but no visit to this Puget Sound metropolis would be complete without dinner at Wild Ginger. This pan-Asian restaurant—the most popular in Seattle at least two years in a row, according to the Zagat Survey—has done much to satisfy the local passion for Pacific Rim flavors. The focal point of the sleekly contemporary two-story dining room is a half-moon shaped saté bar, where nearly a dozen different kinds of tiny Asian kebabs are grilled to order on a massive grill. Saté (pronounced sat-tay) may be part of the American culinary repertory these days, but when the saté bar was pioneered by Wild Ginger in the early 1990s, it was nothing less than revolutionary. I can't think of a more pleasurable light summer meal or a prelude to a more substantial dinner than a sampler of these tiny kebabs.

METHOD:
Direct grilling

ADVANCE PREPARATION:
1 to 2 hours for marinating the pork

INGREDIENTS:
2 stalks lemongrass, trimmed and coarsely chopped (6 to 8 tablespoons), or 3 strips lemon zest (each about 1½ by ½ inch; see Note)
1 large or 2 medium-size shallots, coarsely chopped (about 5 tablespoons)
3 cloves garlic, coarsely chopped
1 to 3 Thai chiles, serrano peppers, or other hot chiles, seeded and roughly chopped (for hotter satés, leave the seeds in)
3 tablespoons sugar
½ cup Asian fish sauce or soy sauce
¼ cup fresh lime juice
4 to 5 tablespoons vegetable oil
1 teaspoon freshly ground black pepper
2 pounds pork loin or tenderloin
Peanut Sauce (recipe follows)
Cucumber Relish (page 85)

YOU'LL ALSO NEED:
About 36 long slender (8- to 12-inch) bamboo skewers; heavy-duty aluminum foil

1 Place the lemongrass, shallot, garlic, chile(s), and sugar in a food processor and pulse to make a coarse paste. Add the fish sauce, lime juice, 3 tablespoons of the oil, and the black pepper and purée until smooth. You can also place all of the marinade ingredients in a blender and purée until smooth.

2 Using a very sharp knife, cut the pork loin crosswise slightly on the diagonal into thin slices (about

⅛ inch thick). Cut each slice lengthwise in half or thirds to create thin strips of meat about 1 inch wide and 3 to 4 inches long. Weave each strip of meat like a ribbon onto a skewer. The meat will bunch up as it goes on the skewer; gently spread it out with your fingers.

3 Arrange 12 of the satés in a single layer in a nonreactive baking dish. Pour a third of the marinade over the satés in the baking dish. Turn the satés to coat both sides with the marinade. Arrange 12 more satés on top of the first layer, pour half of the remaining marinade over these, and turn this layer to coat evenly. Arrange the remaining satés on top of the second layer, pour the remaining marinade over these, and turn to coat evenly. Let the pork mar-

inate in the refrigerator, covered, for 1 to 2 hours.

4 Set up the grill for direct grilling (see page 21 for charcoal or gas) and preheat to high.

5 When ready to cook, brush and oil the grill grate. Tear off a piece of heavy-duty aluminum foil that is roughly as long as the grill is wide. Fold the piece of aluminum foil in half lengthwise. Place the folded aluminum foil flat on the grate at the edge closest to you. Arrange the satés on the grate so that they are over the fire but the exposed ends of the skewers are on top of the foil shield to keep them from burning. Depending upon the size of the grill, you may need to cook the satés in batches. Grill the satés until cooked through, 1 to 2 min-

Flames leap at Wild Ginger's saté bar.

utes per side, basting them with vegetable oil. Transfer the grilled satés to a platter or hand them to your guests right off the grill. Serve with tiny dishes of Peanut Sauce for dipping and the Cucumber Relish.

YIELD:

Makes about 36 satés

NOTE: You can use a vegetable peeler to remove the oil-rich, yellow outer rind of the lemon in strips of zest. Be careful to leave behind the bitter white pith.

Satés—hot off the grill and served by the fistful.

Peanut Sauce

Peanut sauce is the traditional Southeast Asian condiment for satés, but there's at least one precedent for it in the Americas—a Haitian peanut sauce called *mamba,* which coincidentally, was born on the island of Hispanola, the birthplace of barbecue. Peanut sauces have become firmly implanted in the American mainstream. In the event you haven't tried pairing peanut butter with grilled meat, you're in for a revelation.

INGREDIENTS:

¾ **to 1 cup chicken stock, light cream, or unsweetened coconut milk**

¾ **cup peanut butter**

1 large clove garlic, minced

1 Thai chile or serrano pepper, seeded and minced (for a hotter sauce, leave the seeds in)

3 tablespoons soy sauce, or more to taste

2 tablespoons chopped fresh cilantro

1½ tablespoons sugar, or more to taste

2 teaspoons minced or grated peeled fresh ginger

1 teaspoon ground coriander

½ **teaspoon freshly ground black pepper, or more to taste**

Place ¾ cup of the stock in a saucepan over medium heat. Add the peanut butter, garlic, chile, soy sauce, cilantro, sugar, ginger, coriander, and black pepper and gradually bring to a simmer, whisking as needed to blend. Let the sauce simmer until richly flavored, about 5 minutes, whisking occasionally. The sauce should be thick but pourable; add the remaining ¼ cup stock if necessary. Taste for seasoning, adding more soy sauce, sugar, and/or black pepper as necessary; the sauce should be highly seasoned. The sauce can be served warm or at room temperature. It will keep in the refrigerator, covered, for several days. Stir to recombine and bring to room temperature before serving.

YIELD:

Makes about 1¾ cups

Cucumber Relish

Think of this easy relish as Pacific Rim pickles or coleslaw. Like a conventional slaw, its purpose is to provide refreshment and crunch. (If you like, you can turn up the heat by adding a serrano pepper.) What some people call Kirby and other people call pickling cucumbers tend to be crunchier and less watery than conventional cucumbers. They're my choice for this relish.

INGREDIENTS:

2 to 4 Kirby (pickling) cucumbers, or 1 regular cucumber (about 9 ounces)
½ small red onion, thinly sliced
1 serrano pepper (optional), seeded and thinly sliced (for a hotter relish, leave the seeds in)
1 tablespoon sugar, or more to taste
1 scant teaspoon coarse salt (kosher or sea), or more to taste
3 tablespoons rice vinegar, or more to taste
½ teaspoon freshly ground black pepper

1 If using Kirby cucumbers, cut them lengthwise in half, then thinly slice them crosswise (you don't need to peel them). If using a regular cucumber, peel it, cut it in half, scrape out the seeds with a melon baller or spoon, then thinly slice each half crosswise. Place the sliced cucumber and the onion and serrano in a nonreactive mixing bowl and toss with the sugar and salt. Let stand for 10 minutes.

2 Add the rice vinegar and black pepper and toss to mix. Taste for seasoning, adding more sugar, salt, and/or vinegar as necessary; the relish should be highly seasoned. You can serve the relish right away, or you can make it several hours ahead and refrigerate it, covered. It's OK to serve the relish cold.

YIELD:

Makes about 1½ cups

WALL OF FLAME

WILD GINGER

When Ann and Rick Yoder opened Wild Ginger, it had what was very likely the first saté bar in North America. Enjoy a couple of these small kebabs as an appetizer or nibble an entire meal from bamboo skewers—there are seven signature grilled satés to choose from, not to mention the innovative grilled main courses.

1401 Third Avenue
Seattle, Washington
(206) 623-4450

Miami, Fla.

PORTOBELLO MUSHROOM SATES

When I was growing up, no one had ever heard of portobello mushrooms. Today, we can't seem to live without this giant version of the *Agaricus bisporus* (the white button mushroom). The most common way to cook portobellos is whole; their broad expanse makes them ideal for grilling. My stepson, Miami-born chef Jake, has devised a striking alternative method. He cuts the caps lengthwise into strips and grills them on bamboo skewers as satés. Button mushrooms can be marinated and grilled in a similar fashion (leave the mushrooms whole).

METHOD:
Direct grilling

ADVANCE PREPARATION:
**30 minutes to 1 hour for marinating
    the mushrooms**

INGREDIENTS:
**4 portobello mushrooms (each about
    4 inches across and 8 to 10 ounces)**
¼ cup honey
¼ cup red wine vinegar
**¼ cup sherry (preferably cream sherry,
    but any will do)**
¼ cup walnut oil (see Note)
3 tablespoons soy sauce
2 cloves garlic, minced
Freshly ground black pepper

YOU'LL ALSO NEED:
**16 long slender (8- to 12-inch) bamboo
    skewers; heavy-duty aluminum foil**

1 Trim the stems off the portobellos, using a paring knife. Wipe the caps clean with a damp paper towel. Using a serrated knife, cut each portobello into 4 even strips. Stick each strip lengthwise on a bamboo skewer. Stand the satés upright, mushroom end down, in a straight-sided bowl or soufflé dish.

2 Place the honey, vinegar, sherry, walnut oil, soy sauce, and garlic in a nonreactive mixing bowl and whisk to mix. Season generously with pepper to taste. Pour this marinade into the bowl with the mushroom strips, making sure that the mushrooms are completely submerged. Let the mushrooms marinate for 30 minutes to 1 hour.

3 Set up the grill for direct grilling (see page 21 for charcoal or gas) and preheat to high.

4 When ready to cook, drain the marinade from the satés and set it aside. Brush and oil the grill grate. Tear off a piece of heavy-duty aluminum foil that is roughly as long as the grill is wide. Fold the piece of aluminum foil in half lengthwise. Place the folded aluminum foil flat on the grate at the edge closest to you. Arrange the satés on the grate so that they are over the fire but the exposed ends of the skewers are on top of the foil shield to keep them from burning. Depending upon the size of the grill, you may need to cook the satés in batches. Grill the satés until the portobellos are browned and very tender, 1 to 2 minutes per side (4 to 8 minutes in all). Brush the satés with some of the marinade as they cook. Transfer the grilled satés to a platter or serve them hot off the grill, basting them one last time with marinade before serving.

YIELD:

Makes 16 satés

NOTE: Walnut oil is available at gourmet shops and health food stores. You can substitute hazelnut, sesame, or extra-virgin olive oil.

Seattle, Wash.

COCONUT CURRY CHICKEN SATES

Here's the third of our trio of tiny Amer-Asian kebabs known as satés. This recipe was also inspired by Seattle's Wild Ginger, but similar versions turn up at Thai and Malaysian restaurants throughout North America. The part of the chicken traditionally used for satés is the thigh—an economical cut with considerably more flavor and less tendency to dry out than a skinless, boneless chicken breast. Breasts are quicker and easier to handle, however, so you can use them if you prefer. Note the use of an aluminum foil shield to protect the bamboo skewers from burning.

METHOD:
Direct grilling

ADVANCE PREPARATION:
1 to 2 hours for marinating the chicken

INGREDIENTS:
2 cloves garlic, coarsely chopped
1 piece (1 inch) fresh ginger, peeled and coarsely chopped
1 to 2 Thai chiles, serrano peppers, or other hot chiles, seeded and coarsely chopped (for hotter satés, leave the seeds in)
2 teaspoons curry powder
1 teaspoon coarse salt (kosher or sea), or more to taste
1 teaspoon freshly ground black pepper, or more to taste
¼ cup unsweetened coconut milk
1 tablespoon fresh lime juice
½ cup finely chopped fresh cilantro
3 pounds chicken thighs, or 2 pounds skinless, boneless chicken breasts
1 to 2 tablespoons vegetable oil

TIPS

Creamlike in consistency, coconut milk is widely available canned and bottled (probably even at your local supermarket). Just be sure to buy an unsweetened one. Otherwise, look for it at ethnic markets or see Mail-Order Sources on page 742. Remember to shake the can or bottle well before opening.

TIPS

The Peanut Sauce and Cucumber Relish on pages 84 and 85 make great accompaniments for these chicken satés.

YOU'LL ALSO NEED:

About 36 long slender (8- to 12-inch) bamboo skewers; heavy-duty aluminum foil

1 Place the garlic, ginger, chile(s), curry powder, salt, pepper, coconut milk, and lime juice in a blender and purée until smooth. Add ¼ cup of the cilantro and gently pulse the blender to mix (don't overblend or the marinade will turn green).

2 Rinse the chicken under cold running water and blot it dry with paper towels. If using chicken thighs, pull off and discard the skin and cut the meat off the bones. Using a very sharp knife, cut each thigh into flat strips about ⅛ inch thick, 3 inches long, and 1 to 2 inches wide. If using chicken breasts, trim off and discard any excess fat, then pull off the tenders, if any. Cut the tendons off the tenders (the easiest way to do this is to pinch the tendon between the knife and the cutting board and cut it off in a sawing motion; for more on trimming chicken breasts, see page 395). Cut each tender in half lengthwise and set aside. Holding your knife on the diagonal, thinly slice the chicken breasts, cutting them on the diagonal of the grain to create strips that are about ⅛ inch thick, 3 inches long, and 1 inch wide. Weave each strip of chicken, including the tender halves, like a ribbon onto a skewer. The chicken will bunch up as it goes on the skewer; gently spread it out with your fingers.

3 Arrange 12 of the satés in a single layer in a nonreactive baking dish. Pour one third of the marinade over the satés in the baking dish, leaving the exposed part of the skewers bare. Turn the satés to coat both sides with the marinade. Arrange 12 more satés on top of the first layer, pour half of the remaining marinade over these, and turn this layer to coat evenly. Arrange the remaining satés on top of the second layer, pour the remaining marinade over these, and turn to coat evenly. Let the chicken marinate in the refrigerator, covered, for 1 to 2 hours.

4 Set up the grill for direct grilling (see page 21 for charcoal or gas) and preheat to high.

5 When ready to cook, brush and oil the grill grate. Tear off a piece of heavy-duty aluminum foil that is roughly as long as the grill is wide. Fold the piece of aluminum foil in half lengthwise. Place the folded aluminum foil flat on the grate at the edge closest to you. Arrange the satés on the grate so that they are over the fire but the exposed ends of the skewers are on the foil shield to keep them from burning. Depending upon the size of the grill, you may need to cook the satés in batches. Grill the satés until cooked through, 1 to 2 minutes per side, basting them with oil. Transfer the grilled satés to a platter and sprinkle the remaining ¼ cup of cilantro over them.

YIELD:

Makes about 36 satés

Aspen, Colo.

LAMB ANTICUCHOS

Shish kebab. Tandoori. Saté. The culinary melting pot of the United States is filled with foreign grill specialties that have come to have distinctly American flavors. What's next? My hunch is *anticuchos*. These tiny kebabs are the street food of Peru, where they're made with diced beef hearts, marinated with chiles, basted with spiced oil, grilled over charcoal, and served with a fiery chile sauce. *Anticuchos* are turning up on cutting-edge grill menus all across America. Not keen on beef heart? Chef Nobu Matsuhisa, who opened one of the first of his many restaurants in Lima, Peru, uses Colorado lamb for the *anticuchos* he serves at his Aspen restaurant. His version reflects his Japanese heritage. The combination of Asian and South American flavors—of miso and chiles—is stunning. Here's how I imagine he makes them.

METHOD:
Direct grilling

FOR THE LAMB AND CHILE SAUCE:
½ teaspoon dried oregano
½ teaspoon ground cumin
2 cloves garlic, minced
Coarse salt (kosher or sea) and
    freshly ground black pepper

½ cup red or white miso
3 tablespoons aji panca paste, or 2
    tablespoons ancho chile powder
3 tablespoons fresh lemon juice
2 tablespoons sake or sherry
2 tablespoons grapeseed oil
    or vegetable oil
1 pound boneless leg or loin of lamb

FOR THE BASTING MIXTURE:
3 tablespoons grapeseed oil
    or vegetable oil
1 clove garlic, minced
½ teaspoon dried oregano

YOU'LL ALSO NEED:
About 2 dozen small (6-inch) bamboo
    skewers; heavy-duty aluminum foil

1 MAKE THE CHILE SAUCE: Crumble the oregano through your fingers into a nonreactive mixing bowl (crumbling releases the scent). Add the cumin and garlic and ½ teaspoon each of salt and pepper. Mash these together with the back of a wooden spoon. Mix in the miso and *aji panca* paste. Add the lemon juice, sake, and grapeseed oil and stir or whisk until a thick but pourable sauce forms. Taste for seasoning, adding more salt and/or pepper as necessary. Pour half of the chile sauce into several small, attractive nonreactive serving bowls and set aside.

2 Cut the lamb into ½-inch cubes. (Use a ruler if you have to. The cubes of meat should be tiny so they stay tender.) Thread the lamb cubes onto skewers, leaving part of each skewer exposed for a handle. Place the kebabs in a nonreactive baking dish and season with salt and pepper. Brush

TIPS

■ To prepare *anticuchos* the way they do in Lima, you need *aji panca*, a moderately spicy Peruvian red chile commonly sold as a piquant paste in jars. You can find it at Peruvian and Latino markets and at an increasing number of gourmet shops, or see Mail-Order Sources on page 742. In a pinch you could substitute ancho chile powder.

■ Red miso is a salty paste made from fermented soybeans and barley. Miso is available at most natural foods stores and many supermarkets. If you can't find red miso, use white.

the meat on all sides with the remaining chile sauce and let it marinate while you make the basting mixture and set up the grill.

3 MAKE THE BASTING MIXTURE: Combine the oil, garlic, and oregano in a small bowl and mix with a fork. The *anticuchos* can be prepared to this stage up to 3 hours ahead.

4 Set up the grill for direct grilling (see page 21 for charcoal or gas) and preheat to high.

5 When ready to cook, brush and oil the grill grate. Tear off a piece of heavy-duty aluminum foil that is roughly as long as the grill is wide. Fold the piece of aluminum foil in half lengthwise. Place the folded aluminum foil flat on the grate at the edge closest to you. Arrange the *anticuchos* on the grate so that they are over the fire but the exposed ends of the skewers are on top of the foil shield to keep them from burning. Depending upon the size of the grill, you may need to cook the *anticuchos* in batches. Grill the lamb until cooked through, about 1 minute per side (2 to 3 minutes in all). Because the *anticuchos* grill so quickly, you'll need to turn them in the same order that you placed them on the grill. Brush the lamb with the basting mixture as it cooks.

6 Transfer the grilled *anticuchos* to a platter or plates and serve with the bowls of chile sauce on the side for dipping.

YIELD:
Makes about 24 *anticuchos*

Anticuchos *originated in Peru, but their popularity is growing in this country.*

The Southwest

GRILLED SHRIMP COCKTAIL

Shrimp cocktails are such a classic at North American steakhouses, we forget that they're popular throughout the Americas—from Chile to the Yucatán. The Mexican version starts with the familiar ketchup-based sauce, then ups the ante with orange juice (or orange soda), onions, cilantro, and smoky chipotle peppers. That's not a bad starting point, I reasoned, but imagine how much more flavor you would get if you grilled the shrimp over mesquite. The result is a Southwestern shrimp cocktail that electrifies an old standby.

METHOD:
Direct grilling

ADVANCE PREPARATION:
30 minutes for marinating the shrimp

FOR THE SHRIMP AND MARINADE:
24 jumbo shrimp (1½ to 2 pounds), peeled and deveined (see page 522)
3 tablespoons chopped fresh cilantro or flat-leaf parsley
2 cloves garlic, minced
1 teaspoon minced canned chipotle pepper, plus 1 to 2 teaspoons of the juices from the can

2 tablespoons olive oil
2 tablespoons fresh lime juice
Coarse salt (kosher or sea) and cracked black pepper

FOR THE COCKTAIL SAUCE:
1 cup ketchup
¼ cup fresh orange juice
2 tablespoons fresh lime juice, or more to taste
1 tablespoon Worcestershire sauce
1 to 2 canned chipotle peppers, minced, plus 1 to 2 teaspoons of the juices from the can
Coarse salt (kosher or sea) and freshly ground black pepper

FOR SERVING:
3 tablespoons diced white onion
6 sprigs fresh cilantro

YOU'LL ALSO NEED:
24 long slender (8- to 12-inch) bamboo skewers; 2 cups wood chips or chunks (preferably mesquite), unsoaked; heavy-duty aluminum foil

1 PREPARE THE SHRIMP: Rinse the shrimp under cold running water, then blot dry with paper towels. Place the cilantro, garlic, and chipotle with its juices in a nonreactive mixing bowl and toss to mix. Stir in the olive oil and lime juice, season with salt and cracked pepper to taste. Add the shrimp and let them marinate in the refrigerator, covered, for 30 minutes.

2 MAKE THE COCKTAIL SAUCE: Place the ketchup, orange juice, lime juice, Worcestershire sauce, and chipotle(s) with their juices in a nonreactive mixing bowl and whisk to

■ Since shrimp cocktails are usually served cold, you can grill the shrimp ahead of time when you're cooking other things. But you could also serve the shrimp hot off the grill, in which case, I'd use the cocktail sauce as a dip.

■ You can also serve the grilled shrimp in martini glasses, as described in Step 4 of the Volcanic Shrimp Cocktail recipe on page 93.

mix. Taste for seasoning, adding more lime juice as necessary and salt and pepper to taste. Place the sauce in a ramekin or small serving bowl and set aside.

3 Thread each shrimp onto a skewer, inserting it near the head and tail ends so that the shrimp curls like the letter C.

4 Set up the grill for direct grilling (see page 21 for gas or charcoal) and preheat to high. If using a gas grill, place all of the wood chips or chunks in the smoker box or in a smoker pouch (see page 24) and run the grill on high until you see smoke. If using a charcoal grill, preheat it to high, then toss all of the wood chips or chunks on the coals.

5 When ready to cook, brush and oil the grill grate. Tear off a piece of heavy-duty aluminum foil that is roughly as long as the grill is wide. Fold the piece of aluminum foil in half lengthwise. Place the folded aluminum foil flat on the grate at the edge closest to you. Arrange the skewered shrimp on the hot grate so that the shrimp are over the fire but the exposed ends of the skewers are on top of the foil shield to keep them from burning. Depending upon

Fresh shrimp wait their turn for a trip to the scale.

the size of the grill, you may need to cook the shrimp in batches. Grill the shrimp until just cooked through, about 2 minutes per side. When done the shrimp will turn a pinkish white and will feel firm to the touch.

6 To serve, place the bowl of sauce on a platter and arrange the grilled shrimp, still on their skewers, around it. Sprinkle the onion and cilantro sprigs over the sauce and serve at once.

YIELD:

Makes 24 kebabs

Indianapolis, Ind.

VOLCANIC SHRIMP COCKTAIL

I can't tell you who serves the world's best shrimp cocktail. But I can sure tell you who serves the world's hottest. That distinction goes to St. Elmo Steak House in downtown Indianapolis. Every day St. Elmo's kitchen grates several cases of fresh horseradish to make a cocktail sauce so diabolically fiery, it's been known to bring tears to patron's eyes. Much as I love St. Elmo's cocktail sauce, I've never much cared for cold boiled shrimp. After all, if you're going to cook shrimp, why not give it some real flavor by grilling it? So here's a shrimp cocktail that has smoke to back up the heat of the horseradish.

METHOD:
Direct grilling

ADVANCE PREPARATION:
30 minutes to 1 hour for marinating the shrimp

INGREDIENTS:
24 jumbo shrimp (1½ to 2 pounds), peeled and deveined (see page 522)
Coarse salt (kosher or sea) and cracked or coarsely ground black pepper

1 to 3 teaspoons hot red pepper flakes
1 tablespoon dried oregano
2 cloves garlic, minced
3 tablespoons extra-virgin olive oil
4 strips lemon zest (each 1½ by ½ inch; see Notes)
3 tablespoons fresh lemon juice
Volcanic Cocktail Sauce (recipe follows)

YOU'LL ALSO NEED:
2 cups wood chips or chunks (optional; preferably oak), unsoaked; 4 (or 6) martini glasses

1 Rinse the shrimp under cold running water, then blot them dry with paper towels. Place the shrimp in a nonreactive bowl and toss with plenty of salt and black pepper. Add the hot red pepper flakes, oregano, and garlic and toss to mix. Stir in the olive oil, lemon zest, and lemon juice. Let the shrimp marinate in the refrigerator, covered, for 30 minutes to 1 hour.

2 Set up the grill for direct grilling (see page 21 for gas or charcoal) and preheat to high. If using a gas grill, place all of the wood chips or chunks, if desired, in the smoker box or a smoker pouch (see page 24) and run the grill on high until you see smoke. If using a charcoal grill, preheat it to high, then toss all of the wood chips or chunks, if desired, on the coals.

3 When ready to cook, brush and oil the grill grate. Place the shrimp on the hot grate and grill until just cooked through, about 2 minutes per side (see Notes). When done the

TIPS

■ When serving shrimp cocktail, be generous—buy the largest ones you can find. And if you leave the tails on when you peel the shrimp, it makes it easier to dip them in the sauce with your fingers.

■ You can grill the shrimp over gas or charcoal, but for a truly unforgettable cocktail, build a wood fire (see Grilling over a Wood Fire on page 20). At the very least, toss some wood chips on the fire. Because I want a light smoke flavor, I don't bother to soak the chips.

WALL OF FLAME

ST. ELMO STEAK HOUSE

St. Elmo's boasts the world's hottest shrimp cocktail (made with volcanic doses of freshly grated horse-radish; you'll find my version on this page) and prime ribs that tip the scale at 32 ounces. Steaks come in all the usual cuts—filet mignon, New York strip, rib eye—thick, juicy, and charred just the way you like them.

127 South Illinois Street
Indianapolis, Indiana
(317) 635-0636
www.stelmos.com

shrimp will turn a pinkish white and will feel firm to the touch. Transfer the grilled shrimp to a plate and let cool to room temperature. Tightly cover the shrimp with plastic wrap to keep them from drying out, then refrigerate until cold.

4 To serve, divide the Volcanic Cocktail Sauce among 4 (or 6) martini glasses. Drape 6 (or 4) shrimp over the edge of each glass, so that their tail ends hang down over the side.

YIELD:

**Serves 4 very generously or
    6 as a start to a large meal**

NOTES:

■ You can use a vegetable peeler to remove the oil-rich, yellow outer rind of the lemon in strips of zest. Be careful to leave behind the bitter white pith.

■ Threading the shrimp on skewers will make them easier to turn.

Volcanic Cocktail Sauce

This isn't like any cocktail sauce you've ever tasted. It's ornery. It's mean. It's downright misanthropic. And it's about to establish your reputation as a grill jockey who means business. But to achieve the full effect, you must use freshly grated horseradish. When grating the horseradish, don't breathe in the fumes from its volatile oils or put your nose near the grater or food processor; a whiff can be a painful experience.

INGREDIENTS:

**1 piece (6 to 8 ounces) fresh
    horseradish root (6 to 8 inches
    long, depending upon the
    thickness)
1¼ cups ketchup
2 tablespoons fresh lemon juice
Freshly ground black pepper**

1 Peel the horseradish. If using a food processor, cut the horseradish into $1/2$-inch cubes and finely grate using the metal blade. If using a box grater, grate the root on the side with the smallest holes. You should have about $3/4$ cup of grated horseradish.

2 Place the ketchup and lemon juice in a nonreactive mixing bowl. Stir in the horseradish and season with pepper to taste. You can serve the cocktail sauce right away, in which case it will be hot. If you let it sit for a few hours before serving, it will be really hot. The cocktail sauce can be refrigerated, covered, for several days, although after the second day its heat will be less. Bring to room temperature before serving.

YIELD:

Makes about 2 cups

Charlestown, R.I.

GRILLED CLAMS
With Sambuca and
Italian Sausage

L ike most Rhode Islanders, Tim Gilchrist loves clams. A lot. So much that he invented a device to facilitate grilling them—a shellfish grate. The problem with grilling clams and oysters, of course, is that the shells tip, dumping the luscious briny juices onto the fire. The metal frame of Gilchrist's grate holds the bivalves steady, so the juices stay in the shell. This recipe for grilling clams pays homage to Rhode Island's sizeable Italian American population by including sambuca, which adds an unexpected taste of licorice, and Italian sausage.

METHOD:
Direct grilling

INGREDIENTS:
½ pound hot or mild Italian bulk
    sausage
4 tablespoons (½ stick) unsalted
    butter
1 small onion, finely chopped
    (about ½ cup)
½ green bell pepper, finely chopped
    (about ½ cup)
½ red bell pepper, finely chopped
    (about ½ cup)
1 clove garlic, minced

2 cups fresh bread crumbs
    (preferably homemade)
¼ cup sambuca
1 teaspoon Worcestershire sauce
Coarse salt (kosher or sea) and
    freshly ground black pepper
36 littleneck clams
Lemon wedges, for serving
Your favorite hot sauce,
    for serving

YOU'LL ALSO NEED:

Shellfish rack or fish or vegetable grate
    (optional)

1 Heat a nonstick skillet over medium heat. Add the sausage and fry it until lightly browned and crumbly, breaking it up with the edge of a wooden spoon, about 5 minutes. Transfer the cooked sausage to a strainer to drain. Discard the fat from the pan.

2 Melt the butter in the frying pan over medium heat. Add the onion,

TIPS

One way to make shucking easier is to place the clams in the freezer until the shells start to gap. Or ask your fishmonger to do the shucking, reserving the juices.

A freshly shucked littleneck ready for the grill.

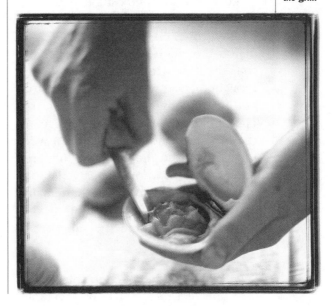

TIPS

To find out where you can order one of Gilchrist's shellfish grates (they're called GreatGrates), see Mail-Order Sources on page 742.

green and red bell peppers, and garlic and cook until lightly browned, 3 to 5 minutes. Stir in the bread crumbs and sauté them until they are lightly browned, about 3 minutes. Stir in the cooked sausage and the sambuca and Worcestershire sauce. Season with salt and black pepper to taste; the sausage mixture should be highly seasoned. The recipe can be prepared to this stage up to a day ahead and refrigerated, covered.

3 Scrub the clams with a stiff brush under cold running water to remove any grit. Discard any clams with cracked shells or shells that fail to close when tapped.

4 Set up the grill for direct grilling (see page 21 for charcoal or gas) and preheat to high.

5 Open a clam, using an oyster knife or blunt paring knife and taking care to spill as little of the juices as possible; Hold the clam in a kitchen towel and, working over the sausage stuffing to catch any juices that spill, insert the blade at the edge where the shell is widest. Pull the blade straight back toward the hinge; stop cutting once you have severed the clam's two adductor muscles. Discard the top shell and place the clam with its juices on the shellfish grate or carefully arrange it on a fish or vegetable grate, if using. Repeat with the remaining clams. Place a spoonful of the sausage mixture in each shell, on top of the clam.

6 When ready to cook, place the shellfish rack or fish or vegetable grate with the clams in it on the hot grate or arrange the clams directly on the grate, positioning them so that the bars hold the shells level. Cover the grill and cook the clams until the juices boil and the shellfish are just cooked through, 3 to 6 minutes (covering the grill ensures that the clams cook from the top as well as the bottom). When done, the clams will be slightly opaque and firm to the touch. Transfer the grilled clams to a platter or plates, taking care not to spill the juices. Serve at once, with lemon wedges and hot sauce on the side.

YIELD:

Serves 6 as an appetizer

VARIATION: Oysters are every bit as good prepared this way. You'll have enough filling for two dozen.

Rhode Island

CLAMS
With Garlic, Pepper, and Parsley

Daunted by the prospect of shucking fresh clams? This recipe is for you. The clam shells pop open all on their own thanks to the heat of the grill. The addition of olive oil, garlic, and hot red pepper flakes reflects Rhode Island's Italian American heritage, and if you choose to use wood chips, they'll add a barbecue-country smoke flavor.

METHOD:
Direct grilling

INGREDIENTS:
4 tablespoons (½ stick) salted butter

4 cloves garlic, minced

¼ cup finely chopped fresh
    flat-leaf parsley

1 to 3 teaspoons hot red pepper flakes

1 teaspoon finely grated lemon zest

¼ cup extra-virgin olive oil

1 cup dry white wine

24 clams (littlenecks or cherrystones)

Lemon wedges, for serving

Crusty bread, for serving

YOU'LL ALSO NEED:
1 cup wood chips or chunks (optional;
    preferably oak or apple), soaked for
    1 hour in water to cover, then drained

1 Melt the butter in a large nonreactive saucepan over high heat on the stove or on the side burner of your grill. Add the garlic, parsley, hot red pepper flakes, and lemon zest and let sizzle until the garlic has lost its rawness but has not quite started to brown, about 3 minutes. Add the olive oil and wine, bring to a boil, and let boil until the wine has lost its raw alcohol flavor and the sauce tastes mellow, 3 to 6 minutes. Remove the saucepan from the heat. The recipe can be prepared to this stage several hours ahead; reheat the broth just before serving.

2 Scrub the clams with a stiff brush under cold running water to remove any grit. Discard any clams with cracked shells or shells that fail to close when tapped.

3 Set up the grill for direct grilling (see page 21 for charcoal or gas) and preheat to high. If using a gas grill, place all of the wood chips or chunks, if desired, in the smoker box or in a smoker pouch (see page 24) and run the grill on high until you see smoke. If using a charcoal grill, preheat it to high, then toss all of the wood chips or chunks, if desired, on the coals.

4 When ready to cook, arrange the clams on the hot grate, positioning them so that the bars hold the shells level. Grill until the shells open, 5 to 8 minutes. Add the clams to the broth as they open. When all are done,

TIPS

Use either littlenecks or cherrystones when making Clams with Garlic, Pepper, and Parsley. Larger clams are too tough for grilling.

Littlenecks and cherrystones should be tightly closed when you buy them.

TIPS

Arnold serves the marrowbones sawed in half lengthwise, which makes for an impressive presentation. Your chief challenge will be finding a butcher who sells marrowbones and is willing to cut them on his meat saw. The bones should be 6 to 8 inches long. If you live in Colorado, you may be able to buy buffalo bones, but beef bones are delectable prepared this way, too.

stir well, then transfer the clams and broth to serving bowls. Serve with lemon wedges and crusty bread.

YIELD:

Serves 4 as an appetizer

Denver, Colo.

"PRAIRIE BUTTER" (Fire-Roasted Marrowbones)

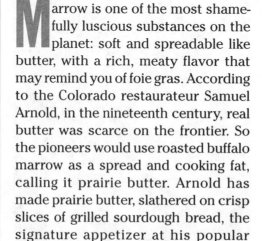

Marrow is one of the most shamefully luscious substances on the planet: soft and spreadable like butter, with a rich, meaty flavor that may remind you of foie gras. According to the Colorado restaurateur Samuel Arnold, in the nineteenth century, real butter was scarce on the frontier. So the pioneers would use roasted buffalo marrow as a spread and cooking fat, calling it prairie butter. Arnold has made prairie butter, slathered on crisp slices of grilled sourdough bread, the signature appetizer at his popular Denver restaurant, The Fort. I've enjoyed marrow on both sides of the

Atlantic (it's a popular if somewhat retro appetizer in France), but Arnold's buffalo bones are my favorite. Of course, I just had to figure out how to cook them on a grill.

METHODS:

Indirect grilling for the marrowbones; direct grilling for the bread

INGREDIENTS:

8 beef or buffalo marrowbones, sawed in half lengthwise
Coarse salt (kosher or sea) and cracked black pepper
8 slices (each ½ inch thick) sourdough bread

1 Set up the grill for indirect grilling (see page 22 for charcoal or gas) and preheat to high. If using a charcoal grill, place a large drip pan in the center.

2 When ready to cook, generously season the marrowbones with salt and pepper. Place the bones, cut side up, in the center of the hot grate, over the drip pan and away from the heat. Cover the grill and cook until the marrow is cooked through (it will look translucent) but not so long that it's melted, 6 to 10 minutes. Transfer the grilled marrowbones to a platter or plates and cover them loosely with aluminum foil to keep warm.

3 Place the bread slices on the grate directly over the fire and grill until nicely toasted on both sides, 1 to 2 minutes per side. Place the toasts on plates or in a basket. Serve the marrowbones with the toasts. To eat, scoop the marrow out of the bones with a butter knife and spread it on the bread. A smooth sipping bourbon makes a good beverage to serve with the marrow.

YIELD:
Serves 8 as an appetizer, 4 as a light main course

Minneapolis. Minn.

GRILLED CHILLED DILLED TOMATO SOUP

I've always been intrigued by the notion of grilled soups. Nothing could be more improbable than cooking a dish whose very essence is its liquidity on a utensil defined by its perforations. But the grill grate can be a great ally for the soup maker—fire roasting corn, fish, and tomatoes produces explosively flavorful chowders, cioppinos, and gazpachos. A case in point is this grilled tomato soup flavored with that most Swedish American flavoring, dill. It was inspired by a tomato soup I had at the Aquant restaurant in Minneapolis. Served with a shot of iced aquavit or Peppar vodka, it's the ultimate summer refresher.

METHOD:
Direct grilling

INGREDIENTS:
1 red bell pepper
3 pounds luscious ripe red tomatoes (preferably plum tomatoes)
1 medium-size red onion, quartered
3 cloves garlic, skewered on a wooden toothpick
1 cucumber, peeled, halved, and seeded (scrape out the seeds with a melon baller)
2 to 3 tablespoons finely chopped fresh dill, plus 6 sprigs for garnish
¼ cup extra-virgin olive oil
2 tablespoons red wine vinegar, or more to taste
Coarse salt (kosher or sea) and freshly ground black pepper

YOU'LL ALSO NEED:
2 cups wood chips or chunks (preferably oak), soaked for 1 hour in water to cover, then drained

The best source for the very ripest tomatoes is your local farm stand.

TIPS

For the ultimate flavor, grill the vegetables over an oak or other wood fire (see Grilling over a Wood Fire on page 20). At the very least, toss some wood chips on the coals.

1 Set up the grill for direct grilling (see page 21 for gas or charcoal) and preheat to high. If using a gas grill, place all of the wood chips or chunks in the smoker box or in a smoker pouch (see page 24) and run the grill on high until you see smoke. If using a charcoal grill, preheat it to high, then toss all of the wood chips or chunks on the coals.

2 When ready to cook, place the bell pepper, tomatoes, onion, garlic, and cucumber on the hot grate. Grill the bell pepper, tomatoes, onion, and garlic until they are blackened on all sides, 4 to 6 minutes per side (16 to 24 minutes in all) for the bell pepper, 3 to 4 minutes per side (12 to 16 minutes in all) for the tomatoes, 3 to 4 minutes per side (9 to 12 minutes in all) for the onion quarters, and 2 to 4 minutes per side (4 to 8 minutes in all) for the garlic. Grill the cucumber just until lightly browned, 3 to 4 minutes per side (6 to 8 minutes in all).

3 Place the grilled bell pepper in a bowl or baking dish, cover with plastic wrap, and let cool to room temperature (the steam trapped by the plastic wrap helps loosen the skin from the pepper). Transfer the rest of the grilled vegetables to a cutting board and let cool. Scrape any really burnt skin off the bell pepper, tomatoes, onion, and garlic, but leave a little of it on; the dark spots will add color and character. Cut the vegetables into 1-inch pieces, place in a food processor, and process to a fine purée. Add the dill and pulse to mix. With the motor running, slowly add the olive oil and vinegar through the feed tube. Add enough water for the soup to be thick but pourable. Season with salt and black pepper to taste; the soup should be highly seasoned.

4 Refrigerate the soup until serving; it should be served cold (if you want to serve it right away, you could add ice cubes instead of water). Try to serve the soup within a few hours of its being made as its virtue lies in its freshness. If the soup has sat for a few hours, taste it for seasoning before serving, adding more salt, black pepper, and/or vinegar as necessary. To serve, ladle the soup into bowls and garnish each with a sprig of dill. Or you can serve the soup as a shooter in a shot glass; in this case you'll have about 32 servings of $1\frac{1}{2}$ ounces. One more alternative would be to serve the soup in disposable plastic wine glasses.

YIELD:

Makes 6 cups

VARIATION: To make a yellow tomato soup, use yellow tomatoes and peppers and yellow squash instead of the cucumber.

The South

PINK LEMONADE

Pink lemonade is a staple on the barbecue circuit in the United States, and I'm probably the only customer who ever asks if it's home-made. It usually isn't. That's a shame, because few beverages are more refreshing than lemonade that's been made from scratch—especially when you use both the sour juice and the fragrant zest. There's no such thing as a pink lemon, of course, so the color here comes from a shot of grenadine.

INGREDIENTS:

6 lemons
½ cup sugar, or more to taste and for serving (optional)
1 tablespoon grenadine
Ice cubes, for serving

1 Rinse all of the lemons and blot them dry with paper towels. Using a vegetable peeler, remove the zest in strips from 3 of the lemons. Be careful to leave behind the bitter white pith. Set all of the lemons aside. Combine the lemon zest, sugar, and 1 cup of water in a nonreactive saucepan over medium-high heat and bring to a boil. Reduce the heat to medium and let the mixture simmer for 10 minutes. Strain this lemon syrup into a pitcher and let cool.

2 Cut 5 of the lemons in half and squeeze the juice from them to

TIPS

When choosing lemons, avoid fruits with knobby ends (they tend to be dry) or ones with a greenish tinge (they tend to be sour—even for lemons).

make 1 cup. Add the lemon juice, 4 cups of water, and the grenadine to the lemon syrup and stir. Taste for sweetness, adding more sugar as necessary.

3 Serve the lemonade in tall glasses filled with ice cubes. Cut the remaining lemon into wedges or slices for garnish. For a fancier presentation, rub the rim of each glass with cut lemon and dip it in sugar before filling it. The lemonade can be made 2 days ahead and stored in the pitcher in the refrigerator, but it is best served the day it is made.

YIELD:

Makes about 6 cups

TIPS

■ Sometimes diced or puréed melon is added to "Rice-Ade." You can also add fresh berries, orange segments, or other fruit.

■ To give this beverage a Pacific Rim twist, use jasmine or basmati rice.

The Southwest

"RICE-ADE" (Rice, Almond, and Cinnamon Cooler)

Lemonade and limeade are favorite thirst quenchers at American barbecues. Hispano-Americans (especially those with roots in Mexico and Central America) enjoy an equally refreshing beverage—a cool milky blend of rice, almonds, and spices called *orchata*. This recipe is a compilation of *orchatas* I've enjoyed in southern California and the Southwest. I'm not saying it will ever replace beer, but it's mighty tasty.

ADVANCE PREPARATION:

12 hours for the "Rice-Ade" to sit

INGREDIENTS:

½ cup white rice
¼ cup slivered almonds
1 cinnamon stick
   (about 2 inches long)
3 cloves
3 allspice berries
2 strips lemon zest
   (each ½ by 2 inches; see Note)
2 strips orange zest
   (each ½ by 2 inches; see Note)
¼ cup sugar, or more to taste
½ teaspoon vanilla extract
1 cup diced or puréed melon
   or whole berries or 1 large
   orange, peeled and segmented
   (optional)

1 Combine the rice, almonds, cinnamon stick, cloves, allspice berries, lemon and orange zests, sugar, and vanilla with 5 cups of water in a pitcher and let sit overnight in the refrigerator, covered.

2 Remove and discard the cinnamon stick from the rice mixture. Stir the mixture well and purée it in a blender, working in several batches. Pour the mixture through a fine-meshed strainer into a pitcher. Taste for sweetness, adding more sugar as necessary. Stir in the melon, berries, or orange segments, if using. The "Rice-Ade" will keep for several days in the refrigerator.

YIELD:
Makes about 1 quart

NOTE: You can use a vegetable peeler to remove the oil-rich outer rind of the lemon and oranges in strips of zest. Be careful to leave behind the bitter white pith.

Detroit, Mich.

NOT YOUR AVERAGE SWEET TEA

Sweet tea (highly sweetened iced tea) is the beverage of choice for barbecue in many parts of the South, often surpassing beer in popularity. (This isn't as surprising as it may seem, given the deep roots of barbecue in abstemious religious communities.) But the best iced tea I ever tasted was not in the South, but in the Frost Belt— Detroit, to be more precise—which is home to a large Middle Eastern community. Iced tea sometimes comes perfumed with rose water in these parts, and I'd be hard pressed to name a more invigorating drink on the planet.

INGREDIENTS:
2 tablespoons loose black tea, or 4 tea bags
3 tablespoons sugar, or more to taste
2 tablespoons pine nuts
About 1 teaspoon rose water
Ice cubes, for serving

1 Bring 1 quart of water to a boil in a large pot over high heat. Remove the pot from the heat and add the tea and sugar. Stir until the sugar dissolves and let steep for 5 minutes, then taste the tea and add more sugar if necessary.

2 Strain the tea into a pitcher (if using a glass pitcher, place a metal spoon in it first to absorb the heat). Let cool to room temperature. Stir in the pine nuts and add rose water to taste. Refrigerate until serving; the tea will keep for several days. Serve in tall glasses with ice cubes.

YIELD:
Makes about 1 quart

TIPS

■ Rose water is a perfumed flavoring sold at Middle and Near Eastern markets. There's no substitute, but an equal amount of orange flower water will add a similar perfumy quality.

■ If you want to make this sweet tea in a hurry, instead of brewing the tea you could use instant iced tea mix (that's what lots of barbecue folks do in the South).

Iced tea is utterly transformed by a few drops of rose water.

Maryland

GINGER ALE AND MILK

You must use whole milk for this recipe, as skim milk may curdle.

My Grammie Sarah wasn't a great cook and she certainly wasn't much of a grill jockey. (She did fire up a mean broiler and there was no limit to her enthusiasm for lamb chops.) Her contribution to this book is a curious beverage that was beloved in our family and that I still drink to this day: ginger ale and milk. The combination may sound strange, even possibly repulsive—until you stop to think about a Coke or root beer float. You'll find this one of the most bracing beverages ever to slake a thirst at a cookout.

INGREDIENTS:

¾ cup cold milk

¾ cup cold ginger ale

Pour the milk into a cold mug or tall glass. Gradually add the ginger ale, stirring gently to mix.

YIELD:

Serves 1; can be multiplied as desired

VARIATION: For variety, substitute an equal amount of root beer, cola, or even orange soda for the ginger ale.

Santa Fe, N.Mex.

CHIMAYO COCKTAIL

To experience the Spanish Southwest, visit a town like Chimayó with its adobe churches and apple orchards planted by Spanish missionaries. Chimayó's superlative apple cider was the inspiration for this cocktail served at the Coyote Cafe in Santa Fe.

INGREDIENTS:

1 large apple, rinsed

6 tablespoons fresh lime juice

6 cups fresh apple cider

¾ cup (6 ounces) tequila

6 tablespoons (3 ounces) crème de cassis

2 cups ice cubes, plus more for serving

1 Core the apple and cut it into 8 wedges. Put the apple wedges in a small nonreactive bowl and toss with 1 tablespoon of the lime juice.

2 Just before serving, combine the cider, tequila, crème de cassis, and the remaining 5 tablespoons of lime juice in a pitcher with the 2 cups of ice. Stir well until all the ingredients are mixed. Pour the Chimayó Cocktail into ice-filled highball glasses. Press an apple wedge onto the rim of each glass for garnish and serve at once.

YIELD:

Serves 8

Texas

TEQUILA WITH SANGRITA (A Spicy Tomato Juice and Vegetable Chaser)

When I was growing up, tequila was pretty much something you drank to get drunk. Few people knew about *reposados* or *añejos* (wood-aged tequilas). No one approached tequila with the sort of connoisseurship traditionally reserved for single-malt scotch or small-batch whisky. Times have changed; now high-end Mexican restaurants in Texas, California, and even Chicago routinely serve top-shelf sipping tequilas the traditional way—with *sangrita,* a spicy chaser made with tomato, orange and/or lime juice and often a little chile powder or pickled pepper juice for punch. Frequently a few radishes, scallions, or jicama slices are served alongside to munch on. I can't think of a better prelude to fajitas or other Tex-Mex barbecue.

INGREDIENTS:

¾ cup tomato juice

½ cup fresh orange juice

3 tablespoons fresh lime juice,
    or more to taste,
    plus 1 or 2 lime wedges

1 to 2 tablespoons juice from
    pickled jalapeño peppers, or
    more to taste

1 to 2 tablespoons finely grated onion
    with its juices (optional)

¼ cup pure chile powder

9 ounces tequila

1 bunch radishes, stemmed, rinsed,
    and cut in half, for serving

1 medium-size jicama, peeled and
    thinly sliced, for serving

YOU'LL ALSO NEED:

12 large shot or cordial glasses

1 Place the tomato juice, orange juice, lime juice, jalapeño juice, and onion, if using, in a pitcher and mix them together. Taste for seasoning, adding more lime juice and/or jalapeño juice as necessary; the *sangrita* should be highly seasoned. The *sangrita* can be made to this point several hours ahead.

2 Spread the chile powder in a shallow bowl. Using the lime wedge(s), moisten the rims of 6 of the glasses. Turn over a lime-moistened glass and dip it in the chile powder to coat the rim. Repeat with the 5 remaining moistened glasses. Pour the *sangrita* into the chile-dusted glasses. Divide the tequila evenly among the remaining 6 glasses. Arrange the radishes and jicama on a platter. Invite everyone to sip the tequila and *sangrita* alternately, munching on the radishes and jicama between bites.

YIELD:

Serves 6

TIPS

To best enjoy this, serve a fine, well-aged tequila, preferably one made with 100 percent agave cactus. By law, tequila need contain only 51 percent agave, but the best brands contain more. Good brands of 100 percent agave tequila include Don Julio, Po, Patrón, and Sauza Hornitos.

TEXAS BARBECUE

This is a story of moist smoky briskets, crackling crisp goat, and ribs tender enough to pull apart with your fingers. It's a tale of hot sweaty days, smoke-filled nights, burning ambition, cruel betrayal, and single-minded obsession. In other words, it's a story about a Texan's favorite food: barbecue. Like cowboy boots and the Alamo, barbecue lies at the very heart of the Texas psyche. Texans love barbecue so much, they routinely eat it for breakfast (Louie Mueller's in Taylor, for example, opens its doors at 10 A.M.). Few other foods have such power to stir emotions and make mouths water. Of course, no two Texans can agree on what the perfect barbecue is, but they'll fight for all they're worth to defend it against what passes for barbecue in Memphis, Kansas City, or North Carolina.

It's easier to say what Texas barbecue isn't than what it is. While pork, chicken, and even *cabrito* (goat) turn up at Texas barbecue joints, beef is the undisputed king. Brisket is the meat on which the state's great pit masters stake their reputations, but almost any cut of beef is fair game for the pit, including clod (beef shoulder), sirloin roast, rib roast, prime rib, and even tenderloin.

If you're expecting a lot of fancy rubs or marinades, go to Memphis or California. The basic seasonings for Texas barbecue are salt, pepper, and perhaps a little cayenne. "It's not what you put on," says Rick Schmidt, owner of the Kreuz Market in Lockhart. "It's what you leave off." (For more about the Kreuz Market see page 166.)

Likewise, if your vision of barbecue involves oceans of sweet sticky barbecue sauce, you've come to the wrong place. At most Texas barbecue joints, the sauce is an afterthought—a little ketchup mixed with vinegar, water, and meat drippings. At Kreuz Market, the granddaddy of all Texas barbecue joints, they don't serve barbecue sauce, period. "We let our meat speak for itself," Schmidt says.

Elsewhere in the United States, sweet baked beans, coleslaw, and corn on the cob may be an integral part of the barbecue experience. In Texas they're at best superfluities and often simply omitted. As for the niceties of tableware, well, a lot of great Texas barbecue joints serve on butcher paper, and it's considered good manners to eat with your fingers.

It's hard to define precisely what Texas barbecue is because the fuels, cookers, and cooking times vary dramatically from

In Texas, even the frying pans go over the fire.

region to region and pit boss to pit boss. The native woods and pecan are popular in the eastern part of the state; oak in central Texas; and mesquite in the west. The traditional Texas barbecue pit looks like a long, rectangular brick box with a fire at one end, a chimney at the other, and counterweighted metal panels serving as covers. But upright pits of the sort used in Kansas and Missouri can be found in the state (at the original Sonny Bryan's in Dallas, for example—to read more about Sonny Bryan's, see page 624), and

at least one highly regarded establishment uses motorized, thermostatically controlled electric cookers.

But, the moment you get good barbecue in Texas, you'll know it—whether it's served on paper or on a plate; at a roadside shack or a restaurant. The meat will be as dark and shiny as a lump of coal on the outside and tender and moist within. The arresting aroma of wood smoke will be omnipresent and the meat will be so flavorful, you won't even need a sauce.

Where's the best barbecue? You can find passable, even superior, barbecue in big cities, like Dallas and Houston, but the very best is served in small towns and in the countryside. And the absolute best is to be found within a hundred mile radius of Austin. With a little perseverance and some serious time behind the steering wheel, you can visit four in a single day. One word of warning: Many Texas barbecue restaurants open and close early (just after lunch) and are closed on Sunday, so call ahead for hours to avoid disappointment.

WHERE TO EAT TEXAS BARBECUE

City Market
633 East Davis
Luling
(210) 875-9019

———

Cooper's Old Time Pit
B-B-Que
604 West Young
(Texas Highway 29)
Llano
(915) 247-5713
www.coopersbbq.com

Kreuz Market
619 North Colorado
Street
Lockhart
(512) 398-2361
www.kreuzmarket.com

Louie Mueller's
Barbecue
206 West 2nd Street
Taylor
(512) 352-6206

———

The Salt Lick
18300 Farm to
Market Road 1826
Driftwood
(512) 858-4959
www.saltlickbbq.net

———

Sam's Bar-B-Cue
2000 East
12th Street
Austin
(512) 478-0378

Sonny Bryan's
Smokehouse
(original location)
2202 Innwood Road
Dallas
(214) 357-7120
www.sonnybryans
bbq.com

———

Goode Co. Texas
BBQ
5109 Kirby Drive
Houston
(713) 522-2530
www.goodecompany.
com

Live-Fire

Raichlen's rule holds that if something tastes good baked, fried, sautéed, steamed, or even raw, it probably tastes even better grilled—which brings us to grilled salads. The smoke and sizzle of a live fire electrify salad ingredients, be they bell peppers, calamari, or even lettuce. Grilling adds a whole new dimension to salads—if you don't believe me, check out the grilled Caesar salad or the tomato and hearts of palm salad with grilled corn. Many of the ingredients can be grilled in advance, leaving you the time and energy to focus on the main course. Of course, no barbecue is complete without coleslaw, and in this chapter you'll find five—everything from an Arkansan slaw with apples to a spicy jicama slaw from the Southwest. No, I'm not suggesting you grill the slaws; I like my cabbage to crunch. But for just about anything else, when it comes to salads, fire up the grill.

Salads

TIPS

To get the full effect of this salad, you need the taste of wood—preferably oak. Instructions for Grilling over a Wood Fire are found on page 20. Alternatively, you can use wood chips in a charcoal or gas grill.

Walt's Wharf is the birthplace of grilled Caesar salad.

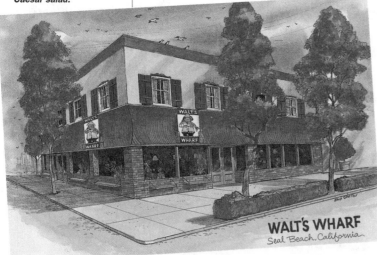

WALT'S WHARF
Seal Beach, California

Seal Beach, Calif.

GRILLED CAESAR SALAD

Caesar salad originated in Tijuana, Mexico, in 1924, the invention of a genial Italian restaurateur named Caesar Cardini. It reaches its apotheosis at Walt's Wharf in Seal Beach, California. The owners of this popular fish house pass two of the traditional ingredients, romaine lettuce and croutons, over a blazing oak fire for a few minutes—just long enough to singe the lettuce and impart the heady aroma of wood smoke. The grilled romaine is served in halves and crowned with the creamy, cheesy, anchovy-spiked dressing that has made the Caesar America's favorite salad.

METHOD:
Direct grilling

INGREDIENTS:

3 medium-size heads romaine lettuce
12 thin slices French bread,
    cut sharply on the diagonal
2 tablespoons extra-virgin olive oil
About ¾ cup Creamy Caesar Dressing
    (recipe follows)
12 anchovy fillets, drained and
    blotted dry (optional)
1 chunk (8 ounces) Parmesan cheese,
    (see Note) for shaving over
    the salad
Freshly ground or cracked black
    peppercorns

YOU'LL ALSO NEED:

2 cups wood chips or chunks
    (preferably oak), soaked for
    1 hour in water to cover,
    then drained

1 Strip any blemished or wilted leaves off the heads of lettuce. Cut each head in half lengthwise, leaving the stem end attached. Place the cut side under cold running water and rinse it thoroughly, gently separating the leaves with your fingers but leaving them attached to the stem. Rinse all of the lettuce until clean, a process that may take 5 or 10 minutes (you can also rinse the lettuce in a large bowl, using several changes of cold water). Holding each lettuce half by the stem, gently shake it over the sink, then place the lettuce halves in a salad spinner and spin dry.

2 Lightly brush the bread slices with the olive oil. The recipe can be prepared to this stage a couple of hours ahead. Keep the lettuce refrigerated.

3 Set up the grill for direct grilling (see page 21 for charcoal or gas) and preheat to high. If using a charcoal grill, preheat it to high, then toss all of the wood chips or chunks directly on the coals. If using a gas grill, place all of the wood chips or chunks in the smoker box or in a smoker pouch (see page 24) and run the grill on high until you see smoke.

4 When ready to cook, brush and oil the grill grate. Place the lettuce halves, cut side up, and bread slices on the hot grate, and grill until the lettuce leaves are slightly wilted and singed (the inside should remain crisp) and the bread is a deep golden brown, 1 to 3 minutes per side.

5 Transfer the grilled lettuce halves to a platter or plates, cut side up. Cut off and discard the stem ends. Spoon the dressing over the lettuce. Place a slice of grilled bread on either side of each lettuce half and arrange 2 anchovy fillets, if using, in an X on top of each. Using a cheese slicer or vegetable peeler, shave large thin slices of the cheese over the salad. Sprinkle it with pepper and serve at once.

YIELD:
Serves 6

NOTE: Cardini made his Caesar salad with Parmesan cheese. I grew up using Romano, a tangy sheep's milk cheese that's a little saltier and sharper than Parmesan. Either will work just fine.

Creamy Caesar Dressing

Caesar salad was the first dish I ever learned to prepare. (My teacher was Mr. Lewis, a venerable maître d' at the late 3900 Restaurant in Baltimore.) The genius of its dressing lies in combining seemingly discordant ingredients—garlic, anchovies, sharp Parmesan cheese—into a harmonious whole. In the old days, the creamy consistency came from a raw or coddled egg. That's how I still make it, but knowing the reluctance of some folks to eat uncooked eggs, sometimes I'll use an egg substitute, which is pasteurized. This makes more dressing than you need for Grilled Caesar Salad, but it's always good to have extra on hand; you can use it for the Grilled Caesar Salad Pizza (page 157).

INGREDIENTS:

2 cloves garlic, coarsely chopped

3 anchovy fillets, coarsely chopped (optional)

2 ounces Parmesan cheese, coarsely chopped

1 tablespoon Dijon mustard

1 tablespoon Worcestershire sauce

1 large egg

¾ cup extra-virgin olive oil

3 tablespoons fresh lemon juice, or more to taste

1 tablespoon red wine vinegar

½ teaspoon coarse salt (kosher or sea), or more to taste

½ teaspoon freshly ground black pepper, or more to taste

WALL OF FLAME

WALT'S WHARF

Welcome to Walt's, home of the grilled artichoke (see page 589), the grilled Caesar salad— today one of Walt Babcock's signature dishes—and the grilled banana split. As for fish, try the white sea bass or lemongrass-marinated local swordfish smokily charred on a red-oak–burning grill; fish doesn't get much fresher.

201 Main Street
Seal Beach, California
(562) 598-4433
www.waltswharf.com

1 Place the garlic, anchovies, if using, cheese, mustard, Worcestershire sauce, and egg in a blender or food processor and purée to a smooth paste. With the motor running, gradually add the olive oil, lemon juice, and vinegar.

2 Add the salt and pepper and process until a smooth, creamy dressing forms. Taste for seasoning, adding more salt, pepper, and/or lemon juice as necessary. The dressing can be refrigerated, covered, for up to 3 days.

YIELD:
Makes 1½ cups

TIPS

For most of my life, hearts of palm have come in cans. In the last decade, I've noticed that fresh hearts of palm are turning up in gourmet shops in Florida and New York City. Fresh hearts of palm aren't cheap, but their crisp texture and sweet, nutty taste are well worth the investment.

Florida

TOMATO AND HEARTS OF PALM SALAD
With Grilled Corn

What's now my home state, Florida, is the only place in the continental United States where fresh hearts of palm are harvested commercially. Their delicate nutty flavor was the inspiration for this colorful salad. Palm hearts make a perfect counterpoint to the smoky sweetness

of grilled corn, and the tomatoes add a fruity acidity. In the unlikely event that you have leftover grilled corn, this is a great way to use it up. (I always grill a few extra ears, but they seem to disappear pretty quickly at our house.)

METHOD:
Direct grilling

INGREDIENTS:

2 ears sweet corn, shucked

**5 tablespoons extra-virgin olive oil
   (see Notes)**

**Coarse salt (kosher or sea) and
   freshly ground black pepper**

1 clove garlic, minced

1 tablespoon Dijon mustard

1 teaspoon brown sugar

1 tablespoon fresh lime juice

**1 tablespoon red wine vinegar,
   or more to taste**

**1 fresh or pickled jalapeño pepper,
   seeded and minced (optional)**

**¼ cup finely chopped fresh cilantro or
   flat-leaf parsley**

**12 ounces fresh hearts of palm, or
   1 can (14 ounces) hearts of palm,
   drained and rinsed**

**1 pint grape or cherry tomatoes,
   rinsed and stemmed (see Notes)**

**1 head Boston or Bibb lettuce, broken
   into leaves, rinsed, and spun dry**

1 Set up the grill for direct grilling (see page 21 for charcoal or gas) and preheat to high.

2 When ready to cook, brush the corn with 2 tablespoons of the olive oil and season generously with salt and pepper. Place the corn on the hot grate and grill until the kernels are nicely browned on all sides, 2 to 3 minutes per side (8 to 12 minutes in all).

3 Transfer the corn to a cutting board and let cool. Cut the kernels off the cobs, using lengthwise strokes of a chef's knife. You should have about 1⅓ cups.

4 In a nonreactive mixing bowl, combine the garlic, mustard, brown sugar, lime juice, vinegar, and jalapeño. Add ½ teaspoon salt and ¼ teaspoon pepper. Whisk until the salt dissolves. Whisk in the remaining 3 tablespoons of olive oil in a thin stream, then add the corn kernels and cilantro. You can also put the ingredients for the dressing in a jar and shake to mix. Taste for seasoning, adding more salt, pepper, and/or vinegar as necessary; the dressing should be highly seasoned.

5 Cut the hearts of palm length wise into halves or quarters (cut small ones in half, large ones in quarters). If using cherry tomatoes, cut each one in half; grape tomatoes can be left whole. Line 4 salad plates or a platter with lettuce leaves. Arrange the hearts of palm and tomatoes in alternating rows on top. Just before serving, spoon the dressing on top and serve at once.

YIELD:
Serves 4

NOTES:
▪ You can use 2 tablespoons melted butter in place of the 2 tablespoons olive oil to brush the corn.

▪ Grape tomatoes are tiny, sweet tomatoes that are even smaller than cherry tomatoes.

New York, N.Y.

GRILLED PITA BREAD SALAD

Say *fattoush* to Arab-Americans, and their eyes will light up with pleasure. This popular pita bread salad turns up at Middle Eastern restaurants around the United States. And no one makes it better than Al Bustan in Manhattan. *Bustan* is the Arabic word

TIPS

This salad is a great way to use up stale or leftover pita bread. You can grill the pita well ahead—even the night before.

Fresh pita bread, hot from the oven.

for orchard, and an autumn fruit is one of the secrets of a truly exceptional pita bread salad: the sweet-sour, juicy, ruby red seeds of the pomegranate. Coupled with smoky grilled pieces of pita and a colorful assortment of crisp vegetables, you've got a salad that fairly explodes with flavor. Add grilled shrimp or chicken to turn it into a light entrée.

METHOD:
Direct grilling

INGREDIENTS:
4 pita breads
⅓ cup extra-virgin olive oil
1 clove garlic, cut in half
1 luscious, ripe, red tomato, cut into
    ½-inch dice, with its juices
1 pomegranate, broken into seeds,
    with its juices (see Notes)
1 cucumber, peeled, seeded,
    and cut into ½-inch dice
    (see Notes)
½ red bell pepper, cored, seeded,
    and cut into ½-inch dice
½ green bell pepper, cored, seeded,
    and cut into ½-inch dice
8 romaine lettuce leaves, rinsed,
    spun dry, and thinly sliced
    crosswise
3 scallions, white and green parts,
    trimmed and finely chopped
¼ cup chopped fresh flat-leaf parsley
¼ cup chopped fresh spearmint or
    other mint
2 tablespoons fresh lemon juice
1 tablespoon red wine vinegar, or
    more to taste
Coarse salt (kosher or sea) and
    freshly ground black pepper

1 Set up the grill for direct grilling (see page 21 for charcoal or gas) and preheat to high.

2 When ready to cook, lightly brush the pitas with a little of the olive oil. Place the pitas on the hot grate and grill until toasted and browned on both sides, 1 to 3 minutes per side. Transfer the grilled pitas to a platter and let cool. The recipe can be prepared to this stage up to 24 hours ahead.

3 Not more than 20 minutes before serving, rub the inside of a nonreactive salad or mixing bowl with the cut garlic. Rub the grilled pitas with the cut garlic. Break or tear the pitas into bite-size pieces and place in the bowl. Add the tomato, pomegranate, cucumber, bell peppers, lettuce, scallions, parsley, mint, lemon juice, vinegar, and the remaining olive oil. Season with salt and pepper and toss to mix. Taste for seasoning, adding more salt and/or vinegar as necessary; the salad should be highly seasoned. Serve the salad at once.

YIELD:
Serves 4 to 6

NOTES:
■ To remove the seeds from a pomegranate, cut the fruit in half lengthwise. Using your fingers, break the halves into sections, then remove the individual seeds. Work over a bowl to catch the juices.

■ To seed a cucumber, cut it in half lengthwise. Scrape out the seeds with a melon baller or spoon.

San Francisco, Calif.

SOURDOUGH BREAD SALAD

Bread salads are part of San Francisco's Italian heritage, invented by frugal peasants as a way to utilize stale loaves and embraced by contemporary chefs to show off the Bay Area's extraordinary artisanal bakeries. Sourdough is the granddaddy of San Francisco breads—a staple in the days of the gold rush, when a jar of starter was almost as prized as a pickax or sack of gold dust. It's a remarkable loaf indeed, darkly browned, handsomely crosshatched, with a crisp crust, a chewy center, and a distinctive tang that makes it one of America's best breads. Actually, legend credits a Frenchman, not an Italian, with the creation of the distinctive San Francisco bread, and the company founded by Isidore Boudin at the time of the gold rush still makes sourdough today (the other big Bay Area bakery is Acme). This grilled bread salad offers a contemporary twist on a California-Italian classic, not to mention a great way to use up any stale sourdough.

Plant manager Fernando Padilla with freshly baked sourdough at San Francisco's Boudin Bakery.

TIPS

You can make this salad with fresh sourdough, but it's even better if the bread is slightly stale. San Francisco sourdough bread is available at many gourmet shops around the country, but you can order it by mail from Boudin (see Mail-Order Sources on page 742). But you don't have to use bread from San Francisco; chances are there's an artisanal bakery in your area that makes a good sourdough bread.

METHOD:
Direct grilling

INGREDIENTS:
4 thick slices (each ¾ inch thick)
    sourdough bread
4 plum tomatoes
2 torpedo onions (see Notes),
    cut in half lengthwise
⅓ cup plus 2 tablespoons
    extra-virgin olive oil
2 ribs celery, thinly sliced
1 cucumber, peeled, seeded,
    and cut into ½-inch dice
    (see Notes)
12 black olives (kalamata or Italian)
¼ cup fresh flat-leaf parsley leaves
12 fresh basil leaves, thinly
    slivered, plus 4 whole sprigs
    for garnish
1 tablespoon drained capers
3 tablespoons red wine vinegar,
    or more to taste
Coarse salt (kosher or sea) and
    freshly ground black pepper

1 Set up the grill for direct grilling (see page 21 for charcoal or gas) and preheat to high.

2 Lightly brush the bread slices, tomatoes, and onions with olive oil, using about 2 tablespoons in all. Let the bread slices sit on a rack to dry out for a few minutes, while you grill the tomatoes and onions.

3 When ready to cook, brush the grill grate. Place the tomatoes and onions on the hot grate and grill until darkly browned; the tomato skins should be blistered. This will take 2 to 3 minutes per side (8 to 12 minutes in all) for the tomatoes and 3 to 4 minutes per side (6 to 8 minutes in all) for the onion halves. Transfer the grilled vegetables to a cutting board and let cool.

4 Place the bread slices on the hot grate and grill until toasted and brown on both sides, 1 to 3 minutes per side. Transfer the bread to the rack to cool.

5 Cut the grilled bread and tomatoes into ¾-inch cubes, reserving the tomato juices. Thinly slice the onions. Place the bread, tomatoes with the reserved juices, and onions in an attractive nonreactive serving bowl. Add the celery, cucumber, olives, parsley, slivered basil, capers, vinegar, and the remaining ⅓ cup olive oil and toss to mix. Taste for seasoning, adding more vinegar as necessary and salt and pepper to taste; the salad should be highly seasoned. You can serve the salad right away, but it will be better if you let it sit for half an hour or so to let the bread absorb the juices. Toss again just before serving. Garnish with the basil sprigs and serve.

YIELD:
Serves 4 generously

NOTES:
■ A torpedo onion is an elongated, slender onion that tapers at the ends. It's great for grilling because its shape

... you've got a salad that explodes with flavor

maximizes the surface area that's exposed to the fire. If unavailable, you can use a red onion cut lengthwise into quarters.

■ To seed a cucumber, cut it in half lengthwise. Scrape out the seeds with a melon baller or spoon.

Chicago, Ill.

CHARLIE TROTTER'S BEEF & ROQUEFORT SALAD

So what do the superstar chefs grill when they're cooking at home? As it turns out, the same uncomplicated dishes that you or I would make. This salad was inspired by Chicago's legendary Charlie Trotter, who has written a very user-friendly book on home cooking, *Charlie Trotter Cooks at Home*. Using a minimal number of ingredients, Trotter plays to all taste buds with a pucker of fresh lemon juice, a salty blast of blue cheese, and the earthy oniony tones of a shallot. I've tinkered

with the master's recipe, adding a few of my own touches, like the balsamic vinegar and toasted walnuts.

METHOD:
Direct grilling

ADVANCE PREPARATION:
20 minutes for marinating the beef

INGREDIENTS:
½ **teaspoon coarse salt**
    (kosher or sea)
½ **teaspoon freshly ground**
    black pepper
½ **teaspoon grated lemon zest**
3 **tablespoons fresh lemon juice**
2 **tablespoons balsamic vinegar**
1 **cup extra-virgin olive oil**
1 **shallot, minced**
    (3 to 4 tablespoons)
1 **piece center-cut beef tenderloin**
    (about 12 ounces), or 12 ounces
    tenderloin tips
6 **cups baby spinach leaves,**
    rinsed and spun dry
6 **ounces Roquefort cheese,**
    crumbled (about ¾ cup)
¼ **cup walnut halves or pieces,**
    lightly toasted (see page 584)

1 Place the salt, pepper, lemon zest, lemon juice, and vinegar in a nonreactive mixing bowl and whisk until the salt dissolves. Whisk in the olive oil in a thin stream. Stir in the shallot.

2 Place the beef in a nonreactive baking dish and pour about ⅓ cup of the vinaigrette over it, turning to coat all sides. Set the remaining vinaigrette aside for dressing the salad. Let the beef marinate in the

TIPS

You could go out and buy center-cut beef tenderloin for this recipe, but you'll save money if you can find tenderloin tips. Not only are they cheaper, but because of their tapered shape they char up great on the grill. For that matter, the salad would be perfectly delicious prepared with thinly sliced grilled flank steak or skirt steak.

WALL OF FLAME

CHARLIE TROTTER'S

Chicago chef Charlie Trotter has received countless distinctions, but I wager the last one he's expecting is a *BBQ USA* Wall of Flame award. Yet, how else do you honor a celebrated culinary superstar who not only grills prime meats and exotic game over wood, but varies the wood from season to season, using robust oak in the winter and grapevine trimmings and herbs in spring and summer?

816 West Armitage Ave
Chicago, Illinois
(773) 248-6228
www.charlietrotters.com

Award-winning Chicago chef Charlie Trotter has the heart of a pit master.

derloin, 2 to 3 minutes per side (6 to 9 minutes in all) for medium-rare tenderloin tips.

6. Transfer the grilled beef to a cutting board and let rest for 3 minutes. Meanwhile, spoon half of the remaining vinaigrette over the spinach mixture and gently toss to mix. Mound the salad on a platter or plates. Thinly slice the beef on the diagonal and arrange it over the spinach. Spoon the remaining vinaigrette over the salad and garnish with the remaining cheese.

YIELD:
Serves 4

refrigerator, covered, for 20 minutes, turning several times so that it marinates evenly.

3. Place the spinach leaves, two thirds of the Roquefort, and the walnuts in a nonreactive mixing bowl, but don't toss.

4. Set up the grill for direct grilling (see page 21 for charcoal or gas) and preheat to high.

5. When ready to cook, brush and oil the grill grate. Place the beef on the hot grate and grill until cooked to taste, 3 to 4 minutes per side (12 to 16 minutes in all) for a medium-rare center-cut piece of ten-

Louisiana

CHICKEN SALAD
With Spicy Cajun Dressing

Just about everyone loves chicken salad, but this isn't your everyday variety—not with chicken that is brashly seasoned with homemade Cajun spice mix, marinated in buttermilk, and dished up with an electrified variation on ranch dressing. The

Louisiana roots of the recipe are obvious. What you may not know is that ranch dressing was the creation of the Henson family in the 1950s. The ranch in question was their Hidden Valley dude ranch, located near Santa Barbara, California.

METHOD:
Direct grilling

ADVANCE PREPARATION:
30 minutes for marinating the chicken

INGREDIENTS:
1½ pounds chicken tenders or skinless,
    boneless chicken breasts
2 teaspoons coarse salt
    (kosher or sea)
½ teaspoon garlic powder
½ teaspoon onion powder
½ teaspoon dried thyme
½ teaspoon dried oregano
½ teaspoon freshly ground
    black pepper
½ teaspoon sweet paprika
¼ to ½ teaspoon cayenne pepper
1 cup buttermilk
Spicy Cajun Dressing (recipe follows)
8 cups mesclun (mixed baby salad greens),
    rinsed and spun dry
3 tablespoons currants or raisins
½ cup toasted pecans
    (page 584)

1 Trim any excess fat or sinews off the chicken and discard. Rinse the chicken under cold running water, then drain and blot dry with paper towels. Put the chicken in a baking dish.

2 Combine the salt, garlic powder, onion powder, thyme, oregano, black pepper, paprika, and cayenne in a small bowl and stir to mix. Set aside 1½ teaspoons of this rub for the Spicy Cajun Dressing. Sprinkle the remaining rub over the chicken on all sides, patting it onto the meat with your fingertips. Pour the buttermilk over the chicken and let marinate in the refrigerator, covered, for 30 minutes, turning it once or twice so that it marinates evenly.

3 Place the dressing in a large nonreactive mixing bowl. Place the mesclun, currants, and ¼ cup of the pecans on top, but don't toss.

4 Set up the grill for direct grilling (see page 21 for charcoal or gas) and preheat to high.

5 When ready to cook, brush and oil the grill grate. Place the chicken on the hot grate and grill until just cooked through, 2 to 3 minutes per side for tenders, 4 to 6 minutes per side for breasts. To test for doneness, poke the chicken in the thickest part with your finger; it should feel firm to the touch. If using chicken breasts, transfer them to a cutting board and let rest for 1 minute, then cut them sharply on the diagonal into ½-inch strips.

6 Toss the salad and mound it on a platter or plates. Place the strips of grilled chicken on top. Sprinkle the remaining ¼ cup pecans over the salad and serve at once.

YIELD:
Serves 4

The chicken tender (a.k.a. finger) is a slender muscle found on the bone side of a chicken breast. Sometimes chicken tenders are sold by themselves at the supermarket. If you can't find them, prepare the recipe with skinless, boneless chicken breasts.

Spicy Cajun Dressing

Most of us forget that salad dressing didn't always come in bottles at the supermarket. Here's a homemade version of ranch dressing that owes its richness to mayonnaise, sour cream, and buttermilk, and its spice to Cajun seasoning. It takes no time to mix it up.

INGREDIENTS:

¼ **cup mayonnaise**

¼ **cup sour cream**

½ **cup buttermilk**

1 **tablespoon cider vinegar,**
    or more to taste

2 **tablespoons chopped fresh flat-leaf**
    parsley or another herb

1 **scallion, white and green parts,**
    trimmed and minced

1 **clove garlic, minced**

½ **teaspoon grated lemon zest**

1½ **teaspoons rub reserved from**
    Cajun Chicken

Freshly ground black pepper and
    coarse salt (kosher or sea)

Place the mayonnaise and sour cream in a nonreactive mixing bowl and whisk to mix. Whisk in the buttermilk, vinegar, parsley, scallion, garlic, lemon zest, and rub. Taste for seasoning, adding more vinegar as necessary, pepper, and perhaps a little salt to taste.

YIELD:

Makes 1 cup

Miami, Fla.

SHRIMP SALAD With Grapefruit Adobo

Hang around Spanish Caribbean cooks in Miami long enough and you'll hear the term *adobo*. The piquant mixture of garlic, cumin, and citrus juice is used to marinate everything from chicken to pork to seafood. My choice for the citrus here is grapefruit, and the adobo doubles as a salad dressing. To prevent cross-contamination, keep the adobo used to marinate the shrimp separate from what you'll use as the dressing—something you should do whenever you want to serve a marinade as a sauce.

METHOD:

Direct grilling

ADVANCE PREPARATION:

30 minutes to 1 hour for marinating the shrimp

IINGREDIENTS:

3 cloves garlic, minced

1 teaspoon coarse salt (kosher or sea)

1 teaspoon ground cumin

1 teaspoon dried mint

½ teaspoon freshly ground black pepper

¾ cup fresh grapefruit juice

¼ cup extra-virgin olive oil

12 jumbo shrimp (about 1 pound), rinsed, peeled, and deveined (leave the tail shells on)

2 grapefruits

5 to 6 cups mesclun, rinsed and spun dry

1 Place the garlic, salt, cumin, mint, and pepper in a mortar and mash to a paste with a pestle or place them in a nonreactive mixing bowl and mash with the back of a wooden spoon. Whisk in the grapefruit juice and the olive oil. You can also purée all of these ingredients in a blender. Transfer half of this mixture to a nonreactive mixing bowl and stir in the shrimp. Let the shrimp marinate for 30 minutes to 1 hour in the refrigerator, covered, stirring once or twice so that they marinate evenly. Set the remaining grapefruit juice mixture aside to use as a salad dressing.

2 Peel the grapefruits, removing all of the white pith. Working over a bowl to catch the juices, cut in between the membranes to release the grapefruit sections. Remove any seeds with a fork. Mound the mesclun in the center of a platter or 4 plates and place the grapefruit segments on top. The salad can be prepared up to 2 hours ahead to this stage and refrigerated, covered.

3 Set up the grill for direct grilling (see page 21 for charcoal or gas) and preheat to high.

4 When ready to cook, brush and oil the grill grate. Drain the marinade from the shrimp and discard it. Place the shrimp on the hot grate and grill until cooked through (it will be firm and white), 2 to 3 minutes per side. Arrange the grilled shrimp on top of the salad and spoon the reserved salad dressing over all. Serve at once.

YIELD:

Serves 4

San Francisco, Calif.

CALAMARI SALAD
With White Beans and Bitter Lettuce

At the risk of sounding older than I care to, I remember when squid was taboo, when the mere mention of this tentacled sea fare was enough to blunt appetites and stop conversations. Today we can't get

TIPS

As with so many things, the smaller the squid, the more tender. A good fishmonger may be able to get you squid about the size of your forefinger. If squid still doesn't catch your fancy after everything I've just written, this salad is almost as tasty made with shrimp.

When buying calamari, clear eyes denote freshness.

When I grill squid, I like it to have a gentle smoke flavor, so I either grill it over wood (see **Grilling over a Wood Fire on page 20**) or toss some oak chips on the fire. I don't bother to soak the chips—you want a light wood flavor, not heavy smoke.

enough of the mild white mollusk now familiarly known as calamari. The name change helps; calamari sounds a lot more appetizing than squid. And squid, a great source of pure, virtually fat-free protein, has a mild flavor that's perfect for absorbing the irresistible scent of wood smoke. If you haven't tried squid, you should, and if your experience is limited to fried calamari, this grilled salad will give you a new perspective. The smoky squid is a perfect foil for the earthy flavor of the white beans and bitter lettuce. The recipe was inspired by a wonderful Mediterranean restaurant in San Francisco called Delfina.

METHOD:
Direct grilling

ADVANCE PREPARATION:
30 minutes for marinating the squid

INGREDIENTS:

**1 pound cleaned small squid (have your
fishmonger do the cleaning)**
1 clove garlic, minced
**1 teaspoon coarse salt (kosher or sea),
or more to taste**
**½ teaspoon hot red pepper flakes,
or more to taste**
1 teaspoon grated lemon zest
Freshly ground black pepper
¼ cup fresh lemon juice, or more to taste
¾ cup extra-virgin olive oil
**3 tablespoons chopped fresh flat-leaf
parsley, plus 1 cup parsley sprigs**
**1½ cups cooked cannellini beans
(cooked from scratch or from
a 15-ounce can; see Notes)**
12 cherry tomatoes, cut in half
**4 cups bite-size pieces frisée or lettuce
(see Notes)**

YOU'LL ALSO NEED:
**1 cup wood chips or chunks
(preferably oak), unsoaked**

1 Rinse the squid inside and out, under cold running water, then blot dry, inside and out, with paper towels. If the squid comes with the tentacles separated, you may wish to skewer them on a slender bamboo skewer so they don't fall through the grate. Place the squid in a nonreactive bowl or baking dish.

2 Place the garlic, salt, hot red pepper flakes, and lemon zest in a large nonreactive mixing bowl, add ½ teaspoon black pepper, and mash to a paste with the back of a wooden spoon. Add the lemon juice and whisk until the salt dissolves. Whisk in the olive oil and chopped parsley. Taste for seasoning, adding more salt, hot red pepper flakes, and/or lemon juice as necessary. Pour half this mixture over the squid, stirring to coat each piece. Set the remaining mixture aside in the mixing bowl for dressing the salad. Let the squid marinate in the refrigerator, covered, for 30 minutes.

3 Place the beans, tomatoes, frisée, and parsley sprigs in the bowl with the remaining dressing, but don't toss.

4 Set up the grill for direct grilling (see page 21 for charcoal or gas) and preheat to high. If using a charcoal grill, preheat it to high, then toss all of the wood chips or chunks on the coals. If using a gas grill, place all of the wood chips or chunks in the smoker box or in a smoker pouch (see page 24) and run the grill on high until you see smoke.

5 When ready to grill, place the squid on the hot grate and grill until cooked through (the squid will turn white), 1 to 2 minutes per side.

6 Toss the bean salad and mound it on 4 plates. Decoratively prop 3 or 4 grilled squid upright on each salad. Grind a little black pepper over the top and serve at once.

YIELD:
Serves 4

NOTES:
■ If using canned beans, rinse them well in a colander under cold running water, then let drain.

■ Frisée is a slender, jagged, pale green salad green with a pleasantly bitter flavor.

The South

GRILLED OKRA SALAD

Okra is the vegetable many Americans love to hate. We hate it on account of its tendency to become slimy when overcooked, which is usually how okra is served. (Actually, unless you grew up in the South, you may never have tasted okra, and if you have, you've probably voluntarily done so only once.) This is a shame, because okra possesses a fine flavor—with hints of asparagus, green beans, even fiddlehead ferns—but it's more aristocratic than all three. Grilling is about the best way I know to cook the finger-shaped pods: The searing heat brings out the okra's sweetness, while at the same time minimizing the slime factor. In this colorful salad, the taste of smoke is reinforced by the addition of grilled corn and red bell pepper. The combination of okra and corn is certainly Southern in spirit, although I doubt that any Southerner, belle or otherwise, has served a grilled okra salad. But maybe you won't want to tell people what they're eating—at least not until they've cleaned their plates.

METHOD:
Direct grilling

TIPS

The salad is served cold, so you may want to grill the vegetables a day or two ahead of time, when you're grilling something else.

For a delicious flavor, grill the okra over a wood fire (see Grilling over a Wood Fire on page 20). At the very least, toss some wood chips on the fire.

The ultimate way to buy okra—from a roadside farm stand.

INGREDIENTS:

1 pound fresh okra (see Note)

About 4 teaspoons plus ¼ cup extra-virgin olive oil

Coarse salt (kosher or sea) and freshly ground black pepper

2 ears sweet corn, shucked

3 scallions

1 red bell pepper

3 tablespoons chopped fresh flat-leaf parsley, plus 4 parsley sprigs

1½ tablespoons tarragon vinegar or cider vinegar, or more to taste

1 large ripe tomato, thinly sliced (12 slices)

YOU'LL ALSO NEED:

1 cup wood chips or chunks (preferably oak or hickory), unsoaked

1 Rinse the okra under cold running water, then blot dry with paper towels. Trim the tips off the stems of the okra but do not cut into the pods. Place the okra in a mixing bowl, toss with 2 teaspoons of the olive oil, and season with salt and pepper. Lightly brush the ears of corn with olive oil, using about 1 teaspoon per ear, and season them with salt and pepper.

2 Set up the grill for direct grilling (see page 21 for charcoal or gas) and preheat to high. If using a charcoal grill, preheat it to high, then toss all of the wood chips or chunks on the coals. If using a gas grill, place all of the wood chips or chunks in the smoker box or in a smoker pouch (see page 24) and run the grill on high until you see smoke.

3 When ready to cook, brush the grill grate. Place the okra, corn, scallions, and bell pepper on the hot grate (position the okra and scallions so that they are perpendicular to the bars). Grill the vegetables until nicely browned on all sides, 2 to 4 minutes per

side (4 to 8 minutes in all) for the okra, 3 to 5 minutes per side (6 to 10 minutes in all) for the scallions, 2 to 3 minutes per side (8 to 12 minutes in all) for the corn, and 3 to 5 minutes per side (12 to 20 minutes in all) for the bell pepper.

4 Place the grilled bell pepper in a bowl or baking dish and cover with plastic wrap. Let the pepper cool to room temperature, about 20 minutes (the steam trapped by the plastic wrap helps loosen the skin from the pepper). Transfer the remaining grilled vegetables to a cutting board and let cool. Cut the okra crosswise into ½-inch slices. Trim and chop the scallions. Cut the kernels off the corn cobs, using lengthwise strokes of a chef's knife. Pull any burnt skin off the bell pepper, core and seed it, then cut the flesh into ½-inch dice. Place the okra slices, chopped scallions, corn kernels, and diced bell pepper in a nonreactive mixing bowl with the chopped parsley, the remaining ¼ cup of olive oil, and the vinegar. Toss to mix, seasoning the salad with salt and pepper to taste. Taste for seasoning, adding more vinegar as necessary; the salad should be highly seasoned.

5 Place 3 tomato slices on each of 4 salad plates. Evenly divide the okra salad among the 4 plates, mounding it in the center of each. Garnish each salad with a parsley sprig and serve at once.

YIELD:
Serves 4

NOTE: When buying okra, look for small, springy green pods. Avoid large or dark okra, which tend to be tough and stringy. Trim off the very end of the stem, but be careful you don't cut into the cap: Exposure to air makes okra slimy, so it's important to keep the pod intact.

VARIATION: Sometimes I leave the grilled okra pods whole, arranging them in rows or in a starburst pattern atop the tomato slices. If you want to do this, combine the corn kernels, diced bell pepper, and scallions in a nonreactive bowl with the ¼ cup of olive oil and the vinegar, season with salt and pepper, and stir to mix. Spoon this mixture over the okra and tomatoes.

Miami, Fla.

SLAW THE JOE'S STONE CRAB WAY

My all-time favorite coleslaw comes not from a barbecue joint but from Miami's legendary crab house, Joe's Stone Crab. It's an easy vinegar-based slaw that would be right at home in North Carolina, and it goes great with any sort of fatty barbecue, from brisket and ribs to a whole hog. Joe's family (now in its fifth generation at the restaurant) has served this tart, sweet, tooth-squeakingly crisp slaw—

with its signature garnish of sliced tomato, mayonnaise, and relish—to adoring multitudes since 1913.

FOR THE DRESSING:

⅓ **cup cider vinegar**

3 **tablespoons sugar, or more**
    to taste

1 **teaspoon salt, or more to taste**

½ **teaspoon freshly ground black pepper**

FOR THE SLAW:

½ **medium-size head green cabbage**
    (about 16 ounces)

2 **large ripe tomatoes, cut crosswise**
    into ¼-inch slices

4 **tablespoons mayonnaise**
    (preferably Hellmann's)

2 **tablespoons sweet pickle relish**

1 MAKE THE DRESSING: Combine the vinegar, sugar, salt, and pepper in a large nonreactive mixing bowl and whisk until the sugar and salt dissolve. Taste for seasoning, adding sugar or salt as necessary; the dressing should be highly seasoned.

2 MAKE THE SLAW: Remove the core from the cabbage and discard it. Cut the cabbage into 4 chunks. Finely shred the cabbage in a food processor using the shredding disc or using a mandoline. Work in batches so as not to overcrowd the processor bowl. You'll have about 5 cups of cabbage.

3 Add the shredded cabbage to the bowl with the dressing, stir to mix, then let stand for 10 minutes. Mound the slaw on a platter or plates. Lean the tomato slices against the coleslaw. Garnish with dollops of mayonnaise,

placing a spoonful of relish in the center of each.

YIELD:
Serves 4

Texas

FIRECRACKER SLAW

I created this fiery slaw for a Super Bowl barbecue story I wrote for *USA Today*. The pyrotechnics came from the addition of fresh and pickled jalapeño peppers. The slaw will send you lunging for your beer.

FOR THE DRESSING:

1½ **teaspoons coarse salt**
    (kosher or sea), or more
    to taste

1 **clove garlic, minced**

½ **cup cider vinegar**

⅓ **cup sugar, or more to taste**

2 **tablespoons Dijon mustard**

2 **tablespoons vegetable oil**

2 **tablespoons pickled jalapeño pepper**
    juice, or more vinegar

1 **to 2 teaspoons of your favorite**
    hot sauce, such as
    Tabasco

½ **teaspoon freshly ground**
    black pepper

½ **teaspoon celery seed**

TIPS

The secret to the slaw is to cut the cabbage into paper-thin shreds. Joe's uses a meat slicer. At home, you could use a mandoline (see Mail-Order Sources on page 742) or the thinnest shredding disc of your food processor.

The slaw will send you lunging for your beer.

FOR THE SLAW:

1 medium-size head green cabbage
(2 to 2¼ pounds)
2 carrots, peeled and grated
or shredded
½ red bell pepper, thinly slivered
½ green bell pepper, thinly slivered
1 to 3 fresh jalapeño peppers,
seeded and thinly sliced
(for a hotter slaw, leave
the seeds in)
1 to 3 tablespoons sliced pickled
jalapeño peppers

1 MAKE THE DRESSING: Place the salt and garlic in a large nonreactive mixing bowl and mash to a paste with the back of a wooden spoon. Add the vinegar, sugar, mustard, oil, jalapeño pepper juice, hot sauce, black pepper, and celery seed and whisk until the sugar and salt dissolve. Taste for seasoning, adding more salt and/or sugar as necessary; the dressing should be highly seasoned.

2 MAKE THE SLAW: Remove the core from the cabbage and discard it. Cut the cabbage into 8 chunks. Finely shred the cabbage in a food processor using the shredding disc or using a mandoline. Work in several batches so as not to overcrowd the processor bowl. You'll have 8 to 10 cups of cabbage.

3 Add the shredded cabbage, the carrots, red and green peppers, and fresh and pickled jalapeños to the dressing and toss to mix. Let the slaw stand for at least 10 minutes, but not more than 3 hours before serving.

YIELD:
Serves 8 to 10

Arkansas

ARKANSAS SLAW
With Apples and Celery

Skip Steele calls it the best coleslaw in America. That's no mean compliment, coming from one of the top barbecue guns in St. Louis— winner of a Memphis in May Whole Hog Championship and co-founder of Missouri's supersuccessful Super Smokers restaurants. Skip was born in Arkansas, and whenever he gets anywhere near his old stamping grounds he makes a pilgrimage to a cinder block barbecue shack in Devalls Bluff called Craig's. Its coleslaw is a masterpiece of balance: The tartness of the vinegar is offset by just the right touch of sugar, with an audible crunch supplied by cabbage, apple, and celery. Here's how I imagine Craig's makes it.

WALL OF FLAME

CRAIG'S BAR-B-QUE

Go for smoky and spicy ribs, pork shoulder tender enough to cut with a fork (not that anyone would actually eat barbecue with a fork), and appley cole slaw that a friend of mine drives 150 miles just to buy in bulk.

Highway 70 West
Devalls Bluff, Arkansas
(870) 998-2616

TIPS

The easiest way to achieve the fine-chopped texture of the original is with a food processor fitted with a chopping blade.

FOR THE DRESSING:

½ cup mayonnaise

3 tablespoons cider vinegar, or more to taste

3 tablespoons sugar

1 teaspoon celery salt, or more to taste

1 teaspoon black pepper

FOR THE SLAW:

1 small or ½ large head green cabbage, cored and cut into 1-inch pieces (about 1½ pounds)

1 small onion, quartered

1 Red Delicious apple, peeled, cored, and cut into 1-inch pieces

2 ribs celery, cut into 1-inch pieces

1 MAKE THE DRESSING: Combine the mayonnaise, vinegar, sugar, celery salt, and pepper in a large nonreactive mixing bowl and whisk until the sugar and salt dissolve.

2 MAKE THE SLAW: Finely chop the cabbage, onion, apple, and celery in a food processor by pulsing the motor (this is a chopped, not sliced or shredded, slaw). Work in batches so as not to overcrowd the processor bowl.

3 Add the chopped cabbage, onion, apple, and celery to the dressing and toss to mix. Taste for seasoning, adding more vinegar and/or celery salt as necessary. Let the slaw stand for at least 10 minutes before serving. The slaw can be refrigerated, covered, for several days.

YIELD:
Serves 8

Barbecue is a family affair at the Memphis in May Barbecue Cooking Contest.

The Southwest

SPICY JICAMA SLAW

J icama is a tan-skinned, white-fleshed, turnip-shaped root vegetable with a snappily crisp texture and an earthy flavor that lies midway between potato and apple. Most people associate it with Southwestern cooking, and to play this up I've added poblano and serrano peppers. The result is a slaw that's perfect with everything from rotisserie chicken to barbecued pork to grilled fish.

INGREDIENTS:

1 large jicama, peeled
4 carrots, trimmed and peeled
1 red or yellow bell pepper,
    cored and seeded
1 poblano pepper, or ½ green
    bell pepper
1 to 3 serrano or jalapeño peppers,
    seeded and minced
1 piece (1 inch) fresh ginger,
    peeled
1 tablespoon sugar, or more
    to taste
1 clove garlic, minced

¼ cup rice vinegar, or more
    to taste
1½ tablespoons Asian (dark)
    sesame oil
¼ cup chopped fresh cilantro
3 scallions, white and green parts,
    trimmed and finely chopped
Coarse salt (kosher or sea) and
    freshly ground black pepper

1 Cut the jicama, carrots, bell pepper, poblano and serrano peppers, and ginger into matchstick slivers (fine julienne) in a food processor using the shredding disc or using a mandoline.

2 Place the sugar and garlic in a large nonreactive serving bowl and mash to a paste with the back of a wooden spoon. Add the vinegar and whisk until the sugar dissolves. Add the sesame oil, cilantro, scallions, and julienned vegetables and toss to mix. Season with salt and pepper to taste. The slaw can be made to this stage up to 2 hours ahead, and refrigerated, covered.

3 Just before serving, taste for seasoning, adding more salt, sugar, and/or vinegar as necessary; the slaw should be a little sweet and a little sour.

YIELD:
Serves 8

TIPS

■ Once you had to go to an ethnic market to find jicama; today it's probably available at your local supermarket. Look for a firm, heavy root free of wrinkles.

■ The easiest way to julienne the vegetables for the slaw is to use a mandoline or the shredding disc of a food processor.

SUPER SMOKERS

And the Rebirth of St. Louis Barbecue

SUPER SMOKERS

1711 West Highway 50
O'Fallon, Illinois
(618) 624-6742
(and other locations)

It sure seems like the Gateway City would have terrific barbecue. After all, there's a St. Louis–cut rib (a spare rib with the brisket removed from the underside). And one of the most famous barbecue sauces in the Midwest—Maull's—is manufactured there. But most Americans, even most hog-a-maniacs, would be hard pressed to name a single landmark St. Louis barbecue restaurant. Certainly, there's no place with the stature or history of an Arthur Bryant's in Kansas City or Charlie Vergos Rendezvous in Memphis. In fact, during my first eating tour of St. Louis, in 1997, I visited a half-dozen barbecue joints with local reputations in the sort of neighborhoods tourists are discouraged from visiting. None served barbecue I would voluntarily order again.

To be sure, there's a very sweet, slightly acidic, sticky, tomato-based barbecue sauce (usually made without liquid smoke) I've come to associate with St. Louis. I've also sampled a distinctive pork side dish, snoots (deep-fried pig snouts), which are sufficiently sui generis to qualify as a regional classic. But St. Louis ribs tended to be soft, even saccharine, and more often than not are braised in the oven, not smoked in a pit. (One local formula calls for briefly grilling the ribs, then baking them all afternoon drowned in sauce—hardly what I'd call true barbecue.)

THE BIG THREE

Enter three hog-o-holics—Terry Black, Skip Steele, and Ron Skinner—who founded the St. Louis–based Super Smokers Bar-B-Que in 1995. Black is the operation's front man, an Arkansas-born smoke meister who once offered the following description of his occupation: "I don't have a job. I party every day and get paid for it." He and his former college roommate, Skip Steele (now the company's director of operations), began competing in barbecue contests in 1987. The third musketeer, Ron Skinner, is a former human resources manager and a veritable surgeon when it comes to trimming and serving up whole hog.

The Super Smokers business plan articulated an ambitious goal: "to redefine St. Louis barbecue." In less than a decade, the company has evolved from a two-guy catering operation to a four-branch restaurant chain with 170 employees. Super Smokers now runs barbecue boutiques in the local supermarket chain Dierbergs and concessions at the Edward Jones Dome (home of the St. Louis Rams) and Busch Stadium (the Cardinals' home). Along the way, they've virtually reinvented the St. Louis rib.

But ask the trio about their proudest moment, and they won't talk restaurant openings or sales growth. No, the apotheosis of a lifetime in barbecue took place at

Super Smokers (left to right) Terry Black, Skip Steele, and Ron Skinner charm a judge at the Memphis in May barbecue competition.

the 2000 Memphis in May World Championship Barbecue Cooking Contest, when the Super Smokers were proclaimed world champions in the whole hog category.

At their restaurants, the Super Smokers have followed some St. Louis barbecue traditions and reinvented others. For example, their championship barbecue sauce is modeled on the city's sweet, tomato-based sauce (the master touch here is a shot of apple juice and liquid cayenne). And in keeping with the local preference for pork, the Super Smokers bestsellers are top loin ribs and pork shoulders. On the other hand, the Super Smokers make extensive use of rubs and spice mixes to add a depth of flavor not traditionally found in St. Louis barbecue. For example, their baby backs are cured overnight in a thick crust of brown sugar, salt, and black pepper. Pork shoulders receive a three-day soak in Italian dressing and mustard.

NAMING THE PITS

All of Super Smokers' meats are lengthily smoked in a pit (smoke has not played a major role in traditional St. Louis barbecue). The second of the Super Smokers restaurants, located in O'Fallon, Illinois, and today the corporate headquarters, boasts two of the largest smokers ever manufactured by Ole Hickory Pits. Christened "Hogzilla One" and "Hogzilla Two," these mammoth pits burn apple wood, which the St. Louis smoke meisters believe is the secret to their meats.

In a city accustomed to eating spareribs, the Super Smokers pioneered the use of top loin—baby back—ribs. "Whenever we try to put St. Louis–cut spareribs on the menu, our customers vote with their wallets for baby backs," observes Terry Black. In one year, the Super Smokers can dish up more than 125 tons of ribs, slow-cooked to perfection. "Take a bite and what do you see? Tooth marks," says Steele. "A proper rib will have some chew to it: It shouldn't fall off the bone."

The trio has succeeded in turning St. Louis on to the virtues of pork shoulders, which they smoke for fourteen to sixteen hours. "Last year, we sold more than a half million pounds of shoulders," Black says. Super Smokers also serves brisket, not to mention a Kansas City–style smoky barbecue sauce and a Carolina-style sweet mustard sauce. Ever eager to broaden the barbecue horizons of their fellow St. Louisans, the Super Smokers are succeeding handily.

> "I don't have a job.
> I party every day and get
> paid for it."
>
> TERRY BLACK
> ARKANSAS-BORN SMOKE MEISTER

Breads and

B read on the grill? Sounds preposterous. But the grill was the original toaster and it still provides an incredibly delicious and effective way to prepare bread dishes. In this chapter you'll find suggestions for toasting bread on the grill—from garlic bread slathered with Parmesan cheese, chives, and butter to an Arawak cassava bread. There are also recipes for doughs and breads you can actually cook on the grill, including Canadian Indian bannock and Navajo grilled fry bread. Along the way, you'll be treated to glorious grilled flat breads and pizzas. If you're looking for bread that's delectably different, head for the grill.

Pizzas

Little Italy, U.S.A.

GRILLED GARLIC BREAD #5
With Parmesan and Chives

Grilled garlic bread is a staple in the Raichlen household. I love the way bread soaks up smoke flavors when you toast it over the fire. I love the variety of possible toppings, from melted or creamed butter to olive oil or an oil flavored with herbs. I serve grilled bread at virtually every barbecue I host. The version here features a golden topping of garlic butter and freshly grated Parmesan cheese, and it's truly irresistible. Why am I calling this #5? It's the fifth variation of garlic bread in the *Barbecue! Bible* series. I just can't stop going back for more.

METHOD:
Direct grilling

INGREDIENTS:
12 tablespoons (1½ sticks) salted butter, at room temperature
4 cloves garlic, minced
¼ cup freshly grated Parmesan cheese
3 tablespoons finely chopped fresh chives
½ teaspoon freshly ground black pepper
1 loaf supermarket French bread

1 Place the butter, garlic, cheese, chives, and pepper in a bowl and beat to mix. Set the garlic butter aside.

2 Using a serrated knife, cut the bread sharply on the diagonal into ½-inch-thick slices. Using a spatula, spread a thin layer of the garlic butter on both sides of the bread slices. The bread can be prepared ahead to this stage; press the buttered slices back together as if reassembling the loaf and wrap them with plastic wrap. The buttered bread can be refrigerated for up to 6 hours.

3 Set up the grill for direct grilling using a two-zone fire (see page 22 for charcoal or gas); preheat one zone to medium-high and leave the other zone unlit so you can move the bread over it if it starts to burn.

4 When ready to cook, brush and oil the grill grate. Place the bread slices over the medium-high zone of the grill and toast them until golden brown, 1 to 3 minutes per side. Don't take your eyes off the grill for a second, as the bread can burn quickly. Serve the garlic bread hot off the grill.

YIELD:
Makes about 20 slices

VARIATIONS: Substitute ¾ cup extra-virgin olive oil for the butter. Add some minced prosciutto and/or lemon zest. To make Caribbean grilled garlic bread, omit the cheese, use cilantro instead of chives, and add a little minced Scotch bonnet chile.

TIPS

■ This is one time when a loaf of cheap supermarket French bread will work just as well as an artisanal baguette.

■ When making a lot of grilled garlic bread, cut the loaves in half the long way and butter both sides of each half loaf. (It's easier to turn a half loaf than a batch of slices.)

Santa Maria, Calif.

SANTA MARIA GARLIC BREAD

S ample barbecue in Santa Maria, California, and along with the tri-tips (see page 183) and the pinquito beans (see page 641), you'll almost always find garlic bread. And the soft, oversize loaves of "French" bread sold in supermarkets are perfect for grilling (in other words, don't worry if you can't find artisanal baguettes for this recipe). While they don't usually use parsley when they make garlic bread in the Santa Maria Valley, I like the way it looks and tastes. For a full description of barbecue in the Santa Maria Valley, see page 186.

METHOD:
Direct grilling

INGREDIENTS:

10 tablespoons (1¼ sticks) salted butter

3 cloves garlic, finely chopped

3 tablespoons finely chopped fresh flat-leaf parsley

1 loaf supermarket French bread

1 Melt the butter in a saucepan over medium heat. Add the garlic and parsley and cook until the garlic is fragrant but not brown, about 2 minutes. Remove the saucepan from the heat.

2 Using a serrated knife, cut the bread sharply on the diagonal into ½-inch-thick slices. Lightly brush some of the garlic butter on both sides of each slice of bread. Work with a light touch; if you soak the bread the dripping butter will catch fire.

3 Set up the grill for direct grilling using a two-zone fire (see page 22 for charcoal or gas); preheat one zone to medium-high and leave the other zone unlit so you can move the bread over it if it starts to burn.

4 When ready to cook, brush and oil the grill grate. Place the buttered bread slices over the medium-high zone of the grill and toast them until golden brown, 1 to 3 minutes per side. Don't take your eyes off the grill for a second,

French bread for grilling—artisanal baguettes or supermarket loaves both work great.

... a golden topping of garlic butter ...

as the bread can burn quickly. Transfer the grilled bread to a basket and serve at once.

YIELD:
Makes about 20 slices

Detroit, Mich.

GRILLED PITAS
With Sesame Seeds and Cracked Pepper

Pita bread is the traditional accompaniment for bell pepper and eggplant dips. And some of the best pita bread in the United States comes from Detroit, home to a large Middle Eastern community. There it's often baked the traditional way—in a wood-burning oven. That was my inspiration for these grilled pita wedges. I like to grill them with a slather of olive oil and a sprinkling of sesame seeds and cracked peppercorns.

METHOD:
Direct grilling

INGREDIENTS:
4 pita breads
2 to 3 tablespoons olive oil
2 tablespoons sesame seeds
2 teaspoons cracked black peppercorns

TIPS

For even more flavor, grill the pitas over a wood fire (see page 20 for instructions on how to do this).

1 Set up the grill for direct grilling (see page 21 for charcoal or gas) and preheat to high.

2 When ready to cook, brush the pita breads on both sides with olive oil and sprinkle the sesame seeds and peppercorns over them. Place the pita breads on the hot grate and toast them until lightly browned, 1 to 3 minutes per side. Don't take your eyes off the grill for a second, as the pitas can burn quickly. Transfer the grilled pitas to a cutting board, cut into wedges, and serve in a basket.

YIELD:
Makes 4 pitas

Puerto Rico

GRILLED CASSAVA BREAD

Forget about johnnycake. The first bread in the Americas was cassava. The Arawak Indians of the Caribbean made it by grating fresh cassava root, which they patted into flat cakes, dried in the sun, and then toasted over the fire. Cassava bread remains a staple in Puerto Rico and the Spanish Caribbean, not to mention in Hispanic neighborhoods in the United States, like those of Miami. The common way to cook cassava bread is by toasting it on a griddle, but it is much more interesting grilled. While it doesn't taste like all that much on its own, brushed with olive oil and hot off the fire, it turns into a crackling, crisp finger food that is unique in the annals of barbecue. Fire brings out cassava's earthy sweetness, and the grilled bread shatters into a thousand tasty shards when you take a bite.

METHOD:
Direct grilling

INGREDIENTS:

½ **cup olive oil**

3 cloves garlic, minced

3 tablespoons chopped fresh cilantro or
      flat-leaf parsley

Coarse salt (kosher or sea) and
      freshly ground black pepper

2 pieces cassava bread

1 Combine the olive oil, garlic, and cilantro in a bowl and stir to mix. Season the garlic oil with salt and pepper to taste. Generously brush the cassava bread on both sides with the garlic oil.

2 Set up the grill for direct grilling using a two-zone fire (see page 22 for charcoal or gas); preheat one zone to medium-high and leave the other zone unlit so you can move the bread over it if it starts to burn.

3 When ready to cook, brush and oil the grill grate. Place the cassava bread over the medium-high zone of the grill and toast it until nicely browned, 30 to 60 seconds per side. You want the bread to be crisp and golden brown. Don't take your eyes off the grill for a second, as the bread can burn quickly.

4 Transfer the grilled cassava bread to a basket or platter, breaking it into pieces for serving, or let your guests break it—that's half the fun of eating this singular Caribbean treat.

YIELD:
Makes 2 cassava breads

VARIATION: Brush the cassava bread with melted butter instead of olive oil.

Look for cassava bread at Hispanic markets or in the ethnic food section of the supermarket. The bread is sold in flat rounds that are about twelve inches across and one-quarter inch thick and come wrapped in paper, two to four to a package. Once you find it, stock up; like hardtack, it keeps forever.

Cassava bread starts with a tropical root that's painstakingly peeled by hand.

TIPS

As the name suggests, the traditional method for cooking fry bread is frying. If you have a side burner on your grill, you can do this outside (you'll find instructions in the Variation at right). Being the live fire fanatic that I am, one day I decided to try grilling the flat bread—after all, the dough is quite similar to that of *naan*, a grilled bread popular in India. The results were amazing, and that's the recipe you'll find here.

New Mexico

GRILLED "FRY" BREAD

Visit a pueblo in New Mexico and this is what you'll find: a crackling campfire; oil heating in a cast-iron skillet over it; and soft, puffy circles of flat bread frying in that sizzling oil. Fry bread is believed to have originated with the Navajos, but today it's enjoyed throughout the Southwest. Powdered milk gives the bread a malty sweetness, while rolling out the soft dough at the last minute keeps it tender. Fry bread is traditionally served with *picadillo* (a Southwestern-style hash), but it also makes a terrific accompaniment for smoked brisket, ribs—even steak. It's good as is, spread with softened butter, drizzled with honey, or sprinkled with cinnamon sugar.

METHOD:
Direct grilling or frying

Fry bread cooked the traditional way—in the hearth.

ADVANCE PREPARATION:

30 minutes for the dough to rest

INGREDIENTS:

**2 cups all-purpose flour, plus
more for rolling out the
dough**

2 tablespoons powdered milk

2 teaspoons baking powder

**1 teaspoon coarse salt
(kosher or sea)**

**2 tablespoons vegetable shortening,
such as Crisco**

**2/3 cup hot water, or more
as needed**

**2 to 3 tablespoons vegetable oil,
or 2 to 3 tablespoons butter,
melted**

1 Place the flour, powdered milk, baking powder, and salt in a mixing bowl and whisk or stir to mix. Add the shortening, cutting it in with two knives; the mixture should be the texture of cornmeal. Add enough hot water to obtain a soft, pliable dough. Turn the dough onto a lightly floured work surface and knead it for 5 minutes. Wrap the dough in plastic wrap and let it rest at room temperature for 30 minutes.

2 Divide the dough into 6 even pieces and roll each piece into a ball. Working on a lightly floured cutting board, roll a ball into a thin disk 5 to 6 inches across. Place the disk on a lightly floured baking sheet, then repeat with the remaining pieces of dough. Keep the rolled-out dough covered with a damp cloth until you are ready to grill it.

3 Set up the grill for direct grilling (see page 21 for charcoal or gas) and preheat to high.

4 When ready to cook, brush and oil the grill grate. Brush the top of each disk with oil. Place a few of the rolled-out disks, oiled side down, on the hot grate (to do so, hold the dough by the edge and gently lay it on the grill). Brush the top side of the dough with oil. After 2 or 3 minutes, the bread will start to puff and blister and the bottom will become golden brown. Turn the bread with tongs and grill the other side, 2 to 3 minutes longer. If you serve the grilled breads at once, they'll be soft and puffy. If you let them sit for 5 to 10 minutes, they'll become delectably crisp.

YIELD:

Makes 6 breads

VARIATION: To make traditional Indian fry bread, prepare the bread dough as described in Steps 1 and 2. You will need 2 to 3 cups of vegetable oil for deep-frying the bread. Pour oil to a depth of 1 inch in a heavy frying pan, place over medium-high heat, and preheat to 350°F (use a deep-fry thermometer or a candy thermometer to tell when the oil has reached 350°F). One at a time, carefully place the disks of dough in the hot oil and fry them until they are puffed and golden brown, 1 to 3 minutes per side, turning them with tongs. Transfer the fried breads to a plate lined with paper towels to drain. Serve each fried bread as soon as it is done; if not eaten immediately it becomes tough and heavy.

WALL OF FLAME

ROQUE'S CARNITAS

Roque Garcia's stainless steel chuck wagon is a Santa Fe institution. From it, he dishes up *carnitas,* thinly sliced strips of marinated prime beef steak, grilled along with *cebolla* (onion) and *chile verde* (green chile), and serves it on a flour tortilla with homemade salsa. It comes in a foil package to help keep you from spilling the ingredients down your shirtfront—a measure that may even occasionally work. Open from April through October.

Washington Street,
around the corner
from the Plaza
Santa Fe, New Mexico

TIPS

Traditionally, you wrap a bannock around one or more sticks and cook it over a campfire. If you choose this method, you'll need smooth straight sticks—scrape off any bark or bumps with a pocketknife. Broom handles work well, too, as do thick, clean dowels. Be sure to grease the wood well with shortening or lard. If you're lucky enough to slide the bread off in one piece, you can insert a grilled hot dog in the center. You can also fry the bannock in lard or oil, preferably in a cast-iron skillet over a campfire (you'll find instructions for doing this in the Variations at right).

North-Central Canada

BANNOCK (Ojibwa Grilled Bread)

I first heard about bannock as a Cub Scout in the 1960s. Not the Scottish oat bread or the New England corn bread—this bannock was made by winding a sort of biscuit dough around a stick and grilling it over a campfire. I searched in vain for a recipe for or reference to the dish for the next forty years and finally found it in, of all places, one my favorite cartoons, "For Better or For Worse," by Lynn Johnston. According to Lynn, bannock is a specialty of the Ojibwa Indian tribe of north-central Canada, and it can be grilled on a stick or fried in lard in a skillet. In berry season, you can add blueberries, or for a New England touch, fresh cranberries.

METHOD:
Direct grilling

INGREDIENTS:

2 cups all-purpose flour

1 tablespoon baking powder

1 teaspoon coarse salt
(kosher or sea)

6 tablespoons cold lard or shortening,
cut into ½-inch pieces, plus
several tablespoons for greasing
the sticks

YOU'LL ALSO NEED:

Straight green wood sticks (each
¾ to 1 inch in diameter) or
wooden broomsticks, 20 to 24 inches
long if cooking on a grill, 3 to 4 feet
long if cooking over a campfire;
3 bricks wrapped in aluminum foil
(optional)

1 To make the dough by hand: Place the flour, baking powder, and salt in a large bowl and stir to mix. Add the pieces of lard and cut them in with two knives until the largest pieces are about the size of peas. Stir in about ⅔ cup of water, a little at a time; use enough to create a soft, pliable dough. It should be the consistency of biscuit dough; do not let it become too sticky.

To make the dough with a food processor: Place the flour, baking powder, and salt in a processor fitted with the metal blade and pulse briefly to combine. Add the pieces of lard and pulse until the largest pieces are about the size of peas. Add about ⅔ cup of water, a little at a time, pulsing to combine. Use only as much water as you need to create a soft, pliable, but not sticky dough.

2 Set up the grill for direct grilling (see page 21 for charcoal or gas) and preheat to medium-high or build a campfire and let the flames burn down to glowing embers.

3 Generously grease the sticks with lard. Pinch off large balls of dough and mold them around the sticks to form a layer about ¼ inch thick that covers all but about 2 inches at the ends of each stick.

4 If cooking on a grill: Place 2 of the aluminum foil–wrapped bricks at opposite sides of the grate so that they are not quite as far apart as the sticks are long and suspend the sticks between them by resting the ends of the sticks on the bricks. Place the remaining brick on top of the sticks at one end to keep them from rolling.

If cooking over a campfire: Hold the sticks about 18 inches above the fire or suspend them between 2 forked sticks placed at opposite sides of the fire.

5 Cook the bannock until nicely browned on the outside and cooked through, rotating the sticks every few minutes to ensure even cooking, 8 to 12 minutes in all.

6 Place the bannock on a platter or baking sheet and let cool for a few minutes, then gently slide it off the sticks. If it doesn't slide off easily, break it off in pieces.

VARIATIONS:

■ Here's how to make fried bannock (if your grill has a side burner, you can fry the bannock outdoors). Prepare the bannock dough as described in Step 1. Roll the bannock dough out to a thickness of about ¾ inch and cut it into 2½-inch biscuits or pinch off pieces of dough and roll them into balls about 1 inch in diameter. Melt about ½ pound lard in an 8- or 10-inch cast-iron skillet over medium heat or pour vegetable oil to a depth of ½ inch in the skillet (1 to 2 cups). Preheat the lard or oil to

Bannock— so easy a child can make it.

350°F (use a deep-fry thermometer or a candy thermometer to tell when the fat has reached 350°F). Carefully place the dough pieces in the skillet and fry the bannock until golden brown, 2 to 3 minutes per side, turning with a wire skimmer or slotted spoon. Transfer the fried bannock to a plate lined with paper towels to drain, then serve at once.

■ For an even richer bannock, substitute an equal amount of buttermilk or heavy cream for the water.

■ To make bannock with blueberries or cranberries, gently stir in 1 cup after you have cut the lard into the dry ingredients, then stir in the water by hand.

YIELD:
Serves 8

Cleveland, Ohio

"CLAY" BREADS

The word *fire* has deep meaning for us barbecue guys. Especially for Douglas Katz, the owner of Cleveland's sizzling restaurant Fire. Katz does most of his cooking on the grill, in a tandoor (the Indian equivalent of a very hot barbecue pit), or in a wood-burning oven—with the flames fully visible in the open kitchen. (The Clevelander reminds us that *fire* is also the word used by chefs to instruct the staff to start cooking an order.) These flat breads—a Fire specialty—are loosely modeled on Indian *naan* and are cooked in Katz's oak-burning tandoor (an oven made out of clay, hence the name "clay" bread). But the breads are equally terrific grilled; the fire forms a crackling crust, leaving the center moist and puffy. The breads are fun to cook (stretching the dough and grilling it makes an entertaining show for your guests), so they're great to serve as an appetizer while people are standing around your grill.

Doug Katz, the man who brought Fire to Cleveland.

METHOD:
Direct grilling

ADVANCE PREPARATION:
1 hour to 2 hours for the dough to rise

INGREDIENTS:
2 packages active dry yeast (about 4½ teaspoons)
1 tablespoon sugar
1 cup warm water
⅔ cup plain yogurt, preferably whole milk
Coarse salt (kosher or sea)
Extra-virgin olive oil
About 4 cups all-purpose flour
Feta and Cucumber Dip (optional; at right)

1 To make the dough with a stand mixer: Place the yeast, sugar, and water in the mixer bowl. Using the dough hook, mix well, then let stand for 10 minutes until foamy. Add the yogurt, 2 teaspoons of salt, 1 tablespoon of olive oil, and 4 cups of flour and mix at the low speed until a smooth dough forms, 8 to 10 minutes. The dough should be soft and moist, but not sticky; if too wet, add a little more flour.

To make the dough with a food processor: Place the yeast, sugar, and water in a measuring cup and mix well with a fork. Let stand for 10 minutes. Using a food processor fitted with the metal blade, place 4 cups flour and 2 teaspoons of salt in the processor and pulse to mix. Add the yeast mixture, the yogurt, and 1 tablespoon of olive oil and process to obtain a smooth dough, about 3 minutes. Add more flour if the dough is too wet.

2 Place the dough in an oiled bowl, turning to coat all sides. Cover the bowl with plastic wrap and set in a warm place. Let the dough rise until doubled in size. You can do this at room temperature 1 to 2 hours before you plan to grill the bread or you can make the dough the night before and let it rise overnight in the refrigerator.

3 Turn the dough out onto a cutting board and divide it into 20 to 24 pieces. Roll each piece into a 2-inch ball. Arrange the balls on a lightly oiled baking sheet about 1 inch apart. Cover with a damp dish towel. The dough balls can be refrigerated, covered with the damp dish towel, for up to 3 hours.

4 Set up the grill for direct grilling (see page 21 for charcoal or gas) and preheat to high.

5 Bring the dough balls, a second baking sheet, a bottle or dish of olive oil, and a bowl of salt to the grill side. Pour a little olive oil on the baking sheet. Lightly oil your hands. Place a ball of dough on the baking sheet and press it into an oval shape. Using the palm of your hand, stretch out the dough to form an oval 6 to 8 inches long, 3 to 4 inches wide, and 1/8 to 1/4 inch thick. Repeat with a few more balls of dough, adding olive oil to the baking sheet as needed. The ovals of dough should be lightly oiled and shiny on both sides, but not dripping with oil. Lightly sprinkle the top of each dough oval with salt.

6 When ready to cook, brush and oil the grill grate. Place a couple of the flattened dough ovals on the hot grate and grill until golden brown and blistered on the bottom and puffed on the top, 1 to 3 minutes. Turn the breads over and grill until the second

FETA AND CUCUMBER DIP

A sort of puréed Greek salad, this tangy dip is what the restaurant Fire, in Cleveland, Ohio, serves with its signature "clay" breads. While the mixture of feta cheese and cucumber suggests the Middle East, the idea of puréeing them to make a dip is uniquely American.

INGREDIENTS:

6 ounces feta cheese,
    drained and crumbled
    (about 1 1/2 cups)
1 large cucumber, peeled, seeded
    (see Note), and diced (about
    1 cup)
3 tablespoons chopped sweet
    onion or scallions
1 clove garlic, minced
1 teaspoon dried oregano
1/2 teaspoon freshly ground
    black pepper
1/2 teaspoon cayenne pepper
2 tablespoons extra-virgin olive oil
1 tablespoon fresh lemon juice
Coarse salt (kosher or sea;
    optional)

Place the feta, cucumber, onion, garlic, oregano, black pepper, and cayenne in a food processor. Process to a coarse purée. With the motor running, add the olive oil and lemon juice through the feed tube. Season with salt to taste. The dip can be refrigerated, covered, for 2 days, but it is best served the day it's made.

YIELD:

Makes about 2 cups

NOTE: To seed a cucumber, cut it in half lengthwise. Scrape out the seeds with a melon baller or spoon.

side is golden brown, 1 to 3 minutes longer. Continue making ovals and grilling them until all of the balls of dough are cooked.

7 Transfer the breads to a bread basket and serve them by themselves or with the Feta and Cucumber Dip. Don't be surprised when people ask for seconds and thirds.

YIELD:

Makes 20 to 24 breads

T I P S

It's tempting to want to smoke roast the spoon bread, but the grilled corn gives you plenty of live-fire flavor, and a heavier smoke would overpower the delicate taste of the bread. So if you do cook this spoon bread on the grill, don't use wood chunks or chips. If your grill is otherwise occupied, you can bake the spoon bread in the oven (I do not often give you license to cook indoors, so enjoy it).

White Sulphur Springs, W.Va.

KATE'S MOUNTAIN SPOON BREAD

A West Virginia pig pickin' just isn't complete without spoon bread. A buttery cornmeal and egg concoction that's a cross between a pudding and corn bread, spoon bread has been a staple here for centuries. This one comes from The Greenbrier resort pit master Ethan Hileman. The lodge at Kate's Mountain serves as home base for many a Greenbrier barbecue and as the "campus" for my Barbecue University. Ethan cooks his spoon bread in a cast-iron skillet that's the size of a manhole cover, but you could also use a baking dish or even an aluminum foil drip pan. Being congenitally unable to follow any recipe without making a few changes, I've boosted the corn flavor here by adding some grilled corn kernels, although you could leave these out.

METHOD:
Indirect grilling

INGREDIENTS:

2 cups whole milk

1¾ cups cold water

4 tablespoons (½ stick) unsalted butter, cut into ½-inch pieces

1 cup yellow cornmeal

2 tablespoons sugar

1½ teaspoons coarse salt (kosher or sea)

4 large eggs

1½ teaspoons baking powder

1 cup Grilled Corn kernels (from 2 to 3 ears; optional; recipe follows)

YOU'LL ALSO NEED:

A 10-inch cast-iron skillet or 8 by 12-inch aluminum foil drip pan sprayed with vegetable oil spray

1 Place the milk, water, butter, cornmeal, sugar, and salt in a large heavy pot and whisk until well blended, with no lumps of cornmeal. Gradually bring the cornmeal mixture to a boil over high heat, whisking often. Let the cornmeal mixture boil for 2 minutes; it will thicken. Remove the pot from the heat and let the mixture cool to lukewarm.

2 Place the eggs, baking powder, and grilled corn kernels, if using, in a bowl and whisk or beat with a fork to mix. Whisk this mixture into the cornmeal mixture. Transfer the batter to the greased skillet or aluminum foil pan.

... a cross between a pudding and corn bread ..

3 Set up the grill for indirect grilling (see page 22 for charcoal or page 23 for gas) and preheat to medium-high or preheat the oven to 375°F.

4 When ready to cook, place the spoon bread in the center of the hot grate, away from the heat, and cover the grill or place the spoon bread in the oven. Grill or bake the spoon bread until it is puffed, lightly browned, and cooked through, 30 to 40 minutes. When done, a metal or bamboo skewer inserted in the center of the spoon bread will come out clean. Serve the spoon bread right out of the skillet or pan.

YIELD:

Makes 1 spoon bread

Grilled Corn

Grilled corn is a delicacy in its own right but it also makes a terrific flavoring, especially when grilled without the husk, so the fire intensifies the sweetness of the kernels. The next time you fire up your grill, toss on a few ears of corn. The grilled kernels will keep for several days in the refrigerator or you can even freeze them. It's good to have them on hand for adding to breads, salads, and sauces.

INGREDIENTS:

4 ears sweet corn, shucked
2 tablespoons (¼ stick) butter,
**   melted, or 2 tablespoons olive oil**
**   or vegetable oil**
Coarse salt (kosher or sea) and
**   freshly ground black pepper**

1 Set up the grill for direct grilling (see page 21 for charcoal or gas) and preheat to high.

2 When ready to cook, brush the grill grate. Lightly brush the corn with some of the butter and season it with salt and pepper. Place the corn on the hot grate and grill it until nicely browned, 2 to 3 minutes per side (8 to 12 minutes in all), basting it with the remaining butter.

3 Transfer the grilled corn to a cutting board and let cool. Cut the kernels off the cobs, using lengthwise

West Virginia spoon bread cooked the traditional way in a cast-iron skillet.

TIPS

■ When making corn sticks choose large ears of corn with fresh-looking bright green husks. You'll need the husks of four or five ears of corn but the kernels from only two ears. Save the remaining corn for grilling, following one of the recipes on pages 600 through 604.

■ If wrapping the corn stick batter in corn husks seems like too much trouble, you can put it in an 8-inch cake pan or skillet and grill it for about thirty minutes over medium-high heat using the indirect method (see page 22 for charcoal or page 23 for gas) or bake it in an oven preheated to 400°F for the same length of time.

strokes of a chef's knife. You should have about 1⅓ cups. The grilled corn will keep in an airtight container for several days in the refrigerator or several weeks in the freezer.

YIELD:
Makes about 1⅓ cups of kernels

The West Indies

A NEW CORN STICK
(Corn Bread Grilled in the Husk)

The first written account of barbecue in the Americas appears in the writings of the Spaniard Gonzalo Fernandez de Oviedo y Valdes. Explorer, adventurer, administrator, chronicler, even gold miner, Oviedo was one of the best-traveled men of the sixteenth century, making six trips to the New World. His *Natural History of the West Indies,* published in 1526, gave Europe one of its first glimpses of the customs and foodways of the New World. This recipe was inspired by his account of how the natives of Hispaniola cooked corn bread—in the corn husks (you'll find

a full account of the history of American barbecue starting on page 5).

METHOD:
Direct grilling

INGREDIENTS:
5 ears sweet corn
1 cup stone-ground white cornmeal
1 cup all-purpose flour
2 tablespoons sugar
2 teaspoons baking powder
1 teaspoon coarse salt
  (kosher or sea)
1 cup milk
1 large egg, beaten with a fork
6 tablespoons (¾ stick) salted butter,
  melted

YOU'LL ALSO NEED:
18 to 20 pieces of butcher's string
  (each 12 inches long)

1 Cut the tip and base off an ear of corn (remove about ½ inch from each end of the cob). Carefully peel off the husks in large pieces and set aside. Remove and discard the corn silk. Repeat with the remaining ears of corn. Cut the kernels off 2 of the cobs, using lengthwise strokes of a chef's knife. Set aside the 3 remaining ears of corn for another use.

2 Place the cornmeal, flour, sugar, baking powder, and salt in a mixing bowl and whisk to mix. Add the milk, egg, butter, and corn kernels and stir until a thick batter forms.

3 Place a piece of corn husk flat on your work surface with the skinny end toward you. Place about

2 tablespoons of the batter on the husk a couple of inches from that end and fold the top half over the batter. Place a second piece of husk on the work surface, again with the skinny end toward you. Position the filled husk on top of this husk so that the folded edge is at the bottom of the second husk and the open end is at the center. Fold over the second husk to enclose the open end of the filled husk. (the natural curl of the husks will effectively seal the sides of the packet.) Tie the packet closed with butcher's string, crisscrossing the string as you would when tying a ribbon around a package, so that all 4 edges are secured. Repeat with the remaining batter and corn husks. The corn packets can be assembled several hours ahead and refrigerated.

4 Set up the grill for direct grilling (see page 21 for charcoal or gas) and preheat to high.

5 When ready to cook, arrange the corn packets on the hot grill grate. Grill until the husks are darkly browned and slightly puffed and the corn sticks are cooked through, about 4 minutes per side. To test for doneness, press the top of a packet; it should feel firm but springy.

6 Transfer the corn packets to a heatproof platter and snip and discard the strings. Let your guests unwrap their own corn sticks before eating.

YIELD:
Makes 18 to 20 corn sticks

Corn stone ground by hand, much as it would have been in pre-Columbian times.

"The Indian women grind [the corn], with the full strength of their arms, in a concave stone with another round stone which they hold in their hands, just as painters are accustomed to grind their colors. As they grind, from time to time they pour in a little water. . . . This produces a paste-like dough. A small portion of the dough is wrapped in a leaf which is used for this purpose or in a corn husk. Then it is placed in the coals of the fire and baked."

— Gonzalo Fernández de Oviedo y Valdes

■ For years I puzzled over how The Pit made its fried biscuits, and I tried frying just about every biscuit recipe I could find. Nothing came close. One day, a staffer confided the secret to me: The Pit uses store-bought biscuit dough—the sort that comes in a cardboard tube in your supermarket dairy case. I normally shy away from processed foods, but I make no apologies for the following recipe. These fried biscuits really taste like The Pit's (no pun intended).

■ If your grill has a side burner, do the frying outside. It keeps the mess out of your kitchen— and you'll be sure to serve the biscuits piping hot.

Tamiami Trail, Fla.

FRIED BISCUITS

"**W**hat do you think is worse for you—the fat on the ribs or the fried biscuits?" It seemed an odd question, coming from a man with a belly the size of a wine barrel. We were standing at the take-out window of a rib joint called The Pit on the Tamiami Trail (the road once connected Tampa and Miami). Here, on the outskirts of Miami, stands a quintessential Southern-style barbecue joint. It's the sort of place that slow smokes meats over Georgian black oak and serves them with the honey mustard sauce so beloved by Southerners. Good as the barbecue is here—and it's very good—my favorite dish at The Pit is actually a side dish: the ethereal pillows of dough known as fried biscuits.

INGREDIENTS:

3 to 4 cups vegetable oil for
    deep-frying
1 tube (12 ounces) bake-and-serve
    biscuit dough
Honey (optional), for serving

YOU'LL ALSO NEED:

A deep-fry thermometer or
    candy thermometer

1 Pour oil to a depth of 2 inches in a deep saucepan or frying pan, place it over medium-high heat, and preheat to 350°F (use a deep-fry thermometer or a candy thermometer to tell when the oil has reached 350°F).

2 Break open the tube of biscuit dough and separate the individual biscuits. Carefully place a few of the biscuits in the hot oil and fry them until they are puffed and golden brown, 2 to 4 minutes per side, turning with a wire skimmer or slotted spoon. Repeat with the remaining biscuits.

3 Transfer the fried biscuits to a wire rack or a plate lined with paper towels to drain, then serve at once. They must be eaten immediately. If you want an accompaniment, try a drizzle of honey.

YIELD:
Makes 10 biscuits

If you enjoy biscuits this way, wait until you try them fried.

Hornbeak, Tenn.

GRILLED-CORN HUSH PUPPIES

You just about always find hush puppies at Southern barbecues, and nobody makes them better than the Genuswine Cookers barbecue team from Hornbeak, Tennessee. This fact was made blissfully apparent to me at the Memphis in May international barbecue contest, where Genuswine occupied the site next to the team I was cooking with. Forget the smoke and barbecue: The fact is, these freshly fried hush puppies darn near drove us crazy.

INGREDIENTS:

2 cups yellow cornmeal

$\frac{1}{2}$ cup self-rising flour

$\frac{1}{4}$ cup sugar

1 teaspoon baking powder

1 teaspoon coarse salt (kosher or sea)

1 small onion, minced (about $\frac{1}{2}$ cup)

$\frac{1}{4}$ cup drained minced pickled
    jalapeño peppers

$\frac{2}{3}$ cup grilled corn kernels (from about
    2 ears; optional; page 145)

About $\frac{1}{2}$ cup buttermilk

1 small can (8.5 ounces) creamed corn

1 large egg, lightly beaten

3 to 4 cups canola oil, for frying

YOU'LL ALSO NEED:

A deep-fry thermometer or
    candy thermometer

The Genuswine Cookers
with their many trophies.
Hush puppies anyone?

1 Place the cornmeal, flour, sugar, baking powder, and salt in a mixing bowl and whisk to mix. Stir in the onion, jalapeños, and grilled corn, if using. Add $\frac{1}{2}$ cup of buttermilk and the creamed corn and egg. Stir with a wooden spoon just to mix. The consistency should be rather like that of soft ice cream; add more buttermilk if necessary.

2 Pour oil to a depth of at least 2 inches in a deep saucepan or frying pan, place it over medium-high heat, and preheat to 350°F (use a deep-fry thermometer or candy thermometer to tell when the oil has reached 350°F). Using two spoons, carefully place $\frac{3}{4}$-inch balls of batter in the hot oil. Position the spoons or scoop no more than 1 inch above the hot oil so the hush puppies drop into the oil without it splashing. Fry the hush puppies until they are golden brown, 3 to 4 minutes in all, turning them with a wire skimmer or slotted spoon.

3 Transfer the hush puppies to a plate lined with paper towels to drain, then serve at once.

YIELD:

Makes about 4 dozen 1-inch hush puppies

TIPS

Should you find yourself craving hush puppies but not have any grilled corn on hand, these are still pretty terrific made without it.

AL FORNO

And the Birth of Grilled Pizza

AL FORNO

577 South Main Street
Providence, Rhode Island
(401) 273-9760

"The discovery of a new dish does more for human happiness than the discovery of a new star," wrote the great nineteenth-century French gastronome Brillat-Savarin. That would make George Germon and Johanne Killeen the grand astronomers of barbecue. The two run the perennially popular Al Forno restaurant in Providence, Rhode Island, and they're the people who came up with one of the most unlikely dishes ever to come off a gridiron: grilled pizza.

Like many remarkable dishes, grilled pizza was born by accident (or at least out of a misunderstanding). The year was 1981. George, a professor at the Rhode Island School of Design, and Johanne, an art student, had just celebrated the first anniversary of their thirty-two-seat Al Forno. One day, a fish purveyor told George about an unusual dish he had sampled in Italy: grilled pizza. "I was fairly sure he meant pizza baked in a wood-burning oven," recalls George, "but I was sufficiently intrigued to attempt cooking pizza dough on the grill."

The obstacles were daunting. How do you cook the crust without burning it? How do you put the toppings on, keep them on, and cook them without burning the crust even more? George attacked the problem logically, building a two-zone fire so he could sear the crust on the hotter side and move it to the cooler side while he added the toppings. He started with a moist dough

Al Forno, where grilled pizza started.

"That's the beauty of grilling; some parts burn, some parts become smoky."

that he stretched into a rectangle on a liberally oiled sheet pan. He reasoned that the oil would form a barrier between the dough and the fire and keep the crust from sticking. "Besides, I've always liked an oily pizza," George confides.

CHEESE FIRST

To solve the topping challenge, George put the cheese on first so it would have time to melt, followed by a garnish of grilled vegetables. Unlike with a conventional pizza, the sauce went on last; after all, it was already cooked, and only needed to be warmed through.

Today Al Forno sells something on the order of four hundred grilled pizzas a week. Toppings range from classic tomato and cheese to caramelized onion, prosciutto, and fig, all arranged sparingly, even pointillistically, so as not to detract from the crust. That crust comes handsomely blistered and is delectably chewy in some spots, and crackling crisp in others. "That's the beauty of grilling; some parts burn, some parts become smoky," explains George. "It's not a uniform heat."

If George has been good to pizza, grilled pizza has been very good for Al Forno. Today, the James Beard Award–winning restaurant occupies a handsome brick building, formerly a

Grilled vegetables ready to top a pizza.

nineteenth-century stable, with two floors of cozy dining amid soft lamplight, Connecticut bluestone, and a massive hearth that blazes in the winter. The restaurant now seats 110, serving 400 on a typical Saturday night.

George and Johanne remain passionate about live fire, cooking 90 percent of the menu on one of the restaurant's vintage, natural lump charcoal–burning Montague grills or in a wood-burning oven. Among the more notable Al Forno specialties are a "dirty steak" that's grilled right on the embers (the recipe for it is in my book *Beer-Can Chicken*) and churned-to-order ice cream for dessert. You'll find recipes for grilled pizza on pages 152 through 159.

Johanne Killeen and George Germon—grilled pizza royalty.

Putting together grilled pizzas at Fresco by Scotto in New York City.

TIPS

I've given directions for a simple homemade uncooked tomato sauce in the pizza Margherita recipe, but you could certainly use a cooked sauce—your favorite homemade one or a commercial brand. Or you can substitute sliced ripe red tomatoes.

New York, N.Y.

GRILLED PIZZA MARGHERITA With Two Cheeses

Al Forno in Providence, Rhode Island, may be the "birthplace" of grilled pizza (read about its birth on page 150), but at least one restaurant in New York has made it a signature appetizer. To visit Manhattan without trying the grilled pizza at Fresco by Scotto would be to miss a classic Big Apple food experience. Fresco by Scotto's pizza comes off the grill wafer-thin, cracking crisp, and smoky as a day spent next to a barbecue pit. Here's my adaptation of their classic Margherita pizza, topped with tomato, basil, and Fontina and Pecorino Romano cheese.

METHOD:
Direct grilling

INGREDIENTS:
Pizza Dough (recipe follows)
1 can (28 ounces) plum tomatoes, drained
¼ cup extra-virgin olive oil
½ cup fresh basil leaves
3 cloves garlic, minced (for 1 tablespoon)
Coarse salt (kosher or sea) and freshly ground black pepper
3 cups mixed grated Fontina and Pecorino Romano cheese (5 to 6 ounces of each)
⅓ cup finely chopped flat-leaf parsley
Extra-virgin olive oil

1 Make the pizza dough and when it is almost finished rising, continue with the pizza recipe.

2 Purée the tomatoes in a food processor until no large chunks remain. With the processor running, add the olive oil, basil, and garlic. Season the sauce to taste with salt and pepper and set aside. (This may make a little more than you need. Serve any left over with pasta.)

3 Set up the grill for direct grilling using a two-zone fire (see page 22 for charcoal or gas) and preheat one zone to high and the other zone to medium. Set up an oiled baking sheet and a cruet of oil on a side table next to the grill. Set the tomato sauce, cheese, and parsley in bowls within reach.

4 When ready to cook, brush and oil the grill grate. Working on the oiled baking sheet, flatten a ball of dough with the palm of your hand, then, starting at the top, stretch it out flatter. Rotate the dough disk and continue stretching away from the center, using plenty of oil, until you have a very thin 12-inch oval.

5 Gently lift the dough oval, taking care not to tear it, and drape it on the hot grate over the hot zone of the fire. The dough should start to rise and blister immediately. Grill the crust until the bottom is golden brown all over, about 2 minutes (lift the edge of the dough with a spatula to check it).

6 Turn the crust over, moving it to the medium zone of the grill. Lightly brush the top with some olive oil and sprinkle with ½ cup of the mixed cheeses (the cheese should go all the way to the edge of the crust). Place 8 or 10 dollops of the tomato sauce (about 1 tablespoon each) on top of the pizza in random spots. Sprinkle 1 tablespoon of the chopped parsley and drizzle 1 tablespoon of the olive oil over the pizza.

7 Gently slide the pizza back over the hot zone of the grill. Cook until the cheese is melted and the bottom of the crust is golden brown, rotating the pizza as needed to cook the crust evenly. If the crust starts to burn on the bottom, move the pizza back to the medium zone of the grill for a minute for the crust to finish browning. Serve at once. Stretch, grill, and assemble the rest of the pizzas the same way.

YIELD:
Makes 6 individual pizzas

Pizza Dough

This dough is exceedingly easy to make, but it may be wetter than you're used to. The easiest way to make it is in an electric stand mixer fitted with a dough hook. You can use a food processor, but if you do, you may need to add a little more flour.

Throughout this chapter are instructions for grilling the pizza dough along with the recipes for Grilled Pizza Margherita (at left), Grilled Asiago, Rosemary, and Garlic Pizzas (see page 154), Bacon, Onion, and Potato Pizzas (see page 156), and Grilled Caesar Salad Pizzas (see page 157).

ADVANCE PREPARATION:
**1 hour and 20 minutes to
1 hour and 40 minutes
for the dough to rise**

INGREDIENTS:
**1¾ cups warm water
2 packages active dry yeast
(about 4½ teaspoons)
1 tablespoon molasses
2 teaspoons coarse salt
(kosher or sea)
3 tablespoons extra-virgin olive oil
3½ cups unbleached all-purpose flour,
or more if necessary
½ cup whole wheat flour, or more
all-purpose flour**

1 Place the water, yeast, and molasses in the bowl of a stand mixer, stir to mix, and let stand until slightly foamy, 5 to 10 minutes.

TIPS

To remove the leaves from a sprig of fresh rosemary hold it by the tip with one hand. Strip the leaves off the stem by grasping it with the fingertips of your other hand and running them gently down its length.

2 Add the salt and 2 tablespoons of the olive oil and mix with a dough hook on the low speed until combined, about 2 minutes. Add the all-purpose and whole wheat flours and mix on the low speed until a smooth dough forms and pulls away from the side of the mixer, 8 to 10 minutes. The dough should be soft and moist but not sticky. If the dough is too wet, add a little more flour. The dough can also be made in a food processor; in this case, add the flour and salt first, followed by the yeast mixture and 2 tablespoons of olive oil.

3 Use the remaining 1 tablespoon of olive oil to oil the inside of a large bowl. Gather the dough into a ball and place it in the bowl, turning to coat all sides. Cover the bowl with plastic wrap and let the dough rise until doubled in size, 1 to 1½ hours at room temperature or overnight in the refrigerator.

4 Remove the dough from the bowl and place on a lightly floured board. Knead the dough a few times with your hands, until it has reduced to its original size.

5 Divide the dough into 6 even balls about 3 inches in diameter. Place the balls of dough on a lightly oiled baking sheet and brush each with a little oil. Cover the dough with plastic wrap and let rise at room temperature until soft and puffy, 20 to 40 minutes.

YIELD:

Makes enough dough for 6 individual pizzas

Providence, R.I.

GRILLED ASIAGO, ROSEMARY, AND GARLIC PIZZAS

Here's the perfect appetizer pizza— a crisp, smoky wafer of dough topped with fresh rosemary, sautéed garlic, and Asiago cheese. My model for this pizza was a pie I had at Al Forno, in Providence. Asiago is a hard grating cheese with the nutty sweetness of Parmigiano-Reggiano but without the hefty price tag.

METHOD:
Direct grilling

INGREDIENTS:
Pizza Dough (page 153)
Extra-virgin olive oil
6 cloves garlic, finely chopped
⅓ cup fresh rosemary leaves
3 cups grated Asiago cheese
  (8 to 10 ounces)
1 tablespoon cracked or coarsely
  ground black peppercorns

1 Make the pizza dough and when it is almost finished rising, continue with the pizza recipe.

2 Place 3 tablespoons of olive oil in a small skillet over medium heat. Add the garlic and rosemary and cook until the garlic just begins to brown, about 3 minutes. Transfer the garlic-rosemary mixture to a heatproof bowl.

3 Set up the grill for direct grilling using a two-zone fire (see page 22 for charcoal or gas) and preheat one zone to high and the other to medium. Set up an oiled baking sheet and a cruet of oil on a side table next to the grill. Set the garlic-rosemary mixture, cheese, and peppercorns in bowls within reach.

4 When ready to cook, brush and oil the grill grate. Working on the oiled baking sheet, flatten a ball of dough with the palm of your hand, then, starting at the top, stretch it out flatter. Rotate the dough disk and continue stretching away from the center, using plenty of oil, until you have a very thin 12-inch oval.

5 Gently lift the dough oval, taking care not to tear it, and drape it on the hot grate over the hot zone of the fire. The dough should start to rise and blister immediately. Grill the crust until the bottom is golden brown all over, about 2 minutes (lift the edge of the dough with a spatula to check it).

6 Turn the crust over, moving it to the medium zone of the grill. Lightly brush the top with some olive oil and spread one sixth of the garlic-rosemary mixture on top. Sprinkle ½ cup of the cheese and ½ teaspoon of the cracked pepper over the crust.

7 Gently slide the pizza back over the hot zone of the grill. Cook until the cheese is melted and the bottom of the crust is golden brown, rotating the pizza as needed to cook the crust evenly. If the crust starts to burn on the bottom, move the pizza back to the medium zone of the grill for a minute for the crust to finish browning. Serve at once. Stretch, grill, and assemble the rest of the pizzas the same way.

YIELD:
Makes 6 individual pizzas

A grilled pizza outpost in Manhattan.

Making a crust for grilled pizza— it's all in the stretching.

In the interest of nutritional sobriety, I call for the bacon fat in this pizza to be drained off after you fry the bacon. Between you and me, I'd leave it in and slather it on the pizza crust instead of olive oil.

Providence, R.I.

BACON, ONION, AND POTATO PIZZAS

The *flammekueche* of Alsace is the inspiration for this curious pizza. But the earthy garnish of bacon, onion, and potatoes would be at home at Providence's Al Forno. For the best results, use a smokehouse bacon like that from Neuske's Hillcrest Farm (see Mail-Order Sources, page 742) and Yukon Gold potatoes. If you want to be completely over the top, grill the onion.

METHOD:
Direct grilling

INGREDIENTS:
Pizza Dough (page 153)
1 pound potatoes, peeled
   and cut into ¼-inch dice
Coarse salt (kosher or sea)
1 tablespoon butter
6 slices of bacon,
   cut crosswise into
   ¼-inch pieces
1 large red onion,
   finely chopped
Olive oil
2 cups grated Muenster
   cheese (6 to 8 ounces)
1 tablespoon cracked or
   coarsely ground black
   peppercorns

1 Make the pizza dough and when it is almost finished rising, continue with the pizza recipe.

2 Place the potatoes and 2 quarts cold salted water in a large pot over medium heat and bring to a boil. Cook until the potatoes are just tender, about 5 minutes. Drain the potatoes in a colander, rinse under cold water, and drain again.

3 Melt the butter in a heavy skillet over medium heat. Add the bacon and onion and cook until both are nicely browned, about 4 minutes. Stir in the boiled potatoes and cook until lightly browned, about 3 minutes. Transfer the potato mixture to a strainer over a bowl to drain off the excess bacon fat.

earthy garnish of bacon, onion, and potatoes

4 Set up the grill for direct grilling using a two-zone fire (see page 22 for charcoal or gas), preheat one zone to high and the other zone to medium. Set up an oiled baking sheet and a cruet of oil on a side table next to the grill. Set the potato mixture, cheese, and peppercorns in bowls within reach.

5 When ready to cook, brush and oil the grill grate. Working on the oiled baking sheet, flatten a ball of dough with the palm of your hand, then, starting at the top, stretch it out flatter. Rotate the dough disk and continue stretching away from the center, using plenty of oil, until you have a very thin 12-inch oval.

6 Gently lift the dough oval, taking care not to tear it, and drape it on the hot grate over the hot zone of the fire. The dough should start to rise and blister immediately. Grill the crust until the bottom is golden brown all over, about 2 minutes (lift the edge of the dough with a spatula to check it).

7 Turn the crust over, moving it to the medium zone of the grill. Lightly brush the top with some olive oil and spread one sixth of the potato mixture on top. Sprinkle ⅓ cup of the cheese and ½ teaspoon of the pepper on top.

8 Gently slide the pizza back over the hot zone of the grill. Cook until the cheese is melted and the bottom of the crust is golden brown, rotating the pizza as needed to cook the crust evenly. If the crust starts to burn on the bottom, move the pizza back to the medium zone of the grill for a minute for the crust to finish browning. Serve at once. Stretch, grill, and assemble the rest of the pizzas the same way.

YIELD:
Makes 6 individual pizzas

Tampa, Fla.

GRILLED CAESAR SALAD PIZZAS

Two of America's favorite ethnic foods come together here, although each is now so deeply enmeshed in our culture, you'd

T I P S

Caesar salad pizza is a little involved. All right, it's a lot involved. But, you can grill the chicken ahead of time. The dressing, too, can be made several days in advance. For that matter, the dough can be made the night before, too.

hardly call either of them ethnic. Despite its ubiquity north of the border, Caesar salad actually originated in Mexico, where it was invented in 1924 by an Italian restaurateur named Caesar Cardini. As for pizza, it arrived here at the turn of the century via Sicilian immigrants and eventually became a $30-billion-a-year industry. The idea of combining the two comes from Marty Blitz, chef-owner of Mise en Place in Tampa. I think you'll find the combination of crusty dough, salty Gorgonzola, smokily grilled chicken, and creamy Caesar dressing to be sufficiently irresistible to warrant the multiple steps required to make this fabulous pizza.

METHOD:
Direct grilling

INGREDIENTS:
Pizza Dough (page 153)
1 pound skinless, boneless chicken
breast halves
Creamy Caesar Dressing (page 111)
1 medium-size red onion,
cut lengthwise into quarters
Olive oil
1 large or 2 small heads romaine lettuce,
rinsed and broken into leaves
8 ounces Gorgonzola cheese, crumbled

YOU'LL ALSO NEED:
4 small bamboo skewers
(each 6 inches long)

1 Make the pizza dough and when it is almost finished rising, continue with the pizza recipe.

2 Trim any sinews or excess fat off of the chicken breasts and discard.

The best of both worlds: Caesar salad and grilled pizza.

Rinse the breasts under cold running water, then drain and blot dry with paper towels. Place the chicken breasts on a plate and pour 1/3 cup of the Caesar salad dressing over them, spreading it on both sides of each breast with the back of a spoon. Secure each onion quarter on a skewer and brush with olive oil.

3 Set up the grill for direct grilling using a two-zone fire (see page 22 for charcoal or gas) and preheat one zone to high and the other to medium. Set up an oiled baking sheet and a cruet of oil on a side table next to the grill.

4 When ready to cook, brush and oil the grill grate. Place the chicken breasts and onion on the grate over the hot zone and grill until the chicken is cooked through and the onion is charred and soft, 4 to 6 minutes per side (8 to 12 minutes in all) for the chicken, and 3 to 4 minutes per side (9 to 12 minutes in all for the onion quarters). To test the chicken for doneness, poke a breast in the thickest part with your finger; it should feel firm to the touch.

5 Transfer the grilled chicken and onion to a cutting board but let the fire continue to burn in the grill. Finely chop the chicken and onion. Place about 6 lettuce leaves one atop the other and slice crosswise into 1/2-inch ribbons. Repeat with the remaining leaves. Toss the lettuce with about 3/4 cup of the salad dressing. Place the chopped chicken and onion, the dressed lettuce, and the cheese in bowls and set them within reach of the grill.

6 Working on the oiled baking sheet, flatten a ball of dough with the palm of your hand, then, starting at the top, stretch it out flatter. Rotate the dough disk and continue stretching away from the center, using plenty of oil, until you have a very thin 12-inch oval.

7 Gently lift the dough oval, taking care not to tear it, and drape it on the hot grate over the hot zone of the fire. The dough should start to rise and blister immediately. Grill the crust until the bottom is golden brown all over, about 2 minutes (lift the edge of the dough with a spatula to check it).

8 Turn the crust over, moving it to the medium zone of the grill. Spread 1 tablespoon of the salad dressing and one sixth of the Gorgonzola and chopped chicken and onion on top.

9 Gently slide the pizza back over the hot zone of the grill. Cook until the cheese is melted and the bottom of the crust is golden brown, rotating the pizza as needed to cook the crust evenly. If the crust starts to burn on the bottom, move the pizza back to the medium zone of the grill for a minute for the crust to finish browning.

10 Transfer the pizza to a platter. Mound one sixth of the dressed lettuce on top and serve at once. Stretch, grill, and assemble the rest of the pizzas the same way.

YIELD:
Makes 6 individual pizzas

Kansas City
BARBECUE

I f Kansas City is considered the nation's barbecue capital (a fact that will be disputed by more than a few Carolinians, Tennesseeans, or Texans, but readily acknowledged by just about everyone else), it's largely due to Arthur Bryant. From 1930 to 1980, the bespectacled black man wrought miracles with brisket and transformed spareribs into staffs of redemption.

WHERE TO EAT BARBECUE IN KANSAS CITY

Arthur Bryant's Barbecue
1727 Brooklyn Avenue
(816) 231-1123

Danny Edwards Famous Kansas City Barbecue
1227 Grand Avenue
(816) 283-0880

BB's Lawnside Bar-B-Q
1205 East 85th Street
(816) 822-7427

Oklahoma Joe's Barbecue
47th and Mission Road
(913) 722-3366

KC Masterpiece Barbecue & Grill
4747 Wyandotte Street
(the Plaza)
(816) 531-3332
(and other locations)

Arthur Bryant worked his miracles with little more than spices and wood smoke in a nondescript storefront in an equally drab neighborhood. Harry Truman dined at his restaurant, so did Jimmy Carter. No sooner did I land in Kansas City for the first time, than I headed for Arthur Bryant's. But first a little background.

Barbecue is Kansas City's official dish—not to mention its obsession. Missourians debate the merits of hickory versus oak, short ends versus long ends, burnt edges versus rib tips, with the passion usually reserved for politics or sports teams. More than seventy-five barbecue joints, ranging from grease houses to white tablecloth restaurants complete with Tiffany lamps, vie for the diner's attention in this sprawling city on the Missouri River.

The most essential ingredient in the local barbecue may be patience—we're talking slow. The KC Masterpiece restaurant cooks its baby back ribs for ten hours, for example; its briskets for twelve hours; and its pork shoulders for sixteen. The leisurely barbecuing renders tough cuts of meat, like spareribs and brisket, tender enough to cut with a fork. The resulting smoke flavor is as intense

Barbecue legend Arthur Bryant with some of his pit-smoked ribs.

and complex as the finest whisky or smoked salmon from Scotland.

Tradition holds that Kansas City barbecue began with Henry Perry, a black man born in 1875 in Shelby County, Tennessee, who sold ribs and briskets that he slow roasted over a hickory and oak fire and served without ceremony wrapped in newspaper. When business boomed, Perry hired George Gates, founder of the popular Kansas City restaurant chain that bears his name, and two brothers, Charlie and Arthur Bryant, who went on to open the legendary Arthur Bryant's.

That's the official story anyway, but *Kansas City Star* reporter Doug Worgul has unearthed an even earlier barbecue pioneer,

Henry "Poppa" Miller, son of a Cherokee Indian and an African-born former slave. Somewhere on his travels, Miller learned to cook barbecue. He arrived in Kansas City in 1890—seventeen years *before* Henry Perry—and cooked at The Hotel Savoy, Coates House, and the old Wishbone Restaurant. (He claims to have invented Wishbone salad dressing—a popular barbecue marinade in Kansas City to this day.) Throughout his long life, Miller sold barbecue—first from his back porch, then from a gas station, and eventually from his own restaurant.

Kansas City barbecue achieved international culinary superstardom when native son and *New Yorker* columnist Calvin Trillin declared, Arthur Bryant's to be the best restaurant in the world. Today, Kansas City is home of one of the world's largest barbecue contests, the American Royal, as well as the Kansas City Barbecue Society, with more than 3,000 members.

The style of Kansas City barbecue reflects the city's central geographic location. Like Carolinians and Mississippians, Missourians are avid pork eaters, but they're broad minded enough to share the Texas enthusiasm for beef. Barbecued chicken is accorded a respect here that is often lacking

elsewhere in the barbecue belt. Like Memphians, Missouri pit masters rub their meats with a dry rub (a mixture of salt, paprika, and other spices) before cooking. They may or may not use a mop sauce.

Missourians take an equally accommodating approach to sauces. Some are smoky, in the style of Texas sauces; others, hot and vinegary, like the pulled pork sauces of North Carolina. Perhaps the most typical Kansas City sauce is KC Masterpiece, created by child psychologist–turned barbecue mogul Rich Davis (for more on Davis, see page 696).

You're probably expecting me to tell you about the single best barbecue joint in Kansas City. I made a happy discovery after several days of round-the-clock feasting: It simply doesn't exist. That is to say, there is no supreme temple of barbecue—each establishment has its standout dishes.

No one can surpass the mountain of greasy, crusty burnt edges at Arthur Bryant's on a good day or the smoky brisket at Danny Edwards Famous Kansas City Barbecue; and BB's Lawnside dishes up some of the best imaginable rib tips and smoked sausage. Oklahoma Joe's, which shares space with a gas station, serves a pulled pork that would do a North Carolinian proud. KC Masterpiece is highfalutin enough to offer barbecued prime rib, but down home enough to serve pork shoulder and ribs. The truth is, it's virtually impossible to get bad barbecue in Kansas City. And that's good news to me.

Gloriously

The polls are in and the winner is . . . beef. Research shows that steak is our favorite food to cook on the grill. But which steak will depend on where you come from—in the following pages you'll find New York Jewish–style Romanian garlic steaks, Koreatown rib-eyes, Philly cheese steaks, and Miami-Cubano garlic oregano steaks with grilled onions. Of course, steak is just a beginning, for if you come from Texas or Oklahoma, barbecue is virtually synonymous with smoke-roasted, slow-cooked brisket. The American barbecued beef tradition also includes juicy tri-tips from California, Baltimore pit beef, and crusty barbecued ribs from Manhattan. Wherever there's smoke, there's fire, and chances are, wherever there's fire, there's beef. This chapter celebrates America's love affair with beef in all its sanguine glory.

Grilled Beef

TIPS

The chief challenge in preparing this recipe will be finding the clod—a cut from the beef shoulder. Plan on ordering it from a butcher shop well in advance of the time you want to serve it. If you can't find clod, or you want to grill a smaller cut of beef, you can follow the basic recipe to create another Kreuz Market specialty: barbecued rib roast. You'll find instructions for doing this in the Variation on the opposite page.

Lockhart, Tex.

TEXAS CLOD (Barbecued Beef Shoulder)

The clod is the ultimate measure of a Texas pit master's mettle. The reason is simple: Beef shoulder is a lot leaner than brisket, so it requires just the right amount of heat and wood smoke to transform this tough cut into something tender enough to tear apart with your fingers. Barbecued clod is revered in Texas and ignored just about everywhere else. And even in the Lone Star State, it's rare to find a pit boss who serves it. Which is all the more reason you should make a pilgrimage to the town many aficionados consider to be the end-all of Texas barbecue—Lockhart, home of Kreuz Market. (You can read at length about Kreuz Market on page 166.)

The Kreuz family, and their successors, the Schmidts, have been in the barbecue business for more than a century, so they've had time to master cooking beef shoulder. Their clod comes off the pit dark and shiny as a lump of coal, crusty as the end cut of a prime rib, salty as a bite of beef jerky (at least on the outside), and so carnivorously beefy, it may make you rethink your allegiance to brisket. What's all the more remarkable is that the clod is seasoned with only three

ingredients: salt, black pepper, and cayenne. For extra richness, Kreuz Market keeps the clod warm and moist in a pan of melted tallow (rendered beef fat). A brushing of butter or bacon fat will achieve the same effect.

METHOD:
Indirect grilling

INGREDIENTS:
¾ cup salt
¼ cup cracked black peppercorns
2 to 3 tablespoons cayenne pepper
1 beef clod (13 to 15 pounds)
Kreuz's Sides (see page 167)

YOU'LL ALSO NEED:
15 cups wood chips or chunks (preferably oak), soaked for 1 hour in water to cover, then drained

1 Place the salt, peppercorns, and cayenne in a small bowl and stir to mix. (Actually, your fingers work better for mixing the rub than a spoon or whisk does.)

2 Generously sprinkle the rub over all sides of the clod, patting it onto the meat with your fingertips.

3 Set up the grill for indirect grilling (see page 23 for gas or page 22 for charcoal) and preheat to medium-low. If using a gas grill, place 4 cups of the wood chips or chunks in the smoker box or in a smoker pouch (see page 24) and run the grill on high until you see smoke, then reduce the heat to medium-low. If using a charcoal grill, place a large drip pan in the center, pre-heat the grill to medium-low, then toss 1½ cups of the wood chips or chunks on the coals.

4 When ready to cook, place the clod, fat side up, in the center of the hot grate, over the drip pan and away from the heat. Cover the grill and cook the clod until darkly browned and cooked through, 8 to 9 hours. To test for doneness, use an instant-read meat thermometer: The internal temperature should be between 190° and 195°F for well-done, which is the way clod is usu-ally served. If the outside starts to burn, cover it loosely with aluminum foil. If using a gas grill, every 2 hours you'll need to add 4 cups of wood chips or chunks. If using a charcoal grill, every

hour you'll need to add 12 fresh coals and ¾ cup of wood chips or chunks to each side.

5 Transfer the grilled clod to a cutting board and let it rest for 10 to 15 minutes, then thinly slice it across the grain with a sharp knife.

YIELD:
Serves 25 to 30

VARIATION: You can also grill a boneless rib roast this way. Use about 2 to 3 tablespoons of the rub to season a 4- to 5-pound one. It will take 1½ to 2 hours for it to cook using the indirect method. The rub you have left over will keep for at least 6 months stored in an airtight jar away from heat and light.

TIPS

Kreuz Market cooks its clod at a relatively high heat over blazing embers of oak. The best way to approximate this at home is to fire your pit or kettle grill with oak logs or chunks (see Grilling over a Wood Fire on page 20). You can light oak logs in the firebox of an offset smoker or, to burn oak chunks in a kettle grill, light them in a chimney starter and transfer the embers to the side baskets of the grill. If your grill doesn't have side baskets, rake the embers into two piles at opposite sides of the grill. Another way to get a wood flavor is to use oak chips to generate wood smoke in a charcoal or gas grill.

The counter at Kreuz, in an uncharacteristic quiet moment, stands ready to greet the day's customers.

THE KREUZ MARKET

in Lockhart, Texas

THE KREUZ MARKET

619 North Colorado
Lockhart, Texas
(512) 398-2361
www.kreuzmarket.com

The first stop on any barbecue pilgrimage is the Kreuz Market in Lockhart, Texas, founded in 1900 by a German immigrant named Charles Kreuz (rhymes with brights). Kreuz ran a grocery store and at the end of each day, he would cook off any unsold meat over wood fire and sell it at bargain prices. In 1924, Kreuz built a cavernous storefront on Commerce Street. By then, his barbecue had become so popular, he installed a massive brick pit with a 35-foot brick chimney and a table-size chopping block for portioning the meat.

In 1948, Kreuz sold the market to one of the employees, Edgar "Smitty" Schmidt. In 1984, Smitty sold the business to his two sons, Don and Rick Schmidt, and left the building to his daughter when he passed away in 1990. Sadly, a family feud erupted, forcing Rick to move the business to a new location on September 1, 1999.

I must confess, I was apprehensive as I drove to Lockhart this time. How could the barbecue possibly be as good in a new establishment, I pondered, where the pits weren't seasoned with 75 years' worth of smoke and grease? The last time I'd visited the Kreuz Market, it still occupied the 1924 storefront, with knives chained to the tables in the original dining room, as in the old days, and the bare-bones main dining room still painted a sickly green. You entered the market through the kitchen and got your toes warmed by the pit

The calm before the storm at the Kreuz Market.

Rick Schmidt, the King of Clod.

NOW ABOUT THOSE SIDES

An establishment as relentlessly carnivorous as Kreuz Market doesn't give a lot of thought to side dishes. You won't find potato salad or coleslaw here. Nonetheless, over the years, a series of accompaniments have come to be associated with Kreuz—the legacy of its origins as a grocery store. All would have been part of the stock, including "rat's cheese," a slab of orange Wisconsin cheddar—the preferred cheese in these parts for baiting mouse traps! None of these requires cooking. If you want to be completely legitimate when preparing Texas Clod (page 164), just arrange everything that follows in bowls or on trays and serve them along with the beef:

Puffy white bread
 (Kreuz Market
  serves ButterKrust)

Saltine crackers

Sour pickles

Sweet pickles

Pickled jalapeños

Thick slices of white
 onion

Slices of peeled avocado

Slices of tomato

Thin (1/4-inch) slabs of
 orange Wisconsin
 cheddar cheese or
 jalapeño Jack cheese

while you waited for barbecue that was sliced to order, priced by the pound, and shoved at you on a sheet of red butcher paper.

The huge, modern, barnlike structure of the new restaurant did little to reassure me, nor did the seating for 550. My spirits brightened, however, at the pungent scent of wood smoke in the parking lot: The new Kreuz Market smelled just like the old one. The brisket was every bit as moist and flavorful as I remembered it, and the smoked prime rib has remained the exemplar of the species. As for the clod (barbecued beef shoulder), well, Kreuz Market is one of the few establishments in Texas that still serves it, and one bite of the coalblack crust banished my worries forever.

EMBERS ON PARADE

When Rick Schmidt moved to the new location, he towed a tub full of burning embers from the original pit through the streets of Lockhart. Four police cars blocked traffic and two TV crews followed the procession. The move was painful, but at least he could take comfort in the fact that the post oak logs used to fire his new pits would be lit by embers from the original Kreuz Market.

"Of course, we weren't happy about moving," says Schmidt, "but I knew we could duplicate the food." The move enabled Schmidt to add grease traps and taller chimneys to the pits, which otherwise follow the design of the original. As at the old location, the accompaniments are still limited to items you'd find in a grocery store, and there's still no barbecue sauce. But the Kreuz Market now makes bottles of Louisiana hot sauce available for those customers who want it. And you still don't get a fork. "God put two of them at the ends of your arms," Schmidt explains.

TIPS

■ The garlic should be fresh and finely chopped (don't use the horrid prechopped garlic in oil). The easiest way to chop garlic is in a food processor or minichopper, adding the pepper and salt when the garlic is mostly chopped.

■ Boneless prime rib is one of the most amiable roasts sold at the butcher shop: luxuriously beefy; tender while still having some chew; and generously marbled, so the exterior crisps while the center stays moist and succulent as it cooks. The only drawback is its hefty price. You could also prepare this recipe with more affordable top round or, for the ultimate extravagance, with a whole prime rib.

Pittsburgh, Pa.

GARLIC PEPPER RIB ROAST

The Pittsburgh airport was the last place I expected to find superlative roast beef. But as I dashed to the gate for my flight, my neck whiplashed at the sight of a roast beef on a carving board, its exterior dark and shiny as anthracite, its center as rosy as a Matisse odalisque. The place was a Samuel Adams tavern, and one of America's premier brewers rewarded me with a roast beef sandwich that made a day of delayed flights worth the wait. Even more remarkable: The stunning flavor of the beef was achieved with three simple seasonings—fresh garlic, cracked black peppercorns, and salt. I've made the roast a bit more upscale, substituting a boneless rib roast for the less expensive top round, and of course, I cook the roast on the grill. I don't generally bother adding wood chips; the garlic-pepper flavor is so vibrant, you don't really need the smoke.

METHOD:
Indirect grilling

INGREDIENTS:
8 cloves garlic
2 tablespoons cracked black peppercorns

2 tablespoons coarse salt (kosher or sea)
1 boneless rib roast (4 to 5 pounds)
2 tablespoons olive oil
Pit Beef Horseradish Sauce
   (page 171), for serving
Kaiser rolls (optional), for serving

1 Finely chop the garlic in a food processor or minichopper. Add the peppercorns and salt and process in short bursts just to mix (do not over-process or the ingredients will become pasty).

2 Rub the roast on all sides with the olive oil. Sprinkle the garlic mixture over all sides of the roast, patting it onto the meat with your fingertips. Let the roast cure at room temperature while you light the grill.

3 Set up the grill for indirect grilling (see page 22 for charcoal or page 23 for gas) and preheat to medium-high. If using a charcoal grill, place a large drip pan in the center.

4 When ready to cook, place the roast in the center of the hot grate, over the drip pan and away from the heat. Cover the grill and cook the roast until done to taste, 1¼ to 1½ hours for medium-rare. To test for doneness, use an instant-read meat thermometer: The internal temperature should be about 140°F for medium-rare. If using a charcoal grill, after 1 hour you'll need to add 12 fresh coals to each side.

5 Transfer the grilled roast to a cutting board and let rest for 10 minutes, then thinly slice it across the grain. Cut the ends into slivers, so everyone gets a piece. There are two ways to serve the beef: uptown style, with the sauce on the side, or down-home style, doused with sauce and piled on a kaiser roll.

YIELD:
Serves 8

Baltimore, Md.

BALTIMORE PIT BEEF

Baltimore's pit beef is part of a hallowed American culinary tradition that includes Texas clod (page 164) and Santa Maria tri-tips (page 183). Unlike a lot of barbecue in the United States, the meat is grilled but not smoked, which keeps the emphasis on the flavor of the beef. Moreover, the meat can be served rare, something you certainly can't do with brisket. Yet another distinguishing feature of pit beef is the sauce—creamy horseradish instead of red barbecue sauce. Pair the sauce with the beef and you get an unexpected party dish that would be great for a Super Bowl party or your monthly poker game.

METHOD:
Direct grilling

ADVANCE PREPARATION:
4 hours or longer for curing the beef

FOR THE BEEF:
**3 to 4 tablespoons Pit Beef Rub
(recipe follows)
1 piece top round (about 3 pounds; ask the
butcher to cut you a thick chunk)**

FOR SERVING:
**8 kaiser rolls, or 16 slices of rye bread
Pit Beef Horseradish Sauce (recipe follows)
1 large sweet white onion,
sliced as thinly as possible
2 ripe red tomatoes, thinly sliced
Iceberg lettuce, thinly sliced**

WALL OF FLAME
BIG AL'S

Not much on formality, but the rosy, moist, fragrant beef at this roadside stand with picnic tables comes sliced properly paper-thin and piled mountain high on bread.

**7926 Pulaski Highway
Baltimore, Maryland
(410) 574-3030**

■ Most Baltimore pit bosses use what I call the modified direct method of grilling: They grill the beef directly over the fire, but position the grate high above the coals, so the meat roasts as much as it grills. To achieve this effect on a home grill, indirect grill the roast using a medium fire.

■ To make a pit beef sandwich like a pro, you'd slice it on a meat slicer—thin slices cut across the grain reduce top round, a traditionally tough cut of beef, to close to fork tenderness. If you don't have a meat slicer, you can use the slicing disc of a food processor, as I've suggested here.

Baltimore pit beef is pretty much a no-frills dining experience. Bring cash and don't expect lavish service.

1 Sprinkle the rub all over the beef, patting it onto the meat with your fingertips. For maximum flavor, place the meat in a baking dish, cover it with plastic wrap, and let cure for at least 4 hours or as long as 3 days in the refrigerator, turning once a day; the longer it cures, the richer the flavor.

2 Set up the grill for direct grilling (see page 21 for charcoal or gas) and preheat to medium.

3 When ready to cook, brush and oil the grill grate. Place the beef on the hot grate and grill until the outside is crusty and dark golden brown (even black), and the meat is cooked to taste, 30 to 45 minutes, turning the beef often with tongs. To test for doneness, use an instant-read meat thermometer. The internal temperature should be about 125°F for rare, 145°F for medium-rare, or 160°F for medium.

4 Transfer the grilled beef to a cutting board and let it rest for 10 minutes. Put all the other ingredients in bowls or on platters on the table for serving. To slice the beef in a food processor, cut it with the grain into chunks small enough to fit in the feed tube, then use the processor to slice across the grain. Or slice the beef by hand as thinly as possible across the grain, using a sharp knife. To serve, have everyone pile slices of beef high on a roll or slice of bread thickly slathered with horseradish sauce and garnish these with onion, tomato, and lettuce. Eat the sandwiches while they're hot.

YIELD:
Serves 8

Pit Beef Rub

Here's the basic rub used by Baltimore's Big Fat Daddy's pit master (or as close as I can get to it). You'll need about ¼ cup for the Pit Beef. Save the rest for steaks and roast beef. (For more about Big Fat Daddy's, see page 172.)

INGREDIENTS:
**½ cup seasoned salt, such as
    Season-All (see Note)**
¼ cup sweet paprika
4 teaspoons garlic powder
4 teaspoons dried oregano
2 teaspoons freshly ground black pepper

Place the seasoned salt, paprika, garlic powder, oregano, and pepper in a small bowl and stir to mix. (Actually your fingers work better for mixing than a spoon or whisk does.) Store the rub in a sealed jar away from heat or light. It will keep for at least 6 months.

YIELD:
Makes about 1 cup

NOTE: Season-All is a commercial spice mix. Look for it in your supermarket.

Pit Beef Horseradish Sauce

Here's the basic horseradish sauce served at Baltimore's pit beef parlors. To kick up the heat, use a half cup of freshly grated horseradish in place of the prepared. Start with a 4-inch peeled piece of root and grate it or finely chop it in a food processor, but be careful not to breathe in the intense fumes.

INGREDIENTS:
**1 cup mayonnaise
    (preferably Hellmann's)**
**½ cup prepared white horseradish,
    or more to taste**
**1 tablespoon fresh lemon juice,
    or more to taste**
**Coarse salt (kosher or sea) and
    freshly ground black pepper**

Combine the mayonnaise, horseradish, and lemon juice in a nonreactive bowl and whisk to mix. Taste for seasoning, adding more horseradish or lemon juice as necessary and salt and pepper to taste. The horseradish sauce will keep in the refrigerator, covered, for several days.

YIELD:
Makes about 1½ cups

WALL OF FLAME

**CHAPS
PIT BEEF**

The oldest and most substantial of the Pulaski Highway pit beef palaces, with four solid walls and a roof, which come in handy when you want to eat a pit beef sandwich on a rainy or snowy day.

5801 Pulaski Highway
Baltimore, Maryland
(410) 483-2379

Baltimore
PIT BEEF

I spent the first eighteen years of my life in Baltimore. Not once did I eat pit beef. I'm not particularly proud of this fact, but it does reflect the intense parochialism of food in Baltimore. I grew up in the northwest suburb of Pikesville, and the foods of my childhood embraced the four Cs of Baltimore gastronomy: crab, corned beef, coddies (leaden cakes of codfish and potatoes eaten with mustard on saltine crackers), and chocolate tops (cookies crowned with a rosette of chocolate icing). Pit beef came from a working class neighborhood on the east side of town, which might as well have been another planet.

Pit beef is Baltimore's version of barbecue—beef grilled so it's crusty on the outside and served rare and juicy inside, heaped high on a sandwich. Several things make it unique in the realm of American barbecue.

For starters, pit beef is grilled, not smoked, so it lacks the heavy hickory or mesquite flavor characteristic of Texas- or Kansas City–style barbecue. It's also served rare, in full sanguine glory, which would be unthinkable for Texas-style brisket. Baltimore pit bosses use top round, not brisket, and to make this flavorful but tough cut of beef tender, they shave it paper-thin on a meat slicer.

Then there's the bread; it's not the simple slab of white bread you'd get throughout the South. No, the proper way to serve pit beef is on a kaiser roll, or more distinctively, on rye bread. The caraway seeds in the rye are an indication of the Eastern European ancestry of many Baltimoreans on the east side of town and add an aromatic, earthy flavor to the beef.

Finally, there's the sauce, which most Americans wouldn't even identify as barbecue sauce. There's no ketchup, brown sugar, and liquid smoke, as you'd find in Kansas City. No Texas-style chili hellfire or thin, piquant vinegar sauce in the style of North Carolina. The proper condiment for Baltimore pit beef is horseradish sauce—as much as you can bear without crying. And speaking of crying, you need some slices of raw, crisp, pungent white onion to make the sandwich complete.

THE LONG AND PITTED ROAD

The epicenter of Baltimore pit beef is an industrial thoroughfare called the Pulaski Highway. As

WHERE TO ENJOY BALTIMORE PIT BEEF

Big Al's
7926 Pulaski Highway
(410) 574-3030

Big Fat Daddy's
8014 Pulaski Highway
(410) 238-2223

Chaps Pit Beef
5801 Pulaski Highway
(410) 483-2379

You can also get pit beef at Baltimore's Camden Yard Stadium

you drive west out of the city toward the suburb of Rosedale, you pass by truck stops, strip clubs, factories, tractor dealerships, and inexpensive motels. Nestled among these are simple roadside eateries—most are little more than huts or tents—and that's where you find pit beef.

You could stop at the granddaddy of these establishments, Chaps, a simple white cinder-block building with black windows and picnic table–style seating, which has been cooking pit beef the old-fashioned way, over blazing charcoal, since 1987. Or you could head for Big Al's, where every pit beef sandwich comes with a nugget of hot Italian sausage. There's no dining room, only picnic tables outdoors.

Then, there's Big Fat Daddy's, located next to a country-western dance hall called Little Texas. To call it a restaurant would be a stretch. The "dining room" is a yellow and red tent with plastic siding. The pit (actually, a gas and lava stone grill) is housed in a cinder-block building not much bigger than a closet. You place your order at the window and dine at one of a half dozen oilcloth-covered picnic tables, watching the traffic rumble by on the highway.

THERE IS A DADDY AND HE'S LARGE

Big Fat Daddy's takes its name from a ruddy, blue-eyed, thirty something cook-turned-barbecue entrepreneur named Brian Schafer.

He's a big boy, all right. (He tips the scales at 280 pounds.) But he's shed 65 pounds since he opened the eatery in 1996, the result of working one hundred hours a week running the restaurant and a catering business that will take him to three states in one weekend.

Schafer rubs his beef with a tangy mixture of seasoned salt, pepper, oregano, garlic powder, and paprika and, to let the flavor permeate the beef, he cures the meat for three full days before grilling it. (Most Baltimore pit beef is grilled without a rub.) When Schafer makes a sandwich, he takes the time to slice up a few burnt edges (the charred crust) to mix with the rare beef to add smoke and crunch and flavor.

Most of the pit beef places on Pulaski Highway serve bottled prepared horseradish, but Schafer makes his own sauce, a rich creamy combination of horseradish and mayonnaise.

Regulars may miss the old days, when Big Fat Daddy's grilled its beef over charcoal. (Schafer switched to gas a few years ago, because "we got tired of looking like we cooked in

a coal mine.") "The truth is that you get as much if not more flavor when the dripping meat juices hit the lava stones," says Schafer.

These small touches from a large man have brought the eatery big success. In the summer, Big Fat Daddy's goes through 40 top rounds a week (each weighing 25 pounds)—enough for 3,000 to 4,000 sandwiches. His catering business takes him from North Carolina to New York. On a recent weekend, for example, he served 6,000 people at simultaneous street fairs in Delaware and Pennsylvania. But even in the dead of winter, on a snowy day, Big Fat Daddy's does a lively business. "We install a portable heater," says Schafer. "The snow plow crews come here for pit beef before they go out plowing."

Stop at Big Fat Daddy's for pit beef along Baltimore's Pulaski Highway.

Fargo, N.Dak.

CLAY B'S RED RIVER VALLEY BRISKET

North Dakota is a big cattle producer, explains barbecue buff Clay Olson, but most folks in the Red River Valley have never tasted barbecued brisket. So the Fargo-based pit master delights in introducing his neighbors to the pleasures of smoke and fire. He starts with a 12-pound brisket and he cuts it in thirds to maximize the surface area exposed to spice and wood smoke. Even more iconoclastic are his serving instruc-

Barbecue from the back of a truck. Clay Olson doesn't need a restaurant.

tions, which I feel obliged to quote verbatim: "Now the hard part. At this point, the meat is done. But to make it even better, *if* [my emphasis] you can stand it, put all of it in the refrigerator until tomorrow. The next day, when you're ready to serve up some really great barbecue, preheat your oven to 350°F and warm the still-wrapped brisket for an hour or so." Talk about pleasure interruptus! I'll leave that last step optional.

METHOD:
Indirect grilling or smoking

ADVANCE PREPARATION:
12 hours for curing the brisket

FOR THE RUB:
1/2 **cup garlic salt**
1/2 **cup granulated sugar**
1/4 **cup firmly packed dark**
      brown sugar
1/4 **cup sweet paprika**
      2 **tablespoons chili powder**
      1 **teaspoon dry mustard**
      1 **teaspoon ground cumin**
      1 **teaspoon onion powder**
      1 **teaspoon lemon pepper**

FOR THE BRISKET:
1 **beef brisket**
      (10 to 12 **pounds;**
      see the facing page)
2 **cups apple cider**
10 to 12 **hamburger buns**
"**Ninth Revision"**
      Barbecue Sauce
      (optional; recipe follows)

YOU'LL ALSO NEED:

4 cups wood chips or chunks (preferably oak; see Note page 176), soaked for 1 hour in water to cover, then drained; spray bottle; heavy-duty aluminum foil

1 MAKE THE RUB: Combine the garlic salt, granulated sugar, brown sugar, paprika, chili powder, mustard, cumin, onion powder, and lemon pepper in a bowl and stir to mix. (Actually your fingers work better for mixing the rub than a spoon or whisk does.) Set aside roughly one third of the rub.

2 Trim the outer layer of fat on the brisket so that about ¼ inch remains. If there is a pocket of fat between the flat and the cap, cut it out and discard it. Cut the meat into 3 equal-size pieces. (I've tried the recipe with whole brisket and I'm pleased to report that it's excellent that way also.) Sprinkle two thirds of the rub all over both sides of the pieces of brisket, dividing it evenly among them and patting it onto the meat with your fingertips. Wrap the meat in plastic wrap and let cure 12 hours in the refrigerator.

3 Pour the cider into the spray bottle and set aside.

4 Set up the grill for indirect grilling (see page 23 for gas or page 22 for charcoal) and preheat to low. If using a gas grill, place all of the wood chips or chunks in the smoker box or in a smoker pouch (see page 24) and run the grill on high until you see smoke, then reduce the heat to low. If using a charcoal grill, place a large drip pan in the center, preheat the grill to low, then toss

ANATOMY OF A BRISKET

The brisket is a tough, flavorful muscle from the underbelly of the steer. A whole brisket is a massive, flattish piece of meat that weighs 14 to 16 pounds. It consists of three parts: the cap, the flat (center cut), and the point. The cap is a fatty, fibrous muscle that sits on top of the wide end of the flat. The flat is a lean rectangular muscle an inch or so thick that tapers to a pointed end, called the point.

When cooking a whole brisket, you need to first trim off the layer of fat covering the meat to a thickness of ¼ inch. (I like to leave a fair amount of fat on my brisket—it melts as the brisket cooks, basting and moisturizing the meat.) Next, cut out the pocket of fat between the cap and the flat. Even with trimming, there's a lot of waste to a whole brisket. Figure on ¾ to 1 pound per person of cooked meat.

Whole briskets are the stock and trade of barbecue restaurants and competition pit masters. They're a little formidable for home cooks, so most supermarkets sell a portion of the flat or point without the cap. These cuts are leaner than whole brisket, so they need to be draped with bacon or wrapped in foil midway through the cooking process to keep them moist. The number of servings you get from a piece of flat is higher—figure on 8 to 10 ounces per person.

Like Carolina pulled pork or Kansas City ribs, brisket tastes best cooked and served well-done (an internal temperature of about 190°F). However, the brisket must be brought to this temperature very slowly, or it will be tough. That's why brisket is traditionally cooked low and slow—at a low temperature for as long as 16 hours. This is what's required to keep the meat moist and tender.

1 cup of the wood chips or chunks on the coals.

If using a smoker, fire it up according to the manufacturer's instructions.

5 When ready to cook, place the brisket in the center of the hot grate, fat side up, over the drip pan and away from the heat, and cover the grill. Cook the brisket until handsomely browned, about 3 hours. Spray the meat every hour with apple cider. Turn over

TIPS

■ Clay Olson cooks his brisket in an offset barrel smoker, using oak as his only fuel—no charcoal. I call for using oak chips or chunks here, but if you have a smoker and access to oak logs, by all means use them.

■ Wrapping the brisket in aluminum foil halfway through the cooking process keeps the meat incredibly moist and tender.

"Art is long, life short . . ."

the meat and cook for 1 more hour. If using a charcoal grill, every hour you'll need to add 12 fresh coals and ½ cup of wood chips or chunks to each side.

6 Spray each piece of meat one more time with apple cider. Sprinkle the reserved rub all over the pieces of meat, dividing it evenly among them, then wrap each piece in heavy-duty aluminum foil. Return the wrapped meat to the grate, cover the grill, and continue cooking the brisket until very tender, another 3 to 4 hours, for a total of 7 to 8 hours. This will be easy in a smoker. It's a little more challenging to maintain such a low heat in a gas or charcoal grill; work at a higher heat if you have to but shorten the cooking time. Partially unwrap one of the briskets to test for doneness; it should be very dark and very tender and have an internal temperature of about 190°F. If using a charcoal grill, you'll need to add 12 fresh coals to each side every hour (no more chips are necessary).

7 Transfer the grilled brisket to a cutting board and let rest for 20 minutes. You can serve the brisket right away (slice it thinly across the grain) or you can refrigerate it overnight and reheat it in a 350°F oven for about 1 hour. Clay serves his brisket on a bun with his "Ninth Revision" Barbecue Sauce on the side. Whichever day you choose to serve it, you come out a winner. "The only complaint I ever hear is 'Put more meat on my next one,'" he writes.

YIELD:

Serves 10 to 12

NOTE: If using wood chunks in a smoker, you'll need 2 quarts.

"Ninth Revision" Barbecue Sauce

"**A**rt is long, life short," observed the poet Goethe. Pit master Clay Olson has spent half a lifetime perfecting this sweet lemony sauce, which is now in its ninth revision. Clay likes to serve it with brisket, but it also goes well with chicken and pork.

INGREDIENTS:

3 cups ketchup
⅔ cup distilled white vinegar,
    or more to taste
¼ cup yellow mustard
    (like French's mustard)
¼ cup Worcestershire sauce
6 very thin slices lemon, seeded and
    finely diced with rind on
1 small onion, minced
1 cup firmly packed dark brown sugar,
    or more to taste
2 tablespoons chili powder
1 teaspoon garlic salt, or more to taste
1 teaspoon black pepper
1 teaspoon ground ginger
¼ to ½ teaspoon cayenne pepper

1 Combine the ketchup, vinegar, mustard, Worcestershire sauce, lemon, onion, brown sugar, chili powder, garlic salt, black pepper, ginger, cayenne, and 1 cup of water in a heavy nonreactive saucepan and slowly bring to a boil over medium heat.

2 Reduce the heat to medium and let the sauce simmer gently until thick and full-flavored, about 30 minutes, adding a little more water if it gets too thick. Taste for seasoning, adding more brown sugar, garlic salt, and/or even vinegar, as necessary, to taste; the sauce should be very flavorful.

3 Clay strains the sauce before serving, but I like the pointillistic pleasure of biting into flavorful bits of lemon and onion. In either case, transfer the sauce to clean jars and refrigerate until serving. The sauce can be refrigerated, covered, for several weeks.

YIELD:

Makes 4½ to 5 cups

Yukon, Okla.

SMOK-LA-HOMA BRISKET

Larry Willrath lives in Yukon (Oklahoma, not Alaska). We met through my Web site, where the

Larry Willrath cooks his brisket in a smoker fashioned from a 500-gallon propane tank, taking the concept of "low and slow" to a whole new level. (Low? How about 190°F? Slow? How about 24 hours?) You simply can't cook at this temperature or for this length of time on a charcoal or gas grill, so I've raised the temperature and shortened the cooking time. But if you have a smoker that runs on low heat, you can certainly try Larry's method.

*A man and his pit—
Oklahoma smoke
master Larry Willrath.*

The Oklahoma pit master starts smoking the brisket over a mixture of oak, pecan, and hickory, switching to apple wood midway through.

talk often turns to how to smoke the perfect brisket. Given Oklahoma's central location, it's not surprising that an Okie brisket would combine elements from Texas and Kansas City. The rub, for example, boasts the Tex-Mex tingle of chili powder, cayenne, and cumin. In Kansas City style, the meat is basted with a sweet-sour mixture of apple cider and vinegar.

Of course, Larry adds a few twists of his own, like marinating the brisket in a paste of brown sugar and mustard. The result is a brisket bursting with regional personality, with a complex layering of flavor that just won't quit. Just keep in mind that you've got to start the brisket marinating first thing in the morning since it cooks for at least 7 hours.

METHOD:

Indirect grilling or smoking

Have pit, will travel.

ADVANCE PREPARATION:

2 to 4 hours for marinating the brisket

FOR THE BRISKET AND THE SEASONING PASTE:

1 beef brisket (10 to 12 pounds; see page 175)

½ cup firmly packed dark brown sugar

½ cup Dijon mustard

2 cloves garlic, minced

2 tablespoons apple juice or cider, or more as needed

FOR THE RUB:

¼ cup sweet paprika

3 tablespoons garlic powder

3 tablespoons celery salt

2 tablespoons coarse salt (kosher or sea)

2 tablespoons dark brown sugar

2 tablespoons ground cumin

2 tablespoons pure chile powder

1 tablespoon granulated sugar

1 tablespoon dried oregano

1 tablespoon freshly ground black pepper

1 tablespoon ground white pepper

2 teaspoons cayenne pepper

FOR THE MOP SAUCE:

1 quart apple juice or apple cider

1 cup cider vinegar

1 tablespoon coarse salt (kosher or sea)

1½ cups of your favorite barbecue sauce

YOU'LL ALSO NEED:

4 cups wood chips or chunks (preferably oak; see Note), soaked for 1 hour in water to cover, then drained

1 Trim the outer layer of fat on the brisket so that about ¼ inch remains. If there is a pocket of fat between the flat and cap, cut it out and discard it. Place the brisket in an aluminum foil or ceramic roasting pan.

2 MAKE THE SEASONING PASTE: Place the brown sugar, mustard, and garlic in a nonreactive mixing bowl. Stir in enough apple juice to obtain a thick paste. (How thick? Like wallpaper paste, says Larry.) Spread half of this paste over the brisket on both sides with a rubber spatula or your fingers. Let sit for 15 minutes. Spread the remaining paste over the brisket on both sides and let sit for another 15 minutes.

3 MAKE THE RUB: Place the paprika, garlic powder, celery salt, coarse salt, brown sugar, cumin, chile powder, granulated sugar, oregano, black pepper, white pepper, and cayenne in a bowl and stir to mix. (Actually, your fingers work better for mixing a rub than a spoon or whisk does.) Sprinkle the rub all over the brisket on both sides, patting it onto the meat with your fingertips. Let the brisket cure in the refrigerator, covered, for 2 to 4 hours.

4 MAKE THE MOP SAUCE: Place the apple juice, vinegar, and coarse salt in a large nonreactive bowl and whisk until the salt dissolves.

5 Set up the grill for indirect grilling (see page 23 for gas or page 22 for charcoal) and preheat to low. If using a gas grill, place all of the wood chips or chunks in the smoker box or in a smoker pouch (see page 24) and run the grill on high until you see smoke, then reduce the heat to low. If using a charcoal grill, place a large drip pan in the center, preheat the grill to low, then toss 1 cup of the wood chips or chunks on the coals.

If using a smoker, fire it up according to the manufacturer's instructions.

6 When ready to cook, place the brisket in the center of the hot grate, fat side up, over the drip pan and away from the heat, and cover the grill. Cook the brisket until handsomely browned, 3½ to 4 hours. Use an instant-read meat thermometer to determine when it's time to wrap it in aluminum foil: The internal temperature should be about 165°F. Mop or baste the meat every hour with some of the mop sauce. If using a charcoal grill, every hour you'll need to add 12 fresh coals and ½ cup of wood chips or chunks to each side.

7 Generously brush the brisket on both sides with the barbecue sauce and tightly wrap it in heavy-duty aluminum foil. Return the wrapped meat to the grate, cover the grill, and continue cooking the brisket until very tender, another 3½ to 4 hours, for a total of 7 to 8 hours. This will be easy in a smoker. It's a little more challenging to maintain such a low heat in a gas or charcoal grill; work at a higher heat if you have to, but shorten the cooking time. Partially unwrap the brisket to test for doneness, taking care not to spill the juices; the meat should be very dark and very tender and have an internal temperature of about 190°F. If using a charcoal grill, you'll need to add 12 fresh coals to each side every hour (no more chips are necessary).

8 Open the aluminum foil wrapping at one end and pour the meat juices into a bowl. Transfer the grilled brisket to a cutting board and let rest for 20 minutes. Thinly slice the meat across the grain. Spoon the reserved juices over the brisket and serve at once. You could accompany the meat with more of your favorite barbecue sauce, but if you do so, serve it on the side. The brisket will be so phenomenal, you shouldn't distract the first taste with sauce.

YIELD:

Serves 10 to 12

NOTE: If using wood chunks in a smoker, you'll need 2 quarts.

Columbus, Ohio

MILLIONAIRE BRISKET
With Coffee and Beer Mop Sauce

High-wheeling investment advisor by day (his minimum portfolio is one million dollars), award-winning barbecue champ by night and on the weekends, Jim Budros has parlayed a lifelong passion for smoke and fire into a respected and highly profitable business. In 1997, his team won the American Royal Barbecue championship for brisket. He's also the co-owner of one of the best barbecue

Smoked meats that cook long and low are the specialty at City in Columbus.

restaurants in Ohio, City Barbeque in Columbus. Jim stresses the basics of good barbecue: "cook low and slow," "use real hardwood," and "don't go overboard with the smoke." He's adamant about the importance of conscientious basting to keep the meat from drying out. Above all, Jim insists, don't sauce the meat until the final minutes of cooking. So is this the recipe that Jim and his team used to win the award in Kansas? Pit masters never tell, but I can assure you, it will become a winner in your repertory.

METHOD:
Indirect grilling

ADVANCED PREPARATION:
4 to 24 hours for marinating the brisket (optional)

FOR THE RUB AND BRISKET:
¼ cup coarse salt (kosher or sea)
¼ cup firmly packed light brown sugar
¼ cup sweet paprika
2 tablespoons pure chile powder
2 tablespoons freshly ground black pepper
1 tablespoon onion powder
1 tablespoon garlic powder
½ teaspoon dried oregano
1 center-cut piece beef brisket (5 to 6 pounds; see page 175)

FOR THE MOP SAUCE:
1 cup beer
1 cup apple cider
⅓ cup cider vinegar
⅓ cup coffee
⅓ cup beef or chicken stock (preferably homemade)
¼ cup vegetable oil

¼ cup Worcestershire sauce
2 tablespoons Tabasco sauce or another hot sauce
2 teaspoons coarse salt (kosher or sea), or more to taste
1 teaspoon freshly ground black pepper

6 slices of bacon (optional)
Jim's Really Easy and Really Good Barbecue Sauce (recipe follows)

YOU'LL ALSO NEED:
4 to 6 cups wood chips or chunks (preferably hickory or apple), soaked for 1 hour in water to cover, then drained

1 MAKE THE RUB: Place the salt, brown sugar, paprika, chile powder, pepper, onion and garlic powders, and oregano in a small bowl and stir to mix. (Actually your fingers work better for mixing than a spoon or whisk does.)

2 In the unlikely event your brisket comes covered with a thick layer of fat, trim it to a thickness of ¼ inch. Place the brisket in a roasting pan and generously sprinkle both sides with the rub, using about 3 tablespoons per side and patting it onto the meat with your fingertips. (You'll have about ¾ cup more rub than you need for the brisket. The leftover rub will keep for several months in a jar.) You can cook the brisket right away, but it will be better if you let it cure with the rub in the refrigerator, covered, for several hours, or even a day ahead.

3 MAKE THE MOP SAUCE: Place the beer, cider, vinegar, coffee, stock, oil, Worcestershire sauce, Tabasco

T I P S

Jim normally cooks a whole brisket, which weighs 14 to 16 pounds. This may be more than the average backyard barbecuer wants to wrestle with, so I call for a 6-pound center-cut piece, which you should be able to find at your local supermarket. Don't let the butcher trim off the fat—that's what will keep the brisket moist while it smokes. Should you start with a really lean brisket, I suggest draping bacon slices over the meat to keep it from drying out. (Jim does not do this, but then again, a whole brisket has plenty of fat built in.)

WALL OF FLAME

CITY BARBEQUE

Come for slow-smoked brisket and Boston butts, lovingly rubbed with proprietary spice blends. Unless you request otherwise, the barbecue sauce will be served on the side. "If you have to put the sauce on the meat, you have something to hide," observes co-owner Jim Budros.

2111 West
Henderson Road
Columbus, Ohio
(614) 538-8890

sauce, salt, and pepper in a nonreactive bowl and whisk to mix. Taste for seasoning, adding more salt as necessary.

4 Set up the grill for indirect grilling (see page 23 for gas or page 22 for charcoal) and preheat to medium-low. If using a gas grill, place all of the wood chips or chunks in the smoker box or in a smoker pouch (see page 24) and run the grill on high until you see smoke, then reduce the heat to medium-low. If using a charcoal grill, place a large drip pan in the center, preheat the grill to medium-low, then toss 1 cup of the wood chips or chunks on the coals.

5 When ready to cook, place the brisket in the center of the hot grate, fat side up, over the drip pan and away from the heat. Drape the bacon slices, if using, over the top of the meat, then cover the grill. Cook the brisket until very tender, 5 to 6 hours (the cooking time will depend on the size of the brisket and the heat of the grill). To test for doneness, use an instant-read meat thermometer: The internal temperature should be about 190°F. Generously mop or baste the meat on both sides with the mop sauce once an hour for the first 5 hours. If the brisket starts to brown too much, generously baste it with mop sauce, wrap it in aluminum foil, and continue cooking until done. If using a charcoal grill, every hour you'll need to add 12 fresh coals and ½ cup of wood chips or chunks to each side.

6 Transfer the grilled brisket to a cutting board and let rest for 10 minutes. Thinly slice across the grain, using an electric knife or sharp carving knife. Transfer the sliced meat to a platter. Spoon the barbecue sauce over the meat or, better yet, serve it on the side.

YIELD:
Serves 8 to 10

Jim's Really Easy and Really Good Barbecue Sauce

Q uick and easy to prepare, this is what I call a "doctor sauce." You start with a commercial barbecue sauce and doctor it with other ingredients. Hey, if it works for Jim, it works for me.

INGREDIENTS:

2 cups of your favorite commercial barbecue sauce, such as Bull's-Eye or KC Masterpiece
1 to 2 cups commercial salsa, mild or hot—your choice
¼ cup cider vinegar, or more to taste
Coarse salt (kosher or sea) and freshly ground black pepper

C ombine the barbecue sauce, salsa, and vinegar in a nonreactive saucepan over medium heat, bring to a simmer, and let cook until thick and flavorful, 5 to 8 minutes. Season with salt and pepper to taste. The sauce can be served hot or at room temperature and may be refrigerated, covered, for up to 48 hours. Bring to room temperature before serving.

YIELD:
Makes about 3½ cups

Santa Maria, Calif.

SANTA MARIA TRI-TIP
With All the Fixin's

Barbecue in southern California means tri-tip, and in the Santa Maria Valley, about three hours north of Los Angeles, this slab of bottom sirloin turns up at all manner of public celebrations and backyard cookouts, seasoned with garlic and spiced pepper, then oak grilled, and thinly sliced. Unlike Texas brisket, the meat is tender enough to serve rare or medium-rare, so it combines the smoke flavor of true slow-cooked barbecue with the sanguine succulence of steak. In Santa Maria, tri-tip is usually served with salsa, toasted French bread, and pinquito beans—distinctive, small, pink-red beans that are unique to these parts. (For a full discussion of Santa Maria tri-tips, see page 186.)

Tri-tips make magnificent party fare—the accompaniments can be cooked ahead and the beef grilled at the last minute. (A tri-tip is large enough to be fairly forgiving in terms of timing. If it comes off the grill too rare, you can simply put it back on for more cooking.) You carve it to order, basking in the admiring gazes of your company. It's slam-dunk barbecue, because just about everyone loves beef, beans, bread, and salsa. Although it's customary for the tri-tip to be seasoned only with salt, garlic salt or garlic powder, and black pepper, I also like to add dried oregano and rosemary.

TIPS

The first thing you'll need to make this recipe is a tri-tip, of course—a thick, flavorful slab of meat cut from the bottom of the sirloin. If you live on the West Coast, you can probably find tri-tip at your local supermarket. If not, ask your butcher to cut a 2- to 3-inch thick slab of meat from the bottom sirloin.

A parking lot pit master tends to his tri-tips.

WALL OF FLAME

THOUSAND OAKS MEAT LOCKER

On a good day, you can smell the Thousand Oaks Meat Locker before you actually see it. At 8 A.M. they fire up the mesquite charcoal–burning brick pit out front; at 9 A.M. the first tri-tips, beef ribs, chickens, and sausages go on the grate. The aroma reaches its crescendo around 11 A.M., when the darkly browned meats are carved and served, first come, first served, until the supply runs out.

2684 East Thousand Oaks Boulevard
Thousand Oaks, California
(805) 495-3211
www.webbq4u.com

METHOD:
Direct grilling

FOR THE RUB AND TRI-TIP:
**2 teaspoons coarse salt
    (kosher or sea)
2 teaspoons freshly ground
    black pepper
2 teaspoons garlic powder
2 teaspoons dried rosemary,
    crumbled between your fingers
1 teaspoon dried oregano
1 tri-tip (2¼ to 2½ pounds),
    or 1 piece bottom sirloin
    (2 to 2½ inches thick and
    2¼ to 2½ pounds)**

FOR SERVING:
**Santa Maria Garlic Bread
    (page 135)
Santa Maria–Style Salsa
    (recipe follows)
Santa Maria Pinquito Beans
    (page 641)**

YOU'LL ALSO NEED:
**Red oak chunks or logs for building
    your fire, or 3 to 4 cups wood
    chips or chunks (preferably oak),
    unsoaked**

1 MAKE THE RUB: Combine the salt, pepper, garlic powder, rosemary, and oregano in a small bowl and stir to mix. (Actually, your fingers work better for mixing than a spoon or whisk does.) Place the tri-tip in a baking dish and sprinkle the rub on all sides, patting it onto the meat with your fingertips. Let the meat cure in the refrigerator, covered, while you set up the grill.

2 Set up the grill for direct grilling using a two-zone fire (see page 22 for gas or charcoal). If using a gas grill, place all of the wood chips or chunks in the smoker box or a smoker pouch (see page 24) and run two burners on high until you see smoke, then reduce the heat of one burner to medium-high and the other to medium. If using a charcoal grill, preheat one zone to medium-high and one zone to medium. Toss all of the wood chips or chunks on the coals once they are preheated.

3 When ready to cook, brush and oil the grill grate. Place the tri-tip over the medium-high zone of the grill and grill until cooked to taste, about 10 minutes per side for medium-rare. If the meat starts browning too quickly, move it to the medium zone. To test for doneness, insert an instant-read meat thermometer through the side of the tri-tip. The internal temperature should be 140° to 145°F for medium-rare.

4 Transfer the grilled tri-tip to a cutting board and let rest for 5 minutes, then thinly slice it crosswise across the grain. Serve the meat slices with the grilled bread (you can make a sandwich if you like), salsa, and pinquito beans.

YIELD:
Serves 6

Santa Maria–Style Salsa

The tri-tip experience simply isn't complete without salsa. The Santa Maria version is enriched with celery, oregano, and Worcestershire sauce. Here's the official recipe, provided by the Santa Maria Valley Chamber of Commerce—well, almost: The lime juice is my own contribution.

INGREDIENTS:

3 luscious, ripe red
   medium-size tomatoes,
   finely chopped with their juices

2 ribs celery, finely chopped
   (about ½ cup)

3 scallions, both white and green parts,
   trimmed and finely chopped
   (about ½ cup)

2 to 3 Anaheim chiles,
   seeded and finely chopped
   (about ½ cup),
   or 1 to 2 jalapeño peppers,
   seeded and chopped

¼ cup chopped fresh cilantro

2 tablespoons fresh lime juice

1 tablespoon distilled white vinegar,
   or more to taste

1 teaspoon Worcestershire sauce

½ teaspoon dried oregano

½ teaspoon Tabasco sauce
   or another hot sauce,
   or more to taste

Garlic salt and freshly ground
   black pepper

Combine the tomatoes, celery, scallions, chiles, cilantro, lime juice, vinegar, Worcestershire sauce, oregano, and hot sauce in an attractive nonreactive serving bowl and stir to mix. Taste for seasoning, adding more vinegar and/or hot sauce as necessary, and season with garlic salt and black pepper to taste; the salsa should be highly seasoned. It tastes best served within several hours of being made.

YIELD:

Makes about 3 cups

Here I am readying a grill for cooking tri-tip at Barbecue University at The Greenbrier.

SANTA MARIA BARBECUE

And the Birth of the Tri-Tip

AUTUMN ARTS
GRAPES & GRAINS
FESTIVAL

Santa Maria Valley Visitor
& Convention Bureau
(800) 331-3779
www.santamaria.com

Larry Viegas says, "Let's get one thing straight. I didn't invent the tri-tip." I'm sitting with the octogenarian electrical engineer turned butcher—now retired—at one of the most celebrated steak houses in central California, Jocko's (where, curiously, tri-tip isn't served—more on that later). I've come to the sprawling agricultural town of Santa Maria, 170 miles north of Los Angeles, to learn about one of America's best-kept barbecue secrets. But Viegas isn't making it easy.

In other parts of the country, bragging and tall tale telling are as much a part of the barbecue tradition as spice rubs and wood smoke. Here I am, across the table from the guy who was very likely the first person ever to grill a tri-tip, and he makes it sound as though he was an accidental by-stander, not the co-creator of California's favorite barbecued beef.

So just for the record, here's how Viegas tells it: The year was 1952. The place, an old Safeway store, long since razed, on the corner of Mill and Vine Streets in Santa Maria. Filling in for the reg-ular butcher, who was on vaca-tion, Viegas was busy butchering beef loins, separating the tender-loins from the top block sirloins. As was the practice in those days, he trimmed off the fibrous, trian-gular tip of the sirloin and set it aside to be ground into hamburg-ers or cut into stew beef.

Only the meat department already had more ground beef and stew meat than it could sell that day, so the meat department man-ager—a one-armed butcher named Bob Schutz—told Viegas to put the tip of the sirloin on the rotisserie. "Are you nuts?" replied the latter. "It'll be tough as hell."

At Schutz's urging, he seasoned the meat with salt, pepper, and garlic powder and threaded it onto the turnspit. What a surprise when the two men tasted it! Spit roasting kept the meat moist; cut-ting it into thin slices across the grain kept it tender; and it had the rich, sanguine flavor of costlier sirloin.

CAUGHT IN THE ACT

The store manager came into the meat department just as the two men were sampling the meat. "What the hell's that?" he asked,

Santa Maria barbecue is a communal (and mostly fraternal) affair.

Japanese farmers, making for an ethnic diversity that continues to this day. After changing its name and boundaries several times and surviving a devastating fire, the town officially became known as Santa Maria in 1885.

EARLY GATHERINGS

The first barbecues began in the mid-nineteenth century as communal feasts, where ranchers fed large crowds of ranch hands and farmers. Early black-and-white photographs in the Santa Maria historical archives show huge pits fueled with blazing wood. The meat—a flavorful loin cut called top block sirloin—was skewered on long steel rods and spit roasted over the open fire. The seasonings were kept simple—salt, pepper, garlic powder or garlic salt, perhaps a little dried parsley—to keep the emphasis on the taste of the meat.

not thrilled that his employees were lunching on Safeway merchandise. "Tri-tip," blurted out Schutz, mindful of the cut's triangular shape. "What the hell's a tri-tip?" grumbled the manager. "It's not in the meat cutter's handbook." It was hardly an auspicious start for a regional barbecue classic.

I wish I could say it was an overnight success. The fact is, if it hadn't been for the enthusiasm of budget-minded salesmen from a nearby used car dealership, the tri-tip probably would have gone the way of the eight-track audio tape. But word gradually spread of this inexpensive cut that tasted liked high-priced steak. A few years later, Schutz opened his own butcher shop and actively began promoting tri-tip. Airmen from nearby Vandenberg Air Force Base acquired a taste for it

and spread the word further. Today, tri-tip is found throughout central California—indeed, when Santa Marians, many Santa Barbarans, and even Angelinos speak of barbecue, tri-tip is frequently what they mean.

Actually, Santa Maria barbecue predates the invention of the tri-tip. The Spanish likely brought cattle here in the late eighteenth century. The valley's first American settler was William Benjamin Foxen, a cattle rancher, who purchased the Rancho Tinaquaic in 1842. The early cattle ranchers were joined by Swiss dairy men and Danish, Portuguese, and

A cranked pulley allows the pit masters to control the cooking temperature.

Slow-roasting the meat leaves plenty of time for conversation.

In time, the accompaniments came to include a distinctive small, pinkish local bean of Hispanic origin—the pinquito. Stewed with tomatoes, onions, and spices, it became the Santa Maria version of baked beans (the dish is considerably less sweet). A Mexican influence can be seen in the salsa traditionally served with Santa Maria barbecue, while the obligatory accompanying green salad and grilled garlic bread are pure California. Top block sirloin continues to be grilled at restaurants and community barbecues staged by fraternal organizations. Home cooks and weekend pit masters prefer the more manageably sized tri-tip.

DRIVE & DINE

But don't take my word for it. Drive down Broadway, the main drag of Santa Maria, on a weekend in barbecue season (late spring and early summer) and you'll find dozens of pit masters serving up freshly grilled tri-tip. They arrive early, towing the local version of a barbecue pit—a giant black metal box with an adjustable grate you raise and lower with the turn of a crank or tug on a pulley. These giant grills are part of what distinguish barbecues in Santa Maria from the heavily smoked meats found elsewhere on the American barbecue trail. Adding a touch of local pride, the pits are often branded with the names of their owners, cut from steel in bold silhouette.

The fuel, local red oak, is the second distinguishing feature of Santa Maria–style barbecue. Don't expect the heavy smoke flavor associated with the barbecue of the American South. No, the open pits impart a light, delicately aromatic wood flavor that's now synonymous with California grilling.

Most of these weekend barbecues are staged as local fundraisers. During a recent visit, I met pit masters drumming up money for a local little league team, a college scholarship fund, and a Filipino American civic group. And Santa Maria's ethnic diversity remains very much in evidence at these parking lot barbecues. A Mexican American team, for example, bolstered their salsa with prodigious quantities of jalapeños.

The best way to sample Santa Maria–style barbecue is to stop wherever you see smoke. In October the city stages a barbecue cook-off as part of its Autumn Arts Grapes & Grains Festival. For information and dates see the box on page 186.

In the old days, tri-tip was roasted over an ember-filled hole in the ground.

New Orleans, La.

CAJUN "HUNGER KILLER"

Whenever I teach a grilling class, I leave my students with a homework assignment—create a variation on one of the dishes I demonstrated. This is how the following recipe came to be, thanks to the imagination of a budding grill master from New Orleans. The model was a *matambre,* Argentina's infamous "hunger killer." But instead of stuffing and rolling the flank steak with the traditional South American flavorings, my student had the idea to use tasso ham, andouille sausage, and other Louisianan flavorings. And to give it another distinctly American twist, the meat is smoked as well as grilled using the indirect method.

METHOD:
Indirect grilling

INGREDIENTS:

1 beef flank steak (1½ to 1¾ pounds)

1 tablespoon Cajun Rub (page 420) or
    your favorite commercial brand

1 andouille sausage (about 6 ounces)

1 slice tasso ham (about ½ inch thick
    and 6 ounces)

1 slice aged Provolone cheese (about
    ½ inch thick and 6 ounces; see Notes)

1 red bell pepper, cored and seeded

1 green bell pepper, cored and seeded

1 long carrot, trimmed and peeled

3 hard-cooked eggs (see Notes), peeled

4 slices of bacon

YOU'LL ALSO NEED:
**Butcher's string; 2 cups wood chips or
    chunks (preferably hickory or oak),
    soaked for 1 hour in water to cover,
    then drained**

1 BUTTERFLY THE FLANK STEAK: Trim the edges of the flank steak so that they are straight and the meat is an even rectangle. Place the flank steak at the edge of the cutting board, with a short side closest to you. Using a long slender knife, make a horizontal cut through a long side, slicing the meat almost in half (stop about ½ inch from the opposite side). Open the steak up like a book, then pound the center flat with a meat pounder or the side of a cleaver. Sprinkle the Cajun Rub all over the flank steak on both sides, patting it onto the meat with you fingertips.

2 Cut the andouille sausage in half lengthwise, then cut each half in half lengthwise; you will have 4 strips. Cut the tasso ham and the Provolone into ½-inch-wide strips. Cut each bell pepper lengthwise into ½-inch-wide strips. Cut the carrot into quarters lengthwise. Cut the hard-cooked eggs into quarters lengthwise; you will have 12 egg quarters.

3 Put the seasoned butterflied flank steak on a cutting board so that a short side is closest to you. Starting at the edge of the meat nearest you, arrange the ingredients for the filling in neat, narrow, alternating rows in the

TIPS

■ Although this recipe may look complicated, it can be assembled in 15 minutes. When people see the results, they'll think you've been working for hours. The only even remotely tricky part is butterflying the flank steak, and if you're not comfortable with your knife skills, ask your butcher to do it for you.

■ If you haven't already encountered them, andouille is a smoky Cajun sausage and tasso is a spicy Cajun ham. They are available at specialty food shops and from butchers, or see Mail-Order Sources on page 742.

following order: 2 andouille sausage strips, placed end to end; some of the red bell pepper strips; some of the Provolone strips; a piece of carrot; some of the green bell pepper strips; some of the strips of tasso; then 6 quarters of hard-cooked egg. You want the rows of filling to be positioned parallel to the grain of the meat; continue until all of the filling has been used. Leave the last 2 or 3 inches of meat bare. Starting with the edge of meat closest to you, roll up the flank steak into a tight cylinder. Carefully move it to the side.

4 Cut four 15-inch pieces of butcher's string. Position the strings on the cutting board, so that they are parallel to each other and roughly 2 inches apart. Place 1 slice of bacon across the center of the strings so that it is perpendicular to them.

5 Place the rolled meat on top of the slice of bacon so that it is perpendicular to the strings. Place a slice of bacon lengthwise on top of the rolled meat. Press the remaining 2 slices of bacon against either side of the rolled flank steak. Tie the pieces of string together around the meat so that they hold the slices of bacon tightly against it. The flank steak can be prepared several hours ahead to this stage. Refrigerate it, covered.

6 Set up the grill for indirect grilling (see page 23 for gas or page 22 for charcoal) and preheat to medium. If using a gas grill, place all of the wood chips or chunks in the smoker box or in a smoker pouch (see page 24) and run the grill on high until you see smoke, then reduce the heat to medium. If using a charcoal grill, place a large drip pan in the center, preheat the grill to medium, then toss all of the wood chips or chunks on the coals.

7 When ready to cook, place the rolled steak in the center of the hot grate, over the drip pan and away from the heat, and cover the grill. Grill the flank steak until darkly browned and cooked through, 1½ to 2 hours. To test for doneness insert an instant-read meat thermometer into an end of the hunger killer: The internal temperature should be about 190°F. If the roast isn't completely browned on the outside, move it directly over the fire the last 10 to 15 minutes of cooking, rotating it every 3 to 4 minutes. If using a charcoal grill, after 1 hour you'll need to add 12 fresh coals to each side.

8 Transfer the grilled flank steak to a cutting board and let rest for 10 minutes. Remove and discard the strings, cut the roll crosswise into ½-inch slices, and serve at once.

YIELD:

**Serves 8 to 10 as an appetizer,
    4 to 6 as a main course**

NOTES:

■ If you can't find hard, aged Provolone, use another hard cheese, such as Pecorino Romano.

■ You'll find instructions on the best way to hard cook eggs on page 38.

New York, N.Y.

ROMANIAN GARLIC SKIRT STEAKS

If you like the sanguine flavor of beef and the nose-tweaking pungency of garlic, you'll adore this garlicky skirt steak, inspired by Sammy's Roumanian in New York City. Sammy's is Manhattan's most famous (some would say most infamous) Jewish-style restaurant: Dinner at this Lower East Side landmark is like attending a boisterous bar mitzvah that happens to be open to the public. Sammy's gives both skirt steaks and veal chops the royal garlic treatment. My own contribution to the recipe is a blast of oregano and hot paprika.

METHOD:
Direct grilling

ADVANCE PREPARATION:
2 to 4 hours for marinating the steaks

INGREDIENTS:
1½ pounds skirt steaks
Coarse salt (kosher or sea) and
    freshly ground black pepper
Hungarian hot paprika
2 tablespoons olive oil
4 to 6 cloves garlic (see Note),
    finely chopped
1 tablespoon dried oregano

1 Place the steaks in a baking dish. Generously season them on both sides with salt, pepper, and paprika. Drizzle the steaks on both sides with the olive oil, patting it on with your fingertips. Sprinkle the garlic and oregano over the steaks, again patting them on with your fingertips. Let the steaks marinate in the refrigerator, covered, for 2 to 4 hours. Be sure you tightly cover the baking dish with plastic wrap.

2 Set up the grill for direct grilling (see page 21 for charcoal or gas) and preheat to high.

Go to Sammy's—a classic Lower East Side Jewish restaurant—for a boisterous, belt-loosening dining experience.

TIPS

■ Skirt steak is a flat, stringy steak from the underbelly of the steer. This may not sound very appetizing, but it's loaded with flavor, and if you slice it thinly across the grain it will be as tender as you could wish for.

■ This steak has a kick and I don't just mean from the garlic. If hot paprika burns your tongue too much, you can substitute mild or sweet. Just be sure to use an imported Hungarian paprika: One good kind comes from the region of Szeged.

3 When ready to cook, brush and oil the grill grate. Place the steaks on the hot grate and grill until cooked to taste, 3 to 4 minutes per side for medium-rare. When ready to turn, the steaks will be nicely browned on the bottom. To test for doneness, use the poke method; the meat should be gently yielding for medium-rare. Transfer the steaks to a platter or plates and let rest for 2 minutes, then serve at once.

YIELD:
Serves 4

NOTE: How many garlic cloves you use depends on how intense a garlic flavor you want. I go for broke.

Miami, Fla.

CUBANO STEAKS
With Grilled Onions

Floridians joke that Miami is Cuba's northernmost province. That's not stretching the truth much: Miami has more Cubans than any other city except Havana. It's not surprising that steak here should have a Latin accent: seasoned with an aromatic blend of garlic, oregano, and sour orange juice.

So, next time you hunger for steak that's a little different, try this.

METHOD:
Direct grilling

ADVANCE PREPARATION:
4 hours for marinating the steaks

INGREDIENTS:
**1 large or 2 medium-size sweet or
    white onions, cut crosswise into
    1/2-inch slices
1 1/2 pounds skirt steaks
4 cloves garlic, finely chopped
3 tablespoons chopped fresh oregano,
    or 2 teaspoons dried oregano
Coarse salt (kosher or sea) and
    coarsely ground black pepper
1/3 cup fresh sour orange juice
    (see Note) or lime juice
6 tablespoons extra-virgin olive oil**

YOU'LL ALSO NEED:
**6 to 8 small (6-inch) bamboo skewers
    or long wooden toothpicks**

1 Skewer the onion slices crosswise with skewers or toothpicks to hold them together during grilling. Place half of the onions over the bottom of a non-reactive baking dish just large enough to hold the steaks.

2 Sprinkle the steaks on both sides with the garlic and oregano and season both sides with salt and pepper. Place the steaks on top of the onions in the baking dish. Pour the sour orange juice over the steaks, turning to coat both sides. Repeat with 4 tablespoons of the olive oil. Place the remaining onions on top. Let the steaks marinate in the refrigerator, covered, for 4 hours.

3 Set up the grill for direct grilling (see page 21 for charcoal or gas) and preheat to high.

4 When ready to cook, drain the marinade from the steaks and onion slices and discard the marinade. Brush and oil the grill grate. Arrange the steaks and onions on the hot grate, placing them on a diagonal to the bars. Grill the steaks until cooked to taste, 3 to 4 minutes per side for medium-rare; grill the onions until they are golden brown and tender, 3 to 4 minutes per side. When ready to turn, the steaks will be nicely browned on the bottom. To test for doneness, use the poke method; the meat should be gently yielding. Baste the steaks and onions with the remaining 2 tablespoons of olive oil as they grill.

5 Transfer the grilled steaks to a platter or plates and let rest for 2 minutes. Top with the grilled onions (remove the skewers). Serve at once.

YIELD:
Serves 4

NOTE: A sour orange *(naranja agria)* is an orange-like citrus fruit with juice that is sour like that of a lime. Fresh lime juice makes an acceptable substitute.

Dallas, Tex.

DRUNKEN STEAK

Since the earliest days of our nation, beef and bourbon have been keeping one another company. There's something about the sweetness of sipping whiskey that enhances the rich, meaty flavor of beef. Especially when that beef is a uniquely American preparation: London broil. (No, despite its name, it doesn't come from England.) The idea for this recipe

> The traditional steak for Cubano Steaks is *palomilla*, a thin, tough, flavorful cut from the top round; it's pounded to make it tender. I find that the flavorings go great with another popular Latino cut of beef: skirt steak.

In the old days, the butcher shop came to you.

(see Grilling over a Wood Fire, page 20).

■ For maximum flavor, you'd grill over blazing oak or mesquite embers (see Grilling over a Wood Fire, page 20). Or you can use wood chips with a charcoal or gas grill to give you a light smoke flavor.

■ Note the use of a two-zone fire here: You sear the steak over the hot zone and move it to the medium zone to finish cooking.

comes to me from one David Ashmore of Dallas, Texas. He came to see me at a book signing one evening, eager to share his prized family recipe. David learned it from his grandfather, a meat-and-potatoes guy from Iowa, who used to work for Heinz. I'd keep the accompaniments pretty simple here. Perhaps some grilled asparagus (see page 592) and barbecued potatoes (see page 619).

METHOD:
Direct grilling

ADVANCE PREPARATION:
4 hours for marinating the steak

FOR THE MARINADE:
1 cup bourbon
1 cup soy sauce (preferably Kikkoman)
3 tablespoons Asian (dark) sesame oil
2 tablespoons sugar
2 cloves garlic, minced
1 tablespoon minced peeled fresh ginger

FOR THE STEAK:
1 beefsteak (1¼ to 1½ inches thick and 1¾ to 2 pounds), cut from the top or bottom round
Coarse salt (kosher or sea) and freshly ground black pepper
1 tablespoon cold salted butter

YOU'LL ALSO NEED:
1 cup wood chips or chunks (preferably oak or hickory), soaked for 1 hour in water to cover, then drained

1 MAKE THE MARINADE: In a mixing bowl, combine the bourbon, soy sauce, sesame oil, sugar, garlic, and gin-

ger. Whisk until the sugar dissolves. Place the steak in a roasting pan just large enough to hold it. Pour the marinade over it, turning the steak once or twice to coat it evenly with the marinade. Let the steak marinate for 4 hours in the refrigerator, covered, turning it once more.

2 Set up the grill for direct grilling using a two-zone fire (see page 22 for gas or charcoal). If using a gas grill, place all of the wood chips or chunks in the smoker box or in a smoker pouch (see page 24) and run the grill on high until you see smoke, then lower one burner to medium. If using a charcoal grill, preheat one zone to high and the other to medium, then toss all of the wood chips or chunks on the coals.

3 When ready to cook, brush and oil the grill grate. Drain the marinade off the steak and discard the marinade. Place the steak on the hot grate and grill until cooked to taste, 6 to 8 minutes per side for medium-rare. Start by searing the steak over the hot zone for about 2 minutes, then move it over the medium zone. Repeat on the other side. To test for doneness, insert an instant-read thermometer in the side of the beef: The internal temperature should be 140° to 145°F for medium-rare. Generously season the steak with salt and pepper as it cooks.

4 Transfer the grilled steak to a cutting board. Stick the piece of butter on the end of a fork and rub it over the top of the beef. Let the steak rest for about 3 minutes.

5 Using a sharp knife, carve the beef into broad thin slices, holding the knife blade at a 45 degree angle to the top of the meat. Pour the juices over the slices and serve at once.

YIELD:

Serves 4

Tuscon, Ariz.

TUCSON "TUSCAN" PORTERHOUSE

The porterhouse is the most aristocratic steak ever to sizzle on a grill grate. This bible-thick slab of meat combines two steaks in one—a tender filet mignon and a flavorful New York strip, which are connected by a T-bone. New York's infamous trencherman, Diamond Jim Brady, is said to have dined on porterhouse daily (eating several at a single seating), and this plate-burying steak has been the signature dish at the legendary Peter Luger Steak House in Brooklyn for more than a century. Here's an Arizonan version, spiced up with a chile powder and mustard rub and anointed with

cilantro-serrano oil. So why's it called Tucson "Tuscan?" Well, porterhouse is also the steak specialty of Tuscany, Italy, where it goes by the name of *bistecca alla fiorentina*. This recipe uses the Tuscan method to produce a porterhouse that explodes with Southwestern flavors.

METHOD:
Direct grilling

FOR THE STEAK AND RUB:
**1 porterhouse steak
    (1½ to 2 inches thick and
    1¾ to 2 pounds)**
**1 teaspoon coarse salt
    (kosher or sea)**
**1 teaspoon cracked black
    peppercorns**
1 teaspoon pure chile powder
1 teaspoon dry mustard
1 teaspoon dried oregano
½ teaspoon garlic powder
½ teaspoon ground cumin
¼ teaspoon ground cinnamon

FOR THE CILANTRO-SERRANO OIL:
5 tablespoons extra-virgin olive oil
**3 tablespoons chopped fresh
    cilantro**
**1 to 2 serrano or small jalapeño peppers,
    thinly sliced**
1 to 2 cloves garlic, thinly sliced

YOU'LL ALSO NEED:
**1 cup wood chips or chunks
    (preferably mesquite),
    soaked for 1 hour in water
    to cover, then drained**

1 Place the steak in an oval baking dish.

TIPS

■ A Tuscan pit master would grill over oak. For a real Southwest flavor, build your fire with mesquite logs or chunks—or at the very least use mesquite chips (see Grilling over a Wood Fire on page 20).

■ Due to the thickness of a porterhouse steak, you should work over a two-zone fire. Use the hot zone for searing the steak; the medium zone for cooking it through.

2 MAKE THE RUB: Place the salt, peppercorns, chili powder, mustard, oregano, garlic powder, cumin, and cinnamon in a bowl and stir to mix. (Actually, your fingers work better for mixing than a spoon or whisk does.) Sprinkle the rub all over the steak on both sides, patting it onto the meat with your fingertips.

3 MAKE THE CILANTRO-SERRANO OIL: Heat the olive oil in a small saucepan over medium heat. Add the cilantro, serranos, and garlic and cook until fragrant, about 2 minutes. Do not let the garlic brown. Remove the pan from the heat.

4 Set up the grill for direct grilling using a two-zone fire (see page 22 for gas or charcoal). If using a gas grill, place all of the wood chips or chunks in the smoker box or in a smoker pouch (see page 24) and run the grill on high until you see smoke, then lower one burner to medium. If using a charcoal grill, preheat one zone to high and the other to medium, then toss all of the wood chips or chunks on the coals.

5 When ready to cook, brush and oil the grill grate. Arrange the steak on the grate over the hot zone, placing it on a diagonal to the bars. Grill for about 2 minutes, then move the steak to the medium zone, rotating it a quarter turn to create an attractive cross-hatch of grill marks. Let grill for 6 to 8 minutes longer.

6 Turn the steak over, placing it over the hot zone of the grill and on a diagonal to the bars. Let this side sear for about 2 minutes, then move the steak to the medium zone, rotating it a quarter turn. Let the steak continue to grill until cooked to taste, another 6 to 8 minutes for medium-rare. Brush the top of the steak with some of the cilantro-serrano oil as it cooks. To test for doneness, insert an instant-read meat thermometer in the side of the porterhouse. The internal temperature should be 140° to 145°F for medium-rare.

7 Transfer the grilled porterhouse to a deep platter and pour the remaining cilantro-serrano oil over it. Let the steak rest for about 3 minutes, turning it several times in the oil to baste both sides.

When it comes to grilling steak, you can't beat the perfume of wood smoke.

8 To carve and serve the porterhouse, cut the two steaks off either side of the T-bone. Cut each crosswise into ¼-inch-thick slices. Pour the juices in the platter over the slices and serve at once.

YIELD:
Serves 2 very hungry people or 3 to 4 people with more moderate appetites

San Antonio, Tex.

TEX-MEX RIB EYES
Con Mucha Cerveza

Mi Tierra is a San Antonio landmark—very nearly as much so as the Alamo. For decades, this lively restaurant, located in the central market, has defined the local Mexican dining experience. Tourists and locals alike flock here for two-fisted margaritas (served from a manorial mahogany bar), guacamole made the old-fashioned way (in a *molcajete*—a lava stone mortar and pestle), and plate-burying grilled chops and steaks. This brings us to the following rib eye, which is dished up with grilled scallions, jalapeño peppers, and salsa. The *mucha cerveza* (much beer) marinade is my own contribution to a dish that has kept San Antonians coming to Mi Tierra for half a century.

METHOD:
Direct grilling

ADVANCE PREPARATION:
2 hours for marinating the steaks

FOR THE STEAKS:
4 rib eye steaks (each about 1 inch thick and 8 to 10 ounces)
Coarse salt (kosher or sea) and freshly ground black pepper
3 tablespoons olive oil

FOR THE MUCHA CERVEZA MARINADE:
1 bottle (8 ounces) dark Mexican beer
¼ cup fresh lime juice
1 medium-size onion, finely chopped
3 cloves garlic, finely chopped
1 to 2 jalapeño peppers, seeded and finely chopped (for hotter steaks, leave the seeds in)
¼ cup chopped fresh cilantro

FOR SERVING:
2 bunches scallions, trimmed
4 to 8 jalapeño peppers
4 flour tortillas
Lime wedges
El Paso Picante (page 688) or your favorite salsa in an attractive serving bowl

YOU'LL ALSO NEED:
2 cups wood chips or chunks (preferably mesquite or oak), soaked for 1 hour in water to cover, then drained

1 Generously season the steaks on both sides with salt and black pepper. Place the steaks in a nonreactive

■ Rib eye is one of my favorite steaks, being generously marbled, uncommonly tender, and as flavorful as prime rib. But you could certainly substitute a leaner steak, like a strip steak or a T-bone.

■ In keeping with the Texas origins of this dish, I'd suggest grilling the steaks over mesquite wood (see Grilling over a Wood Fire, page 20). Mesquite chips will generate wood smoke if you are using a gas or charcoal grill. You could also use oak.

baking dish just large enough to hold them and drizzle the olive oil over them. Turn the steaks a couple of times, rubbing them with your fingertips to coat with oil.

2 MAKE THE *MUCHA CERVEZA* MARINADE: Combine the beer, lime juice, onion, garlic, chopped jalapeño(s), and cilantro in a nonreactive mixing bowl and stir to mix. Pour the marinade over the steaks and let them marinate in the refrigerator, covered, for 1 to 2 hours, turning them a couple of times so that they marinate evenly.

3 Set up the grill for direct grilling (see page 21 for gas or charcoal) and preheat to high. If using a gas grill, place all of the wood chips or chunks in the smoker box or in a smoker pouch (see page 24) and run the grill on high until you see smoke. If using a charcoal grill, preheat it to high, then toss 1 cup of the wood chips or chunks on the coals.

4 When ready to cook, brush and oil the grill grate. Place the scallions and whole jalapeños on the hot grate and grill until nicely browned on all sides. This will take 2 to 3 minutes per side (6 to 9 minutes in all) for the jalapeños and 3 to 4 minutes per side (6 to 8 minutes in all) for the scallions. Transfer the grilled vegetables to a plate.

5 Remove the steaks from the marinade and drain, discarding the marinade. If using a charcoal grill, toss the remaining 1 cup of wood chips or chunks on the coals. Place the marinated steaks on the hot grate and grill

until cooked to taste, 4 to 6 minutes per side for medium-rare, rotating each steak a quarter turn after 2 minutes on each side to create an attractive cross-hatch of grill marks. Season the steaks on both sides with salt and pepper. To test for doneness, use the poke method; the meat should be gently yielding. Transfer the grilled steaks to plates or a platter and let rest for 3 minutes.

6 Warm the tortillas on the grill, about 15 seconds per side, and transfer them to a cloth-lined basket. Serve the steaks with the grilled jalapeños, scallions, and tortillas and salsa on the side. To eat, wrap bite-size pieces of steak in a tortilla with some of the scallions, jalapeños, and salsa.

YIELD:
Serves 4

Toronto, Canada

ROLL IN THE HAY STEAKS

Maybe it's the result of drinking too much beer—or inhaling too many charcoal fumes—but grilling seems to bring out eccentricity in its practitioners. (Think of beer-can chicken or sweet potatoes roasted in

the embers.) One of the most individu-
alistic grill masters I know is the
Toronto-based Ted Reader, author,
along with Kathleen Sloan, of an ingenious book called *The Sticks & Stones
Cookbook.* Ted offers up lots of oddball
barbecuing techniques, including
grilling with vines, boards, and stones.
One of his more outlandish creations
is steak wrapped in hay and seared on
the grill. The hay actually catches fire,
creating a crisp crust (that's putting it
mildly) and imparting an irresistible
smoke flavor. I've simplified Ted's
recipe to keep the focus on the taste
that the smoldering hay imparts.

METHOD:
Direct grilling

ADVANCE PREPARATION:
30 minutes for soaking the hay

INGREDIENTS:
**About 2 gallons of hay
    (enough to half fill a 4-gallon
    household bucket)
3 bottles (12 ounces each) beer,
    or 1 quart water
4 boneless strip steaks
    (8 to 10 ounces each)
Coarse salt (kosher or sea) and
    cracked black peppercorns
¼ cup molasses
½ cup chopped fresh herbs,
    including parsley, sage,
    rosemary, thyme, and/or
    basil
3 cloves garlic, minced
2 tablespoons extra-virgin olive oil
    or melted butter
Pepper Herb Butter
    (optional; recipe follows)**

*Hay-grilled steaks and grilled shrimp cocktail prepared
by Canadian grill master Ted Reader.*

1 Place the hay in a bucket or bowl
and douse with the beer. Let soak
for 30 minutes, then drain.

2 Place the steaks on a platter.
Season them very generously on
both sides with salt and cracked peppercorns. Brush the steaks on both
sides with the molasses. Combine the
herbs and garlic in a small bowl and
stir to mix. Sprinkle the herb mixture
over the steaks, patting it onto the
meat with your fingertips to make a
thick crust.

3 Grab a good-size handful of hay.
Lay it flat on a baking sheet,

TIPS

The hardest part of
preparing this recipe
will be finding hay.
Try a farm stand,
tack shop, or riding
school. If you
can't find hay, the
herb and molasses
crust still makes a
compelling steak. If
you don't use hay,
you don't need to
cover the grill.

TIPS

This is a very theatrical way of grilling, and it produces lots of smoke and fire. Never grill a steak in hay on an apartment balcony or closed-in porch. In fact, you should only attempt it on an open patio or in a backyard, well away from all buildings or trees. If you have long hair, tie it back, and if you're wearing loose sleeves, roll them up. Also, the timing can be a little tricky, so I suggest you try the recipe by yourself first, before attempting it in front of a crowd.

spreading it out to form a rectangle the same length and about 3 times the width of a steak. Place a steak at the bottom of the rectangle (the longest side of the steak should be parallel to the short side of the rectangle). Roll up the steak in the hay. Repeat with the remaining steaks and hay.

4 Set up the grill for direct grilling (see page 21 for charcoal or gas) and preheat to high.

5 When ready to cook, brush the grill grate. Lay the hay-wrapped steaks on the hot grate and cover the grill. Grill the steaks for about 3 minutes. Uncover the grill and continue grilling for 1 minute. Expect a lot of smoke and flames as the hay catches fire.

6 Turn the steaks and scrape any unburned hay off the tops onto the grill grate next to the meat. It will catch fire, creating further smoke for the steaks. Brush the tops of the steaks with 1 tablespoon of the olive oil. Cover the grill and continue grilling for 3 minutes.

7 Turn the steaks again and scrape any unburned hay off the tops onto the grill grate next to the meat. Brush the tops of the steaks with the remaining 1 tablespoon of olive oil. Continue grilling the steaks until cooked to taste, another minute or so per side for medium-rare. To test for doneness, use the poke method; the meat should be gently yielding.

8 Brush off any ash with a pastry brush and transfer the steaks to a platter or plates. Place rounds or dollops of the Pepper Herb Butter on top, if desired, and serve at once.

YIELD:
Serves 4

Pepper Herb Butter

Ted likes to serve Roll in the Hay Steaks with this fragrant herb butter. It isn't absolutely essential because the steaks are plenty flavorful by themselves. But why not go all the way? This will make twice as much herb butter as you need for the Roll in the Hay Steaks. It would be equally delicious on grilled salmon, pork chops, or chicken breasts.

INGREDIENTS:

**8 tablespoons (1 stick) salted butter,
    at room temperature**
**2 tablespoons chopped fresh herbs,
    including parsley, sage, rosemary,
    thyme, and/or basil**
1 shallot, minced fine as dust
1½ teaspoons cracked black peppercorns
1½ teaspoons balsamic vinegar

1 Place the butter in a large bowl and beat with a wooden spoon or whisk until light and creamy. Beat in the herbs, shallot, cracked peppercorns, and vinegar.

2 Place a 12-inch-square piece of plastic wrap or parchment paper on your work surface. Put the flavored butter at the bottom edge and roll the butter into a log, twisting the ends to make a Tootsie Roll–like tight cylinder. Refrigerate or freeze until firm. The flavored butter can be refrigerated for up to 5 days or frozen for 3 months.

3 To serve, unwrap the butter and cut it crosswise into ½-inch slices. Place 1 slice of flavored butter on each steak.

YIELD:
Makes about ½ cup

San Antonio, Tex.

"UGLY TACOS" (Tex-Mex Steak and Eggs)

El Milagrito (the Little Miracle), in San Antonio, Texas, is the sort of eatery every traveler dreams of stumbling upon—a neighborhood hole-in-the-wall with a black-and-white checkered linoleum floor and colorful Mexican pennants on the walls. It's the sort of joint where you can eat yourself silly for breakfast and still get change from a $10 bill. The *taco feo* (ugly taco) is El Milagrito's answer to the traditional American steak and

Barbecue is more than just food in Texas. It's a religion.

egg breakfast, and a glorious creation it is: a flour tortilla piled high with scrambled eggs, refried beans, sliced grilled steak, *pico de gallo* (a simple but fiery salsa made with tomatoes, onions, and jalapeños), and a second fiery Tex-Mex salsa. It's the sort of breakfast you might cook over a fire when you're camping.

METHOD:
Direct grilling

ADVANCE PREPARATION:
30 minutes for marinating the steaks

TIPS

■ This recipe looks a good deal more complicated than it really is. You can certainly make the refried beans from scratch, but canned will work just fine for this recipe. Ditto for the salsa. In fact, you probably have an interesting salsa of some sort in your refrigerator already.

■ You have to be pretty die-hard to fire up your grill for breakfast, but "ugly tacos" make a great, theatrical Sunday brunch, especially if your grill has a side burner for scrambling the eggs. If it doesn't, you can heat a cast-iron skillet right on the grate.

FOR THE STEAK:

1½ pounds strip steak or sirloin steak
　(about ½ inch thick)
1 teaspoon coarse salt (kosher or sea)
1 teaspoon freshly ground black pepper
1 to 3 teaspoons pure chile powder
2 limes, each cut in half

FOR THE PICO DE GALLO:

½ cup finely diced white onion
½ cup finely diced ripe tomato
½ cup finely chopped fresh cilantro
2 to 4 jalapeño peppers, seeded and
　diced (for a hotter pico de gallo,
　leave the seeds in)

FOR THE TACOS:

1½ cups refried beans
2 cups El Paso Picante (page 688;
　see Note) or your favorite salsa
6 large eggs
Coarse salt (kosher or sea) and
　freshly ground black pepper
5 tablespoons butter or lard
6 flour tortillas (8 inches each)
Lime wedges, for serving

1 Generously season the steak on both sides with salt, black pepper, and chile powder. Squeeze the limes over the meat and let marinate for 30 minutes.

2 MAKE THE *PICO DE GALLO:* Combine the onion, tomato, cilantro, and jalapeños in an attractive nonreactive serving bowl and stir to mix.

3 Heat the refried beans in a skillet or saucepan over medium-high heat, 3 to 5 minutes, or in a glass bowl in a microwave. Keep the refried beans warm until ready to serve.

4 Place 1½ cups of the El Paso Picante in an attractive nonreactive serving bowl. Place the remaining ½ cup of El Paso Picante in a nonreactive mixing bowl and beat in the eggs. Add salt and black pepper to taste. Melt 3 tablespoons of the butter in a skillet over medium heat. Brush a little butter on each tortilla.

5 Set up the grill for direct grilling (see page 21 for charcoal or gas) and preheat to high.

6 When ready to cook, brush and oil the grill grate. Place the steak on the hot grate and grill until cooked to taste, 3 to 4 minutes per side for medium. (Tex-Mex steak tends to be served medium or even medium-well, rather than medium-rare.) To test for doneness, use the poke method; the meat will yield only slightly at the touch when cooked to medium. Transfer the grilled steak to a cutting board and let rest for 3 minutes. Meanwhile, toast the buttered tortillas on the grill until warm but not quite crisp, 30 seconds per side. Transfer the toasted tortillas to a platter or plates. Spread ¼ cup of the refried beans on each tortilla.

7 Place a frying pan on the grill or on the grill's side burner over medium heat, add the remaining 2 tablespoons of butter, and let it melt. Add the egg mixture and cook until scrambled, stirring with a wooden spoon (I like my eggs fairly loose— this will take 2 to 3 minutes). Divide the scrambled eggs evenly among the tortillas, spooning them over the refried beans. Thinly slice the steak on the diagonal and arrange the slices on top of the eggs. Spoon a little of the *pico de gallo* over the steak, followed by some of the El Paso Picante. Serve the remaining salsas on the side, along with the lime wedges. This is the sort of breakfast or brunch that should last you until dinner; it's that good.

YIELD:
Serves 6

NOTE: This El Paso Picante is a tasty homemade salsa, not to be confused with the commercial salsa bottled under the Old El Paso label.

Los Angeles, Calif.

KOREATOWN RIB EYES
With Sweet Sesame Marinade

Soot Bull Jeep may be the best kept restaurant secret in Los Angeles—a Koreatown barbecue joint so authentic, each table comes equipped with its own charcoal-burning hibachi. This means you get to enjoy the eye-stinging smoke and spark-spitting coals of a backyard barbecue with someone else prepping the food and clearing the tables. And what food! Gorgeously marbled rib eye steaks, sliced wafer-thin, marinated in a sweet, nutty-tasting mixture of sugar, sesame oil, and soy sauce. Grilled at the table by you or your waitress, the steaks are served with all the trimmings, which in this case means the colorful panoply of pickled vegetables and salads that the Koreans call *kimchi*. If you're familiar with Korean food, you may know steaks fixed this way by their Korean name—*bool kogi*—and if you don't, it's high time you tried them, for rarely does such a quick, easy preparation result in such extraordinary taste.

WALL OF FLAME

SOOT BULL JEEP

Half the fun at Soot Bull Jeep is grilling dinner on your own hibachi, and the other half is eating the *bool kogi,* Korean sweet-salty rib eye, or *kalbi kui,* butterflied grilled short ribs, with a tongue-tingling assortment of *kimchis* (Korean pickles). Come with friends so you'll have a whole table to yourselves.

3136 West 8th Street
Los Angeles, California
(213) 387-3865

Korean restaurants often deliver the ultimate grilling experience thanks to a charcoal-burning hibachi built right into the table.

TIPS

Tradition calls for *bool kogi* to be made with rib eye steaks sliced very thin (1/8 to 1/4 inch thick), so the meat cooks through quickly enough that the sugar in the marinade does not burn. If you live in or near a Korean neighborhood or you have a good butcher, you may be able to have the rib eye custom sliced on a meat slicer. Barring this, you can buy a normal size rib eye (3/4 to 1 inch thick) and, using a very sharp knife and holding the blade parallel to the cutting board, slice the steak across the grain into three or four thin slices. This will feel a little awkward at first, but it becomes second nature with practice.

METHOD:
Direct grilling

ADVANCE PREPARATION:
30 minutes to 1 hour for marinating the steaks

FOR THE BEEF AND MARINADE:
2¼ to 2½ pounds rib eye steaks
3 scallions, both white and green parts, trimmed and thinly sliced
3 cloves garlic
1 piece (1 inch) fresh ginger, peeled and cut into ¼-inch slices
¼ cup sugar
2 tablespoons toasted sesame seeds (see page 584)
⅓ cup Asian (dark) sesame oil
¾ cup soy sauce
1 to 3 teaspoons chile oil or hot paprika (see Note)
½ teaspoon freshly ground black pepper

FOR SERVING:
2 tablespoons toasted sesame seeds (see page 584)
Kimchi (optional)
Romaine lettuce (optional)

1 Carefully cut the rib eyes crosswise (through the thickness) on a meat slicer (or using a very sharp knife) into slices no more than ¼ inch thick. Place the beef slices in a baking dish.

2 MAKE THE MARINADE: Set aside 3 tablespoons of the scallion greens for garnish. Place the garlic, ginger, sugar, sesame seeds and the remaining scallions in a food processor and finely chop. Add the sesame oil, soy sauce, chile oil, and pepper and process to mix. Pour the marinade over the beef slices, turning them to coat. Let the beef marinate for 30 minutes to 1 hour in the refrigerator, covered.

3 Set up the grill for direct grilling (see page 21 for charcoal or gas) and preheat to high.

4 When ready to cook, brush and oil the grill grate. Drain the marinade from the beef and discard the marinade. Place the beef on the hot grate and grill until nicely browned, 1 to 2 minutes per side for medium, the degree of doneness served at most Korean restaurants. Sprinkle the reserved scallion greens and the sesame seeds on top, then serve. Korean Americans would eat *bool kogi* with *kimchi* (pickled vegetables), wrapping them together in romaine lettuce leaves and serving steamed rice on the side.

YIELD:
Serves 6

NOTE: Chile oil is a hot pepper oil sold in Asian markets. Most brands are Chinese.

Indianapolis, Ind.

BLOODY MARY STEAKS

Steak and Bloody Marys have been inseparable companions almost since the birth of the American steak house. Few places make the two better than the venerable Indianapolis steak emporium St. Elmo. Founded in 1902, the restaurant has raised the commonplace shrimp cocktail to the level of art (see page 93), and its Bloody Marys are invigorated with volcanic doses of freshly grated horseradish. That set me thinking. Since the two are such steady companions, why not marinate the beef in a Bloody Mary mix? What follows is destined to become a new American classic. Be sure to make up an extra batch of Bloody Mary mix so you have something to sip on while the grill preheats.

METHOD:
Direct grilling

ADVANCE PREPARATION:
1 to 2 hours for marinating the steaks

INGREDIENTS:
4 large filets mignons (each 1½ inches thick and 6 to 8 ounces)
3 to 4 tablespoons extra-virgin olive oil
2 cups tomato juice or V8 juice
¼ cup vodka (preferably Absolut Peppar) or gin
2 tablespoons fresh lime juice
4 teaspoons Worcestershire sauce, or more to taste
1 tablespoon freshly grated horseradish or prepared white horseradish
1 to 2 teaspoons Tabasco sauce, or to taste (less if you're using Peppar vodka)
½ teaspoon celery salt
½ teaspoon freshly ground black pepper
Tomato Horseradish Butter (optional; recipe follows)

1 Place the steaks in a nonreactive baking dish and pour the olive oil over them. Turn the steaks a couple of times to coat with oil.

2 Place the tomato juice, vodka, lime juice, Worcestershire sauce, horseradish, Tabasco sauce, celery salt, and pepper in a nonreactive mixing bowl and whisk to mix. Taste for seasoning, adding more Worcestershire sauce as necessary. Pour this Bloody Mary marinade over the steaks and let them marinate in the refrigerator, covered, for 1 to 2 hours, turning the steaks a couple of times so that they marinate evenly.

3 Set up the grill for direct grilling (see page 21 for charcoal or gas) and preheat to high.

4 When ready to cook, drain the marinade from the steaks and discard the marinade. Brush and oil the grill grate. Arrange the steaks on the hot grate, placing them on a diagonal to the bars. Grill until cooked to taste, 4 to 6 minutes per side for filets

TIPS

The secret to this recipe is the horseradish, and unless you're willing to make a commitment to scraped knuckles and burning nasal passages (that is, unless you're willing to grate it from scratch), you won't enjoy the steaks at their very best. But prepared horseradish will give you pretty good results, too—without the fumes.

T·I·P·S

As I do with many steaks, I like to top these filet mignons with a compound butter—in this case, a colorful one flavored with sun-dried tomatoes and more horseradish. To simplify the recipe, I've made the butter optional, but I urge you to try it.

For more than a century, black-jacketed workers have served up some of Indiana's best steaks at St. Elmo.

mignons cooked to medium-rare. To test for doneness, use the poke method, the meat should be gently yielding. Rotate each steak a quarter turn after 2 minutes on each side to create an attractive crosshatch of grill marks. Using tongs, turn the steaks on their sides to brown the edges.

5 Transfer the grilled steaks to a platter or plates and let rest for about 3 minutes. If using the Tomato Horseradish Butter, cut it into rounds and place one round on top of each steak.

YIELD:
Serves 4

Tomato Horseradish Butter

Loaded as it is with garlic, sun-dried tomatoes, and tongue-torturing doses of freshly grated horseradish, this simple compound butter has color and flavor aplenty. You could cheat and use bottled horseradish, but you won't get the full effect.

INGREDIENTS:
2 sun-dried tomatoes, soaked for 30 minutes in hot water, then drained (see Note)
1 clove garlic, minced
8 tablespoons (1 stick) salted butter, at room temperature
1 to 2 tablespoons freshly grated horseradish or prepared horseradish
2 teaspoons fresh lime juice
1/2 teaspoon freshly ground black pepper

1 Mince the soaked tomatoes. Place them in a food processor, add the garlic and butter, and process until light and creamy, about 2 minutes. Add the horseradish, lime juice, and pepper.

2 Place a 12-inch-square piece of plastic wrap or parchment paper on your work surface. Put the flavored butter at the bottom edge and roll the butter into a log, twisting the ends to make a Tootsie Roll–like tight

cylinder. Refrigerate or freeze until firm, about 2 hours.

3 To serve, unwrap the butter and cut off 4 slices, each ½-inch thick. This makes about twice the amount of butter that you'll need for the Bloody Mary Steaks. The remainder can be refrigerated for up to 5 days or frozen for 3 months.

YIELD:

Makes about ½ cup

NOTE: You could also use 2 oil-packed sun-dried tomatoes; you won't need to soak these.

Grain-fed Nebraska beef with all the fixin's.

Nebraska

PEPPERED FILETS MIGNONS
With Mushroom Bourbon Sauce

When I was in college, I briefly dated a girl from Nebraska. This was back in the 1970s— the height of the tofu and alfalfa sprout era—yet once a month, my girlfriend's parents would ship her a giant cooler full of steaks. Meaty strip steaks, lusciously marbled rib eyes, filets mignons so tender you could cut them with a fork—beef designed to keep their daughter from wasting away in the seafood-rich and vegetarian-rife Pacific Northwest.

As a frequent beneficiary of their largesse, I can rightly say that Nebraskans have reason to be proud of their grain-fed beef. Indeed, one family has built it into a business that makes close to $300 million a year. I'm talking, of course, about Omaha Steaks, founded by a Latvian immigrant named J. J. Simon in 1917. Now in its fifth generation, Omaha has 1.5 million customers and has become synonymous with Midwestern, dare I say American, beef. Which brings us to the following filets mignons, painted with mustard, thickly crusted with peppercorns, and smokily seared on the grill. The sauce is loosely inspired by a recipe developed for Omaha Steaks by James Beard.

METHOD:
Direct grilling

FOR THE MUSHROOM BOURBON SAUCE:
12 ounces mushrooms
3 tablespoons butter
2 shallots, finely chopped
(about 6 tablespoons)
½ cup dry white wine
¾ cup beef or chicken stock
1 cup heavy (whipping) cream
2 tablespoons bourbon
1 teaspoon Dijon mustard
Coarse salt (kosher or sea) and
freshly ground black pepper

FOR THE STEAKS:
4 large filets mignons
(each 1½ inches thick and
6 to 8 ounces)
2 tablespoons Dijon mustard
2 tablespoons cracked black
peppercorns
2 tablespoons cracked white
peppercorns (or more black
peppercorns)
Coarse salt (kosher or sea) and
freshly ground black pepper

1 MAKE THE MUSHROOM BOURBON SAUCE: Trim the ends off the mushroom stems. Wipe the mushrooms clean with a damp paper towel (don't rinse them or they'll become soggy). Pick out 4 of the largest, best-looking mushroom caps and cut the stems off at the base. Thinly slice the rest of the mushrooms.

2 Melt the butter in a heavy saucepan over medium heat. Brush a little of the melted butter (about 1 tablespoon) over the whole mushroom caps and set them aside.

3 Add the shallots to the saucepan and cook until soft and translucent, but not brown, about 3 minutes. Increase the heat to high and add the sliced mushrooms. Stirring with a wooden spoon, sauté the mushrooms until they are nicely browned and all the mushroom juices have evaporated, 3 to 5 minutes. Stir in the wine, bring to a boil, and let boil until the liquid is reduced by half, 3 to 5 minutes. Stir in the stock, bring to a boil, and let boil until reduced by two thirds, 3 to 5 minutes. Stir in the cream, bring to a boil, and let boil until reduced by one third (the sauce should be thick and creamy), 4 to 6 minutes. Add the bourbon bring to a boil, and let boil for 1 minute. Whisk in the mustard and season with salt and pepper to taste; the sauce should be highly seasoned. Set the sauce aside while you prepare the steaks (it will keep for several hours; reheat it before serving).

4 Brush each filet mignon on all sides with the mustard. Combine the peppercorns and 1 tablespoon of salt in a shallow bowl and stir to mix. Thickly crust the steaks with the peppercorn mixture, concentrating it on the tops and bottoms and patting it onto the meat with your fingertips.

TIPS

■ The easiest way to crack the peppercorns is with a cast-iron skillet: Wrap the peppercorns in a clean cotton dishcloth and crush them with the edge of the skillet—or use a hammer or meat pounder. You can also buy already cracked peppercorns.

■ For the mushrooms, you could use standard button mushrooms, shiitakes, or other mushrooms, or a combination of these.

5 Set up the grill for direct grilling (see page 21 for charcoal or gas) and preheat to high.

6 When ready to cook, brush and oil the grill grate. Place the filets mignons on the hot grate and grill until cooked to taste, about 3 to 4 minutes per side for rare; 4 to 6 minutes per side for medium-rare; or 7 to 8 minutes per side for medium. To test for doneness; for rare the meat will be soft; for medium-rare it will be gently yielding. Using tongs, turn the steaks on their sides to brown the edges.

7 Once the steaks are on the grill, season the reserved mushroom caps with salt and pepper, place them on the grate, and cook them until they are browned and soft, 2 to 3 minutes per side.

8 Transfer the grilled filets mignons and mushroom caps to a platter or plates and let rest for 2 minutes. Meanwhile, reheat the sauce if necessary. Taste for seasoning, adding more salt and/or pepper as necessary. Spoon the sauce over the filets mignons. Top each one with a grilled mushroom cap and serve at once.

YIELD:
Serves 4

Philadelphia, Pa.

PHILLY CHEESE STEAKS ON THE GRILL

Pat's or Geno's? A simple question, but it's been known to spark hours of fiery polemic. I'm talking, of course, about that glory of Philadelphia gastronomy, the cheese steak. The City of otherwise Brotherly Love is fiercely divided on who makes the best: Pat's or Geno's. Both are located in lively South Philly, and both are perennially packed with hordes of loyal customers. Local legend has it that the cheese steak sandwich was invented in 1930 by Pat Olivieri of Pat's King of Steaks restaurant, where the meat (thinly sliced rib eye) and onions were flash fried on a griddle (the melted cheese would have to wait until 1948). I've always maintained that if something tastes great griddled or panfried, it probably tastes even better grilled. So here's a not strictly traditional, but eminently satisfying, cheese steak you can serve sizzling hot off the grill. I can't think of a better sandwich for Super Bowl Sunday.

METHOD:
Direct grilling

TIPS

■ Tradition calls for the steak to be sliced paper-thin, a technique that speeds up the cooking and tenderizes the meat. I'm using slightly thicker steaks here, which are more practical for grilling. (The easiest way to cut the steaks is on a meat slicer—ask your butcher to do it.)

■ For even more flavor, the mushrooms, bell peppers, and onion are grilled too.

Geno's in Philly makes great cheese steaks—even without a grill.

INGREDIENTS:

8 large button mushrooms

1 large sweet onion, cut into
    1/2-inch-thick slices

4 tablespoons olive oil, plus more
    for brushing the steaks

Coarse salt (kosher or sea) and
    freshly ground black pepper

2 green or red bell peppers

2 tablespoons balsamic vinegar,
    or more to taste

1 1/4 pounds boneless rib eye steaks,
    cut into 4 slices each about
    1/2 inch thick

Garlic salt

4 slices aged Provolone cheese
    (4 to 6 ounces)

4 hoagie rolls or long, soft Italian rolls

Mayonnaise, mustard, ketchup,
    and/or the condiment of
    your choice

YOU'LL ALSO NEED:

6 to 8 small (6-inch) bamboo skewers or
    wooden toothpicks

1 Trim the ends off the mushroom stems. Wipe the mushrooms clean with a damp paper towel (don't rinse them or they'll become soggy). Skewer the onion slices crosswise with skewers or toothpicks to hold them together during grilling. Lightly brush the mushrooms and onion slices with about 2 tablespoons of the olive oil and season them generously with coarse salt and black pepper.

2 Set up the grill for direct grilling (see page 21 for charcoal or gas) and preheat to high.

3 When ready to cook, brush and oil the grill grate. Place the bell peppers on the hot grate and grill until charred on all sides, 4 to 6 minutes per side (16 to 24 minutes in all). After about 8 minutes, add the mushrooms and onion slices and grill until golden brown, 3 to 4 minutes per side (6 to 8 minutes in all). Transfer the grilled bell peppers, mushrooms, and onion slices to a cutting board and let cool. Let the fire continue to burn in the grill. Peel, core, seed, and thinly slice the bell peppers. Thinly slice the mushrooms. Unskewer the onion slices. Place the vegetables in a bowl, add the vinegar, and 2 tablespoons of the olive oil, and stir to mix. Season with coarse salt and black pepper to taste; the mixture should be highly seasoned.

4 Generously brush the steak slices with olive oil and season with garlic salt and black pepper. Brush and oil the grill grate. Place the steak slices on the hot grate and grill until cooked to taste, 2 to 3 minutes per side for medium-rare. Place the Provolone slices on top of the steaks after turning them over, then cover the grill to melt the cheese.

5 Place the steak slices and melted cheese on hoagie rolls you've generously slathered with mayonnaise or other condiments. Mound the vegetable mixture on top of the steak and cheese. Serve the cheese steaks at once.

YIELD:
Serves 4

New York, N.Y.

SALT & PEPPER BEEF RIBS

It takes a master to dare to put a dish of such startling simplicity on a menu. Or several masters in this case: Manhattan restaurateurs Danny Meyer, Michael Romano, and David Swinghamer, who redefined barbecue for New Yorkers with their much talked about barbecue emporium, Blue Smoke. Pork ribs are the house specialty, crusty, smoky baby backs cooked in the style of Danny Meyer's

native St. Louis. But Blue Smoke also serves beef ribs, and if you've never had these dark, meaty, Brobdingnagian bones, you're about to have a life-changing experience. The boys keep the seasonings simple, just coarse salt and cracked black peppercorns. That way you get to appreciate the beef in all its smoky glory. (For more about Blue Smoke, see page 214.)

METHOD:
Indirect grilling

INGREDIENTS:
1 rack of beef ribs
    (2½ to 3½ pounds)
Coarse salt (kosher or sea)
Cracked or coarsely ground black pepper
Your choice of barbecue sauce,
    for serving

YOU'LL ALSO NEED:
3 cups wood chips or chunks
    (preferably apple or hickory),
    soaked for 1 hour in water to cover,
    then drained

1 Very generously season the beef ribs on both sides with salt and pepper.

2 Set up the grill for indirect grilling (see page 23 for gas or page 22 for charcoal) and preheat to medium-low. If using a gas grill, place all of the wood chips or chunks in the smoker box or in a smoker pouch (see page 24) and run the grill on high until you see smoke, then reduce the heat to medium-low. If using a charcoal grill, place a large drip pan in the center, preheat the grill to medium-low, then toss 1½ cups of the wood chips or chunks on the coals.

Beef ribs are available at most butcher shops and at an increasing number of supermarkets; some are meatier than others. The sort of ribs I use for this recipe are roughly 6 to 8 inches long and come in racks of seven. Figure on 2 to 3 ribs per person if there's a good amount of meat on the bone.

3 When ready to grill, place the seasoned ribs in the center of the hot grate, meat side up, over the drip pan and away from the heat. Cover the grill and cook the ribs until dark brown (almost black), very crisp on the outside, and tender enough to pull apart with your fingers, 2 to 2½ hours. If using a charcoal grill, every hour you'll need to add 12 fresh coals and ¾ cup of wood chips or chunks to each side.

4 Transfer the grilled ribs to a cutting board and cut the rack into individual ribs. Serve with your favorite barbecue sauce on the side (there is a great St. Louis–style sauce on page 666).

YIELD:
Serves 2 or 3

Pine Bluff, Ark.

SMOKY MEAT LOAF

Like all good Arkansans, Candy Weaver loves the evocative, smoky flavor of barbecue. So it comes as no surprise that her family has created a new form of fuel: the BBQr's Delight smoking pellet. The Weavers, whose company headquarters are in Pine Bluff, Arkansas, were in the business of manufacturing wood pellets for home heating. But a few unseasonably warm winters led them to look for another revenue source, and the smoking wood pellet was born.

The pellets are made with pure hardwood sawdust pressed into tiny cylinders and they have several advantages over conventional wood chips or chunks. First, you need less (a third of a cup versus two) and pellets don't require advance soaking. The pellets take up less room than wood chunks and they don't attract bugs or mold and they work well on gas grills. But don't take my word for it: Memphis barbecue legend John Willingham is said to use nothing but these pellets in his smokers. All of which is a lengthy prologue to a meat loaf the likes of which you've probably never tasted, transformed by smoke roasting to an unforgettable standout. And it's just as good cold as it is hot.

METHOD:
Indirect grilling

INGREDIENTS:
1½ pounds lean ground beef
½ cup dried bread crumbs
1 large egg, beaten
1 small onion, finely chopped
1 rib celery, finely chopped
1 clove garlic, minced
¼ cup homemade red barbecue sauce
     (pages 666 through 675) or
     a good commercial brand,
     or more to taste, plus more
     barbecue sauce for serving
2 tablespoons balsamic vinegar

TIPS

This recipe calls for ground beef, but you could also use ground veal or turkey or even a mixture of these meats. To make a low fat meat loaf, use lean ground turkey breasts and two egg whites in place of the whole egg.

1½ teaspoons coarse salt (kosher or sea),
    or more to taste
½ teaspoon freshly ground black pepper,
    or more to taste
Cooking oil spray

YOU'LL ALSO NEED:
One 8-by-4-by-3-inch aluminum foil loaf
    pan (4½ to 5 cups capacity);
    5 tablespoons BBQr's Delight wood
    pellets (preferably sassafras or
    black walnut) or 2 cups conventional
    wood chips or chunks (preferably
    sassafras or hickory), soaked for
    1 hour in water to cover, then
    drained

1 Combine the beef, bread crumbs, egg, onion, celery, garlic, barbecue sauce, vinegar, salt, and pepper in a nonreactive mixing bowl and mix well with your hands or a wooden spoon (I find that hands work best). To test the mixture for seasoning, fry a little patty in a nonstick frying pan or grill it on the end of metal skewer. Add more barbecue sauce, salt, and/or pepper, as necessary. Spray the loaf pan with oil and add the meat loaf mixture. Tap the pan a few times on the work surface to knock out any air bubbles.

2 Set up the grill for indirect grilling (see page 23 for gas or page 22 for charcoal) and preheat to medium. If using a gas grill, place all of the wood chips or chunks or the wood pellets in the smoker box or in a smoker pouch (see page 24) and run the grill on high until you see smoke, then reduce the heat to medium. If using a charcoal grill, preheat it to medium, then toss all of the wood chips or chunks on the coals, if using wood pellets, wrap them in a foil pouch, make a tiny hole in the top, and place the packet on the coals.

3 When ready to cook, place the meat loaf in the center of the hot grate, away from the heat, and cover the grill. Grill the meat loaf until cooked through, about 1 hour. To test for doneness, use an instant-read meat thermometer: The internal temperature should be about 160°F.

4 Transfer the grilled meat loaf to a platter and let rest for 5 minutes, then unmold by inverting the pan. Cut into slices and serve with more barbecue sauce.

YIELD:
Serves 4 to 6

BLUE SMOKE

BLUE SMOKE

**116 East 27th Street
New York, New York
(212) 447-7733**

The Flatiron district in Manhattan is about the last place you'd come looking for great barbecue. But life for Big Apple rib addicts got a lot brighter with the opening of Blue Smoke. Brainchild of restaurateur Danny Meyer (of Union Square Cafe, Eleven Madison Park, and Gramercy Tavern fame), Blue Smoke brings down-home barbecue to an increasingly fashionable part of the city. The dining room may have the Soho loft chic of slate grays and blacks, exposed ventilation, and industrial lighting, but the place smells as smoky as a back alley barbecue joint.

As well it should. Meyer was born in St. Louis, and taken to rib parlors from the time he could walk. One of his partners, David Swinghamer, comes to barbecue through his love of music—his contribution to the operation is a popular jazz club, Jazz Standard, located in the basement. The third partner, Michael Romano, may be European trained, but when it came to finding a consulting pit master, he had the good sense to hire Mike Mills.

Mills will be known to anyone who follows competition barbecue. In the 1990s, his Apple City barbecue team won three Memphis in May barbecue contest Grand Championships—a feat unique in the event's history (for more about Memphis in May, see page 229). Mike commuted to Manhattan for months to help his city-slicker friends launch Blue Smoke. It wasn't easy.

The stainless steel Ole Hickory barbecue pit had to be trucked in from Texas. The fire department required an industrial-strength exhaust fan and fifteen-story chimneys to carry the smoke away from the sensitive noses of neighbors. And you can't exactly go to your local restaurant supply house to order split, seasoned apple wood for burning in the pit. Three years elapsed between the initial dream of Blue Smoke and its opening in March 2002.

ST. LOUIS MEETS NEW YORK

Blue Smoke's menu is ecumenical enough to include Texas-style brisket, grill-smoked salmon (served with steamed broccoli, no less), and even smoked foie gras

Michael Romano chows down on ribs at Blue Smoke.

The stainless steel Ole Hickory barbecue pit had to be trucked in from Texas.

Salt & Pepper Beef Ribs as smoky as you could wish for.

with jalapeño jelly. But there's no mistaking the focal point of the restaurant: pork. There are St. Louis–cut spareribs, dry-rubbed baby backs, and a sliced pork shoulder that would do any pit master proud. The ribs are incredibly tender—the result of five hours of smoking—but not so soft they fall off the bone. (Be suspicious of fall-off-the-bone tender ribs; they've probably been boiled.) If you're used to sweet, sticky Kansas City ribs, these smoky, crusty dry ribs will come as a revelation. Not the least amazing thing about them is that, beneath the spice, you can still actually taste the pork.

There are lots of other St. Louis touches at Blue Smoke:

"Toasted" (breaded, fried) shrimp ravioli reminiscent of the fried ravioli you find on The Hill (St. Louis's Italian district). Smoked bologna sandwiches made with genuine Usinger's bologna. A "Marshall Field" (a smoked turkey, Swiss cheese, and bacon sandwich served under a rib-sticking cream sauce). And to wash them down, you can order a Fitz's root beer—imported direct from St. Louis.

It's not every Danny Meyer restaurant that serves deviled eggs, "burnt ends" chili (made with brisket trimmings), and barbecued potato chips. To keep things authentic, Meyer used his grandmother Rosetta "Grandma Rosie" Harris's recipes for the potato and egg salad and the mashed potatoes with fried onions. The proper way to eat the mashed potatoes is off the end of a spare rib, Meyer says. As at any self-respecting barbecue joint in the South, the meats come with a pile of white bread, but here it's semolina loaf that's specially baked for Blue Smoke. The "napkins" are cloth dish towels and galvanized buckets are thoughtfully provided for the bones.

On the line at Blue Smoke.

The proper way to eat the mashed potatoes is off the end of a spare rib.

Miami, Fla.

SHIRLEY'S DILLED VEAL MEAT LOAF

Veal is not a meat most of us associate with barbecue, but as a delicately flavored one it readily soaks up smoke flavors. This recipe comes from my friend, Miami resident Shirley Drevich, who learned it from her Polish-born mother. (The Polish influence is apparent in the flavorings: garlic and dill.) Mama Drevich wouldn't have used a grill, of course, but I'm sure she would have approved of the smoke flavor. A shot of club soda acts as a leavening agent, producing an uncommonly light meat loaf. If you've always thought of meat loaf as a plebian dish incapable of elegance, wait until you taste this.

METHOD:
Indirect grilling

INGREDIENTS:
2 slices white bread
1½ pounds ground veal
1 large egg, plus the white of 1 large egg,
      lightly beaten together with a fork
3 cloves garlic, minced
1 medium-size onion, diced
      (about ¾ cup)
3 tablespoons finely chopped fresh
      flat-leaf parsley
3 tablespoons finely chopped fresh dill
⅓ cup club soda
1 teaspoon coarse salt (kosher or sea),
      or more to taste
½ teaspoon freshly ground black
      pepper, or more to taste
Cooking oil spray

YOU'LL ALSO NEED:
One 8-by-4-by-3-inch aluminum foil
      loaf pan; 2 cups conventional
      wood chips or chunks
      (preferably sassafras or
      hickory), soaked for 1 hour in
      water to cover, then drained

1 Soak the bread in warm water to cover in a large mixing bowl for 3 minutes. Pour off the water, then squeeze the bread in your fingers to wring out the liquid; discard the liquid. Stir in the veal, eggs, garlic, onion, parsley, and dill. Mix well with your hands or a wooden spoon (I find that hands work best). Stir in the club soda, salt, and pepper. To test the mixture for seasoning, fry a little patty in a nonstick frying pan or grill it on the end of a metal skewer. Add more salt and/or pepper as necessary. Spray the loaf pan with oil and add the meat loaf mixture. Tap the pan a few times on the work surface to knock out any air bubbles.

2 Set up the grill for indirect grilling (see page 23 for gas or page 22 for charcoal) and preheat to medium. If using a gas grill, place all of the wood chips or chunks in the smoker box or in a smoker pouch (see page 24) and run the grill on high until you see smoke, then reduce the heat to medium. If using a charcoal grill, preheat it to medium, then toss all of the wood chips or chunks on the coals.

3 When ready to cook, place the meat loaf in the center of the hot grate, away from the heat, and cover the grill. Grill the meat loaf until cooked through, about 1 hour. To test for doneness, use an instant-read meat thermometer: The internal temperature should be about 160°F.

4 Transfer the grilled meat loaf to a platter and let rest for 5 minutes, then unmold by inverting the pan. Cut into slices for serving.

YIELD:
Serves 4

Miami, Fla.

JAKE'S BARBECUED VEAL BRISKET

Readers of my books are familiar with my stepson chef, Jake. Growing up in Florida, he began barbecuing with me, but quickly became a grill meister in his own right. Consider the following veal brisket—

Jake's smoky contribution to a Rosh Hashanah (Jewish New Year) dinner. (It's traditional to eat brisket at the New Year's feast.) Although smaller in size, veal brisket has a lot in common with beef brisket: Tough and stringy but flavorful, it's a perfect meat for smoking. It's considerably more delicate than beef, however, so Jake has taken care to create a rub and mop sauce that aren't overpowering. The rub plays the pungency of cumin against the sweetness of brown sugar and cinnamon. The mop sauce features the delicate piquancy of vinegar made from Champagne.

METHOD:
Indirect grilling

ADVANCE PREPARATION:
30 minutes for curing the brisket

FOR THE BRISKET:
1 veal brisket (about 3½ pounds)
¼ cup Cinnamon and Cumin Veal Rub
    (recipe follows)
Champagne Vinegar Mop Sauce
    (page 220)

FOR THE BARBECUE SAUCE:
Drippings from the brisket
1 to 1½ cups veal, chicken, or
    beef stock, preferably homemade
3 tablespoons reserved Champagne
    Vinegar Mop Sauce
½ cup cane syrup or dark corn syrup,
    or more to taste
3 tablespoons tomato paste
3 tablespoons Dijon mustard
2 teaspoons Cinnamon and
    Cumin Veal Rub (recipe follows)
Coarse salt (kosher or sea) and
    freshly ground black pepper

YOU'LL ALSO NEED:

**3 cups wood chips or chunks
(preferably apple, cherry,
pear, or peach), soaked for 1 hour
in water to cover, then drained**

1 Place the brisket in a roasting pan. Sprinkle each side with 2 tablespoons of the rub, patting it onto the meat with your fingertips. Let the brisket cure in the refrigerator, covered, for 30 minutes.

2 Set up the grill for indirect grilling (see page 23 for gas or page 22 for charcoal) and preheat to medium-low. If using a gas grill, place all of the wood chips or chunks in the smoker box or in a smoker pouch (see page 24) and run the grill on high until you see smoke, then reduce the heat to medium-low. If using a charcoal grill, place a large drip pan in the center, preheat the grill to

medium-low, then toss 1½ cups of the wood chips or chunks on the coals.

3 Set aside 3 tablespoons of the Champagne Vinegar Mop Sauce for the barbecue sauce.

4 When ready to cook, place the brisket in the center of the hot grate, fat side up, over the drip pan and away from the heat, and cover the grill. Cook the brisket until nicely browned, 2 hours. Mop or baste it with some of the mop sauce during grilling. If using a charcoal grill, after the first hour you'll need to add 12 fresh coals to each side and toss the remaining wood chips or chunks on the coals.

5 Mop the brisket one more time, wrap it in aluminum foil (this seals in the juices and keeps the meat moist), and return it to the grill. Cook the brisket 2 to 2½ hours longer (4 to 4½ hours in all). To test for doneness, use an instant-read meat thermometer: The internal temperature should be about 190°F and the meat should be tender enough to pull into shreds with your fingers. If using a charcoal grill, after the second and third hour you'll need to add 12 fresh coals to each side (no more chips are necessary).

6 Transfer the grilled veal to a cutting board and let rest while you make the barbecue sauce.

7 MAKE THE BARBECUE SAUCE: In a 2-cup or larger heatproof measuring cup, combine any veal drippings

Split, seasoned hardwood is the secret to great barbecue.

from the aluminum foil wrapping with enough stock to make 1½ cups of liquid. Transfer this mixture to a saucepan and add the reserved 3 tablespoons of the mop sauce and the cane syrup, tomato paste, mustard, and Cinnamon and Cumin Veal Rub. Place the saucepan over medium-high heat, bring the sauce to a simmer, and let simmer until richly flavored and slightly thickened, 5 to 10 minutes. Taste for seasoning, adding more cane syrup as necessary and salt and pepper to taste.

8 To serve, thinly slice the brisket across the grain and arrange on a platter. Add any accumulated juices to the barbecue sauce. Spoon half of the barbecue sauce over the sliced brisket and serve the remainder on the side.

YIELD:
Serves 6

VARIATION: For an uptown version of this dish, you can grill a rack of veal instead of a brisket. The rack of veal is analogous to a prime rib on a steer. Most racks of veal are cut into veal chops, so you'll probably need to specially order one from your butcher. A 4- or 5-pound one will serve six to eight. Prepare the rack following the instructions for the veal brisket. If you use a grill, preheat it to medium-high; the cooking time will be about 1½ hours. If you cook it in a smoker, follow the manufacturer's directions for setting it up; the total cooking time at 275°F will be 2½ to 3 hours.

Cinnamon and Cumin Veal Rub

Jake created this aromatic rub for veal, but it goes well with all light meats, from poultry to pork. This makes twice as much rub as you'll actually need for the veal brisket and mop sauce, but it's so good, you'll want to have extra for other barbecue.

INGREDIENTS:

1 tablespoon dried rosemary
½ cup firmly packed dark brown sugar
¼ cup coarse salt (kosher or sea)
3 tablespoons freshly ground black pepper
2 tablespoons ground cumin
2 tablespoons dried oregano
1 tablespoon ground cinnamon

1 Crumble the rosemary between your fingers into a small bowl.

2 Add the brown sugar, salt, pepper, cumin, oregano, and cinnamon to the rosemary and stir to mix. (Actually, your fingers work better for mixing than a spoon or whisk does.) Store the rub in an airtight jar away from heat and light; it will keep for several months.

YIELD:
Makes about 1 cup

T I P S

■ Veal brisket can be found at Jewish grocery stores and butcher shops. A trimmed brisket weighs about 3½ pounds. The brisket should be trimmed, but not scalped: Ask the butcher to leave a ¼-inch layer of fat (this melts during the cooking, tenderizing the veal).

■ Veal isn't as strongly flavored as beef, so you'll want to smoke it with a mild wood, like apple, cherry, pear, or peach.

Champagne Vinegar Mop Sauce

Champagne vinegar gives this mop a gentle piquancy and uncommon depth of flavor. Look for Champagne vinegar at gourmet shops and upscale supermarkets, or you can substitute white wine vinegar or distilled white vinegar. The pink peppercorn is a tiny aromatic berry from Madagascar and Réunion; you'll find it at gourmet shops. This makes enough mop sauce for the veal brisket, but it would also be delicious on any slow-cooked meat—brisket, ribs, or pork shoulder.

INGREDIENTS:

½ teaspoon pink peppercorns
1¼ cups Champagne vinegar
1 shallot, finely chopped
    (about 3 tablespoons)
3 tablespoons dark brown sugar
2 tablespoons Cinnamon and Cumin
    Veal Rub (page 219)
½ teaspoon coarse salt
    (kosher or sea)

1 Crush the pink peppercorns in a mortar with a pestle or wrap them in a clean cotton dishcloth and crush them with the edge of a cast-iron skillet, a hammer, or a meat pounder.

2 Place the crushed peppercorns and the vinegar, shallot, brown sugar, rub, and salt in a nonreactive mixing bowl and whisk until the brown sugar and salt dissolve.

YIELD:
Makes about 1½ cups mop sauce

San Francisco, Calif.

OLIVE GRILLED VEAL CHOPS

Tapenade (an olive paste) may have been born on the south coast of France, but it reaches its apotheosis in California. The two places are kindred spirits—both produce olives and fruity olive oil and both welcome the brash flavors of garlic, capers, and anchovies. Bay Area grilling enthusiast Mary Frances Dedrick set me to thinking about how these would taste with veal, and these thick, meaty, and vibrantly flavorful chops are the result.

METHOD:
Direct grilling

ADVANCE PREPARATION:
30 minutes to 2 hours for marinating
    the chops

INGREDIENTS:
1 cup pitted kalamata or other black olives,
    or ¾ cup olive paste

1 tablespoon capers, drained

1 to 2 anchovy fillets (optional),
    coarsely chopped

2 cloves garlic, coarsely chopped

1 teaspoon hot red pepper flakes

1 tablespoon Dijon mustard

2 to 3 tablespoons extra-virgin olive oil

Freshly ground black pepper and
    coarse salt (kosher or sea)

4 veal chops (each about 1 inch thick
    and 10 to 12 ounces)

Grilled Polenta, for serving
    (optional; page 650)

1 Place the olives, capers, anchovies, if using, garlic, hot red pepper flakes, and mustard in a food processor fitted with the metal blade and finely chop. With the motor running, add enough olive oil to obtain a thick but spreadable paste. Season this tapenade with black pepper and perhaps just a little salt to taste.

2 Spread half of the tapenade on both sides of the veal chops and let marinate in the refrigerator, covered, for 30 minutes to 2 hours (the longer the better). Set the remaining tapenade aside.

3 Set up the grill for direct grilling (see page 21 for charcoal or gas) and preheat to high.

4 When ready to cook, brush and oil the grill grate. Oil it especially well to keep the tapenade from sticking. Place the marinated chops on the hot grate and grill until the outsides are crusty and sizzling and the meat is

cooked to taste, 5 to 8 minutes per side for medium. (I like my veal cooked medium, not medium-rare.) To test for doneness, use the poke method; the meat should be firm and only very gently yielding. Transfer the grilled chops to a platter or plates and top each with a generous spoonful of the reserved tapenade. Grilled polenta makes a good accompaniment.

YIELD:
Serves 4

VARIATION: I call for the olive paste to be spread and grilled on veal chops here, but it would be equally tasty with steak, pork, and lamb chops. To make a delectable crust for rack of lamb, spread it generously over two 1-pound racks and grill them using the indirect method for about 30 minutes—awesome.

TIPS

You can buy ready-made tapenade at gourmet shops, or you can make your own as described in Step 1.

Mary Frances Dedrick at her day job—Dedrick's in Placerville, California.

Of course, you could grill the veal over gas or charcoal, but to get the maximum flavor, you should use wood. Charcoal grillers will find this as easy as making a trip to their local grill shop or Home Depot to buy a bag of oak chunks. (Gas grillers will have to use unsoaked oak chips in a smoker box or smoker pouch. Grilling over a Wood Fire is explained in full on page 20.)

New York, N.Y.

MARIO'S VEAL CHOPS
With Lemon Oregano Jam

Mario Batali is one of our most respected and beloved Italian-American chefs. But the pony-tailed, short pants–wearing Food Network celebrity is no slouch when it comes to barbecue. Grilling is one of the focal points of his restaurant, Babbo. Consider these smokily grilled veal chops, served with an electrifying lemon oregano "jam."

METHOD:
Direct grilling

ADVANCE PREPARATION:
30 minutes for marinating the chops

INGREDIENTS:
4 veal chops (each about 1 inch thick
    and 10 to 12 ounces)
1 to 2 tablespoons extra-virgin
    olive oil
Coarse salt (kosher or sea) and
    freshly ground black pepper
1 lemon, halved and seeded
2 tablespoons chopped fresh
    oregano
Lemon Oregano Jam (recipe follows)

YOU'LL ALSO NEED:
2 cups wood chips or chunks
    (preferably oak), unsoaked

1 Lightly brush or rub the chops with olive oil and season generously with salt and pepper. Place the chops in a nonreactive baking dish and squeeze the lemon juice over them. Sprinkle the oregano on both sides of the chops, turning them several times to coat them evenly. Let the chops marinate for 30 minutes.

2 Set up the grill for direct grilling (see page 21 for gas or charcoal) and preheat to high. If using a gas grill, place all of the wood chips or chunks in the smoker box or in a smoker pouch (see page 24) and run the grill on high until you see smoke. If using a charcoal grill, preheat it to high then toss all of the wood chips or chunks on the coals.

3 When ready to cook, brush and oil the grill grate. Place the marinated chops on the grate and grill until cooked to taste, 5 to 8 minutes per side for medium, rotating the chops a quarter turn after 3 minutes to create an attractive crosshatch of grill marks. To test for doneness, use the poke method; the meat should be firm and just gently yielding.

4 Transfer the grilled chops to a platter or plates and let rest for about 3 minutes, then serve with the Lemon Oregano Jam on the side.

YIELD:
Serves 4

Lemon Oregano Jam

Savory "jams" became popular in the 1990s as American chefs sought to get away from complicated Eurocentric sauces and emphasize simply grilled meats and seafoods. This lemon and oregano jam, sweet, sour, and salty, makes a perfect foil for a wood-grilled veal chop, managing to be electrifying without being overpowering. It wouldn't be half bad with grilled chicken, lamb, or seafood, either. The recipe makes more jam than average people will need for serving with four veal chops (but then again, I like to eat it with a spoon).

INGREDIENTS:

2 large lemons (preferably with thin rinds)
¼ cup sugar, or more to taste
1½ teaspoons coarse salt (kosher or sea), or more to taste
¾ teaspoon freshly ground black pepper, or more to taste
2 tablespoons extra-virgin olive oil
2 tablespoons finely chopped fresh oregano leaves

1 Scrub the lemons under cold running water, then pat dry with paper towels. Cut each lemon into 8 pieces and remove and discard the seeds.

2 Place the lemon pieces and the sugar, salt, and pepper in a food processor and process to a coarse purée. With the motor running, add the olive oil in a thin stream; the mixture should emulsify, becoming honeylike in consistency. Add the oregano, pulsing to mix. The jam can be prepared up to this stage and kept, refrigerated, for several weeks. Transfer it to a clean glass jar, placing a piece of plastic wrap between the top of the jar and the lid to keep the lid from corroding. Bring to room temperature before serving, stir to recombine, and taste for seasoning, adding more sugar, salt, and/or pepper as necessary.

YIELD:
Makes ¾ cup

New York, N.Y.

CALF'S LIVER
With Onions, Pancetta, and Mushrooms

Liver and onions is an American classic that, sadly, is getting harder and harder to find. Perhaps this is due to our obsession with fat grams and cholesterol, perhaps due to our general lack of enthusiasm for organ meats. I say it's high time to rehabilitate this luncheonette standby, and there's no better way to do this than to grill it. This is the way calf's liver is served at Peasant restaurant in New York City. Chef-owner Franco de Carlo has updated the dish, cooking the liver

TIPS

■ You'll probably need to go to a butcher shop for the calf's liver. Do insist on calf's liver, which has a delicate flavor—beef liver would be too strong. Ask the butcher to slice the liver very thin.

■ Pancetta is an unsmoked Italian bacon. Look for it at Italian markets, gourmet shops, and in the deli case of some supermarkets. Or substitute bacon.

on a wood-burning grill and topping it with a savory sauté of onions, mushrooms, and pancetta (Italian bacon). A splash of Marsala adds a touch of sweetness. You won't mistake this for the blue plate special.

METHOD:
Direct grilling

INGREDIENTS:

3 tablespoons butter
4 thin slices pancetta (about 2 ounces),
    cut into ¼-inch slivers
1 large onion, finely chopped
2 tablespoons chopped fresh sage leaves,
    or 2 teaspoons crumbled dried sage
8 ounces button mushrooms, trimmed,
    wiped clean with a damp paper towel,
    and thinly sliced
½ cup Marsala, cream sherry,
    or vin santo
Coarse salt (kosher or sea) and
    freshly ground black pepper
1½ tablespoons extra-virgin olive oil
4 thin slices calf's liver
    (each ¼ to ½ inch thick and
    6 to 8 ounces)
4 whole fresh sage leaves,
    for garnish (optional)

YOU'LL ALSO NEED:
2 cups wood chips or chunks
    (preferably oak), unsoaked

1 Melt 1 tablespoon of the butter in a frying pan over medium heat. Add the pancetta and cook until the fat starts to render, about 2 minutes. Add the onion and cook until it and the pancetta are golden brown, 4 to 6 minutes longer, adding the chopped sage leaves after 2 minutes. Increase the heat to high and add the mushrooms. Cook until most of the mushroom liquid has evaporated and the mushrooms are nicely browned, about 3 minutes longer. Add the Marsala, let it come to a boil, and boil until reduced by half. Stir in the remaining 2 tablespoons of butter and remove the frying pan from the heat. Season with salt and pepper to taste; the onion mixture should be highly seasoned. The onion mixture can be prepared several hours ahead and reheated just before serving.

2 Drizzle the olive oil over both sides of the liver, rubbing it on with your fingertips or painting it on with a pastry brush. Season the liver generously with salt and pepper.

3 Set up the grill for direct grilling (see page 21 for gas or charcoal) and preheat to high. If using a gas grill, place all of the wood chips or chunks in the smoker box or in a smoker pouch (see page 24) and run the grill on high until you see smoke. If using a charcoal grill, preheat it to high, then toss all of the wood chips or chunks on the coals.

4 When ready to cook, brush and oil the grill grate. Arrange the liver slices on the grate on the diagonal and grill until cooked to taste, 2 to 3 minutes per side for medium-rare.

5 Transfer the grilled liver to a platter or plates. Spoon the onion mixture over the liver, then garnish with the whole sage leaves, if using.

YIELD:
Serves 4

Nipomo, Calif.

GRILLED SWEETBREADS

Grilled sweetbreads are one of the best-kept secrets in barbecue. But don't only take my word for it: Oak-grilled sweetbreads are a specialty at one of the most venerable barbecue restaurants in central California—Jocko's in Nipomo. "Sweetbreads are naturally salty, so we don't even bother to season them," says Jocko's pit master, Josh Sprouts. But he does provide a bowl of clarified butter for dipping the sweetbreads in.

METHOD:
Direct grilling

INGREDIENTS:
¾ cup (1½ sticks) salted butter
1½ pounds veal sweetbreads

YOU'LL ALSO NEED:
2 cups wood chips or chunks
    (preferably oak), soaked for 1 hour
    in water to cover, then drained;
    toothpicks (optional)

1 CLARIFY THE BUTTER: Melt the butter in a saucepan over medium heat, then pour it into a heatproof measuring cup. Let it stand for about 2 minutes. Using a spoon, carefully skim off the white foam on the top of the melted butter. Carefully pour the clear yellow melted butter into 4 small ramekins, leaving behind the milky layer of water and sediment at the bottom of the measuring cup. Put the ramekins in a shallow pan of hot water to keep the butter warm.

2 Trim off and discard any veins and gristle from the sweetbreads. Rinse the sweetbreads under cold running water to remove any blood (we barbecue guys skip the classic French practice of blanching and pressing the sweetbreads). Butterfly the sweetbreads by cutting them almost in half through the side and open them up, like a book.

3 Set up the grill for direct grilling (see page 21 for gas or charcoal) and preheat to medium-high. If using a gas grill, place all of the wood chips or chunks in the smoker box or in a smoker pouch (see page 24) and run the grill on high until you see smoke, then reduce the heat to medium-high. If using a charcoal grill, preheat it to medium-high, then toss all of the wood chips or chunks on the coals.

4 When ready to cook, brush and oil the grill grate. Place the sweetbreads on the hot grate and grill until crusty, golden brown, and cooked through, 5 to 8 minutes per side. When done they will be firm when pressed with your finger.

5 Serve the sweetbreads with the bowls of clarified butter on the side for dipping. Or cut the sweetbreads into ½-inch pieces, stick these on tooth-

■ Sweetbreads are the thymus gland of the calf. Look for them in butcher shops and upscale supermarkets.

■ This recipe contains only two ingredients; to get the full effect, you need wood smoke. Grill the sweetbreads over an oak fire (see page 20) or use wood chips to generate the requisite smoke flavor.

JOCKO'S

JOCKO'S

125 N. Thompson Avenue
Nipomo, California
(805) 929-3686

Ask a Los Angeles food sophisticate like baker-to-the-stars Nancy Silverton her favorite barbecue joint and she's quick to name Jocko's. For half a century this unassuming eatery in the hamlet of Nipomo, California, has served some of the best grilled steaks, chops, sausages, and sweetbreads this side of the Continental Divide. Unassuming? Well, if you blink at the wrong moment, you could drive right by the one-story cinder-block box of a building. If the dining room, with its cream-colored walls, wood ceiling, and Formica tables, were any more spartan, it could double as a jail cell. But take one forkful of a phone book–thick steak or softball-size lamb chop and you'll understand why Jocko's draws connoisseurs like Silverton all the way from Los Angeles.

Jocko's began as a saloon built in 1886 by Emery Knotts in downtown Nipomo. He was assisted in the business by his eight sons, including one particularly colorful lad nicknamed Jocko. During Prohibition, Jocko ran a service station (where he was rumored to sell bootleg out of the trunk of a car). When alcohol became legal again, Jocko's Cage, as it was now called, became a popular local watering hole.

In the 1950s, Jocko's sons Fred and George took over the business and began serving barbecue on the weekends. Soon oak-grilled meats became the star attraction of the restaurant. The current building and pit date from 1962. Around the perimeter of the ceiling you can still see the cattle brands of the local ranchers, including that of Captain William G. Dana, the original owner of the 38,000-acre Nipomo Ranch.

THE STAR OF THE SHOW

The focal point of the restaurant is an open brick pit in a courtyard, manned when I was there by Josh Sprouts, a twenty-something pit master with a wispy goatee and black baseball hat. Like most pit masters in these parts, Sprouts stokes the pit with blazing red oak and controls the heat by raising and lowering the grate. On a typical Saturday night, he'll grill something on the order of five hundred steaks: meaty strip steaks, rich-flavored top sirloins, and the house specialty, an admirably marbled Spencer—a rib eye trimmed of its fatty tail and served in 13- or 18-ounce portions. And for something a bit unusual, there are the silk-textured sweetbreads with the perfect outer crust (see page 225).

picks, and serve them with the melted butter for dipping—these make great hors d'oeuvres.

YIELD:

Serves 6 to 8 as an appetizer, or 4 as a main course

St. George, Utah

CHILE-RUBBED ELK STEAKS

The Red Mountain Spa is a place where people come to lose weight and get healthy. But executive chef Jim Gallivan's food has so much flavor, you'd never dream it could be low in cholesterol, carbohydrates, and fat. Of course the location, near St. George, Utah, makes his task easier, as the southwest fairly explodes with flavorful ingredients—fresh and dried chiles, nopal and prickly pear cacti, not to mention a bounty of wild game, especially elk. Lean, dark, rich elk meat gets a triple blast of flavor here: first from a red chile rub, then from flash charring on the grill, and finally from an offbeat barbecue sauce made with prickly pears.

METHOD:
Direct grilling

FOR THE RED CHILE RUB:
2 tablespoons sweet paprika
2 teaspoons coarse salt (kosher or sea)
2 teaspoons coarsely ground black pepper
2 teaspoons brown sugar
1 teaspoon ancho or other pure chile powder
1/8 to 1/4 teaspoon cayenne pepper

FOR THE STEAKS:
4 elk steaks (each 1/2 to 3/4 inch thick and 6 to 8 ounces)
1 1/2 to 2 tablespoons extra-virgin olive oil
Prickly Pear Barbecue Sauce (recipe follows)

1 MAKE THE RUB: Place the paprika, salt, black pepper, brown sugar, chile powder, and cayenne in a small bowl and stir to mix. (Actually, your fingers work better for mixing than a spoon or whisk does.)

2 Sprinkle the rub all over the elk steaks, patting it onto the meat with your fingertips. Let the steaks cure while you set up the grill.

3 Set up the grill for direct grilling (see page 21 for charcoal or gas) and preheat to high.

4 When ready to cook, lightly brush the steaks on both sides with olive oil or drizzle the oil over the steaks, rubbing it onto the meat with your fingertips. Brush and oil the grill grate. Place the steaks on the hot grate and grill until cooked to taste, 3 to 5 minutes per side for medium-rare. To test for doneness, use the poke method; the meat should be gently yielding.

TIPS

So where do you find elk steaks? If you live in the West, you may hunt for elk yourself or know a hunter. Otherwise, look for elk at a good butcher shop. In a pinch, you could substitute beef fillets.

TIPS

■ Depending upon what part of the country you're in, prickly pears are in season fall through spring. The fruit is distributed by Melissa's; prickly pear purée can be ordered from The Perfect Purées of Napa Valley (see Mail-Order Sources on page 742 for both).

■ The recipe makes more than you'll need for serving with the Chile-Rubbed Elk Steaks, but the sauce is so tasty you'll want to have extra on hand. It would also be great with pork ribs, pulled pork, brisket, and barbecued chicken—to name just a few.

5 Transfer the steaks to a platter or plates and let rest for 2 minutes. Serve with the Prickly Pear Barbecue Sauce on the side.

YIELD:

Serves 4

Prickly Pear Barbecue Sauce

Prickly pears, the sweet, pinkish or greenish, oval fruit of flat-paddled cacti that grow through-out the American Southwest, are the desert's *dessert*. The flavor is mild and vaguely reminiscent of honeydew melon. (see the Tip at left for sources); if they're not available, you can substitute honeydew.

INGREDIENTS:

1 cup ketchup
¹⁄₂ cup cider vinegar, or more to taste
3 tablespoons vegetable oil
¹⁄₄ cup Worcestershire sauce
3 ribs celery, finely chopped
¹⁄₄ small onion, finely chopped
(2 to 3 tablespoons)
1 clove garlic, peeled and gently crushed with the side of a cleaver
3 bay leaves
1 teaspoon pure chile powder
1 teaspoon sweet paprika
¹⁄₂ teaspoon freshly ground black pepper

About 1 cup prickly pear purée (see Note)
Juice and finely grated zest of 1 lemon
1 to 2 tablespoons light brown sugar or honey (optional)
Coarse salt (kosher or sea; optional)

1 Place the ketchup, vinegar, oil, Worcestershire sauce, celery, onion, garlic, bay leaves, chile powder, paprika, and pepper in a heavy nonreactive saucepan over medium heat. Bring to a simmer and let simmer gently until the celery and onion are tender and the mixture is highly flavorful, 20 to 30 minutes.

2 Strain the mixture into another nonreactive saucepan. Stir in the prickly pear purée, lemon zest, and lemon juice. Place the saucepan over medium heat, bring to a simmer, and let simmer until thick and richly flavored, 4 to 6 minutes. If a sweeter sauce is desired, whisk in the brown sugar. Taste for seasoning, adding more vinegar as necessary or salt, if desired. The sauce may be refrigerated, covered, for up to 1 week.

NOTE: To make prickly pear purée, stick a fruit on the end of a fork to secure it, then cut the ends off with a paring knife. Remove and discard the skins. Cut the fruit into ¹⁄₂-inch dice, place these in a food processor, and pulse until puréed. Strain the purée to remove the hard seeds. You'll need about 1³⁄₄ pounds of prickly pears to make roughly 1 cup of purée; 4 to 5 prickly pears should be enough.

YIELD:

Makes about 2¹⁄₂ cups

THE BARBECUE "SUPER BOWL"

They come from Texas, Alabama, Kentucky, Virginia, and from as far away as County Clare, Ireland, Thailand, and Abidjan in the Ivory Coast. They arrive with smokers, generators, industrial-strength sound systems, trailers, and enough building materials to erect a small city. They converge on Tom Lee Park along the banks of the Mississippi River in Memphis for three days of round-the-clock cooking, feasting, beer drinking, and carousing.

MEMPHIS IN MAY

**Tom Lee Park
Memphis, Tennessee
(901) 525-4611**

Welcome to the Memphis in May World Championship Barbecue Cooking Contest, the self-proclaimed barbecue Super Bowl that lends new meaning to the phrase *living high on the hog.*

Founded in 1978 and listed in the *Guinness Book of Records,* the Memphis cook-off is the world's largest barbecue festival. In a typical year, some 275 teams from thirty-five states and three or four countries compete for $60,000 worth of cash prizes before 100,000 spectators. Contestants vie for trophies in fifteen divisions, including a Miss Piggy contest (featuring large men dressed in swine drag), a hog-calling contest (won one year by the Hampton Hawgs rap group), and a best-cooker contest (aced one year by a team sporting a smoker in the shape of a giant teapot).

Contestants strive to outdo each other not only in cooking but in sheer outlandishness. Witness the team names, which range from

A passion for barbecue transcends gender, and even blurs it.

Jurassic Pork and Great Boars of Fire, to Swine and Dine and The Pit and the Pigulum. The team mottoes reflected the general tenor of the event. "We cook the right butt, baby," boast the Sporty Porkers from Hawkinsville, Georgia. "Our butts will tickle your ribs," promises the Joe Drilling Barbecue Team from Little Rock. Crispy Critters team captain Lee Pope sums up the rationale behind the event perfectly: "This is the only hobby I know of that requires you to drink vast quantities of beer, eat vast quantities of barbecue, and stay up partying all night."

The contestants begin arriving on a Monday. By Thursday, the park resembles a city built by Barnum & Bailey. There are hillbilly shacks and desert encampments with tons of sand and palm trees, courtesy of

the Sultans of Swine from Jackson, Mississippi. Elvis sightings occur hourly. During a showmanship contest, the King's alter ego, Tarz-Elvis, can be heard crooning such classics as "Don't Leave Me Hungry" and "Whole Hog Hotel."

EYE ON THE PRIZE

Despite the silliness, participants are deadly serious about their cooking. Prizes are awarded for the best ribs, shoulder, and whole hog. The Anything But category, for best nonpork barbecue, features anything from zebra to rattlesnake. The grand championship comes with an $11,000 purse and a four-foot-high trophy crowned with a silvery meat cleaver.

Each team, of course, has its own secret formulas and procedures. Some cooks swear by hickory, others by pecan, cherry, or mesquite. Some smoke the meat first, then cook it; others do the opposite. The Bryce Boar Blazers toss forty pounds of onions on the coals to provide their pig with extra flavor and moistness.

Spice rubs are an integral part of Memphis-style barbecue. The rubs are massaged into the meat with an affection that borders on lust. One team uses five different kinds of pepper "to hit all the different parts of your taste buds."

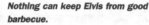

Nothing can keep Elvis from good barbecue.

Basting mixtures range from beer and cider to sorghum molasses and even Coca-Cola.

But the most important ingredient is time. Teams go to extraordinary lengths to keep the cooking low and slow. The Good, the Bad, and the Swine team from Memphis cooks its ribs for 24 hours, its pork shoulders for 36. "If we ever entered the whole hog contest, we'd have to start cooking the week before," quips team captain, Ken Johnson.

ABOUT THOSE SMOKERS

The smokers are works of art in themselves. Most are constructed from 500-gallon metal propane or furnace oil tanks. The tanks are fitted with fireboxes, wire racks for holding the meat, and doors or a coffinlike lid. Then they're personalized. The smoker of a Florida-based team, Papa G's Porkers from Paradise, sports a metal snout, curly wire tail, and porcine pink paint job. Among the more outlandish devices I've witnessed at Memphis in May are the life-size, locomotive-shaped smoker used by Choo-Chew Bar-B-Que from Louisville, Kentucky, and a smoker built from an old postal truck by the U.S. Porkmasters of Memphis. Most of the smokers are built on trailers to facilitate travel to barbecue festivals around the United States.

A simple smoker might cost $1,500 to build, and many teams spend $10,000 on the more elaborate rigs. Some teams have corporate sponsors, but most raise their own money to pay for the smoker, meat, transportation, lodging, and $350 contest entrance fee. But don't despair if you don't have an expensive rig to enter in the contest. The Patio Porkers division is designed for individuals using home-style equipment.

DOWN TO BUSINESS

By Friday night, all the booths are set up and the smokers are stoked and loaded. Night falls over a scene reminiscent of a rock festival. The air is thick with plumes of smoke. Music blares from sound systems, and the beer flows almost as fast as the mighty Mississippi. The riverside park has become a thirty-three-acre block party.

The mood is very different on Saturday morning, and not just because of the hangovers. Eleven A.M. marks the start of the judging for the first of the three main categories: whole hog, ribs, and shoulders. The burly, beer-guzzling barbecue buffs tie on aprons, wield whisk brooms and mops, and set tables with a fastidiousness normally associated with Michelin-starred restaurants. Smokers are decorated with garlands of flowers and fruit baskets. After all, the teams will be judged not only on the taste of their barbecue, but on the creativity and attractiveness of their presentation.

"Hamming" it up at Memphis in May.

More than four hundred judges fan out across the fairground. Some will participate in blind tastings. Others will visit the team areas. In order to be certified, the judges attend a $40, day-long seminar at Pork University. "Just because you can eat barbecue doesn't mean you can judge it," explains Mike Potter, a Memphis banker when he's not a barbecue judge. When asked about his qualifications, Potter points to his ample waistline.

The first thing Potter considers is the barbecue site: Its overall appearance and cleanliness. After the welcome formalities, Potter will proceed to the smoker, where the captain begins an elaborate dissertation on the team's philosophy, smoker construction, and techniques. The spokesmen are graded on their ingenuity, sincerity, and conviction. It helps to have a sense of humor and a penchant for tall tales.

Finally, the judge is led to the table for the actual tasting. He first tastes the meat "naked" (without sauce), then the sauce alone, and finally the two together. The ultimate grade is determined by the color, tenderness, doneness, and flavor of the meat. Each contestant starts with the highest score, 10. Points are deducted for toughness, greasiness or lumps of fat, or other imperfections.

The scores from the blind tasting and on-site inspections are tabulated by Pricewaterhouse accountants. Winners are announced at an ebullient ceremony on Saturday evening. The grand champion is chosen from the winners of the ribs, shoulder, and whole hog divisions. The winners rejoice; the losers reflect on how to improve their chances for next year; and everyone leaves Memphis overfed, overdrunk, overtired, and eager to return the next year.

Going

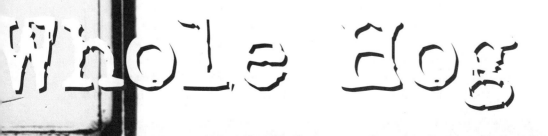

For many Americans—especially if you come from the South or Midwest—barbecue means pork. Memphis-style ribs. Carolina pulled pork shoulder. Iowa pork chops. Sizzling St. Louis pork steaks. Long before the United States was a nation, we loved to roast entire hogs over log fires and swab pork shoulders with spicy vinegar sauces, so it's no surprise that the pig is the icon of American barbecue. What is surprising is just how diverse the art of grilling pork has become. In addition to the classics, in the following pages you'll find Hawaiian Filipino-style pork tenderloin kebabs, Jamaican American jalapeño jerk baby back ribs, Miami's Cuban *lechon asado* (roast pork shoulder), and even a "pig in an orchard" (apple-stuffed, chile-glazed pork loin) from South Dakota. And for a truly grand finale, try your hand at grilling a whole hog West Virginia style, following the step-by-step instructions. This chapter invites you to make a metaphorical pig of yourself, hogging all the kudos at your next cookout.

Whole Hog

PULLED PORK

ulled pork is a uniquely American contribution to the world of barbecue. You find it in the South, and sometimes in the Midwest, but virtually nowhere else on the planet. Pulled pork is practically synonymous with barbecue in North Carolina, which can rightfully be called its birthplace. And, when people speak of barbecue in South Carolina and parts of Georgia, they mean pulled pork, although the sauces they use are completely different.

Pulled pork turns up as far north as Virginia and as far west as Missouri and Kansas, making frequent appearances in Alabama, Mississippi, Kentucky, and Tennessee, and it's beginning to make inroads in other parts of the country. I've had excellent renditions at Blue Smoke in Manhattan and the East Coast Grill in Cambridge, Massachusetts, and even as far west as Oakland, California. Indeed, I predict that the time is not far off when pulled pork will achieve the sort of all-American recognition that Texas-style brisket and Kansas City ribs enjoy already.

At its most elemental, pulled pork consists of a whole hog or pork shoulder roasted to fall-off-the-bone tenderness in a smoky pit. How tender? Real tender. The traditional way to serve the pork is torn by hand into thin meaty shreds of edible bliss—hence the name pulled pork.

DECISIONS, DECISIONS

ulling is the basic procedure, although a lot of pulled pork in the Carolinas is actually chopped with a meat cleaver or in a motorized commercial chopper (a buffalo chopper). But, as in all great barbecue, there are a myriad variations on what you pull. Do you start with pork shoulder, fresh ham, or a whole hog? Do you include rib meat? Is your rub a complex mix of spices or do you season with just salt and pepper? Do you cook the pork over charcoal, gas, or wood? In a metal cooker or a brick pit? Should the sauce be drizzled on, slathered over, or blended into the shredded meat?

And what *is* the proper sauce for pulled pork? Here, too, controversy and regional chauvinism run deep. In North Carolina, the condiment of choice is a thin, spicy, peppery vinegar sauce, but even here it varies depending on whether

you live in the eastern or western part of the state. (In general, folks in the east prefer a clear vinegar sauce, while folks in the west redden their sauce with ketchup.) The requisite condiment in South Carolina is a sharp, tangy mustard sauce, while in Kansas City the sauce runs sweet and smoky.

As for serving, do you eat the pork by itself off a sheet of waxed paper? Piled on a bun or on a slab of white bread? What are the proper accompaniments? Coleslaw? Pickles? Baked beans? Hush puppies? And what do you wash it down with? Cherry soda or beer?

In the recipes on pages 235 through 252 we'll explore some of the regional variations on this American barbecue classic. Diversity is a beautiful thing.

Goldsboro, N.C.

CLASSIC PULLED PORK (Made with Fresh Ham)

The eastern North Carolina style is probably the oldest version of pulled pork. I say this for four reasons—the type of meat, the cooking method, the sauce, and the fact that eastern North Carolina was settled earlier than the west.

If you want to experience eastern North Carolina pulled pork in one of its purest manifestations, visit Wilber's in Goldsboro. For well nigh a half century, this rambling barbecue joint has been preparing pulled pork the time-honored way: slow roasting whole hogs over an open pit filled with glowing hickory embers. (For more about Wilber's, see page 238.)

By starting with a whole hog, you get to enjoy three different parts of the pig—the meaty ham, the well-marbled shoulder, and the robustly flavored ribs—in a single sandwich. (In this recipe we use the richest part of the hog—the ham.) Cooked over burning embers in an open pit, the pork is seared as much as smoked, and as a result the smoke flavor is less overpowering than in barbecue elsewhere in the United States (the smoke remains an accent, not the dominant taste). The sauce is probably pretty similar to what Americans served with barbecued pork two centuries ago—vinegar, salt, and pepper—as the tomato ketchup used in western North Carolina barbecue sauce wouldn't have been available until the late 1800s. Pair this with the pork and you have a dish steeped in history that's spectacular in taste.

METHOD:
Indirect grilling

TIPS

I call here for a cut of meat that's larger and more robust than a shoulder, but smaller and more manageable than a whole hog: a fresh ham. A fresh ham comes from the hind quarter of the pig. It's not cured.

In many parts of the country barbecue is synonymous with pulled pork.

PEPSI-COLA

say "Pepsi please"

BARBECUE

PLATE	6.00
POUND	7.00
WITH BREAD AND SLAW	8.00
BRUNSWICK PT	3.25
SANDWICHES	2.50
COMBINATION	6.25
WHITE MEAT .50	EXTRA
HALF DARK CH	5.00

TIPS

You can cook the ham with the skin on, partially removed, or off. The advantage of leaving the skin on is that it ultimately gives you "brownies," tiny bits of smoky pork rind. The disadvantage is that the rind blocks out some of the seasonings and smoke. My compromise is to remove part of the skin. If you want to try this, using a sharp knife in a sawing motion, cut off half the skin, removing it in long two-inch-wide strips. Leave two inches of skin between each strip.

INGREDIENTS:

1 fresh ham (15 to 18 pounds)
Salt and freshly ground black pepper
Eastern North Carolina–Style Vinegar
    Sauce (recipe follows)
20 to 24 hamburger buns
North Carolina–Style Coleslaw
    (page 239)

YOU'LL ALSO NEED:

6 to 8 cups wood chips or chunks
    (preferably hickory), soaked for 1 hour
    in water to cover, then drained

1 Generously, and I mean generously, season the ham all over with salt and pepper. You'll need 3 to 4 tablespoons of each.

2 Set up the grill for indirect grilling (see page 23 for gas or page 22 for charcoal) and preheat to medium-low. If using a gas grill, place 3 cups of the wood chips or chunks in the smoker box or in a smoker pouch (see page 24) and run the grill on high until you see smoke, then reduce the heat to medium-low. If using a charcoal grill, place a large drip pan in the center, preheat the grill to medium-low, then toss 1 cup of the wood chips or chunks on the coals.

3 When ready to cook, place the ham, skin side up, in the center of the hot grate, over the drip pan and away from the heat, and cover the grill. Cook the ham until darkly browned on the outside and cooked through and very tender inside, 7 to 8 hours. To test for doneness, use an instant-read meat thermometer: The internal temperature of the ham should be about 195°F. (Yes, this is very well-done—that's how you get meat tender enough to pull.) If the ham starts to brown too much (and it probably will), cover it loosely with aluminum foil, but remember that those browned bits are good, too. If using a charcoal grill, have an extra bag of charcoal on hand; every hour you'll need to add 12 fresh coals and ½ cup of wood chips or chunks to each side. If using a gas grill, after 3 hours add 3 more cups of wood chips or chunks. To do this, remove the ham from the grill and add the wood chips or chunks to the smoker box or replace the smoker pouch with a new one. Run the grill on high until you see smoke, reduce the heat to medium-low, then return the ham to the grate.

4 Transfer the cooked ham to a cutting board, cover it loosely with aluminum foil, let it rest for 20 minutes, then pull off any skin and finely chop it with a cleaver. Pull the pork into large pieces, discarding any bones or lumps of fat (you'll probably want to wear latex gloves or even heavy-duty insulated rubber gloves to do this). Using your fingertips or a fork, pull each piece of ham into thin shreds. Or use a cleaver to finely chop it. Transfer the ham to a large aluminum foil pan and stir in 3 cups of the vinegar sauce—enough to keep the meat moist. If you are not quite ready to serve, cover the pan with aluminum foil and place it on a warm—not hot—grill or in an oven turned on low to keep warm.

5 To serve, have your guests mound the ham onto hamburger buns. Top with coleslaw and let everyone add additional vinegar sauce to taste.

YIELD:

Serves 20 to 24

VARIATIONS:

■ If the prospect of cooking a 15- to 18-pound chunk of ham intimidates you, a 5-pound pork shoulder or Boston butt is equally tasty fixed this way. It will feed up to a dozen people. If you use one of these, it will take 4 to 6 hours to grill. Now, if you're feeling really ambitious, you'll want to make this dish with a whole hog. Instructions for grilling whole hogs can be found on page 300.

■ Fresh hams can also be cooked in a smoker. Set it up and preheat it following the manufacturer's instructions. You'll probably be cooking at a temperature of 250° to 275°F, so be prepared to add several hours to the cooking time.

Lemonade, Philly steaks, and pulled pork—a cross section of American tastes.

... pulled pork the time-honored way ...

WILBER'S
In Goldsboro

Wilber Shirley certainly puts his money where his mouth is. When I arrived at his landmark restaurant, the septuagenarian barbecue king, recognizable by his silver-gray hair and copper bracelet, was sitting at a counter worn smooth by generations of elbows, eating a plate of chopped pork with vinegar sauce—just like he's done for the last half century. Welcome to one of the most venerable and distinguished barbecue joints in North Carolina, Wilber's.

Wilber's serves the quintessential eastern Carolina barbecue—whole hog, not just pork shoulder, cooked over an old-fashioned open pit, doused with chile-stung vinegar sauce with nary a drop of ketchup. Like all true North Carolina barbecue, it's served

WILBER'S BARBECUE

4172 U.S. Highway 70 E.
Goldsboro, North Carolina
(919) 778-5218
(and other locations)
www.esn.net/wilbers/

with slaw (chopped cabbage with vinegar sauce) to provide a crunchy counterpoint to the tender, moist pork. The potato salad is properly mustardy, even if the hush puppies are a little dense.

It's not much to look at—what barbecue joint is? But there's a homey comfort to the cozy dining rooms with their pine paneling

and red checkered tablecloths. Background "music" is provided by the roar of F-16s from the air base next door.

What makes Wilber's so extraordinary is the smokehouse. And if you ask real politely, you just might finagle a glimpse. What you'll see is darn near as old as North Carolina barbecue itself. Wilber favors the old-fashioned open pit—a sort of trough made of cinder blocks. On the metal crossbars over the pit, split whole pigs are cooked to smoky perfection. The pit boss arrives at the end of the day: For the next twelve hours, he'll patiently burn hickory in the fire box, shovel the coals under the hogs, and turn them at just the right moment to obtain skin as crisp as cracklings and meat as tender as pot roast. On a typical weekend, twenty-five pigs will be thus transformed into the fork-tender stuff of legend.

Eastern North Carolina–Style Vinegar Sauce

If American barbecue sauces had an extreme division, this mouth-puckering condiment—all vinegar and fire—would lead the pack. It's not for licking off your fingers, but the sharp acidity mellows when mixed with fatty pork. The recipe makes roughly six cups; some to flavor the pulled pork, some to dress the coleslaw, and what's left gets served on the side.

INGREDIENTS:

5 cups distilled white vinegar

3 tablespoons salt, or more to taste

3 tablespoons sugar

3 tablespoons freshly ground black pepper

2 tablespoons hot red pepper flakes,
    or more to taste

3 tablespoons hot sauce,
    such as Tabasco or Texas Pete

Put the vinegar, salt, sugar, black pepper, hot red pepper flakes, and hot sauce in a large nonreactive bowl, add 1 cup of water, and whisk until the salt and sugar dissolve. Or, place the ingredients in a large jar and shake to mix. Taste for seasoning, adding more salt and/or hot red pepper flakes as necessary. The sauce can be refrigerated for several weeks. Bring it to room temperature before using.

YIELD:

Makes about 6 cups

North Carolina–Style Coleslaw

North Carolina coleslaw is coleslaw at its most elemental. No onions. No carrots or peppers. No mayonnaise. Just cabbage and peppery vinegar sauce. It may seem almost austere, but nothing goes better with North Carolina pulled pork.

INGREDIENTS:

1 large head green or savoy cabbage
    (2½ to 3 pounds)

1½ cups Eastern North Carolina–Style
    Vinegar Sauce (at left), or
    more to taste

Salt (optional)

1. Remove the core from the cabbage and discard it. Cut the cabbage into 8 chunks. Finely chop the cabbage in a food processor using the metal blade and pulsing the motor (this is a chopped, not sliced or slivered, slaw). Work in several batches so as not to overcrowd the processor bowl.

2. Place the cabbage in a large nonreactive bowl and stir in the vinegar sauce. Taste for seasoning, adding more vinegar sauce as necessary. Let stand for 10 minutes, then taste again, adding more vinegar sauce and/or salt as necessary. The coleslaw can be made up to 4 hours ahead. Store it in the refrigerator, covered.

YIELD:

Makes 6 to 8 cups

MONK'S SANCTUARY

The five tall, smoke-belching chimneys of Lexington Barbecue are visible from a distance. The jam-packed parking lot of the huge, white barnlike structure indicates what the locals think of the food. And the fact that the first person I met when I entered the restaurant was its founder, Wayne Monk, spoke volumes about how he runs his business.

Lord knows, after forty years at this location, Monk is probably

LEXINGTON BARBECUE

**Highway 29-70 South
Lexington, North Carolina
(336) 249-9814**

famous enough to let other people run his restaurant. But on a Saturday afternoon, he set up trays, dished out barbecue, and shuttled between the kitchen and the dining room.

Monk led me to a brick wall with five huge brick pits that spew out a half ton of smoked pork shoulders a day. It's not a complicated operation: Huge oak and hickory logs are reduced to glowing red embers in a fire box built into the wall of the pit. Heavily seasoned pork shoulders are lined up on a smoke-darkened rack in the pits. Thick metal doors, warped with heat, keep the temperature of the pit at 275°F. Every hour, the pit master tosses a shovel full of glowing coals under the meat. The shoulders spend three hours on the face (the meat side), three hours on the back (the skin side), then two hours back on the face. By

the time the pork emerges from the pit, it's tender enough to pull apart by hand.

And that's precisely what Monk and his acolytes do—sort of. Chunks of meat are fed into a buffalo chopper (Monk switched to machine chopping a few years ago when the sheer volume of his business made it impossible to chop all the pork by hand.) They generally discard the skin, unless a customer orders some "brownies." Then a bit of chopped skin is added—I strongly recommend trying it that way.

Piled on a warm hamburger bun, splashed with vinegar sauce, and crowned with a mound of vinegary coleslaw, what you have is a symphonic play of flavors, temperatures, and textures: the pork hot and meaty, the bun soft and warm, the sauce piquant but edged with the sweetness of ketchup, and the slaw cool and crisp. The hush puppies (the traditional accompaniment to barbecue in these parts) are delectably oniony. I washed my meal down with Cheerwine (a sugary cherry soda) and ended with a crumbly canned-peach cobbler.

All this, and you still get change from a sawbuck!

LEXINGTON BARBECUE

Lexington, N.C.

LEXINGTON PULLED PORK SHOULDER

This is it—the ultimate pork shoulder. My inspiration is no less than the pulled pork sandwich at Lexington Barbecue (formerly the Honey Monk) in Lexington, North Carolina. This furniture-manufacturing town of twenty-thousand is reputed to have more barbecue joints per capita than any other city in North America. The most popular of all is the gargantuan restaurant run by Wayne Monk. If you want to know what western North Carolina barbecue is all about, just bite into one of his pulled pork sandwiches—piled high with meat from a patiently smoked pork shoulder, chopped to a fine confetti, available with or without "brownies" (crisp bits of chopped pork rind), and served with a kick-ass vinegar sauce that owes its reddish hue and hint of sweetness to a fillip of ketchup. Pork shoulders are easier to cook than the fresh ham on page 235, so there's no excuse for not trying this recipe.

METHOD:
Indirect grilling or smoking

FOR THE RUB:
4 teaspoons sweet paprika
1 tablespoon brown sugar
1 tablespoon salt
1 teaspoon black pepper
1 teaspoon white pepper
1 teaspoon dry mustard
1 teaspoon garlic powder
¹/₂ to 1 teaspoon cayenne pepper

FOR THE PORK:
1 Boston butt (bone-in pork shoulder roast; 5 to 7 pounds)
Lexington Vinegar Sauce (recipe follows)
10 to 12 hamburger buns
Lexington Slaw (page 243)

YOU'LL ALSO NEED:
4 to 6 cups wood chips or chunks (preferably hickory), soaked for 1 hour in water to cover, then drained

1 MAKE THE RUB: Place the paprika, brown sugar, salt, black pepper, white pepper, mustard, garlic powder, and cayenne in a small bowl and stir to mix. (Actually, if you don't have sensitive skin, your fingers work better for mixing a rub than a spoon or whisk does.) Set aside 1¹/₂ tablespoons of the rub for the Lexington Vinegar Sauce. Sprinkle the remaining rub all over the pork, patting it onto the meat with your fingertips.

2 Set up the grill for indirect grilling (see page 23 for gas or page 22 for charcoal) and preheat to medium-low. If using a gas grill, place all of the wood chips or chunks in the smoker box or in a smoker pouch (see page 24) and run the grill on high until you see smoke, then reduce the heat to medium-low. If

TIPS

A whole pork shoulder (which contains both the shoulder and upper part of the foreleg) weighs about fourteen pounds. What I call for here is a roughly five-pound shoulder roast, sometimes called a Boston butt. Of course, if you're feeling ambitious, and want to feed twice as many people, you could always cook a whole shoulder, in which case add a couple more hours to the cooking time and double the sauce and slaw.

using a charcoal grill, place a large drip pan in the center, preheat the grill to medium-low, then toss 1 cup of the wood chips or chunks on the coals.

3 When ready to cook, place the pork, skin side up, if there is one, in the center of the hot grate, over the drip pan and away from the heat, and cover the grill. Cook the pork until darkly browned on the outside and very tender inside, 4 to 6 hours. To test for doneness, use an instant-read meat thermometer: The internal temperature of the pork should be about 195°F. (Yes, this is very well-done—that's how you get pork tender enough to pull.) If the pork starts to brown too much (and it probably will), cover it loosely with aluminum foil, but remember that those browned bits are good, too. If using a charcoal grill, every hour you'll need to add 12 fresh coals and ½ cup of wood chips or chunks to each side.

4 Transfer the cooked pork to a cutting board, cover it loosely with aluminum foil, let it rest for 20 minutes, then pull the pork into large pieces, discarding any bones or lumps of fat (you'll probably want to wear latex gloves or even heavy-duty insulated rubber gloves to do this). Using your fingertips or a fork, pull each piece of pork into thin shreds. Or use a cleaver to finely chop it. Transfer the pulled pork to a large aluminum foil pan and stir in 1 to 1½ cups of the vinegar sauce—enough to keep the meat moist. If you are not quite ready to serve, cover the pan with aluminum foil and place it on a warm—not hot—grill or in an oven turned on low to keep warm.

. . . the pork hot and meaty, the bun soft and warm, the sauce piquant . . .

Shoveling the embers from the firebox to the pit at Lexington Barbecue.

5 To serve, have your guests mound the pulled pork onto hamburger buns. Top with coleslaw and let everyone add additional vinegar sauce to taste.

YIELD:
Serves 10 to 12

Lexington Vinegar Sauce

Where do you stand in the great eastern North Carolina versus western North Carolina sauce fight? Folks in the eastern part of the state like a sauce that's based on vinegar, while in the west they prefer a sauce that's slightly sweeter and tinted red with ketchup, like the one here. Both kinds of sauces are thin and mouth-puckeringly tart; they go perfectly with rich pork shoulder. Try each for yourself to pick your favorite (you'll find the eastern version on page 239).

INGREDIENTS:

2¹/₂ cups cider vinegar

¹/₂ cup ketchup

2 tablespoons brown sugar

1 tablespoon hot sauce
    (preferably Crystal hot sauce)

4 teaspoons salt

4 teaspoons hot red pepper flakes

1 teaspoon freshly ground black pepper

1 teaspoon white pepper

1¹/₂ tablespoons rub reserved from
    Lexington Pulled Pork Shoulder,
    or your favorite barbecue rub

Combine the vinegar, ketchup, brown sugar, hot sauce, salt, hot red pepper flakes, black pepper, white pepper, and rub in a large nonreactive bowl with ¹/₂ cup of water. Whisk until the sugar and salt dissolve. Alternatively, place the ingredients in a large jar and shake to mix. Stored in a jar in the refrigerator the sauce will keep for several weeks. Bring to room temperature before using.

YIELD:
Makes about 3¹/₂ cups

Lexington Slaw

Once again, a simple vinegary slaw serves as a counterpoint for rich pulled pork. Save the more elaborate slaws you'll find on pages 125 through 129 for serving as side dishes.

INGREDIENTS:

1 medium-size head green cabbage
    (about 2 pounds)

1 cup Lexington Vinegar Sauce
    (at left), or more to taste

Coarse salt (kosher or sea; optional)

1 Remove the core from the cabbage and discard it. Cut the cabbage into 8 chunks. Finely chop the cabbage in a food processor using the metal blade and pulsing the motor (this is a chopped, not sliced or slivered, slaw). Work in several batches so as not to overcrowd the processor bowl.

WALL OF FLAME

THE BARBECUE CENTER

The Barbecue Center, located in a 1950s style drive-in, serves a tasty chopped pork sandwich with the ketchup-reddened vinegar sauce that's popular in these parts. Curbside service is available for no extra charge. But barbecue is only half the story—the soda fountain dishes up what may be the largest banana split in North Carolina.

900 North Main Street
Lexington, North Carolina
(336) 248-4633
www.barbecuecenter.com

2 Place the cabbage in a large non-reactive bowl and stir in the vinegar sauce. Taste for seasoning, adding more vinegar sauce as necessary. Let stand for 10 minutes, then taste again for seasoning, adding more vinegar sauce and/or salt as necessary. The coleslaw can be made up to 4 hours ahead. Store it in the refrigerator, covered.

YIELD:
Makes 5 to 6 cups

South Carolina

SOUTH CAROLINA SMOKED PORK SHOULDER
With Mustard Sauce

Mustard country begins in southern North Carolina and runs through South Carolina to parts of Georgia, Alabama, and Mississippi. I'm not talking about the places where the spicy yellow stuff grows or is manufactured but about where mustard-flavored barbecue sauce reigns supreme. The pork shoulder here is fixed a bit more elaborately than what you'd find at your average South Carolina roadside barbecue joint—I've added a mustard rub and a mustard

mop. Depending upon where you are in South Carolina, the pork will be pulled, chopped, or even sliced (my choice for this recipe). Some pit masters add slaw, others sliced pickles. I call for pickles, but you could always make a mustard slaw by mixing chopped cabbage with the South Carolina Mustard Barbecue Sauce on page 246.

METHOD:
Indirect grilling

FOR THE RUB AND BOSTON BUTT:
2 teaspoons dry mustard
2 teaspoons sweet paprika
2 teaspoons salt
1 teaspoon freshly ground black pepper
1 teaspoon ground white pepper
1 teaspoon garlic powder
1 teaspoon onion powder
1/2 to 1 teaspoon cayenne pepper
1 Boston butt (bone-in pork shoulder roast; 5 to 7 pounds)

FOR THE MOP SAUCE:
2 cups distilled white vinegar
1/2 cup Dijon mustard
1 tablespoon salt
2 teaspoons freshly ground black pepper

FOR SERVING:
10 to 12 hamburger buns
3 tablespoons butter (optional), melted
South Carolina Mustard Barbecue Sauce (recipe follows)
Thinly sliced sweet or dill pickles

YOU'LL ALSO NEED:
4 to 6 cups wood chips or chunks (preferably hickory), soaked for 1 hour in water to cover, then drained; barbecue mop (optional; see page 288)

TIPS

Mop sauces are thin, spicy liquids swabbed on pork shoulders and other slow-roasting meats. Mops serve at least two purposes: They keep the meat moist and they add an extra layer of flavor. The implement of choice for swabbing is a barbecue mop; you'll find more information about these on page 292.

1 MAKE THE RUB: Place the mustard, paprika, salt, black pepper, white pepper, garlic powder, onion powder, and cayenne in a bowl and stir to mix. (Actually, if you don't have sensitive skin, your fingers work better for mixing a rub than a spoon or whisk does.) Sprinkle the rub all over the pork, patting it onto the meat with your fingertips. Let the pork cure at room temperature while you make the mop sauce.

2 MAKE THE MOP SAUCE: Combine the vinegar, mustard, salt, and black pepper in a large nonreactive mixing bowl, add 1/2 cup of water, and whisk until the salt dissolves.

3 Set up the grill for indirect grilling (see page 23 for gas or page 22 for charcoal) and preheat to medium-low. If using a gas grill, place all of the wood chips or chunks in the smoker box or in a smoker pouch (see page 24) and run the grill on high until you see smoke, then reduce the heat to medium-low. If using a charcoal grill, place a large drip pan in the center, preheat the grill to medium-low, then toss 1 cup of the wood chips or chunks on the coals.

4 When ready to cook, place the pork, skin side up, if there is one, in the center of the hot grate, over the drip pan and away from the heat, and cover the grill. Cook the pork until darkly browned on the outside and very tender inside, 4 to 6 hours. To test for doneness, use an instant-read meat thermometer: The internal temperature of the pork

Pork lovingly pulled into tender shreds— Carolina barbecue at its finest.

should be about 195°F. (Yes, this is very well-done—that's how you get pork tender enough to chop or pull.) If the pork starts to brown too much (and it probably will), cover it loosely with aluminum foil, but remember that the browned bits are good, too. Every hour for the first 4 hours, swab the pork with some of the mop sauce, using a barbecue mop or basting brush. If using a charcoal grill, every hour you'll need to add 12 fresh coals and 1/2 cup of wood chips or chunks to each side.

5 Transfer the cooked pork to a cutting board, cover it loosely with aluminum foil, and let it rest for 20 minutes. You could pull or chop the pork, but I like to thinly slice it across the grain (the practice of many South Carolina pit masters). Place the pork slices in an aluminum foil pan. If you

are not quite ready to serve, cover the pan with aluminum foil and place it on a warm—not hot—grill or in an oven turned on low to keep warm.

6 If you're feeling fancy, brush the hamburger buns with the melted butter and lightly toast them on the grill (work directly over the coals or a lit burner). Otherwise, skip the butter and simply serve the buns without toasting. Load each bun with sliced pork and slather with mustard sauce. Top the pork and sauce with pickle slices and serve at once.

YIELD:
Serves 10 to 12

South Carolina Mustard Barbecue Sauce

Mustard sauce has the same goal as a North Carolina vinegar sauce—to cut the fattiness of the pork. The mustard and sugar make this thicker and saucier than one made with vinegar (you could dip your bread in it or lick the spoon, for example— something you wouldn't do with a vinegar sauce). Tradition calls for an inexpensive yellow mustard, but I like a mellower, more refined condiment, like Dijon-style Grey Poupon.

INGREDIENTS:
1 tablespoon butter
1 small onion, finely chopped
1 clove garlic, minced
1 cup Dijon mustard
¾ cup firmly packed brown sugar
¾ cup distilled white vinegar
1 tablespoon hot sauce
 (preferably Crystal), or more to taste
Coarse salt (kosher or sea) and
 freshly ground black pepper

1 Melt the butter in a heavy non-reactive saucepan over medium heat. Add the onion and garlic and cook until soft but not brown, about 3 minutes.

2 Stir in the mustard, brown sugar, vinegar, and hot sauce and add ½ cup of water. Let the sauce simmer, uncovered, until thick and richly flavored, 6 to 10 minutes. Taste for seasoning, adding more hot sauce as necessary and seasoning with salt and pepper to taste. Let the sauce cool to room temperature before serving. In the unlikely case you have any mustard sauce left, store it in a clean jar in the refrigerator. It will keep for at least a week; bring it to room temperature before using.

YIELD:
Makes about 3 cups

VARIATION: You could use a different sweetener, substituting honey or molasses for the brown sugar. Use ¾ of a cup of honey. If substituting molasses, start with ¾ of a cup, but taste for sweetness—you may need to add a little more, since molasses is not as sweet as brown sugar.

Memphis, Tenn.

MEMPHIS 'QUE (Pulled Pork with Mustard Slaw)

Mention Memphis outside of Tennessee and most people will think of dry ribs. But to locals, the term *barbecue* refers to pork shoulder, pit roasted to a melting tenderness, pulled or chopped into meaty bits, and piled high on a bun with mustardy coleslaw. That's how Leonard Heuberger made it when he opened Leonard's Pit Barbecue back in 1922. And that's how pork shoulder is still prepared at this legendary Memphis pit stop today.

METHOD:
Indirect grilling

INGREDIENTS:

1 Boston butt (bone-in pork shoulder
    roast; 5 to 7 pounds)
Coarse salt (kosher or sea) and
    freshly ground black pepper
10 to 12 hamburger buns
Memphis Mustard Slaw
    (recipe follows)
Your favorite tomato-based barbecue
    sauce (optional; I like The Doctor's
    Medicine on page 680)

1 Generously season the pork all over with salt and pepper.

2 Set up the grill for indirect grilling (see page 22 charcoal or page 23 for gas) and preheat to medium. To be strictly authentic, you'd use charcoal, but the recipe will also work on a gas grill. If using a charcoal grill, place a large drip pan in the center.

3 When ready to cook, place the pork, skin side up, if there is one, in the center of the hot grate, over the drip pan and away from the heat, and cover the grill. Cook the pork until very tender, 4 to 5 hours. To test for doneness, use an instant-read meat thermometer: The internal temperature of the pork should be about 195°F (the cooking time will depend on the size of the Boston butt and heat of the grill). If the pork starts to brown too much (and it probably will), cover it

TIPS

You may be surprised by the lack of wood smoke in this recipe, but Memphis pork shoulders are traditionally cooked over charcoal, not wood. The pit is set up for a sort of modified direct grilling: The shoulders are positioned directly over the fire, but about three feet above the coals. The result is more akin to indirect grilling, which is what I call for here, than to direct.

Leonard's uses a bare-bones seasoning: salt and pepper, but no spice rub.

loosely with aluminum foil, but remember that those browned bits are good, too. If using a charcoal grill, every hour you'll need to add 12 fresh coals to each side.

4. Transfer the cooked pork to a cutting board, cover it loosely with aluminum foil, if you have not done so already, and let it rest for 10 minutes. Pull off the brown skin and finely chop it with a cleaver (these crisp bits are called "brownies" and they're indispensable for a proper Memphis pork sandwich). Pull the pork into large pieces, discarding any bones or lumps of fat (you'll probably want to wear latex gloves or even heavy-duty rubber gloves to do this). Using your fingertips or a fork, pull each piece of pork into thin shreds. Or use a cleaver to finely chop it.

5. To serve, pile the pulled pork and brownies on the hamburger buns. Top each with a mound of mustard slaw and, if desired, a dollop of barbecue sauce. Serve at once.

YIELD:
Serves 10 to 12

Memphis Mustard Slaw

Memphis coleslaw is characterized by a tangy, sharp, sweet mustard dressing. Here's how it's been made at Leonard's for more than eighty years. Well, almost:

. . . pit roasted to a melting tenderness . . .

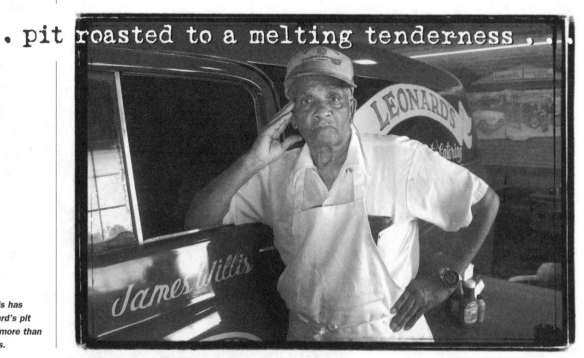

James Willis has been Leonard's pit master for more than six decades.

Leonard's uses canned red peppers, but I prefer the sweet crunch of fresh, which I call for here.

FOR THE SLAW:

1 small or ½ large head green cabbage (about 1½ pounds)

½ red bell pepper

FOR THE DRESSING:

¼ cup yellow mustard

¼ cup mayonnaise

¼ cup sugar

¼ cup distilled white vinegar

½ teaspoon celery seed

½ teaspoon freshly ground black pepper, or more to taste

Salt

1 Remove the core from the cabbage and discard it. Cut the cabbage into 8 chunks. Finely chop the cabbage in a food processor using the metal blade and pulsing the motor (this is a chopped, not sliced or slivered, slaw). Work in several batches so as not to overcrowd the processor bowl.

2 Cut the bell pepper into the finest possible dice.

3 MAKE THE DRESSING: Place the mustard, mayonnaise, and sugar in a nonreactive mixing bowl and whisk until smooth. Whisk in the vinegar, celery seed, and black pepper. Add the chopped cabbage and diced bell pepper and stir to mix. Taste for seasoning, adding salt and more pepper as necessary. The slaw can be made up to 1 day ahead.

YIELD:

Makes 5 to 6 cups

What's more formidable, the server or the sandwich?

Lawrenceville, N.J.

PULLED PORK
With Espresso
Barbecue Sauce

N ew Jersey may not be renowned for its barbecued pork shoulder, but while taping a TV segment in Lawrenceville, I ate a pulled pork sandwich that made me sit up and take notice. It was slathered with coffee barbecue sauce. This isn't as strange as it sounds—there's a long-standing tradition in the United States of serving ham or pork with coffee (think redeye gravy). Although the recipe here was inspired by Chambers Walk Café, the rub, mop, and sauce are all my own inventions.

Chambers Walk serves its pork on kaiser rolls with red cabbage slaw and coffee barbecue sauce. You'll find a quick slaw recipe here, but you could use any of the slaws on pages 125 through 129.

METHOD:
Indirect grilling

FOR THE RUB:
2 teaspoons ground coffee
2 teaspoons sweet paprika
2 teaspoons sugar
2 teaspoons coarse salt (kosher or sea)
2 teaspoons freshly ground black pepper

FOR THE MOP SAUCE:
1 cup brewed coffee
½ cup distilled white vinegar
4 tablespoons (½ stick) salted butter
1 tablespoon rub reserved from above

FOR THE PORK:
1 Boston butt (bone-in pork shoulder roast;
**   5 to 7 pounds)**
Espresso Barbecue Sauce (recipe follows)
10 to 12 kaiser rolls
Quick Red Slaw (see the facing page)

YOU'LL ALSO NEED:
4 to 6 cups wood chips or chunks
**   (preferably hickory), soaked for 1 hour**
**   in water to cover, then drained;**
**   barbecue mop (optional; see page 292)**

1 MAKE THE RUB: Place the ground coffee, paprika, sugar, salt, and pepper in a small bowl and stir to mix. (Actually, your fingers work better for mixing a rub than a spoon or whisk does.) Set aside 1 tablespoon of the rub for the mop sauce. Sprinkle the remaining rub all over the pork, patting it onto the meat with your fingertips. Set aside.

2 MAKE THE MOP SAUCE: Place the brewed coffee, vinegar, butter, and the reserved 1 tablespoon of rub in a nonreactive bowl and whisk to mix.

3 Set up the grill for indirect grilling (see page 23 for gas or page 22 for charcoal) and preheat to medium-low. If using a gas grill, place all of the wood chips or chunks in the smoker box or in a smoker pouch (see page 24) and run the grill on high until you see smoke, then reduce the heat to medium-low. If using a charcoal grill, place a large drip pan in the center, preheat the grill to medium-low, then toss 1 cup of the wood chips or chunks on the coals.

4 When ready to cook, place the pork, skin side up, if there is one, in the center of the hot grate, over the drip pan and away from the heat, and cover the grill. Cook the pork until darkly browned on the outside and very tender inside, 4 to 6 hours. To test for doneness, use an instant-read meat thermometer: The internal temperature of the pork should be about 195°F. If the pork starts to brown too much (and it probably will), cover it loosely with aluminum foil, but remember that those browned bits are good, too. Every hour for the first 4 hours swab the pork with the mop sauce. If using a charcoal grill, every hour you'll need to add 12 fresh coals and ½ cup of wood chips or chunks to each side.

5 Transfer the cooked pork to a cutting board, cover it loosely with aluminum foil, and let it rest for 20 minutes, then pull the pork into large pieces, discarding any bones or lumps of fat (you'll probably want to wear latex gloves or even heavy-duty insulated rubber gloves to do this). Using your fingertips or a fork, pull each piece of pork into thin shreds. Or use a cleaver to finely chop it. Transfer the pulled pork to a large aluminum foil pan and stir in about half of the Espresso Barbecue Sauce—enough to keep the meat moist. If you are not quite ready to serve, cover the pan with aluminum foil and place it on a warm—not hot—grill or in an oven turned on low to keep warm.

6 To serve, mound the pulled pork onto the kaiser rolls. Top with Quick Red Slaw and let everyone add additional barbecue sauce to taste.

YIELD:
Serves 10 to 12

Espresso Barbecue Sauce

There's something outrageous about brewing a sauce from a beverage you usually associate with breakfast. Here, you'll be able to sense the coffee without actually tasting it.

INGREDIENTS:
¾ **cup espresso or strong brewed coffee**
¾ **cup ketchup**
6 **tablespoons heavy (whipping) cream**
½ **cup honey**
⅓ **cup Dijon mustard**
¼ **cup firmly packed brown sugar,**
   or more to taste
3 **tablespoons cider vinegar,**
   or more to taste

3 **tablespoons Worcestershire sauce**
1 **tablespoon Tabasco sauce or your**
   favorite hot sauce, or more to taste
Coarse salt (kosher or sea) and
   freshly ground black pepper

1 Combine the espresso, ketchup, cream, honey, mustard, brown sugar, vinegar, Worcestershire sauce, and Tabasco sauce with 3 tablespoons of water in a large heavy nonreactive saucepan. Gradually bring to a boil over medium-high heat.

2 Reduce the heat to medium and let the sauce simmer gently until thick and richly flavored, 6 to 10 minutes. Taste for seasoning, adding more brown sugar, vinegar, and/or Tabasco sauce as necessary and season with salt and pepper to taste. If necessary, add a little more water to thin and mellow the sauce. The sauce can be served hot or at room temperature and may be refrigerated, covered, for up to 1 week. Bring it to room temperature and stir to recombine before serving.

YIELD:
Makes about 3¼ cups

Quick Red Slaw

Most slaws are made with green cabbage. The yuppified roots of this one are evident in the red cabbage, the balsamic vinegar, and the extra-virgin olive oil. Golden raisins add bursts of fruity sweetness.

WALL OF FLAME

HAROLD'S BARBECUE

If your idea of heaven is a crusty pork shoulder smoked in a traditional brick pit over smoldering hickory until it's meltingly tender, consider this paradise found. Harold's Barbecue chops its pork by hand and piles it on slices of white bread browned over a shovelful of embers.

171 McDonough
   Boulevard, SE
Atlanta, Georgia
(404) 627-9268

INGREDIENTS:

1 tablespoon Dijon mustard
2 tablespoons balsamic vinegar
4 tablespoons extra-virgin olive oil
Coarse salt (kosher or sea) and
**   freshly ground black pepper**
1 small or ½ large head red cabbage
**   (1½ to 2 pounds)**
½ cup golden raisins

1 Place the mustard in a large, attractive, nonreactive bowl and whisk in the vinegar and olive oil. Season with salt and pepper to taste; the dressing should be highly seasoned.

2 Remove the core from the cabbage and discard it. Cut the cabbage into 8 chunks. Thinly slice the cabbage in a food processor fitted with the slicing disc. Work in batches so as not to overcrowd the processor bowl.

3 Stir the sliced cabbage into the dressing, then add the raisins. Taste for seasoning, adding more salt and/or pepper as necessary. Serve the slaw within 5 hours of making it.

YIELD:
Makes about 6 cups

Hawaii

KALUA PIG

No survey of regional American barbecued pork would be complete without Hawaii's kalua pig. If

Unearthing Hawaii's kalua pig.

you've ever been to a luau, you've probably sampled this porcine masterpiece, with meat moist as stew and tender enough to eat with your fingers (which, of course, is what you're meant to do). To achieve this, Hawaiians have traditionally cooked whole pigs underground in pits. A similar effect can be achieved by wrapping a pork shoulder in banana leaves and grilling it using the indirect method.

METHOD:
Indirect grilling

ADVANCE PREPARATION:
12 hours for curing the pork

FOR THE PORK:
1 pork shoulder (5 to 7 pounds)
2 to 3 tablespoons coarse salt (kosher or sea)
1 to 2 tablespoons freshly ground
black pepper
2 tablespoons liquid smoke (optional)
2 banana leaves
1 medium-size onion, thinly sliced (optional)
1 piece (3 to 4 inches) fresh ginger
(optional), peeled and thinly sliced
6 cloves garlic (optional), thinly sliced
Lime wedges, for serving

FOR SERVING, ANY OF THE FOLLOWING:
Taro root
Sweet potatoes
Butter
Buns or bread
4½ cups (1½ batches) Pineapple
Barbecue Sauce (optional; page 293)
Passion Fruit Applesauce
(optional; recipe follows)

YOU'LL ALSO NEED:
Butcher's string

1 Using a sharp knife, make 6 to 8 shallow (½-inch-deep) cuts running the length of the pork shoulder. Sprinkle the salt, pepper, and liquid smoke, if using, all over the pork, patting them onto the surface of the meat and into the cuts with your fingertips.

2 Wrap the pork shoulder in the banana leaves: If using fresh banana leaves, soften them by holding them with tongs for a minute or so over the lit burner of your stove or over a lit grill. Let cool slightly, then place a banana leaf on your work surface. Put half of the onion, ginger, and garlic slices, if using, on the leaf toward the center. Place the pork shoulder in the center of the banana leaf on top of the onion, ginger, and garlic slices, if using, then place the remaining onion, ginger, and garlic slices on top of the pork. Draw the ends of the banana leaf up over the pork to enclose it. Place the banana leaf–wrapped pork on the second banana leaf so that the leaves are at a right angle to each other. Draw the second leaf up over the first and tie the leaves in place with butcher's string. Place the wrapped pork in the refrigerator and let cure overnight.

3 Set up the grill for indirect grilling (see page 22 for charcoal or page 23 for gas) and preheat to medium-low. If using a charcoal grill, place a large drip pan in the center.

4 When ready to cook, place the wrapped pork in the center of the hot grate, over the drip pan and away from the heat. Cover the grill and cook the pork until very tender, 5 to 6 hours.

TIPS

■ Being a nut for flavor, I like to place sliced onion, ginger, and garlic between the pork and the banana leaves. But for most Hawaiians, less is more when it comes to preparing this classic dish; they use only salt and, perhaps, liquid smoke as seasonings.

■ If you live in Hawaii or Florida, you may have banana trees growing in your garden, but don't use leaves from a plant that's been treated with pesticides. Frozen banana leaves can be found in Mexican, Caribbean, or Southeast Asian markets. If banana leaves aren't available, you can wrap the pork shoulder in aluminum foil.

TIPS

Passion fruit has a sharp, musky flavor that epitomizes the tropics. Many gourmet shops and supermarkets carry fresh passion fruit, which look like wrinkly purple balls and are filled with fragrant orange pulp. You can also buy frozen passion fruit pulp at a Hispanic market or look for passion fruit nectar.

To test for doneness, insert an instant-read meat thermometer through the banana leaves into the pork, but not so that it touches a bone: The internal temperature should be about 190°F.

5 Transfer the cooked pork to a cutting board and let it rest for 10 minutes, then unwrap it, discarding the banana leaves and string. Tear the pork into chunks or shreds, discarding any bones or lumps of fat (you'll probably want to wear latex gloves or even heavy-duty insulated rubber gloves to do this). Serve at once. The traditional Hawaiian accompaniment is sweet potatoes and poi (puréed taro root). You can roast taro root and sweet potatoes in the embers, then peel the taro root and break open the sweet potatoes and serve both with butter. You could also serve the pork on buns or bread as a sandwich. Serve the Pineapple Barbecue Sauce and Passion Fruit Applesauce alongside.

YIELD:
Serves 10 to 12

Passion Fruit Applesauce

Applesauce is the traditional accompaniment to pork in many parts of the United States. Hawaiian mega-chef Roy Yamaguchi puts a tropical spin on his applesauce by adding a perfumed shot of passion fruit. The acidity of the passion fruit makes this the perfect foil for Kalua Pig.

INGREDIENTS:
**6 apples (any variety you fancy; about 3 pounds), peeled, quartered, and cored
¾ cup strained passion fruit juice, pulp, or nectar (see Note)
½ vanilla bean, split
2 slices peeled fresh ginger (each ¼ inch thick), gently crushed with the side of a cleaver
½ cup mirin (sweet rice wine)
3 tablespoons honey, or more to taste**

1 Place the apples, passion fruit juice, vanilla bean, ginger, mirin, and honey in a heavy nonreactive saucepan over medium heat. Cover the saucepan and cook until the apples are very soft, 10 to 15 minutes. Lower the heat if the apple mixture starts to boil over. Remove the saucepan from the heat and fish out and discard the vanilla bean and ginger slices.

2 Transfer the apple mixture to a food processor and purée to a smooth sauce. Taste for sweetness, adding more honey as necessary.

YIELD:
Makes about 5 cups

NOTE: If you can find fresh passion fruit, you'll need 12 to 16 to make ¾ cup of pulp. Cut the fruit in half, scrape out the pulp, and press it through a strainer with the back of a wooden spoon.

MIAMI'S LECHON ASADO
Cuban Pig Roast

The day before Christmas, Miami's sky is filled with smoke from a thousand backyard barbecues. Not just any smoke: It's the fragrant aroma of *lechon asado,* pork marinated in a garlicky adobo, wrapped in banana leaves, and slow roasted over an ember-filled pit. It's the quintessential smell of Miami this time of year, and everywhere you turn preparations are under way for *la Noche Buena,* the traditional Cuban Christmas Eve feast.

In South Florida, the Cuban Americans jokingly refer to Miami as the fifteenth province of Cuba. And at Christmas, Miami's Cuban roots are at their most visible—and most festive. Butcher shops advertise young pigs, while supermarket produce sections bulge with yucca, sour oranges, and ripe plantains. Bakeries are crowded with customers buying *buñuelos* (syrup-soaked fritters) and a nougatlike candy called *turron.*

Catholics around the world honor Christmas Eve, but Latin Americans—particularly Cubans— have made it one of the most festive days (or more accurately, nights) of the year. The holiday begins with a late-night feast, followed by dancing and socializing. At midnight, people attend a *misa del gallo,* literally a rooster mass, so called because it's said to end around the time the first rooster crows. A Cuban Noche Buena celebration in Miami combines the belt-loosening largesse of American Thanksgiving with the conviviality of a Fourth of July barbecue.

My own initiation into the Noche Buena festivities came from a man who knows a thing or two about pig roasts. Octogenarian Efrain Veiga Sr., whom my wife and I call Papi, was a butcher in Havana and con-

tinued to work in the meat industry after immigrating to the United States in 1959. (His son, also named Efrain, opened the nation's first *Nuevo Latino* restaurant, YUCA.) The family invited me to participate in a traditional Noche Buena—and help with everything from buying the pig to eating it.

PICKING A PIG

My alarm clock went off at 6 A.M. After fortifying ourselves with steaming cups of *café con leche,* Papi and I drove to Cabrera's in Hialeah Gardens, a blue cinder block building on the outskirts

Building the pit with cinder blocks, chicken wire, and rebar.

of Miami. Even at this very early hour, we found a line at the rough-and-tumble slaughterhouse. We waited our turn to get our pig, a forty-nine-pound *macho* (male) that Papi had selected on account of its plumpness. On a normal day, Cabrera's will process three hundred pigs; right before Christmas, they process twelve hundred in a single day! It's customary for the whole family to come along to Cabrera's when the pig is selected for a Noche Buena dinner. The honor of making the choice is given to the grandfather. Thanks to our early arrival, we left forty-five minutes later with *el macho* safely stowed in the trunk.

PREPARING THE PIG

Once back home, our first task was to soak the pig in a tangy marinade called adobo. Adobo turns up throughout the Spanish-speaking world, varying widely from country to country. Mexico's

The skin is as crisp as a potato chip.

adobo, for example, is a spicy paste of ancho chiles and orange juice. Cuban adobo pits the breath-wilting pungency of fresh garlic (lots of it) against the fragrance of cumin and oregano, with a greenish fruit called *naranja agria* (sour orange) providing a snappy acidity.

Papi supervised the digging of the pit, a rectangular hole, about one foot deep, three feet wide, and four feet long, dug at the end of the driveway. When the dimensions of the hole were just right, Papi lined the pit with a sheet of galvanized steel, then built a fire with a couple of bags of charcoal.

As the coals blazed down to embers, Papi raked them into an area roughly the size of *el macho*, with extra coals at either end to cook the shoulders and hams more quickly. We placed the pig, skin side down, on a grate fashioned from rebars and chicken wire. We splashed on more adobo and covered the pig with banana leaves. The leaves will hold in the moisture and smoke while imparting a distinctive flavor, Papi explained.

Meanwhile, Esther "Mami" Veiga worked on the accompaniments, for no Noche Buena would be complete without a trio of classic Cuban side dishes: *moros y christianos, yuca con mojo,* and fried plantains. The first, literally Moors and Christians, is a Cuban

Banana leaves are placed over the pig to hold in the smoke and moisture.

Cubano roast pig with all the fixin's.

box, close it, and shovel coals on the top. The box acts like a giant oven and produces pork of extraordinary succulence. You can buy *cajas chinas* at hardware stores in Miami. But Papi and I agreed that we'd miss the live fire flavor that comes from roasting the pig over a pit.

FELIZ NAVIDAD

By nightfall, *el macho* was as shiny and dark as mahogany and tender enough to pull apart with your fingers, precisely what Papi invited me to do. The table sagged under the weight of *lechon asado* and its various accompaniments. We splashed garlicky *mojo* over the pork and licked our fingers. At the end, Mami brought out a shimmering flan delicately flavored with lemon and cinnamon for dessert.

Cooking a whole pig can be challenging if you're an apartment dweller—or even if you're an accomplished griller. On page 258, you'll find a recipe for making *lechon asado* with a more manageable cut, pork shoulder. Like the pig, the roast marinates in garlicky adobo, and for additional flavor you can poke holes in the meat so it absorbs even more marinade. But if you're ever in Miami on Christmas Eve, try to get yourself invited to a Noche Buena dinner. You won't regret it.

staple consisting of soupy black beans ladled over white rice. Yucca is Cuban comfort food, a starchy white tuber that tastes vaguely buttery but mostly bland. It's enjoyed the way Anglos eat boiled or mashed potatoes, but instead of adding a mere pat of butter, Cubans use an explosively flavorful sauce called *mojo,* made with fried garlic, cumin, and sour orange juice. The same sauce will be slathered over the grilled pork. As for plantains, these jumbo cooking bananas are another mainstay of the Cuban table and Mami took great pains to procure the softest, blackest, ripest plantains she could find, for these will be delectably sweet.

Like all great barbecue, *lechon asado* requires bursts of intense activity, followed by lots

of sitting around watching the pig roast. As we sipped beer, Papi recalled his last Noche Buena in Cuba. He and his friends cooked an enormous pig, which they strung between two palm trees like a hammock. They swung it back and fourth over the fire until the skin was as crisp as a potato chip. "But Castro changed all that," Papi said and sighed.

After two hours, we turned the pig over, its skin now brown and crackling. We added enough fresh coals for an additional hour and a half of roasting. Our talk turned to another artifact of a Cuban Noche Buena: the *caja china,* or Chinese box. This is a metal crate a bit larger than a steamer trunk, which many Cubans use in place of a barbecue pit. You place the pig in the

Lechon asado is traditionally served with sweet fried plantains. I like plantains grilled even better, and on page 615 you'll find an easy-to-make recipe.

Miami, Fla.

LECHON ASADO (Cuban Citrus and Garlic Roast Pork)

No trip to Miami would be complete without *lechon asado*. The term means many things in the casual Spanish of Miami's Cubans: roast suckling pig, baked pork shoulder, barbecued whole hog, not to mention a roast pork and *mojo* sandwich that's one of the glories of Cuban American cooking. *Lechon asado* is enjoyed daily in Miami's Little Havana, but the dish assumes almost mythic proportions when served on December 24, the night of the feast the Cubans call Noche Buena (see page 255 for a description). Tradition calls for cooking a whole pig, but pork shoulder comes out very nearly as splendid and is a lot easier to work with.

METHOD:
Indirect grilling

ADVANCE PREPARATION:
12 to 24 hours for marinating the pork

INGREDIENTS:
1 head garlic, broken into cloves
   and finely chopped
1 tablespoon coarse salt
   (kosher or sea)
2 teaspoons ground cumin
2 teaspoons dried oregano
1 teaspoon freshly ground black pepper,
   plus pepper for seasoning the roast
2 cups sour orange juice (see Note),
   or 1½ cups fresh lime juice
   (from 18 limes) and ½ cup fresh
   orange juice (from 3 oranges)
1 tablespoon olive oil
1 pork shoulder (5 to 7 pounds)
Coarse salt (kosher or sea) and
   freshly ground black pepper
2 cups Mojo (recipe follows),
   for serving
Grilled plantains (optional; page 615),
   for serving

1 Place the garlic and salt in a mortar and, using a pestle, pound to a paste, or place them in a bowl and mash them with the back of a wooden spoon. Add the cumin, oregano, pepper, sour orange juice, and olive oil and stir to combine thoroughly. Alternatively, you can use a food processor: Add the garlic, salt, cumin, oregano, and pepper and pulse to make a paste. With the motor running, add the sour orange juice and olive oil through the feed tube. The marinade should be the consistency of salad dressing.

2 Using the tip of a chef's knife, make ½-inch-deep slits all over the pork, 2 inches apart. Place the pork in a nonreactive baking dish. Pour the marinade all over the pork, massaging the marinade into the slits with your fingertips. Let the pork marinate in the refrigerator for 12 to 24 hours, turning it several times so that it marinates evenly. Keep the pork securely covered with plastic wrap to hold in the garlic fumes.

3 Set up the grill for indirect grilling (see page 22 for charcoal or page 23 for gas) and preheat to medium.

4 When ready to cook, drain the marinade from the pork and discard the marinade. Season the pork generously on all sides with salt and pepper. Place the pork, fat side up, in the center of the hot grate, over the drip pan and away from the heat. Cover the grill and cook the pork until nicely browned and cooked through, 3 to 4 hours. To test for doneness, use an instant-read meat thermometer: The internal temperature should be about 195°F (Cubans like their pork more well-done than do most Americans). If the pork starts to brown too much (and it probably will), reduce the heat to medium-low and cover the pork loosely with aluminum foil. If using a charcoal grill, every hour you'll need to add 12 fresh coals per side.

5 Transfer the cooked pork to a cutting board and let it rest for 10 minutes. Slice it and serve with the *Mojo* and grilled plantains.

YIELD:
Serves 10 to 12

NOTE: Sour oranges are greenish-orange fruits that look like oranges but taste like limes. They are available at most Miami supermarkets and elsewhere at Hispanic and West Indian grocery stores. You'll need about 9 sour oranges for 2 cups of juice and about 6 for 1⅓ cups of juice.

Mojo (Cuban Citrus and Garlic Sauce)

First things first. The name of this sauce is pronounced MO-ho, not mo-joe. And it's hard to think of a Cuban grilled or roast meat that *isn't* served with this garlicky, cumin-flavored citrus sauce. Every food market (super or otherwise) in Miami sells bottled *mojo,* but the end product is infinitely tastier if you make your own from scratch. The sauce lives and dies by its main ingredient—fresh garlic.

INGREDIENTS:

1 cup olive oil
12 cloves garlic, thinly sliced crosswise
1⅓ cups fresh sour orange juice
    (see Note at left), or 1 cup
    fresh lime juice (from 12 limes)
    and ⅓ cup fresh orange juice
    (from 2 oranges)
2 teaspoons coarse salt (kosher or sea),
    or more to taste
2 teaspoons ground cumin
1 teaspoon freshly ground black pepper,
    or more to taste
1 teaspoon dried oregano
½ cup chopped fresh cilantro

1 Heat the olive oil in a deep non-reactive saucepan over medium heat. Add the garlic and cook until fragrant and a pale golden brown, 2 to 3 minutes. Do not let the garlic brown too much or it will become bitter.

2 Stir in the sour orange juice, salt, cumin, pepper, and oregano, and

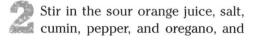

2/3 cup of water. Stand back as you do this; the sauce may sputter. Raise the heat to medium-high and let the sauce come to a rolling boil. Taste for seasoning, adding more salt and/or pepper as necessary. Let the sauce cool to room temperature, then stir in the cilantro. Serve the *mojo* in a nonreactive bowl; be sure to stir it well before using. The sauce can be made up to 3 hours ahead; do not add the cilantro until just before using. If it sits, taste for seasoning again, adding more salt and/or pepper as necessary.

YIELD:

Makes 3 cups, enough for the Lechon Asado and the grilled plantains on page 615.

El Paso, Tex.

BOURBON AND APRICOT SPIT-ROASTED HAM

Park Kerr is a founder of the El Paso Chile Company. This alone should endear him to barbecue buffs, but he also hosts a zany television cooking show called *Let's Get Cooking* (think of it as the Galloping Gourmet meets MTV). Some time ago, I joined him at his home in El Paso to tape a show on Floridian grilling. Between takes, Park prepared this spit-roasted

fresh shoulder ham, which would make an offbeat centerpiece for an Easter barbecue—or any cookout. The bourbon-apricot barbecue sauce caramelizes while it grills, forming a crisp, candy-sweet crust.

METHOD:
Rotisserie grilling

FOR THE RUB:
2 cups firmly packed light brown sugar
1/4 cup dry mustard
1 tablespoon ground ginger
1/2 teaspoon ground cloves

FOR THE BOURBON AND APRICOT BARBECUE SAUCE:
2 cups apricot preserves
3/4 cup Dijon mustard
1/2 cup bourbon
1 tablespoon grated peeled fresh ginger
2 cloves garlic, minced

FOR THE HAM:
1 boneless fresh shoulder ham (about 3 pounds)
Coarse salt (kosher or sea) and freshly ground black pepper
1/2 cup Dijon mustard

YOU'LL ALSO NEED:
2 cups wood chips or chunks (optional), soaked for 1 hour in water to cover, then drained

1 MAKE THE RUB: Place the brown sugar, dry mustard, ground ginger, and cloves in a large bowl and stir to mix. (Actually, your fingers work better for mixing a rub than a spoon or whisk does.) Set the rub aside.

2 MAKE THE BOURBON AND APRICOT BARBECUE SAUCE: Combine the apricot preserves, ¾ cup mustard, the bourbon, grated ginger, and garlic in a large heavy nonreactive saucepan and bring to a boil over medium-high heat, whisking to mix. Reduce the heat to medium and let the sauce simmer until thick and flavorful, 5 to 8 minutes. Set the barbecue sauce aside.

3 Set up the grill for rotisserie grilling, following the manufacturer's instructions, and preheat to medium-high. If using a gas grill, place all of the wood chips or chunks, if desired, in the smoker box or in a smoker pouch (see page 24) and run the grill on high until you see smoke, then reduce the heat to medium-high. If using a charcoal grill, preheat it to medium-high, then toss 1 cup of the wood chips or chunks, if desired, on the coals.

4 Generously season the ham all over with salt and pepper. Skewer it on the turnspit. Brush the ham on all sides with the ½ cup mustard and thickly crust it with the rub, patting the rub onto the ham with your fingertips.

5 When ready to cook, attach the spit to the rotisserie mechanism by inserting the pointed end of the spit into the rotisserie motor socket. If your rotisserie spit has a counterweight, position it so that it counterbalances the ham. Turn on the motor and grill the ham until the outside is handsomely browned and the ham is cooked through, 1¼ to 1½ hours. To test for doneness, use an instant-read meat thermometer: The internal temperature should be about 160°F. After the ham has grilled for 45 minutes, baste it with some of the barbecue sauce, continuing to baste it with some of the barbecue sauce every 15 minutes. If using a charcoal grill, after 1 hour you'll need to add 12 fresh coals to each side and toss the remaining 1 cup of wood chips or chunks, if using, on the coals (½ cup per side).

6 Unspit the ham onto a platter or cutting board and let it rest for 10 minutes. Thinly slice the ham, serving the remaining barbecue sauce on the side.

YIELD:

Serves 6 to 8

VARIATION: If you don't have a rotisserie, you can grill the pork using the indirect cooking method.

Fresh shoulder hams come from the forequarters of the pig. Take care to buy a ham that is not cured or salted. You could also use a pork loin. It will take 1 to 1½ hours to cook.

THE EL PASO CHILE CO.

DOWNTOWN EL PASO, TEXAS

There are lots of
possibilities for rubs
to use here: The
Cold Mountain Rub
on page 701, the
Four, Three, Two,
One Rub on page
703, or your favorite
commercial brand
will all produce good
results.

Tennessee

TENNESSEE PORK LOIN
With Whiskey, Brown Sugar, and Mustard

What constitutes Tennessee barbecue? I posed this question during my travels on the barbecue trail and got about as many answers as the number of people I asked. For some it was synonymous with the dry rub used on the ribs at the Rendezvous in Memphis. For others, it was characterized by the sweet, vinegary tomato sauces slathered on barbecue in and around Nashville. One pit master mentioned a pork shoulder that was cut in half, stuffed with brown sugar and mustard, and slowly smoked over hickory. Another spoke lovingly of a pork roast that was swaddled in bacon and barbecued in a pit. And, of course, no Tennessee barbecue should be without a shot of whiskey—on this point everyone agreed.

After pursuing all these regional variations, I decided it might just be easier to incorporate them into a single recipe. This pork loin plays pinball on your taste buds, offering the sweetness of brown sugar, the tang of

... no Tennessee

mustard, and the rich smoke flavor of bacon (the bacon also helps keep the meat moist). And just for polish, there's a Tennessee whisky glaze.

METHOD:
Indirect grilling

FOR THE PORK:
1 center-cut piece of pork loin
   (2½ to 3 pounds)
3 tablespoons Tennessee whiskey
2 tablespoons of your favorite barbecue rub
   (see Tip at left)
3 tablespoons Dijon mustard
½ cup firmly packed brown sugar
4 slices bacon

FOR THE GLAZE:
3 tablespoons salted butter
3 tablespoons brown sugar
3 tablespoons Dijon mustard
3 tablespoons Tennessee whiskey

Nashville Sweet barbecue sauce
   (optional; page 669), for serving

YOU'LL ALSO NEED:
Butcher's string; 2 cups wood chips or
   chunks (preferably hickory), soaked for
   1 hour in water to cover, then drained

1 BUTTERFLY THE PORK LOIN: Using a very sharp knife, cut the roast almost in half lengthwise through one side (stop about 1 inch from the opposite side). Open the roast up as you would a book. Sprinkle the inside of the roast with 1 tablespoon of the whiskey and let it marinate for 5 minutes.

arbecue should be without a shot of whiskey . . .

Sprinkle a third of the rub over the inside of the roast. Spread the mustard on top with a spatula, then sprinkle the brown sugar on top of the mustard. Sprinkle the remaining 2 tablespoons of whiskey on top of the brown sugar. Fold the roast back together (like closing a book) and sprinkle the remaining rub over the outside.

2 Cut four 12-inch pieces of butcher's string. Position the pieces of string on the work surface so that they are parallel and roughly 2 inches apart. Place a slice of bacon across the strings so that it is perpendicular to and in the center of them. Set the roast on top of the bacon, positioning its long side parallel to the bacon. Place a slice of bacon on top of the roast. Press the remaining 2 slices against the long sides of the roast. Tie each piece of string together around the roast so that they hold the slices of bacon against it. Set the pork roast aside.

3 MAKE THE GLAZE: Combine the butter, brown sugar, mustard, and whiskey in a saucepan and boil until syrupy, 4 to 6 minutes. Set the glaze aside.

4 Set up the grill for indirect grilling (see page 23 for gas or page 22 for charcoal) and preheat to medium. If using a gas grill, place all of the wood chips or chunks in the smoker box or in a smoker pouch (see page 24) and run the grill on high until you see smoke, then reduce the heat to medium. If using a charcoal grill, place a large drip pan in the center, preheat the grill to medium, then toss all of the wood chips or chunks on the coals.

5 When ready to cook, place the pork roast on the hot grate, over the drip pan and away from the heat and cover the grill. Cook the roast until cooked through, 1 to 1½ hours. To test for doneness, insert an instant-read meat thermometer into the side of the roast: The internal temperature should be about 160°F. Start basting the roast with some of the glaze after 30 minutes and continue basting every 15 minutes. If you are using a charcoal grill and the pork is not done after 1 hour, you'll need to add 12 fresh coals to each side.

6 Transfer the cooked roast to a cutting board and let it rest for 5 minutes, then remove and discard the strings. Slice the roast crosswise and drizzle any remaining glaze over it. If you like, serve the Nashville Sweet barbecue sauce alongside.

YIELD:
Serves 6

VARIATION: I've written this recipe for a pork loin roast, which is readily available, quick to prepare, and easy to serve. But you can certainly use a pork shoulder. If you do, you'll need to increase the cooking time by 1½ to 2 hours on a grill or 3 to 4 hours in a smoker.

TIPS

If making a tunnel through the pork loin seems too intimidating, you can butterfly the loin: Using a very sharp knife, cut it almost in half lengthwise through one side (stop about one inch from the opposite side). Open the loin up as you would a book. Spread the stuffing inside, fold the loin closed, and tie it closed in three or four places with butcher's string.

Sioux Falls, S.Dak.

PIG IN AN ORCHARD (Apple-Stuffed, Chile-Glazed Pork Loin)

Pity Omer "Mike" Nelson. It isn't easy being a smoke master in Sioux Falls, South Dakota. To most Dakotans, barbecue means hamburger mixed with barbecue sauce— what the rest of us would call a sloppy joe. As for pit cooking and smoke roasting, they're simply not part of the landscape. That's starting to change,

Mike Nelson, the South Dakota pig meister.

reports Omer, but a couple decades ago, when the twenty-one-year radio veteran wanted to experience true 'que, he had to venture to Kansas City. His contribution to South Dakota's emerging barbecue culture is the poetically named Pig in an Orchard, a pork loin stuffed with honey-laced dried apples, glazed with jalapeño jelly, and slow smoked over apple wood. I'd say Omer has made up for lost time, and he certainly does South Dakota proud.

METHOD:
Indirect grilling

INGREDIENTS:
1 center-cut piece of pork loin
    (2½ to 3 pounds)
1 package (4 ounces) dried apples
    (about 1⅓ cups)
½ teaspoon ground cinnamon
½ teaspoon ground nutmeg
¼ teaspoon ground allspice
Coarse salt (kosher or sea) and
    freshly ground black pepper
2 to 3 tablespoons honey
1 tablespoon olive oil
¼ cup red jalapeño pepper jelly
    (see Note)
Spicy Apple Glaze (optional; recipe follows)

YOU'LL ALSO NEED:
2 cups wood chips or chunks
    (preferably apple), soaked for 1 hour
    in water to cover, then drained

1 Make a tunnel through the center of the loin: The easiest way to do this is to insert a long (12- to 14-inch) slender carving knife in one end of the loin, pushing it all the way through to the other. If you don't have a knife that long, insert a slender knife into one end of the roast and a second slender knife into the other end until the knife tips touch in the middle. Then widen the slit into a tunnel: Insert the handle of a wooden spoon into the slit and wiggle it in all directions to make a larger hole. Set the loin aside.

2 Place the dried apples in a bowl. Add the cinnamon, nutmeg, allspice, and a little salt and pepper and toss to mix. Stir in enough honey to moisten the apples. Insert the honeyed apples in the tunnel in the pork loin, using the handle of a wooden spoon to push them to the center. Insert some of the apples from one end, some from the other (the idea is to fill the pork loin). Lightly brush the loin with the olive oil and season very generously on all sides with salt and pepper.

3 Set up the grill for indirect grilling (see page 23 for gas or page 22 for charcoal) and preheat to medium. If using a gas grill, place all of the wood chips or chunks in the smoker box or in a smoker pouch (see page 24) and run the grill on high until you see smoke, then reduce the heat to medium. If using a charcoal grill, place a large drip pan in the center, preheat the grill to medium, then toss all of the wood chips or chunks on the coals.

4 When ready to cook, place the loin in the center of the hot grate, over the drip pan and away from the heat. Cover the grill and cook the roast until nicely browned and almost cooked through, 1 to 1 1/4 hours. At this point, if you insert an instant-read meat thermometer into the meat, the internal temperature should be about 165°F. If using a charcoal grill, you'll need to add 12 fresh coals to each side.

5 Brush the loin on all sides with the jalapeño jelly. Cover the grill again and continue cooking for 10 to 15 minutes longer. When done, the internal temperature of the pork should be about 160°F.

6 Transfer the cooked loin to a cutting board and let rest for 10 minutes. To serve, carve the loin crosswise into 1/2-inch slices. Fan these out on a platter or plates. Spoon the Spicy Apple Glaze, if using, over the slices of pork and serve at once.

YIELD:
Serves 6

NOTE: Red jalapeño pepper jelly is available at specialty food stores, or see Mail-Order Sources on page 742.

Spicy Apple Glaze

Gild the lily with a sauce containing only three ingredients: apple jelly, Thai chile sauce, and lime juice. The electrifying combination perfectly suits the fruit-stuffed pork.

INGREDIENTS:

¾ cup apple jelly

**¼ cup Thai sweet chile sauce
    (nuoe cham ga; see Note)**

1 tablespoon fresh lime juice

Place the apple jelly, chile sauce, and lime juice in a heavy nonreactive saucepan over medium heat. Let cook until the jelly is melted, 3 to 5 minutes, stirring the glaze with a wooden spoon. Keep the glaze over low heat until ready to use.

YIELD:

Makes about 1 cup

NOTE: Sweet Thai chile sauce (*nuoe cham ga*) is available at Asian markets and in the foreign food section of some supermarkets.

Kentucky

COFFEE-CRUSTED PORK TENDERLOINS
With Redeye Barbecue Sauce

Some years ago I served as an interpreter for a French chef on a teaching tour in the United States. I'll never forget his astonishment when one of our hosts ordered coffee to drink with dinner. Coffee is woven deeply into America's social fabric, and cowboys drank it with meat around a campfire long before anyone heard of Starbucks. Coffee is a traditional ingredient in at least one classic Southern pork dish: country ham with redeye gravy, a dish I last enjoyed in Louisville. Kentucky ham isn't quite as well-known as that from Virginia, but it's every bit as tasty and it gave me the idea for this coffee-crusted pork tenderloin served with a coffee barbecue sauce.

METHOD:

Direct grilling

ADVANCE PREPARATION:

4 to 12 hours for marinating the tenderloins

INGREDIENTS:

**1½ pounds pork tenderloin
    (2 to 3 tenderloins)**

3 tablespoons ground coffee

1 tablespoon coarse salt (kosher or sea)

1 tablespoon dark brown sugar

2 teaspoons sweet paprika

1 teaspoon freshly ground black pepper

1 teaspoon garlic powder

1 teaspoon onion powder

½ teaspoon ground cumin

½ teaspoon ground coriander

½ teaspoon unsweetened cocoa powder *or cinn*

2 tablespoons canola oil

Redeye Barbecue Sauce (recipe follows)

YOU'LL ALSO NEED:

**Butcher's string; 2 cups wood chips or
    chunks (preferably oak or mesquite),
    soaked for 1 hour in water to cover,
    then drained**

TIPS

These tenderloins aren't smoked per se, but the wood chips tossed on the coals impart a whiff of wood smoke.

1 Place a tenderloin on your work surface. Remove the silver skin (the thin, translucent, sinewlike covering on the outside) by using a knife to trim it away from the meat. About 3 inches from the end of the "tail" (the skinny end), make a crosswise cut, slicing about halfway through the meat. This will enable you to fold the "tail" back over the rest of the roast, giving the tenderloin a roughly cylindrical shape, which will help it to cook more evenly. Tie the "tail" in place with butcher's string. Repeat with the remaining tenderloin(s). Place the tenderloins in a baking dish.

2 Place the coffee, salt, brown sugar, paprika, pepper, garlic and onion powders, cumin, coriander, and cocoa in a small bowl and stir to mix. (Actually, your fingers work better for mixing a rub than a spoon or whisk does.) Sprinkle this rub all over the tenderloins, patting it onto the meat with your fingertips. Drizzle the oil over the pork and rub it on well. Let the pork marinate in the refrigerator, covered, for at least 4 hours or as long as overnight.

3 Set up the grill for direct grilling (see page 21 for gas or charcoal) and preheat to medium-high. If using a gas grill, place all of the wood chips or chunks in the smoker box or in a smoker pouch (see page 24) and run the grill on high until you see smoke, then reduce the heat to medium-high. If using a charcoal grill, preheat it to medium-high, then toss all of the wood chips or chunks on the coals.

4 When ready to cook, brush and oil the grill grate. Place the pork tenderloins on the hot grate and grill until cooked through, 3 to 4 minutes per side (12 to 16 minutes in all). To test for doneness, insert an instant-read meat thermometer into the meat: The internal temperature should be about 160°F.

5 Transfer the grilled pork to a cutting board and let rest for about 3 minutes. Remove and discard the strings, then slice the tenderloins crosswise on a diagonal and serve at once with Redeye Barbecue Sauce on the side.

YIELD:
Serves 4

VARIATION: You could also grill a larger, fattier cut of pork, like Boston butt or pork shoulder using the coffee rub. In this case, I'd use the indirect method of grilling and medium heat. A 5-pound pork shoulder will take 3 to 4 hours to cook.

TIPS

I don't generally bother to trim the fat off pork tenderloin; it helps baste the meat as it cooks. But I do like to score and fold over the "tail" to obtain a cylindrical roast that will grill evenly. You'll find instructions for doing this in Step 1.

Redeye Barbecue Sauce

Inspired by the redeye gravies of the American South, this barbecue sauce contrasts the bittersweet flavor of coffee with the richness of bacon and cream. I bet you can't eat just a single spoonful.

INGREDIENTS:

1 tablespoon butter

1 slice bacon, finely chopped

**1/2 medium-size onion,
     finely chopped**

1 clove garlic, minced

**3/4 cup brewed strong coffee or
     espresso**

3/4 cup ketchup

1/4 cup Worcestershire sauce

1/4 cup heavy (whipping) cream

2 tablespoons Dijon mustard

2 tablespoons molasses

2 tablespoons brown sugar

**Coarse salt (kosher or sea) and
     freshly ground black pepper**

1 Melt the butter in a heavy saucepan over medium heat. Add the bacon, onion, and garlic and cook until lightly browned, about 3 minutes. Stir in the coffee, ketchup, Worcestershire sauce, cream, mustard, molasses, and brown sugar and let the mixture gradually come to a boil.

2 Reduce the heat slightly and let the sauce simmer until thick and richly flavored, about 10 minutes, whisking from time to time. Season with salt and pepper to taste. You can serve the sauce hot or at room temperature. It can be made up to 2 days ahead and refrigerated, covered. Bring the sauce to room temperature before serving.

YIELD:

Makes about 2 cups

Florida

SOY-GLAZED GRILLED PORK TENDERLOINS

Pork has a natural affinity for soy sauce and vinegar—a fact appreciated by anyone who's enjoyed Asian-style grilled pork in Hawaii or Vancouver. The idea of combining them comes from a Franco-Hispano grill man named Eziquiel "Kelo" d'Andre. Kelo's garlicky soy and vinegar marinade is equally remarkable for its simplicity and its mouth-filling flavor. I've used it with the tenderloins here, but it's also pretty terrific with pork chops, lamb, and even beef.

METHOD:

Direct grilling

ADVANCE PREPARATION:

4 to 12 hours for marinating the pork

INGREDIENTS:

**1 1/2 pounds pork tenderloin
     (2 to 3 tenderloins)**

1 cup soy sauce

1/2 cup red wine vinegar

1 tablespoon vegetable oil

1 tablespoon minced fresh garlic

2 teaspoons dried oregano

1 teaspoon cracked black peppercorns

YOU'LL ALSO NEED:

Butcher's string

1 Place a tenderloin on your work surface. Remove the silver skin (the thin, translucent, sinewlike covering on the outside) by using a knife to trim it away from the meat. About 3 inches from the end of the "tail" (the skinny end), make a crosswise cut, slicing about halfway through the meat. This will enable you to fold the "tail" back over the rest of the roast, giving the tenderloin a roughly cylindrical shape, which will help it to cook more evenly. Tie the "tail" in place with butcher's string. Repeat with the remaining tenderloin(s). Place the tenderloins in a baking dish.

2 Place the soy sauce, vinegar, oil, garlic, oregano, and peppercorns in a nonreactive bowl and whisk to mix. Pour this marinade over the pork and let it marinate in the refrigerator, covered, for at least 4 hours, preferably overnight, turning the tenderloins several times so that they marinate evenly.

3 Drain the marinade from the pork, place it in a saucepan, and bring to a boil over medium-high heat. Boil for 2 minutes. You'll use this for basting the pork.

4 Set up the grill for direct grilling using a two-zone fire (see page 22 for charcoal or gas) and preheat one zone to high and the other to medium.

5 When ready to cook, brush and oil the grill grate. Place the tenderloins over the hot zone of the grill to sear the outsides, 1 to 2 minutes per side (4 to 8 minutes in all). Transfer the pork to the medium zone of the grill and continue cooking it until done, about 2 minutes per side longer (about 12 to 16 minutes in all) for medium. To test for doneness, insert an instant-read meat thermometer into the meat: The internal temperature should be about 160°F. Baste each side twice with some of the boiled marinade.

6 Transfer the grilled pork to a cutting board and let it rest for about 3 minutes. Baste the tenderloins once more with any remaining marinade, then slice them crosswise on a diagonal and serve at once.

YIELD:
Serves 4

Barbecue on the hoof.

Tradition calls for adobos to be stewed, not grilled, but using the sauce as a marinade gives pork a terrific flavor and it cooks down to make an interesting barbecue sauce. You could also marinate pork chops the same way.

Tongs at the ready, this vendor serves up grilled pork kebabs.

Hawaii

GRILLED PORK KEBABS With Hawaiian Filipino Adobo

Filipino cuisine is one of the world's best-kept food secrets. Even if you live in a city with a large Asian community, like San Francisco or Seattle, I bet you'd be hard pressed to name a single Filipino dish. This is a shame, because Filipino cooks draw on two rich culinary traditions—the Iberian cuisine of its Spanish colonizers and the vibrant flavors of the Far East.

Consider the following pork tenderloin adobo. As the adobo moved from Spain to the Philippines, it picked up Asian seasonings, such as ginger and soy sauce, a combination that's hard to resist. This recipe comes not from the Philippines, but from Hawaii—home to a large Filipino community and one of the few places in the United States where Filipino cuisine is accorded the respect it deserves.

METHOD:
Direct grilling

ADVANCE PREPARATION:
2 to 8 hours for marinating the pork

INGREDIENTS:
1½ pounds pork loin or tenderloin (2 to 3 tenderloins)
Coarse salt (kosher or sea) and freshly ground black pepper
1 medium-size onion, thinly sliced
3 cloves garlic, thinly sliced
1 piece (1 inch) fresh ginger, peeled and cut into matchstick slivers
2 scallions, trimmed, white parts minced, green parts thinly sliced
1 cup soy sauce
⅔ cup rice vinegar or white wine vinegar, or more to taste
1 tablespoon sweet paprika
3 bay leaves
2 tablespoons Asian (dark) sesame oil
1 large onion, peeled
2 tablespoons (¼ stick) butter
2 tablespoons vegetable oil

YOU'LL ALSO NEED:
8 long bamboo or metal skewers (12 inches each)

1 Place a tenderloin on your work surface. Remove the silver skin (the thin, translucent, sinewlike covering on the outside) by using a knife to trim it away from the meat. Cut the meat into 1-inch cubes and place these in a nonreactive baking dish.

2 Generously season the pork on all sides with salt and pepper, rubbing them onto the meat with your fingertips. Add the sliced onion, garlic, ginger, scallion whites, soy sauce, vinegar, paprika, bay leaves, and sesame oil to the baking dish. Turn the pork several times to coat it with the marinade. Let the pork marinate in the refrigerator, covered, for at least 2 hours or as long as 8, stirring the cubes several times so that they marinate evenly.

3 Cut the large onion lengthwise into quarters, then cut each quarter in half crosswise. Break the onion pieces into individual layers (this will give you flattish pieces for threading onto the kebabs).

4 Drain the marinade from the pork, place it in a saucepan, and bring to a boil over medium heat. Let simmer briskly until the mixture is reduced by about a third and syrupy, about 5 minutes. After 3 minutes, add the butter. Stir the sauce as it cooks. Taste for seasoning, adding salt and pepper, plus a splash of vinegar if necessary; the sauce should be piquant and highly seasoned. Keep the sauce warm until serving.

5 Thread the marinated pork cubes onto skewers, placing a piece of onion between each cube.

6 Set up the grill for direct grilling (see page 21 for charcoal or gas) and preheat to high.

A pushcart grill for urban 'que heads.

7 When ready to cook, brush and oil the grill grate. Place the pork kebabs on the hot grate and grill until golden brown and cooked through, 2 to 3 minutes per side (8 to 12 minutes in all). Baste the kebabs with the vegetable oil as they cook. During the last 2 minutes of grilling, brush the kebabs with a little of the sauce.

8 Transfer the kebabs to a platter or plates and spoon the remaining sauce on top (or spoon sauce on plates and arrange the pork on top). Sprinkle the scallion greens over the kebabs and serve at once.

YIELD:
Serves 4

Lockhart, Tex.

"RACK" OF PORK
In the Style of Kreuz Market

Pork is the last thing you'd expect to find at the legendary Kreuz Market in Lockhart, Texas. Beef is the name of the game in these parts— crusty briskets, meaty clods (beef shoulders), prime ribs dark and glistening with wood smoke. Their "rack" of pork originated back in the days when Kreuz was a meat market. Some cost-minded butcher must have decided it would be better to cook a leftover rack of pork chops in the pit, rather than to leave it unsold. Even today rack of pork is something of an afterthought. "We put some on the pit," explained Kreuz Market's owner, Don Schmidt. "When we sell out of it, well, that's that." There are afterthoughts and there are afterthoughts, and despite its lack of sauces or special seasonings, Kreuz's dark, smoky, moist rack of pork remains one of the most glorious ways you can eat this meat. It's so good, you don't even need a sauce. (For more about Kreuz Market, see page 166.)

METHOD:
Indirect grilling

The cavernous Kreuz Market stands ready to serve barbecue to the multitudes.

FOR THE "RACK":

1 tablespoon salt

¹/₂ tablespoon cracked black peppercorns

2 teaspoons cayenne pepper

1 rack of pork (5 to 5¹/₂ pounds; see Note)

FOR SERVING, ANY OF THE FOLLOWING:

Saltine crackers or white bread

Sweet or sour pickles

Pickled jalapeño peppers

Diced onion

Diced avocado

YOU'LL ALSO NEED:

**Butcher's string; 2 cups wood chips
or chunks (preferably oak),
soaked for 1 hour in water to cover,
then drained**

1 Place the salt, peppercorns, and cayenne in a small bowl and stir to mix. (Actually, if you do not have sensitive skin, your fingers work better for mixing a rub than a spoon or whisk does.) Generously sprinkle the rub all over the pork, patting it onto the meat with your fingertips. Tie a piece of butcher's string lengthwise around the rack to hold the chops together.

2 Set up the grill for indirect grilling (see page 23 for gas or page 22 for charcoal) and preheat to medium-high. If using a gas grill, place all of the wood chips or chunks in the smoker box or a smoker pouch (see page 24) and run the grill on high until you see smoke, then reduce the heat to medium-high. If using a charcoal grill, place a large drip pan in the center, preheat the grill to medium-high, then toss 1 cup of the wood chips or chunks on the coals.

3 When ready to cook, place the pork in the center of the hot grate, with the ends of the bones pointing up, over the drip pan and away from the heat. Cover the grill and cook the pork until nicely browned and cooked through, 1¹/₂ to 2 hours. To test for doneness, insert an instant-read meat thermometer through the side of the rack but not so that it touches a bone. The internal temperature should be about 160°F. If using a charcoal grill, after 1 hour you'll need to add 12 fresh coals to each side and toss the remaining 1 cup of wood chips or chunks (¹/₂ cup per side) on the coals.

4 Transfer the cooked pork to a cutting board and let rest for 5 minutes, then remove the string and cut the rack into chops. Kreuz Market serves the pork with your choice of saltine crackers or white bread, sweet or sour pickles, pickled jalapeño peppers, and diced onion or avocado. Just don't serve it with sauce.

YIELD:

Serves 6

NOTE: A "rack" of pork is a roast made up of chops (either rib or loin). Kreuz Market uses pork T-bones—chops with the tenderloin attached. This is not a roast commonly sold at the supermarket (stores get more money by selling the pork as individual chops), so you'll need to go to a butcher shop and specially order a 6-chop rack. Ask the butcher to

TIPS

Kreuz Market cooks all its meats at a relatively high heat over oak. To most closely approximate the flavor they get, fire your pit or kettle grill with oak chunks or logs (see page 20 for instructions for grilling over a wood fire). Or, you can use wood chips with a charcoal or gas grill.

cut through the chine bone between the chops to facilitate carving when the rack is cooked.

VARIATION: In the best of all worlds, you'd grill over oak logs in an offset smoker or over oak chunks in a kettle grill. If you use a kettle grill, light the chunks in a chimney starter and transfer the embers to the side baskets or rake them into 2 piles at opposite sides of the grill.

New England

CIDER-GRILLED PORK PORTERHOUSE

Pork is often served with apples. The reason is simple: The fruity tartness of an apple makes the perfect counterpoint to the fatty richness of pork. And pork gets a double blast of apple flavor in this recipe: first from the apple marinade, then from the suave, sweet cider sauce. As a side dish, I'd serve honey-glazed Apple "Steaks"; as a beverage, sweet or hard cider. The New England roots of this recipe are obvious—in both the use of apple cider and in the presence of sage, a traditional Yankee seasoning for everything from turkey stuffing to cheese.

TIPS

I originally conceived of this dish as being grilled in a fireplace. To achieve a similar result on the grill, grill the chops directly over apple wood chunks in a charcoal grill (see Grilling over a Wood Fire, page 20) or add some apple wood chips to your gas grill.

METHOD:
Direct grilling

ADVANCE PREPARATION:
2 to 4 hours for marinating the pork

INGREDIENTS:
4 pork "porterhouse steaks" or
    loin chops (each 1 inch thick
    and 10 to 12 ounces)
1 cup apple cider
4 tablespoons Asian (dark) sesame oil,
    walnut oil, or olive oil
2 tablespoons honey
2 tablespoons soy sauce
2 strips lemon zest (each about 2 by
    ½ inch; see Note)
2 tablespoons fresh lemon juice
8 fresh sage leaves, or 1 teaspoon
    dried sage
2 scallions, white parts gently
    crushed with the side of a cleaver,
    green parts finely chopped
2 cloves garlic, peeled and gently
    crushed with the side of a cleaver
2 slices fresh ginger (¼ inch thick),
    peeled and gently crushed with
    the side of a cleaver
2 tablespoons unsalted butter
Coarse salt (kosher or sea) and
    freshly ground black pepper
Apple "Steaks" (optional; page 628)

YOU'LL ALSO NEED:
1 cup wood chips or chunks
    (optional; preferably apple),
    soaked for 1 hour in water to cover,
    then drained

1 Trim any excess fat off the pork chops. Place the chops in a nonreactive baking dish just large enough to hold them or in a resealable plastic bag.

2 Combine the cider, 3 tablespoons of the sesame oil, the honey, soy sauce, lemon zest and juice, sage, scallion whites, garlic, and ginger in a nonreactive mixing bowl and stir until well mixed. Pour this marinade over the pork chops and let them marinate in the refrigerator, covered, for 2 to 4 hours, turning the chops several times so that they marinate evenly.

3 Drain the marinade from the chops, place it in a heavy nonreactive saucepan, and bring to a boil over high heat. Let boil until thick, syrupy, and reduced to about 1 cup, 6 to 10 minutes. Whisk in the butter and season to taste with salt and pepper. This will serve as your sauce.

4 Set up the grill for direct grilling (see page 21 for gas or charcoal) and preheat to high. If using a gas grill, place all of the wood chips or chunks, if desired, in the smoker box or in a smoker pouch (see page 24) and run the grill on high until you see smoke. If using a charcoal grill, preheat it to high, then toss all of the wood chips, if desired, on the coals.

5 When ready to cook, blot the chops dry with paper towels. Brush the chops on both sides with the remaining 1 tablespoon of sesame oil and season generously with salt and pepper. Brush and oil the grill grate. Grill the chops until cooked through, about 6 minutes per side, rotating them a quarter turn after 3 minutes to create an attractive crosshatch of grill marks. When ready to turn, the chops will be nicely browned

Select your cut for barbecue pleasure.

on the bottom. To test for doneness, use the poke method; the meat should be firm but just gently yielding. Or insert an instant-read meat thermometer sideways into a chop: The internal temperature should be about 160°F.

6 Transfer the grilled pork to a platter or plates and let rest for 2 minutes, then spoon the cider sauce on top. Serve with the Apple "Steaks," if desired.

YIELD:
Serves 4

NOTE: You can use a vegetable peeler to remove the oil-rich, yellow outer rind of the lemon in strips of zest. Be careful to leave behind the bitter white pith.

VARIATION: Pork "porterhouse steaks" are the most lavish cut you can use in this recipe, but you could certainly use a rib chop or even a boneless chop, in which case the cooking time would be about 4 minutes per side.

TIPS

A pork "porterhouse" is a loin chop with the tenderloin attached.

TIPS

■ Where do you find double-thick pork chops? Ask your butcher to cut a rack of pork into chops with two or even three bones each.

■ Hal smokes his chops in a souped-up Ole Hickory Pit, a large boxlike stainless steel commercial cooker, but the recipe is great cooked on a charcoal grill or in a backyard smoker. Most gas grills don't put out enough wood smoke to achieve the full effect.

Cheyenne, Wyo.

CHEYENNE PORK CHOPS (Spiced, Smoked, and Double Thick)

What's a nice Jewish boy from Brooklyn doing dishing up pork chops in Cheyenne, Wyoming? Good question! Hal Ginsberg acquired his love of smoke in his native New York. He may have been the only grill jockey on Manhattan's Upper East Side to have five Weber Smokey Mountain smokers on his terrace (he changed boroughs after he got married). But a visit to Wyoming convinced him that the wide open spaces of the West were a better place to raise a family. So Ginsberg moved kith and kin to Cheyenne and followed the path of many a pit master: He opened a catering company called Hal's Backyard Bar-B-Que. Local sporting events, rodeos, and bike and motorcycle rallies just aren't complete without his two-fisted, double-thick pork chops, which tip the scales at 14 to 22 ounces—each! Like most grillers, Hal keeps his rub formula pretty close to his vest, so what follows is my rendition of the dish that's made his name.

METHOD:
Indirect grilling

ADVANCE PREPARATION:
4 hours for curing the chops (optional)

INGREDIENTS:
1 tablespoon sweet paprika
1 tablespoon brown sugar
1 tablespoon granulated sugar
1 tablespoon seasoned salt (Smelling Salts, page 707 or your favorite commercial brand)
2 teaspoons freshly ground black pepper
2 teaspoons ground cumin
1 teaspoon MSG (optional)
½ to 1 teaspoon cayenne pepper
4 double- or triple-thick pork chops (each 14 to 16 ounces), cut as described in the Tip at left
Your favorite barbecue sauce (see Note), for serving

YOU'LL ALSO NEED:
2 cups wood chips or chunks (preferably hickory), soaked for 1 hour in water to cover, then drained

1 Place the paprika, brown and granulated sugars, salt, black pepper, cumin, MSG, if using, and cayenne in a small bowl and stir to mix. (Actually, if you don't have sensitive skin, your fingers work better for mixing a rub than a spoon or whisk does.) Sprinkle this rub on the chops on all sides, patting it onto the meat with your fingertips. You can smoke the chops right away or, for an even richer flavor, let them cure in the refrigerator, covered, for 4 hours.

2 Set up the grill for indirect grilling (see page 23 for gas or page 22 for charcoal) and preheat to medium. If using a gas grill, place all of the wood chips or chunks in the smoker box or a smoker pouch (see page 24) and run the grill on high until you see smoke, then reduce the heat to medium. If using a charcoal grill, place a large drip pan in the center, preheat the grill to medium, then toss all of the wood chips or chunks on the coals.

3 When ready to cook, place the chops in the center of the hot grate, over the drip pan and away from the fire, and cover the grill. Cook the chops until cooked though, 1¼ to 1¾ hours. To test for doneness, use the poke method; the meat should be firm but just gently yielding. Or insert an instant-read meat thermometer sideways into a chop: The internal temperature should be about 160°F. If using a charcoal grill, after 1 hour you'll need to add 12 fresh coals to each side.

4 Transfer the cooked chops to a platter or plates and let them rest for 2 minutes. Serve the chops, in all their plate-burying glory, with barbecue sauce.

YIELD:
Serves 4 very hungry people

NOTE: A sweet red or a mustard barbecue sauce will be particularly good with these chops.

Canada

MAPLE MUSTARD PORK CHOPS

I've always maintained that there's no such thing as a mistake in cooking, just a new recipe waiting to be discovered. My Web master, Benjamin Wilchfort, agrees. "We once forgot to pack barbecue sauce on a camping trip," recalls the man who keeps my barbecuebible.com Web site humming. "So we slathered our steaks with maple syrup and the results were fantastic." (Benjamin grew up in Toronto, where maple syrup is a traditional sweetener and is often paired with pork.) Intrigued by the idea, I marinated some pork chops in mustard

Pit-smoked barbecue—by the plate or by the pound.

T I P S

Maple syrup has
become quite
expensive in recent
years, especially
the highest grades,
Fancy and A. Grade
B may be darker
and less expensive,
but it actually
possesses a richer
maple flavor, so you
can save money and
get better results.

powder, soy sauce, and maple syrup. I
figured that pork would show off the
maple syrup even better than steak,
and it did, which goes to show just how
felicitous an improvisation can be.

METHOD:
Direct grilling

ADVANCE PREPARATION:
30 minutes for marinating the chops

INGREDIENTS:
4 pork chops ($\frac{1}{2}$ to $\frac{3}{4}$ inch thick
     and 6 to 7 ounces each for
     boneless chops or 8 to
     10 ounces each for bone-in
     chops)
Coarse salt (kosher or sea) and
     freshly ground black pepper
About 3 tablespoons dry mustard
About 3 tablespoons soy sauce
$\frac{1}{2}$ cup maple syrup
3 tablespoons vegetable oil
Maple Mustard Barbecue Sauce
     (optional; recipe follows)

1 Place the pork chops in a baking
dish and season generously on both
sides with salt and pepper. Sprinkle the
pork chops on both sides with the mustard powder, using about 1 teaspoon
per side and rubbing it onto the meat
with a fork or your fingertips. Drizzle
the soy sauce over the chops, patting it
onto the mustard with a fork to make a
flavorful paste. Place the maple syrup
and oil in small bowl and stir with a fork
to mix. Pour this mixture over the
chops, turning to coat both sides, and
let marinate in the refrigerator, covered,
for 30 minutes.

2 Set up the grill for direct grilling
(see page 21 for charcoal or gas)
and preheat to high.

3 When ready to cook, brush and oil
the grill grate. Drain the marinade
from the chops and discard the marinade. Arrange the chops on the hot
grate, placing them on a diagonal to
the bars. Grill the chops until cooked
through, 4 to 6 minutes per side, depending on the thickness of the chops.
Rotate the chops a quarter turn after 2
minutes to create an attractive crosshatch of grill marks. When ready to
turn, the chops will be nicely browned
on the bottom. To test for doneness,
use the poke method; the meat should
be firm but gently yielding. Or insert an
instant-read meat thermometer sideways into a chop: The internal temperature should be about 160°F.

4 Transfer the grilled chops to a
platter or plates and let rest for
2 minutes. Serve the chops with the
Maple-Mustard Barbecue Sauce, if
desired.

YIELD:
Serves 4

VARIATION: Beef steaks, particularly strip steaks, are also good prepared this way.

Maple Mustard Barbecue Sauce

Canada, a major producer of maple syrup, meets the Carolinas in this tangy mustard sauce—a twist on a classic South Carolina barbecue sauce. It's great with all sorts of pork.

INGREDIENTS:

1 tablespoon butter
2 slices bacon, cut into ¼-inch slivers
1 small onion, finely chopped (about ¾ cup)
1 clove garlic, minced
1 tablespoon tomato paste
¾ cup maple syrup
6 tablespoons Dijon mustard
2 tablespoons cider vinegar, or more to taste
**Coarse salt (kosher or sea) and
    freshly ground black pepper**

1 Melt the butter in a nonreactive saucepan over medium heat. Add the bacon, onion, and garlic and cook until golden brown, 4 to 5 minutes. Stir in the tomato paste and cook for 1 minute.

2 Stir in the maple syrup, mustard, and vinegar and let the sauce simmer until thick and flavorful, about 10 minutes. Taste for seasoning, adding salt and pepper to taste and more vinegar as necessary. You can serve the sauce hot or at room temperature. It can be made up to 2 days ahead and refrigerated, covered. Bring the sauce to room temperature before serving.

YIELD:
Makes about 1¼ cups

Newton, Iowa

IOWA PORK CHOPS
With Maytag Blue

The Hawkeye State produces fine cattle, but as the locals know, the real specialty here is pork. An Iowa pork chop is everything you want a chop to be: generously marbled, bible thick, with a rich, meaty flavor that just doesn't quit. My colleague, Iowa-based food editor Nancy Byal, likes to pair the hometown pork with another Iowa specialty: Maytag Blue. This is a semifirm, pleasantly creamy blue cheese from the town of Newton, and its brisk flavor has more than a passing kinship with fine European blues, like Cabrales or Stilton. Put Iowa pork and Maytag Blue together and you get a quick and easy pork dish.

METHOD:
Direct grilling

TIPS

For years, Americans have been taught to cook pork to death, a throwback to an age when pigs were fed garbage and undercooked pork could give you trichinosis. Modern livestock rearing techniques have all but eliminated this risk today, and in any case, cooking pork to 160°F removes the risk of trichinosis (if you want to take a chop's temperature, just insert an instant-read meat thermometer through the side). So treat these pork chops more like you would veal chops— that is grill them until crusty on the outside but still moist and a little pink within.

FOR THE BLUE CHEESE BUTTER:

**4 tablespoons (½ stick) unsalted butter,
    at room temperature**
**1 ounce Maytag Blue cheese,
    crumbled, at room temperature**
**1 tablespoon chopped toasted walnuts
    (see page 584)**
1 tablespoon thinly slivered fresh basil
**Coarse salt (kosher or sea) and
    freshly ground black pepper**

FOR THE PORK:

**4 bone-in pork loin chops
    (each about 1¼ inches thick and
    8 to 10 ounces)**
2 cloves garlic, cut in half crosswise
**Coarse salt (kosher or sea) and
    freshly ground black pepper**

1 MAKE THE BLUE CHEESE BUTTER: Place the butter and blue cheese in a mixing bowl and mash together with a fork. Stir in the walnuts and basil and season with salt and pepper to taste (add just a little salt; the cheese is already quite salty). The blue cheese butter can be kept refrigerated, covered, for 5 days or frozen for 3 months.

2 Set up the grill for direct grilling (see page 21 for charcoal or gas) and preheat to high.

3 When ready to cook, rub both sides of each pork chop with a half clove of garlic, then season the chops generously with salt and pepper. Brush and oil the grill grate. Place the chops on the hot grate and grill until cooked through, 6 to 8 minutes per side. When ready to turn, the chops will be nicely browned on the bottom. To test for doneness, use the poke

method; the meat should be firm but gently yielding. Or insert an instant-read meat thermometer sideways into a chop: The internal temperature should be about 160°F.

4 Transfer the grilled chops to a platter or plates and let rest for 2 minutes. Top each with a dollop of the blue cheese butter and serve.

YIELD:
Serves 4

VARIATION: For a showier effect, you can roll the butter in plastic wrap, chill the resulting log, and cut it into slices for topping the chops with. I like the rustic look of dollops, but if you want to make a butter roll, you'll find instructions on page 198.

Vancouver, Canada

ARMANDO'S SWEET AND SALTY PORK CHOPS

Armando Bacani holds no elected office, but this affable vendor could be hailed as the mayor of Vancouver. Everyone, and I mean

Armando Bacani, butcher to the grillers of Vancouver.

everyone, knows him. The microbiologist turned butcher left the city of Baguio in the Philippines in the 1980s to seek his fortune in Canada. He wound up in Vancouver, where he opened a meat stall in the Granville Island market. Since then, Armando has become something of a local celebrity, and his booming business now employs three generations of family members.

A lot of that business involves satisfying Vancouver's insatiable hunger for barbecue. Like most of the butchers here, Armando sells dozens of meats that have been marinated and are ready for grilling. The most distinctive is a Canadian twist on *tocino,* one of the national

dishes of the Philippines. *Tocino* means bacon in Spanish, but the Filipino version features thin slices of pork cured with salt, sugar, pepper, paprika, and garlic. In the old days, the curing would be done at room temperature, with saltpeter added as a preservative. Armando cures the meat in the refrigerator, omitting the saltpeter. When the pork comes off the grill, it is as sweet as proverbial candy, and the curing keeps what is often a dry cut of meat deliciously moist.

METHOD:
Direct grilling

ADVANCE PREPARATION:
1 to 3 days for curing the pork

INGREDIENTS:
½ cup sugar
1 tablespoon coarse salt (kosher or sea)
1 tablespoon sweet paprika
2 teaspoons freshly ground black pepper
6 cloves garlic, minced
4 boneless pork chops (each ½ to ¾ inch thick and 6 to 7 ounces), or 1½ pounds pork loin (2 to 3 tenderloins)
2 tablespoons vegetable oil
Rice, for serving (optional)

1 Place the sugar, salt, paprika, pepper, and garlic in a small mixing bowl and stir to mix. (Actually, your fingers work better for mixing a rub than a spoon or whisk does.)

Traditionally, the pork for *tocino* is sliced paper-thin, which is easy to do if you have a meat slicer. I like to use boneless pork loin chops, which don't require slicing and are easier to grill.

🔥🔥🔥🔥🔥
WALL OF FLAME

GRANVILLE ISLAND PUBLIC MARKET

The butchers and meat vendors of the Granville Island Public Market proudly supply Vancouverites with a dazzling array of grill-ready marinated meats and preskewered kebabs. Go to Armando's for Filipino and Asian style meats or try the marinated chops and kebabs brimming with Mediterranean flavors at Tenderland Meats.

1689 Johnston Street
Vancouver
British Columbia
Canada
(604) 666-5784

2 If using pork loin, cut it crosswise into ½-inch-thick slices. Place the pork in a baking dish and sprinkle the rub all over both sides, patting it onto the meat with your fingertips. Let the meat cure in the refrigerator, covered, for at least 24 hours or as long as 3 days (the longer the meat cures, the stronger the flavor). You can also cure the spice-rubbed pork in a resealable plastic bag (this is what I do, as it takes up less room in the refrigerator).

3 Set up the grill for direct grilling (see page 21 for charcoal or gas) and preheat to high.

4 When ready to grill, brush and oil the grill grate. Using a rubber spatula, scrape most of the rub off the pork. Lightly brush the chops on both sides with the oil. Place the chops on the hot grate and grill until browned on the outside and cooked through, 2 to 3 minutes per side. To test for doneness, use the poke method; the meat should be firm but gently yielding.

5 Transfer the grilled pork to a platter or plates, let it rest for 2 minutes, then serve. Rice makes a good accompaniment.

YIELD:
Serves 4

St. Louis, Mo.

ST. LOUIS PORK STEAKS

Mention St. Louis barbecue to most Americans and what comes to mind is ribs. Indeed, there's even a St. Louis rib cut—spareribs with the brisket removed. But visit a typical St. Louis backyard in the summertime and you'll likely find something very different sizzling away on the grill: pork shoulder steaks slathered with Maull's, a local tomato-based barbecue sauce. These steaks, frequently referred to as blade steaks, are unique in the annals of American barbecue. They're cut not from the leg or loin but from the shoulder, so they're very generously marbled. (That's putting it mildly.) The fat keeps the steaks from drying out during grilling, which is more than you can expect from your average pork chop. On the down side, the dripping fat makes pork shoulder steaks prone to flare-ups. So don't crowd the grill, and if you do get flames, simply move the meat to another section of the grate.

METHOD:
Direct grilling

When the pork comes off the grill,
it is as sweet as proverbial candy.

INGREDIENTS:

St. Louis Barbecue Sauce (recipe follows),
    or 2 cups Maull's barbecue sauce

4 pork shoulder steaks (each about 1/2 inch
    thick and 6 to 8 ounces)

2 to 3 teaspoons garlic powder

2 to 3 teaspoons dried oregano

Coarse salt (kosher or sea) and
    freshly ground black pepper

1 Place 1/2 cup of the barbecue sauce in a cup for basting the pork steaks. Place the remaining 1 1/2 cups in a bowl for serving. Set both aside.

2 Generously season the pork steaks on both sides with garlic powder, oregano, salt, and pepper.

3 Set up the grill for direct grilling (see page 21 for charcoal or gas) and preheat to high.

4 When ready to cook, brush and oil the grill grate. Arrange the steaks on the hot grate, placing them on a diagonal to the bars. Grill the steaks until cooked through, 4 to 6 minutes per side, rotating the steaks a quarter turn after 2 minutes to create an attractive crosshatch of grill marks. To test for doneness, use the poke method; the meat should be firm but just gently yielding. As the steaks finish grilling, brush them on both sides with the 1/2 cup of barbecue sauce. Sizzle the sauce on each side for about 15 seconds. Transfer the grilled steaks to a platter or plates and serve with the remaining barbecue sauce on the side.

YIELD:

Serves 4

St. Louis Barbecue Sauce

St. Louisians have been pouring a slightly sweet, slightly tart, mildly spicy red sauce on barbecue since 1926. Invented by an itinerant grocer named Louis Maull, the classic sauce differs from most American barbecue sauces in that it contains no liquid smoke. If you live in St. Louis, you'd buy a bottle of Maull's at your local supermarket (heck, you probably already have a bottle in your refrigerator). Being a made-from-scratch sort of guy, I created the following barbecue sauce modeled on Maull's.

INGREDIENTS:

1 1/2 cups tomato purée

1/3 cup distilled white vinegar

3 tablespoons dark corn syrup

2 tablespoons brown sugar

2 tablespoons Worcestershire sauce

1 1/2 tablespoons molasses

1/2 teaspoon grated lemon zest

3 tablespoons fresh lemon juice

1 tablespoon thawed orange juice
    concentrate

2 teaspoons A.1. steak sauce

2 teaspoons soy sauce

1 teaspoon Tabasco sauce or
    other hot sauce

1 1/2 teaspoons coarse salt (kosher or sea),
    or more to taste

1 teaspoon onion powder

1 teaspoon garlic powder

1/2 teaspoon freshly ground black pepper,
    or more to taste

1/4 teaspoon ground cloves

TIPS

It's easy to find pork shoulder steaks in St. Louis, less so in other parts of the country. If you can't find them, use shoulder chops; they'll grill for the same length of time. Or buy a whole pork shoulder and ask your butcher to slice it on his band saw crosswise into 1/2-inch slices.

1 Combine the tomato purée, vinegar, corn syrup, brown sugar, Worcestershire sauce, molasses, lemon zest and juice, orange juice concentrate, steak sauce, soy sauce, Tabasco sauce, salt, onion powder, garlic powder, pepper, and cloves in a large deep heavy nonreactive saucepan over medium-high heat. Gradually bring to a boil, whisking often.

2 Reduce the heat to medium and let the sauce simmer until thick and richly flavored, 6 to 10 minutes, whisking occasionally. Taste for seasoning, adding more salt and/or pepper as necessary.

YIELD:

Makes about 2 cups

TIPS

Bruno uses what I call modified direct grilling to cook his ribs. The coals and wood burn directly under the meat, as in direct grilling, but the grate is positioned so high above them that the result is a modest temperature more characteristic of smoking. To approximate the effect, I smoke cook the ribs using the indirect method, then move them over the fire for the last five minutes to brown the outside.

Indianapolis, Ind.

LORD OF THE 'QUE SPARERIBS

For some guys barbecue is a calling. Every weekend, Carl Bruno barbecues for friends and family at backyard cookouts, dishing up ribs and chicken wings for everyone who stops by. Bruno seasons his ribs in a two-step process. First comes a rub made with seasoned salt, brown sugar, and garlic powder. Then comes a "squirt," a Worcestershire-based basting mixture sprayed on the ribs from a spray bottle. To this, add the sweet smoke of Indiana red oak or apple wood, and you've got high-octane ribs that will trash the competition. Of course, few rib masters will disclose their actual recipes. Here's how I imagine Bruno puts it all together.

METHOD:

Indirect grilling

FOR THE RIBS AND RUB:

4 racks spareribs
(12 to 15 pounds total)
3 tablespoons seasoned salt
(Smelling Salts, page 707,
or use a commercial brand,
such as Lawry's)
3 tablespoons brown sugar
1 tablespoon freshly ground black pepper
1 tablespoon onion powder
1 tablespoon garlic powder

FOR THE "SQUIRT":

1/2 cup Worcestershire sauce
3 tablespoons honey
3 tablespoons distilled white vinegar
2 tablespoons ketchup
2 teaspoons liquid smoke
1 teaspoon Tabasco sauce

St. Louis Red (page 666) or your favorite
commercial barbecue sauce

YOU'LL ALSO NEED:

3 cups wood chips or chunks
(preferably oak or apple), soaked
for 1 hour in water to cover, then
drained; spray bottle or mister;
rib rack (optional; see page 288)

1 Remove the thin, papery membrane from the back of each rack of ribs: Turn a rack meat side down. Insert a sharp implement, such as the tip of a meat thermometer, under the membrane (the best place to start is right next to the first rib bone). Using a dishcloth or pliers to gain a secure grip, pull off the membrane. Repeat with the remaining racks.

2 MAKE THE RUB: Place the seasoned salt, brown sugar, pepper, onion powder, and garlic powder in a small bowl and stir to mix. (Actually, your fingers work better for mixing a rub than a spoon or whisk does.) Sprinkle the rub all over the ribs on both sides, patting it onto the meat with your fingertips.

3 MAKE THE "SQUIRT": Place the Worcestershire sauce, honey, vinegar, ketchup, liquid smoke, and Tabasco sauce in a nonreactive mixing bowl, add 3 tablespoons of water, and stir until well mixed. Place the "squirt" in a spray bottle or mister and set aside.

4 Set up the grill for indirect grilling (see page 23 for gas or page 22 for charcoal) and preheat to medium-low. If using a gas grill, place all of the wood chips or chunks in the smoker box or in a smoker pouch (see page 24) and run the grill on high until you see smoke, then reduce the heat to medium-low. If using a charcoal grill, place a large drip pan in the center, then toss 1 cup of the wood chips or chunks on the coals.

5 When ready to cook, place the ribs, preferably on a rib rack, in the center of the hot grate, over the drip pan and away from the heat. Cover the grill and cook the ribs until tender, 2½ to 3 hours. When the ribs are done, they'll be handsomely browned and the meat will have shrunk back about ¼ inch from the ends of the bones. If the ribs begin to darken too much, wrap them in aluminum foil until they finish cooking. Spray the ribs with the "squirt" every 30 minutes. If using a charcoal grill, every hour you'll need to add 12 fresh coals and ½ cup of wood chips or chunks to each side.

6 About 5 minutes before the ribs are done, move them directly over the fire, removing them from the rib rack, if using. Leave the grill uncovered and cook the ribs until browned and sizzling, about 3 minutes per side.

7 Transfer the cooked ribs to a platter or cutting board. Cut the racks in half or carve them into individual ribs. Serve them with the barbecue sauce on the side or slather the sauce over the ribs.

YIELD:
Serves 8 to 12

TIPS

I first tried this recipe with rib tips. Here I call for larger, meatier spareribs (you'll find a description of all the various kinds of ribs beginning on page 286). If you're working on a conventional backyard grill (as opposed to a professional smoker), get yourself a rib rack (see page 288), which will hold the ribs vertically, so you can fit more on the grate.

RIBS, RIBS, RIBS
Down to the Bone

The rib is probably the most perfect morsel ever to emerge from a barbecue pit. This statement will be disputed by a few Texans (well, possibly more than a few), who swear by brisket, and by North Carolinians, who insist that the only true barbecue is whole hog or smoke-roasted pork shoulder. But ribs are king in Memphis and Kansas City, and in most other parts of the United States a barbecue simply isn't complete without them. Many a chain restaurant has achieved national success with ribs—even without a smoker or pit on the premises.

There's good reason for the rib's preeminence. The meat is generously marbled, which gives it a rich taste and keeps it moist as it cooks. The melting fat crisps the meat fibers, naturally basting the meat. The bones themselves impart additional flavor (meat next to the bone always has more flavor), while literally providing physical support—a gnawable rack on which to cook the meat. Finally, ribs not only can but must be eaten with your fingers. And there's nothing like the primal pleasure of devouring your meal using your hands.

There are many different types of ribs to choose from. Geography plays a part: A St. Louis–style rib will be quite different from one from Kansas City or Memphis. So here's a scorecard to help you know the various players.

PORK RIBS

The pork rib is king in American barbecue, served up dry in Memphis, sweet and sticky in Kansas City, and just about every way you can think of in the rest of the country. The pig supplies four basic types: baby backs, spareribs, rib tips, and country-style ribs.

BABY BACK RIBS, sometimes called top loin ribs, are short, succulent, well-marbled ribs cut from the center section of the loin. They come from the upper part of the pig's rib cage directly adjacent to the chine (backbone). Their high fat content and remarkable tenderness—not to mention

Judging ribs at a barbecue contest is serious business.

Rib masters strut their stuff.

the relatively short time they take to cook—make them America's favorite rib. The weight of a rack of baby backs can vary from 1 to 2½ pounds. While imported baby backs generally weigh about 1 pound, domestic racks tip the scale at between 1½ and 2½ pounds. A 1-pound rack makes a generous serving for one. Figure on a 1½- to 2-pound rack feeding two people with average appetites. Baby backs' singular deliciousness is reflected in the expression "eating high off the hog."

SPARERIBS come from lower down on the rib cage (from the sides and upper belly of the pig). Larger and longer than baby backs, they contain more connective tissue, so spareribs are a little tougher. On the plus side, they're also more flavorful. A rack of spareribs can weigh from 2½ to 4 pounds. The smaller the sparerib, the more tender. Thus, connoisseurs look for a 3½ down, a rack of ribs that weighs 3½ pounds or less. Spareribs are sold both with and without the brisket, the flap of meat on the inside. In meat packer parlance, St. Louis–style ribs have both the brisket and rib tips removed. One rack of spareribs will be enough for two to three people.

If you look at a full rack of spareribs, you'll see that one end (the shoulder end) is wider than the other. In Kansas City people make much of the respective virtues of the two ends, and at any respectable rib parlor you can specify which end you want. Long ends are the wide, lean foresection of a rack of spareribs; short ends are the narrower, fattier, meatier hind section. Both have their partisans.

RIB TIPS come from the gristly cartilaginous part of the pig that connects the two racks of spareribs in its underbelly. They're not much to look at and a little tough to chew, but rib tips are so loaded with flavor, they're the preferred choice of many barbecue cognoscenti. You find them in Cincinnati and at Kansas City rib emporiums. Rib tips are also popular with Chinese American chefs.

COUNTRY-STYLE RIBS are the meatiest ribs of all, mini pork chops cut from the blade end of the loin. Purists consider them chops, not ribs. The Memphis in May World Championship Barbecue Cooking Contest, for example, will not allow country-style ribs to be used in its competitions. Country-style ribs can be grilled as well as smoked.

BEEF & LAMB RIBS

Beef ribs each measure eight to ten inches long (in my family we call them dinosaur bones). They're what's left over when the butcher cuts out a rib roast. Each side of beef has seven ribs. Beef ribs can be cooked any way you'd prepare pork ribs.

When the ribs are cooked, the ends of the bones will be bare.

BEEF SHORT RIBS come from the lower end of the rib roast. Short ribs are thicker, tougher, and fattier than regular beef ribs, so they need prolonged cooking at a low heat. Korean Americans have a particularly ingenious way of preparing short ribs—they slice the meat in long, continuous, paper-thin strips and grill these on a hot hibachi or brazier.

LAMB RIBS AND RIBLETS are cut from the lower side of the rib cage. They're delectable barbecued and are tender enough to cook on the grill. You'll probably need to place a special order for them from your butcher.

TO SKIN OR NOT TO SKIN

Pork and lamb ribs come with a papery membrane on the back (the concave side). The world of barbecue is divided as to whether

Spareribs can be grilled directly over charcoal.

or not to remove this skin. Advocates of peeling ribs argue that the membrane makes the ribs slightly tougher and impedes the absorption of smoke flavor. Naturalists hold that leaving the membrane on helps hold the ribs together during cooking. To put the issue in perspective, most competition barbecuers skin their ribs but few restaurants do. I always skin my ribs, and I've found that baby back ribs are easier to peel than spareribs.

To remove the membrane, loosen one corner of it from the meat using a slender, blunt, round object, like the tip of a meat thermometer or a clean Phillips head screwdriver. Insert the point just under the membrane next to one of the ribs and wiggle it. Grab the membrane with a paper towel or the end of a dish towel or even a pair of pliers—it's slippery, and this will give you a secure grip. Gently but firmly pull the membrane away from the ribs; it should come away in a single sheet. Even easier, ask your butcher to remove the membrane for you.

HOW TO COOK RIBS

In North America, ribs are generally cooked by barbecuing or indirect grilling. The idea here is that the low heat and slow cooking help dissolve the tough connective tissue. I cook my baby backs at 325° to 350°F, a slightly higher temperature

than is traditional. This results in a crisp, crusty rib with a minimum of fat. You can also grill baby back ribs directly over moderate heat; this is the technique used by the Rendezvous restaurant in Memphis. You can even cook baby backs on the rotisserie. Over medium heat, a one-pound rack of baby backs will take about an hour to be fully cooked; a larger rack will be done after about an hour and a half. Spareribs grilled over medium-low heat take from two and a half to three hours.

When fully cooked, ribs should be tender enough to pull apart with your fingers (beware of fall-off-the-bone tender ribs, however; they've probably been boiled or baked). You'll find recipes for grilling pork ribs on page 284 and pages 289 through 298 and one for grilling beef ribs on page 211.

RIB RACKS

For many backyard barbecuers the chief challenge to cooking ribs is fitting them on the grill. This is not a problem if you have a smoker, but it will be if you use a charcoal kettle grill or some gas grills. There's an easy way to quadruple your grill's rib capacity: Use a rib rack. These wire racks look like old-fashioned toast holders, and they enable you to cook four racks of ribs in an upright position, freeing up valuable space. Rib racks are sold at grill stores and many cookware shops or can be ordered by mail (see page 742).

St. Louis, Mo.

SUPER SMOKERS
Sweet and Smoky Dry Rub Ribs

The Super Smokers burst upon the St. Louis barbecue scene in 1995, and their rise to barbecue stardom has been steady and unstoppable. This band of friends turned competition barbecue team has shown an unwavering devotion to great barbecue from their first regional win to their Grand Championship in the whole hog category at Memphis in May 2000 (to read more about the Super Smokers, see page 130). The ribs here, modeled on the Super Smokers recipe, demonstrate how a few simple ingredients and a little patience will give you barbecue that's out of this world.

METHOD:
Indirect grilling

ADVANCE PREPARATION:
4 hours for curing the ribs

INGREDIENTS:
**4 racks baby back pork ribs
(6 to 8 pounds total)**
2 cups firmly packed brown sugar
1 cup coarse salt (kosher or sea)
¼ cup freshly ground black pepper

St. Louis Red barbecue sauce (page 666), for serving

YOU'LL ALSO NEED:
2 cups wood chips or chunks (preferably apple), soaked for 1 hour in water to cover, then drained; rib rack (optional; see opposite page)

1 Remove the thin, papery membrane from the back of each rack of ribs: Turn a rack meat side down. Insert a sharp implement, such as the tip of a meat thermometer, under the membrane (the best place to start is right next to the first rib bone). Using a dishcloth or pliers to gain a secure grip, pull off the membrane. Repeat with the remaining racks. Place the ribs on baking sheets.

2 Place the brown sugar, salt, and pepper in a bowl and stir to mix well. (Actually your fingers work better for mixing a rub than a spoon or whisk does.) Sprinkle this rub all over the ribs on both sides, patting it onto the meat with your fingertips. Cover the ribs with plastic wrap and let cure in the refrigerator for 4 hours.

3 Set up the grill for indirect grilling (see page 23 for gas or page 22 for charcoal) and preheat to medium. If using a gas grill, place all of the wood chips or chunks in the smoker box or smoker pouch (see page 24) and run the grill on high until you see smoke, then reduce the heat to medium. If using a charcoal grill, place a large drip pan in the center, preheat the grill to medium, then toss all of the wood chips or chunks on the coals.

T I P S

Peeling the ribs isn't absolutely mandatory, but it will make them more tender (for more about ribs, see page 286).

TIPS

If you have a smoker, you'll be able to smoke the ribs at 250°F; it will take two to two and a half hours. If you have a grill, you'll have to work at a higher temperature, but your ribs will still be quite good. (F.Y.I., the Super Smokers use only apple wood for smoking. "You can't oversmoke a rib with apple," says pit boss Skip Steele.)

The Super Smokers, Ron Skinner, Terry Black, and Skip Steele, and a couple of their trophies in front of the St. Louis Gateway Arch.

4 When ready to cook, using a rubber spatula, scrape the excess rub off the ribs. Place the ribs, preferably on a rib rack, in the center of the hot grate, over the drip pan and away from the heat. Cover the grill and cook the ribs until tender, 1¼ to 1½ hours. When the ribs are done, they'll be handsomely browned and the meat will have shrunk back about ¼ inch from the ends of the bones.

5 Transfer the cooked ribs to a platter or cutting board. Serve them as whole racks, cut the racks into pieces, or carve them into individual ribs. Serve them with the St. Louis–style barbecue sauce.

YIELD:

Serves 4 really hungry people or 8 folks with average appetites

Pan-American

JALAPEÑO JERK BABY BACK RIBS

I first tasted these fantastic ribs at the Memphis in May World Championship Barbecue Cooking Contest, but their tropical roots are obvious. The pineapple glaze and barbecue sauce evoke the cookouts of Hawaii, while the jerk rub will resonate with Jamaican communities (and Jamaican barbecue fanatics) from Manhattan to Miami. The idea is to play the sweetness of pineapple juice against the heat of the jerk seasoning and jalapeño peppers.

METHOD:
Indirect grilling

ADVANCE PREPARATION:
2 to 3 hours for marinating the ribs

FOR THE RIBS:
**4 racks baby back pork ribs,
    (6 to 8 pounds total)**
1 quart pineapple juice
**1 bunch fresh cilantro, washed and
    coarsely chopped**
4 to 8 jalapeño peppers, thinly sliced

FOR THE GLAZE:
2 cups pineapple juice
1/2 cup rice vinegar or cider vinegar

3 tablespoons brown sugar
3 tablespoons butter
1/2 teaspoon freshly ground black pepper

FOR THE SEASONING:
**Dry Jerk Seasoning (recipe follows),
    or 1/2 cup of your favorite
    commercial brand**
**Pineapple Barbecue Sauce
    (page 293)**

YOU'LL ALSO NEED:
Rib rack (optional; see page 288)

1 Remove the thin, papery membrane from the back of each rack of ribs: Turn a rack meat side down. Insert a sharp implement, such as the tip of a meat thermometer, under the membrane (the best place to start is right next to the first rib bone). Using a dishcloth or pliers to gain a secure grip, pull off the membrane. Repeat with the remaining racks.

2 Place the ribs in a large nonreactive roasting pan. Pour the 1 quart of pineapple juice over them and add the cilantro and jalapeños. Let the ribs marinate in the refrigerator, covered, for 2 to 3 hours.

3 MAKE THE GLAZE: Place the 2 cups pineapple juice, the vinegar, brown sugar, butter, and black pepper in a heavy saucepan over high heat and bring to a boil. Let the glaze boil until syrupy and reduced to about 1 cup, 10 to 15 minutes, stirring occasionally with a wooden spoon. Set the glaze aside.

4 Drain the marinade off the ribs and discard the marinade. Blot

If you've got the time, you can make the dry jerk seasoning from scratch (you'll find the recipe on page 292), but you could certainly use a commercial one.

the ribs dry with paper towels, then sprinkle the jerk seasoning all over them on both sides, patting it onto the meat with your fingertips.

5 Set up the grill for indirect grilling (see page 22 for charcoal or page 23 for gas) and preheat to medium. If using a charcoal grill, place a large drip pan in the center.

6 When ready to cook, place the ribs, preferably on a rib rack, in the center of the hot grate, over the drip pan and away from the heat. Cover the grill and cook the ribs until tender, 1¼ to 1½ hours. When the ribs are done, they'll be handsomely browned and the meat will have shrunk back about ¼ inch from the ends of the bones. After 45 minutes brush the ribs with the glaze and brush them two or three more times before serving. If using a charcoal grill, after 1 hour you'll need to add 12 fresh coals to each side.

7 Transfer the cooked ribs to a platter or cutting board. Serve them as whole racks, cut the racks into pieces, or carve them into individual ribs. Serve the barbecue sauce alongside.

YIELD:
Serves 4 really hungry people or 8 folks with average appetites

VARIATION: While I'm calling for the ribs to be grilled using the indirect method here, you can also smoke them. It will take 2½ to 3 hours of cooking time at 250°F.

MOPPING UP

They look really cool, and there's nothing better for applying a thin sauce or a liquid flavoring agent to ribs or pork butts. I'm talking, of course, about the barbecue mop, which looks like a miniature floor mop (actually, when pro pit bosses grill large quantities of meat, they use full-size floor mops—clean ones). Barbecue mops are available at grill shops and many hardware and cookware shops, or see Mail-Order Sources on page 742. But yes, you could always use a basting brush instead.

Dry Jerk Seasoning

Here's a quick dry jerk seasoning, one you can make from scratch, and unlike many store-bought versions it contains no MSG. For a mail-order source for habañero chile powder, see page 742.

INGREDIENTS:
3 tablespoons dark brown sugar
1½ tablespoons coarse salt (kosher or sea)
1½ tablespoons ground coriander
1½ teaspoons freshly ground black pepper
1½ teaspoons garlic powder
1½ teaspoons onion powder
1½ teaspoons dried thyme
1½ teaspoons ground allspice
1 teaspoon ground cinnamon
½ to 1 teaspoon habañero chile powder or cayenne pepper

ombine the brown sugar, salt, coriander, black pepper, garlic powder, onion powder, thyme, allspice, cinnamon, and habañero chile powder in a small bowl and stir to mix. (Actually, your fingers work better for mixing a rub than a spoon or whisk does.) Store the rub in an airtight jar away from heat and light; it will keep for at least 6 months.

YIELD:

Makes about ½ cup

Who needs a fork when you've got your fingers?

Pineapple Barbecue Sauce

ineapple juice makes a fitting base for a barbecue sauce. After all, barbecue originated in the West Indies and so did the pineapple (it was found by Columbus in 1493 on the island of Guadeloupe). In Colonial times, the pineapple became an American symbol of hospitality and appeared as a decorative motif, carved, for example, into moldings and banisters. The fruit's sweet, musky acidity makes it a perfect foil for pork.

INGREDIENTS:

2 cups pineapple juice

1 to 2 jalapeño peppers, seeded and minced

2 tablespoons chopped fresh cilantro

1 tablespoon minced peeled fresh ginger

¾ cup ketchup

3 tablespoons cider vinegar

2 tablespoons Worcestershire sauce

2 tablespoons brown sugar

1 tablespoon soy sauce

Coarse salt (kosher or sea) and freshly ground black pepper

1 Place the pineapple juice, jalapeño(s), cilantro, and ginger in a heavy non-reactive saucepan over high heat and bring to a boil. Let boil until the liquid is reduced by half.

2 Add the ketchup, vinegar, Worcestershire sauce, brown sugar, and soy sauce to the saucepan and stir. Let the sauce simmer until richly flavored and slightly thickened, about 10 minutes. Season to taste with salt and pepper (go easy on the salt). The sauce can be refrigerated, covered, for up to 1 week. Bring to room temperature before serving.

YIELD:

Makes about 3 cups

Murphysboro, Ill.

APPLE CITY CHAMPIONSHIP RIBS

Apple City was the sort of competition barbecue team that was talked about in reverential whispers among smoke masters (active in the 1990s, the team has now retired). The guys from Murphysboro, Illinois, had the unbelievable good fortune (and more important, the skill) to win three—count 'em—three Grand World Championships at the Memphis in May international barbecue contest. One year their ribs fetched a perfect score. Murphysboro is situated in the heart of Illinois apple country and, not surprisingly, apples played a big part in the winning recipe. The ribs are marinated in and sprayed with apple cider, smoked over apple wood, and served with an apple-based barbecue sauce. To this add "Magic Dust" (the ingredients of this rub are "so top secret," explains former team captain Mike Mills, tongue firmly planted in cheek, that "no single person knows the whole recipe"), and you have a championship recipe. No self-respecting barbecue team would disclose its actual prize-winning formula, of course, so what follows is my best guess at how they do it.

METHOD:
Indirect grilling

ADVANCE PREPARATION:
**4 to 12 hours for marinating the ribs
plus 4 hours for curing the ribs**

FOR THE RIBS:
**4 racks baby back pork ribs
(9 to 12 pounds total)
2 quarts plus ¾ cup apple cider**

FOR THE "MAGIC DUST":
**¼ cup sweet paprika
3 tablespoons dark brown sugar
2 tablespoons freshly ground black pepper
1 tablespoon pure chile powder
2 teaspoons garlic powder
2 teaspoons dry mustard
2 teaspoons celery salt
1 teaspoon coarse salt (kosher or sea)
1 teaspoon cayenne pepper**

Apple Barbecue Sauce (recipe follows)

YOU'LL ALSO NEED:
**2 cups wood chips or chunks
(preferably apple), soaked for
1 hour in water to cover, then drained;
spray bottle or mister; rib rack
(optional; see page 288)**

1 Remove the thin, papery membrane from the back of each rack of ribs: Turn a rack meat side down. Insert a sharp implement, such as the tip of a meat thermometer, under the membrane (the best place to start is right next to the first rib bone). Using a dishcloth or pliers to gain a secure grip, pull off the membrane. Repeat with the remaining racks.

2 Place the ribs in a large nonreactive roasting pan or in a clean plastic garbage bag and pour 3 quarts of the apple cider over them. Place the remaining 1 cup of cider in a spray bottle or mister for basting and refrigerate until ready to use. Let the ribs marinate in the refrigerator, covered (twist tie the garbage bag closed, if using), for at least 4 hours or as long as overnight, turning the ribs several times so that they marinate evenly.

3 MAKE THE "MAGIC DUST": Place the paprika, brown sugar, black pepper, chile powder, garlic powder, mustard, celery salt, coarse salt, and cayenne in a small bowl and stir to mix. (Actually, if you don't have sensitive skin, your fingers work better for mixing a rub than a spoon or whisk does.) Set the rub aside.

4 Drain the cider from the ribs, reserving 2 cups. Pat the ribs dry with paper towels. Sprinkle about 9 tablespoons of the "Magic Dust" all over the ribs on both sides (you'll need about 1 tablespoon per rack; set aside the remainder). Rub the "Magic Dust" onto the meat with your fingertips. Let the ribs cure in the refrigerator, covered, for 4 hours.

5 Set up the grill for indirect grilling (see page 23 for gas or page 22 for charcoal) and preheat to medium-low. Place a large drip pan in the center, if there is not already one there, and add the 2 cups of cider reserved from the marinade. If using a gas grill, place all of the wood chips or chunks in the smoker box or in a smoker pouch (see page 24) and run the grill on high until you see smoke, then reduce the heat to medium-low. If using a charcoal grill—and this is what I prefer—preheat the grill to medium-low, then toss 1 cup of the wood chips or chunks on the coals.

6 When ready to cook, place the ribs, preferably on a rib rack, in the center of the hot grate, over the

When you lay siege to a world championship recipe, you need a lot of planning and patience. Start this recipe the day before you plan to grill, so the ribs have time to marinate and cure.

It takes a whole team to make championship barbecue.

drip pan and away from the heat. Cover the grill and cook the ribs until tender, 1½ to 2 hours. When the ribs are done, they'll be handsomely browned and the meat will have shrunk back about ¼ inch from the ends of the bones. Spray the ribs with cider every 30 minutes. During the last 30 minutes, brush each rack with some of the barbecue sauce to give it a sheen. If using a charcoal grill, after 1 hour you'll need to add 12 fresh coals to each side and toss the remaining 1 cup of wood chips or chunks (½ cup per side) on the coals.

7 Transfer the cooked ribs to a cutting board and sprinkle 4 tablespoons of the remaining rub over them (you'll have a little rub left over; save it for another use). Serve the ribs as whole racks or carve them into individual ribs and serve the remaining barbecue sauce on the side.

YIELD:
Serves 4 really hungry people or 8 folks with average appetites

Apple Barbecue Sauce

There's apple flavor aplenty in this barbecue sauce—from freshly grated apple, applesauce, and cider vinegar. It's delectable with any type of grilled or smoked pork, and it's not half bad with poultry, too.

INGREDIENTS:
2 cups ketchup
¼ cup applesauce
¼ cup cider vinegar
¼ cup Worcestershire sauce
2 tablespoons soy sauce
1½ teaspoons liquid smoke
1 tablespoon brown sugar, or more to taste
1 teaspoon garlic powder
1 teaspoon freshly ground white pepper
1 tablespoon grated peeled fresh ginger, or 1 teaspoon ground ginger
1 Golden Delicious apple, peeled, cored, and finely grated
1 small onion, finely grated (about ½ cup)
1 jalapeño pepper, seeded and minced, or a 2-inch piece green bell pepper, minced

1 Place the ketchup, applesauce, vinegar, Worcestershire sauce, soy sauce, liquid smoke, brown sugar, garlic powder, white pepper, ginger, apple, onion, and jalapeño in a heavy nonreactive saucepan over medium heat and bring to a simmer. Let simmer gently until the sauce is thick and flavorful, 20 to 30 minutes. Taste for sweetness, adding more brown sugar as necessary.

2 For a smooth sauce, pass it through a strainer. For a more coarsely textured sauce, serve it as is. Either way, serve the sauce at room temperature. It can be refrigerated, covered, for several days. Bring to room temperature before serving.

YIELD:
Makes about 3 cups

WALL OF FLAME

17TH STREET BAR & GRILL

Mike Mills' Apple City Bar-B-Que team has won *four* Memphis in May world championships and was the only team in the contest's history ever to fetch a perfect score. Come to his 17th Street Bar and Grill for crusty pork shoulder, a lip-smacking blackened rib eye, and some of the most exquisite baby back ribs on the planet.

32 North 17th Street
Murphysboro, Illinois
(618) 684-3722
www.4-17th-rib.com

Memphis, Tenn.

"THE ORIGINAL" MEMPHIS DRY RUB RIBS

W et or dry? Three simple words, but to barbecue fanatics they speak volumes. Wet is the way most people in the United States eat ribs—smoky, tender, and dripping with sweet, sticky barbecue sauce. But if you really want to savor pork bones, you must journey to Memphis to sample the dry rub ribs at the restaurant Rendezvous. For more than half a century, the Vergos (pronounced Vargus) family has been dishing up baby back ribs that are crustily grilled over charcoal, mopped with vinegar sauce, and thickly coated with a dry rub just before serving. The irony is that this, the most famous barbecue in Memphis, technically speaking, may not be barbecue at all. Not if you define barbecue as meats roasted low and slow in a pit with plenty of wood smoke. The Rendezvous grills its ribs over an open charcoal fire, with nary a log or hickory chip in sight. (For more about the Rendezvous, see page 36.)

METHOD:
Direct grilling

FOR THE MOP SAUCE:
1 cup distilled white vinegar
1 tablespoon salt
2 tablespoons Memphis Dry Rub (recipe follows)

FOR THE RIBS:
4 racks baby back pork ribs (6 to 8 pounds)
Salt and ground black pepper
Memphis Dry Rub (recipe follows)

YOU'LL ALSO NEED:
Rib rack (optional; see page 292); barbecue mop (optional; see page 288)

1 MAKE THE MOP SAUCE: Place the vinegar, salt, and rub in a nonreactive bowl, add 1 cup of water, and whisk until the salt dissolves. Set aside.

2 Remove the thin, papery membrane from the back of each rack of ribs: Turn a rack meat side down. Insert a sharp implement, such as the tip of a meat thermometer, under the membrane (the best place to start is right next to the first rib bone). Using a dishcloth or pliers to gain a secure grip, pull off the membrane. Repeat with the remaining racks. Generously season the ribs all over with salt and pepper.

3 Set up the grill for direct grilling (see page 21 for charcoal or gas) and preheat to medium.

4 When ready to cook, brush the grill grate. Place the ribs on the hot grate, bone side down, and grill until that side is sizzling and golden brown, about

TIPS

Many Memphians like to eat their dry rub ribs with red barbecue sauce. I don't share their preference, but if you do like sauce with these ribs, serve it on the side so everyone can try them in all their dry spice glory first.

TIPS

Duplicating
Rendezvous ribs at
home is virtually
impossible—first
because they're
cooked in a one-of-a-
kind pit using what
I call modified direct
grilling (the ribs
are cooked directly
over the fire, but
the grates are
positioned so high
above the coals that
the result is more
like that of using
the indirect method,
and this keeps the
meat from burning).
Then there's the
Rendezvous rub, the
formula for which is
a closely guarded
family and trade
secret. So what
you'll find here is
my approximation
of the original
Rendezvous ribs.
    If you want to
compare these to
the real McCoy,
you can order
Rendezvous's own
ribs by mail (see
Mail-Order Sources
on page 742).

35 minutes. Turn the ribs and grill meat side down until that side is sizzling and golden brown, about 25 minutes longer. When fully cooked, the ribs will be nicely browned and tender enough to pull apart with your fingers. The dripping fat may cause flare-ups; if this happens, move the ribs to another spot on the grate.

5 Transfer the grilled ribs to a platter or cutting board. Generously brush or mop the ribs on both sides with the mop sauce. Thickly sprinkle the meat side with the remaining rub to form a crust. You can use all of the rub or just a part, depending on your fondness for spice. I like a crust that's about ⅛ inch thick. Serve the ribs as whole racks, cut the racks into pieces, or carve them into individual ribs and serve any remaining rub on the side.

YIELD:
**Serves 4 really hungry people or 8 folks
    with average appetites**

Memphis Dry Rub

Here's my version of the Rendezvous spice rub. It may make more rub than you'll need for "The Original" Memphis Dry Rub Ribs, but don't worry, you'll find plenty of other uses for it.

INGREDIENTS:
**3 tablespoons sweet paprika
3 tablespoons pure chile powder
1 tablespoon salt
2 teaspoons freshly ground black pepper**

**2 teaspoons garlic powder
2 teaspoons onion powder
2 teaspoons dried thyme
2 teaspoons dried oregano
2 teaspoons yellow mustard seeds
1 teaspoon ground coriander
1 teaspoon celery seed
1 teaspoon cayenne pepper**

Place the paprika, chile powder, salt, black pepper, garlic and onion powders, thyme, oregano, mustard seeds, coriander, celery seed, and cayenne in a bowl and stir to mix. (Actually, if you don't have sensitive skin, your fingers work better for mixing a rub than a spoon or whisk does.) Store the rub in an airtight jar away from heat and light; it will keep for at least 6 months.

YIELD:
Makes ¾ cup

Baltimore, Md.

GRILLED HAM STEAKS With Grilled Pineapple

My mother wasn't much of a cook (that's putting it mildly), but she knew her way around a grill. Steaks would come off the rickety old charcoal grill in our Baltimore back-yard the perfect "Pittsburgh rare" (coal black outside; red, almost moo-ing inside). Her ham steaks were dark with the caramelization that makes sweet cured meats such a thrill to grill—and to eat. Ham steak has fallen somewhat out of fashion in these days of uptown pork T-bones and tender-loins. I say it's time to bring it back. My mother wouldn't have grilled pineap-ple, of course (this *was* the 1950s), but she was just wacky enough to appreci-ate how the burnt sugar sweetness of the pineapple could counterpoint the salty tang of the ham.

METHOD:

Direct grilling

FOR THE GLAZE:

4 tablespoons (½ stick) unsalted butter

1 clove garlic, finely chopped

¼ cup pineapple juice

¼ cup dark rum

¼ cup firmly packed brown sugar

1 tablespoon ketchup

½ teaspoon ground cinnamon

¼ teaspoon ground cloves,
**   or 4 whole cloves**

Coarse salt (kosher or sea) and
**   freshly ground black pepper**

FOR THE HAM STEAKS:

4 ham steaks (each about ½ inch thick
**   and 6 to 8 ounces)**

4 slices fresh pineapple (each about
**   ½ inch thick), rind and core removed**

1 MAKE THE GLAZE: Place the butter and garlic in a heavy nonreactive saucepan over medium heat and cook until the butter is melted and the garlic

begins to brown, about 3 minutes. Stir in the pineapple juice, rum, brown sugar, ketchup, cinnamon, and cloves. Boil until thick and syrupy, about 5 min-utes, then season with salt and pepper to taste. The glaze can be prepared sev-eral hours ahead and refrigerated, covered. Bring to room temperature before using.

2 Set up the grill for direct grilling (see page 21 for charcoal or gas) and preheat to high.

3 When ready to cook, brush and oil the grill grate. Place the ham steaks and pineapple slices on the hot grate and grill until nicely browned and heated through, 3 to 6 minutes per side, basting with the glaze after about 2 min-utes. Transfer the grilled ham steaks to a platter or plates, top with the pineapple, and drizzle any remaining glaze on top.

YIELD:

Serves 4

This recipe calls for the supermarket variety of ham steak—one cut from a cooked ham. If you want to get fancy, you could grill slices of Smithfield, Virginia, or honey baked ham. Look for them in gourmet shops or Asian markets. Smithfield steaks are quite salty, so you may need to soak them in water first to remove some of the excess salt before grilling.

Frances Raichlen: ballet dancer and barbecue mom.

How to Barbecue
A WHOLE HOG

A whole hog is the Mount Everest of barbecue—the ultimate challenge, the feat that separates the men from the boys (or the women from the girls) and tests your mettle as a pit master. Every serious grill jockey should attempt cooking one at some point in his or her life. The gratifying result more than outweighs the momentary queasiness of coming eyeball to eyeball with an entire pig or the strategizing it takes to meet the task's formidable logistical challenges. Learn how they do it in West Virginia on page 302.

No matter which method you use, roasting a whole hog presents two immediate challenges: acquiring that hog and finding a cooker or digging a pit large enough to cook it in. A pig can be ordered from most butcher shops if you give a few days' notice. This is especially true if you live in the South or Midwest. If you live on the East or West Coast and your regular butcher can't help you, often a Latino meat market can deliver the goods. Otherwise, look in the Yellow Pages under meat packers or ask your favorite local barbecue joint to order a whole pig for you.

SMALLER THAN YOU THINK

The mention of a whole hog in most barbecue circles evokes the image of a 150-pound behemoth, but you can find whole pigs that are as small as 40 or 50 pounds. These are certainly easier to manage and they'll still serve a

Philadelphia pit master Jack McDavid shows off a whole hog.

respectable crowd. As a rough rule, you'll need one pound of pig for every person you plan to serve.

You can make roasting a hog more manageable by dividing and conquering it. Greenbrier pit master Ethan Hileman has his hogs cut in half the long way, after having the head and legs removed. It's a lot easier to handle a trimmed half hog than a whole one, and there's also much less waste. Of course, you lose the spectacle of presenting an entire hog with its head on, but sometimes the convenience is worth it.

Bear in mind that, unless you have a gigantic refrigerator, you'll need to pick up the pig the day you want to barbecue it. If that's not feasible, an impromptu refrigerator can be created by placing the pig in a very large cooler or even in a clean plastic trash can and filling it with ice.

NOW YOU'RE SMOKING

The next challenge will be procuring a large enough cooker, and while I fully hope that everyone will go out and buy a competition-size rig to haul behind his or her SUV or pickup truck after reading this book, I realize that most folks have only family-size gas grills or kettle grills. Many party supply houses rent smokers and cookers: The common 55-gallon drum model is large enough to handle a 40- to 50-pound pig or half of a 75-pound

HOG TIPS

At some point every serious pit master wants to go whole hog. But just how long does it take to smoke an entire pig and how can you tell when it's done? For that matter, how many people will that pig feed? Each pig is unique. And don't forget the weather factor—it takes a lot longer for the pig to be done on a cool night than on a sunny afternoon. My barbecue buddy Rick Malir, of City Barbeque in Columbus, Ohio, has cooked more than a few hogs in his day. He shared the following guidelines.

COOKING TIME: Figure on 1 hour for every 5 to 6 pounds of pig barbecued in a smoker burning at 225°F; this time is based on a dressed pig with head on.

HOW TO TELL WHEN IT'S DONE: A pig is fully cooked when the internal temperature taken in the deepest part of the thigh or shoulder registers about 190°F. Use an instant-read meat thermometer to take the temperature, taking care that it does not touch a bone.

YIELD: About 40 percent of a dressed whole hog, with the head on, is edible meat. That means a 100-pound hog will give you about 40 pounds of meat. Figure on 2½ to 3 servings per pound of cooked pork.

Just for the record, Rick's idea of heaven is cooking a 90-pound pig at 225°F in a smoker for about sixteen hours. (Pit masters differ in the cooking temperatures and times they prefer.)

animal. Once, when we needed to bring in the heavy artillery for a beach barbecue in Miami, we found a local party planner and caterer who was willing to arrange the rental of five mammoth Southern Pride rotisserie-smokers (the sort you hitch on the back of a truck).

Another source for smokers is a local barbecue restaurant or a barbecue team; for a listing of these, contact the folks at the Kansas City Barbecue Society, (800) 963-5227, or Memphis in May, (901) 525-4611. The advan-

tage to taking this route is that when you rent the smoker, you might also get some expert advice at the same time.

Of course, some of you may want to make the ultimate commitment to barbecue and invest in that full-size cooker. The classified ads of the *National's Barbecue News* and the *Kansas City Bullsheet* are full of good deals on these. Who knows, you may even wind up competing at the Jack Daniel's World Championship Invitational Barbecue or Kansas City's American Royal Barbecue!

TIPS

Ethan normally cooks a 150-pound hog. You can certainly do this (add two to three hours to the cooking time indicated here), but you can feel equally proud of yourself if you cook the more manageable eighty- to one hundred-pound pig called for here. Ethan has a nifty trick for making any whole hog easier to handle. He has the butcher remove the head and legs and cut the hog in half with a band saw. It's a lot easier to lift two forty-pound halves than one eighty-pound pig.

White Sulphur Springs, W.Va.

ETHAN'S WHOLE HOG

W e always start the opening night of Barbecue University at The Greenbrier with a traditional West Virginia pig pickin' on Kate's Mountain. As anyone from the Carolinas knows, a pig pickin' is a communal feast centered around a smoke-roasted hog. Ours is prepared by Greenbrier banquet chef and pit master extraordinaire Ethan Hileman. Being a West Virginian, Ethan does things a little differently than his Carolina neighbors. For starters, he seasons the hog with "pig paste," a mudlike mixture of fresh herbs and spices, instead of the traditional dry rub. His sauce is based on a North Carolina vinegar one that's reddened and sweetened Kansas City style with ketchup and brown sugar.

The fixin's have a decidedly West Virginian cast, too, running from skillet spoon bread (see page 144) to grilled grits with country ham (see page 647). As for Kate's Mountain, both the mountain itself and a huge stone and wood lodge were named for an early pioneer who survived an Indian attack that took her husband's life. It's the "campus" of Barbecue University. (Kate became the first white settler on the mountain.) This is my take on Ethan's basic recipe.

METHOD:
Indirect grilling

ADVANCE PREPARATION:
3 to 24 hours for marinating the pig (optional)

FOR THE PIG PASTE:
1½ cups peeled garlic cloves (about 8 ounces)
About 2 quarts tightly packed stemmed fresh herbs, including rosemary, thyme, sage, and/or parsley (8 to 12 bunches)
4 cups vegetable oil, or as needed
1 cup coarse salt (kosher or sea)
1 cup sweet paprika
¾ cup sugar
¾ cup freshly ground black pepper
¼ cup hot red pepper flakes
2 tablespoons ground mace

FOR THE PIG:
1 pig (80 to 100 pounds), head and legs removed, body sawed in half lengthwise; ask your butcher do this
Hamburger buns on white bread
Kate's Mountain Vinegar Sauce (recipe follows)

YOU'LL ALSO NEED:
A large smoker; 8 to 10 hickory logs, or 10 to 12 cups wood chips or chunks (preferably hickory), soaked for 1 hour in water to cover, then drained

1 MAKE THE PIG PASTE: Coarsely chop the garlic. Place one quarter of the herb mixture and one quarter of the chopped garlic in a food processor and process to a fine paste. With the motor running, add 1 cup of the oil through the feed tube. Transfer the herb paste to a large bowl. Repeat in batches with the remaining herbs, garlic, and oil, transfering the herb paste to the bowl. Stir in the salt, paprika, sugar, black pepper, hot red pepper flakes, and mace. If necessary, add more oil to create a thick but spreadable paste the consistency of Dijon mustard.

2 Spread the pig paste all over both halves of the pig (inside and out). If you have a place to keep the pig cold, you can do this several hours or even a day ahead to give the meat more of the herb flavor. But the pig will also taste great if you apply the pig paste just prior to cooking.

3 Set up the smoker, following the manufacturer's instructions. For example, if you're using a 55-gallon drum-style smoker, light the charcoal in 2 piles, one at each end of the barrel; use about 5 pounds of charcoal for each pile. Place a log, 2 cups of wood chips or 3 to 4 wood chunks on each pile of coals. If you're using a gas smoker, place a log, 2 cups of wood chips, or 3 or 4 wood chunks in the smoker box. If the smoker does not have a smoker box, you may need to place a metal pan filled with lit charcoal in it and place a log on top (that's what Ethan does with his smoker). The important thing is to adjust the smoker so that it maintains a temperature of about 250°F and has a constant source of wood smoke.

4 When ready to cook, place the pig halves, bone side down, on the grate and cover the smoker. Smoke roast the pig until darkly browned and cooked through, 7 to 9 hours. To test for doneness, use an instant-read meat thermometer: Insert it into the thickest part of a thigh but not so that it touches the bone. The internal temperature should be about 190°F. If the outside of the pig starts to burn, cover it loosely with aluminum foil. Every hour for the first 5 hours you'll need to add 1 log, 2 cups wood chips, or 2 wood chunks to each pile of coals. If using a charcoal smoker, every hour you'll need to add fresh coals to each pile.

5 Transfer the cooked pig halves to a work table or chopping block and let rest for 20 to 40 minutes. Pull the pork into large pieces, discarding any bones or lumps of fat (you'll probably want to wear latex gloves or even heavy-duty rubber gloves to do this). Using your fingertips or a fork, pull each piece of pork into thin shreds or use a cleaver to finely chop it. Ethan likes to serve the pulled pork in the browned, hollowed pig skin; pour and scrape any excess pork fat out first. Have

ETHAN HILEMAN
CATERING CHEF

TIPS

In case you were wondering, mace is a sweet spice made from the dried outer covering of nutmeg kernels.

your guests mound the pulled pork onto hamburger buns or bread and add Kate's Mountain Vinegar Sauce to taste.

YIELD:

Serves 70 to 80

Kate's Mountain Vinegar Sauce

This piquant sauce bridges north and south, east and west, as befits a sauce born in the mountains of West Virginia. Like the sauces of the Carolinas, it's vinegar based with hot pepper flakes for punch, but it also contains ketchup and brown sugar and white sugar, like the sauces of the Midwest and North.

INGREDIENTS:

1 gallon cider vinegar
8 cups ketchup
3 cups dark brown sugar, or more to taste
1 cup granulated sugar
1/2 cup salt, or more to taste
1/2 cup freshly ground black pepper
1/4 cup crushed hot red pepper flakes, or more to taste

1 Combine the vinegar, ketchup, brown sugar, granulated sugar, salt, black pepper, and hot red pepper flakes with 1 quart of water in a large heavy nonreactive pot over medium-high heat and gradually bring to a boil. Reduce the heat to medium and let the sauce simmer gently until the sugars and salt dissolve and the flavors are blended, 15 to 20 minutes. The sauce should be fairly liquid (much thinner than a red barbecue sauce), but not quite watery; look for the consistency of light cream. Add more water as needed. Taste for seasoning, adding more brown sugar, salt, and/or hot red pepper flakes as necessary.

2 Let the sauce cool to room temperature before serving. It may be refrigerated, covered, for up to 1 week. Bring the sauce to room temperature before serving.

YIELD:

Makes about 1 1/2 gallons; serves 75 to 100

MEMPHIS BARBECUE

There are lots of reasons to come to Memphis—the blues clubs on Beale Street, the National Civil Rights Museum, the obligatory pilgrimage to Graceland. But for me, the main attraction in this lively metropolis on the Mississippi River is barbecue: ribs of all shapes and sizes, with myriad flavors and frequently so succulent that the juices dribble down your chin when you eat them; pork shoulders so tender, they all but fall apart when you touch them, served pulled, chopped, or sliced as thin as parchment; and weird stuff most people wouldn't even think of barbecuing, like bologna. Why, Memphians are so obsessed they even have barbecue pizza and spaghetti.

Blues and barbecue are the soul of Memphis.

Ask locals what constitutes authentic Memphis barbecue and you might be surprised that they probably won't mention ribs. Among the natives, the real test of a pit master's mettle is the pork sandwich. Few people make them better than Dan Brown, the owner of Leonard's Pit Barbecue since 1993. Founded by Leonard Heuberger, the restaurant is the oldest continuously operating barbecue business in the city.

Leonard's has moved several times since it opened in 1922, but the house specialty—barbecued pork shoulder slow roasted over charcoal and served chopped on hamburger buns with tangy mustard slaw piled on top—has remained the same.

Dan Brown was a fifteen-year-old high school student when he came to work at Leonard's. The year was 1962, and the restaurant was at its most celebrated loca-

tion, 1140 South Bellevue. Brown recalls humongous fifteen-pound pork shoulders cooked thirty at a time in an ancient brick pit with a twenty-foot chimney. "We laid a twenty-pound sack of lump charcoal in the bottom of the pit, and when the coals burned down we put the pork on iron grates about three feet over the glowing embers." The heat was controlled by moving coals around with a garden hoe. Pork shoulders cooked for nine to eleven hours. It took a pitchfork to turn them.

Brown has one pit master who's still going strong after more than sixty years in the business. Once a week, James Willis, eighty-six at this writing, returns to Leonard's to tend the pits—a profession he has plied since he started with Leonard Heuberger in 1938. The Center for the Study of Southern Culture at the University of Mississippi recently honored Willis with a Keeper of the Flame award for his lifetime commitment to barbecue.

Barbecue seasonings were minimal—perhaps a little salt and pepper (Leonard's still cooks its pork shoulders without any seasonings at all). And curiously, wood smoke never entered the Memphis barbecue equation in the old days and still doesn't at such landmark establishments as the Rendezvous, Cozy Corner, and Corky's Bar-B-Q. "We always cooked directly over lump charcoal," says Brown. "I never saw a stick of hardwood." According to Brown, Memphis pit masters only started using hickory and other woods in the 1980s.

What makes traditional Memphis pork shoulder so great is the way it's served, either as "pulled white"—shreds of moist, light-colored meat from the inside; as "brown chopped"—crusty bits of chopped fire-seared exterior; or as "mixed meat"—a combination of the two. Added to the sandwich is a mound of mustardy coleslaw. Even the sauce, a dulcet amalgam of ketchup, vinegar, chili powder, paprika, and barbecue spices that was called sweet sauce—not barbecue sauce—in the old days, is optional.

WAIT, THERE'S MORE

That's just the beginning of barbecue in Memphis. In the late 1940s, another legendary Memphis pit master, Charlie Vergos, pioneered the dish Memphis is identified with today—dry-spiced baby back ribs (you can read more about these on page 297). Vergos didn't set out to make barbecue history. He was looking for a way to express his appreciation for a case of ribs he received free of charge from a zealous meat salesman. Like Heuberger, Vergos cooked over lump charcoal. His stroke of genius was to apply a thick, explosively flavorful rub after the ribs were cooked, slathering a vinegar mop sauce on the ribs first to provide another layer of flavor and to keep the rub on the ribs.

Well, shoulders and ribs are pretty standard barbecue fare, but only in Memphis do you find barbecue spaghetti, barbecue pizza, *and* barbecue nachos. The spaghetti is believed to have originated in the 1950s at a legendary barbecue joint: Brady and Lil's on South Parkway. Brady would combine spaghetti sauce, barbecue sauce, and a pinch of sugar for sweetness and smoke this mixture in a hickory-fired pit. He'd toss spaghetti noodles with the smoked sauce and chopped barbecued pork. Spaghetti is still prepared this way at Frank Vernon's Bar-B-Que Shop; Vernon learned the recipe from Brady Vinson, the Brady in Brady and Lil's.

As for barbecue pizza, according to the Memphis *Commercial Appeal* food writer Christine Arpe Gang, it was created in the 1950s by Horest Coletta, son of Emil Coletta. In 1923, Emil opened a sandwich shop and ice cream parlor called

The popular Corky's Bar-B-Q—turn in at the sign of the smiling pig.

Coletta's. Horest carried on the family business. "When my dad started selling pizza, very few people knew what it was," recalls Horest's son, Jerry. "To stimulate interest in it, he started topping pizza with something every Memphian could relate to: chopped pork shoulder." Elvis was a big fan of Coletta's barbecue pizza, and it remains one of the pasta parlor's most popular dishes.

It was only a matter of time until someone had the idea to combine barbecue and nachos. Christine Gang credits the invention to Robert Garcia, the general manager of Ovations Food Service, which runs the food and beverage concessions at AutoZone Park. Garcia had the idea to combine Memphis's favorite food with one of America's favorite snacks for a Redbirds game in 1999. "Today, it's our top seller," reports Garcia, who buys the barbecued pork from that Memphis landmark, Charlie Vergos Rendezvous.

AN EMBARRASSMENT OF RICHES

Now there are more than forty barbecue restaurants in Memphis. No survey of the city's barbecue would be complete without mentioning four more establishments: Jim Neely's Interstate Bar-B-Que, Corky's Bar-B-Q, Cozy Corner, and The Bar-B-Q Shop. Interstate was founded in 1980 by an insurance man turned pit master, Jim Neely. The most popular

WHERE TO ENJOY MEMPHIS BARBECUE

THE BAR-B-Q SHOP
1782 Madison Ave.
(901) 272-1277

CHARLIE VERGOS RENDEZVOUS
52 South Second St.
(901) 523-2746
Mail-order:
(888) 464-7359

COZY CORNER
745 North Parkway
(901) 527-9158

CORKY'S BAR-B-Q
5259 Poplar Ave.
(901) 685-9744
(and other locations)
Mail-order:
(800) 926-7597

GERMANTOWN COMMISSARY
2290 S. Germantown Rd.
(901) 754-5540

JIM NEELY'S INTERSTATE BARBECUE
2265 South Third St.
(901) 775-2304
Mail-order:
(888) 227-2793

LEONARD'S PIT BARBECUE
5465 Fox Plaza Dr.
(901) 360-1963

NEELY'S BAR-B-QUE
670 Jefferson St.
(901) 521-9798
(and other locations)

TOPS BAR-B-Q
Serves pork shoulder sandwiches only
1286 Union Ave.
(901) 725-7527
(and other locations)

dish at the Interstate is the chopped pork sandwich. Neely also gets consistent kudos for his baked beans.

In commercial terms, Corky's Bar-B-Q is Memphis's most successful barbecue enterprise, having grown from a single eatery in 1984 to a veritable chain, with franchises in Mississippi, Illinois, and several other states. Daily rib consumption is measured in tons, not pounds. Corky's was founded by Don Pelts, a former furniture salesman. He runs the operation with his son, Barry. Today you can find Corky's barbecue sauce and even their frozen ribs at a growing number of supermarkets. You can also order them by mail.

Of course, for many aficionados, Memphis barbecue tastes best at small, family-run, strictly local, one-of-a-kind restaurants like the Cozy Corner and The Bar-B-Q Shop. (read more about each of these establishments on pages 430 and 356). The Cozy Corner is famed for its barbecued game hens, of all things, while The Bar-B-Q Shop serves up a mean barbecued bologna and barbecue spaghetti.

Elvis sang "Love Me Tender." One thing's for sure, as long as there's a Memphis, tender barbecue (especially pork shoulders slow roasted over charcoal, served with a pugnacious mustard slaw on a bun) will be king!

Lamb with

Lamb isn't the first meat most Americans think of throwing on the grill. (Unless you happen to come from Owensboro home of Kentucky's distinctive barbecued mutton—or Washington, D.C., with its large Middle-Eastern diplomatic corps.) So, you may be surprised to learn that barbecued lamb was a favorite of the Founding Fathers—a love that continues at cutting-edge restaurants today. The robust flavor of lamb is well suited to grilling, the perfect foil for the fragrant scent of wood smoke and the sizzle of the grill. In this chapter you'll find everything from lamb on the rod (Pennsylvania-style shish kebab) to smoked lamb shanks with mint barbecue sauce to a spectacular mega-ginger butterflied grilled leg of lamb. If you love lamb on the bone, look for the 'Que Queens Parmesan pepper chops or the wine-marinated chops that feature a sauce made with mustard and Oregon Pinot Noir. Lamb is one of the best meats ever to face the fire, as this chapter amply proves.

Sizzle

TIPS

Laurence Butler
describes cooking
a whole lamb, but
a butterflied leg—
one that is split
open and has the
bones removed—is
more manageable
for most backyard
grillers. It's easier
to carve and
produces stunning
results. You'll find
a description of
the technique on
the facing page or
ask your butcher
to butterfly the leg
of lamb for you.

Virginia

SPIT-ROASTED LAMB
With Butter & Salt

What was the first American barbecue? What did it look like? How did it taste? I've pondered this question frequently since I began writing this book. One early version was described by a gentleman named Laurence Butler in a letter to his compatriots back in England when he visited Virginia in the 1780s.

Barbique . . . is a Lamb or Mutton & indeed sometimes a Beef splitt into & stuck on spitts & then they have a large Hole dugg in the ground where they have a number of Coals made of the Bark of Trees, put in this Hole, & then they lay the Meat over that within about six inches of the Coals, & then they Keep basting it with Butter & Salt & Water & turning it every now & then, untill its done.

The modern grill master will recognize two essential elements here: the use of wood (in this case tree bark) to flavor the meat with smoke and the frequent basting. Pit masters throughout the Americas still use melted butter to keep meat moist—you'll find this at steak houses like Ruth's Chris. But as for the salt water, as far as I know,

the technique is no longer used in the United States. I can tell you, though, that if you try and duplicate this method it makes for some extraordinary spit roasting. You'll see for yourself when you make the crusty, succulent boneless leg of lamb below.

METHOD:
Rotisserie grilling

ADVANCE PREPARATION:
1 hour for soaking the wood chips

INGREDIENTS:
**1 butterflied leg of lamb
(3 to 4 pounds;
see the facing page)
8 tablespoons (1 stick)
unsalted butter
2 tablespoons coarse salt
(kosher or sea)
1 tablespoon freshly ground
black pepper (optional)
½ cup fresh lemon juice or red
wine vinegar (optional)**

YOU'LL ALSO NEED:
**2 cups wood chips or chunks
(preferably oak); long-handled
basting brush or sauce mop;
butcher's string (optional)**

1 Tie the lamb into a tight cylinder or have your butcher do this. Skewer the lamb on the turnspit.

2 Melt the butter in a small saucepan over medium heat. Combine 2 cups warm water and the salt in a large nonreactive bowl and whisk until the salt dissolves. Whisk in the pepper and lemon juice or vinegar, if using.

BUTTERFLYING A LEG OF LAMB

Butterflying is a technique used to reduce the thickness and increase the surface area of a piece of meat for grilling. The technique shortens the cooking time and helps create a savory crust. To butterfly a leg of lamb, slice it almost in half through the side. Once the meat is spread open, you can remove the bone, winding up with a broad, thin sheet of meat that is perfect for direct grilling. Or you can roll the butterflied leg of lamb into a compact cylinder to roast. Butterflying a leg of lamb isn't difficult, but if the task seems too daunting, most butchers will be happy to do it for you.

3 Set up the grill for rotisserie grilling following the manufacturer's instructions and preheat to medium-high. Place a large drip pan in the center of the grill, under where the lamb will turn. If using a gas grill, place all of the wood chips or chunks in the smoker box or smoker pouch and run the grill on high until you see smoke, then reduce the heat to medium-high. If using a charcoal grill, preheat it to medium-high, then toss all of the wood chips or chunks on the coals.

4 When ready to cook, attach the spit to the rotisserie motor mechanism by inserting the pointed end of the spit into the rotisserie's motor socket. If your rotisserie spit has a counterweight, position it so that it counterbalances the lamb. Turn on the motor and spit roast the lamb until golden brown on the outside and cooked to taste, 1 to 1½ hours for medium (see Note). To test for doneness, use an instant-read thermometer: The internal temperature should be about 160°F. After 10 minutes, baste the lamb with the salt water; after another 10 minutes, baste it with the melted butter. Repeat until the lamb is done.

5 Remove the grilled lamb from the spit and transfer it to a platter. Brush it one last time with melted butter, then let it rest for 5 minutes. Slice the lamb crosswise and serve.

YIELD:
Serves 6 to 8

NOTE: Lamb tends to be served medium to medium-well done in traditional American barbecue.

In keeping with Butler's "recipe," I call for butter and salt water, but the lamb will be even tastier if you spice up the brine with some black pepper and vinegar or lemon juice—ingredients that would have been common in eighteenth-century Virginia.

Not lamb but mutton is the meat of choice in Owensboro, Kentucky (see page 331).

TIPS

Legs of lamb vary in size depending on the butcher, region, and time of year. This recipe calls for a 2½ to 3-pound leg. For a larger leg (4 to 5 pounds) increase the cooking time by 3 to 6 minutes per side.

If you can't get to the Rendezvous, you can always mail-order.

Memphis, Tenn.

NICK VERGOS'S GREEK LEG OF LAMB

You may be surprised to find a Greek-style lamb recipe from one of the scions of Memphis's first family of barbecue. But when Rendezvous restaurant co-owner Nick Vergos isn't busy cooking Memphis-style baby back ribs, he's apt to reach for the seasonings of his Greek ancestors—olive oil, vinegar, oregano, and garlic. Nick originally created the marinade for pork loin or tenderloin, but the flavors are right on for lamb.

METHOD:
Direct grilling

ADVANCE PREPARATION:
4 to 12 hours for marinating the lamb

FOR THE LAMB:
**1 butterflied leg of lamb
    (2½ to 3 pounds; see page 311)
Coarse salt (kosher or sea) and
    freshly ground black pepper**

FOR THE MARINADE:
**⅔ cup extra-virgin olive oil
⅓ cup red wine vinegar
1 tablespoon dried oregano
6 cloves garlic, finely chopped**

FOR THE BASTING MIXTURE:
**4 tablespoons (½ stick)
    salted butter
2 tablespoons fresh lemon juice**

1 Generously, and I mean generously, season the lamb on both sides with salt and pepper. You should use roughly twice as much salt as pepper. Place the lamb in a nonreactive baking dish just large enough to hold it.

2 MAKE THE MARINADE: Combine the oil, vinegar, oregano, and garlic in a nonreactive bowl and whisk to mix. Pour the marinade over the lamb, turning it to coat both sides. Let the lamb marinate, covered, in the refrigerator for at least 4 hours or as long as overnight, turning it once or twice so that it marinates evenly.

3 MAKE THE BASTING MIXTURE: Put the butter and lemon juice in a small nonreactive saucepan and cook

Not since Adam has a rib been this famous.

1-888-HOGS FLY

CHARLES VERGOS' Rendezvous CHARCOAL RIBS

Ribs from The Rendezvous in Memphis fly tonight. Check the ordering info on the back, and slap a world-famous slab on somebody's table tomorrow.

over medium heat until the butter is melted. Keep warm until ready to use.

4 Set up the grill for direct grilling using a two-zone fire (see page 22 for charcoal or gas) and preheat one zone to high and the other to medium.

5 When ready to cook, drain the marinade from the lamb and discard the marinade. Brush and oil the grill grate. Place the lamb on the grate over the hot zone of the grill. Sear one side for about 2 minutes, then move the lamb to the cooler (medium) zone of the grill and cook for 6 to 8 minutes. When the bottom side is crusty and brown, turn the lamb over, placing it on the hot zone to sear the second side for 2 minutes, then move the lamb to the medium zone for another 6 to 8 minutes. Once you have turned the lamb over, begin basting it with the butter and lemon mixture as it grills. The total cooking time will be about 8 minutes per side for medium-rare, 10 to 12 minutes per side for medium. To test for doneness, use an instant-read meat thermometer: When cooked to medium-rare, the internal temperature will be about 145°F; when cooked to medium, the internal temperature will be 160°F.

6 Transfer the grilled lamb to a cutting board and let it rest for 5 minutes. Thinly slice it on the diagonal across the grain. Place the slices on a platter, drizzle any remaining basting mixture over them, and serve at once.

YIELD:
Serves 6

Washington, D.C.

GRACE'S GINGER LEG OF LAMB

Lamb and fresh ginger are made for each other—something anyone who has sampled the combination at an Indian, Southeast Asian, or Chinese restaurant will appreciate. That got me thinking about flavoring a leg of lamb with a uniquely American beverage, ginger ale. The concept is just bizarre enough to be interesting, but not so strange as to taste weird. So what's the connection to Washington, D.C.? When I was in my twenties, a friend's mother, Grace Orlansky, who lives in the Washington suburbs, served a similar butterflied leg of lamb. The only thing missing was the ginger ale.

METHOD:
Direct grilling

ADVANCE PREPARATION:
4 to 12 hours for marinating the lamb

FOR THE LAMB:
½ leg of lamb, butterflied (about 2½ pounds; see page 311)
1 piece (1½ inches) fresh ginger, peeled and cut into matchstick slivers
2 cloves garlic, cut into matchstick slivers

TIPS

To boost the flavor, I stud the lamb with slivers of fresh ginger and garlic. If you're in a hurry, you can omit this step; thanks to the marinade, your lamb will still be very flavorful.

FOR THE MARINADE:

1 piece (2 inches) peeled fresh ginger,
    coarsely chopped
2 cloves garlic, coarsely chopped
3 scallions, trimmed, white parts
    coarsely chopped, green parts
    finely chopped
½ cup ginger ale or ginger beer
    (see Notes)
6 tablespoons soy sauce
3 tablespoons Asian (dark)
    sesame oil
2 tablespoons honey
1 to 3 teaspoons Thai hot sauce
    (Sriracha; see Notes) or your
    favorite hot sauce
1 teaspoon Chinese five-spice powder
½ teaspoon freshly ground
    black pepper

1 Using the tip of a slender paring knife, make small ½-inch-deep slits all over the lamb about 1 inch apart. Insert ginger slivers in half of the holes, garlic slivers in the remainder. Place the lamb in a baking dish or roasting pan just large enough to hold it.

2 MAKE THE MARINADE: Place the chopped ginger and garlic and the scallion whites, ginger ale, soy sauce, sesame oil, honey, hot sauce, five-spice powder, and pepper in a blender or food processor and blend to a coarse purée. Pour the marinade over the lamb, turning it to coat both sides evenly. Let the lamb marinate in the refrigerator, covered, for at least 4 hours or as long as overnight, turning it once or twice so that it marinates evenly.

3 Set up the grill for direct grilling (see page 21 for charcoal or gas) and preheat to medium.

4 When ready to cook, drain the marinade from the lamb and discard the marinade. Brush and oil the grill grate. Arrange the lamb on the hot grate so that it is slightly on a diagonal to the bars. Grill the lamb until cooked to taste, 10 to 12 minutes per side for medium, rotating the lamb a quarter turn after 5 minutes of grilling on each side to create an attractive crosshatch of grill marks. Turn the lamb over when the bottom side is crusty and brown. To test for doneness, use an instant-read meat thermometer: When cooked to medium-rare, the internal temperature will be about 145°F; when cooked to medium, the internal temperature will be 160°F.

5 Transfer the grilled lamb to a cutting board and let it rest for 5 minutes. Slice the lamb on the diagonal across the grain and serve with the chopped scallion greens sprinkled on top.

YIELD:
Serves 4 to 6

NOTES:

■ Ginger beer is a West Indian soft drink with a stronger, sharper ginger flavor than ginger ale.

■ Thai hot sauce is sweet and hot, like turbo-charged ketchup.

DREAMLAND BARBECUE

Legend has it that brick mason John "Big Daddy" Bishop Sr. prayed to God to show him an easier way to make a living. The answer came in a dream: Open a barbecue joint. So Bishop built a cinder-block eatery with his own hands, block by block, in the rough-and-tumble Tuscaloosa neighbo hood of Jerusalem Heights and christened it Dreamland.

As befits any proper barbecue joint, the open brick pit was the focal point. Big Daddy cooked his ribs (flavorful spareribs) over glowing hickory embers, and they came off the grill with just the right amount of chew and wood smoke. No fall-off-the-bone-tender ribs, these. No, these ribs were meant for gnawing.

Today, Dreamland is a big business, with outlets in Birmingham, Mobile, and Atlanta. The newer outposts serve barbecued chicken and pork and side dishes. The original Tuscaloosa location, serves only the ribs that made Dreamland famous.

Whichever location you isit, you'll find that the ribs are tender, smoky, grilled over hickory fire, and slathered with a distinctive vinegary, hot, red barbecue sauce—just the way Big Daddy dreamt they should be.

5535 15th Avenue East
Tuscaloosa, Alabama
(205) 758-8135

1427 14th Avenue South
Birmingham, Alabama
(205) 933-2133

(and other locations)
www.dreamlandbbq.com

If barbecue is the stuff of dreams, this is the Posturepedic.

TIPS

I like to use double-thick chops (1 to 1½ inches thick) for this recipe. To make a double-thick rib chop, cut a rack of lamb into 4 or 5 chops, each with two ribs, then cut off one of the rib bones. All the more meat to sink your teeth into.

Louisiana

LAMB CHOPS With Creole Cream Sauce

Here's a quick, easy lamb chop recipe that's bursting with Louisiana flavors. The chops are rubbed with Cajun seasoning and garlic. The sauce owes its punch to spicy Creole mustard. One good brand is Zatarain's, and it's available at most supermarkets. If you can't find Creole mustard, substitute Dijon, although the flavor won't be quite the same.

METHOD:
Direct grilling

FOR THE LAMB CHOPS:
8 double-thick lamb rib chops
   (3 to 4 ounces each)
2 tablespoons Cajun Rub (page 420)
   or your favorite commercial brand
4 cloves garlic, minced
2 tablespoons extra-virgin olive oil

FOR THE MUSTARD SAUCE:
¼ cup Creole mustard
2 tablespoons mayonnaise
2 tablespoons sour cream
1 tablespoon Worcestershire sauce
1 shallot, minced (3 to 4 tablespoons)
Coarse salt (kosher or sea) and
   freshly ground black pepper

1 Place the lamb chops in a baking dish and sprinkle the Cajun Rub and garlic all over both sides. Drizzle the oil over both sides of the chops, patting it onto the meat with your fingertips. Let the chops marinate in the refrigerator, covered, for 1 hour.

2 MAKE THE MUSTARD SAUCE: Place the mustard, mayonnaise, sour cream, Worcestershire sauce, and shallot in a nonreactive mixing bowl and whisk to mix. Season with salt and pepper to taste.

3 Set up the grill for direct grilling (see page 21 for charcoal or gas) and preheat to high.

4 When ready to cook, brush and oil the grill grate. Place the lamb chops on the hot grate and grill until cooked to taste, about 4 minutes per side for medium-rare. Rotate the chops a quarter turn after 2 minutes on each side to create an attractive crosshatch of grill marks. If the rib bones start to burn, slide a folded piece of aluminum foil beneath them as a shield. To test for doneness, use an instant-read meat thermometer: When cooked to medium-rare, the internal temperature will be about 145°F; when cooked to medium, the internal temperature will be 160°F. Transfer the grilled chops to a platter or plates and let them rest for 3 minutes before serving. Spoon or drizzle the mustard sauce over them and serve at once.

YIELD:
Serves 4

Portland, Ore.

LAMB CHOPS
With Mustard
Pinot Noir Sauce

When I went to Reed College in Portland in the 1970s, Oregon's wine industry was in its infancy. Imagine my surprise, attending a college function twenty years later, when I was served world-class wines from the Willamette Valley, where I used to hike as a freshman. Oregon's mild, damp Pacific climate is particularly well suited to the Pinot Noir grape, and if you haven't tasted a wine from Ponzi or Eyrie Vineyards, it's worth a special trip to your local liquor store. All of which is a lengthy prologue to these loin lamb chops, which are marinated in Pinot Noir and rosemary and served with a simple tangy sauce made with mustard and more red wine. Pinot Noir possesses an earthy, red berry–like flavor, which makes it a good partner for lamb.

METHOD:
Direct grilling

Long-smoked meats cut the old-fashioned way—by hand on a time-worn butcher block.

ADVANCE PREPARATION:
2 to 3 hours for marinating the chops

INGREDIENTS:
8 loin lamb chops (about 2 inches thick and 6 to 8 ounces each)
Coarse salt (kosher or sea) and freshly ground black pepper
1/2 cup extra-virgin olive oil
2 cups Pinot Noir (preferably from Oregon)
4 sprigs fresh rosemary
2 cloves garlic, peeled and gently crushed with the side of a cleaver
4 juniper berries, gently crushed with the side of a cleaver
Mustard Pinot Noir Sauce (recipe follows)

1 Trim any excess fat off the chops (leave a little) and generously season them on both sides with salt and

I call for loin chops here, but you could certainly use rib chops, in which case I'd suggest double-thick chops (you'll find a description of these in the Tip on the facing page). For that matter, you could marinate and grill a whole rack of lamb or even prepare filets mignons of beef in this fashion.

pepper. Place the chops in a nonreactive baking dish. Pour the oil over the chops, turning them a couple of times to coat both sides well. Add the wine, rosemary, garlic, and juniper berries. Let the chops marinate for 2 to 3 hours in the refrigerator, covered, turning them several times so they marinate evenly.

2 Set up the grill for direct grilling (see page 21 for charcoal or gas) and preheat to high.

3 When ready to cook, brush and oil the grill grate. Drain the marinade from the chops and discard the marinade. Place the chops on the hot grate and grill until cooked to taste, 5 to 8 minutes per side for medium-rare. Rotate the chops a quarter turn after 3 minutes on each side to create an attractive crosshatch of grill marks. Turn the chops on their sides and briefly grill the edges. To test for doneness, use the poke test; when cooked to medium-rare, the meat should be gently yielding. Transfer the grilled chops to a platter or plates and let them rest for 3 minutes before serving with the Mustard Pinot Noir Sauce alongside.

YIELD:
Serves 4

TIPS

The wine needn't break the bank, but you should use a Pinot Noir you wouldn't mind drinking.

Mustard Pinot Noir Sauce

Simplicity itself, this sauce contains only two main ingredients, but it never fails to bring down the house.

INGREDIENTS:

1 cup dry red wine, preferably Pinot Noir
¾ cup Dijon mustard
Coarse salt (kosher or sea) and lots of freshly ground black pepper

Place the wine in a heavy nonreactive saucepan over high heat and bring to a boil, swirling the wine in the pan to prevent scorching. Let boil until the wine is reduced to about ¼ cup. Let the wine cool to room temperature, then whisk in the mustard. Season with salt and pepper to taste. Serve the sauce warm or at room temperature. The sauce may be refrigerated, covered, for up to a week.

YIELD:
Makes about 1 cup

Kansas City, Mo.

BBQ QUEENS' PARMESAN PEPPER RACK OF LAMB

W ho says Kansas City is all about smoky ribs and brisket? Not the BBQ Queens, an association of female Kansas City food professionals and barbecue buffs that includes a caterer, a cookbook author, a restaurateur, a mystery writer, and the nation's largest distributor of barbecue books.

The 'Que Queens have fielded a barbecue team at the American Royal in Kansas City and manufacture their own sauce (the proceeds from which go to charity). While they originally created this Parmesan and herb paste for strip steaks, the garlic and pepper also go exceedingly well with lamb.

METHOD:
Indirect grilling

INGREDIENTS:
2 racks of lamb (1½ pounds each), frenched
½ cup finely grated Parmesan cheese
2 cloves garlic, minced
2 tablespoons dried basil
2 tablespoons dried oregano
1 tablespoon cracked black peppercorns
4 to 6 tablespoons extra-virgin olive oil
Coarse salt (kosher or sea)
Lemon wedges

TIPS

Rib bones that have been frenched burn easily. If you see this starting to happen, slip a doubled sheet of aluminum foil underneath the bones to protect them from the flames.

The 'Que Queens in full regalia give fans the royal wave.

1 Trim off the flap of fat covering the outside of each frenched rack of lamb.

2 Place the cheese, garlic, basil, oregano, and peppercorns in a bowl and stir to mix. Stir in enough oil to create a thick paste. Generously season the racks on both sides with salt. Spread the herb paste on the racks on both sides, using the back of a spoon. Let the racks marinate for 15 minutes at room temperature while you light the grill.

3 Set up the grill for indirect grilling (see page 22 for charcoal or page 23 for gas) and preheat to medium-high.

4 When ready to cook, brush and oil the grill grate. Be exceptionally generous with the oil, as the cheese in the herb paste tends to stick to the grate. Place the racks in the center of the hot grate, meat side up, over the drip pan and away from the heat, and cover the grill. Cook 25 to 40 minutes per side for medium-rare, about 145°F on an instant-read meat thermometer (the cooking time will depend on the size of the racks). Transfer the racks to a platter and let them rest for 3 minutes. Carve the lamb into chops and serve with lemon wedges for squeezing over the meat.

YIELD:
Serves 4

Illinois

SMOKED LAMB SHANKS
With Mint Barbecue Sauce

When I was growing up, there was nothing fashionable about lamb shanks. The tough, sinewy, but immensely flavorful cut was the unheralded cousin of rack of lamb and loin chops. If you wanted to sample it, you had to go to a Greek neighborhood, like Chicago's Greektown or Central Square in Cambridge, Massachusetts. Today, the lowly shank turns up at trendy restaurants across the United States, cherished by chefs for its soulful flavor and its reasonable cost. The traditional way to cook lamb shanks is to braise them: The meat needs the slow, low, moist heat to make it tender. But lamb shanks I ate in Chicago's Greektown set me thinking about another long, slow cooking method dear to my heart—smoking. Noting how well mint goes with lamb, I added dried mint to the rub and mint jelly to the barbecue sauce. Think of this as barbecued lamb osso buco.

METHOD:
Indirect grilling

INGREDIENTS:

4 teaspoons olive oil

4 lamb shanks (12 to 14 ounces each)

1 tablespoon coarse salt

1 tablespoon dried mint (see Note)

2 teaspoons garlic powder

1 teaspoon freshly ground black pepper

Mint Barbecue Sauce (recipe follows)

YOU'LL ALSO NEED:

1½ cups wood chips or chunks (preferably oak), soaked for 1 hour in water to cover, then drained

1 Drizzle the oil over the lamb shanks, rubbing it onto the meat with your fingertips. Place the salt, mint, garlic powder, and pepper in a small bowl and stir to mix. (Actually, your fingers work better for mixing a spoon or whisk does.) Sprinkle this rub all over the lamb shanks, patting it onto the meat with your fingertips.

2 Set up the grill for indirect grilling (see page 22 for charcoal or page 23 for gas) and preheat to medium-low. If using a charcoal grill, place a large drip pan in the center, preheat the grill to medium-low, then toss the wood chips or chunks on the coals. If using a gas grill, place the wood chips or chunks in the smoker box or in a smoker pouch (see page 24) and run the grill on high until you see smoke, then reduce the heat to medium-low.

3 When ready to cook, place the lamb shanks, on their side, in the center of the hot grate, over the drip pan and away from the heat, and cover the grill. Smoke-roast the lamb shanks for 1 hour.

4 Wrap each shank in aluminum foil and continue cooking until very tender, 45 minutes to 1¼ hours more. When the shanks are fully cooked, the meat will have pulled back from the shank bone and will be tender enough to pull apart with your fingers. To test for doneness, insert an instant-read meat thermometer into the thickest part but not so that it touches the bone: The temperature should be about 185°F. During the last 15 minutes, unwrap the shanks and brush them with some of the Mint Barbecue Sauce. Then, rewrap and finish smoking. If using a charcoal grill, after 1 hour you'll need to add 12 fresh coals to each side.

5 Brush the shanks with some of the Mint Barbecue Sauce, then transfer them to a platter or plates and serve with the remaining sauce.

YIELD:

Serves 4

NOTE: If you don't have dried mint, simply tear open a mint tea bag.

VARIATION: You can also cook the shanks in a smoker. Following the manufacturer's instructions, preheat it to low (250° to 275°F). Add 1 cup wood chips when you put on the lamb and 1 cup after 1 hour. Smoke the shanks until very tender and the internal temperature is 180°F, 1½ hours unwrapped and 1 to 1½ hours wrapped—2½ to 3 hours in all.

TIPS

■ Once the province of ethnic markets, lamb shanks can be purchased at many supermarkets (it helps to give the butcher advance notice). If not, look for them at a Greek or Italian market.

■ This recipe uses a technique borrowed from competition brisket jocks—wrapping the smoked lamb shanks halfway through smoking to keep them from drying out.

Mint Barbecue Sauce

If you like your barbecue sauce meaty and not too sweet, this is for you. Mustard and mint make it tangy. Thanks to the corn syrup (one of the least sugary of traditional sweeteners), it's not overly sweet.

INGREDIENTS:

1 cup veal, beef, or chicken stock

3 tablespoons dark corn syrup

2 tablespoons red wine vinegar

2 tablespoons tomato paste

2 tablespoon Dijon mustard

2 tablespoons chopped fresh mint leaves

Coarse salt (kosher or sea) and
freshly ground black pepper

Place the stock, corn syrup, vinegar, tomato paste, mustard, and mint in a nonreactive saucepan over medium-high heat and bring to a simmer. Reduce the heat to medium and let the sauce simmer until richly flavored and slightly thickened, 5 to 10 minutes. Season with salt and pepper to taste. Serve hot or at room temperature. The sauce will keep, covered, for several days in the refrigerator.

YIELD:
Makes about 1 cup

Lamb has a natural affinity for mint.

PACIFIC RIM SMOKED LAMB SHANKS

While we're on the subject of lamb shanks, sometimes I prepare them with a Chinese spice rub and an Asian barbecue sauce inspired by a visit to San Francisco's Chinatown. If you don't know about them already, let me introduce you to a few of the ingredients. Five-spice powder is a Chinese spice mix that often includes star anise, fennel seeds, pepper, cinnamon, and cloves. Hoisin sauce is a thick, sweet Chinese table sauce made primarily of fermented soybean paste and sugar. There are several options for rice wine: You can use brown Chinese rice wine or the clear Japanese sake, or you could even use a Spanish sherry (dry or cream). Thai hot sauce is a sort of chile-laced ketchup; one good kind is Sriracha. To mix things up a little, this recipe also includes a tomato-based hot sauce. Put these all together with lamb and you've got a delectable synergy. Think of it as Grant Avenue meets Memphis.

ADVANCE PREPARATION:
1 hour for soaking the wood chips

METHOD:
Indirect grilling

FOR THE LAMB AND RUB:

4 tablespoons Asian (dark) sesame oil

4 lamb shanks (12 to 14 ounces each)

1 tablespoon coarse salt (kosher or sea)

1 tablespoon sugar

1 teaspoon Chinese five-spice powder

1 teaspoon freshly ground black pepper

FOR THE HOISIN BARBECUE SAUCE:

1½ cups tomato-based barbecue sauce
    such as St. Louis Red
    (page 666) or your favorite
    commercial brand

½ cup hoisin sauce

¼ cup rice wine

2 tablespoons Thai hot sauce
    (Sriracha) or your favorite
    hot sauce

YOU'LL ALSO NEED:

1½ cups wood chips or chunks
    (preferably oak), soaked for 1 hour
    in water to cover, then drained

1 Drizzle the oil over the lamb shanks, rubbing it onto the meat with your fingertips.

2 Place the salt, sugar, five-spice powder, and pepper in a small bowl and stir to mix. (Actually, your fingers work better for mixing a rub than a spoon or whisk does.) Sprinkle the rub all over the lamb shanks, patting it onto the meat with your fingertips.

3 MAKE THE HOISIN BARBECUE SAUCE: Place the barbecue sauce, hoisin sauce, rice wine, and hot sauce in a nonreactive saucepan over medium heat, bring to a simmer, and let simmer until thick and richly flavored, 10 to 15 minutes. Set the sauce aside.

4 Set up the grill for indirect grilling (see page 22 for charcoal or page 23 for gas) and preheat to medium-low. If using a charcoal grill, place a large drip pan in the center, preheat the grill to medium-low, then toss the wood chips or chunks on the coals. If using a gas grill, place the wood chips or chunks in the smoker box or in a smoker pouch (see page 24) and run the grill on high until you see smoke, then reduce the heat to medium-low.

5 When ready to cook, place the lamb shanks, on their side, in the center of the hot grate, over the drip pan and away from the heat, and cover the grill. Smoke roast the lamb shanks for 1 hour.

6 Wrap each shank in aluminum foil and continue cooking until very tender, 45 minutes to 1¼ hours more. When the shanks are fully cooked, the meat will have pulled back from the shank bone and will be tender enough to pull apart with your fingers. To test for doneness, insert an instant-read meat thermometer into the thickest part but not so that it touches the bone: The temperature should be about 180°F. During the last 15 minutes or so, unwrap the shanks and brush them with some of the sauce. If using a charcoal grill, after 1 hour you'll need to add 12 fresh coals to each side.

7 Transfer the grilled lamb shanks to a platter or plates and serve with the remaining barbecue sauce.

YIELD:

Serves 4

TIPS

As we've seen elsewhere in this chapter, lamb goes well with mint—an affinity appreciated by the British, who accompany it with mint jelly, and by people throughout the Middle and Near East, who season it with dried or fresh mint leaves. I've never actually seen anyone place fresh mint leaves on a shish kebab, but I think you'll find the practice irresistible.

Pennsylvania

LAMB ON A ROD

Leave no lead unfollowed and no dish untasted. Such is my motto, and it's led me to some pretty phenomenal barbecue. It's also sent me on some wild-goose chases. Which is how I found myself in a rather hardscrabble town in northwestern Pennsylvania in search of lamb on a rod. My informant spoke lovingly of a Lebanese family restaurant, of a whole crackling crisp lamb turning slowly over a charcoal fire. Of freshly baked Middle Eastern–style bread and nose-tweakingly pungent garlic sauce. After much driving, I finally found the "restaurant," which hadn't been owned by Lebanese for more than a decade. As for the magisterial lamb on a rod, it turned out to be commonplace shish kebab. But the afternoon wasn't a complete waste, for it set me dreaming how I would like to make lamb on a rod.

METHOD:
Direct grilling

ADVANCE PREPARATION:
30 minutes for marinating the lamb

INGREDIENTS:
1½ pounds boneless leg of lamb,
    cut into 1-inch cubes
2 teaspoons dried mint
1 teaspoon coarse salt (kosher or sea)

1 teaspoon freshly ground black pepper
6 cloves garlic, peeled and gently
    crushed with the side of a cleaver
2 tablespoons extra-virgin olive oil
1 bunch fresh mint leaves,
    rinsed and shaken dry
Garlic Lemon Sesame Sauce
    (recipe follows)
8 to 12 pickled peppers
Pita bread

YOU'LL ALSO NEED:
4 long (10-inch) or 8 short (6-inch)
    metal skewers

1 Place the lamb in a mixing bowl and sprinkle the dried mint, salt, and black pepper over it. Toss the meat with your fingers to mix. Stir in the garlic and oil and let marinate in the refrigerator, covered, for 30 minutes.

2 Thread the marinated lamb on skewers, placing a fresh mint leaf between each piece of meat.

3 Set up the grill for direct grilling (see page 21 for charcoal or gas) and preheat to high.

4 When ready to grill, brush and oil the grill grate. Place the kebabs on the hot grate and grill until cooked to medium, 2 to 3 minutes per side (8 to 12 minutes in all). To test for doneness, use the poke test, the lamb will feel firmly yielding.

5 Unskewer the lamb onto a platter or plates. (Don't eat the lamb off

nose-tweakingly

the hot metal skewers, or you'll burn your lips.) Serve the lamb with the Garlic Lemon Sesame Sauce, pickled peppers, and pita bread.

YIELD:
Serves 4

Garlic Lemon Sesame Sauce

Lebanese *taratoor* (garlic tahini sauce) was the inspiration for this creamy garlic sauce. You must use fresh garlic for this recipe; the pre-chopped garlic sold in oil just doesn't have the same flavor.

INGREDIENTS:
5 cloves garlic, coarsely chopped
¹/₃ cup tahini
¹/₃ cup fresh lemon juice, or more to taste
¹/₃ cup extra-virgin olive oil
**1 teaspoon coarse salt (kosher or sea),
    or more to taste**
¹/₂ teaspoon freshly ground black pepper

Place the garlic, tahini, lemon juice, oil, salt, and pepper in a blender or food processor and purée until a smooth sauce forms. Add enough cool water to make the sauce pourable (you'll probably need about ¹/₃ cup). Taste for seasoning, adding more lemon juice and/or salt as necessary; the sauce should be highly seasoned. The

pungent garlic

sauce can be refrigerated, covered, for several days. Stir before serving.

YIELD:
Makes about 1¹/₃ cups

Massachusetts

GREEKTOWN KEBABS
With Greek Salad "Salsa"

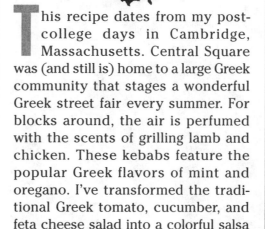

This recipe dates from my post-college days in Cambridge, Massachusetts. Central Square was (and still is) home to a large Greek community that stages a wonderful Greek street fair every summer. For blocks around, the air is perfumed with the scents of grilling lamb and chicken. These kebabs feature the popular Greek flavors of mint and oregano. I've transformed the traditional Greek tomato, cucumber, and feta cheese salad into a colorful salsa to serve with the kebabs.

METHOD:
Direct grilling

ADVANCE PREPARATION:
1 hour for marinating the lamb

These kebabs are also great made with 1½ pounds of chicken (for best flavor use dark meat; for greatest convenience, use boneless breasts). Or you can season and grill whole chicken breasts the same way (in that case, I'd grill the onion in wedges and the peppers whole).

INGREDIENTS:

1½ pounds boneless lamb leg or shoulder,
    cut into 1-inch pieces
2 teaspoons dried mint
2 teaspoons dried oregano
1 teaspoon coarse salt (kosher or sea)
1 teaspoon freshly ground black pepper
4 cloves garlic, peeled and crushed with
    the side of a cleaver
5 tablespoons extra-virgin olive oil
5 tablespoons fresh lemon juice
1 medium-size red onion, peeled
1 green bell pepper, seeded and
    cut into 1-inch squares
1 yellow bell pepper, seeded and
    cut into 1-inch squares
Steamed rice or pita bread
Greek Salad "Salsa" (recipe follows)

YOU'LL ALSO NEED:

About 4 metal skewers

*Lamb kebabs
are the food
of choice at
Greek street
fairs.*

1 Place the lamb pieces in a nonreactive mixing bowl and toss with the mint, oregano, salt, and black pepper. Stir in the garlic, 3 tablespoons of the oil, and 3 tablespoons of the lemon juice and let marinate in the refrigerator, covered, for 1 hour.

2 Combine the remaining 2 tablespoons oil and 2 tablespoons lemon juice in a small nonreactive bowl and beat with a fork to combine.

3 Cut the onion in half crosswise. Cut each half into quarters. Separate each wedge of onion into layers. Thread the lamb pieces onto skewers, alternating them with pieces of onion and bell pepper.

4 Set up the grill for direct grilling (see page 21 for charcoal or gas) and preheat to high.

5 When ready to cook, drain the marinade from the lamb and discard the marinade. Brush and oil the grill grate. Place the lamb kebabs on the hot grate and grill until cooked to medium, 2 to 3 minutes per side (8 to 12 minutes in all). After 4 minutes, start basting the kebabs with the lemon-oil mixture. To test for doneness, use the poke test; the lamb will feel firmly yielding.

6 Serve the lamb kebabs over rice or with pita bread, with the Greek Salad "Salsa" on the side.

YIELD:
Serves 4

Greek Salad "Salsa"

Here's a barbecue twist on a classic Greek salad—a salsa you can spoon over the lamb. You can have all the ingredients diced ahead of time, but don't mix them together until serving time.

INGREDIENTS:

1 cucumber

2 luscious, ripe red tomatoes, seeded and cut into ¼-inch dice

1 small green bell pepper, seeded and cut into ¼-inch dice

¼ cup kalamata olives, pitted—and diced if you have the patience

¼ cup diced red onion

3 tablespoons chopped fresh flat-leaf parsley

3 tablespoons extra-virgin olive oil

2 tablespoons red wine vinegar (or to taste)

1 teaspoon dried oregano

2 ounces feta cheese, crumbled

Coarse salt (kosher or sea) and freshly ground black pepper

1 Using a vegetable peeler, partially peel the cucumber (remove the peel in lengthwise strips, leaving a little green showing for color). Cut the cucumber in half lengthwise, scrape out the seeds with a melon baller or spoon, and cut the flesh into ¼-inch dice.

2 Combine the cucumber, tomatoes, bell pepper, olives, onion, parsley, oil, vinegar, and oregano in an attractive nonreactive serving bowl and toss to mix. Just before serving, gently stir in the feta cheese and season with salt and pepper to taste. The salsa ingredients can be prepared up to 1 hour ahead, but wait to mix it until just before serving.

YIELD:
Serves 4

Hawaii

PINEAPPLE GINGER LAMB KEBABS

If you like lamb with a tropical twist, you'll love these colorful kebabs, seasoned with two of Hawaii's favorite flavorings: pineapple juice and fresh ginger. To reinforce the pineapple flavor, I like to thread fresh pineapple chunks on the skewers along with the lamb (choose a golden pineapple—a supersweet fruit with a yellow or gold rind). The marinade boils down to make a sizzling, sweet-salty glaze.

METHOD:
Direct grilling

ADVANCE PREPARATION:
3 to 4 hours for marinating the lamb

WALL OF FLAME

LA SHISH EAST

Detroit's most famous Middle Eastern restaurant specializes in *tawook* (marinated chicken breast), *kafta* (Middle Eastern sausage), lamb, swordfish, shrimp, and vegetables that are spitted on swords and charcoal grilled. Served in a flaming tower that is ceremoniously carried through the dining room, it never fails to cause whiplash at the other tables.

12918 Michigan Avenue
Dearborn, Michigan
(313) 584-4477
www.lashish.com
and other locations

TIPS

■ Hawaii is a major world ginger producer, and Hawaiians have the good fortune of being able to buy young ginger at their local supermarkets. Young ginger is so tender and sweet, you don't even need to peel it. But even the tougher, older ginger found in mainland supermarkets will produce explosively flavorful lamb.

■ A common fuel for grilling in Hawaii is kiawe (mesquite). To replicate its flavor I suggest using mesquite charcoal or tossing some unsoaked mesquite chips on the fire.

FOR THE MARINADE:

1 piece (2 inches) fresh ginger, peeled and roughly chopped
3 cloves garlic, coarsely chopped
3 scallions, trimmed, white part coarsely chopped, green part finely chopped
1 jalapeño pepper, seeded and coarsely chopped (for a hotter marinade, leave the seeds in)
¼ cup chopped fresh cilantro
1½ cups pineapple juice
½ cup soy sauce
¼ cup Asian (dark) sesame oil
2 strips lemon zest (each about ½ by 1½ inches; see Note)
2 tablespoons fresh lemon juice
½ teaspoon freshly ground black pepper

FOR THE LAMB AND KEBABS:

2¼ pounds boneless lamb leg or shoulder, cut into 1-inch pieces
1 ripe pineapple, peeled, cored, and cut into 1-inch chunks
¼ cup chopped fresh cilantro

YOU'LL ALSO NEED:

6 long (10-inch) or 12 short (6-inch) metal or bamboo skewers; 2 cups wood chips or chunks (preferably mesquite)

1 MAKE THE MARINADE: Place the ginger, garlic, scallion whites, jalapeño, cilantro, pineapple juice, soy sauce, oil, lemon zest and juice, and pepper in a blender and purée until smooth. To use a food processor, finely chop the ginger, garlic, scallion whites, jalapeño, cilantro, and lemon zest first through the feed tube in the processor. Then, with the motor running, add the pineapple juice, soy sauce, oil, lemon

juice, and pepper. Transfer the marinade to a nonreactive bowl and stir in the lamb. Let marinate in the refrigerator, covered, for 3 to 4 hours.

2 Drain the marinade from the lamb through a strainer into a heavy nonreactive saucepan. Bring to a boil over high heat and let boil until thick, syrupy, and reduced by half, about 10 minutes. Set aside to use as a glaze.

3 Thread the marinated lamb and the pineapple chunks onto skewers, alternating pieces of meat and fruit.

4 Set up the grill for direct grilling (see page 21 for charcoal or gas) and preheat to high. If using a charcoal grill, preheat it to high, then toss all of the wood chips or chunks on the coals. If using a gas grill, place all of the chips or chunks in the smoker box or in a smoker pouch (see page 24) and run the grill on high until you see smoke.

5 When ready to cook, brush and oil the grill grate. Place the kebabs on the hot grate and grill until cooked to taste, 2 to 3 minutes per side (8 to 12 minutes in all) for medium. Each time you turn the kebabs, baste them with some of the glaze. To test for doneness, use the poke test; the lamb will feel firmly yielding. When cooked to medium-rare the internal temperature will be about 145°F.

6 Unskewer the grilled kebabs onto a platter or plates. Drizzle the remaining glaze over them. Sprinkle the scallion greens and cilantro on top and serve at once.

YIELD:

Serves 6

NOTE: You can use a vegetable peeler to remove the oil-rich, yellow outer rind of the lemon in strips. Be careful to leave behind the bitter white pith.

Owensboro, Ky.

OWENSBORO BARBECUED MUTTON

Owensboro, Kentucky, is unique in the national pantheon of barbecue—mutton is the preferred meat here, and it's slow roasted over a smoky hickory fire in an old-fashioned pit the way it's been done for nearly two centuries. If you're not from Owensboro, mutton can be intimidating, and hard to find. So here you'll also find instructions for barbecuing a more benign leg of lamb.

METHOD:

Indirect grilling

FOR THE MUTTON:

1 piece mutton shoulder or leg
    (about 5 pounds)
Coarse salt (kosher or sea) and
    freshly ground black pepper

FOR THE BASTING SAUCE:

1 cup cider vinegar
²/₃ cup Worcestershire sauce
5 tablespoons coarse salt (kosher or sea)
2 tablespoons fresh lemon juice
¹/₂ teaspoon freshly ground black pepper

FOR THE DIPPING SAUCE:

¹/₄ cup Worcestershire sauce
¹/₄ cup cider vinegar
2 teaspoons fresh lemon juice
1¹/₂ teaspoons brown sugar
1 teaspoon freshly ground black pepper
¹/₂ teaspoon coarse salt (kosher or sea)
¹/₂ teaspoon onion salt
¹/₂ teaspoon garlic powder
¹/₄ teaspoon MSG (optional)
¹/₄ teaspoon ground allspice

10 to 12 hamburger buns, or 20 to 24
    slices white bread (optional)

YOU'LL ALSO NEED:

4 cups wood chips or chunks
    (preferably hickory), soaked for 1 hour
    in water to cover, then drained

1 Generously season the mutton with about 1 tablespoon each of salt and pepper. Set aside.

2 MAKE THE BASTING SAUCE: Combine the vinegar, Worcestershire sauce, salt, lemon juice, and pepper with 1¹/₂ cups water in a nonreactive saucepan and bring to a boil over high heat.

3 MAKE THE DIPPING SAUCE: Combine the Worcestershire sauce, vinegar, lemon juice, brown sugar, pepper, coarse and onion salts, garlic powder, MSG, if using, allspice, and 2 cups water in a large nonreactive

TIPS

■ Depending upon where you live, you may or may not be able to buy mutton. Don't despair if you can't find it. Simply barbecue a leg of lamb instead (you'll find cooking instructions for this in the Variation at the end of the recipe).

■ Don't be put off by the large amount of salt in the basting sauce. It not only flavors the meat, but helps form a wonderful, flavorful crust. The dipping sauce isn't really the sort of sauce you'd want to dunk your bread in, but it tastes great with the lamb.

saucepan, bring to a boil over high heat, and cook until richly flavored and slightly reduced, about 5 minutes. Transfer the sauce to a nonreactive serving bowl to cool.

4 Set up the grill for indirect grilling (see page 22 for charcoal or page 23 for gas) and preheat to medium-low. If using a charcoal grill, preheat it to medium, then toss 1 cup of the wood chips or chunks on the coals. If using a gas grill, place all of the wood chips or chunks in the smoker box or in a smoker pouch (see page 24) and run the grill on high until you see smoke, then reduce the heat to medium.

5 When ready to cook, place the mutton, fat side up, in the center of the hot grate, over the drip pan and away from the heat, and cover the grill. Cook the mutton until it is fall-off-the-bone tender, 4 to 6 hours. To test for doneness, insert an instant-read meat thermometer into the thickest part of the mutton but not touching the bone: The internal temperature should be about 190°F. Baste the mutton with the basting sauce every half hour. If the mutton starts to burn, cover it loosely with aluminum foil. If using a charcoal grill, every hour you'll need to add 12 fresh coals and ½ cup of the wood chips or chunks to each side.

6 Transfer the grilled mutton to a cutting board and let it rest for 5 minutes. Slice the mutton thinly across the grain or finely chop it with a cleaver. Spoon half of the dipping sauce over the meat. Serve the mutton on toasted or grilled hamburger buns or slices of white bread or all by itself, passing the remaining dipping sauce on the side.

YIELD:
Serves 8 to 10

VARIATION: You can substitute a 5- pound leg of lamb for the mutton. The cooking time will be closer to 4 hours. To test for doneness, insert an instant-read meat thermometer into the thickest part of the leg but not touching the bone: The internal temperature should be about 190°F.

Ken Bosley, second-generation owner of the legendary Moonlite.

THE BARBECUED MUTTON

Of Owensboro, Ky.

If you want to know about barbecue in Owensboro, Kentucky, just ask Harl Foreman Jr. what he thinks about lamb. "Don't much care for it," says the fourth generation owner of the Old Hickory Bar-B-Q. "It's just too darned bland."

Lamb has been called lots of things, but not bland. What makes lamb a distant fourth among the meats Americans eat isn't its lack of flavor, but its assertiveness. You'd never accuse it of being bland—unless you come from Owensboro, a city of 60,000 on the southern banks of the Ohio River at the northwest edge of Kentucky. Here the meat of choice for barbecue is not pork, not beef, not chicken, not even lamb. No, only one meat will do: mutton.

Folks in these parts have been eating smoked ewe at least since July 4, 1834, the first record of the mutton barbecue that's become a yearly ritual. The practice probably began even earlier, as Owensboro was settled by Dutch sheep farmers in the early 1800s. Harl's great-grandfather, Charles "Pappy" Foreman, was a blacksmith, so he was used to toiling over a smoky fire. In 1918, he swapped forge for barbecue pit, setting up shop at the corner of 25th and Frederica Streets, across from where the restaurant is today. He cooked his

BARBECUED MUTTON IN OWENSBORO

Old Hickory Bar-B-Q
338 Washington Avenue
(270) 926-9000

Moonlite Bar-B-Q Inn
2840 W. Parrish Avenue
(270) 684-8143

mutton the time honored way—over an open, hickory-fired pit, swabbing the meat with a blackish dip made with Worcestershire sauce, vinegar, and allspice. It was a winning formula then; it's a winning formula now; and Old Hickory sells something on the order of 10,000 pounds of mutton a week.

Old Hickory Bar-B-Q may be the oldest barbecue joint in Owensboro, but for sheer numbers of customers (7,000 weekly), no place beats the Moonlite Bar-B-Q. Hugh and Catherine Bosley took it over in 1963. "We never had any previous restaurant experience, so we just pretended we were having company," Catherine recalls. Hugh's pit-roasted mutton and Catherine's country-style vegetables made a winning combination.

The focal point of the Moonlite is a sprawling buffet, where in addition to barbecued mutton, you can sample home-cooked turnip greens, corn pudding, and copper pennies (candied carrots).

But the very best way to taste barbecued mutton is to come to the Owensboro International Bar-B-Q Festival, held the first or second week of May. Each year since 1978 local pit masters erect cinderblock pits in the streets. The smokefest draws some 70,000 visitors to savor the barbecue of the winners. For information, go to www.bbqfest.com. Barbecued mutton is relentlessly regional; to enjoy it outside of your own home you must journey to Owensboro. And in this age of homogenized culture, I find that notion rather comforting.

> The meat of choice for barbecue is not pork, not beef, not chicken, not even lamb... it's mutton.

Burgers, Dogs

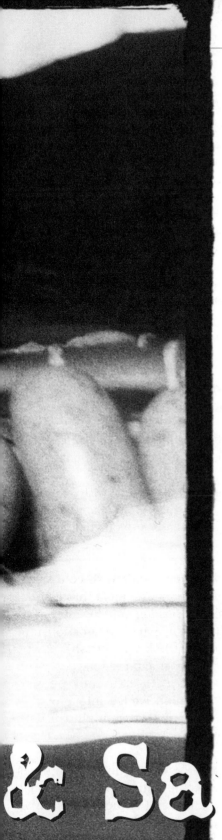

can't tell you who cooked the first hamburger. But, I can tell you the best way to cook one: on the grill. There's nothing like live fire for searing meat, melting out fat, and imparting that signature smoke flavor that goes so perfectly with ground beef. But don't stop there, because as every tailgate picnicker knows, the ultimate way to cook hot dogs and sausages is to sizzle them on the grill.

This chapter covers the fine points of grilling all manner of burgers and sausages, even bologna. From Car Wash Burgers (the specialty of a Detroit barbecue joint located, yes, in a car wash) to my take on the classic Cincinnati chili dog, *BBQ USA* has you covered.

& Sausages

TIPS

If the health risks associated with ground beef are so grave these days, how does Louis' Lunch get away with serving hamburgers rare? The answer is simple: They grind their own beef each morning. If you have a meat grinder, you can try this (food processors do a poor job of grinding meat). Otherwise, buy your ground beef from a reputable butcher. If you do use supermarket beef, be sure to cook it medium or medium-well done.

New Haven, Conn.

THE ULTIMATE HAMBURGER

For historic continuity, ferociously loyal community support, and an atmosphere that you could spread with a knife, you can't beat the hamburger joint Louis' Lunch, in New Haven, Connecticut. Since 1898, the Lassen family has been grinding its own beef daily, hand shaping patties to order, and grilling burgers on antique cast-iron broilers in front of live flames. (This answers the question once and for all—the proper way to cook a hamburger is by grilling, not by frying it on a griddle.) And as any regional American culinary landmark should be, Louis' Lunch is sufficiently quirky to allow melted processed cheese but militantly prohibit ketchup and mustard as accompaniments to its signature burgers. Here, then, is the granddaddy of all burgers; it's the next best thing to elbowing your way up to the counter at Louis' (to learn more about Louis' Lunch and the history of the hamburger, see page 336).

METHOD:
Direct grilling

INGREDIENTS:
1¼ pounds ground chuck

1¼ pounds ground sirloin
Coarse salt (kosher or sea) and
　　freshly ground black pepper
½ medium-size onion, cut into
　　8 thin wedges
16 slices sandwich bread
3 tablespoons butter, melted
　　(optional)
1 large or 2 medium-size gorgeous,
　　luscious, ripe red tomatoes,
　　thinly sliced
8 Boston lettuce leaves or
　　iceberg lettuce slices
Cheese Sauce (optional;
　　recipe follows)

1 Set up the grill for direct grilling (see page 21 for charcoal or gas) and preheat to high.

2 Place the chuck and sirloin in a large mixing bowl and mix with a wooden spoon, or mix the meat in a stand mixer fitted with a dough hook. If possible, avoid mixing the meat with your hands so your fingers don't warm it.

3 Wet your hands with cold water and divide the meat into 8 equal portions. Working quickly and with a light touch, pat each portion into a ½-inch-thick squarish patty. Generously season each patty on both sides with salt and pepper. Press an onion wedge into one side of each patty so that it's flush with the meat.

4 Lightly brush the bread slices with the butter, if using. Arrange the tomatoes and lettuce leaves on an attractive serving platter.

5 When ready to cook, brush and oil the grill grate. Place the burgers on the hot grate, onion side down. Grill the burgers until cooked to taste, 3 to 4 minutes per side for medium-rare. To test for doneness, insert an instant-read meat thermometer through the side of a burger into the center. The internal temperature should be about 145°F for medium-rare or, if using commercial ground beef, cook it to at least medium, 160°F.

6 Meanwhile, place the bread slices on the hot grate and grill until lightly toasted, 1 to 2 minutes per side.

7 To serve, place a lettuce leaf on top of a slice of toast. Top with a burger, tomato slice, and Cheese Sauce, if using. Slap a piece of toast on top and serve at once.

YIELD:
Makes 8 burgers

Cheese Sauce

The Grilling Guru has a moral dilemma. To be strictly faithful to Louis' Lunch, he should tell you to top your hamburger with a liquid processed cheese, like Cheez Whiz. The Grilling Guru doesn't use Cheez Whiz himself, however, so he feels awkward about calling for it. So he's created a made-from-scratch cheese sauce that will satisfy the purist, while remaining faithful to the lurid orange cheese topping used by Louis'.

INGREDIENTS:
½ clove garlic
1 cup beer
2 cups (about 8 ounces) coarsely grated Colby cheese or orange cheddar cheese
2 teaspoons cornstarch
2 teaspoons prepared mustard
Coarse salt (kosher or sea) and freshly ground black pepper

1 Rub the bottom and side of a heavy saucepan with the cut garlic. Place the garlic clove in the pan, add the beer, and bring to a boil over high heat.

2 Meanwhile, place the cheese and cornstarch in a bowl and toss to mix. Sprinkle the cheese into the boiling beer, stirring it with a wooden spoon. Let the sauce come back to a boil; it will thicken.

3 Reduce the heat slightly, stir in the mustard, and season the sauce with salt and pepper to taste. Let the sauce simmer gently until smooth and rich-tasting, 3 to 5 minutes, stirring steadily with the wooden spoon. The purist can fish out and discard the garlic clove; otherwise, one lucky person will get to eat it.

YIELD:
Makes about 1¼ cups

To make a light cheese sauce, use an inexpensive lager-style mass-marketed canned beer. For a darker, richer sauce with a pleasantly bitter edge, use a dark beer.

LOUIS' LUNCH

And the Birth of the Hamburger

LOUIS' LUNCH

261-263 Crown Street
New Haven, Connecticut
(203) 562-5507

Let's get one thing straight: Louis' Lunch did not invent the hamburger. There, I've said it. But while this simple assertion may win the approbation of a few food historians, it's likely to get me tarred and feathered in New Haven, Connecticut. Never mind that the legendary New York City restaurant Delmonico's listed hamburger steak on its menu as early as 1834 (it sold for 10 cents; twice the price of roast beef), the first burger with any personality was created by Louis Lassen in 1898. A blacksmith by trade and a preacher by vocation, Lassen immigrated from Denmark to New Haven. To make ends meet, he set up a tiny lunch wagon called Louis' Lunch on Meadow Street near Union Station in 1895.

Why did he come up with his celebrated burger? There are two theories. The first holds that the frugal Dane couldn't bear discarding meat scraps left over from his popular steak sandwiches, so he chopped them into patties. The second cites a customer who dashed into Louis's shop (by now housed in a tiny luncheonette) in search of a quick meal to eat on the run. So Lassen slapped a broiled beef patty between two slices of bread and the modern hamburger was born.

Did I say broiled? This brings us to the first of four things that make Louis' Lunch's America's most distinctive hamburgers. Now, as then, the burgers are cooked in an ancient gas-fired, cast-iron, vertical Bridge Beach Co. broiler. (This part of New Haven had gas long before electricity, quips the restaurant's wry current owner, Louis's grandson, Ken Lassen.) The antique broiler, which hasn't been manufactured for half a century, looks like a giant old-fashioned toaster, with upright metal

Louis' Lunch—
a hamburger landmark.

... the first establishment in the United States to grill a hamburger.

cages that hold the burgers in front of vertical gas flames. This meets the definition of live fire cooking in my book, making Louis' Lunch the first recorded establishment in the United States to grill a ham-burger. McDonald's take note: The vertical roasting has a real advantage—it drains off all the fat.

ABOUT THAT BEEF

The second thing is the burger itself, made from beef ground fresh each day on the premises. Lassen won't disclose what "parts of the moose" he uses, but I wouldn't be surprised if the rich-flavored blend contains both chuck and sirloin. Ken's white-haired wife, Lee, hand shapes the meat and squarish patties to order. These are salted and peppered just prior to being inserted in the antique broiler.

The third thing that distinguishes Louis' Lunch's burgers is that they're served not on buns, but between two slices of toasted white bread. And, the final factor is the accompaniments, a thin wedge of onion pressed into the meat and cooked with it, a slice of tomato, a lettuce leaf, and an optional squirt of melted cheese. Conspicuously and militantly absent are ketchup or mustard. The Lassens are adamant about this—there's even a sign in the tiny dining room showing a ketchup bottle with a diagonal slash through it. "Teenagers use ketchup to help get their food down," explains Lassen. "Our burgers are so good, you don't need it."

For most of the last century, Louis' Lunch occupied a small, squat, square building, a former tannery, on Temple Street. When the wrecker's ball threatened the property in 1975 to make way for a high-rise, Louis fans from all across the country united to protect this tiny landmark. The restaurant was moved part and parcel to its current location on Crown Street and granted national historic landmark status. And just to make sure the structure wouldn't be forced to move again, Ken Lassen rebuilt it with bricks sent by well-wishers the world over. He'll proudly point to stones from the Parthenon, the Colosseum, and even the Great Wall of China.

Today, the restaurant is officially run by Louis's great-grandson, Jeff, although the "retired" Ken Lassen still works at a pace that would leave most of us breathless. The low ceilings, brick walls, and pew-like wooden seats remain as they have for decades. So do the burgers, which are remarkable for their crisp broiled crust, soft juicy center, and beefy, dare I say sanguine, taste.

Contented customers have ranged from Charles Lindbergh to band leader Artie Shaw to the elder and younger George Bush.

SAY WHAT?

Given the tiny dimensions of the dining room and the huge number of patrons who come here each day, a sort of verbal shorthand has been developed to speed up the ordering process. Thus, if you hear someone walk up to the counter and bark "Gimme two cheese works, a Californian, a salad, and a birch," what he's actually saying is "May I please have two original hamburgers with cheese, tomato and onion, cooked medium-rare and served on toast; a hot dog with cheese, relish, and onion; an order of potato salad; and an ice-cold birch beer."

Whatever you order, just don't ask for ketchup.

TIPS

■ **Maytag Blue is available at gourmet shops and a growing number of supermarkets. Of course, you could substitute another blue cheese, from Gorgonzola to Roquefort.**

■ **For the beef, I like a half-and-half mixture of ground chuck and sirloin (the chuck for flavor, the sirloin for finesse), but you can certainly use just one kind.**

Newton, Iowa

INSIDE-OUT BLUE CHEESE BURGERS

Cheeseburger. Cheeseburger. Cheeseburger. Here's a new take on an American icon. The salty tang of blue cheese makes a terrific counterpoint to ground beef—especially when it's the refined, creamy Maytag Blue cheese from Iowa. What's unusual is that the cheese is mashed with a little butter and tucked inside the burgers. This enables you to cook the burgers through, but still keep the meat moist thanks to the melting blue cheese and butter. It's so juicy, the burger might even squirt when you take a bite.

METHOD:
Direct grilling

ADVANCE PREPARATION:
1 hour for freezing the flavored butter

FOR THE BURGERS:
2 ounces blue cheese,
    such as Maytag Blue
2 tablespoons unsalted butter,
    at room temperature
1/2 teaspoon cracked black peppercorns
1 1/2 pounds ground chuck and/or sirloin
Coarse salt (kosher or sea) and
    freshly ground black pepper

FOR SERVING:
4 hamburger buns or kaiser rolls
2 tablespoons butter, melted
Lettuce leaves
Tomato slices
Paper-thin sweet onion slices
Mustard, ketchup, mayonnaise, relish,
    or whatever other condiment you
    may fancy

1 Place the cheese in a shallow bowl and mash it with a fork. Mash in the butter and peppercorns. Spoon the butter mixture onto a sheet of plastic wrap and roll it into a cylinder about 2 inches long and 1 1/2 inches wide. Place the butter roll in the freezer and freeze until firm, about 1 hour. The butter can be frozen for up to 3 months.

2 Unwrap the butter roll and cut it crosswise into 4 even pieces.

3 Wet your hands with cold water and divide the ground beef into 4 equal portions. Working quickly and with a light touch, pat each portion into a thick patty. Make a depression in the center of each patty with your thumbs and place a disk of blue cheese butter in it. Mold the ground beef around the blue cheese butter to encase it. Place the patties on a plate lined with plastic wrap and refrigerate, covered, while you set up the grill.

4 Set up the grill for direct grilling (see page 21 for charcoal or gas) and preheat to high.

5 When ready to cook, brush and oil the grill grate. Generously season the burgers with salt and pepper, then place them on the hot grate. Grill the burgers until cooked through, 5 to 7 minutes per side for medium. To test for doneness, insert an instant-read meat thermometer though the side of a burger into the center: The internal temperature should be about 160°F for medium.

6 Meanwhile, brush the buns with the melted butter and toast them on the grill, 1 to 2 minutes per side.

7 Place each of the grilled burgers on a bun with some lettuce leaves and tomato and onion slices. Serve with the condiments of your choice and plenty of ice-cold beer.

YIELD:
Makes 4 burgers

Pontiac, Mich.

CAR WASH BURGERS

It was such a logical idea, I'm surprised more people hadn't thought of it. Satisfy two of modern man's basic needs in a single location, and the public will beat down your door. That's precisely what happened when Chuck Jackson set up a barbe-

cue pit at a car wash in Pontiac, Michigan. A retired General Motors employee, Jackson was born in Rolling Fork, Mississippi, and he's been barbecuing all his life.

Retired now, Jackson exercised his art on a cooker fashioned from an old furnace-oil tank in a tiny shed next to the car wash. His place is under different management now, and the menu has changed, but in its heyday, his ribs, chicken, and pork steaks were cooked to smoky perfection in a pit blackened with age and creosote. The most distinctive dish that came out of Jackson's pit was a hamburger so large, it could double as a meat loaf. Perhaps someone has eaten a whole one, but that's a feat that requires an appetite far more formidable than mine. My interpretation of the car wash burger has been

Cars and barbecue, a Michigan tradition.

TIPS

■ Jackson uses what
I call the hybrid
grilling method: The
food is positioned
directly over the
fire, as in direct
grilling, but high
above the coals, so
the heat is more like
indirect grilling. To
achieve a similar
effect on a home
grill, I suggest using
the indirect method,
then moving the
burgers directly over
the flames for the
last few minutes to
crisp the exterior.

■ The addition of
wood chips to the
fire is my own
contribution to
Jackson's burger;
I like the way the
smoke flavor rounds
out the meaty taste
of the burger.

enriched with oatmeal and eggs and studded with onion and bell peppers. It's an awe-inspiring burger that only a barbecue fanatic could concoct. Ribs are common currency in and around Detroit, but I know of only one barbecued burger.

METHOD:
Indirect grilling

FOR THE BURGERS:
**2 pounds ground chuck
(you must use chuck)
1 cup quick-cooking oatmeal
(not instant oatmeal)
1 medium-size onion, finely chopped
½ green bell pepper, finely chopped
½ red bell pepper, finely chopped
2 cloves garlic, minced
2 teaspoons coarse salt
(kosher or sea)
1 teaspoon freshly ground black pepper
1 teaspoon dried oregano
2 large eggs, lightly beaten
with a fork**

FOR SERVING:
**Hamburger buns or sliced white bread
Pickle slices
Onion slices
Your favorite barbecue sauce**

YOU'LL ALSO NEED:
**2 cups wood chips or chunks
(preferably hickory), soaked for
1 hour in water to cover,
then drained**

1 Place the chuck, oatmeal, onion, green and red bell peppers, garlic, salt, black pepper, oregano, and eggs in a mixing bowl and mix well with a

wooden spoon. Wet your hands with cold water and divide the beef mixture into 4 equal portions. Working quickly and with a light touch, pat each portion into a very thick patty. Place the patties on a plate lined with plastic wrap and refrigerate, covered, while you set up the grill.

2 Set up the grill for indirect grilling (see page 23 for gas or page 22 for charcoal) and preheat to medium. If using a gas grill, place all of the wood chips in the smoker box or in a smoker pouch (see page 24) and run the grill on high until you see smoke, then reduce the heat to medium. If using a charcoal grill, place a large drip pan in the center, preheat the grill to medium, then toss all of the wood chips or chunks on the coals.

3 When ready to cook, place the burgers in the center of the hot grate, over the drip pan and away from the heat. Cover the grill and cook the burgers until cooked to taste, 30 to 40 minutes for medium-well-done (this is the way Jackson serves them). To test for doneness, insert an instant-read thermometer through the side of a burger into the center: The internal temperature should be about 170°F for medium-well-done (160°F for medium). During the last few minutes, move the burgers directly over the fire to sear the outside. Serve at once on buns or slices of bread, with pickles, onions, and barbecue sauce.

YIELD:
Makes 4 mammoth burgers

Minnesota

VEAL BURGERS
With Onion and Dill

What do you get when you cross a Swedish meatball with an American hamburger? An uptown burger made with ground veal and perfumed with fresh dill, coriander, and onion. The recipe was inspired by Minnesota's Swedish American community, although it's likely that it exists only in my imagination. What's very real is the exquisite contrast of flavors you get when you expose a delicate

Grilling burgers: the job of American moms and dads for half a century.

meat like veal to fire and wood smoke. In keeping with the Scandinavian theme, I serve the burgers with a mustard and dill sauce.

METHOD:
Direct grilling

ADVANCE PREPARATION:
2 hours for chilling the meat (optional)

INGREDIENTS:

2 slices white bread
1/2 cup milk or water
1 1/2 pounds ground veal
1 small onion, finely chopped (about 1/2 cup)
1 clove garlic, minced
3 tablespoons finely chopped fresh dill
1 large egg, lightly beaten with a fork
1 teaspoon coarse salt (kosher or sea), or more to taste
1 teaspoon ground coriander
1/2 teaspoon freshly ground black pepper, or more to taste
4 hamburger buns (preferably topped with poppy seeds)
2 tablespoons butter, melted
Lettuce leaves
Tomato slices
Onion slices
Mustard Dill Sauce (recipe follows)

YOU'LL ALSO NEED:

1 cup wood chips or chunks (optional; preferably oak or hickory), unsoaked

1 Cut off and discard the crusts of the slices of bread, then cut the bread

TIPS

■ Ground veal is available at butcher shops and many supermarkets. Because it tends to be lean, I add a little bread soaked in milk or water.

■ You want a fairly light smoke flavor here, so I've called for using unsoaked wood chips. For a more pronounced smoke flavor, soak the chips in cold water for an hour and then drain them before using. Or if you're in a hurry, omit the wood chips entirely—the burgers will still be very tasty.

WALL OF FLAME

GOODE CO. TEXAS BAR-B-Q

What brings me back again and again to this Houston institution is the homemade jalapeño cheese bread, smoky Czech-style sausage, and meats with smoke rings as pink as cherubs' cheeks. Goode's also serves items you seldom see on Texas barbecue menus, such as sweet water duck and Brazos Bottom pecan pie. After lunch, visit the Hall of Flame store across the street, which carries a wide range of barbecue sauces, rubs, and gadgets.

5109 Kirby Drive
Houston, Texas
(713) 522-2530
(and other locations)

into cubes. Place these in a bowl and stir in the milk. Let soak for 3 minutes, then squeeze the bread with your fingers to wring out the excess liquid. Place the soaked bread in a mixing bowl and stir in the veal, onion, garlic, dill, egg, salt, coriander, and pepper. Mix well with a wooden spoon. To taste for seasoning, grill or fry a little ball of the veal mixture; add more salt and/or pepper as necessary. You can make the burgers right away, but they'll be easier to shape if you chill the meat mixture, covered, for 2 hours.

2 Wet your hands with cold water and divide the veal mixture into 4 equal portions. Working quickly and with a light touch, pat each portion into a thick round patty. Place the patties on a plate lined with plastic wrap and refrigerate, covered, while you set up the grill. The burgers can be prepared up to this stage several hours ahead.

3 Set up the grill for direct grilling (see page 21 for gas or charcoal) and preheat to high. If using a gas grill, place all of the wood chips or chunks, if desired, in the smoker box or in a smoker pouch (see page 24) and run the grill on high until you see smoke. If using a charcoal grill, preheat it to high, then toss all of the wood chips or chunks, if desired, on the coals.

Fresh dill, indispensable for these Scandinavian-inspired burgers.

4 When ready to cook, brush and oil the grill grate. Place the burgers on the hot grate and grill until cooked through, 4 to 6 minutes per side for medium. (If you like, rotate the burgers a quarter turn halfway through cooking on each side to create an attractive crosshatch of grill marks.) To test for doneness, insert an instant-read meat thermometer though the side of a burger into the center: The internal temperature should be about 160°F for medium.

5 Meanwhile, brush the buns with the melted butter and toast them on the grill, 1 to 2 minutes per side. Place each of the grilled burgers on a bun with some lettuce leaves, tomato and onion slices, and a dollop of Mustard Dill Sauce. Serve the remaining sauce on the side.

YIELD:
Makes 4 burgers

Mustard Dill Sauce

Most Scandinavian mustard sauces are sweet, which may taste great with smoked and grilled fish but would be jarring with a burger. Here's a mustard sauce free of the distraction of sugar.

INGREDIENTS:

⅔ **cup mayonnaise (preferably Hellmann's)**

⅓ **cup Dijon or grainy mustard (not a sweet mustard)**

2 **tablespoons chopped fresh dill, plus a whole sprig for garnish**

½ **teaspoon ground coriander**

½ **teaspoon finely grated lemon zest**

1 **tablespoon fresh lemon juice, or more to taste**

Coarse salt (kosher or sea) and freshly ground black pepper

Place the mayonnaise, mustard, dill, coriander, and lemon zest and juice in a nonreactive mixing bowl and whisk to mix. Taste for seasoning, adding more lemon juice as necessary and salt and pepper to taste. The sauce will keep for 3 days, covered and refrigerated. Let the sauce return to room temperature before using.

YIELD:
Makes about 1 cup

Toronto, Canada

LAMB BURGERS

I discovered lamb burgers at a popular Toronto restaurant called Jerusalem. Founded by a Greek-born, Jerusalem-raised chef named Romeo Vazdekis, the restaurant pays homage to Romeo's Mediterranean roots in a combination of meats and seasonings served in pita bread—what Middle Easterners would recognize as *kofta*. But Romeo prepares his *kofta* patty style, like hamburgers. The results hum with electrifying flavors.

METHOD:
Direct grilling

FOR THE BURGERS:
12 ounces ground lamb
12 ounces ground beef
1 small onion, finely chopped
3 tablespoons finely chopped fresh flat-leaf parsley
3 tablespoons chopped fresh mint, or 2 teaspoons dried mint
1 teaspoon coarse salt (kosher or sea)
1 teaspoon freshly ground pepper

FOR SERVING:
4 pita breads
Lettuce leaves
Cucumber slices
Tomato slices
Paper-thin red onion slices (optional)
Yogurt Garlic Mint Sauce (optional; recipe follows)

T·I·P·S

Fresh mint is available at most supermarkets. If you can't find it, simply open a mint tea bag.

WALL OF FLAME

REINDEER SAUSAGE VENDORS

Reindeer are plentiful in northern Alaska and herds are regularly culled to prevent overpopulation, so you'll find lots of pushcarts in Anchorage selling juicy, garlicky reindeer sausage. The best is Auntie's, a cart operated by Colombian-born Eugenia "Tia" Buitrago. Look for a pushcart with a green umbrella, a gas grill bolted to its back, and the largest crowd of customers (if you want to try this Alaskan treat at home, see Mail-Order Sources on page 742).

Fourth Street between F and G Streets (near the old Federal Building) Anchorage, Alaska

1 MAKE THE BURGERS: Place the lamb, beef, chopped onion, parsley, mint, salt, and pepper in a mixing bowl and stir with a wooden spoon to mix. Wet your hands with cold water and divide the meat mixture into 4 equal portions. Working quickly and with a light touch, pat each portion into a large round patty. Place the patties on a plate lined with plastic wrap and refrigerate, covered, while you set up the grill.

2 Set up the grill for direct grilling (see page 21 for charcoal or gas) and preheat to high.

3 When ready to cook, brush and oil the grill grate. Place the burgers on the hot grate and grill until cooked to taste, 4 to 6 minutes per side for medium. To test for doneness, insert an instant-read meat thermometer through the side of a burger into the center: The internal temperature should be about 160°F for medium. (Middle Eastern–style lamb burgers are usually served medium to well-done.) Place the pita breads on the grill to warm them, 30 to 60 seconds per side. Watch them carefully so they don't burn.

4 Cut a slit in each pita bread and insert a burger. Insert a lettuce leaf and a few cucumber and tomato slices, and onion slices, if using. Pour a couple spoonfuls of sauce on top and serve at once.

YIELD:
Makes 4 burgers

Yogurt Garlic Mint Sauce

Modeled on a Middle Eastern yogurt dip, this tangy sauce is eminently refreshing on a hot summer day. The main challenge will be finding unsweetened, unflavored whole milk yogurt—if your supermarket doesn't have it, look for it at a natural foods store or Middle Eastern or Greek grocery store.

INGREDIENTS:
1 clove garlic, minced
1/2 teaspoon coarse salt (kosher or sea), or more to taste
1 cup plain whole milk yogurt
2 tablespoons extra-virgin olive oil
1 tablespoon chopped fresh mint, or 1 teaspoon dried mint
Freshly ground black pepper

Place the garlic and salt in the bottom of a mixing bowl and mash to a paste with the back of a spoon. Stir in the yogurt, olive oil and mint. Season with pepper to taste, then taste for seasoning adding more salt as necessary; the sauce should be highly seasoned.

YIELD:
Makes about 1 cup

California

"SUSHI" BURGERS

Sushi has become such a part of the American diet, it's hard to imagine a time when most Americans would have been horrified by the notion of eating seaweed and raw fish. Today the *tekka maki* (literally gambler's roll), raw tuna wrapped in vinegared rice and nori and dipped in a tongue-blasting tincture of soy sauce and wasabi, is hardly more exotic than a hamburger. The comparison is apt—like the sandwich, *tekka maki* was supposedly created for an inveterate gambler, so he could eat it with his fingers while playing cards. Sushi morphed into tuna burgers in California in the 1980s. The burgers here feature such traditional sushi seasonings as soy sauce, sesame seeds, wasabi, scallion, *shiso,* and pickled ginger. Think of them as sushi for people who like their fish cooked.

METHOD:
Direct grilling

INGREDIENTS:

1 tablespoon wasabi powder

1½ pounds superfresh ahi tuna

4 teaspoons toasted sesame seeds
   (see page 584)

4 teaspoons finely chopped gari or peeled
   fresh ginger

2 shiso leaves, or 4 large fresh basil
   leaves, or 8 mint leaves, thinly slivered

2 scallions, both white and green parts,
   trimmed and finely chopped

1½ to 2 tablespoons soy sauce,
   or more to taste

½ teaspoon freshly ground black pepper,
   or more to taste

About 1 tablespoon Asian (dark) sesame oil

4 hamburger buns

Wasabi Cream Sauce (optional; page 480)

1 Place the wasabi in the bottom of a mixing bowl. Add 1 tablespoon water and stir to make a paste. Let stand for 5 minutes.

2 Finely chop the tuna by hand (you'll get the best consistency this way) or in a food processor. If using a food processor, cut the tuna into ½-inch chunks, don't fill the processor bowl more than a quarter full, and process in short pulses. Add the chopped tuna to the wasabi paste and stir in the sesame seeds, *gari, shiso,* scallions, soy sauce, and pepper. Taste for seasoning, adding more soy sauce and/or pepper as necessary (it's OK to taste tuna raw).

3 Oil your hands with a little sesame oil. Divide the tuna mixture into 4 equal portions and shape these into hamburger-like patties.

4 Set up the grill for direct grilling (see page 21 for charcoal or gas) and preheat to high.

5 When ready to cook, brush and oil the grill grate. Place the tuna burgers on the hot grate and grill until

TIPS

There may be some unfamiliar ingredients in this "Sushi" Burger recipe. Wasabi is a root that is frequently referred to as Japanese horseradish and most commonly sold in powdered form. You mix a little of the pale green powder with water to make a thick fiery paste. *Gari* is thinly shaved pickled ginger. It, like wasabi, is served as an accompaniment to sushi. If it's not available, you can use fresh ginger. *Shiso* (also known as perilla or beefsteak leaf) is a Japanese herb that tastes like a cross between mint and basil. Look for it at Japanese markets and specialty greengrocers, but if you can't find it, substitute mint or basil.

cooked to taste, about 3 minutes per side for medium-rare, or until the burgers are cooked at the edges but still pink in the center when tested with the tip of a knife (unlike hamburgers, it's safe to serve tuna burgers medium-rare). Lightly brush the buns with sesame oil and toast them on the grill, 1 to 2 minutes per side. Serve the grilled tuna burgers on the buns. Wasabi Cream Sauce makes a good accompaniment.

YIELD:

Makes 4 burgers

Hawaii

"POKE" BURGERS

Long before the first trendy new American restaurant served tuna tartare, Hawaiians were enjoying poke (pronounced PO-key). This refreshing combination of diced uncooked ahi tuna, seaweed, sesame oil, and sea salt (or soy sauce) has been a Hawaiian staple for centuries, and you find it at fancy dining establishments, private homes, and just about everywhere in between. Traditional poke (the uncooked version) would make a great appetizer at a barbecue, but I decided to take the idea one step further. Why not use the

unique counterpoint of salty and nutty flavors to jazz up a tuna burger? The result is nontraditional but extremely delicious and roaring with Hawaiian flavors.

METHOD:

Direct grilling

INGREDIENTS:

1½ pounds superfresh ahi tuna

2 tablespoons Asian (dark) sesame oil plus more for your hands and for brushing the nori and buns

4 teaspoons toasted sesame seeds (see page 584)

4 teaspoons soy sauce, or more to taste

2 scallions, white and green parts, trimmed and finely chopped

1 Thai or serrano chile pepper, seeded and minced

½ teaspoon freshly ground black pepper

¼ cup limu seaweed or hiyashi wakame, or 2 sheets nori (optional)

4 hamburger buns

Wasabi Whipped Cream (optional; page 695)

1 Finely chop the tuna by hand (you'll get the best consistency this way) or in a food processor. If using a food processor, cut the tuna into ½-inch chunks, don't fill the processor more than a quarter full, and process in short pulses. Place the chopped tuna in a mixing bowl and stir in the sesame oil, sesame seeds, soy sauce, scallions, chile, and black pepper. If using limu or hiyashi wakame, finely chop it and stir it into the tuna mixture.

TIPS

Traditionally, poke is made with tuna and *limu* seaweed. *Limu* is a softly crisp, briny seaweed that is widely available in Hawaii and just about impossible to find anywhere else. One possible substitute is a prepared mixed seaweed salad called *hiyashi wakame*, which is sold at many supermarkets, natural foods stores, and Japanese markets. Another is to crumble a few sheets of toasted nori into the burger—an even less traditional option that happens to look and taste great.

2 If using nori, lightly brush it with sesame oil and toast it over a lit burner or your grill if it is lit (hold it about 3 inches above the flame or heating element and cook until crinkly and crisp, 1 to 2 minutes per side). Let the nori cool, then crumble it into the tuna mixture and stir to mix. Taste the tuna mixture for seasoning, adding more soy sauce as necessary (it's OK to taste tuna raw).

3 Oil your hands with a little sesame oil. Divide the tuna mixture in 4 equal portions and shape these into hamburger-like patties.

4 Set up the grill for direct grilling (see page 21 for charcoal or gas) and preheat to high.

5 When ready to cook, brush and oil the grill grate. Place the tuna burgers on the hot grate and grill until cooked to taste, about 3 minutes per side for medium-rare, or until the burgers are cooked at the edges but still pink in the center when tested with the tip of a knife (unlike hamburgers, it's safe to serve tuna burgers medium-rare). Lightly brush the buns with sesame oil, if desired, and toast on the grill, 1 to 2 minutes per side. Serve the grilled tuna burgers on the buns with Wasabi Whipped Cream, if desired.

YIELD:
Makes 4 burgers

Hawaii

LOMI LOMI TUNA BURGERS

Similar to poke, but flavored with onions, tomatoes, and ginger, *lomi lomi* is a Polynesian raw fish dish. (Don't forget, Hawaii marks the westernmost boundary of Polynesia.) *Lomi lomi,* too, is great grilled—my contribution to the tradition.

METHOD:
Direct grilling

INGREDIENTS:
1½ pounds superfresh ahi tuna
½ cup finely diced sweet onion
1 medium-size ripe red tomato, peeled, seeded, and cut into ¼-inch dice (see Note)
1 scallion, both white and green parts, trimmed and finely chopped
1 tablespoon minced peeled fresh ginger
1 tablespoon toasted sesame seeds (see page 584)
3 tablespoons Asian (dark) sesame oil, plus more for your hands and for brushing the buns
½ teaspoon freshly ground black pepper
4 hamburger buns

1 Finely chop the tuna by hand or in a food processor. If using a food processor, cut the tuna into ½-inch

SOUTHSIDE MARKET & BBQ

No place makes hot guts—a peppery, smoky beef sausage—better than Southside Market in the town of Elgin. It turns out about 35,000 pounds of the stuff a week, burning four cords of Texas oak to smoke it.

1212 Highway 290 West
Elgin, Texas
(512) 285-3407
www.sausage.cc

chunks, don't fill the processor more than a quarter full, and process in short pulses. Place the chopped tuna in a mixing bowl and stir in the onion, tomato, scallion, ginger, sesame seeds, sesame oil, and pepper.

2 Oil your hands with a little sesame oil. Divide the tuna mixture into 4 equal portions and shape these into hamburger-like patties.

3 Set up the grill for direct grilling (see page 21 for charcoal or gas) and preheat to high.

4 When ready to cook, brush and oil the grill grate. Place the tuna burgers on the hot grate and grill until cooked to taste, about 3 minutes per side for medium-rare, or until the burgers are cooked at the edges but still pink in the center when tested with the tip of a knife (unlike hamburgers, it's safe to serve tuna burgers medium-rare). Lightly brush the buns with sesame oil, if desired, and toast them on the grill, 1 to 2 minutes per side. Serve the grilled tuna burgers on the buns.

YIELD:
Makes 4 burgers

NOTE: To peel a tomato, using a paring knife, cut a shallow X on the end opposite the stem. Plunge the tomato into 1 quart of boiling water until the skin loosens, 30 to 60 seconds. Rinse the tomato under cold water, then pull off the skin. To seed the tomato, cut it in half crosswise. Holding a tomato half cut side down, gently squeeze it to wring out the seeds.

Cincinnati, Ohio

CINCINNATI CHILI DOGS

You may be familiar with Cincinnati chili, which is as remarkable in the annals of American gastronomy for its unexpected flavorings (cinnamon and cocoa powder) as for the bizarre way it's served (over spaghetti and kidney beans, with oyster crackers). Like much great American lunch counter food, Cincinnati chili originated with an immigrant.

Athanas Kiradjieff settled in this lively town on the Ohio River in the 1920s. Kiradjieff's stroke of genius was to add the sweet spices of his native Macedonia (cinnamon, cloves, allspice) to a savory hash of ground beef, onions, and peppers. Kiradjieff and subsequent chili masters, like Nicholas Lambrinides (founder of Cinci's current reigning chili champ, the Skyline), served the chili over hot dogs, not just spaghetti—a practice continued today. However, the hot dogs were boiled, resulting in a pathetically anemic platform for a truly remarkable chili. My remedy will be predictable: Keep the chili, but grill the hot dog.

METHOD:
Direct grilling

FOR THE CHILI:

2 tablespoons vegetable oil

1 large onion, finely chopped

3 cloves garlic, minced

1 pound lean ground beef

½ cup tomato sauce

3 tablespoons ketchup

1 tablespoon red wine vinegar

1 tablespoon pure chile powder

1 teaspoon ground cinnamon,
    or more to taste

1 teaspoon dried oregano

1 teaspoon unsweetened cocoa powder

1 teaspoon ground cumin

¼ teaspoon ground cloves

¼ teaspoon ground allspice

Coarse salt (kosher or sea) and
    freshly ground black pepper

FOR THE HOT DOGS:

1½ cups canned kidney beans,
    drained and warmed in a saucepan

1 medium-sweet onion, finely diced

1½ cups finely grated orange
    cheddar cheese

8 beef hot dogs

3 tablespoons butter, melted

8 hot dog buns

1 MAKE THE CHILI: Heat the oil in a heavy skillet over medium heat. Add the chopped onion and garlic and cook until lightly browned, 3 to 4 minutes. Increase the heat to high, add the beef, and cook until browned, 3 to 5 minutes, crumbling the beef with a wooden spoon. Stir in the tomato sauce, ketchup, vinegar, chile powder, cinnamon, oregano, cocoa powder, cumin, cloves, and allspice. Add ½ cup of water and season with salt and pepper to taste. Bring the chili to a boil, reduce the heat to medium and let sim-

mer gently until thick and flavorful (the chili should be moist, even wet, but not soupy), 20 to 30 minutes. Taste for seasoning, adding more cinnamon, salt, and/or pepper as necessary. The chili should be highly seasoned and should have a hint of sweetness. The recipe can be prepared ahead to this stage and refrigerated, covered, for 3 days or frozen for 1 month.

2 Set up the grill for direct grilling (see page 21 for charcoal or gas) and preheat to high.

3 Reheat the chili, if necessary. Place the chili, beans, diced onion, and cheese in attractive serving bowls.

4 When ready to cook, brush and oil the grill grate. Lightly brush the hot dogs with a little of the melted butter (this will give them a crisp skin). Place the hot dogs on the hot grate and grill until handsomely browned, about 2 minutes per side (8 minutes in all). Lightly brush the insides of the buns with the remaining butter and toast them on the grill, 1 to 2 minutes per side. (In Cincinnati hot dogs are never served on toasted buns, but I prefer them toasted.) Place the grilled hot dogs on the buns and let each person add chili, beans, onion, and cheese to taste. Serve any left over chili over spaghetti with oyster crackers.

YIELD:
Makes 8 chili dogs

TIPS

Cincinnati chili parlors tend to favor pork hot dogs, but for my money, nothing can beat the flavor of kosher beef franks.

WISCONSIN BRATS

BRAT STOP

12304 75th Street
(Highway 50 and I-94)
Kenosha, Wisconsin
(262) 857-2011

Some years ago, a book tour took me from Chicago to Milwaukee. The moment we crossed the Wisconsin border, my tour escort brought us to a screeching halt at the Brat Stop. It wasn't a question of my being hungry (I had dined at Charlie Trotter's earlier that evening), and it certainly wasn't a question of sightseeing—the Brat Stop stands amid a hideous cluster of fast food outlets on one of the ugliest thoroughfares in the Midwest. No, the stop was prompted by pure civic pride in Wisconsin's most beloved dish. Then and there, that very minute, my escort explained, I had to taste a brat.

Butcher Ralph F. Stayer founded a bratwurst empire.

Brat (pronounced braht) is short for bratwurst, of course, and no other sausage in the United States inspires such fervor. There are brat appreciation societies and brat festivals (the largest, Bratwurst Days, now in its fiftieth year, takes place the first weekend in August in America's self-declared brat capital, Sheboygan); and there are heated debates on the Internet (not to mention in football stadium parking lots) as to the proper way to prepare a brat.

The sausage even shapes linguistics, for in local parlance, barbecue takes on a German name: *brat-fry*.

Bratwurst was brought to Wisconsin by German and Austrian immigrants in the late 1800s. Brats are enjoyed from one end of the Badger State to the other, but the *real* brat capital is Johnsonville, a rural village named for President Andrew Johnson that's little more than a country crossroads. It was here that a first-generation Austrian American butcher named

Ralph F. Stayer, armed with a century-old family recipe, founded Johnsonville Sausage in 1945.

What makes a brat a brat? In general terms, there's the meat (pork), the grind (coarse), the casing (natural), and the seasonings (which include salt, pepper, and for a touch of sweetness, nutmeg or mace). Ralph C. Stayer isn't about to go into the particulars, but he does remember the moment his father realized that bratwurst was the family calling. He recalls his father saying, "One day a customer came in and ordered forty pounds of hamburger and ten pounds of bratwurst. When he returned the following week and ordered forty pounds of bratwurst and ten pounds of hamburger, we knew we had something special." Today bratwurst is big business, and Johnsonville Sausage sells seven different brat varieties (cheddar or roasted garlic anyone?) in all fifty states and as far abroad as Japan. Last year, the company sold something on the order of 400 million brats!

And what is the best way to cook brats? Here's the younger Stayer's method: "I make a vodka gimlet and light my charcoal. When the gimlet is finished, I rake out the coals. I make a second gimlet, and I put the brats on the grill." Stayer believes in working over a moderate fire. By the time the second gimlet is finished, the bratwurst is cooked.

Talk to other Wisconsinites, and you soon realize that there's a wide divergence of opinion on the proper way to cook and serve brats. Some people like to parboil the sausages in beer or wine—with or without sliced onion—before grilling. Others like to brush the brats with oil or melted butter to make the casings extra crisp. Onions are generally considered to be essential, but debate rages over whether they should be raw, sautéed, or grilled (and for that matter minced, diced, or sliced).

ON A ROLL

There's little disagreement that the proper roll for a brat is a Sheboygan hard roll (a.k.a. hearth roll), sometimes called by its German name *semmel*, a roll that's crusty on the outside, soft on the inside, and often dusted with cornmeal. "You only find it in Wisconsin and it's highly perishable," says

Sheboygan's New York Street becomes Mustard Mall in honor of Bratwurst Days.

Stayer. "If we could figure out how to give it an extended shelf life, we'd sell millions." But do you butter the roll, toast it, or both? Stayer favors toasting the roll, then slathering it with a dark, stone-ground, German-style mustard, like Plochman's. He also likes a touch of finely chopped onion. Unlike many of his compatriots, he eschews sauerkraut. Dark mustard is the requisite condiment, but should you be open-minded enough to allow ketchup or relish, too?

One thing is for sure: As long as there are brats, there will be heated debates about the best way to serve them. And that's the way it should be.

On the following pages you'll find instructions for some of the most popular ways to grill brats.

The Johnsonville brat meisters in 1954.

TIPS

Your brat sandwich will only be as good as the sausage on it. Most Wisconsinites swear by Johnsonville sausages (for more about these, see page 350). If you live in an area with a large German American community, you could try the brats at a neighborhood butcher. As for the roll, it should be bakery fresh, soft on the inside, and crusty on the outside. Kaiser rolls work well.

Wisconsin

DOUBLE BRATS

No, they're not obnoxious twins from Sheboygan. The double brat is the Badger State's favorite sandwich and mandatory fare for tailgate parties or lakeside cookouts. The brats in question are bratwursts—coarsely ground, slightly sweet pork sausages—and come rain or shine (or snow or shine), the air in hundreds of towns across Wisconsin is filled with the heady scent of sausages sizzling over charcoal. The perfume is not complete without the piquant aroma of onion, the nostril-flaring pungency of dark mustard, and the brash tang of sauerkraut. Here's what I call the basic brat recipe, followed up by the most widely accepted variations.

METHOD:
Direct grilling

INGREDIENTS:
8 uncooked bratwursts
1 tablespoon vegetable oil (optional)
4 round semels, hard rolls, hearth rolls,
**   or kaiser rolls**
2 to 3 tablespoons butter, melted
**   (optional)**
Dark, spicy, stone-ground German-style
**   mustard**
1 sweet onion, thinly sliced or
**   finely chopped**
About 2 cups sauerkraut, drained (optional)
About 1 cup dill pickle slices (optional)

1 Set up the grill for direct grilling (see page 21 for charcoal or gas) and preheat to medium—I repeat, medium. The key to grilling a highly flammable food like sausage is to use a moderate heat and grill slowly.

2 When ready to cook, lightly brush each sausage on all sides with oil, if desired (this is not generally done in Wisconsin, but I find it gives you a crisper casing). Place the brats on the hot grate so that they are parallel to the bars (the bars will hold the sausages steady). Grill the brats until crisp and handsomely browned on the outside and cooked through, 4 to 6 minutes per side (16 to 24 minutes in all), turning with tongs. In the event that dripping sausage fat causes flare-ups, move the brats to another section of the grill. With time, you'll learn to tell doneness simply by looking at the brat. Beginners can use an instant-read meat thermometer: Insert it in one end to the center of the sausage. The internal temperature should be about 170°F.

3 Meanwhile, lightly brush the inside of the rolls with butter, if using, and toast them briefly on the grill, 1 to 2 minutes per side. This is by no means mandatory—indeed, many brat fans prefer their rolls untoasted.

4 To serve, slather the rolls with mustard. Place 2 brats on each roll. Top with onion and sauerkraut and/or pickles, if using.

YIELD:
Makes 4 sandwiches; serves 4 normal
**   people or 2 Paul Bunyans**

BRAT VARIATIONS

SINGLE BRAT: Grill the brats as described in the master recipe at left, but serve them on smaller elongated rolls, one to a roll (you'll need 8 rolls).

GRILLED ONION BRAT: Cut an onion crosswise into ¼-inch slices. Skewer each slice crosswise with a wooden toothpick to keep it from falling apart. Lightly brush the onion slices with vegetable oil, season them with salt and pepper, and grill them until golden brown, 6 to 8 minutes per side. Remove the toothpicks and serve the grilled onion with the grilled brats.

BRAT REUBEN: Make single brat sandwiches as described above and place 2 thin slices of Swiss cheese on each. Top the cheese with sauerkraut and grilled sliced onion. For a sauce, mix equal parts German-style mustard and Thousand Island dressing. The brat Reuben is the invention of Johnsonville Sausage developmental chef Michael Zeller.

PHILLY CHEESE BRAT: Another Zeller innovation. Make single brat sandwiches, but set the grill up for a two-zone fire (see page 22) with a high and a medium zone. Grill the brats over the medium zone and a red and a green bell pepper over the high zone. It will take 4 to 6 minutes per side (16 to 24 minutes in all) for the

Bratwurst by the yard.

bell peppers to be nicely charred. Peel, core, and seed the peppers then cut them into strips. Arrange the pepper strips on the brats. Add some thinly sliced Provolone and top with Jalapeño Beer Mustard from page 354.

BEER-SIMMERED BRATS: A lot of folks in Wisconsin like to parboil their brats in beer with onions before grilling them. This offers two advantages: The beer and onions add flavor, and parboiling shortens the grilling time. To do this, place at least 2 inches of beer in a large sauté pan. Add 1 thinly sliced medium-size onion. Add the brats and bring the mixture to the gentlest imaginable simmer over medium heat. Let the brats simmer

gently until partially cooked, 6 to 8 minutes. Do not let the brats boil or they will burst. Drain the brats well. Finish cooking the brats by grilling them as described in the master recipe, but reduce the cooking time to 2 to 3 minutes per side. One good beer to use for simmering—and drinking—is Leinenkugel's from northern Wisconsin.

BEER-SIMMERED BRATS ANOTHER WAY: This is a great method for grilling brats during a neck-and-neck football game, when you don't want to leave the TV for a second. Grill the brats ahead of time, as described in the master recipe. Meanwhile, bring at least 3 inches of beer and 1 thinly sliced medium-size onion to a boil in a large pot over high heat. Reduce the heat to medium and let simmer gently for 5 minutes. As the brats come off the grill, place them in the simmering beer, keeping the heat low—just high enough to keep the beer and brats hot. The advantage of this method is that it keeps the brats moist for extended periods. The disadvantage is that the casing loses its crispness.

WINE-SIMMERED BRATS: Substitute a dry white wine for the beer, using either simmering method above.

TWO MUSTARD SAUCES FOR BRATS

Michael Zeller knows a thing or two about bratwurst. For starters, he was born in Sheboygan during the Bratwurst Days festival (see page 350). And he currently works as corporate developmental chef for the world's largest bratwurst manufacturer, the Johnsonville Sausage Company in Wisconsin. When he created the mustard recipes here, his goal was to add character to a brat sandwich without overpowering the sausage itself.

Chef Michael Zeller born on a Bratwurst Day.

Johnsonville, Wisc.

Jalapeño Beer Mustard

Jalapeño mustard is supereasy to make, but remember to start it the night before to give the flavors time to meld. Mustard seeds are available at Indian markets and spice shops, and at most supermarkets.

INGREDIENTS:

- ½ cup dark beer
- 1 tablespoon yellow mustard seeds
- 2 teaspoons ground mustard powder
- 1 teaspoon cider vinegar
- ½ teaspoon hot red pepper flakes
- 1 to 2 fresh jalapeño peppers, seeded and minced (for a hotter mustard, leave the seeds in), or pickled jalapeño peppers, minced
- 1 tablespoon chopped fresh chives or scallion greens
- 1 cup prepared coarse-ground mustard

1 The night before you plan to serve the mustard, place the beer, mustard seeds and powder, vinegar, and hot pepper flakes in a nonreactive saucepan and whisk to mix. Cover and let the ingredients infuse in the refrigerator overnight.

2 The next day, place the saucepan with the beer mixture over medium heat and bring to a boil. Let simmer briskly until reduced by half. Remove the saucepan from the heat, let the beer mixture cool slightly, then stir in the jalapeños, chives, and prepared mustard. Transfer the mustard to a jar and let cool to room temperature, then refrigerate, covered, until serving. The mustard will keep for at least a week.

YIELD:
Makes about 1¼ cups

Johnsonville, Wisc.

Gorgonzola Beer Mustard

Blue cheese, garlic, and beer make this an aromatic, if not downright odoriferous mustard you won't soon forget. There are lots of blue cheeses to choose from. For maximum aroma, go for Italian Gorgonzola.

INGREDIENTS:

1 tablespoon butter
**3 cloves garlic, peeled and gently
    crushed with the side of a cleaver**
1 tablespoon cracked black peppercorns
1 bottle (12 ounces) dark beer
4 ounces Gorgonzola cheese, crumbled
1 cup prepared coarse-ground mustard

1 Melt the butter in a heavy saucepan over medium heat. Add the garlic and cook until very fragrant, but not brown, about 3 minutes. Add the peppercorns and beer, bring to a boil, and let boil until reduced by half. Stir in

the Gorgonzola and cook until melted, whisking to mix.

2 Remove the saucepan from the heat and let cool slightly, then whisk in the mustard. Transfer the mustard to a jar and let cool to room temperature, then refrigerate, covered, until serving. The mustard will keep for at least a week.

YIELD:
Makes about 1½ cups

Memphis, Tenn.

BARBECUED BOLOGNA

Bologna is hardly worthy of an epicurean panegyric. But season it with rub and smoke it for half a day in a pit, and this humble lunch meat becomes the stuff of legend. Just ask Frank Vernon, owner of the celebrated Bar-B-Q Shop in Memphis. Frank serves smoked bologna as part of his appetizer platter (for more about the Bar-B-Q Shop, see page 356). It also makes a great sandwich for feeding the troops at a scout meeting or barbecue competition.

THE BAR-B-Q SHOP

The year 1982 was nerve-racking for Memphis. I'm not talking about race relations or a Mississippi flood or even a dearth (or overabundance) of Elvis sightings. No, this was the year that a couple of upstarts with barely a decade of experience in the restaurant business took over the legendary Brady and Lil's.

Now *that* was a barbecue joint—run by an ancient couple who could turn pork shoulders into the stuff angels eat and ribs into magic wands. Never mind that the new Bar-B-Q Shop owners, Frank and Hazel Vernon, had trained by Mr. Brady's side for months or that they kept the same smoke-blackened pits, spicy rub, and piquant barbecue sauce.

Well, Memphis can breathe a sigh of relief, because the Vernons have remained faithful to Brady's original recipes, while adding a few memorable new dishes of their own. Unlike some of the more famous rib emporiums downtown, The Bar-B-Q Shop is still primarily a local haunt, its green and maroon dining room outfitted with church-pew booths,

THE BAR-B-Q SHOP

1782 Madison Avenue
Memphis, Tennessee
(901) 272-1277

its brick walls hung with photos of the old Brady and Lil's and scenes of vintage Memphis. The scent of wood smoke is everywhere—in the succulent pork shoulders, in the slow-cooked St. Louis–cut ribs, in the barbecued bologna (yes, barbecued bologna, which

Frank deep-fries before serving), and in a dish you'll find only in Memphis, barbecue spaghetti. And it will certainly be in your clothing by the time you finish lunch. Frank and Hazel have a King Solomon–esque solution to the age-old Memphis dilemma: Wet or dry? They offer a half-and-half platter, half the ribs served dry, and half slathered with the house Dancing Pigs Bar-B-Que Sauce.

The kitchen may look spartan, but The Bar-B-Q Shop delivers the goods.

METHOD:
Indirect grilling

INGREDIENTS:
1 whole small beef bologna
(about 3 pounds)
¼ cup of your favorite Memphis-style or
other barbecue rub (see page 698)
Vegetable oil for frying (optional)

YOU'LL ALSO NEED:
4 cups wood chips or chunks
(preferably hickory), soaked for 1 hour
in water to cover, then drained

1 Remove the casing from the bologna. Using the tip of a paring knife, make 4 to 6 lengthwise ¼-inch-deep slits running the length of the bologna. These allow the smoke flavor to penetrate the meat. Sprinkle the bologna with the barbecue rub, patting it into the slits with your fingertips. Let the bologna cure while you set up the grill.

2 Set up the grill for indirect grilling (see page 23 for gas or page 22 for charcoal) and preheat to medium. If using a gas grill, place all of the wood chips or chunks in a smoker box or in a smoker pouch (see page 24) and run the grill on high until you see smoke, then reduce the heat to medium. If using a charcoal grill, place a large drip pan in the center, preheat the grill to medium, then toss 2 cups of the wood chips or chunks on the coals.

3 When ready to cook, place the bologna in the center of the hot grate, over the drip pan and away from the heat, and cover the grill. Grill the bologna until nicely browned on the outside and smoky throughout, 1¼ to 1¾ hours. If using a charcoal grill, after 1 hour you'll need to add 12 fresh coals to each side and toss the remaining 2 cups of wood chips or chunks (1 cup per side) on the coals.

4 Transfer the grilled bologna to a cutting board. Thinly slice the bologna or cut it into ½- to 1-inch-thick slices and cut these into chunks. If you're feeling extra sinful, deep-fry the bologna slices or chunks until crisp, 2 to 3 minutes in oil heated to 350°F.

YIELD:
Serves 12 to 16

Chicago, Ill.

GRILLED KIELBASA
With Sauerkraut

The Polish Americans of Chicago have immeasurably enriched North America's barbecue repertory by sizzling the smoky, garlicky, Polish sausage, kielbasa, on the grill. Kielbasa on a roll is a magnificent sandwich to jack open your jaws for—especially when served under a tangy carpet of sauerkraut.

TIPS

Frank uses an all-beef bologna—available from your supermarket deli department. As an added refinement, he slices and deep-fries the barbecued bologna—a process I've made optional. All this reminds me of my Aunt Linda, who likes to serve hot dogs wrapped in panfried bologna slices.

TIPS

Most of the kielbasa sold in the United States is already cooked, so all you need to do is heat it on the grill. However, many Polish American grill meisters like to plump up the sausage first by simmering it in beer and sauerkraut juice (this certainly gives you a moister, more flavorful kielbasa). That's how I've done it here, but if you're in a hurry, you can skip this step and simply grill a precooked sausage as is.

METHOD:
Direct grilling

INGREDIENTS:
1½ pounds fully cooked kielbasa
1 bottle (12 ounces) beer
1 small onion, thinly sliced
1 pound sauerkraut
4 crusty round rolls or kaiser rolls, split
1 tablespoon butter, melted (optional)
Sharp mustard

1 Cut the kielbasa into 4 equal pieces. Cut each piece almost in half lengthwise (you don't want to cut through the casing at the bottom) then open the kielbasa like a book.

2 Place the beer and onion in a sauté pan or nonstick frying pan. Add most of the sauerkraut juice (leave a little in the kraut to keep it moist). Bring the mixture to a gentle simmer over medium heat. Add the kielbasa, cut side down, and let simmer gently until soft and moist, about 10 minutes. Transfer the kielbasa to a platter. Discard the onion slices and pour out all but 3 tablespoons of the cooking liquid from the sauté pan. Add the sauerkraut to the sauté pan and warm it on the stove or on the side burner of your grill.

3 Set up the grill for direct grilling (see page 21 for charcoal or gas) and preheat to high.

4 When ready to cook, brush and oil the grill grate. Place the kielbasa on the hot grate and grill it until the casing is crisp and the inside is lightly browned, 4 to 6 minutes per side, turning with tongs. If you like your rolls toasted (not everyone does), brush the cut sides with melted butter and place the rolls on the grill for a minute or so.

5 To serve, slather the rolls with mustard, then pile on the grilled kielbasa and sauerkraut.

YIELD:
Serves 4

Cambridge, Mass.

GRILLED GREEK SAUSAGE
With Peppers and Onions

I first tasted *loukanika*, Greek sausage, at the summer block party the Greek Orthodox Church stages each year in my old neighborhood, in Cambridge's Central Square. I was hooked with my first bite. I loved the sweet, citrusy flavor of the orange peel and fennel seeds in the sausage. I loved the grilled onions and peppers piled on top. I even loved the way the grease stained my chin when I took a bite. When it comes to Greek-American grilling, most of us think of gyros or souvlaki. This sausage is a minor miracle—worth the trouble of ferreting it out.

METHOD:
Direct grilling

INGREDIENTS:

1½ pounds fully cooked loukanika (Greek
    sausage flavored with orange peel)
3 to 4 tablespoons olive oil
1 red bell pepper
1 green bell pepper
1 large onion, cut into ½-inch rounds
Coarse salt (kosher or sea) and
    freshly ground black pepper
4 crusty sausage or hoagie rolls
Mustard (optional)

YOU'LL ALSO NEED:

Wooden toothpicks, soaked for
    1 hour in water to cover,
    then drained

1 Cut the sausage almost in half lengthwise (you don't want to cut through the casing at the bottom) then open the sausage like a book. Lightly brush each sausage all over with some of the olive oil. Lightly brush the outside of the bell peppers with some of the olive oil. Skewer each onion slice crosswise with a wooden toothpick to keep it from falling apart and lightly brush it with olive oil. Generously season the bell peppers and onion with salt and black pepper.

2 Set up the grill for direct grilling (see page 21 for charcoal or gas) and preheat to high.

3 When ready to cook, brush and oil the grill grate. Put the bell peppers, onion, and sausage on the hot grate and grill until the bell peppers and onion are nicely browned and cooked through and the sausage is warmed through, 3 to 4 minutes per side (12 to 16 minutes in all) for the bell peppers and 4 to 6 minutes per side (8 to 12 minutes in all) for the onion slices and sausage. Baste the vegetables with any remaining olive oil as they cook.

4 To serve, remove the toothpicks from the onion slices and separate the rings. Core and seed the bell peppers and cut the flesh into strips. Pile the sausage, onion slices, and bell peppers on the rolls and serve at once. Yes, you can slather on some mustard.

YIELD:
Serves 4

New York, N.Y.

KARNATZLACH
(Romanian Grilled Garlic Sausage Patties)

Sammy's Roumanian in New York City occupies a boisterous basement on the Lower East Side, where pitchers of schmaltz (rendered chicken fat) sit on the table to drizzle

The main challenge in making this recipe will be finding the *loukanika*. Look for it at Greek markets (sometimes you'll find it at Middle Eastern markets, too). *Loukanika* comes both fresh and cooked, the former in links, the latter shaped like jumbo knockwurst. Cook fresh *loukanika* the same way you would fresh bratwurst (see page 352); the cooked kind just needs to be split and heated on the grill. As a substitute for cooked *loukanika* you can use kielbasa, adding a little grated orange zest and fennel seed to the oil for basting the sausage.

TIPS

Combining beef and veal in a single sausage is characteristic of the Balkans. The club soda and baking soda are added to make the meat patties light. One more nice thing about these sausages is that you don't need to stuff them into a casing.

over your black bread and the meal ends with complimentary egg creams (a chocolaty soda fountain drink). Along the way, there are plate-burying portions of chicken fricassee, thick garlicky veal chops, and chopped liver so fresh it's mixed at the table. The live entertainment will make you feel like you've stumbled into someone's bar mitzvah. Whenever I eat at Sammy's, the one dish I make sure not to miss is the *karnatzlach* (there spelled *karnatzlack*), a mega-garlicky, free-form Romanian beef sausage; I also make sure to bring an extra tin of breath mints.

METHOD:
Direct grilling

ADVANCE PREPARATION:
1 to 2 hours for chilling the sausage (optional)

INGREDIENTS:
1 pound stew beef, cut into ¾-inch cubes
1 pound veal, cut into ¾-inch cubes
½ cup club soda
½ teaspoon baking soda
8 cloves garlic, minced
2 teaspoons coarse salt (kosher or sea)
1 teaspoon ground cumin
1 teaspoon sweet paprika
½ to 1 teaspoon freshly ground black pepper
¼ cup chopped fresh flat-leaf parsley
Black bread (optional)
Deli mustard (optional)

1 Put the meat twice through a meat grinder or use the metal blade of a food processor to chop it in short pulses (see Note).

2 Place the club soda and baking soda in a mixing bowl and stir in the garlic, salt, cumin, paprika, pepper, and parsley. Add the ground meat and stir with a wooden spoon until mixed. Cover the bowl with plastic wrap and let the sausage rest for 1 to 2 hours in the refrigerator. This "ripens" the sausage. If you're in a hurry, you can skip this step.

3 Wet your hands with cold water and form the meat mixture into elongated patties shaped rather like cigars. Each patty should be about 3 inches long and 1 inch wide. You'll have about 20 patties. Place the patties on a baking sheet lined with plastic wrap and refrigerate, covered, while you set up the grill.

4 Set up the grill for direct grilling (see page 21 for charcoal or gas) and preheat to high.

5 When ready to cook, brush and oil the grill grate. Place the sausages on the hot grate and grill until sizzling, brown, crisp, and cooked through, 3 to 5 minutes per side (6 to 10 minutes in all). Serve at once. Black bread and deli mustard make nice accompaniments.

YIELD:
Serves 8 as an appetizer, 4 to 6 as a main course

NOTE: For the best results, chop the meat in a meat grinder—or have your butcher do it for you. If you must use a food processor, don't fill the processor bowl more than a quarter full and grind the meat in short pulses. Be careful not to overprocess it.

NORTH CAROLINA BARBECUE

Whenever I travel, I love nothing better than to track down out-of-the-way, down-and-dirty barbecue joints where the meat's as smoky as a chimney and as tender as two adolescents in love. This is how I found myself in a Cherokee Six, soaring 3,000 feet over the rolling countryside of central North Carolina. I had only forty-eight hours in the state, and I was determined to spend the majority of those hours eating. The night before I'd met a couple of fellow barbecue addicts at dinner. When I learned they had a private plane, I shamelessly caged a ride—a man with a passion for barbecue will do anything he has to to get his next fix. My destination was Lexington, in the western part of the state. The city boasts at least twenty barbecue restaurants and an annual barbecue festival that draws more than 100,000 people. The festival takes place in October; for more information, call (336) 956-1880 or go to its Web site, www.barbecuefestival.com.

Fact is that North Carolinians have enjoyed barbecue for the better part of three centuries. Pork is king in the Tar Heel state and has been since at least 1728, when chronicler William Byrd observed: "The only business here is raising of hogs, which is managed with the least trouble, and affords the diet [North Carolinians] are most fond of. The truth of it is, the inhabitants of North Carolina devour so much swine's flesh that it fills them full of gross humours [sic]." I didn't see anyone filled with gross humors, but I did see a very large number of people indulging in pork and their humor seemed excellent.

WHERE TO EAT NORTH CAROLINA BARBECUE

Allen & Son Barbecue
6203 Millhouse Road
Chapel Hill
(919) 942-7576

The Barbecue Center
900 North Main Street
Lexington
(336) 248-4633
www.barbecuecenter.com

Lexington Barbecue
10 Highway 29-70 South
Lexington
(704) 249-9814

Wilber's Barbecue
4172 East U.S. 70
Highway, Goldsboro
(919) 778-5218
www.esn.net/wilbers/

North Carolina barbecue is customarily served pulled into meaty shreds or chopped. According to

Pork is king in the Tar Heel state.

Pork shoulders roast over glowing hickory embers.

... long threads of unbelievably moist, tender, succulent meat

Bob Garner, author of *North Carolina Barbecue,* the practice of chopping barbecue may have originated in the dark ages of dentistry, when few people had a full set of teeth for chewing. Today chopping guarantees the maximum absorption of sauce. And sauce is something that makes North Carolina barbecue distinctive. The sauce is a bracingly tart mixture of vinegar and hot peppers, with a little salt for flavor and sometimes a bit of sugar to round out the edges. (A little ketchup is added in the western part of the state—more about that shortly.) It's the original kick-ass sauce, designed to complement pork, not camouflage it.

A great deal has been made of the supposed rivalry between eastern and western North Carolina–style barbecue. Bob Garner quotes from the war of words between two North Carolina journalists in the 1950s: No pig worth its salt should be turned into the "vinegar-tainted, half-burned nonsense" they serve in Goldsboro, wrote Vernon Sechriest, editor of the *Rocky Mount Evening Telegram* in western North Carolina. Rocky Mount barbecue "has some resemblance to mush," retorted his adversary, Henry Belk, then editor of *Goldsboro News-Argus.* Actually, the debate is really so much hot air rising up like smoke from a barbecue pit. But for the use of ketchup and the cut of pork used, the two styles are virtually the same. And both are shamelessly good.

BLISS ON A BUN

What does the perfect North Carolina barbecue taste like? That's why I went to Lexington. The luscious chopped pork sandwiches served at Lexington Barbecue are the epitome of the western North Carolina style. For well nigh forty years, this sprawling restaurant has been Lexington's number one barbecue spot, serving literally thousands of customers every Saturday alone. The four huge chimneys towering over four equally huge brick pits tell part of the story—proprietor Wayne Monk cooks his pork the old-fashioned way: in a sealed brick pit over blazing oak embers (to read more about Lexington Barbecue, see page 240). The preferred cut of meat is pork shoulder. It comes doused with vinegar sauce slightly reddened and sweetened with ketchup.

If Lexington serves definitive western North Carolina barbecue, Goldsboro dishes up classic eastern-style fare. The unassuming community is home to the legendary Wilber's Barbecue and to the state's longest continuously operating barbecue restaurant, Scott's Famous Barbecue. As is typical in eastern North Carolina barbecue, Wilber Shirley smokes whole hogs instead of pork shoulders, using a troughlike open pit as a cooker (for more on Wilber's see page 238). The meat is more intricately flavored and richer than in the west, the result of a combination of fatty shoulder meat; rich, tender rib meat; robustly flavored meat from the hams; and even smoky bits of burnt pork skin. The tartness of a vinegar sauce combined with the unctuous pork gives my tongue a frisson of pleasure. The slaw is a little crisper and sharper here, lending the sandwich a no-nonsense quality in keeping with the plainer sauce.

North Carolina–style "health food."

If barbecue were art, Wayne Monk's Lexington-style barbecue, with its ketchup-sweetened sauce, would have the soft voluptuousness of a Titian. Wilber's vinegary pork would suggest the sharpness and intensity of a Goya. I could gaze on—or rather, eat—both with pleasure for hours, but would be utterly incapable of saying which is best.

A COMMUNITY AFFAIR

Barbecue in North Carolina can be as much a social event as a food. If you're invited to a pig pickin' while you're in the area, don't hesitate to show up. A pig pickin' is North Carolina barbecue done on a community scale—a whole hog roasted over wood or charcoal, lovingly chopped or shredded into fine bits, paired with the obligatory vinegar sauce, coleslaw, and hamburger buns. But, unlike at a restaurant, the hog is the focal point of an event that lasts an entire afternoon and features the best food and hospitality that North Carolina has to offer.

My main man for pig pickin' is David Sparrow. I met the caterer and pit master, whose company is called Pig in the Pen, at a grilling class I was teaching at the Fearrington House in Pittsboro. By the time I arrived at his rambling farmstead at 10 A.M., a 170-pound pig was just finishing a night on a giant cooker fashioned from an old furnace oil tank.

"Look'ee here," said David, tugging on a pork rib with his tongs. The rib pulled away with ease, exposing long threads of unbelievably moist, tender, succulent meat. I ate some and ate some more, then tackled a piece of ham and pork loin, imagining what the pig pickin' would be like that afternoon, with oceans of beer and bluegrass music and a man the likes of David Sparrow as master of ceremonies.

I wish I could wax grandiloquent about *all* North Carolina barbecue. The truth is that traditional barbecue is in trouble. More and more restaurants are abandoning wood- or charcoal-fired pits for gas and even electric cookers. They produce pork that's pleasant enough but utterly devoid of the inimitable flavor of wood smoke, and I'm not sure I'd call it barbecue. The sad truth is that only a handful of pit masters remain who still cook over wood or charcoal. Which makes men like Wayne Monk, Wilber Shirley, and David Sparrow not just experts in their field, but heroes.

Birds on the

Chicken is great grilled. The mild-flavored meat eagerly absorbs fire and smoke flavors, and live fire sizzles the skin till it's crackling crisp. But there's a down side: Chicken breasts tend to dry out and whole chickens (because of their high fat content) can burn or burst into flames on the grill. All too often, poultry goes on the grill with the best intentions and comes off black on the outside but raw within. Relax—this chapter will show you how to grill, smoke, and spit-roast chicken and other birds without fear or tears. From Cajun-style beer-can chicken to Maui-spiced, pineapple-glazed grilled chicken breasts; from paper-thin grilled chicken paillards to Southwestern green or red chile chicken under bricks, we've got you covered. Did I mention Alabama barbecued chicken with an offbeat white barbecue sauce, quail "Little Havana," or turkey breast maple smoked Vermont style? There's even an outlandish Boy Scout classic—trash-can turkey. Whatever you fancy, follow the tips in this chapter and you'll never burn birds on the grill again. Scout's honor.

Barbecue

TIPS

This recipe calls for a roasting chicken, which is bigger than a fryer, so you'll need a large beer can—a sixteen-ounce "tall boy" works perfectly. Or, if you prefer, you could brine a 3½- or 4-pound chicken and cook it on a regular (twelve-ounce) beer can. If you do, reduce the brining time to eight hours and cut the grilling time to 1¼ to 1½ hours.

Alabama

BRANT'S BRINED BEER BUTT BIRD

My enthusiasm for beer-can chicken knows no limits (hey, I wrote a whole book on the subject). Alabama pit master Brant Warren is another devotee of this singular grilling method, and the following bird took first prize at the EGGtoberfest—an event organized by Big Green Egg users in Atlanta. (The Big Green Egg is a *kamado*-style ceramic cooker that has an almost cultlike following—see page 30.) The chicken owes its incredible succulence to an overnight bath in a honey-cinnamon brine, not to mention being smoke roasted on an upright open can of beer. If you've never made beer-can chicken, you're about to become a believer.

METHOD:
Indirect grilling

ADVANCE PREPARATION:
12 hours for brining the chicken

INGREDIENTS:
¾ cup coarse salt (kosher or sea)
¾ cup honey
6 tablespoons red wine vinegar
3 cinnamon sticks (each 2 inches long)
3 bay leaves
1 roasting chicken (6 to 7 pounds)
1 large can (16 ounces) beer
1½ tablespoons sweet paprika
1½ tablespoons dark brown sugar
2 teaspoons dried basil
½ teaspoon cayenne pepper
2 tablespoons butter, melted
2 tablespoons red wine vinegar
1 tablespoon Worcestershire sauce
Your choice of barbecue sauce, for serving

YOU'LL ALSO NEED:
2 cups wood chips or chunks (preferably hickory or oak), soaked for 1 hour in water and/or beer to cover, then drained; vertical chicken roaster (optional)

The Big Green Egg cooker has a cultlike following.

1 Place the salt, honey, vinegar, cinnamon sticks, and bay leaves in a large deep nonreactive pot (one just large enough to hold the chicken and brine). Add 3 quarts of water and bring to a boil over high heat. Let boil for 3 minutes. Remove the pot from the heat and let this brine cool to room temperature. The brine must be completely cool before you add the chicken.

2 Remove the packet of giblets from the body cavity of the chicken and set aside for making stock or another use. Remove and discard the fat just inside the body and neck cavities. Rinse the chicken, inside and out, under cold running water, then drain and blot dry, inside and out, with paper towels. Place the chicken in the pot with the cooled brine. Place a weight, such as a saucepan or plate, on top to keep the bird submerged. You can also brine the bird in a large resealable plastic bag. Let the chicken brine in the refrigerator, covered, for 12 hours.

3 Pop the tab off the beer can. Pour half of the beer (1 cup) over the soaking wood chips or chunks or reserve for another use. If cooking the chicken on the can, using a church key–style can opener, make 2 additional holes in the top. Set the can aside.

4 Place the paprika, brown sugar, basil, and cayenne in a small bowl and stir to mix. (Actually, if you don't have sensitive skin, your fingers work better for mixing a rub than a spoon or whisk does.)

CHICKEN DONE JUST RIGHT

There's nothing like grilling for transforming a commonplace bird into an unforgettable mouthful. But a lot of people have trouble cooking chicken on the grill.

Chickens have a lot of fat and the skin has a tendency to burn. Whether you are preparing chicken pieces or a whole bird, be sure to follow these three simple rules for grilling and the results will be perfect:

1. Work over a moderate, not a hot, fire. To be completely safe, use the indirect grilling method.

2. Don't crowd the grill. Leave plenty of open space on the grate where you can move the chicken to dodge flare-ups, which more than likely will occur.

3. Apply sweet sauces at the end of cooking. If you use them at the beginning, the sugar in the sauce will burn.

5 Drain the chicken, discarding the brine. Blot the chicken dry, inside and out, with paper towels. Sprinkle half of the rub inside the chicken in the body and neck cavities. Brush or rub the outside of the bird with the melted butter and sprinkle with the remaining rub, patting it all over the skin with your fingertips. Let the chicken cure in the refrigerator, covered, for 15 minutes.

6 If cooking the chicken on the beer can, add the vinegar and Worcestershire sauce to the can and, holding the bird upright, with the opening of the body cavity at the bottom, lower it onto the can so the can fits into the body cavity. Pull the chicken legs forward to form a sort of tripod, so the bird stands upright. The rear leg of the tripod is the beer can.

If cooking the chicken on a vertical chicken roaster, fill it with the remaining 1 cup of beer and the vinegar and Worcestershire sauce. Position the chicken on top following the manufacturer's instructions.

 Tuck the wing tips behind the chicken's back.

TESTING CHICKEN FOR DONENESS

The various organizations in the United States that are dedicated to keeping us informed about poultry recommend cooking chickens and turkeys until they are well-done in order to kill any harmful bacteria. This translates to an internal temperature of 170°F for breast meat and 180°F for leg meat (the breast cooks a little more quickly than the leg). Just to play it safe, when cooking a whole bird, I use the leg temperature to ascertain doneness. Not all chefs, particularly those at temples of high gastronomy, cook their birds quite this well-done. The reason is simple—these chefs buy their poultry from small farms, where salmonella and other forms of contamination are not a risk. They can safely serve their chicken or turkey when it's cooked to, say, 160°F. If you are grilling commercial poultry, I suggest you cook it until the higher temperature is reached.

FOR A WHOLE BIRD: To check the temperature, insert an instant-read meat thermometer into the thickest part of the thigh (but not so that it touches the bone) and leave it there for 20 seconds. When the bird is done, it will register about 180°F.

FOR A HALF CHICKEN: Insert the instant-read meat thermometer through the thigh or you can use the poke test: The meat should feel firm when pressed. The poke test also works for spatchcocked chicken or a split turkey breast.

FOR A BONELESS CHICKEN BREAST: To see whether it's done, I generally use the poke test: Again, the meat should feel firm when pressed. Here, too, if you want to be absolutely sure, you can take its temperature by inserting the thermometer in one end.

8 Set up the grill for indirect grilling (see page 23 for gas or page 22 for charcoal) and preheat to medium. If using a gas grill, place all of the wood chips or chunks in the smoker box or in a smoker pouch (see page 24) and run the grill on high until you see smoke, then reduce the heat to medium. If using a charcoal grill, place a large drip pan in the center, preheat the grill to medium, then toss 1 cup of the wood chips or chunks on the coals.

9 When ready to cook, stand the chicken upright in the center of the hot grate, over the drip pan and away from the heat. Cover the grill and cook the chicken until the skin is golden brown and very crisp and the meat is cooked through, 1³⁄₄ to 2 hours. To test for doneness, use an instant-read meat thermometer: Insert it into the thickest part of a thigh but not so that it touches the bone. The internal temperature should be about 180°F. (See box at left for more about testing for doneness.) If the chicken skin starts to brown too much, cover the bird loosely with aluminum foil. If using a charcoal grill, after 1 hour you'll need to add 12 fresh coals to each side and toss the remaining 1 cup of wood chips or chunks (¹⁄₂ cup per side) on the coals.

10 When the chicken is done, if cooking it on a can, using tongs, hold the bird by the can and carefully transfer it in an upright position to a platter. If cooking the chicken on a vertical chicken roaster, use oven mitts or pot holders to remove the bird from the grill while it's still on the vertical roaster.

11 Present the bird to your guests. Let the chicken rest for 5 minutes, then carefully lift it off the support. Take care not to spill the hot beer or otherwise burn yourself. Carve the chicken and serve with your favorite barbecue sauce (there are several dozen in this book to choose from).

YIELD:

Serves 6

VARIATION: Brant cooks his chicken in a Big Green Egg, which he runs at 275°F. If you have a Big Green Egg or a smoker and are cooking at that low a heat, add 1 to 1½ hours to the cooking time given here.

Memphis, Tenn.

CAJUN ROASTIN' CHICKEN ON A BEER CAN

The year was 1996; the place, the Memphis in May World Championship Barbecue Cooking Contest. I'd come to this metropolis on the banks of the Mississippi to learn about competition barbecue. A local barbecue team, the Bryce Boar Blazers, took

me in, taught me, fed me, and introduced me to beer-can chicken. I've been hooked ever since. There are two interesting aspects to their recipe: First, it's made with a large roasting chicken, not a fryer, so you'll need a big beer can, a 16-ounce one. Second, the bird is injected with a liquid seasoning, using a Cajun injector, which looks like a giant hypodermic needle. This keeps the bird squirting moist and tender, despite its hefty size.

METHOD:

Indirect grilling

INGREDIENTS:

1 large can (16 ounces) beer
¼ cup chicken stock (preferably homemade), at room temperature
2 tablespoons salted butter
1 tablespoon brandy
7 teaspoons Cajun Rub (page 420) or a good commercial blend
1 teaspoon fresh lemon juice
1 roasting chicken (6 to 7 pounds)
3 tablespoons melted butter, for basting
Your favorite barbecue sauce, for serving

YOU'LL ALSO NEED:

2 cups wood chips or chunks (preferably hickory or oak), soaked for 1 hour in water and/or beer to cover, then drained; kitchen syringe; vertical chicken roaster (optional)

1 Pop the tab off the beer can. Pour half of the beer (1 cup) over the soaking wood chips or chunks. If cooking the chicken on the can, using a

TIPS

■ Cajun injectors, also called kitchen syringes, can be purchased at cookware shops or ordered by mail (see Mail-Order Sources, page 742).

■ The Blazers used a commercial injector seasoning. You'll find a simple homemade version here.

4 Fill the kitchen syringe with the injector sauce. To do this, push the plunger all the way down, place the tip of the needle in the sauce, and slowly draw the plunger up: The syringe will fill with sauce. Inject the sauce into the breast, thighs, and drumsticks. Don't be surprised if a little sauce squirts out; this is OK. Brush the outside of the bird with 1 tablespoon of the melted butter. Season the outside of the bird with the remaining 1 tablespoon of the Cajun Rub.

5 If cooking the chicken on the beer can, hold the bird upright, with the opening of the body cavity at the bottom, and lower it onto the can so the can fits into the body cavity. Pull the legs forward to form a sort of tripod, so the bird stands upright. The rear leg of the tripod is the beer can.

If cooking the chicken on a vertical chicken roaster, fill it with the remaining 1 cup of beer and position the chicken on top, following the manufacturer's instructions.

6 Tuck the wing tips behind the chicken's back.

7 Set up the grill for indirect grilling (see page 23 for gas or page 22 for charcoal) and preheat to medium. If using a gas grill, place all of

church key–style can opener, make 2 additional holes in the top. Set the can of beer aside.

2 Combine the stock, 2 tablespoons butter, brandy, 1 teaspoon of the Cajun Rub, and the lemon juice in a non-reactive saucepan over medium heat. Warm until the butter is melted, stirring with a fork. Remove the saucepan from the heat and let this injector sauce cool to room temperature.

3 Remove the packet of giblets from the body cavity of the chicken and set aside for making stock or another use. Remove and discard the fat just inside the body and neck cavities. Rinse the chicken, inside and out, under cold running water, then drain and blot dry, inside and out, with paper towels. Sprinkle 1 tablespoon of the Cajun Rub inside the body and neck cavities of the chicken.

the wood chips or chunks in the smoker box or in a smoker pouch (see page 24) and run the grill on high until you see smoke, then reduce the heat to medium. If using a charcoal grill, place a large drip pan in center, preheat the grill to medium, then toss 1 cup of the wood chips or chunks on the coals.

8 When ready to cook, stand the chicken upright in the center of the hot grate, over the drip pan and away from the heat. Cover the grill and cook the chicken until the skin is golden brown and very crisp and the meat is cooked through, 1¾ to 2 hours. To test for doneness, use an instant-read meat thermometer: Insert it into the thickest part of a thigh but not so that it touches the bone. The internal temperature should be about 180°F. (See page 368 for more about testing for doneness.) As it cooks, carefully baste the chicken with the remaining 2 tablespoons of melted butter at 45-minute intervals, taking care not to knock the bird over. If the chicken skin starts to brown too much, loosely cover the bird with aluminum foil. If using a charcoal grill, after 1 hour you'll need to add 12 fresh coals to each side and toss the remaining 1 cup of wood chips or chunks (½ cup per side) on the coals.

9 When the chicken is done, if cooking it on a can, using tongs, hold the bird by the can and carefully transfer the chicken in an upright position to a platter. If cooking the chicken on a vertical chicken roaster, use oven mitts or pot holders to remove the bird from the grill while it's still on the vertical roaster.

10 Present the bird to your guests. Let the chicken rest for 5 minutes, then carefully lift it off the support. Take care not to spill the hot beer or otherwise burn yourself. Carve the chicken and serve it with your favorite barbecue sauce (there are several dozen in this book to choose from).

YIELD:
Serves 6

Florida

PINEAPPLE JALAPENO CHICKEN

Barbecue buffs have hundreds of marinades, but none is as noble as adobo. I mean this quite literally, for the name of this piquant mixture of garlic, cumin, and lime or sour orange juice derives from a medieval legal term, *adobar,* to ennoble. Adobo is the starting point for many of the Hispano-American barbecue recipes

WALL OF FLAME

WEBER GRILL RESTAURANT

Everything at the Weber Grill Restaurant is grilled on oversize, charcoal-burning Weber Ranch grills, from the fire-roasted artichoke and spinach dip, to the twenty-two-ounce T-bone (served with a blue cheese "steak splash"), to what's perhaps the only beer-can chicken you can order in a restaurant. The restaurant is easy to recognize—turn in at the fourteen-foot-tall red Weber kettle grill.

539 North State Street
Chicago, Illinois
(312) 467-9696
(and other locations)
www.weberrestaurant.com

TIPS

For maximum flavor, place the adobo under the chicken skin, as I have described here, so it can perfume the meat. This technique is worth mastering because you can also use it to marinate turkeys, ducks, and game hens. Of course, if it seems like too much trouble, you can just use the adobo as a simple marinade: Place the bird in a resealable plastic bag and pour the adobo over it.

you find in Florida. It flavors anything from chicken to shrimp to steak. An American twist comes from adding fresh pineapple and jalapeño peppers. The results are spectacular with whole chicken and turkey. To complete the theme, serve the chicken with the Pineapple Barbecue Sauce on page 293.

METHOD:
Indirect grilling

ADVANCE PREPARATION:
4 to 12 hours for marinating the chicken (optional)

FOR THE ADOBO:
1 slice fresh pineapple (1 inch thick; 3 to 4 ounces), cored and cut into 1-inch chunks, or 1 can (8¼ ounces) pineapple chunks, drained
1 to 2 shallots, coarsely chopped (about ⅓ cup)
2 cloves garlic, coarsely chopped
1 to 2 jalapeño peppers, seeded and coarsely chopped (for a hotter adobo, leave the seeds in)
½ teaspoon ground cumin
½ teaspoon dried oregano
2 tablespoons Dijon mustard
1 tablespoon fresh lime juice
1 tablespoon olive oil
Coarse salt (kosher or sea) and freshly ground black pepper

FOR THE CHICKEN:
1 roasting chicken (6 to 7 pounds)
Coarse salt (kosher or sea) and freshly ground black pepper
1 tablespoon olive oil

YOU'LL ALSO NEED:
2 cups wood chips or chunks (preferably oak or citrus wood), soaked for 1 hour in water to cover, then drained; butcher's string (optional)

1 MAKE THE ADOBO: Place the pineapple, shallots, garlic, jalapeño(s), cumin, and oregano in a food processor and process to a smooth paste. Gradually add the mustard, lime juice, and olive oil and season with plenty of salt and black pepper to taste; the adobo should be very highly seasoned.

2 Remove the packet of giblets from the body cavity of the chicken and set aside for making stock or another use. Remove and discard the fat just inside the body and neck cavities. Rinse the chicken, inside and out, under cold running water, then drain and blot dry, inside and out, with paper towels.

3 Generously season the inside of the chicken with salt and black pepper. Place 1 tablespoon of the adobo in the body cavity and 1 tablespoon in the neck cavity of the chicken. Loosen the chicken skin from the body: Starting at the top of the neck cavity, tunnel your index finger under the skin. Taking care not to tear it, gently loosen the skin from the meat, inserting additional fingers one at a time until you can use your whole hand to loosen the skin from the breast meat, then the thighs. Spoon the remaining adobo under the skin, spreading it over the breast, thighs, and even the back meat by rubbing your fingers over the outside of the skin. You can cook the chicken right away but the flavor will be richer if you let it marinate in the refrigerator, covered, for at least 4 hours or as long as overnight.

4 Truss the chicken (see box at right for instructions); this is optional, but it will give the bird a more dignified appearance. Brush or rub the outside of the chicken with the olive oil and season it generously with salt and black pepper.

5 Set up the grill for indirect grilling (see page 23 for gas or page 22 for charcoal) and preheat to medium. If using a gas grill, place all of the wood chips or chunks in the smoker box or in a smoker pouch (see page 24) and run the grill on high until you see smoke, then reduce the heat to medium. If using a charcoal grill, place a large drip pan in the center, preheat the grill to medium, then toss all of the wood chips or chunks on the coals.

6 When ready to cook, place the chicken, breast side up, in the center of the hot grate, over the drip pan and away from the heat. Cover the grill and cook the chicken until the skin is gorgeously browned and the meat is cooked through, 1¾ to 2 hours. To test for doneness, use an instant-read meat thermometer: Insert it into the thickest part of a thigh but not so that it touches the bone. The internal temperature should be about 180°F. (See page 368 for more about testing for doneness.) If the chicken skin starts to brown too

TO TRUSS OR NOT TO TRUSS

Many of the chicken, duck, and turkey recipes in this book call for trussing. Does the bird have a hernia? Or a penchant for bondage and dominance?

Actually, poultry is trussed for cosmetic purposes—to give it a handsome, compact appearance. Some chefs argue that a trussed bird roasts more evenly, while others maintain that heat penetrates better when the bird is not trussed. Like most cosmetic surgery, it's elective and the various procedures range from simple to complex.

The easiest way to truss a bird is to tie the drumsticks together with butcher's string. Tuck the wing tips behind the bird's back, so that it can sit steady on the grill. Or you can insert a bamboo skewer crosswise through one leg, pinning it to the body, then pass the skewer through the body cavity and the other leg. The idea here is to pin the legs to the body.

The classic French way to truss poultry involves looping string around the legs and back of the body, over the thighs and over the wings, and then tying it in the back. A variation on this technique involves sewing the legs and wings in place with a trussing needle.

So what happens if you don't truss the bird? The cooking time will be marginally shorter and, blindfolded, you won't be able to taste the difference.

much, loosely cover the bird with aluminum foil. If using a charcoal grill, after 1 hour you'll need to add 12 fresh coals to each side.

7 Transfer the chicken to a platter or cutting board and let rest for 5 minutes, then untruss it, if necessary, carve, and serve.

YIELD:
Serves 6

TIPS

Note how the barbecue sauce is brushed on the bird at the end here: This lets the chicken skin become crisp and prevents the sugar in the sauce from burning.

The South

FOOLPROOF BARBECUED CHICKEN

Chicken is the dish grill jockeys love and hate. They love it because there's nothing like grilling to crisp the skin, smoke the meat, and turn out a bird that's tender and juicy. They hate it because all too often the skin turns out burnt, the meat remains raw in the center, and the flames from the dripping fat cause problems almost the moment you put the bird on the grill. Well, if you have encountered these pitfalls, here's a grilled chicken that's guaranteed foolproof. In fact, you couldn't burn it if you tried!

I've taken all the risk out of the recipe by moving the fire to the sides of the grill—away from where the chicken cooks. You still get that smoky live-fire flavor, but without the risk of the bird burning. Grill jockeys will recognize this technique as indirect grilling, and it produces some of the tastiest barbecued chicken this side of Memphis. And to make you feel like a pro, I've included a mop sauce (a vinegar mixture you apply to the chicken with a barbecue mop), so you can hold your own with the big boys on the barbecue circuit.

METHOD:
Indirect grilling

ADVANCE PREPARATION:
1 to 2 hours for curing the chicken

FOR THE CHICKEN AND RUB:
1 chicken (3½ to 4 pounds)
1½ teaspoons coarse salt (kosher or sea)
1½ teaspoons sweet paprika
1½ teaspoons brown sugar
1 teaspoon freshly ground black pepper
½ teaspoon onion powder
½ teaspoon garlic powder
¼ teaspoon celery seed

FOR THE MOP SAUCE:
½ cup distilled white vinegar
¼ cup Worcestershire sauce
1 tablespoon rub reserved from above

2 cups Dr Pepper Barbecue Sauce (recipe follows) or your favorite commercial sauce

YOU'LL ALSO NEED:
2 cups wood chips or chunks (preferably hickory), soaked for 1 hour in water to cover, then drained; poultry shears

1 Remove the packet of giblets from the body cavity of the chicken and set aside for making stock or another use. Remove and discard the fat just inside the body and neck cavities. Rinse the chicken, inside and out, under cold running water, then drain and blot dry, inside and out, with paper towels. Place the chicken on its breast. Using poultry shears and starting at the neck end, make a lengthwise cut along one side of the backbone to the tail. Make a second lengthwise cut along the other side of the backbone. Discard the backbone or set aside for another use. Open the chicken like a book, skin side up, and lay it flat. Using the poultry shears, cut the chicken in half through the breastbone. This will give you two chicken halves, which will lie flat on the grill. Place the chicken halves in a baking dish.

2 MAKE THE RUB: Combine the salt, paprika, brown sugar, pepper, onion and garlic powders, and celery seed in a small bowl and stir to mix. (Actually, your fingers work better for mixing a rub than a spoon or whisk does.) Set aside 1 tablespoon of the rub for the mop sauce. Sprinkle the remaining rub over the chicken on both sides, patting it onto the meat with your fingertips. Let the chicken cure in the refrigerator, covered, for 1 to 2 hours.

3 MAKE THE MOP SAUCE: Combine the vinegar, Worcestershire sauce, and remaining 1 tablespoon of rub with ½ cup water in a nonreactive mixing bowl and stir until the salt and brown sugar in the rub dissolve.

4 Set up the grill for indirect grilling (see page 23 for gas or page 22 for charcoal) and preheat to medium. If using a gas grill, place all of the wood chips or chunks in the smoker box or in a smoker pouch (see page 24) and run the grill on high until you see smoke, then reduce the heat to medium. If using a charcoal grill, place a large drip pan in the center, preheat the grill to medium, then toss all of the wood chips or chunks on the coals.

5 When ready to cook, place the chicken halves in the center of the hot grate, skin side up, over the drip pan and away from the heat. Cover the grill and grill the chicken until cooked through, 40 to 60 minutes. To test for doneness, use an instant-read meat thermometer: Insert it into the thickest part of a thigh but not so that it touches the bone. The internal temperature should be about 180°F. (See page 368 for more about testing for doneness.) After the first 20 minutes of grilling, using a barbecue mop or basting brush, baste the chicken with the mop sauce every 10 minutes while it cooks. Be sure to baste both sides of the chicken halves.

No mistakes are possible with Foolproof Barbecued Chicken.

6 During the last 3 minutes, brush the chicken with about ½ cup of the barbecue sauce. Move the chicken pieces directly over the fire to sizzle and brown the sauce on both sides.

7 Transfer the grilled chicken halves to a platter or plates and let rest for 3 minutes. Serve the chicken with the remaining barbecue sauce on the side.

YIELD:
Serves 2 to 4

VARIATION: This recipe calls for half chickens, but you could also use chicken quarters or chicken pieces, or even chicken breasts (you'll have to reduce the cooking time accordingly).

The Old Corner Drug Store, birthplace of Dr Pepper.

Dr Pepper Barbecue Sauce

Barbecue sauces flavored with soda are a great American tradition. This one features the granddaddy of American soft drinks—Dr Pepper—which was invented in 1885, a year before Coke. The setting was Waco, Texas, then, also known as Six Shooter Junction. The place was Wade Morrison's Old Corner Drug Store, where a pharmacist named Charles Alderton combined spices, sweeteners, and carbonated water to come up with this uniquely American beverage.

As for the name, it was Wade Morrison's attempt to woo a Virginia girl he was courting (her father was Dr. Charles Pepper). His sweet, tart, aromatic soda possesses just the flavor profile you want in a barbecue sauce.

INGREDIENTS:

1 large juicy lemon
1 clove garlic, peeled and lightly crushed
   with the side of a cleaver
1 thin (¼-inch) slice onion
1 cup Dr Pepper
¾ cup ketchup
3 tablespoons Worcestershire sauce
2 tablespoons A.1. steak sauce
1 tablespoon of your favorite
   hot sauce, or more to taste
1 tablespoon cider vinegar,
   or more to taste
1 teaspoon liquid smoke
½ teaspoon freshly ground black pepper
Coarse salt (kosher or sea)

*Wade Morrison (center)
provided the setting.
Charles Alderton (left)
perfected the blend
for the beverage that
made the Old Corner
Drug Store famous.*

1 Cut the lemon in half cross wise and cut a ¼-inch slice off of one half. Remove any seeds in this slice. Juice the remaining lemon: You should have 2 to 3 tablespoons juice.

2 Place the lemon slice, 2 table spoons of the lemon juice, and the garlic, onion slice, Dr Pepper, ketchup, Worcestershire sauce, steak sauce, hot sauce, vinegar, liquid smoke, and pepper in a heavy nonreactive saucepan and gradually bring to a boil over medium heat.

3 Reduce the heat slightly to main tain a gentle simmer. Let the sauce simmer gently until thick and richly flavored, 10 to 15 minutes. Taste for seasoning, adding more lemon juice, hot sauce, and/or vinegar as necessary and seasoning with salt to taste, if desired. Strain the sauce into a bowl (or clean glass jars) and let cool to room temperature, then refrigerate, covered, until serving. The sauce will keep for several months in the refrigerator. Bring to room temperature before serving.

YIELD:
Makes about 2 cups

BIG BOB

And the Invention of White Barbecue Sauce

BIG BOB GIBSON BAR-B-Q

1715 6th Avenue S.E.
Decatur, Alabama
(256) 350-6969

Barbecue is some of the last truly regional food in the United States, and few other dishes are so strongly associated with a particular place and culture. The barbecued chicken with white sauce of northern Alabama is a case in point. This singular dish was born more than seventy-five years ago at Big Bob Gibson Bar-B-Q in Decatur, Alabama. Today, it is enjoyed within a seventy-five-mile radius of its original birthplace—and just about nowhere else on the planet. As one local wag puts it, "People raised in Decatur just know that barbecue sauce is supposed to be white."

The cooking method is fairly traditional: Half chickens are slowly smoked to fall-off-the-bone tenderness in a hickory-fired pit. What's unique is the sauce; it's not tomato based, not mustard based, not even vinegar based, for gosh sakes, but rather a peppery amalgam of vinegar and mayonnaise that's neither red nor brown nor black, but white.

The Bob in question was a six-foot-four-inch, three-hundred-pound railroad worker from Decatur (easy to see why they called him "Big"). Gibson loved cooking barbecue in his spare time, and in 1925 he set up a makeshift table nailed to a sycamore tree in his backyard. Friends, neighbors, and fellow railroad workers flocked to his stand, and soon Bob was making a better living as a pit master than as a railroad man. Legend has it that Bob concocted his signature white sauce for a customer who hated tomatoes.

A FAMILY AFFAIR

Over the next thirty years, Gibson's expanded and moved dozens of times, but the house specialty remained barbecued chicken with that distinctive white barbecue sauce. In the 1950s, all five of his children became pit masters, and his daughter, Catherine, and her husband, Coy McLemore, took over the original restaurant. The couple added new dishes, such as homemade chocolate, coconut cream, and lemon pies, while sensibly keeping the chicken as star of the show.

BIG BOB GIBSON'S BAR-B-Q
1721 Bee Line 31 So. East — Ph. EL 3-9935

there's the slow smoking over hickory, with a generous basting of vegetable oil—or is the secret ingredient lard? And the cooking time (three and a half hours at 275°F), admittedly long for barbecuing chicken, but one which renders the meat extremely tender. The final element is a bath (for the chicken, not the pit masters) in a creamy tub of white sauce just prior to serving.

Today, Big Bob's is run by the founder's grandson, the patrician-looking Don McLemore and his wife, Carolyn. The business continues to grow matrilineally: Don and Carolyn's daughter, Amy (Big Bob's great-granddaughter) and her husband, Chris Lilly, now run a second Big Bob's on Decatur's South Side.

Often, when a barbecue joint gets to its third or fourth generation, the owners are more versed in the ways of MBAs than pitsmanship, but Don McLemore and son-in-law, Chris Lilly, definitely still walk the walk. Avid competition barbecuers, the pair have won eight state championships and three world championships, including being named the Memphis in May Grand Champions in 2000. And in 1998, these fourth-generation white-barbecue-sauce makers managed to come up with a championship red sauce good enough to be named "The Best Barbecue Sauce on the Planet" at the American Royal barbecue contest.

Big Bob Gibson with enough barbecued chicken to serve an army.

A SECRET'S A SECRET

So what's the secret of barbecued chicken with white sauce? It's no surprise that when it comes to the precise formula, McLemore isn't talking, but he and Chris Lilly did invite me to watch them cook at several barbecue festivals. Part of the technique is the way the chicken is cut (split in half without the backbone or breastbone). The seasoning is simplicity itself: just salt and coarse pepper. Then

Here's the catch: You could follow each step to the letter and your chicken still wouldn't taste like Bob's. Blame the intense regionality of barbecue or the unpredictable mystique of smoke and fire. Whatever the reason, if you want to enjoy barbecued chicken with white sauce the way it's *really* meant to taste, you have to go to Decatur (although the recipe on the next page will give you a good idea).

TIPS

■ My own contribution to the recipe is a blast of prepared horseradish. It isn't traditional, but I like its kick.

■ I've called for two chickens here—as long as you're grilling for almost two hours, you might as well cook two birds. Of course, you could always cut the recipe in half.

Decatur, Ala.

ALABAMA BARBECUED CHICKENS With White Barbecue Sauce

I admit I was skeptical about barbecued chicken with white sauce. I mean, how can you even *call* something barbecue when it lacks a rub and when it contains not a whisper of ketchup, Worcestershire sauce, brown sugar, or molasses? But in northern Alabama barbecue simply isn't worth eating without a tangy white sauce the chief ingredients of which are vinegar, mayonnaise, and black pepper—the way it's served at the popular Big Bob Gibson's in Decatur, Alabama (see page 378). While you can find chicken with white sauce as far away as Birmingham, it's worth making a pilgrimage to its place of birth. You're skeptical, too? One taste of Big Bob's barbecued chicken, smoked to the color of mahogany, then dunked in this creamy, peppery, piquant white sauce, will make you a believer.

METHOD:
Indirect grilling

INGREDIENTS:

2 chickens (each 3½ to 4 pounds)
Coarse salt (kosher or sea) and
    coarsely ground black pepper
2 cups mayonnaise (preferably Hellmann's)
1 cup cider vinegar
½ cup prepared white horseradish
    (optional)
½ teaspoon cayenne pepper,
    or to taste
½ cup lard or butter, melted,
    or vegetable oil or olive oil

YOU'LL ALSO NEED:

2 cups wood chips or chunks
    (preferably hickory), soaked
    for 1 hour in water
    to cover, then drained;
    poultry shears

1 Remove the packet of giblets from the body cavity of each chicken and set aside for making stock or another use. Remove and discard the fat just inside the body and neck cavities. Rinse the chickens, inside and out, under cold running water, then drain and blot dry, inside and out, with paper towels. Place a chicken on its breast. Using poultry shears and starting at the neck end, make a lengthwise cut along one side of the backbone to the tail. Make a second lengthwise cut along the other side of the backbone. Discard the backbone or set aside for another use. Open the chicken like a book, skin side up, and lay it flat. Using the poultry shears, cut the chicken in half through the breastbone. This will give you two chicken halves, which will lie flat on the grill. Repeat with the second chicken. Generously season the chickens all over with salt and pepper.

2 Place the mayonnaise, vinegar, horseradish, if using, 2 teaspoons of salt, 2 teaspoons of black pepper, and the cayenne in a very large nonreactive mixing bowl and whisk to mix. Transfer 1 cup of this white barbecue sauce to an attractive small nonreactive serving bowl and set aside until you are ready to serve the chicken. Leave the remaining sauce in the mixing bowl and set aside.

3 Set up the grill for indirect grilling (see page 23 for gas or page 22 for charcoal) and preheat to medium-low. If using a gas grill, place all of the wood chips or chunks in the smoker box or in a smoker pouch (see page 24) and run the grill on high until you see smoke, then reduce the heat to medium-low. If using a charcoal grill, place a large drip pan in the center, preheat the grill to medium-low, then toss 1 cup of the wood chips or chunks on the coals.

4 When ready to cook, place the chicken halves, skin side up, in the center of the hot grate, over the drip pan and away from the heat, and cover the grill. Let the chickens cook for 1 hour, then baste the skin side of the chickens with lard. Turn the halves over so they're bone side up and baste this side. If using a charcoal grill, add 12 fresh coals to each side and toss the remaining 1 cup of wood chips or chunks ($\frac{1}{2}$ cup per side) on the coals. Continue grilling the chicken, bone side up, until the skin is mahogany brown and the meat is very tender, 30 to 45 minutes. The total cooking time will be $1\frac{1}{2}$ to $1\frac{3}{4}$ hours. To test for

doneness, use an instant-read meat thermometer: Insert it into the thickest part of a thigh but not so that it touches the bone. The internal temperature should be about 180°F. (See page 368 for more about testing for doneness.)

5 Transfer the grilled chicken halves to the large mixing bowl of white barbecue sauce, turning the chicken to coat it completely. Let sit for 2 minutes, then turn the chicken over and let sit for 2 minutes longer. Serve the chicken with the small bowl of barbecue sauce on the side.

YIELD:

Serves 4 to 8

PULLED CHICKEN SANDWICH

Sometimes when I grill Alabama Barbecued Chickens, I serve the meat shredded and on a bun with coleslaw—think of it as a pulled pork sandwich with wings. To make the coleslaw, prepare a half recipe of the white barbecue sauce described in Step 2 at left, and mix half of this with three cups of finely chopped or shredded green cabbage. (Using a food processor is the quickest way to prepare the cabbage. The metal blade will chop it; the slicing disc will shred it.)

Once you've grilled the chickens following the recipe at left, let them rest for about three minutes. Pull the meat and skin off the bones, then tear the meat and skin into shreds with your fingers or finely chop it with a cleaver. If you're shredding by hand, you'll need to wear a pair of insulated rubber gloves. Put the chicken in an aluminum foil pan and mix in the remaining white barbecue sauce. To serve, mound the shredded chicken and coleslaw on hamburger buns. This will make about eight sandwiches.

CORNELL CHICKEN

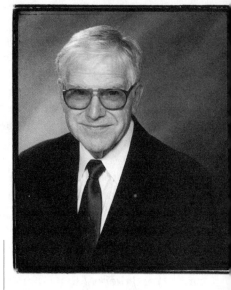

Bob Baker came up with Cornell chicken as a way to help the poultry industry sell more birds.

Cornell chicken is possibly the most famous barbecue you've never heard of—unless you live in upstate New York, near Ithaca or Syracuse, in which case Cornell chicken is quite likely to be your definition of barbecue.

The chicken has a singular history. Most barbecue has been perfected over decades, even centuries, by generations of anonymous pit masters. Cornell chicken was invented for a specific occasion by one man who had a single goal in mind—a goal that had nothing to do with barbecue.

The occasion was a dinner held in 1946 for Pennsylvania governor Edward Martin. The man was Dr. Bob Baker, a young professor of poultry sciences at the University of Pennsylvania. He was asked to come up with something unusual to serve at the function. Baker's goal was to get people to eat more chicken. (In the 1930s and 1940s, the birds were raised commercially in the United States primarily for their eggs, not for eating. Times have changed; today Americans devour about 80 pounds of chicken, per capita, each year.) Baker had an inspiration: You grill steak—why not grill chicken? The recipe he developed for a baste was the key.

BUT WHY CORNELL CHICKEN?

When Baker joined the Cornell University poultry science faculty in 1949, he brought his chicken recipe with him. Two years later his recipe appeared in a university publication and became known as Cornell chicken. Meanwhile, Baker had established a booth at the New York State Fair, in Syracuse, called Bakers' Chicken Coop. Hungry fair-goers flocked, as it were, to buy his chicken. The coop has grown into a regular fixture at the fair and now serves as many as 5,000 chickens a day (mere, er, chicken feed compared to a barbecue Baker once prepared for the whopping 10,000 guests of the Babcock poultry company). As of this writing, Bakers' Chicken Coop just celebrated its fifty-third anniversary; Baker's children and grandchildren now do most of the heavy lifting.

Baker's recipe is unusual in the annals of American barbecue. First of all, it contains not a speck of tomato or any sweet red barbecue sauce. And the bird grills directly over the fire; it's

Cornell chicken is possibly the most famous barbecue you've never heard of.

not smoked in a pit. The ingredients Baker uses for basting—cider vinegar, vegetable oil, poultry seasoning, an egg, a hefty dose of salt, and some black pepper—make a combination that would raise the eyebrows of most pit masters. "The vinegar, salt, and poultry seasoning act to boost flavor," explains Baker. "The oil keeps the bird from burning." As for the egg, it wasn't in the original recipe, but Baker quickly found it helped keep the basting mixture from separating.

In the course of his more than forty years in the poultry sciences, Baker developed at least fifty revolutionary new products, including chicken hot dogs, chicken nuggets, and turkey ham. He eventually became chair of the Department of Poultry and Avian Sciences at Cornell. But upstate New York remembers Baker for the barbecued chicken that, had he been less modest, would rightfully bear his name.

WHERE TO SAMPLE CORNELL CHICKEN

Although Baker is retired, his family still runs a nursery and garden shop on Route 34 between Auburn and Ithaca called Bakers' Acres. Four times a year, the Bakers serve their barbecued chicken at Bakers' Acres Tea Room, which can also be reserved for private groups. For information, call (607) 533-3650. Or, for twelve days at the end of the summer, you can stop by Bakers' Chicken Coop at the New York State Fair in Syracuse. If you want to make the classic version for yourself, you'll find the recipe on the next page.

Bill, Hillary, and Chelsea Clinton pay a visit to Bakers' Chicken Coop.

TIPS

Baker recommends grilling the chicken directly over a charcoal fire that has burned down to glowing embers. You can certainly grill it over gas, provided you work over a moderate flame. Grilling the chicken using the direct method gives you the best searing, but it requires near constant attention. You can also grill the bird indirectly, which doesn't require much of anything. You'll find instructions for this on the opposite page.

Ithaca, N.Y.

THE ORIGINAL CORNELL BARBECUED CHICKEN

This tangy, golden grilled chicken is the creation of Bob Baker, a retired professor of poultry science at Cornell University and one of the early champions of barbecued chicken (on page 382 you can read about the birth of Cornell chicken). The recipe is improbable for at least three reasons: It contains an egg, which you would expect to curdle or scramble during the grilling process. It contains a considerable amount of salt—a whopping three tablespoons in the basting sauce. And it doesn't have a paprika-based rub or tomato-based barbecue sauce, ingredients most Americans associate with barbecued chicken. It was invented in 1946 and to this day country fairs and summer cookouts in upstate New York (and throughout much of the mid-Atlantic) just wouldn't be complete without it. If you like your grilled chicken sizzling and golden brown (not burnt), if you like it tasting like chicken, not like barbecue sauce, this recipe is for you.

METHOD:
Direct grilling

INGREDIENTS:
4 chickens (3½ to 4 pounds each)
1 large egg
1 cup vegetable oil
2 cups cider vinegar
3 tablespoons coarse salt
**   (kosher or sea)**
1 tablespoon poultry seasoning
½ teaspoon freshly ground
**   black pepper**

YOU'LL ALSO NEED:
Poultry shears

1 Remove the packet of giblets from the body cavity of each chicken and set aside for making stock or another use. Remove and discard the fat just inside the body and neck cavities. Rinse the chickens, inside and out, under cold running water, then drain and blot dry, inside and out, with paper towels. Place a chicken on its breast. Using poultry shears and starting at the neck end, make a lengthwise cut along one side of the backbone to the tail. Make a second lengthwise cut along the other side of the backbone. Discard the backbone or set aside for another use. Open the chicken like a book, skin side up, and lay it flat. Using the poultry shears, cut the chicken in half through the breastbone. Repeat with the remaining chickens.

2 Place the egg in a food processor and pulse the motor to beat. With the motor running, add the oil in a thin steam through the feed tube, followed by the vinegar, then add the salt, poultry seasoning, and pepper. Or place the egg in a nonreactive mixing bowl and whisk in the oil in a steady stream. The mixture will thicken. Whisk in the vinegar, salt, poultry seasoning, and pepper. Set the basting mixture aside.

3 Set up the grill for direct grilling using a two-zone fire (see page 22 for charcoal or gas) and preheat one zone to medium and the other to medium-low.

4 When ready to cook, brush and oil the grill grate. Place the chicken halves, skin side down, over the medium zone of the grill. Grill the chicken halves until the skin side is cooked on the surface, about 5 minutes, then turn and grill until the other side is cooked on the surface, about 5 minutes longer.

5 Whisk the basting sauce to recombine, then baste the chicken halves. Continue basting them generously every 3 to 5 minutes and whisking the basting sauce as necessary. Grill the chicken halves until they turn a rich golden brown and the meat is cooked through, 15 to 20 minutes per side. If the chicken starts to burn, move it to the medium-low zone. To test for doneness, use an instant-read meat thermometer: Insert it into the thickest part of a thigh but not so that it touches the bone. The internal temperature should be about 180°F. (See page 368 for more about testing for doneness.) Transfer the grilled chicken to a platter or plates, let rest for 3 minutes, then serve.

YIELD:
Serves 4 to 8

Ithaca, N.Y.

INDIRECT CORNELL CHICKEN

It won't give you quite the same flame-charred flavor as cooking the chicken halves directly over the fire, but using the indirect method to grill Cornell chicken has several advantages. For one thing, you don't need to turn the chickens; for another, there's less risk of them burning.

INGREDIENTS:

4 chickens (each 3½ to 4 pounds)
1 large egg
1 cup extra-virgin olive oil
1 cup fresh lemon juice (from 4 lemons)
1 cup tarragon vinegar or red wine vinegar
3 tablespoons coarse salt (kosher or sea)
3 tablespoons chopped fresh tarragon or
**   rosemary**
3 cloves garlic, minced
½ teaspoon freshly ground black pepper

1 Remove the packet of giblets from the body cavity of each chicken and set aside for making stock or another use. Remove and discard the fat just inside the body and neck cavities. Rinse the chickens, inside and out, under cold running water, then drain and blot dry, inside and out, with paper towels. Place a chicken on its breast. Using poultry shears and starting at the neck end, make a lengthwise cut along one side of the backbone to the tail. Make a second lengthwise cut along the other side of the backbone. Discard the backbone. Fold the chicken open like a book, skin side up, and lay it flat. Using the poultry shears, cut the chicken in half through the breast bone. Repeat with the remaining chickens.

2 Place the egg in a food processor and pulse the motor to mix. With the motor running, add the oil in a thin stream through the feed tube, followed by the lemon juice and vinegar, then

THE CORNELL SCHOOL OF COOKING

Cornell chicken is a recipe, of course, but it's also a method. Its unique egg-based marinade and basting technique can be used with other ingredients to create versions that highlight a wide range of flavors. Here are two variations on the basting sauce. Prepare them following the directions in Step 2 of The Original Cornell Barbecued Chicken recipe on page 384, then grill the chicken as described in the steps that follow. Note: Mustard oil is available at Indian markets.

Cornell Chicken with Mustard Baste

1 large egg
½ cup extra-virgin olive oil
½ cup mustard oil,
    or more olive oil
¼ cup Dijon mustard
2 cups distilled white vinegar
3 tablespoons coarse salt
    (kosher or sea)
1 tablespoon mustard seeds
2 cloves garlic, minced
½ teaspoon freshly ground
    black pepper

Cornell Chicken with Curry Orange Baste

1 large egg
1 cup vegetable oil
1 cup fresh lime juice or
    distilled white vinegar,
    or a mixture of the two
1 cup fresh orange juice
3 tablespoons coarse salt
    (kosher or sea)
1 tablespoon curry powder
2 cloves garlic, minced
½ teaspoon freshly ground
    black pepper

add the salt, tarragon, garlic, and pepper. Or place the egg in a nonreactive mixing bowl and whisk in the oil in a steady stream. The mixture will thicken. Whisk in the lemon juice, vinegar, salt, tarragon, garlic, and pepper.

3 Place the chicken halves in a nonreactive baking dish and add half of the basting sauce, turning the chickens to coat them on all sides. Let the chickens marinate in the refrigerator, covered, for 4 to 12 hours, turning them several times. Refrigerate the remaining basting sauce separately.

4 Set up the grill for indirect grilling (see page 22 for charcoal or page 23 for gas) and preheat to medium-high. If using a charcoal grill, place a large drip pan in the center.

5 When ready to cook, brush and oil the grill grate. Place the chicken halves in the center of the hot grate, bone side down, over the drip pan and away from the heat and cover the grill. Grill the chickens for 15 minutes, then baste the birds with the remaining basting liquid every 5 minutes until the chicken is cooked through. The total cooking time will be 40 to 60 minutes. To test for doneness, use an instant-read meat thermometer: Insert it into the thickest part of a thigh but not so that it touches the bone. The internal temperature should be about 180°F. If you like, move the chicken halves directly over the heat for the last 2½ to 3 minutes of grilling on each side for extra browning.

YIELD:
Serves 4 to 8

A world without
this mahogany-colored bird
would be a sad place.

Palm trees and tiki torches set the stage for Hawaiian barbecue.

Hawaii

HULI HULI CHICKEN
From Paradise

Huli huli chicken may be Hawaii's most significant contribution to American barbecue. A world without this mahogany-colored bird—lacquered with a sweet-salty glaze of soy sauce, ketchup, and honey or brown sugar—would be a sad place to contemplate. *Huli huli* chicken takes its name from the Hawaiian word for *turn,* or *turn often,* and herein lies the secret. The chicken is turned frequently as you baste and grill it, which crisps the skin, sizzles the sauce, and keeps the bird from burning. You'll find three variations on the *huli huli* chicken theme here. This first first recipe was inspired by a Hawaiian pit master who cooks chickens over high heat in a Big Green Egg (a ceramic *kamado*-style cooker). I prefer the control that a more moderate heat provides and suggest you grill the birds over a medium fire. So light your tiki torches and let the party begin!

TIPS

Hawaiian salt has a pinkish tinge and an aromatic flavor, due to the presence of traces of clay. Look for it at gourmet shops or use coarse sea or kosher salt.

METHOD:
Direct grilling

FOR THE CHICKEN:
**2 chickens (each 3½ to 4 pounds),
     quartered
1 to 2 tablespoons Asian (dark)
     sesame oil
Coarse salt (preferably Hawaiian pink)
     and freshly ground black pepper**

FOR THE HULI HULI SAUCE:
**⅓ cup firmly packed dark brown sugar
⅓ cup soy sauce
⅓ cup ketchup
⅓ cup sherry
1 tablespoon rice vinegar or
     distilled white vinegar
½ teaspoon freshly ground black pepper
2 slices (each ¼ inch thick) peeled
     fresh ginger, gently crushed
     with the side of a cleaver
2 cloves garlic, peeled and
     gently crushed with the side
     of a cleaver
1 scallion, trimmed, white part
     gently crushed with the side
     of a cleaver, green part finely
     chopped**

1 Rinse the chicken quarters under cold running water, then blot dry with paper towels. Brush each piece with sesame oil and season generously with salt and pepper.

2 MAKE THE *HULI HULI* SAUCE: Place the brown sugar, soy sauce, ketchup, sherry, vinegar, pepper, ginger, garlic, and scallion white in a heavy nonreactive saucepan and whisk to mix. Add 2 tablespoons of water. Bring

to a simmer over medium heat, then let simmer gently until thick and syrupy, about 5 minutes, whisking to prevent scorching. If the sauce is too thick, add a little more water (the sauce should be pourable). Strain the sauce into a clean nonreactive saucepan and set aside.

3 Set up the grill for direct grilling (see page 21 for charcoal or gas) and preheat to medium.

4 When ready to grill, brush and oil the grill grate. Place the chicken pieces on the hot grate and grill until crisp, brown, and cooked through, 8 to 12 minutes per side, turning several times. To test for doneness, use an instant-read meat thermometer: Insert it into the thickest part of a thigh but not so that it touches the bone. The internal temperature should be about 180°F. (See page 368 for more about testing for doneness.) During the last 2 minutes on each side, brush the chicken with some of the *huli huli* sauce.

5 Transfer the grilled chickens to a platter or plates and drizzle the remaining *huli huli* sauce over them. Let the chickens rest for 5 minutes, then sprinkle the scallion greens over them and serve at once.

YIELD:
Serves 4 to 8

VARIATION: For worry-free and burn-proof chicken pieces, grill them using the indirect method for 30 to 40 minutes.

Hawaii

SPIT-ROASTED HONEY LIME HULI HULI CHICKEN

The original *huli huli* chicken was meant to be cooked on a spit (that's what *huli huli* means—in the words of The Byrds, to "turn, turn, turn"). The gentle rotation of the spit ensures even roasting and bastes the bird internally. Hawaiian grill jockey Elder Ward likes to place thin slices of garlic and fresh thyme leaves under the chicken skin to further perfume the bird.

METHOD:
Rotisserie grilling

FOR THE CHICKEN:
1 chicken (3½ to 4 pounds)
1 clove garlic, thinly sliced crosswise
1 bunch fresh thyme (you won't need all of it, but this is the easiest way to buy it)
Coarse salt (kosher or sea) and freshly ground black pepper
1 tablespoon Asian (dark) sesame oil

Huli Huli *chicken is a Hawaiian church supper favorite.*

FOR THE GLAZE:
½ cup honey
½ cup dark or regular soy sauce
½ cup fresh lime juice
2 tablespoons light brown sugar
2 tablespoons Thai chile sauce
1 clove garlic, peeled and gently crushed with the side of a cleaver
½ teaspoon freshly ground black pepper

1 Remove the packet of giblets from the body cavity of the chicken and set aside for making stock or another use. Remove and discard the fat just inside the body and neck cavities. Rinse the chicken, inside and out, under cold running water, then drain and blot dry, inside and out, with paper towels. Season the inside of the chicken with salt and pepper.

2 Loosen the chicken skin from the body: Starting at the top of the neck cavity, tunnel your index finger

TIPS

■ When grilling on a rotisserie, be sure to place an aluminum foil drip pan under the turning chicken. Not only will it facilitate cleanup, but you can use the chicken fat that drips into it for basting.

■ If you're in a hurry, don't bother to loosen the chicken skin; simply place the flavorings in the chicken cavities.

under the skin. Taking care not to tear it, gently loosen the skin from the meat, inserting additional fingers one at a time until you can use your whole hand to loosen the skin from the breast meat, then the thighs. Place about half of the garlic slices and 6 small sprigs of thyme under the skin over the thighs and breasts. Place the remaining garlic in the body and neck cavities of the chicken, then place 4 small sprigs of thyme in the body cavity and 2 sprigs in the neck cavity. Truss the bird (see page 373 for instructions); this is optional, but it will give the bird a more dignified appearance. Generously season the outside with salt and pepper and brush with sesame oil.

3 MAKE THE GLAZE: Place the honey, soy sauce, lime juice, brown sugar, chile sauce, garlic, and pepper in a heavy nonreactive saucepan over medium-high heat and bring to a simmer. Let the glaze simmer briskly until thick and syrupy, about 5 minutes.

If the smoke gets to you, spit roast the chicken instead.

4 Set up the grill for rotisserie grilling following the manufacturer's instructions and preheat to medium-high.

5 Skewer the chicken on the turn spit from tail to neck (remember to place a prong on the spit first). Slide the second prong onto the spit and make sure the chicken is held snugly in place. Tighten the screw on this prong, gripping it between the tines of a fork for leverage.

6 When ready to cook, attach the spit to the rotisserie mechanism by inserting the pointed end of the spit into the rotisserie motor socket. If your rotisserie spit has a counterweight, position it so that it counterbalances the chicken. Turn on the motor and grill the chicken until golden brown on the outside and cooked through, $1\frac{1}{4}$ to $1\frac{1}{2}$ hours. To test for doneness, use an instant-read meat thermometer: Insert it into the thickest part of a thigh but not so that it touches the bone. The internal temperature should be about 180°F. (See page 368 for more about testing for doneness.) During the last 10 minutes of cooking, baste the bird 3 times with some of the glaze. If using a charcoal grill, after an hour you'll need to add 12 fresh coals to each side.

7 Transfer the grilled chicken to a platter and untruss it, if necessary. Let the chicken rest for 5 minutes, then carve it and serve with the remaining glaze on the side as a sauce.

YIELD:
Serves 2 to 4

Hawaii

PINEAPPLE HULI HULI CHICKEN

Although originally from the Caribbean, the pineapple has been associated with Hawaii for centuries. The Aloha State remains the nation's largest pineapple producer (indeed, at one point, the island of Lanai was one enormous pineapple plantation). Pineapple juice serves as both a marinade and glaze in this version of *huli huli* chicken, which was inspired by Hawaiian grilling enthusiast Mischele Hicks.

METHOD:
Direct grilling

ADVANCE PREPARATION:
4 to 12 hours for marinating the chicken

INGREDIENTS:

1 cup pineapple juice
½ cup chicken stock (preferably homemade)
¼ cup dry white wine or sherry
¼ cup soy sauce
¼ cup ketchup
2 tablespoons Asian (dark) sesame oil
1 tablespoon Worcestershire sauce
2 teaspoons minced or grated peeled fresh ginger
Freshly ground black pepper
1 chicken (3½ to 4 pounds)

Coarse salt (kosher or sea)
Cooked sticky rice (optional; see Note)
Macaroni salad (optional)

YOU'LL ALSO NEED:
Poultry shears

1 Place the pineapple juice, chicken stock, wine, soy sauce, ketchup, sesame oil, Worcestershire sauce, ginger, and ½ teaspoon pepper in a nonreactive mixing bowl and whisk to mix.

2 Remove the packet of giblets from the body cavity of the chicken and set aside for making stock or another use. Remove and discard the fat just inside the body and neck cavities. Rinse the chicken, inside and out, under cold running water, then drain and blot dry, inside and out, with paper towels.

3 Spatchcock the chicken: Place the bird on its breast. Using poultry shears and starting at the neck end, cut out the backbone by making one lengthwise cut on either side of the bone. Remove and discard the backbone or set it aside for making stock or another use. Open the chicken like a book, skin side down. Use a paring knife to cut along each side of the breastbone. Run your thumbs firmly along both sides of the breastbone and white cartilage, then pull these out. Cut off the wing tips and trim off any loose skin. If you are feeling ambitious, turn the bird over (skin side up) and lay it out flat. Make a 1-inch slit in the rear portion of each side of the chicken. Reach under the bird and pull the end of each drumstick through the nearest slit to secure it.

TIPS

This recipe calls for spatchcocking the chicken, a technique that allows you to grill a whole chicken using the direct method. Removing the backbone and breastbone lets you open up the chicken like a book to lay it flat on the grill. You could also cut the chicken into halves or quarters to grill.

4 Season the chicken on all sides with salt and pepper. Place the bird in a nonreactive baking dish just large enough to hold it and pour the marinade/glaze over it. Let the chicken marinate in the refrigerator, covered, for 4 hours or as long as overnight, turning the bird several times so that it marinates evenly.

5 Drain the marinade into a heavy nonreactive saucepan, place over high heat, and bring to a boil. Reduce the heat to medium-high and let the marinade boil until thick, syrupy, and reduced by almost half, 6 to 10 minutes, stirring with a wooden spoon to prevent scorching.

6 Set up the grill for direct grilling (see page 21 for charcoal or gas) and preheat to medium.

7 When ready to cook, brush and oil the grill grate. Place the chicken on the grill and grill until cooked through, 15 to 20 minutes per side, turning several times with a large spatula. To test for doneness, use an instant-read meat thermometer: Insert it into the thickest part of a thigh but not so that it touches the bone. The internal temperature should be about 180°F. (See page 368 for more about testing for doneness.) During the last 2 minutes of cooking on each side, baste the chicken with some of the glaze.

8 Transfer the cooked chicken to a platter. Place the saucepan with any remaining glaze over high heat and bring to a boil. Let boil for 2 minutes, then drizzle the glaze over the chicken.

For an authentic Hawaiian picnic lunch, serve with sticky rice and macaroni salad.

YIELD:
Serves 2 to 4

NOTE: Sticky rice is a Japanese-style short-grain rice that, as the name suggests, sticks together when cooked—it's the sort of rice you get at a Japanese restaurant.

Guam

GUAMANIAN BARBECUED CHICKEN

"**G**uamanians love to party, and whenever we get together a barbecue isn't far behind," observes Guam pit master Rueban Olivas. He should know. Born in California's great barbecue capital, Santa Maria (see page 186), the policeman turned fire chief moved to Santa Rita, Guam, in 1986 and he's never looked back. His first two weeks on the island were feted with nearly nonstop barbecue and beer. According to Olivas, Guamanian barbecue is characterized by a salty tart marinade made with roughly equal parts of soy sauce and vinegar. Onion, garlic, and ginger can be added to suit personal taste. The stuff makes fantastic chicken, and it's pretty terrific on ribs, too. By the way, San Diego has a large Guamanian community that gathers at the local Chamorro clubs. Pay one of them a visit and you might find yourself invited to a barbecue you won't soon forget.

METHOD:
Direct grilling

ADVANCE PREPARATION:
4 to 8 hours for marinating
the chicken

INGREDIENTS:
2 chickens (each 3½ to 4 pounds)
1 medium-size onion, finely chopped
4 cloves garlic, minced
1 piece (1 inch) fresh ginger,
peeled and finely chopped
1 cup soy sauce (preferably Kikkoman)
1 cup distilled white vinegar or
cider vinegar
Cooked rice
Your choice of finadene hot sauce
(page 661)

YOU'LL ALSO NEED:
1½ cups wood chips or chunks
(optional; preferably red oak or
mesquite), unsoaked

1 Remove the packet of giblets from the body cavity of the chickens and set aside for making stock or another use. Remove and discard the fat just inside the body and neck cavities. Rinse the chickens, inside and out, under cold running water, then drain and blot dry, inside and out, with paper towels. Cut each chicken into 8 pieces. Place the chicken pieces in a large nonreactive baking dish.

2 Combine the onion, garlic, ginger, soy sauce, and vinegar in a bowl and stir to mix. Pour this mixture over the chicken, turning the pieces to coat well. Let the chicken marinate in the refrigerator, covered, for 4 to 8 hours, turning the pieces a couple of times so that they marinate evenly.

3 Set up the grill for direct grilling using a two-zone fire (see page 22 for gas or charcoal) and preheat one zone to medium and the other to low. If using a gas grill, place all of the wood chips or chunks, if desired, in the smoker box or in a smoker pouch (see page 24) and run the grill on high until you see smoke, then reduce the heat to medium. If using a charcoal grill, preheat it to medium, then toss all of the wood chips or chunks, if desired, on the coals.

4 When ready to cook, drain the marinade from the chicken and discard the marinade. Brush and oil the grill grate. Place the marinated chicken pieces over the medium zone of the grill, skin side down. Grill until crisp and golden brown on the outside and cooked through, 15 to 20 minutes in all, turning the chicken pieces several times with tongs. To test for doneness, poke a piece of chicken with your finger; it should feel firm to the touch (see page 368 for more about testing for doneness). Should the chicken start to burn or should the fat cause a flare-up,

■ Traditionally Guamanians use distilled white vinegar when barbecuing chicken and cider vinegar with meat.

■ Guamanians usually grill over wood fire; you'll find instructions for doing this on page 20.

Powderpuff Barbeque brought gender equality to Kansas City barbecue.

move the chicken over the low zone of the grill.

5 Transfer the grilled chicken pieces to a platter or plates and serve with cooked rice and one of the *finadene* sauces.

YIELD:
Serves 4 to 6

VARIATION: I've called for chicken pieces here, but you could certainly use chicken halves or even a spatchcocked bird.

Kansas City, Mo.

POWDERPUFF BARBECUED CHICKEN BREASTS

In the 1990s, the all female Powderpuff Barbeque team burst on the Kansas City competition circuit, making tongues wag and mouths water and winning several state championships in the process. One taste of these smoky chicken breasts—seasoned with a celery garlic rub and basted with butter—and you'll see why.

METHOD:
Direct grilling

ADVANCE PREPARATION:
30 minutes to 1 hour for curing the chicken

FOR THE CELERY GARLIC RUB:
2 tablespoons celery salt
2 tablespoons sweet paprika
2 tablespoons garlic powder
1 tablespoon freshly ground black pepper

FOR THE CHICKEN:
6 bone-in half chicken breasts with skin (each half 7 to 8 ounces)
8 tablespoons (1 stick) unsalted butter, melted
Your favorite barbecue sauce, for serving

YOU'LL ALSO NEED:

2 cups wood chips or chunks
(preferably apple) soaked for
1 hour in water to cover,
then drained

1 MAKE THE CELERY GARLIC RUB: Place the celery salt, paprika, garlic powder, and pepper in a small bowl and stir to mix. (Actually, your fingers work better for mixing a rub than a spoon or whisk does.)

2 Trim any sinews or excess fat off the chicken breasts and discard. Rinse the breasts under cold running water, then drain and blot dry with paper towels. Place them in a baking dish. Sprinkle the rub all over the chicken breasts on both sides, patting it onto the meat with your fingertips. Let the breasts cure in the refrigerator, covered, for 30 minutes to 1 hour.

3 Set up the grill for direct grilling using a two-zone fire (see page 22 for gas or charcoal) and preheat one zone to medium and the other to low. If using a gas grill, place all of the wood chips or chunks in the smoker box or in a smoker pouch (see page 24) and run the grill on high until you see smoke, then reduce the heat to medium. If using a charcoal grill, preheat it to medium, then toss all of the wood chips or chunks on the coals.

4 When ready to cook, brush and oil the grill grate. Place the chicken breasts, skin side down, over the medium zone of the grill. Grill the breasts until golden brown and cooked

TRIMMING BONELESS BREASTS

Chicken breasts come in a variety of forms: whole with skin and breastbone, split with skin and bones, boneless but with skin, and so on. The most common and popular form is the skinless, boneless breast. This may or may not come with the tender, a long, skinny, cylindrical strip of meat on the inside of the breast. I like to remove the tender from the breast before grilling (start at the loose end and simply pull it off with your fingers). Then, using a sharp paring knife, trim any visible fat or sinew off the breast and you're ready for grilling.

The chicken tender has a strip of tough, silvery sinew running its length. This should be removed before grilling. Lay the tender on a cutting board, sinew side down. Hold the tip of the sinew against the cutting board with one hand. Holding a knife parallel to the cutting board, slide the blade between the sinew and the meat so that it pinches the sinew against the board. Run the knife along the sinew, cutting it away from the meat. Your chicken tender is now ready for skewering or grilling.

through, 6 to 8 minutes per side. To test for doneness, poke a breast in the thickest part with your finger; it should feel firm to the touch (see page 368 for more about testing for doneness). Lightly baste the chicken breasts with the melted butter as they cook, but don't start until each breast has cooked for 3 minutes on each side. Move the chicken over the low zone of the grill if the dripping fat causes flare-ups.

5 Transfer the grilled chicken breasts to a platter or plates and drizzle any remaining melted butter over them. Serve with the barbecue sauce on the side.

YIELD:
Serves 6

TIPS

I like to use bone-in chicken breasts with the skin still on for this recipe; the skin keeps the meat moist (not to mention the fact that grilled chicken skin is one of the tastiest substances in existence). Grilling the chicken directly over a medium heat sizzles the skin without burning it.

HOW TO GRILL CHICKEN BREASTS WITHOUT DRYING THEM OUT

It's a problem that bedevils grill jockeys from Biloxi to Berkeley: How do you grill chicken breasts and keep them succulent and tender? Grilling, of course, is a dry, high-heat cooking method. Ideal for intensifying flavor, it has a tendency to dry out lean cuts of meat—especially chicken breasts. For this reason, most grillers worldwide prefer to cook chicken thighs or drumsticks. But here in United States, the cut we almost unanimously prefer is the breast. Over the years, I've adopted four strategies for keeping chicken breasts moist and tender during grilling:

• Seal in moistness with rubs and glazes.

• Add succulence by using brines.

• Minimize the cooking time by pounding chicken breasts into wafer-thin sheets called paillards.

• Use the most theatrical grilling technique of all: Grill the chicken breast under a brick or skillet.

RUBBED, GLAZED, OR BRINED

Rubs and glazes, of course, are part of the great American grilling tradition. A rub is nothing more than a mix of herbs and spices, and it can be dry (made with dried or powdered seasonings) or wet (containing oil, vinegar, beer, or another liquid in addition to herbs and spices). Sprinkled on just before grilling, rubs season chicken, much like a seasoned salt. But for an even richer, more complex flavor, you can apply a rub several hours before you plan to grill; this actually cures the meat. Keep the curing time brief—a couple of hours will do it. See the Powderpuff Barbecued Chicken Breasts on page 394 for an example of cooking breasts with rubs.

As for glazes, they're syrupy mixtures of butter or oil; sweeteners, such as brown sugar or honey; and often a spirit, such as rum or bourbon. You apply a glaze to chicken while it grills, and it serves a triple purpose: It seals in succulence, adds an additional layer of flavor, and gives grilled breasts a handsome sheen. For an example of this strategy, check out the Spiced Pineapple-Glazed Chicken on the facing page.

Brines help keep chicken breasts moist through the process of osmosis. A brine is nothing more than a solution of salt and water that can contain seasonings. It works in two steps: First the salt draws the blood and water out of chicken breasts. Then, to reestablish the equilibrium of minerals and liquids, the brine flows into the meat. The basic formula for a brine is a tablespoon of salt and an optional tablespoon of sugar or other sweetener for every cup of water. You can add any other flavorings you like, from herbs to garlic to spirits or even coffee. The typical brining time for chicken breasts is 2 to 4 hours. Overbrining will give the chicken a rubbery texture and make it too salty. The Bourbon-Brined Chicken on page 398 shows how well this method works.

FLATTENED TWO WAYS

If brining provides a "chemical" solution to the drying-out problem, pounding chicken breasts into thin paillards works by the simple law of physics. The process is straightforward: You pound chicken breasts into broad, thin sheets about a quarter of an inch thick. This minimizes the cooking time to about a minute per side, so the breasts don't have time to dry out. To see this technique in action, check out the Tarragon Chicken Paillards on page 403.

Cooking chicken breasts under a brick is a technique I learned in Italy. The basic procedure is to wrap a brick in aluminum foil (shiny side out for aesthetics) and place it atop chicken breasts while they grill. The weight compacts the meat, so you have a crisp crust; it presses the breast against the bars of the grill grate so you get killer grill marks; and it keeps the breasts covered, so they won't dry out. Take a look at the Green Chile Chicken Under Bricks on page 405 for a step-by-step explanation.

Maui, Hawaii

SPICED PINEAPPLE-GLAZED CHICKEN

Maui meets Montego Bay in these quick, easy grilled chicken breasts. The rub is inspired by Jamaica's fiery jerk, while the ginger and sesame oil and the pineapple-rum glaze are pure Hawaiian. Using a rub and a glaze is one of four strategies for keeping chicken breasts from drying out when grilled (for the others, see the opposite page). The Grilled Pineapple Ginger Salsa on page 62 would make a terrific accompaniment to these.

METHOD:
Direct grilling

ADVANCE PREPARATION:
1 hour for curing the chicken

FOR THE RUB:
1 tablespoon brown sugar
1½ teaspoons coarse salt (kosher or sea)
1 teaspoon ground coriander
½ teaspoon freshly ground black pepper
½ teaspoon dried thyme
½ teaspoon ground allspice
½ teaspoon ground cinnamon
¼ to ½ teaspoon cayenne pepper

FOR THE CHICKEN:
2 whole skinless, boneless chicken breasts (each 12 to 16 ounces), or 4 half breasts (each half 6 to 8 ounces)
1 to 1½ tablespoons Asian (dark) sesame oil
2 cloves garlic, minced
1 scallion, trimmed, white part minced, green part finely chopped
1 tablespoon minced peeled fresh ginger

FOR THE PINEAPPLE-RUM GLAZE:
4 tablespoons (½ stick) salted butter
¼ cup firmly packed brown sugar
¼ cup dark rum
¼ cup pineapple juice

1 MAKE THE RUB: Place the brown sugar, salt, coriander, black pepper, thyme, allspice, cinnamon, and cayenne in a small bowl and stir to mix. (Actually, your fingers work better for mixing a rub than a spoon or whisk does.)

2 If using whole chicken breasts, cut each breast in half. Trim any sinews or excess fat off the chicken breasts and discard. Rinse the breasts under cold running water, then drain and blot dry with paper towels. Place the breasts in a baking dish and drizzle just enough sesame oil over them to moisten them without making them oily, rubbing the oil over both sides of the breasts. Sprinkle the rub over the chicken on both sides, followed by the garlic, scallion white, and ginger, patting the seasonings onto the meat with your fingertips. Let the chicken

TIPS

To avoid the risk of bacterial contamination, always brush glazes on chicken breasts after they have been turned over, so the basting brush comes in contact only with meat that is cooked.

cure in the refrigerator, covered, for 1 hour.

3 MAKE THE PINEAPPLE-RUM GLAZE: Combine the butter, brown sugar, rum, and pineapple juice in a heavy nonreactive saucepan over high heat. Let the glaze come to a boil and boil until syrupy, 5 to 8 minutes. Set the glaze aside.

4 Set up the grill for direct grilling (see page 21 for charcoal or gas) and preheat to high.

5 When ready to cook, brush and oil the grill grate. Arrange the chicken breasts on the hot grate, placing them on a diagonal to the bars. Grill the breasts for 2 minutes, then rotate them a quarter turn to create an attractive crosshatch of grill marks. Continue grilling the breasts on that side for about 2 minutes longer. When the bottoms of the breasts are brown and sizzling, turn them over and generously brush the tops with some of the glaze. Grill until cooked through, 4 to 6 minutes longer, again rotating the breasts after 2 minutes to create a crosshatch of grill marks. Turn the chicken breasts over again, brush with glaze, and grill for 1 minute longer. The total cooking time will be 9 to 11 minutes, depending on the thickness of the chicken breasts. To test for doneness, poke a breast in the thickest part with your finger; it should feel firm to the touch (see page 368 for more about testing for doneness).

6 Transfer the grilled chicken breasts to a platter or plates and drizzle any remaining glaze over them. Sprinkle the scallion greens on top and serve at once.

YIELD:
Serves 4

Kentucky

BOURBON-BRINED CHICKEN

Desperate times call for desperate measures. In the past thirty years, all meat in the United States has gotten leaner, and the boneless, skinless chicken breast is no exception. This popular cut is about as low in fat as meat can be. So what's the problem? Well, fat is what carries flavor and it's what keeps meat from drying out during grilling. That's where brining comes in—this traditional American technique puts moisture back in meat. And the bourbon? Well, this distinctly American whiskey adds a smoky sweetness that's perfect for grilled chicken.

METHOD:
Direct grilling

ADVANCE PREPARATION:
2 to 3 hours for brining the chicken

FOR THE BRINE:

¼ cup bourbon

¼ cup coarse salt (kosher or sea)

¼ cup firmly packed brown sugar

4 slices (each ¼ inch thick) lemon

2 cloves garlic, peeled and gently
crushed with the side of a cleaver

1 tablespoon black peppercorns

1 tablespoon mustard seeds

1 tablespoon coriander seeds

FOR THE CHICKEN:

2 whole skinless, boneless chicken
breasts (each 12 to 16 ounces),
or 4 half breasts (each half 6 to
8 ounces)

2 tablespoons melted butter or olive oil

Your favorite barbecue sauce, for serving

YOU'LL ALSO NEED:

2 cups wood chips or chunks (optional;
preferably hickory or oak), soaked for 1
hour in water to cover, then drained

1 MAKE THE BRINE: Combine the bourbon, salt, brown sugar, lemon slices, garlic, peppercorns, and mustard and coriander seeds in a large nonreactive bowl with 4 cups of water and whisk until the salt and brown sugar dissolve.

2 If using whole chicken breasts, cut each breast in half. Trim any sinews or excess fat off the breasts and discard. Rinse the breasts under cold running water, then drain. Place the chicken breasts in a large resealable plastic bag and add the brine. Let the breasts brine in the refrigerator for 2 to 3 hours, turning the breasts twice so that they brine evenly.

3 Set up the grill for direct grilling (see page 21 for gas or charcoal) and preheat to high. If using a gas grill, place all of the wood chips or chunks, if desired, in the smoker box or in a smoker pouch (see page 24) and run the grill on high until you see smoke. If using a charcoal grill, preheat it to high, then toss all of the wood chips or chunks, if desired, on the coals.

4 When ready to cook, drain the brine off the chicken and blot the breasts dry with paper towels. Discard the brine. Lightly brush both sides of the breasts with the melted butter. Brush and oil the grill grate, then arrange the chicken breasts on the hot grate, placing them on a diagonal to the bars. Grill the breasts for 2 minutes, then rotate them a quarter turn to create an attractive crosshatch of grill marks. Continue grilling the breasts on that side for 2 minutes longer. Turn the breasts over and grill until cooked through, 4 to 6 minutes longer, again rotating them after 2 minutes to create a crosshatch of grill marks. The total cooking time will be 8 to 10 minutes, depending on the thickness of the chicken breasts. To test for doneness, poke a breast in the thickest part with your finger; it should feel firm to the touch (see page 368 for more about testing for doneness). Transfer the grilled chicken breasts to a platter or plates and serve at once with your favorite barbecue sauce.

YIELD:

Serves 4

■ "Too much whiskey is just enough," Mark Twain is alleged to have quipped. The same cannot be said for brine. Overbrining will make your chicken rubbery and unpalatably salty. Keep the chicken in the brine for just two to three hours. If space is tight in your refrigerator you can brine the breasts in a resealable plastic bag.

■ Traditionally, brined foods are smoked or grilled using the indirect method (see the Coffee-Molasses Turkey on page 421), but because chicken breasts are so small, they're best grilled using the direct method. To give them a smoke flavor, add wood chips to the fire.

TIPS

I call for sour cherries here, but the chicken is also good with sweet Bings. Now, I realize that pitting cherries and putting them on skewers is totally over the top, but I'm sure no one else on your block has served them this way, so you'll score points for novelty. To help with the pits, you can buy a cherry pitter at a cookware shop.

Traverse City, Mich.

CINNAMON-BRINED CHICKEN With Orange Cherry Barbecue Sauce

Traverse City, Michigan, is the self-proclaimed cherry capital of the world. Every July, America's tables are graced with delectable sour cherries from its orchards. To exploit the theme, flavor the barbecue sauce with cherry jam and grill cherry kebabs as a garnish. The brine gives you an irresistible chicken that is succulent every time.

METHOD:
Direct grilling

ADVANCE PREPARATION:
2 to 3 hours for brining the chicken

FOR THE CHICKEN AND BRINE:
**2 whole skinless, boneless chicken breasts
(each 12 to 16 ounces), or 4 half
breasts (each half 6 to 8 ounces)**
¼ cup coarse salt (kosher or sea)
¼ cup firmly packed dark brown sugar
1 small onion, thinly sliced
2 thin lemon slices
2 cinnamon sticks (each 2 inches long)

FOR THE CHERRIES AND SAUCE:
3 tablespoons granulated sugar
2 teaspoons ground cinnamon
24 sour cherries
2 tablespoons butter, melted
**Orange Cherry Barbecue Sauce
(recipe follows)**

YOU'LL ALSO NEED:
**8 short (6-inch) bamboo skewers
or wooden toothpicks; 2 cups
wood chips or chunks (optional,
see Note; preferably cherry), soaked
for 1 hour in water to cover, then
drained; heavy-duty aluminum foil**

1 If using whole chicken breasts, cut each breast in half. Trim any excess fat or sinews off the chicken breasts and discard. Rinse the breasts under cold running water, then drain and blot dry with paper towels. Place the breasts in a nonreactive baking dish.

2 MAKE THE BRINE: Place the salt and brown sugar in a large nonreactive bowl with 4 cups of cool water and whisk until dissolved. Pour the brine over the breasts, stir in the onion, lemon slices, and cinnamon sticks, and cover the chicken with plastic wrap. Or place in a large resealable plastic bag and add the brine. Let brine in the refrigerator for 2 to 3 hours, turning the breasts twice so that they brine evenly.

3 Place the granulated sugar and cinnamon in a small bowl and stir to mix.

4 Rinse the cherries under cold running water and blot dry with paper towels. Pit the cherries, then place 3 on each of the bamboo skewers. Brush the cherries with the melted butter. Sprinkle the cinnamon and sugar mixture over the cherry kebabs.

5 Set up the grill for direct grilling (see page 21 for gas or charcoal) and preheat to high. If using a gas grill, place all of the wood chips or chunks in the smoker box or in a smoker pouch (see page 24) and run the grill on high until you see smoke. If using a charcoal grill, preheat it to high, then toss all of the wood chips or chunks on the coals.

6 When ready to cook, drain the brine from the chicken and blot the breasts dry with paper towels. Discard the brine. Brush and oil the grill grate. Arrange the chicken breasts on the hot grate, placing them on a diagonal to the bars. Grill the breasts for 2 minutes, then rotate them a quarter turn to create an attractive crosshatch of grill marks. Continue grilling the breasts on that side for 2 minutes longer. Turn the breasts over and grill until cooked through, 4 to 6 minutes longer, again rotating them after 2 minutes to create a crosshatch of grill marks. The total cooking time will be 8 to 10 minutes, depending on the thickness of the chicken breasts. To test for doneness, poke a breast in the thickest part with your finger; it should feel firm to the touch (see page 368 for more about testing for doneness). Transfer the grilled chicken breasts to a platter and cover loosely with aluminum foil to keep warm while you grill the cherry kebabs.

Cherry season spells good eating for Michigan grill buffs.

7 Tear off a piece of heavy-duty aluminum foil that is roughly 12 inches long. Make an aluminum foil shield for the exposed parts of the bamboo skewers by folding the foil in half.

8 Place the foil shield on the hot grate. Arrange the cherry kebabs on the grate so that they are over the fire but the exposed ends of the skewers are on the foil shield to keep them from burning. Grill the cherry kebabs until lightly browned, 1 to 2 minutes per side (2 to 4 minutes in all), turning them with tongs. Transfer the grilled cherry kebabs to the platter with the grilled breasts. Serve the Orange Cherry Barbecue Sauce on the side.

YIELD:
Serves 4

NOTE: I call for wood chips or chunks here to add a smoke flavor to the chicken, but you can certainly grill the breasts without wood.

Orange Cherry Barbecue Sauce

Sweet and tart, this fruity sauce is perfect for any type of poultry. But don't stop there, because grilled pork and even salmon and shrimp shine in its presence.

INGREDIENTS:

1 medium-size orange
1 medium-size lemon
1 cinnamon stick (2 inches long)
¼ teaspoon ground cloves
½ cup sour cherry jam or preserves
1 cup chicken stock (preferably homemade)
½ cup plus 1 tablespoon port wine
¼ cup orange marmalade
1 tablespoon ketchup
2 teaspoons cornstarch
⅛ teaspoon cayenne pepper
Coarse salt (kosher or sea) and
**   freshly ground black pepper**

1 Using a vegetable peeler, remove 2 strips of zest, each 1½ by ½ inches, from the orange and 2 strips of zest, each 1½ by ½ inches, from the lemon. Squeeze the orange and lemon and strain the juice into a medium-size nonreactive saucepan. Add the strips of zest, cinnamon stick, cloves, cherry jam, and stock and gradually bring to a boil over high heat. Reduce the heat to medium and let the mixture simmer until the jam dissolves and the mixture is reduced by a quarter, about 10 minutes. Remove and discard the orange and lemon zests and the cinnamon stick.

2 Add ½ cup of the port, the orange marmalade, and ketchup and let simmer until the marmalade is dissolved and the sauce is richly flavored, about 5 minutes. Dissolve the cornstarch in the remaining 1 tablespoon of port. Whisk this mixture into the sauce and let simmer for 15 seconds; the sauce will thicken. Add the cayenne and season with salt and black pepper to taste. The sauce can be served warm or at room temperature. It can be refrigerated, covered, for up to 3 days. Bring to room temperature before serving.

YIELD:
Makes 2¼ cups

New York, N.Y.

TARRAGON CHICKEN PAILLARDS

If I had to pick a single place for Saturday lunch in Manhattan, it would be Balthazar in SoHo. This jam-packed bistro has it all: a vintage decor, a star-studded clientele (on a recent visit our co-diners included Bono, Yoko Ono, Donna Karan, and ex-mayor Ed Koch), and a menu of solid bistro classics prepared exactly the way they should be and served without the least bit of pretension. You don't normally come to a bistro for barbecue, of course, but Balthazar grills its chicken paillards, and it's easy to see why this is one of their best-sellers. A paillard is a piece of meat that's been pounded paper-thin, so it buries the plate. Besides providing an opportunity for the obvious chest-thumping theatrics of wielding a scallopini pounder or cleaver, pounding tenderizes the meat. The accompanying salad makes this a complete and healthy meal. Here's my rendition of a Balthazar classic.

METHOD:
Direct grilling

ADVANCE PREPARATION:
30 minutes for marinating the chicken

INGREDIENTS:

2 whole skinless, boneless chicken
 breasts (each 12 to 16 ounces),
 or 4 half chicken breasts
 (each half 6 to 8 ounces)
1 clove garlic, minced
½ teaspoon coarse salt (kosher or sea)
½ teaspoon freshly ground black pepper
½ teaspoon hot red pepper flakes
2 tablespoons Dijon mustard
3 tablespoons chopped fresh tarragon
3 tablespoons fresh lemon juice
1 tablespoon balsamic vinegar
1 cup extra-virgin olive oil
1 cup grape or baby cherry tomatoes
 (cut cherry tomatoes in half)
6 to 8 cups mesclun, rinsed and spun dry
 (see Note)
4 fresh tarragon sprigs, for garnish
4 lemon wedges, for serving

YOU'LL ALSO NEED:

2 cups wood chips or chunks
 (optional; preferably oak),
 unsoaked

TIPS

■ The easiest way to pound out the chicken breasts is to use a scallopini pounder or the side of a heavy cleaver (a rolling pin will work in a pinch). Placing the chicken breasts between sheets of plastic wrap allows them to spread and flatten without tearing.

■ Tossing unsoaked wood chips on the fire when you grill the chicken approximates the flavor of grilling over wood.

1   If using whole chicken breasts, cut each breast in half. Trim any sinews or excess fat off the breasts and discard. Rinse the breasts under cold running water, then drain (don't blot dry with paper towels; the breasts should be damp). Place a breast half between two sheets of plastic wrap. Pound it out into a broad flat sheet ¼ to ⅛ inch thick, using a scallopini pounder or the side of a heavy cleaver. Repeat with the remaining breast halves. Place the pounded breasts on a rimmed nonstick baking sheet.

2   Place the garlic, salt, black pepper, and hot red pepper flakes in the bottom of a large nonreactive mixing bowl and mash to a paste with the back of a wooden spoon. Add the mustard, 1 tablespoon of the chopped tarragon, and the lemon juice and vinegar and whisk to mix. Gradually whisk in the olive oil; the mixture will thicken. Pour a quarter of this vinaigrette over the chicken breasts, patting it onto the chicken with a fork. Turn the breasts over, pour another quarter of the vinaigrette on top, and pat it onto the chicken with a fork. Let the chicken marinate in the refrigerator, covered, for 30 minutes. Set the remaining vinaigrette aside. You'll use it to dress the salad.

3   Just before you set up the grill, place the tomatoes, mesclun, and the remaining chopped tarragon, in that order, in the bowl with the remaining dressing, but don't toss them together.

New York's trendy Balthazar serves a memorable grilled chicken paillard.

4 Set up the grill for direct grilling (see page 21 for gas or charcoal) and preheat to high. If using a gas grill, place all of the wood chips or chunks, if desired, in the smoker box or in a smoker pouch (see page 24) and run the grill on high until you see smoke. If using a charcoal grill, preheat it to high, then toss all of the wood chips or chunks, if desired, on the coals.

5 When ready to cook, brush and oil the grill grate. Arrange the paillards on the hot grate, placing them on a diagonal to the bars. Grill the paillards until cooked through, about 2 minutes per side, rotating each a quarter turn after 1 minute to create an attractive crosshatch of grill marks, if desired (use a long, wide spatula to rotate and turn over the paillards). To test for doneness, poke a paillard with your finger; it should feel firm to the touch (see page 368 for more about testing for doneness).

6 Transfer the grilled paillards to a platter or plates. Quickly toss the salad and mound it on top of the paillards. Garnish with the tarragon sprigs and serve at once with the lemon wedges.

YIELD:
Serves 4

NOTE: Mesclun is a mix of baby lettuces. You can buy it ready mixed at most gourmet shops and supermarkets, or you can make your own, using your favorite lettuces.

New Mexico

GREEN CHILE CHICKEN UNDER BRICKS

Mexicans keep chicken breasts moist by grilling them under stones. Here's a New Mexican version, redolent with garlic, cilantro, and lime.

METHOD:
Direct grilling

ADVANCE PREPARATION:
30 minutes to 1 hour for marinating the chicken

INGREDIENTS:
2 whole skinless, boneless chicken breasts (each 12 to 16 ounces), or 4 half breasts (each half 6 to 8 ounces)
Coarse salt (kosher or sea) and cracked or freshly ground black peppercorns
1 teaspoon cumin seeds
3 cloves garlic, finely chopped
1 New Mexico green chile, or 2 to 4 serrano or jalapeño peppers, seeded and finely chopped (for hotter chicken, leave the seeds in)
½ cup chopped fresh cilantro, plus 4 cilantro sprigs for garnish
¼ cup fresh lime juice, plus 4 lime wedges for serving
¼ cup extra-virgin olive oil

TIPS

■ New Mexico green chiles are long, slender green peppers similar in shape to the Anaheim. Their flavor is mild and herbaceous. You could certainly use a hotter chile, like a serrano or jalapeño.

■ A possible sauce for this chicken is Fiery Salsa Verde (see page 58).

YOU'LL ALSO NEED:

**2 bricks, wrapped in aluminum foil
    (shiny side out)**

1 If using whole chicken breasts, cut each in half. Trim any sinews or excess fat off the breasts and discard. Rinse the breasts under cold running water, then drain and blot dry with paper towels. Place the breasts in a non-reactive baking dish.

2 Generously season the breasts on both sides with salt, pepper, and the cumin seeds. Sprinkle both sides of the breasts with the garlic, chile, and chopped cilantro. Pour the lime juice and olive oil over the chicken breasts, turning to coat both sides. Let the chicken marinate in the refrigerator, covered, for 30 minutes to 1 hour.

3 Set up the grill for direct grilling (see page 21 for charcoal or gas) and preheat to high.

4 When ready to cook, brush and oil the grill grate. Arrange the breasts on the hot grate, placing them on a diagonal to the bars. Pour any remaining marinade over them. Place one brick on top of each two breast halves. Grill the breasts for 2 minutes, then rotate them a quarter turn to create an attractive crosshatch of grill marks, if desired. Continue grilling the breasts on that side for 2 minutes longer. Turn the breasts over, place the bricks on top, and grill until cooked through, 4 to 6 minutes longer, again rotating them after 2 minutes to create a crosshatch of grill marks, if desired. The total cooking time will be 8 to 10 minutes. To test for

doneness, poke a breast in the thickest part with your finger; it should feel firm to the touch (see page 368 for more about testing for doneness). Transfer the grilled chicken to a platter or plates. Garnish with the cilantro sprigs and serve with the lime wedges.

YIELD:
Serves 4

New Mexico

RED CHILE CHICKEN UNDER BRICKS

The red chile is another staple of New Mexican cuisine, and unlike the green, it's almost always used dried or powdered. New Mexico red chile powder is moderately spicy, earthy, and very aromatic. You could use another type of pure chile powder, but the results will be more authentic if you use the New Mexico (see Mail-Order Sources, page 742).

METHOD:
Direct grilling

ADVANCE PREPARATION:
**30 minutes to 1 hour for marinating
    the chicken**

FOR THE RUB:

2 tablespoons ground New Mexico
   red chile pepper

2 teaspoons coarse salt (kosher or sea)

1 teaspoon ground cumin

1 teaspoon ground coriander

½ teaspoon freshly ground black pepper

¼ teaspoon ground cinnamon

FOR THE CHICKEN:

2 whole skinless, boneless chicken
   breasts (each 12 to 16 ounces),
   or 4 half breasts (each half
   6 to 8 ounces)

¼ cup extra-virgin olive oil

3 cloves garlic, finely chopped

½ cup chopped fresh cilantro, plus
   4 cilantro sprigs for garnish

¼ cup fresh lime juice, plus 4 lime
   wedges for serving

YOU'LL ALSO NEED:

2 bricks, wrapped in aluminum foil
   (shiny side out)

1 MAKE THE RUB: Combine the red chile powder, salt, cumin, coriander, black pepper, and cinnamon in a small bowl and stir to mix. (Actually, if you do not have sensitive skin, your fingers work better for mixing a rub than a spoon or whisk does.)

2 If using whole chicken breasts, cut each in half. Trim any sinews or excess fat off the breasts and discard. Rinse the breasts under cold running water, then drain and blot dry with paper towels. Place the breasts in a nonreactive baking dish. Sprinkle the rub over the chicken breasts on both sides, patting it onto the meat with your fingertips.

New Mexican red chiles dry in the sun.

3 Drizzle 2 tablespoons of the olive oil over the chicken breasts, rubbing it onto both sides. Sprinkle the breasts with the garlic and chopped cilantro, patting the flavorings onto the chicken with your fingertips. Pour the lime juice and remaining olive oil over the chicken, turning to coat both sides. Let the chicken marinate in the refrigerator, covered, for 30 minutes to 1 hour, turning the breasts once or twice so they marinate evenly.

4 Set up the grill for direct grilling (see page 21 for charcoal or gas) and preheat to high.

5 When ready to cook, brush and oil the grill grate. Arrange the breasts on the hot grate, placing them on a diagonal to the bars. Pour any remaining marinade over them. Place one brick on top of each two breast halves.

Grill the breasts for 2 minutes, then rotate them a quarter turn to create an attractive crosshatch of grill marks, if desired. Continue grilling the breasts on that side for 2 minutes longer. Turn the breasts over, place the bricks on top, and grill until cooked through, 4 to 6 minutes longer, again rotating them after 2 minutes to create a crosshatch of grill marks, if desired. The total cooking time will be 8 to 10 minutes. To test for doneness, poke a breast in the thickest part with your finger; it should feel firm to the touch (see page 368 for more about testing for doneness). Transfer the grilled chicken to a platter or plates. Garnish with the cilantro sprigs and serve with the lime wedges.

YIELD:

Serves 4

Florida

TANGERINE TERIYAKI CHICKEN

Add a touch of Florida to a Japanese classic and you get something of a culinary conundrum. The main flavoring—tangerine—is only in season in the winter, when many people, in the Frost Belt at least, have mothballed their grills for the season. Of course, that's not a problem in Florida, where our prime grilling seasons are autumn and winter (it takes a real diehard to fire up the grill during our steamy summers). Still, whatever the weather, the perfumed, sweet tangerine juice makes a great counterpoint for the salty tang of the soy sauce.

METHOD:
Direct grilling

ADVANCE PREPARATION:
1 to 2 hours for marinating the chicken (optional)

INGREDIENTS:
1 cup fresh tangerine juice (from 3 to 5 tangerines)
½ cup soy sauce
⅓ cup honey
4 strips tangerine zest (each about 1½ by ½ inch; see Note)
2 cloves garlic, peeled and gently crushed with the side of a cleaver
2 scallions, trimmed, white parts gently crushed with the side of a cleaver, green parts thinly sliced
2 slices fresh ginger (each ¼ inch thick), peeled and gently crushed with the side of a cleaver
1 cinnamon stick (2 inches long)
2 to 3 tablespoons Asian (dark) sesame oil
2 whole skinless, boneless chicken breasts (each 12 to 16 ounces), or 4 half chicken breasts (each half 6 to 8 ounces)
1 tablespoon toasted sesame seeds (see page 584)

Florida tangerines and their perfumed cousins, tangelos, are in season November through February. If these are unavailable, oranges will give you highly respectable results.

1 Place the tangerine juice in a nonreactive saucepan over high heat and bring to a boil. Let boil until reduced by half. Add the soy sauce, honey, tangerine zest, garlic, scallion whites, ginger, cinnamon stick, and 1 tablespoon of the sesame oil. Let the mixture boil until thick and syrupy, about 5 minutes. Remove the saucepan from the heat and let cool to room temperature.

2 If using whole breasts, cut each breast in half. Trim any sinews or excess fat off the breasts and discard. Rinse the breasts under cold running water, then drain and blot dry with paper towels. Place the breasts in a nonreactive baking dish.

3 Pour half of the tangerine mixture over the chicken, turning to coat both sides. Set the rest of the tangerine mixture aside; you'll use it as a glaze. Let the chicken marinate for 1 to 2 hours in the refrigerator, covered, turning the breasts once or twice so that they marinate evenly. If you're in a hurry, you can shorten the marinating time or omit it altogether, but the chicken won't be quite as flavorful.

4 Set up the grill for direct grilling (see page 21 for charcoal or gas) and preheat to high.

5 When ready to cook, drain the marinade from the chicken and discard the marinade. Brush and oil the grill grate. Lightly brush each breast with some of the sesame oil. Arrange the chicken breasts on the hot grate, placing them on a diagonal to the bars. Grill the breasts for 2 minutes, then brush them with more sesame oil and rotate them a quarter turn to create an attractive crosshatch of grill marks. Continue grilling the breasts on that side for 2 minutes longer. Turn the breasts over and grill until cooked through, 4 to 6 minutes longer, again rotating them after 2 minutes to create a crosshatch of grill marks. The total cooking time will be 8 to 10 minutes, depending on the thickness of the chicken breasts. To test for doneness, poke a breast in the thickest part with your finger; it should feel firm to the touch (see page 368 for more about testing for doneness). During the last 2 minutes of grilling, using a clean brush, baste the breasts with the reserved glaze.

6 Transfer the grilled chicken breasts to plates or a platter and pour any remaining glaze over them. For a fancier presentation, you can slice the chicken breasts crosswise on the diagonal and fan out the slices. Sprinkle the scallion greens and sesame seeds over the chicken and serve.

YIELD:
Serves 4

NOTE: Use a vegetable peeler to remove the oil-rich outer rind of the tangerine in strips of zest.

TIPS

To toast sesame seeds, place them in a dry skillet over medium heat. Cook them until they are fragrant and just beginning to brown, two to four minutes, shaking the skillet constantly. Immediately transfer the toasted sesame seeds to a heatproof bowl to cool.

TIPS

■ There are mangoes and there are mangoes. If you're lucky enough to get ahold of a Florida mango in June or July, you'll experience a perfume and intensity of flavor you'd have never dreamed possible. Look for Florida mangoes at specialty greengrocers.

■ Some people are allergic to mango sap. If you have sensitive skin, wear rubber gloves when handling mangoes.

Miami, Fla.

MANGO GRILLED CHICKEN

In our back yard we have a mango tree a stone's throw from the grill. The musky fragrance of mango (think peach of the tropics) makes a great foil for grilled chicken—especially when paired with fresh mint in a salsa that does double duty as a marinade. And talk about easy: You're looking at 15 minutes of preparation time, tops. If you're allergic to mango sap, be sure to wear rubber gloves when handling the fruit.

METHOD:
Direct grilling

ADVANCE PREPARATION:
30 minutes to 1 hour for marinating the chicken

INGREDIENTS:
2 whole skinless, boneless chicken breasts (each 12 to 16 ounces), or 4 half breasts (each 6 to 8 ounces)
Coarse salt (kosher or sea) and cracked black peppercorns
1 mango, peeled, seeded, and cut into ¼-inch dice (about 2 cups)
1 cucumber, peeled, seeded, and cut into ¼-inch dice

½ cup diced red onion
1 clove garlic, minced
½ cup chopped fresh mint, plus 4 mint sprigs for garnish
¼ cup fresh lime juice
½ cup extra-virgin olive oil

1 If using whole breasts, cut each breast in half. Trim any sinews or excess fat off the chicken breasts and discard. Rinse the chicken breasts under cold running water, then drain and blot dry with paper towels. Generously season the breasts on both sides with salt and pepper. Place the breasts in a nonreactive baking dish.

2 Combine the mango, cucumber, onion, garlic, and chopped mint in a nonreactive mixing bowl and stir to mix. Stir in the lime juice and olive oil and season with salt and pepper to taste; the mango mixture should be highly seasoned. Pour half of the mango mixture over the chicken breasts, turning to coat both sides. Let the chicken marinate for 30 minutes to 1 hour in the refrigerator, covered, turning the breasts once or twice so that they marinate evenly. Refrigerate the remaining mango mixture, covered; you'll use it as the salsa.

3 Set up the grill for direct grilling (see page 21 for charcoal or gas) and preheat to high.

4 When ready to cook, drain the marinade from the chicken breasts and discard the marinade. Brush and oil the grill grate. Arrange the chicken breasts on the hot grate, placing them on a diagonal to the bars. Grill the chicken breasts until cooked through, 4 to 6 minutes per side. To test for doneness, poke a breast in the thickest part with your finger; it should feel firm to the touch (see page 368 for more about testing for doneness).

5 Transfer the grilled chicken breasts to a platter or plates. Spoon the mango salsa over them and garnish with the mint sprigs. Serve at once.

YIELD:
Serves 4

A turkey and a fledgling smoke master.

New England

THE PERFECT THANKSGIVING TURKEY

Let's face it, a lot of bad turkey gets served every Thanksgiving. The problem has less to do with human error than with avian anatomy. The reason is that the delicate white meat of the turkey breast cooks faster than the dark, rich meat of the legs and thighs. So if you cook a turkey to a safe temperature (180°F), the breast is almost guaranteed to dry out. There is a way around this problem, however: Brine the bird and roast it on the grill. Smoke-roasting a turkey has at least four compelling advantages: The low, slow heat cooks the bird through without drying it out; it provides the haunting flavor of wood smoke; and it takes the fuss and mess outside, liberating your oven for stuffing, roasted chestnuts, and other essential side dishes. It also gives you an excuse to spend the afternoon outdoors, beer in hand, bonding with your barbecue buddies (and if you live in the north, you'll learn who your real friends are). As for brining, this involves nothing more than marinating the bird overnight in salt water, which moisturizes the meat, adding succulence as well as flavor. For a New England touch—and northern earthy sweetness—I like to add a fillip of Vermont maple syrup to the brine.

■ The key to brining is not to overdo it. Excessive soaking will give the turkey the unnatural texture and flavor of commercial lunch meats—twelve to sixteen hours will do it.

■ You'll need a big pot for brining. I use a stockpot (putting a water-filled zipper-top plastic bag on top will keep the bird completely submerged). In a pinch, you could brine the turkey in a clean plastic garbage bag.

METHOD:
Indirect grilling

ADVANCE PREPARATION:
16 hours for brining the turkey

INGREDIENTS:
**1 turkey (about 12 pounds), thawed
    if frozen (see page 417)**
1¼ cups coarse salt (kosher or sea)
1 quart hot water
1 cup maple syrup
1 medium-size onion, thinly sliced
**4 cloves garlic, peeled and crushed
    with the side of a cleaver**
10 black peppercorns
5 bay leaves
**4 strips lemon zest (each about
    1½ by ½ inch; see Note)**
2 whole cloves
**4 to 6 tablespoons (½ to ¾ stick)
    salted butter, melted**
Maple Redeye Gravy (recipe follows)

YOU'LL ALSO NEED:
**3 cups wood chips or chunks
    (preferably hickory), soaked for
    1 hour in water to cover,
    then drained**

1 Remove the packet of giblets from the neck or body cavity of the turkey and set aside for another use. Remove and discard the fat just inside the cavities of the turkey. Rinse the turkey, inside and out, under cold running water, then drain and blot dry, inside and out, with paper towels.

2 Place the salt and hot water in a large deep nonreactive pot and whisk until the salt dissolves. Whisk in 4 quarts of cold water and maple syrup and add the onion, garlic, peppercorns, bay leaves, lemon zest, and cloves. Let the brine cool; it should be no warmer than room temperature when you add the turkey to it. Place a large resealable plastic bag filled with cold water on top to keep the bird submerged. Cover the pot, place in the refrigerator, and let the turkey brine overnight.

3 Set up the grill for indirect grilling (see page 23 for gas or page 22 for charcoal) and preheat to medium. If using a gas grill, place all of the wood chips or chunks in the smoker box or in a smoker pouch (see page 24) and run the grill on high until you see smoke, then reduce the heat to medium. If using a charcoal grill, place a large drip pan in the center, preheat the grill to medium, then toss 1 cup of the wood chips or chunks on the coals.

4 When ready to cook, place the turkey, breast side up, in the center of the hot grate, over the drip pan and away from the heat. Brush the turkey with some of the melted butter, then cover the grill. Grill the turkey until cooked through, 2½ to 3 hours. To test for doneness, use an instant-read meat thermometer: Insert it into the thickest part of a thigh but not so that it touches the bone. The internal temperature should be about 180°F. (See page 418 for more about testing for doneness.) Baste the turkey with melted butter every hour. If the wing tips or skin start to burn or brown too much, cover them loosely with aluminum foil. If using a charcoal grill, every hour you'll need to add 12 fresh coals and ½ cup of wood chips or chunks to each side.

5 Transfer the grilled turkey to a platter, cover it loosely with aluminum foil, if you have not already done so, and let it rest for 10 to 15 minutes before carving. Serve with the Maple Redeye Gravy.

YIELD:
Serves 12 to 14

NOTE: Use a vegetable peeler to remove the yellow outer rind of the lemon in strips of zest. Be careful to leave behind the bitter white pith.

VARIATION: If you use a smoker to cook your turkey, it will take 3½ to 4 hours at a temperature of 275°F.

Maple Redeye Gravy

Turkey is only as good as the gravy you spoon over it. This may be about the best gravy you've ever tasted, enriched as it is with smoked turkey drippings, Madeira, and for an unexpected touch, shots of coffee and maple syrup.

INGREDIENTS:
About 2 cups turkey drippings
   (see Note)
1 to 2 cups turkey or chicken stock
   (preferably homemade)

4 tablespoons (½ stick) salted butter
¼ cup flour
¼ cup Madeira
¼ cup coffee
¼ cup heavy (whipping) cream
2 tablespoons maple syrup
Coarse salt (kosher or sea) and
   freshly ground black pepper

1 Strain the turkey drippings into a fat separator (see Tips). Wait a few minutes, then pour the drippings into a large measuring cup, stopping when the fat starts to come out. Add enough chicken stock to obtain 3 cups.

2 Melt the butter in a heavy saucepan over medium-high heat. Stir in the flour and cook until it's a dark golden brown, 3 to 5 minutes.

3 Remove the pan from the heat and gradually whisk in the Madeira, coffee, cream, maple syrup, and the turkey drippings with stock. Return the pan to the heat and bring to a boil over high heat, whisking steadily. Reduce the heat to medium and let the sauce simmer until richly flavored and reduced to about 3 cups, 6 to 10 minutes. Season with salt and pepper to taste.

YIELD:
Makes about 3 cups

NOTE: To remove the turkey drippings from the grill when the turkey is done, using grill mitts or a grate grabber, lift the grate off the grill. Carefully lift out the drip pan and pour the contents into a heatproof measuring cup or into a fat separator.

TIPS

The easiest way to defat turkey drippings is to use a fat separator. This device looks like a measuring cup, but it has a spout that is attached at the base, not the top. Fat rises, so when you pour off the drippings, the portion without fat will flow out first, leaving the fat behind. You can find fat separators at kitchenware stores.

TRASH-CAN TURKEY

Move over beer-can chicken: Make way for one of the most outrageous preparations every to steal the show at a cookout. I'm talking about a dish so improbable and peculiar, so showstopping and bizarre, you'll probably want to try it this weekend. It's a classic on the Boy Scout circuit—trash-can turkey.

The basic procedure is simple enough: You drive a stake in the ground and stick a turkey on top of it—in the undignified position that's a hallmark of beer-can chicken. Then you place a clean metal garbage can over the bird and arrange glowing charcoals on top of the can and around the sides. The charcoal turns the trash can into a sort of giant oven (think of it as a really, really big Dutch oven).

I'd heard rumors about trash-

Earning your pit master merit badge is easy for some (left) and a dream for others (above).

can turkey for years, but it wasn't until I visited a Scout Masters Camporee at Markham Park in Sunrise, Florida, that I witnessed the singular procedure firsthand. My guide was Jeff Gravenstreter, carpenter for the Broward County school system by day, scoutmaster and extraordinary outdoor cook by night and on weekends. Jeff's main job that weekend was to run a chili cook-off, but he found the time to unearth a clean

> ... a dish so improbable and peculiar, so showstopping and bizarre, you'll probably want to try it this weekend.

garbage can, light the coals, and show me how to trash-can cook a turkey.

"We try to teach kids to keep it simple," observed Jeff, recognizable by his tan shirt, green shorts, red-topped green socks, and hiking boots (although the same sartorial details would describe about five hundred other scoutmasters on the scene). Jeff has been making trash-can turkey for more than a decade and he didn't so much learn the recipe as absorb it from general Boy Scout culture.

WHOSE IDEA WAS THIS ANYWAY?

Where did the dish originate? Jeff hypothesizes that trash-can turkey may have been the brainchild of a hobo or other transient. Or like beer-can chicken or marshmallows roasted on a stick—or even the invention of fire—it may have sprung up in several places simultaneously.

Aside from the novelty, there are at least two advantages to cooking a turkey in this manner. First, because the heat radiates from the top down as well as from the sides inward, the bird cooks quickly. How quick? A 12-pound turkey will be done in two hours or less (compare that to the three hours or more it takes to grill a turkey using the indirect method). And, it's almost impossible to overcook a trash-can turkey—because it cooks in a sealed environment, the meat stays incredibly moist and tender.

To make trash-can turkey, in addition to the turkey and the trash can, you need some sort of seasoning and a lot of charcoal. The seasoning could include any sort of barbecue rub or spice mix, from poultry seasoning to herbes de Provence.

As for charcoal, you'll need a 20-pound bag, and while I usually advocate natural lump charcoal, commonplace briquettes will work just fine for this because the fire remains outside the trash can (the easiest way to light 20 pounds of charcoal is in a kettle grill or other charcoal grill; you can transfer the lit coals to the garbage can with a shovel).

Trash-can turkey produces a bird that's meltingly tender and ineffably succulent. So the next time you're looking to show off at a cookout or at Thanksgiving, look no further than your garage or hardware store. The concept may seem farfetched, but the preparation is guaranteed to bring down the house. You'll find the recipe on the next page.

It's hot work tending a trash-can turkey.

Boy Scout Camps, U.S.A.

TRASH-CAN TURKEY

Awhole turkey roasted upright on a stake under a metal trash can? This sure doesn't sound like the sort of Thanksgiving fare—or barbecue—I grew up on. But I've seen it with my own eyes, and it's a guaranteed showstopper. Even more amazing, the singular procedure produces some of the moistest, tastiest turkey you'll ever eat. A full account of trash-can turkey can be found on page 414. Thanksgiving will never be the same.

METHOD:
**Unlike any you've ever seen
(modified indirect grilling)**

ADVANCE PREPARATION:
**4 to 12 hours for curing the turkey
(optional)**

FOR THE RUB:
**2 tablespoons poultry seasoning
2 tablespoons coarse salt (kosher or sea)
1 tablespoon dry mustard
1 tablespoon freshly ground black pepper
1½ teaspoons garlic powder**

FOR THE TURKEY:
**1 turkey (about 12 pounds), thawed
if frozen (see facing page)
1 tablespoon olive oil**

YOU'LL ALSO NEED:
**1 wood or metal stake (at least 1 inch
thick and 20 inches long); heavy-duty
aluminum foil; 1 clean 20-gallon
metal trash can (see Notes);
shovel; 20 pounds charcoal
(see Notes); heavy-duty insulated
grill gloves**

1 MAKE THE RUB: Place the poultry seasoning, salt, mustard, pepper, and garlic powder in a small bowl and stir to mix. (Actually, your fingers work better for mixing a rub than a spoon or whisk does.)

2 Remove the packet of giblets from the neck or body cavity of the turkey and set aside for another use. Remove and discard the fat just inside the cavities of the turkey. Rinse the turkey, inside and out, under cold running water, then blot dry, inside and out, with paper towels. Season the bird with the rub, placing 1 tablespoon in the neck cavity and 2 tablespoons in the body cavity. Brush or rub the outside of the turkey all over with the olive oil and sprinkle it all over with the remaining rub, patting it onto the skin with your fingertips. You can cook the turkey right away but it will have more flavor if you let it cure in the refrigerator, covered, for 4 hours or even overnight.

3 Clear a 4-foot circle on the ground, using a shovel (do this on dirt, not on your lawn). Cover the circle with heavy-duty aluminum foil. Drive the stake into the ground in the center of the circle, so it sticks up about 16 inches above the ground.

4 Light the charcoal in a grill or in 3 chimney starters. It's OK to light the charcoal in several batches, provided each is ready within 10 to 15 minutes of the one before.

5 Holding the turkey with the neck end at the top, lower it onto the stake. The tail end of the bird should be about 6 inches above the ground. Place the trash can over the turkey, keeping the bird in the center and resting the trash can on the ground. Shovel a third of the coals on top of the trash can and the remainder around the outside; these should come 3 to 4 inches up the sides of the can. This should be enough coals to cook the turkey, but if they burn out before the turkey is done, replenish as needed.

6 Cook the turkey until cooked through, 1½ to 2 hours. Using a shovel, remove the coals and ash from the sides and the top of the can. Wearing heavy-duty insulated grill gloves, lift the can off the turkey. The turkey should be handsomely browned and fall-off-the-bone-tender. To check for doneness, use an instant-read meat thermometer: Insert it in the thickest part of a thigh but not so that it touches the bone. The internal temperature should be about 180°F. (See page 418 for more about testing for doneness.)

7 Using heavy-duty insulated rubber gloves, lift the turkey off the stake and transfer it to a platter. Cover the bird loosely with aluminum foil and let it rest for 10 to 15 minutes, then carve and serve.

HOW TO THAW A TURKEY

Except at holiday time, in many parts of the country supermarket turkeys come frozen (fresh turkeys can be ordered from specialty meat markets). There are two ways to safely thaw a frozen turkey: in the refrigerator and in cold water. Never thaw a turkey at room temperature—you run the risk of it becoming contaminated by bacteria.

To thaw a frozen turkey in the refrigerator (the lazy but longer method), place it in a roasting pan to catch any dripping liquid. To speed up the thawing process, place the bird in a sink or a large pot filled with cold water. You'll need to change the water every thirty minutes; the water must remain cold to avoid the risk of bacterial contamination. You'll find thawing times for both methods below.

THAWING TIMES

WEIGHT OF TURKEY	IN REFRIGERATOR	IN COLD WATER
8 to 12 pounds	1 to 2 days	4 to 6 hours
12 to 16 pounds	2 to 3 days	6 to 8 hours
16 to 20 pounds	3 to 4 days	8 to 10 hours
20 to 24 pounds	4 to 5 days	10 to 12 hours

YIELD:

Serves 12 to 14 hungry scouts or adults

NOTES:

■ Some scout masters recommend using a trash can with crimped, not soldered, seams. The can should be about 3 feet tall.

■ As mentioned earlier, charcoal briquettes, which I usually avoid, work just fine for trash-can turkey.

TURKEY COOKING TIMES

Use an instant-read meat thermometer to test whether a turkey is done. When fully cooked, the breast meat of the turkey should be about 170°F; thigh meat, taking the temperature in the thickest part of thigh (don't let the thermometer touch the bone) should be about 180°F. The times here are for turkeys grilled using the indirect method and medium heat (325° to 350°F). And how big a bird do you need? Figure on roughly a pound person.

WEIGHT OF TURKEY	GRILLING TIME	SERVES
8 to 12 pounds	2¾ to 3 hours	8 to 12 people
12 to 16 pounds	3 to 3¾ hours	12 to 16 people
14 to 18 pounds	3¾ to 4½ hours	14 to 18 people
18 to 20 pounds	4½ to 4¾ hours	18 to 20 people
20 to 24 pounds	4¾ to 5¼ hours	20 to 24 people

Louisiana

BIG EASY BARBECUED TURKEY

Over the years, I've tried dozens of ways of cooking turkey—from baking it wrapped in a blanket (an oddball technique I found in Oregon) to inserting truffles and thinly sliced salt

Talking turkey in the hen house.

pork under the skin (a trick I learned in France). But the method I keep returning to is barbecuing the bird on the grill. No other method keeps turkey quite so moist and flavorful, a plus for a bird that has a natural tendency to dry out. Barbecued turkey can be found all over North America. This version comes from Louisiana, birthplace of the deep-fried turkey. Think of this as fried turkey without the fat.

METHOD:
Indirect grilling

FOR THE INJECTOR SAUCE:
**6 tablespoons chicken stock
    (preferably homemade),
    at room temperature**
1 tablespoon bourbon
1 tablespoon Cajun Rub (recipe follows)

FOR THE TURKEY:
**1 turkey (8 to 10 pounds), thawed
    if frozen (see page 417)**
**4 tablespoons Cajun Rub
    (recipe follows)**
1 tablespoon canola oil

Kitchen syringe; 3 cups wood chips or chunks (preferably hickory or oak), soaked for 1 hour in water to cover, then drained

1 MAKE THE INJECTOR SAUCE: Combine the stock, bourbon, and Cajun Rub in a bowl and whisk to mix.

2 Remove the packet of giblets from the neck or body cavity of the turkey and set aside for another use. Remove and discard the fat just inside the cavities of the turkey. Rinse the turkey, inside and out, under cold running water, then blot dry, inside and out, with paper towels. Season the inside of both cavities with 2 tablespoons of the Cajun Rub.

3 Fill the kitchen syringe with the injector sauce. To do this, push the plunger all the way down, place the tip of the needle in the sauce, and slowly draw the plunger up: The syringe will fill with sauce. Inject the sauce into the turkey breast, thighs, and drumsticks. Don't be surprised if a little sauce squirts out; this is OK. Truss the turkey (see page 373 for instructions); this is optional, but it will give the bird a more dignified appearance. Rub the outside of

the turkey with the oil and sprinkle the remaining 2 tablespoons of Cajun Rub all over it, patting it onto the skin with your fingertips.

4 Set up the grill for indirect grilling (see page 23 for gas or page 22 for charcoal) and preheat to medium. If using a gas grill, place all of the wood chips or chunks in the smoker box or in a smoker pouch (see page 24) and run the grill on high until you see smoke, then reduce the heat to medium. If using a charcoal grill, place a large drip pan in the center, preheat the grill to medium, then toss 1 cup of the wood chips or chunks on the coals.

5 When ready to cook, place the turkey, breast side up, in the center of the hot grate, over the drip pan and away from the heat. Cover the grill and cook the turkey until the skin is nicely browned and the meat is cooked through, 2¼ to 2¾ hours. To check for doneness, insert an instant-read thermometer in the thickest part of a thigh but not so that it touches the bone. The internal temperature should be about 180°F. (See opposite page for more about testing for doneness.) If the wing tips start to burn, cover them loosely with aluminum foil; if the skin starts to brown

TIPS

This recipe calls for the turkey to be injected with bourbon-spiced broth. The oversize syringe used to do this is available at cookware shops, or see Mail-Order Sources on page 742. By the way, it will make you look like a mad scientist. The injector sauce also reduces the turkey's tendency to dry out.

too much, cover the bird loosely with aluminum foil. If using a charcoal grill, every hour you'll need to add 12 fresh coals and ½ cup wood chips or chunks to each side.

6 Transfer the grilled turkey to a platter, cover it loosely with aluminum foil, if you have not already done so, and let it rest for 10 minutes. Untruss the turkey, if necessary, carve, and serve.

YIELD:

Serves 8 to 10

Cajun Rub

Originally used for pan blackening, this pungent spice mix will lend Cajun character to just about any dish you cook on the grill. You'll have more than you need for the Big Easy Barbecued Turkey, but it's sure not to go to waste.

INGREDIENTS:

¼ **cup coarse salt (kosher or sea)**
3 **tablespoons sweet paprika**
2 **tablespoons garlic powder**
2 **tablespoons onion powder**
2 **tablespoons dried thyme**
    (preferably ground)
2 **tablespoons dried oregano**
1 **tablespoon freshly ground**
    black pepper
1 **tablespoon freshly ground**
    white pepper
2 **teaspoons ground dried sage**
    leaves
2 **teaspoons cayenne pepper**

Combine the salt, paprika, garlic and onion powders, thyme, oregano, black pepper, white pepper, sage, and cayenne in a small bowl and whisk to mix or place in a jar, cover it, and shake to mix. Store the rub in an airtight jar away from heat and light; it will keep for at least 1 year.

YIELD:

Makes about 1 cup

Boston, Mass.

COFFEE MOLASSES TURKEY

All too often today, what passes for smoked turkey breast in the deli case is actually a horrid concoction of chopped turkey, water, gelatin, and synthetic flavorings. I say it's high time to resurrect the real thing—a meaty breast that's carved off the bone and has true turkey texture and flavor. Smoking a turkey breast is quicker and easier than you might think, and it can be done on the simplest of grills. The basic procedure is to brine the turkey breast overnight, then grill it indirectly, using plenty of wood chips for smoke. Sliced hot or cold, it's terrific for sandwiches.

Not long ago, I dined in a restaurant located in a former Boston molasses warehouse, and it reminded me of how important this robust sweetener was in nineteenth-century New England. So, the turkey breast here is flavored with a molasses and coffee brine. When you cut into it, you'll know you've done the brotherhood of barbecue proud.

METHOD:
Indirect grilling

ADVANCE PREPARATION:
16 to 24 hours for brining the turkey

FOR THE BRINE:
½ cup hot espresso
½ cup molasses
6 tablespoons coarse salt
(kosher or sea)
3 tablespoons Dijon mustard
1 tablespoon black peppercorns

FOR THE TURKEY:
1 bone-in turkey breast
(about 5 pounds)
Espresso Barbecue Sauce
(optional; page 251),
for serving

YOU'LL ALSO NEED:
1 cup wood chips or chunks
(preferably sassafras or another
fragrant wood, such as hickory),
soaked for 1 hour in water to cover,
then drained

1 MAKE THE BRINE: Combine the espresso, molasses, salt, mustard, and peppercorns with 6 cups of water in a large bowl and whisk until the salt dissolves. Let the mixture cool to room temperature.

2 Rinse the turkey breast under cold running water, then drain and blot dry with paper towels. Lay the turkey breast, skin side down, on a cutting board. Cut out the breastbone and cut the breast in half. Using poultry shears or a large knife, trim off and discard any ribs, flaps of skin, or excess fat. Place the turkey breast halves in a large heavy-duty resealable plastic bag and add the brine. Seal the bag and place it in a large deep bowl in the refrigerator. Let the turkey breast brine for 16 to 24 hours.

TIPS

You can buy turkey breasts that weigh anywhere from four to ten pounds. I find that five pounds is just large enough to be worth the effort and just small enough to be tender.

3 Set up the grill for indirect grilling (see page 23 for gas or page 22 for charcoal) and preheat to medium. If using a gas grill, place all of the wood chips or chunks in the smoker box or in a smoker pouch (see page 24) and run the grill on high until you see smoke, then reduce the heat to medium. If using a charcoal grill, place a large drip pan in the center, preheat the grill to medium, then toss all of the wood chips or chunks on the coals.

4 When ready to cook, drain the brine from the turkey and discard the brine. Place the turkey breast halves, skin side up, in the center of the hot grate, over the drip pan and away from the heat. Cover the grill and cook the turkey until cooked through, 1¼ to 1½ hours. To test for doneness, use an instant-read meat thermometer: The internal temperature should be about 170°F. (See page 418 for more about testing for doneness.) If using a charcoal grill, after 1 hour you'll need to add 12 fresh coals to each side.

5 Transfer the grilled turkey breast halves to a cutting board and let them rest for 5 to 10 minutes. Carve hot or let cool to room temperature, then refrigerate until serving. If you like, serve the smoked turkey with the Espresso Molasses Barbecue Sauce.

YIELD:
Serves 8 to 10

Napa Valley, Calif.

MAYONNAISE BARBECUED TURKEY

Thomas Keller, owner of The French Laundry in the Napa Valley, is one of the top chefs in the United States—possibly the world. Imagine my surprise when, a few years ago, I asked him what he was preparing for Thanksgiving, and was told turkey breast roasted in mayonnaise. "My mother was in the restaurant business, so Thanksgivings were always rushed," Keller recalls. "She'd slather a turkey breast with mayonnaise and roast it in the oven." This is one instance where haste produces great results, because the mayonnaise keeps what is usually the driest part of the turkey incredibly moist, tender, and flavorful (Keller's mother used Hellmann's, but he would probably favor homemade). I recently tried cooking Keller's turkey breast on the grill, using the indirect method to give it a subtle smoke flavor. It's the kind of dish that has barbecue written all over it despite its classical source.

METHOD:
Indirect grilling

INGREDIENTS:
1 large, boneless half turkey breast (2½ to 3 pounds)

2 teaspoons poultry seasoning

**2 teaspoons coarse salt
    (kosher or sea)**

½ teaspoon freshly ground black pepper

**1½ to 2 cups mayonnaise
    (preferably homemade)**

**Hellfire Cranberry Salsa
    (optional; page 686),
    for serving**

YOU'LL ALSO NEED:

**2 cups wood chips or chunks
    (preferably apple, cherry, or
    another fruit wood), soaked for
    1 hour in water to cover, then
    drained; wire rack; aluminum
    foil drip pan**

1 Pull the skin off the turkey breast, using a paring knife. Trim off and discard any excess fat from the breast. Rinse the breast under cold running water, then drain and blot dry with paper towels.

2 In a small bowl, mix together the poultry seasoning, salt, and pepper. Generously season the breast on both sides with this rub. Turn the breast so that what was the skin side is facing down. Spread this side with ½ cup of the mayonnaise. Turn the breast over, place it on a wire rack, and spread the other side with enough mayonnaise to make an even ½-inch-thick layer (the best tool for spreading mayonnaise is a palate knife).

3 Set up the grill for indirect grilling (see page 23 for gas or page 22 for charcoal) and preheat to medium. If using a gas grill, place all of the wood chips or chunks in the smoker box or in

Thomas Keller of the celebrated French Laundry gives you an excuse to fire up the grill.

a smoker pouch (see page 24) and run the grill on high until you see smoke, then reduce the heat to medium. If using a charcoal grill, place a large drip pan in the center, preheat the grill to medium, then toss all of the wood chips or chunks on the coals.

4 When ready to cook, place the turkey breast, still on its rack, in the center of the hot grate, over the drip pan and away from the heat. Cover the grill and cook the turkey until cooked through, 1 to 1¼ hours (the coating will turn quite black and there will be quite a bit of oil in the drip pan). To test for

TIPS

■ According to Thomas Keller, this recipe works best with a half turkey breast laid flat on the grill. The mayonnaise will not adhere properly to a whole breast, which is too rounded. The half breast makes the perfect amount for a small group, say four to six people. For larger gatherings, simply cook two half breasts.

■ The rub is my contribution to the recipe—for the Keller family version, use only salt and pepper to season the breast.

doneness, use an instant-read meat thermometer: The internal temperature should be about 170°F. (See page 418 for more about testing for doneness.)

5 Transfer the grilled turkey breast to a platter and let rest for 5 to 10 minutes. Slice crosswise and serve with Hellfire Cranberry Salsa, if desired.

YIELD:
Serves 4 to 6

Vermont

MAPLE-SMOKED TURKEY BREAST

Here's a Vermont twist on the perennial favorite, smoked turkey breast. The recipe packs a triple whammy of maple flavor: first from the maple sugar used in the rub, then from the maple syrup used for basting, finally from the maple chips that provide the smoke (after all, the Green Mountain State is America's maple sugar and syrup capital).

METHOD:
Indirect grilling

ADVANCE PREPARATION:
12 hours for curing the turkey

FOR THE RUB AND THE TURKEY:
2 tablespoons maple sugar or light brown sugar
1 tablespoon sweet paprika
2 teaspoons freshly ground black pepper
1 teaspoon coarse salt (kosher or sea)
1 teaspoon celery salt
1 teaspoon garlic powder
1 teaspoon onion powder
½ teaspoon cayenne pepper
½ teaspoon dry mustard
1 bone-in turkey breast (about 5 pounds)

FOR THE MAPLE BUTTER BASTING MIXTURE:
¼ cup maple syrup
4 tablespoons (½ stick) salted butter, melted

YOU'LL ALSO NEED:
Poultry shears; 2 cups wood chips or chunks (preferably maple), soaked for 1 hour in cold water to cover, then drained

1 MAKE THE RUB: Place the maple sugar, paprika, black pepper, coarse salt, celery salt, garlic and onion powders, cayenne, and mustard in a small bowl stir to mix. (Actually, if you don't have sensitive skin, your fingers work better for mixing a rub than a spoon or whisk does.)

2 Rinse the turkey breast under cold running water, then drain and blot dry with paper towels. Using poultry shears or a large knife, cut out the ribs so the turkey breast lies flat. Trim off and discard any excess fat. Sprinkle the rub over the turkey on all sides, patting it onto the meat with your fingertips. Place the breast in a covered bowl or resealable plastic bag and let cure overnight in the refrigerator.

3 MAKE THE BASTING MIXTURE: Combine the maple syrup and melted butter in a small saucepan.

4 Set the grill up for indirect grilling (see page 23 for gas or page 22 for charcoal) and preheat to medium. If using a gas grill, place all of the wood chips or chunks in the smoker box or in a smoker pouch (see page 24) and run the grill on high until you see smoke, then reduce the heat to medium. If using a charcoal grill, place a large drip pan in the center, preheat the grill to medium, then toss all of the wood chips or chunks on the coals.

5 When ready to cook, place the turkey breast in the center of the hot grate, over the drip pan and away from the heat. Cover the grill and cook the turkey until cooked through, 1¼ to 1½ hours. To test for doneness, use an instant-read meat thermometer: The internal temperature should be about 170°F degrees. (See page 418 for more about testing for doneness.) After 45 minutes, brush the turkey breast with some of the maple butter basting mixture. Baste the turkey 2 or 3 more times with the maple butter. If using a charcoal grill, after 1 hour you'll need to add 12 fresh coals to each side.

6 Transfer the grilled turkey breast to a cutting board and let it rest for 5 to 10 minutes, then carve. Or refrigerate the turkey until completely chilled and serve it cold.

YIELD:
Serves 8 to 10

VARIATION: While I call for a turkey breast here, you could certainly smoke a whole turkey the same way. For a 10-pound turkey, you'd need a double batch of the rub and basting mixture. The cooking time would be 2½ to 3 hours.

Maple sugar is available at natural foods stores. See Mail-Order Sources (page 742) for maple wood chips.

Tapping sap to make maple syrup— appropriately, the traditional syrup boiler is wood fired.

TIPS

■ Duck breasts are the New York strip steaks of poultry, featuring a rich, dark red meat that's delectable grilled. (Speaking of New York strip, beef is fantastic prepared this way.) Duck breasts are available from specialty butchers and gourmet shops and by mail order from companies like D'Artagnan (see Mail-Order Sources, page 742).

■ Duck skin is quite fatty and thus highly prone to burning. Don't crowd the grill, so you can move the breasts if you get flare-ups. As another precaution, you might want to place an aluminum foil shield on the grill (fold an 18-inch-long piece of foil over three times). If the breasts start to burn, place them on the shield.

Hartford, Conn.

GRILLED DUCK BREASTS
With Vietnamese Seasonings

Connecticut is probably not the first destination you'd think of for great Vietnamese cooking. But going to Hartford without visiting Truc Orient Express would be to miss some of the best Southeast Asian food in New England. Truc owner and chef Bình Duong immigrated to the United States when he was fourteen years old, and he painstakingly re-creates the dishes of his childhood, using the ingredients of his adopted state (he chronicled these dishes in his award-winning cookbook, *Simple Art of Vietnamese Cooking*). When I asked him for a recipe for this book, he obliged with a grilled duck breast that epitomizes the Vietnamese flair for creating complex flavors with just a few simple ingredients—virtually every Vietnamese barbecue recipe features the sweet-salty-sour dialectic of sugar, fish sauce, and lemon or lime juice. Bình's contribution to a classic is the aromatic addition of fried garlic, shallots, and hot peppers.

METHOD:
Direct grilling

ADVANCE PREPARATION:
2 hours for marinating the duck

FOR THE DUCK AND MARINADE:
4 duck breasts (each about 8 ounces)
½ cup fish sauce (see Note)
½ cup fresh lemon juice
¼ cup sugar
3 cloves garlic, peeled and gently crushed with the side of a cleaver
½ teaspoon freshly ground black pepper

FOR THE GARNISH:
1 cup vegetable oil
12 cloves garlic, thinly sliced
4 shallots, thinly sliced
4 to 8 serrano, jalapeño, or other hot peppers, thinly sliced

1 Trim any excess skin off the duck breasts (leave on just enough to cover the top of each breast). Rinse the breasts under cold running water, then drain and blot dry with paper towels. Using a very sharp knife, score the duck skin in a lattice pattern, cutting through the skin but not through the flesh. The cuts should be spaced about every ¼ inch (scoring helps render the duck fat).

2 MAKE THE MARINADE: Combine the fish sauce, lemon juice, sugar, garlic, and black pepper in a large non-reactive mixing bowl and whisk until the sugar dissolves. Add the duck breasts to the marinade, cover, and let marinate for 2 hours in the refrigerator, turning them several times so that they marinate evenly.

3 MAKE THE GARNISH: Heat the oil to 350°F in a small frying pan over medium heat. Fry the sliced garlic until golden brown, 30 to 60 seconds. Using a metal skimmer, transfer the fried garlic to paper towels to drain. Then fry the shallots until golden brown and the serranos until lightly browned, 1 to 2 minutes. Transfer to paper towels to drain. The recipe can be prepared to this stage up to 3 hours ahead.

4 Set up the grill for direct grilling using a three-zone fire (see page 21 for charcoal or gas) and preheat one zone to medium-high and one zone to medium; leave the third zone unlit.

5 When ready to cook, brush and oil the grill grate. Place the duck breasts over the medium-high zone of the grill, skin side down, and spoon the remaining marinade over them. Cook the breasts until the skin is crisp and nicely browned, 4 to 6 minutes. You'll need to move the breasts to the medium zone and even to the unlit one as they grill since the melting fat will cause flare-ups. Turn the breasts over and grill on the other side until cooked to taste, 2 to 3 minutes for medium. To test for doneness, poke a breast in the thickest part with your finger; it should feel gently yielding when the duck is cooked to medium-rare.

6 Transfer the grilled duck breasts to a platter or plates and sprinkle the fried garlic, shallots, and serranos on top. Serve at once. For a fancier presentation, you can thinly slice the duck breasts and fan out the slices.

YIELD:
Serves 4

Miami, Fla.

CHIMICHURRI GAME HENS

You may think of *chimichurri,* the explosively flavorful garlic, parsley, and olive oil sauce that accompanies grilled meats from Managua to Buenos Aires as an Argentinean steak sauce, but I first sampled it at the Nicaraguan restaurant Los Ranchos,

Chimichurri **is customarily served with beef, but it's terrific with grilled poultry, as you'll soon see. I've jazzed up the traditional recipe, adding cilantro and jalapeño peppers.**

Latino-inspired street parades are a common sight in Miami.

TIPS

The game hens here are spatchcocked: The backbones are removed, so you can open the birds flat like a book. This enables you to grill them whole using the direct method. You could also cook chicken in this fashion or, if you don't want to take the time to spatchcock, use skinless, boneless chicken breasts.

in Miami. Here the *chimichurri* is used both as a marinade and a sauce.

METHOD:
Direct grilling

ADVANCE PREPARATION:
1 to 4 hours for marinating the game hens

FOR THE GAME HENS AND RUB:
4 game hens (each about 1 pound)
1½ teaspoons coarse salt (kosher or sea)
1½ teaspoons freshly ground black pepper
1½ teaspoons ground cumin
1½ teaspoons dried oregano
1½ teaspoons hot red pepper flakes
2 tablespoons extra-virgin olive oil

FOR THE CHIMICHURRI AND GARNISH:
¾ cup rinsed, stemmed, and coarsely chopped fresh flat-leaf parsley
¾ cup rinsed, stemmed, and coarsely chopped fresh cilantro
6 cloves garlic, coarsely chopped
1 to 3 jalapeño peppers, seeded and coarsely chopped (for a hotter chimichurri, leave the seeds in)
½ cup white wine vinegar, or more to taste
2 teaspoons coarse salt (kosher or sea), or more to taste
1 teaspoon freshly ground black pepper
1½ cups extra-virgin olive oil

1 luscious, ripe red tomato (optional), seeded and diced

YOU'LL ALSO NEED:
Poultry shears; 2 cups wood chips or chunks (optional; preferably oak), soaked for 1 hour in water to cover, then drained

1 Remove the packet of giblets (if any) from the body cavities of the game hens and set aside for making stock or another use. Remove and discard the fat just inside the body and neck cavities. Rinse the hens, inside and out, under cold running water, then drain and blot dry, inside and out, with paper towels.

2 Spatchcock the game hens: Place a hen on its breast. Using poultry shears and starting at the neck end, cut out the backbone by making one lengthwise cut on either side of the bone. Remove and discard the backbone or set aside for making stock or another use. Open the game hen like a book, skin side down. Use a paring knife to cut along each side of the breastbone. Run your thumbs firmly along both sides of the breastbone and white cartilage, then pull these out. Cut off the wing tips and trim off any loose skin. If you are feeling ambitious, turn the bird over (skin side up) and lay it out flat. Make a 1-inch slit in the rear portion of each side of the hen. Reach under the bird and pull the end of each drumstick through the nearest slit to secure it. Spatchcock the remaining game hens the same way. Place the spatchcocked hens in a nonreactive baking dish.

3 MAKE THE RUB: Place the salt, black pepper, cumin, oregano, and hot red pepper flakes in a small bowl and stir to mix. (Actually, your fingers work better for mixing a rub than a spoon or whisk does.) Sprinkle this rub all over the hens on both sides, dividing it evenly among them. Drizzle the olive oil over the hens, patting it onto the meat with your fingertips. Let the game hens cure while you make the *chimichurri*.

4 MAKE THE *CHIMICHURRI*: Place the parsley, cilantro, garlic, and jalapeño(s) in a food processor and finely chop. Add the vinegar, salt, and black pepper and process to mix. Add the olive oil and ½ cup of water in a thin stream with the machine running; the *chimichurri* should have the consistency of a thin, pourable pesto. Taste for seasoning, adding more salt and/or vinegar as necessary; the *chimichurri* should be highly seasoned. Pour half of the *chimichurri* over the game hens, turning the birds to coat both sides. Let the hens marinate in the refrigerator, covered, for 2 to 4 hours, turning them once or twice so they marinate evenly. Set the remaining *chimichurri* aside.

5 Set up the grill for direct grilling (see page 21 for gas or charcoal) and preheat to medium. If using a gas grill, place all of the wood chips or chunks, if desired, in the smoker box or in a smoker pouch (see page 24) and run the grill on high until you see smoke, then reduce the heat to medium. If using a charcoal grill, preheat it to medium, then toss all of the wood chips or chunks, if desired, on the coals.

6 When ready to cook, drain the marinade from the hens and discard it. Brush and oil the grill grate. Arrange the hens on the hot grate, skin side down and on a diagonal to the bars. Grill the hens until cooked through, 10 to 14 minutes per side, rotating each hen a quarter turn after 5

minutes to create an attractive cross-hatch of grill marks. Turn the hens over when they are golden brown on the bottom. To test for doneness, use an instant-read meat thermometer: Insert it into the thickest part of a thigh but not so that it touches the bone. The internal temperature should be about 180°F.

7 To serve, spoon the remaining *chimichurri* over the bottom of a platter or plates. Place the grilled hens on top and garnish with the diced tomato, if desired.

YIELD:
Serves 4

Miami, Fla.

QUAIL "LITTLE HAVANA"

Just when I think I know the extent of my recipe tester Elida Proenza's culinary repertory, she comes up with some new treasure. Elida found a package of quail in the refrigerator and set to work making "a little something" in her corner of the kitchen. Her delicious quail contrast the smoky char of the fire with the sweetness of a currant and nut stuffing. I've named the dish after the epicenter of Miami's Cuban American community, Little Havana.

COZY CORNER

COZY CORNER

745 North Parkway (at Manassas)
Memphis, Tennessee
(901) 527-9158

In a state that swears by pork, in a city that swears by ribs, the Cozy Corner is an anomaly. The house specialty is that Johnny-come-lately to the American barbecue belt: chicken. And it's not even a proper full-size one. It's a pint-size game hen. But before you decide to take your business elsewhere, let me tell you that this is about the best game hen you'll ever taste—smoky without being overpowering; tender without being soft; spicy, but not so highly seasoned that you can't taste the sweet, mild meat. In short, everything a barbecued game hen should be. And its extraordinary flavor is all the more remarkable for the fact that the pit is fired with charcoal, not wood.

Cozy Corner founder Raymond Robinson. His family carries on the tradition.

The Cozy Corner was the brainchild of Raymond Robinson, an electrician turned pit master, who opened the forty-six-seat restaurant in 1977. His interest in barbecue was originally an issue of self defense. Prior to the Cozy Corner, he worked in Denver. "You couldn't get decent barbecue in Colorado, so I started making my own," he noted. He decided to make it his full-time profession in Memphis.

Robinson built a glassed-in pit next to the restaurant's entrance (you walk by it on the way to the dining room). It was and is a no-nonsense setting, but the public liked what it tasted, and the Cozy Corner has steadily attracted a loyal clientele over the years, including notables such as Danny DeVito and Robert Duvall.

Robinson passed away a few years ago, but his wife, Desiree, daughter Val, and son Ray Jr. carry on the tradition. The menu hasn't changed since the restaurant opened. The plate-burying ribs still come wet or dry; the barbecue spaghetti and barbecued bologna still to stick to your ribs. As for the game hens, well, they remain exemplars of their kind—and living proof that pork's not the only barbecue in Memphis.

The Cozy Corner—one of the best kept barbecue secrets in Memphis—is secret no more.

METHOD:
Indirect grilling

FOR THE STUFFING:

⅔ cup Valencia or Arborio rice

2 tablespoons butter or olive oil

1 small onion, finely chopped

1 clove garlic, minced

3 tablespoons coarsely chopped
  slivered almonds

3 tablespoons coarsely chopped walnuts

¼ cup currants or yellow raisins

3 tablespoons chopped fresh flat-leaf
  parsley

¼ cup dry white wine

1 teaspoon grated lemon zest

¼ cup grated white cheddar cheese
  (mild or medium)

Coarse salt (kosher or sea) and
  freshly ground black pepper

FOR THE QUAIL:

8 quail (about 2 pounds total)

Coarse salt (kosher or sea) and
  freshly ground black pepper

4 slices bacon, cut in half crosswise

YOU'LL ALSO NEED:

Butcher's string; 1 cup wood chips or
  chunks (preferably oak), soaked for
  1 hour in water to cover, then drained

1 MAKE THE STUFFING: Place the rice in a bowl, cover with 2 cups of cold water, and let soak until tender, about 1 hour. Drain well in a strainer.

2 Melt the butter in a nonstick frying pan over medium heat. Add the onion, garlic, almonds, and walnuts and cook until the mixture is just beginning to brown, about 5 minutes. Add the soaked rice, currants, parsley, wine,

and lemon zest and cook until the wine is completely evaporated, about 5 minutes more. Remove the pan from the heat and let the stuffing cool to room temperature. Stir in the cheddar and season with salt and pepper to taste.

3 Remove the wire frames from the quail, if necessary. Rinse the quail under cold running water, then drain and blot dry with paper towels. Season the quail inside and out with salt and pepper. Spoon some of the stuffing into each bird, packing it in quite tightly. Place a strip of bacon over the breast of each quail and tie it in place with butcher's string.

4 Set up the grill for indirect grilling (see page 23 for gas or page 22 for charcoal) and preheat to medium. If using a gas grill, place all of the wood chips or chunks in the smoker box or in a smoker pouch (see page 24) and run the grill on high until you see smoke, then reduce the heat to medium. If using a charcoal grill, place a drip pan in the center, preheat the grill to medium, then toss all of the wood chips or chunks on the coals.

5 When ready to cook, place the quail in the center of the hot grate, over the drip pan and away from the heat. Cover the grill and cook the quail until golden brown on the outside and cooked through, 25 to 35 minutes. Transfer the quail to a platter or plates, remove the strings, and serve at once.

YIELD:
Serves 8 as an appetizer, or 4 as a
  main course

T I P S

■ **These days, most quail are sold partially boned with a wire frame to hold them flat. This makes stuffing and grilling a snap.**

■ **Elida uses short-grain Valencia rice; you could also use Italian Arborio or a short-grain rice from Japan.**

Flame-Seared

When I was young we grilled almost nightly, but we didn't grill fish and no one we knew grilled it either. Today tuna seared in the flames rivals steak in popularity at many restaurants, and grilling and smoking are considered two of the best ways there are to cook fish. This will come as no surprise to people in Washington State, who have smoke-roasted salmon with blazing alder the American Indian way for hundreds of years. Nor will it surprise Asian-inspired Hawaiian grill masters, who char tuna with rice powder; Connecticut fisher folk, who roast shad on oak planks; or Montana sportsmen, who grill bacon-wrapped trout over campfires.

This chapter celebrates grilled fish in all its smoky glory, from sardines that are grilled in grape leaves to a "London broil" of tuna to a Louisiana-style grill-blackened redfish. When it comes to cooking fish, you can't beat live fire.

Bolinas, Calif.

MARTHA'S WEDDING SALMON

My cousin Martha married Steve Wade on a bluff overlooking the Pacific Ocean in the town of Bolinas, north of San Francisco. Everything about the wedding dazzled, including the spectacular setting and the mammoth grill from which the wedding feast was served. For the main course, Martha and Steve chose whole salmon that had been stuffed with herbs, basted with butter, and grilled wrapped in aluminum foil. The virtues of this method are many: A whole fish makes a show-stopping centerpiece, while the foil seals in flavor and moistness and makes the fish easy to turn. I like to open up the foil wrapping during the last twenty or so minutes of grilling to allow some of the fire and smoke flavors to reach the fish.

METHOD:
Direct grilling in aluminum foil

INGREDIENTS:
1 whole salmon, head removed
    (8 to 10 pounds)
Coarse salt (kosher or sea) and
    freshly ground black pepper
12 tablespoons (1½ sticks) butter,
    at room temperature
2 lemons
1 large bunch fresh basil, rinsed,
    shaken dry, and stemmed
    (for about 2 cups packed leaves)
3 cloves garlic, crushed with the side
    of a cleaver
Basil Aioli (recipe follows) or
    mayonnaise for serving

YOU'LL ALSO NEED:
Heavy-duty aluminum foil

1 Rinse the salmon, inside and out, under cold running water and blot it dry, inside and out, with paper towels. Generously season the fish all over with salt and pepper. Rub 4 tablespoons of the butter inside the cavity and where the head was removed. Thinly slice half of 1 lemon; juice the remaining half and the second lemon; you'll have ¼ to ⅓ cup of juice. Sprinkle a tablespoon or so of the lemon juice

I find barbecue everywhere—even at my cousin Martha's wedding to Steve.

inside the cavity, then add the lemon slices, basil, and garlic. Spread 4 tablespoons of the remaining butter onto one side of the fish and season again with salt and pepper.

2 Spread a large piece of heavy-duty aluminum foil on your work surface. The piece of foil should be more than twice as long as the fish. Place the salmon, lengthwise and buttered side down, in the center of the piece of aluminum foil so that it is parallel to the long side of the foil. Spread the remaining 4 tablespoons of butter on top of the fish and season it with more salt and pepper. Fold up the edges of the foil to hold in the liquid, then pour the remaining lemon juice over the fish.

3 Fold the short ends of the foil over the fish and crimp them together. Then crimp the edges of the two long sides together to fully seal the packet. The salmon can be prepared to this stage several hours ahead and refrigerated.

4 Set up the grill for direct grilling (see page 21 for charcoal or gas) and preheat to medium.

5 When ready to cook, place the foil-wrapped salmon on the hot grate. Grill for 30 minutes, then turn the packet over. Using a paring knife, cut open the top piece of foil over the fish (wear oven mitts when you open the foil to protect your hands from the escaping steam). Continue grilling the fish until it is cooked, 20 to 30 minutes longer, basting the fish with the juices

that collect at the bottom of the foil (use a spoon to scoop up the juices). To test for doneness, insert a slender metal skewer into the thickest part of the fish away from the bone for 20 seconds: When it is done, the skewer should come out very hot to the touch. You can also test for doneness by making a slit in the back of the fish; the flesh near the bone should be cooked through; if it is, it will be opaque, not translucent.

6 Serve the salmon in the aluminum foil packet or transfer it to a large platter. To carve, run a knife horizontally along the backbone to separate the top fillet. Cut straight down through the top layer of fish and lift it off the bones in serving portions. Use a fork or spatula to pry out the bones, then cut the remaining fish into serving portions. Serve the Basil Aioli on the side.

YIELD:
Serves about 16

TIPS

Your local fish market or supermarket should be able to get you a whole salmon; just keep in mind that you'll need to order it a few days ahead of time.

Basil Aioli

Aioli is Provençal garlic mayonnaise, but contemporary American chefs have used it as a springboard for all sorts of sauces and condiments. Here's a fragrant basil version that goes great with salmon. It couldn't be easier to make, too, as you start with commercial mayonnaise.

INGREDIENTS:

24 fresh basil leaves, rinsed and blotted dry
4 cups mayonnaise (preferably Hellmann's)
4 to 6 cloves garlic, minced (see Note)
1/3 to 1/2 cup lemon juice
Freshly ground white pepper

1 Stack the basil leaves atop one another and roll them into a tight tube. Thinly slice the basil tube cross-wise to obtain the hair-thin slivers called chiffonade.

2 Place the mayonnaise in a mixing bowl and stir in the garlic, basil slivers, and lemon juice. Season with pepper to taste. The sauce can be refrigerated, covered, for up to 4 days, but tastes best served the same day it's made.

YIELD:

Makes 4½ cups

NOTE: Be sure the garlic is minced really, really fine. I'm not normally a partisan of garlic presses, but this is a good occasion to use one.

Topeka, Kans.

HARVEY HOUSE SALMON

Fred Harvey may not be remembered like Kit Carson, Wyatt Earp, or Wild Bill Hickok, but when it

How the West was won: Fred Harvey's dining rooms set new standards for cleanliness.

came to taming the West, few men had more impact. No, he wasn't a gunslinger or sheriff—his arms were skillet and cutlery. In 1876, Harvey joined forces with the Atchison, Topeka & Santa Fe Railroad to launch the Harvey Houses, a chain of train depot restaurants, starting with one in Topeka. For the first time since the West was opened by the railroads, travelers could count on finding wholesome food served by well-mannered waitresses in clean, well-lighted dining rooms. This may not sound like much of an accomplishment today, but prior to Harvey, Wild West eateries were nearly as deadly as bandits. To staff his eating houses, Harvey hired respectable young women from the East and Midwest, and the growing legions of "Harvey Girls" had as much civilizing effect on the West as the six-shooter.

To experience the sort of simple, wholesome, solidly American food

served at Harvey restaurants, try this grilled salmon, adapted from *From Hardtack to Home Fries* by Barbara Haber.

METHOD:
Direct grilling

ADVANCE PREPARATION:
4 to 12 hours for curing the salmon

INGREDIENTS:
**4 salmon steaks (each 1 inch thick
     and 6 to 8 ounces)**
¼ cup finely chopped fresh dill
2 tablespoons coarse salt (kosher or sea)
2 tablespoons sugar
**½ teaspoon freshly ground black
     or white pepper**
Lemon wedges, for serving

1 Rinse the salmon steaks under cold running water, then blot dry with paper towels. Place the salmon in a non-reactive roasting pan. Combine the dill, salt, sugar, and pepper in a bowl and stir to mix. Sprinkle half of the dill mixture on top of the salmon steaks, pressing it onto the fish with your fingertips. Turn over the salmon, then sprinkle the remaining dill mixture on the second side, again pressing it onto the fish with your fingertips. Cover with plastic wrap and let the fish cure in the refrigerator for at least 4 hours or as long as overnight. (The original recipe calls for the fish to be cured for 36 hours, but this is not necessary with today's salmon.)

2 Set up the grill for direct grilling (see page 21 for charcoal or gas) and preheat to high.

3 When ready to cook, brush and oil the grill grate. Arrange the salmon steaks on the hot grate, placing them on a diagonal to the bars. Grill until cooked through, 4 to 6 minutes per side, rotating each steak a quarter turn after 2 minutes on each side to create an attractive cross-hatch of grill marks, if desired. To test for doneness, press the fish with your finger; it should break into clean flakes. Transfer the grilled salmon to a platter or plates and serve at once with lemon wedges.

YIELD:
Serves 4

TIPS

This salmon recipe may seem familiar—even if you've never tasted it—for the ingredients are virtually the same as the Scandinavian dish called gravlax. As with gravlax, the fish is cured, but grilling gives it a whole new dimension. However, you need to use nice thick salmon steaks, as thin fillets would become too salty.

The Harvey Girls helped tame the Wild West.

How to
GRILL FISH

When it comes to bringing out the flavor of seafood, nothing beats the grill. But fish has a nasty tendency to stick to the bars of the grate. It has an equally frustrating habit of going from under-cooked to overcooked in a matter of seconds. All too often seafood comes off the grill burned on the outside and raw in the center. No wonder so many people are intimidated by grilling it.

Well, take heart, because grilling fish isn't difficult at all. The secret is to choose the most appropriate fish, use the right accessories, and above all, remember the cardinal rules of master grilling.

WHAT KIND OF FISH?

Almost any kind and cut of fish can be grilled, from sardines to swordfish, from whole fish to fillets. Steak fish, such as swordfish, tuna, and salmon, are the easiest to grill. Their dense consistency (and, in the case of salmon, high oil content) helps keep them from sticking to the grate and falling apart when you turn them. The most challenging fish to grill are soft fillets, like those of flounder, sole, and bluefish. But, with a little skill and ingenuity, even these can be grilled successfully.

Whole fish, particularly small ones—snapper and trout, for example—are easy to grill if you use the right techniques. To begin with, make a series of parallel slashes all the way to the bone in each, about an inch apart. This lets the heat penetrate to the thickest part of the flesh, ensuring even cooking.

INVEST IN A FISH BASKET

You can buy hinged wire baskets that are designed to hold a fish while exposing the maximum surface area to the fire. To turn the fish you turn

Conscientious basting prevents the fish from sticking and keeps it moist.

the basket. The fish won't stick to the grate, and it doesn't fall apart. Just don't forget to oil the basket (I do this with spray oil). Fish baskets are available for both whole fish or steaks or fillets; look for them at grill shops.

OR A FISH GRATE

Another useful accessory is the fish grate—a wire or perforated metal plate you place on top of the grill grate. The idea behind a fish grate is that it's smoother and flatter

than a conventional grill grate, which makes it a snap to slide a spatula under fish to turn it. The key to using a fish grate is to preheat it on the grill and oil it well before you put on the fish. Fish grates are also available at grill shops.

THE GRILL MEISTER'S MANTRA

The ultimate test of a grill meister's mettle is to grill fish directly on the grill grate. And to do this, you need to keep three things in mind:

KEEP IT HOT. Starting with a hot grill is paramount. The surface sears quickly when the grill is hot, so the fish is less likely to stick. If your fish sticks, chances are you're not cooking on a hot enough enough, grill grate. When the grill is hot enough you shouldn't be able to hold your hand three inches above the grate for longer than two to three seconds.

KEEP IT CLEAN. Scrub the bars of the grate with a long-handled stiff wire grill brush. This indispensable tool is available at any grill shop or hardware store. In a pinch, you can use a piece of crumpled aluminum foil (hold it with your tongs). The important thing is to scrub the bars of the grate to remove any debris to which the fish could stick.

KEEP IT LUBRICATED. Dip a tightly folded paper towel in vegetable oil and, holding it with long-handled tongs, rub it over the bars of the grate. This pre-

Small whole fish are some of the easiest seafood to grill.

The grill grate:
Keep it hot; keep it clean;
keep it lubricated.

vents sticking, of course, and it also helps give you those killer grill marks that are the signature of master grillsmanship.

As a further precaution against sticking, if the recipe doesn't already call for it, lightly oil fillets before grilling them by squirting a little oil in a metal pan and rolling the fish in it to coat both sides. The operational word here is *lightly*—you don't want to over oil the fish or the dripping oil will cause flare-ups. Another way to lubricate the fish is to brush it

with a little oil on both sides, using a basting brush.

TWO LAST TRICKS. As you place a fillet on the grill, gently slide it forward a half inch or so to keep it from sticking. And when it comes time to turn the fish, flip it onto a section of the grate that has been brushed and oiled but has not yet had a piece of fish on top of it.

Grilling fish is really not difficult. If you practice these techniques, you can grill any kind without it sticking.

TIPS

Summer salmon can be made with either salmon fillets or salmon steaks. If you use fillets, cutting them on the diagonal into broad, thin slices will maximize the surface area exposed to the fire. Steaks have the advantage of holding together better on the grill, but of course you wind up with bones and skin.

Edgartown, Mass.

RAICHLEN'S SUMMER SALMON
With a Bunch of Basil

Grilled salmon is a summer tradition at our house, especially after we've been to our local farmers' market in Edgartown, on Martha's Vineyard. We buy bunches—no, veritable bouquets—of fragrant, fresh summer basil. Think of the marinade here as pesto without the pine nuts and cheese. Long on flavor, short on preparation time, a vivid study in emerald green and salmon pink, this is a perfect fish dish for when basil is in season.

METHOD:
Direct grilling

ADVANCE PREPARATION:
30 minutes to 1 hour for marinating the salmon

INGREDIENTS:
4 pieces skinless salmon fillet (each about 6 ounces), or 4 salmon steaks (each about 1 inch thick and 6 to 8 ounces)
1 bunch fresh basil, rinsed and stemmed (for about ½ cup packed leaves; see Notes), coarsely chopped; reserve 4 small basil sprigs for garnish

3 cloves garlic, coarsely chopped
½ cup extra-virgin olive oil
4 strips lemon zest (each about 2 by ½ inch; see Notes)
3 tablespoons fresh lemon juice (from 1 large lemon), or more to taste
1 teaspoon coarse salt (kosher or sea), or more to taste
½ teaspoon freshly ground black pepper

1 If using salmon fillets, run your fingers over them, feeling for bones. Using needle-nose pliers or tweezers, pull out any you find (you will not need to do this with salmon steaks). Rinse the salmon under cold running water, then blot it dry with paper towels. Cut salmon fillets crosswise sharply on the diagonal into ½-inch-thick slices. Place the salmon in a nonreactive baking dish.

2 Place the chopped basil, garlic, olive oil, lemon zest and juice, salt, and pepper in a blender or food processor and purée until smooth (a blender produces a smoother purée than a food processor, but either way the marinade will work). Taste for seasoning, adding more salt and/or lemon juice as necessary. Pour the marinade over the salmon, turning the fish to coat both sides. Let the salmon marinate in the refrigerator, covered, for 30 minutes to 1 hour, turning it once so that it marinates evenly.

3 Set up the grill for direct grilling (see page 21 for charcoal or gas) and preheat to high.

4 When ready to cook, drain the marinade from the salmon and discard the marinade. Brush and oil the grill grate. Arrange the salmon on the hot grate, placing it on a diagonal to the bars. Grill the salmon until cooked through, about 3 minutes per side for fillet slices, 4 to 6 minutes per side for steaks, rotating each piece a quarter turn halfway through grilling on each side to create an attractive crosshatch of grill marks, if desired. To test for doneness, press the fish with your finger; it should break into clean flakes. Transfer the grilled salmon to a platter or plates, garnish with the basil sprigs, and serve at once.

YIELD:
Serves 4

NOTES:

■ To rinse basil, grab it by the stems and immerse the leaves in a large bowl of cold water. Agitate the leaves as though you were cleaning a paint brush. Change the water several times until it remains clean after you have agitated the basil in it. Shake the water off the basil over the sink and remove the leaves from the stems.

■ You can use a vegetable peeler to remove the oil-rich, yellow outer rind of the lemon in strips of zest. Be careful to leave behind the bitter white pith.

Vermont

MAPLE MUSTARD SALMON

Asia bonds with New England here in a sort of salmon teriyaki flavored with maple syrup, honey mustard, and ginger. The inspiration was a trip to Vermont (where I met my wife, incidentally). Maple syrup is a Green Mountain State delicacy, of course, and every February Vermont's snowy woodlands explode with activity as sugar maples are tapped and drained of their sweet sap.

(There's a live fire connection here, too: The traditional Vermont evaporator is wood fired.) As for honey mustard, New Englanders have always loved the combination of sweet and salty flavors that pair so nicely with the region's smoked meats—and with rich, oily seafoods.

METHOD:
Direct grilling

TIPS

■ You needn't use the most expensive grade of maple syrup, called *Fancy*. In fact, I like the rich caramel flavor of a Grade A dark amber or Grade B syrup.

■ To complete the maple theme, I like to toss a handful of maple chips on the coals before grilling (see Mail-Order Sources, page 742), but this isn't essential.

FOR THE MAPLE MUSTARD GLAZE:

²⁄₃ cup maple syrup

¹⁄₂ cup soy sauce

3 tablespoons honey mustard

2 tablespoons butter

1 tablespoon grated peeled fresh ginger
(see Note)

FOR THE SALMON:

4 pieces skinless salmon fillet
(each about 6 ounces), or 4 salmon
steaks (each about 1 inch thick and
6 to 8 ounces)

1 tablespoon Asian (dark) sesame oil
or canola oil

Coarse salt (kosher or sea) and
freshly ground black pepper

YOU'LL ALSO NEED:

1 cup wood chips or chunks (optional;
preferably maple), soaked for 1 hour
in water to cover, then drained

1 MAKE THE MAPLE MUSTARD GLAZE:
Place the maple syrup, soy sauce,
mustard, butter, and ginger in a small
saucepan and bring to a boil over high
heat. Reduce the heat slightly and let the
glaze simmer briskly until syrupy and
slightly reduced, about 5 minutes, skim-
ming off any foam that rises to the surface and stirring from time to time to
keep the glaze from scorching. The glaze
can be refrigerated, covered, for up to
2 days. Warm it, then divide it in half,
setting half aside for basting the fish and
the other half aside for serving.

2 If using salmon fillets, run your
fingers over them, feeling for
bones. Using needle-nose pliers or
tweezers, pull out any you find (you will
not need to do this with salmon steaks).

Rinse the salmon under cold running
water, then blot it dry with paper towels.
Cut salmon fillets crosswise sharply on
the diagonal into 4 even slices. Brush the
salmon on both sides with the sesame oil
and season with salt and pepper.

3 Set up the grill for direct grilling
(see page 21 for gas or charcoal)
and preheat to high. If using a gas grill,
place all of the wood chips or chunks, if
desired, in the smoker box or in a
smoker pouch (see page 24) and run the
grill on high until you see smoke. If using
a charcoal grill, preheat it to high, then
toss all of the wood chips or chunks, if
desired, on the coals.

4 When ready to cook, brush and oil
the grill grate. Place the salmon on
the hot grate and grill it until cooked
through, about 3 minutes per side for the
fillet slices, 4 to 6 minutes per side for
steaks. Baste the salmon as it grills on
both sides with the glaze reserved for
basting. To test for doneness, press the
fish with your finger; it should break into
clean flakes. Transfer the grilled salmon
to a platter or plates and serve at once,
with the remaining glaze spooned over it
or on the side.

YIELD:

Serves 4

NOTE: Use a Microplane, the fine side
of a box grater, or a Japanese ginger
grater to grate the ginger.

VARIATION: This recipe calls for
salmon, but you could use any rich
fish—especially another New England
delicacy: bluefish.

Florida

GUAVA-GRILLED SALMON

T he guava is one of the most beguiling fruits of the tropics: It's green or yellow and egg-shaped, with a perfume so intense, you can smell it when you enter a home or garden. And guavas grow right here in Florida (my home state). Sunshine Staters love its honeyed, floral, musky, and exotic flavor, which has just the right touch of acidity to balance its sweetness. So why isn't it more popular?

Unfortunately, the pink flesh of the guava is riddled with innumerable, rock hard, tiny seeds, and the overall effect of eating one is rather like gobbling a mouthful of buckshot. For this reason, guava is generally enjoyed in the form of jams, jellies, and nectars. Its distinctive taste is great in barbecue sauce, which is what gave me the idea for pairing it with grilled salmon. Thanks to its rich flavor and abundant oils, salmon goes well with a sweet fruity barbecue sauce. The fish gets a double whammy of guava in this recipe—first in the marinade, then in the sauce.

METHOD:
Direct grilling

ADVANCE PREPARATION:
1 hour for marinating the salmon

INGREDIENTS:

4 pieces skinless salmon fillet (each about 6 ounces), or 4 salmon steaks (each about 1 inch thick and 6 to 8 ounces)
Coarse salt (kosher or sea) and freshly ground black pepper
¾ cup guava nectar (see Notes on page 445)
¼ cup extra-virgin olive oil
Guava Barbecue Sauce (recipe follows)

YOU'LL ALSO NEED:

1 cup wood chips or chunks (optional; preferably oak or cherry), soaked for 1 hour in cold water to cover, then drained

1 If using salmon fillets, run your fingers over them, feeling for bones. Using needle-nose pliers or tweezers, pull out any you find (you will not need to do this with salmon steaks). Rinse the salmon under cold running water, then blot it dry with paper towels. Generously season the salmon on both sides with salt and pepper. Arrange the fish in a baking dish and pour the guava nectar and the olive oil over it. Let the salmon marinate in the refrigerator, covered, for 1 hour, turning the fish several times so that it marinates evenly.

2 Set up the grill for direct grilling (see page 21 for gas or charcoal) and preheat to high. If using a gas grill, place all of the wood chips or chunks, if desired, in the smoker box or in a smoker

The musky fragrance of guava is the essence of the tropics.

The fish gets a double whammy of guava . .

pouch (see page 24) and run the grill on high until you see smoke. If using a charcoal grill, preheat it to high, then toss all of the wood chips or chunks on the coals.

3 When ready to cook, drain the marinade from the salmon and discard the marinade. Brush and oil the grill grate. Arrange the salmon on the hot grate, placing it on a diagonal to the bars. Grill the salmon until cooked through, 3 to 5 minutes per side for fillets, 4 to 6 minutes per side for steaks, rotating each steak a quarter turn halfway through grilling on each side to create an attractive crosshatch of grill marks. To test for doneness, press the fish with your finger; it should break into clean flakes. During the last minute of cooking, brush a little barbecue sauce on the fish. Transfer the salmon to a platter or plates and serve at once, with the remaining barbecue sauce spooned over it.

YIELD:
Serves 4

Guava Barbecue Sauce

The sweet, musty flavor of guava epitomizes the tropics. This distinctive guava sauce is delicious on salmon, shrimp, or pork.

INGREDIENTS:

2 cups guava nectar (see Notes)
4 tablespoons (½ stick) unsalted butter
2 tablespoons tomato paste
1 tablespoon fresh lime juice,
    or more to taste
1 teaspoon Worcestershire sauce,
    or more to taste
1 teaspoon balsamic vinegar,
    or more to taste
½ to 1 teaspoon hot sauce (see Notes),
    or more to taste
1 clove garlic, peeled and gently crushed
    with the side of a cleaver
Coarse salt (kosher or sea) and
    freshly ground black pepper

1 Place the guava nectar in a large heavy nonreactive saucepan over medium-high heat and bring to a boil. Let boil until it's reduced to 1 cup, 5 to 8 minutes. Whisk in the butter, tomato paste, lime juice, Worcestershire sauce, vinegar, hot sauce, and garlic. Let the sauce simmer over medium heat until thick and flavorful, about 5 minutes, whisking from time to time.

2 Taste for seasoning, adding salt and pepper to taste and more lime juice, Worcestershire sauce, vinegar, and/or hot sauce as necessary. Using a fork or a slotted spoon, remove and discard the garlic clove. The sauce can be refrigerated, covered, for several days. Reheat it before serving.

YIELD:
Makes about 1½ cups

NOTES:

■ You can find canned guava nectar in many supermarkets and sometimes in liquor stores. Kern's and Goya are both reliable brands. Be sure to shake the cans vigorously before using the nectar.

■ I like to use a Caribbean-style hot sauce flavored with Scotch bonnet chiles, like any of Trinidadian Matouk's varieties.

Seattle, Wash.

ALDER-GRILLED SALMON
With Citrus Butter

Grilling salmon over alder is a Pacific Northwest tradition. It's also the raison d'être for one of Seattle's most colorful restaurants, Ivar's Salmon House. The Ivar in question was Ivar Haglund, a Scandinavian restaurateur who was smitten by the local Squamish Indian way of roasting salmon next to an alder fire. He made the wood-burning pit the focal point of his lakeside restaurant, one of the most popular and picturesque dining spots in Seattle—go on a sunny day and arrive early so you can get a seat on the terrace. (For more about the restaurant see page 447.) Ivar's grilled salmon isn't so much a recipe as a way of life.

METHOD:
Direct grilling

INGREDIENTS:
**4 pieces skinless salmon fillet
    (each about 6 ounces;
        preferably king or coho salmon)
Coarse salt (kosher or sea)
Lemon pepper (see Note)
1 cup Citrus Butter
    (recipe follows)**

YOU'LL ALSO NEED:
**Alder wood chunks or logs for building a
    fire, or 2 cups alder chips or chunks,
    soaked for 1 hour in water to cover,
    then drained**

1 Run your fingers over the salmon fillets, feeling for bones. Using needle-nose pliers or tweezers, pull out any you find. Rinse the salmon under cold running water, then blot it dry with paper towels. Generously season each piece of fish on both sides with salt and lemon pepper.

2 Set up the grill for direct grilling (see page 21 for gas or charcoal) and preheat to high. In the best of all possible worlds, you'd build a fire with alder logs or chunks. If using a gas grill, place all of the wood chips or chunks in the smoker box or in a smoker pouch (see page 24) and run the grill on high until you see smoke. If using a charcoal grill, toss all of the wood chips or chunks on the coals.

3 When ready to cook, brush and generously oil the grill grate. Arrange the salmon fillets on the hot grate, placing them on a diagonal to the

TIPS

Alder is the traditional wood for grilling in the Pacific Northwest. It has a clean, light, distinctive flavor that's terrific with salmon. So, to get the full effect of this recipe, you need to grill the fish over alder (for Mail-Order Sources, see page 742). If you have a charcoal grill, you can build an alder wood fire (see Grilling over a Wood Fire, page 20). Or you can use alder chips to create the proper smoke flavor by tossing them on the coals of a charcoal grill or placing them in the smoker box of a gas grill.

Landing the catch at the port of Seattle.

Ivar's offers three choices for the salmon: fat, rich king salmon; meaty coho; and *keta* (chub salmon), which locals seem to adore, but which I find a trifle dry and fishy.

bars of the grate. Grill the salmon until cooked through, 3 to 5 minutes per side, rotating the fillets a quarter turn after 1½ minutes on each side to create an attractive crosshatch of grill marks. To test for doneness, press the fish with your finger; it should break into clean flakes. Baste the fish with some of the citrus butter as it cooks. Transfer the grilled salmon to a platter or plates and drizzle a little more citrus butter over it; serve at once.

YIELD:

Serves 4

NOTE: Lemon pepper is a popular barbecue seasoning made with dried lemon zest or lemon oil. One widely available brand is Lawry's.

Citrus Butter

A citrus butter is one of the best bastes I know of for seafood. (I've made this one a separate recipe for the precise reason that you'll want to use it for many other dishes.) Cut the amounts in half if you want just enough for the Alder-Grilled Salmon. When you make it, to get the full effect you must use fresh lemon, lime, and orange juice. Clarifying the butter makes it less likely to burn on the grill. Ivar's uses unsalted butter, but I like the additional flavor you get with salted. You'll have enough for 3 pounds of fish.

INGREDIENTS:

1 cup (2 sticks) salted butter
**⅓ cup fresh orange juice
    (from 1 orange)**
**⅓ cup fresh lemon juice
    (from 2 lemons)**
**⅓ cup fresh lime juice
    (from 2 to 3 limes)**
Freshly ground black pepper

1 Clarify the butter: Melt the butter in a heavy saucepan over medium heat, then pour it into a measuring cup and let it cool for a few minutes. Using a spoon, skim off the impurities that rise to the surface. Carefully pour the clear, yellow melted butter into a bowl, leaving behind the milky layer of water and sediment in the bottom of the measuring cup.

2 Stir the orange, lemon, and lime juices into the clarified butter. Season with pepper to taste. The baste can be refrigerated, covered, for several days. Reheat it to melt the butter before using.

YIELD:

Makes about 2 cups

IVAR'S SALMON HOUSE

IVAR'S SALMON HOUSE

401 NE Northlake Way
Seattle, Washington
(206) 632-0767
www.ivarsrestaurants.com

Ivar Haglund was the Damon Runyon of Seattle restaurateurs—charismatic and larger than life. He's still very much a part of the local restaurant scene, even though he's been dead for more than a decade. The restaurants he founded, Ivar's Salmon House, Ivar's Acres of Clams, and Ivar's Mukilteo Landing, are as busy as ever, and at least one, the Salmon House, is a requisite stop on any journey down the barbecue trail in the United States.

Located on Lake Union and modeled on a traditional Squamish Indian longhouse, Ivar's Salmon House boasts a brick fire pit unique in American barbecue. In it local alder logs are burned to glowing embers, over which king, sockeye, *keta* (chub), and other northwestern fish are smokily charred on the grill. What makes the pit so ingenious is the grill grate—actually a series of hinged steel baskets that span the top of the brick fire box. The chef turns the baskets, not the fish inside, which enables him to eliminate a problem that plagues so many fish grillers—the fillets sticking to the grate.

Ivar's pit has another distinctive design feature: The grate stands perhaps 14 or 16 inches above the fire—far enough away so that the fish smokes as well as grills. This combination of smoking and searing gives Ivar's salmon a smoke flavor that's unique.

Of course, most of the thousands of customers served weekly here don't come for these technical achievements. No, they flock to Ivar's because it's fun. In the summer, you can sit on a deck overlooking the boat traffic on Lake Union. Any time of the year, you can enjoy a sensational waterfront view through the dining room's wall of glass and admire a decor of Native American handicrafts, which include a full-size cedar long-racing canoe suspended from the ceiling.

Incidentally, the sepia-colored photos on the walls depict the region's Squamish Indians and their leader and Seattle's namesake, Chief Sealth. Just in case you wondered who *really* invented barbecued salmon.

Ivar's giant totem pole.

TIPS

■ The salmon here is grilled without so much as a marinade to heighten the impact of the sauce. For the very best results, grill the fish over wood (see page 20). As an alternative, you can use wood chips.

■ If you live on the West Coast, try this recipe with king salmon or coho. East Coasters can use Atlantic salmon.

San Francisco, Calif.

GRILLED SALMON
With San Francisco Salsa Verde

San Francisco's love affair with Italian cuisine began shortly after the arrival of the first immigrants from Genoa in the 1850s. It continues to this day, although the descendents of the Italian fisher folk of Fisherman's Wharf have long since traded their nets for fiber-optic networks and microchips. The recipe here, grilled Pacific salmon served with a gossamer sauce of parsley, mint, anchovy, and capers, a variation on the Italo-American sauce *salsa verde,* will easily show why. The color contrast alone— salmon pink against parsley green—is breathtaking, and you'll love the minty piquancy of the sauce.

METHOD:
Direct grilling

FOR THE SALSA VERDE:
½ cup loosely packed fresh flat-leaf parsley sprigs
¼ cup loosely packed fresh mint leaves
1 anchovy fillet, blotted dry (optional)
1 teaspoon drained capers
½ teaspoon grated lemon zest
1 teaspoon fresh lemon juice, or more to taste
½ cup extra-virgin olive oil
3 to 4 tablespoons boiling water
Coarse salt (kosher or sea) and freshly ground black pepper

FOR THE SALMON:
4 pieces skinless salmon fillet (each about 6 ounces), or 4 salmon steaks (each about 1 inch thick and 6 to 8 ounces)
1 to 2 tablespoons extra-virgin olive oil
Coarse salt (kosher or sea) and freshly ground black pepper

FOR SERVING:
4 lemon wedges
4 fresh flat-leaf parsley sprigs

1 MAKE THE *SALSA VERDE:* Place the parsley, mint, anchovy, if using, capers, lemon zest and juice, and olive oil in a blender or food processor and purée to a paste. Add enough boiling

water to form a smooth purée. Taste for seasoning, adding salt and pepper to taste and more lemon juice as necessary; the sauce should be highly seasoned.

2 If using salmon fillets, run your fingers over them, feeling for bones. Using needle-nose pliers or tweezers, pull out any you find (you will not need to do this with salmon steaks). Rinse the salmon under cold running water, then blot it dry with paper towels.

3 Set up the grill for direct grilling (see page 21 for charcoal or gas) and preheat to high.

4 When ready to cook, lightly brush the salmon pieces on both sides with olive oil and season with salt and pepper. Brush and oil the grill grate. Arrange the fillets on the hot grate, placing them on a diagonal to the bars. Grill the salmon until cooked through, 3 to 5 minutes per side for the fillets, 4 to 6 minutes per side for steaks, rotating each piece a quarter turn halfway through grilling on each side to create an attractive crosshatch of grill marks. To test for doneness, press the fish with your finger; it should break into clean flakes.

5 Spoon the *salsa verde* onto a platter or plates. Place the grilled salmon on top and crown each fillet with a lemon wedge and sprig of parsley. Alternatively, spoon the *salsa verde* over the fish. Serve at once.

YIELD:

Serves 4

Pike Place Market sells some of the freshest fish in Seattle.

Seattle, Wash.

SEATTLE SALMON SALAD With Green and Yellow Beans

Everything about this colorful salmon salad, inspired by one served at Seattle's *über*-chic Dahlia Lounge, screams vibrancy— the vivid colors (the shocking orange of the salmon, the earthy greens and yellows of the beans), the smoky succulence of the salmon, and the unexpected nutty flavor of the hazelnut oil and toasted hazelnuts (hazelnuts grow in nearby Lynden).

METHOD:
Direct grilling

ADVANCE PREPARATION:
**30 minutes for marinating
    the salmon**

**FOR THE SALMON
    AND SALAD:**
**4 pieces skinless salmon fillet
    (each about 6 ounces)**
**Coarse salt (kosher or sea) and
    freshly ground black pepper**
2 tablespoons hazelnut oil (see Notes)
8 ounces green beans, trimmed
**8 ounces yellow beans, or more green
    beans, trimmed**
**1 cup teardrop or cherry tomatoes,
    preferably a mix of red and yellow**

FOR THE DRESSING:
1/2 clove garlic
**1/4 cup heavy (whipping) cream
    or crème fraîche**
1 tablespoon Dijon mustard
3 tablespoons hazelnut oil
1 to 2 tablespoons red wine vinegar
**1 tablespoon fresh lemon juice,
    or more taste**
1/2 teaspoon sugar
**2 tablespoons chopped fresh chives
    or scallion greens**
**Coarse salt (kosher or sea) and
    freshly ground black pepper**

FOR GARNISH:
**1/4 cup peeled, toasted, coarsely chopped
    hazelnuts (see the facing page)**
A few chives cut into 1-inch pieces

Dahlia Lounge owner Tom Douglas uses the most noble and robust of Pacific Northwest seafood: king salmon. If you live on the West Coast, you'll have no trouble finding this. East Coasters can substitute Atlantic salmon, which isn't half bad either.

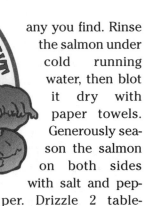

1 Run your fingers over the salmon fillets, feeling for bones. Using needle-nose pliers or tweezers, pull out any you find. Rinse the salmon under cold running water, then blot it dry with paper towels. Generously season the salmon on both sides with salt and pepper. Drizzle 2 tablespoons of the hazelnut oil over both sides of the fish, rubbing it over the fillets with your fingertips. Let the salmon marinate in the refrigerator, covered, for 30 minutes.

2 Bring 4 quarts of water and 2 tablespoons of salt to a rolling boil over high heat. Add the green and yellow beans and cook until crisp-tender, 3 to 5 minutes. Drain in a colander, rinse under cold water until cool, and drain again. Blot the beans dry with paper towels. (See Notes for a grilling alternative.)

3 If using large teardrop or cherry tomatoes, cut them in half. If using baby teardrop tomatoes, leave them whole.

4 MAKE THE DRESSING: Rub the bottom and side of a nonreactive mixing bowl with the cut garlic. Add the cream and mustard and whisk to mix. Gradually whisk in the hazelnut oil, vinegar, lemon juice, sugar, and chopped chives. Taste for seasoning, adding more lemon juice as necessary. Season with salt and pepper to taste; the dressing should be highly seasoned. Place the cooked beans and tomatoes in the bowl with the dressing but don't toss.

5 Set up the grill for direct grilling (see page 21 for charcoal or gas) and preheat to high.

6 When ready to cook, brush and oil the grill grate. Arrange the salmon on the hot grate, placing them on a diagonal to the bars. Grill the salmon until cooked through, 3 to 5 minutes per side for medium, rotating each piece a quarter turn after 1½ minutes on each side to create an attractive crosshatch of grill marks. To test for doneness, press the fish with your finger; it should break into clean flakes.

7 To serve, toss the beans and tomatoes with the dressing. Place the bean salad on a platter or plates and arrange the grilled salmon on top. Sprinkle the chopped hazelnuts and chive pieces on top and serve at once.

YIELD:

Serves 4

NOTES:

■ Hazelnut oil is available at gourmet shops or by mail (see Mail-Order Sources, page 742). In a pinch, you could make your own by frying ¼ cup chopped hazelnuts in 1 cup canola oil. Strain the oil after frying the hazelnuts.

■ If you are really into smoke, you may want to grill the beans rather than boil them, as in Step 2. Use a simple technique I call "rafting." Lay 4 to 6 beans side by side and skewer them crosswise in 2 places with wooden toothpicks. Lightly brush the rafts on both sides with a little hazelnut oil and season them with salt and pepper. Preheat the grill to high, then grill the beans until nicely browned on both sides, 3 to 4 minutes per side. (The beauty of the rafts is that they're easy to turn and they keep the beans from falling through the grate.) Transfer the grilled beans to a platter and let cool, then remove the toothpicks and continue with Step 3 of the recipe.

VARIATION: The salad also makes a great appetizer. Count on it serving 6, so you'll need a half dozen pieces of salmon, each weighing about 4 ounces.

HOW TO TOAST, PEEL, AND CHOP HAZELNUTS

Heat a dry skillet over medium heat (do not use a nonstick skillet for this). Add the hazelnuts and cook until they are aromatic and lightly browned, three to five minutes, shaking the pan to toast them evenly. Transfer the hazelnuts to a large bowl and just as soon as they are cool enough to handle rub them between the palms of your hands to remove the skins (the hotter they are, the easier it will be to do this). You won't be able to get all of the skin off. Don't worry; just remove as much as you can. Let the hazelnuts cool, then coarsely chop them by hand or in a food processor, running the machine in short bursts.

■ For optimal results, you'll want to make this with Alaska salmon, which is widely available in spring and summer on the West Coast and sporadically available in the East. Some of the best comes from the Copper River, and its arrival is heralded with the kind of hype once reserved for Beaujolais Nouveau.

■ Jo Ann Bass uses a hybrid technique to cook the fish—the salmon is grilled using the direct method, but it's set on aluminum foil and the grill is covered. This prevents the fish from sticking and seals in moistness. As you might suspect, I prefer to grill the fish sans foil directly over the fire.

Alaska and Florida

ALASKA SALMON With Brown Sugar and Butter Barbecue Sauce

Can any fish rival Alaska king salmon grilled shortly after it's been caught? Not according to Jo Ann Bass, who as the third-generation owner of Joe's Stone Crab in Miami knows a thing or two about seafood. Jo Ann first tasted this luscious cold-water fish the way God meant it to be prepared—grilled over charcoal in Alaska—and promptly pronounced it the best she had ever eaten. Over the years, she's evolved a barbecue sauce and an Amer-Asian marinade that harmonize beautifully with the rich, fat flesh of the salmon. Here's my take on a dish that has become a bestseller at Joe's.

METHOD:
Direct grilling

ADVANCE PREPARATION:
2 to 4 hours for marinating the salmon

FOR THE SALMON AND MARINADE:
4 pieces salmon fillet (about 6 ounces each; preferably with the skin on; see Notes)
1/4 cup soy sauce
2 tablespoons dry white wine

2 tablespoons sake or sherry
2 tablespoons Worcestershire sauce
2 tablespoons fresh lemon juice
1 to 2 teaspoons Tabasco sauce
3 cloves garlic, minced
2 teaspoons minced peeled fresh ginger (see Notes)
1 teaspoon granulated sugar

FOR THE BROWN SUGAR–BUTTER BARBECUE SAUCE:
8 tablespoons (1 stick) unsalted butter
1/2 cup firmly packed dark brown sugar
2 tablespoons fresh lemon juice
2 tablespoons dry white wine
1 teaspoon Tabasco sauce
1/2 small onion, minced (about 1/4 cup)
1 clove garlic, minced
Coarse salt (kosher or sea) and freshly ground black pepper

Lemon or lime wedges, for serving

YOU'LL ALSO NEED:
2 cups wood chips or chunks (optional; preferably oak or alder), soaked for 1 hour in water to cover, then drained

1 Run your fingers over the flesh side of the salmon fillets, feeling for bones. Using needle-nose pliers or tweezers, pull out any you find. Rinse the salmon under cold running water, then blot it dry with paper towels. Using a sharp paring knife, make 2 or 3 slashes in the skin side of each piece of fish, taking care not to cut all the way through the fillet. Place the fish in a nonreactive baking dish.

2 MAKE THE MARINADE: Place the soy sauce, wine, sake, Worcestershire sauce, lemon juice, Tabasco sauce, garlic, ginger, and granulated sugar in a nonreactive bowl and whisk to mix. Pour the marinade over the salmon, turning the fish to coat on all sides. Let the salmon marinate in the refrigerator, covered, for 2 to 4 hours, turning the fillets once or twice so that they marinate evenly.

3 MAKE THE BROWN SUGAR AND BUTTER BARBECUE SAUCE: Place the butter, brown sugar, lemon juice, wine, Tabasco sauce, onion, and garlic in a heavy nonreactive saucepan and bring to a boil over medium-high heat. Lower the heat to medium and let the sauce simmer until richly flavored and syrupy, 3 to 5 minutes. Season to taste with salt and pepper; the sauce should be highly seasoned. Set the sauce aside.

4 Set up the grill for direct grilling (see page 21 for gas or charcoal) and preheat to high. If using a gas grill, place all of the wood chips or chunks in the smoker box or in a smoker pouch (see page 24) and run the grill on high until you see smoke. If using a charcoal grill, preheat it to high, then toss all of the wood chips or chunks on the coals.

5 When ready to cook, brush and generously oil the grill grate. Arrange the salmon pieces, skin side down, on the hot grate, placing them on a diagonal to the bars. Pour any leftover marinade over the fish. Grill the salmon until cooked through, 3 to 5 minutes per side. To test for doneness, press the fish with your finger; it should break into clean flakes. During the last 2 minutes on each side, baste the salmon with a little of the barbecue sauce.

6 Place the grilled salmon skin side down on a platter or plates and spoon the remaining barbecue sauce on top. Serve with lemon or lime wedges.

YIELD:

Serves 4

NOTES:

■ I like grilled salmon skin. It crisps up like a briny potato chip. It's loaded with flavor and rich in Omega-3 fatty fish oils.

■ Use a Microplane, the fine side of a box grater, or a Japanese ginger grater to grate the ginger.

Pit barbecue Alaska style: salmon grilled over alder.

TILLICUM VILLAGE

TILLICUM VILLAGE

**For information and
reservations, call
(800) 426-1205 or
(206) 933-8600, or visit
www.tillicumvillage.com**

The boat trip from Wharf 55 in downtown Seattle to Blake Island in Puget Sound takes a little less than an hour. But what you see when you arrive will transport you back to a culture that flourished for centuries. Blake Island is the home of Tillicum Village—a cultural center devoted to the arts, architecture, dance, and foods of the Northwest Coast Indians. I hope you're hungry, because you're about to experience one of the most extraordinary manifestations of American barbecue: an authentic Northwest Coast Indian salmon bake.

Actually, the word *bake* is something of a misnomer, as the salmon is roasted on vertical cedar stakes in front of an open fire. Thus, it has more in common with the *barbacoas* of the Arawak Indians in the Caribbean, the planked shad of Connecticut (see page 518), and the early barbecues in Colonial Virginia than with any fish cooked in the oven. This is live-fire cuisine at its finest, and the fragrant scents of alder wood smoke and steaming cedar, magnified in the fresh air, are more potent seasonings than any spices.

Named for the Chinook word for friendly or friendly people, Tillicum Village was the brainchild of a Seattle caterer named Bill Hewitt. The idea was born in 1958, appropriately at a cookout. Hewitt had never before seen a salmon bake, but when he watched a Washington State Fisheries Department employee roast butterflied whole salmon on cedar stakes around a blazing alder wood fire, he instantly grasped the theatrical appeal of this cooking method.

A short time later, Hewitt staged a salmon bake of his own for the Boeing corporation, and the event was so successful, he began looking for a location to build an Indian longhouse–style restaurant. After setbacks too numerous to mention, Tillicum Village opened on Blake Island in Puget Sound the year of the Seattle World's Fair, 1962.

Today, the once shaky venture attracts about 100,000 people annually. Dignitaries who have visited include Julia Child, who pronounced the salmon excellent, and President Bill Clinton, who hosted the

APEC (Asia Pacific Economic Cooperation) leaders meeting here in 1993. The original cedar longhouse has grown to include a state-of-the-art visitors center and theater—the latter home to an acclaimed spectacle of Indian dance and legend called "Dance on the Wind." But for many visitors, the focal point of Tillicum Village remains the barbecue pit.

DON'T TRY THIS AT HOME

A few years ago, I invited Tillicum Village president Mark Hewitt (Bill's son) to stage a salmon bake in Miami. His equipment list will begin to demonstrate the challenge of pulling this off (you probably won't want to try this at home):

- A 6-foot-square open-topped box constructed of four 2-by-12's (build it on the beach)
- 4 to 6 wheelbarrows of clean white sand
- A half cord of alder wood
- A shovel
- A half dozen cedar stakes
- An axe, for splitting the stakes
- Approximately fifty 10-by-¼-by-¼-inch cedar crossbars
- Approximately 75 whole salmon (enough to serve 400 to 500 people; depending on the season, you can use kings or cohos)

The basic procedure runs something like this: Build a giant sandbox on the beach. In the center, light a huge alder log fire and

At Tillicum Village on Blake Island you can experience a traditional Indian salmon bake just a short ferry ride from downtown Seattle.

let it burn down to fiery embers. Meanwhile, cut the heads off the salmon, then open them up through the belly, slicing through the backbone to, but not through, the back. Remove the guts and butterfly the fish, opening them flat like a book (or more appropriately, a magazine).

The next step involves attaching the butterflied fish to the cedar stakes. Each stake is about 5 feet long and 1½ inches square, with a narrow slit cut two thirds of its length. The fish are opened out and inserted in this slit so that the wide end (where the head was) faces down and the stake runs the length of the backbone. Now comes the tricky part: In order to hold the fish open flat so the maximum surface area is exposed to the fire, six to eight cedar crossbars are inserted perpendicular to the stake, in its slit and on either side of the fish.

Finally, you stand the stakes upright with the fish facing the fire and about 18 inches away from it. (The fire must be stoked with fresh alder from time to time to keep it blazing.) Depending on the size of the salmon and intensity of the fire, the cooking time will be about twenty to thirty minutes per side. As the salmon grills, the fat drains out, leaving the skin crackling crisp and the meat perfumed with wood smoke. Hewitt bastes the fish with lemon butter before serving it and accompanies it with boiled clams and sliced whole wheat bread. But it's so intensely flavorful, even these simple accompaniments seem superfluous.

If you're in Seattle, you can travel back in time at Tillicum Village for an afternoon, enjoying a gorgeous boat ride and some of the most singular salmon in the Pacific Northwest.

■ Cedar planks are available at grill and cookware shops (or see Mail-Order Sources, page 742). You could also head to your local hardware store for an untreated cedar shingle. Soaking the plank in water for a couple of hours prevents it from burning, or at least delays this.

■ Some pit masters grill the planked fish fillets directly over the fire, but I find you get better heat control (and fewer conflagrations) if you grill the fish using the indirect method. Either way, after several uses, the plank will become burned beyond recognition. It can still help you make great barbecue; simply break it into pieces to toss on the coals for smoking.

Pacific Northwest

PLANKED SALMON With Mustard and Dill Sauce

For most people, the hardest thing about grilling fish is keeping it from sticking to the grate. The second hardest thing is turning fillets without breaking them. Pacific Northwesters have devised an ingenious solution to these problems—one that adds flavor and theatrics. They grill fish on cedar planks. Planks prevent sticking—heck, you don't even turn the fish—and they impart a haunting spicy flavor that utterly transforms salmon. I've kept the seasonings simple, just a glaze of mustard, dill, and mayonnaise, so you can experience the cedary aromas in the fish.

METHOD:
Grilling on a plank

FOR THE SALMON:
1 salmon fillet, with or without skin
    (about 1½ pounds; ideally cut
    from the end closest to the head;
    see Note)
About 1 tablespoon olive oil
Coarse salt (kosher or sea) and
    freshly ground black pepper

For most Seattleites barbecue means grilled salmon.

FOR THE GLAZE:
½ cup mayonnaise
    (preferably Hellmann's)
⅓ cup Meaux (grainy French) mustard
2 tablespoons chopped fresh dill
½ teaspoon finely grated lemon zest
Coarse salt (kosher or sea) and
    freshly ground black pepper

YOU'LL ALSO NEED:
1 cedar plank (about 6 by 12 inches),
    soaked for 2 hours in water to cover
    (a rimmed baking sheet or large
    roasting pan works well for soaking),
    then drained

1 Run your fingers over the salmon fillet, feeling for bones. Using needle-nose pliers or tweezers, pull out any you find. Rinse the salmon under cold running water, then blot it dry with paper towels. If using salmon with skin, generously brush the skin with olive oil. If using skinless salmon, brush one side of the fish with olive oil. Season both sides with salt and pepper. Place the salmon on the plank, skin side down, if it has one; oiled side down if not.

2 MAKE THE GLAZE: Place the mayonnaise, mustard, dill, and lemon zest in a nonreactive mixing bowl and whisk to mix. Season with salt and pepper to taste.

3 Set up the grill for indirect grilling (see page 22 for charcoal or page 23 for gas) and preheat to medium-high.

4 When ready to cook, spread the glaze mixture evenly over the top and sides of the salmon. Place the salmon on its plank in the center of the hot grate, away from the heat, and cover the grill. Cook the salmon until cooked through and the glaze is a deep golden brown, 20 to 30 minutes. To test for doneness, insert an instant-read meat thermometer through the side of the salmon: The internal temperature should be about 135°F. Another test is to insert a slender metal skewer in the side of the fillet for 20 seconds: It should come out very hot to the touch. Transfer the plank and fish to a heatproof platter and slice the fish crosswise into serving portions. Serve the salmon right off the plank.

YIELD:
Serves 4

NOTE: You can use fish fillets with or without skin—your choice. (My wife finds that the skin makes the salmon taste fishy. I love it.) For that matter, the recipe works well with other rich oily fish fillets, including bluefish and pompano.

Tillicum Village founder, Bill Hewitt, right, and his son Mark, the current village president, demonstrate a traditional Indian salmon bake.

MAKAH DAYS

My first Northwest salmon bake took place in the rustic surroundings of the village of Neah Bay on the Olympic Peninsula. The occasion was Makah Days, an annual festival celebrating Northwest Coast Indian culture on the Makah Indian Reservation. The Makahs are one of the dozens of surviving Indian tribes of the Northwest, and they were joined for the occasion by representatives from the neighboring Tlingit, Kwakwaka' wakw, and Haida tribes.

You may have heard about the Makahs in connection with a controversial whale hunt staged by the village in 1999 (the Makahs are the only Native Americans in the continental United States who have the right, protected by treaty, to whale). It's easy for city folk such as myself to decry killing whales, but when you visit Neah Bay, observe the commitment to the traditional Makah way of life, and learn about the ravages from disease that white settlement in the nineteenth century wrought on the rich local culture, you begin to understand and sympathize with the significance the whale hunt has for this community.

My guide to the ways of a Makah salmon bake was Helen "Auntie" Mable. The process she uses is similar to the one Mark Hewitt showed me (see page 454)—with a few interesting variations. She builds her fire with driftwood, not alder, for example, and she rinses the salmon with sea water prior to grilling it. The seasonings are kept to a bare minimum, just salt and pepper, and the accompaniments run to boiled potatoes and corn.

If you happen to be on the Olympic Peninsula in August, Makah Days offers a fascinating introduction to the ways of the Northwest Coast Indians, complete with a colorful parade (for more information and dates, visit www.makah.com). While there, don't miss the amazing Makah Museum, featuring artifacts from a sixteenth-century Makah village that was buried, Pompei-style, by a mudslide nearly five hundred years ago and recently unearthed.

Roasting salmon on cedar stakes in front of a blazing fire.

San Francisco, Calif.

GRILLED SWORDFISH With Red Onion Jam

Onion jams began appearing on Bay Area menus in the 1990s, a reaction against the heavy Eurocentric sauces of yesteryear. They were as welcome as a cold front on a muggy summer day. Here was a uniquely American way of cooking—electrifying a simply grilled fish steak or veal chop with a highly concentrated, intensely flavorful condiment. At home it's easy to make a big batch of onion jam at the beginning of the summer and stash it in the refrigerator. Come a busy weeknight, throw a piece of fish on the grill and you'll have a great meal in the time it takes to grill the fish.

METHOD:
Direct grilling

ADVANCE PREPARATION:
30 minutes to 1 hour for marinating the swordfish

FOR THE ONION JAM:
2 tablespoons (¼ stick) butter, or 2 tablespoons olive oil
2 medium-size red onions, thinly sliced
⅔ cup balsamic vinegar

⅓ cup red wine
1 tablespoon honey, or more to taste
Coarse salt (kosher or sea) and freshly ground black pepper

FOR THE SWORDFISH:
4 swordfish steaks (each about ¾ inch thick and 6 to 8 ounces)
3 tablespoons extra-virgin olive oil
Coarse salt (kosher or sea) and freshly ground black pepper
1 tablespoon chopped fresh rosemary, plus 4 small rosemary sprigs for garnish
3 tablespoons dry white vermouth or white wine
1 tablespoon fresh lemon juice

1 MAKE THE ONION JAM: Melt the butter in a nonstick skillet over medium-high heat. Add the onions and cook until they soften and look limp, 2 to 3 minutes; do not let them brown. Add the vinegar, wine, and honey and bring to a boil.

2 Reduce the heat to medium and let the onions simmer gently until they have a jamlike consistency; the vinegar and wine should be completely absorbed. This will take 30 to 45 minutes and you'll need to lower the heat to medium-low as the liquid is absorbed and onions caramelize (as the sugar in them breaks down, producing a rich flavor). Stir the onions from time to time to prevent scorching. Taste for sweetness, adding more honey as necessary and season with salt and pepper to taste; the jam should be tart, with a hint of sweetness, and highly seasoned. Transfer to a bowl or jar and let cool.

TIPS

■ I like the color contrast of white swordfish and red onion jam. For an interesting variation, you could make a white onion jam, using Vidalia onions, white wine vinegar, and chardonnay.

■ Onion jam is also delicious with veal and pork chops and with grilled chicken breasts.

Swordfish is the ultimate steak fish, and a challenging catch, too.

fish. Let the swordfish marinate for 30 minutes to 1 hour in the refrigerator, covered, turning the fish once or twice so that it marinates evenly.

4 Set up the grill for direct grilling (see page 21 for charcoal or gas) and preheat to high.

5 When ready to cook, brush and oil the grill grate. Arrange the swordfish steaks on the hot grate, placing them on a diagonal to the bars. Grill the steaks for 2 minutes, then rotate them a quarter turn to create an attractive crosshatch of grill marks. Continue grilling the swordfish until the undersides are nicely browned, about 2 minutes longer. Repeat on the second side. To test for doneness, press one of the swordfish steaks with your finger; it will break into clean flakes when fully cooked. Another test is to insert a metal skewer through the side of one of the steaks for 20 seconds; it should come out very hot to the touch.

The jam can be refrigerated, covered, for several weeks.

3 Rinse the swordfish steaks under cold running water, then blot them dry with paper towels. Place the swordfish steaks in a nonreactive baking dish. Lightly brush them on both sides with a little of the olive oil. Generously season the fish steaks on both sides with salt and pepper and sprinkle the chopped rosemary over them. Combine the remaining olive oil with the vermouth and lemon juice in a small nonreactive bowl and stir with a fork to mix. Pour the marinade over the

6 Transfer the grilled swordfish steaks to a platter or plates. Top each with a spoonful of onion jam or place a little mound on the side, then

. . . steaks of swordfish so fresh it had bee

garnish with a rosemary sprig. For a real California look, insert a rosemary sprig upright in each piece of fish.

YIELD:
Serves 4

Brigantine, N.J.

GRILLED SWORDFISH
With Summer Salsa

I always associate swordfish with shore vacations—like the visits I'd make to Brigantine on the New Jersey shore to the summer home of my aunt and uncle, Linda and Marty Millison. We'd bicycle to the local fish market and buy glorious, glistening, thick steaks of swordfish so fresh, it had been swimming in the ocean earlier that morning. When fish is this fresh, you keep the accompaniments simple: a sprinkle of sea salt, a coarse grind of pepper, maybe a squeeze of fresh lemon juice. By way of a condiment, add a salsa that capitalizes on the inimitable flavors of vine-ripened tomatoes and fresh tarragon. Oh, and some farm stand corn thrown in for color and crunch.

METHOD:
Direct grilling

ADVANCE PREPARATION:
15 to 30 minutes for marinating the swordfish

INGREDIENTS:
**4 swordfish steaks (each about
    ¾ inch thick and 6 to 8 ounces)**
**Coarse salt (kosher or sea) and
    freshly ground black pepper**
2 tablespoons fresh lemon juice
2 tablespoons extra-virgin olive oil
Summer Salsa (recipe follows)
Fresh tarragon sprigs, for garnish

1 Rinse the swordfish steaks under cold running water, then blot them dry with paper towels. Place the swordfish in a nonreactive baking dish and season generously on both sides with salt and pepper. Sprinkle the lemon juice over the fish, turning to coat both sides. Drizzle the olive oil over both sides of the swordfish. Let the swordfish marinate in the refrigerator for 15 to 30 minutes.

2 Set up the grill for direct grilling (see page 21 for charcoal or gas) and preheat to high.

TIPS

Whenever I grill fish, I let freshness, not species, guide my shopping. Should you find another fish that looks fresher than the swordfish, by all means buy it instead (tuna or bluefish would be obvious choices for this recipe).

...wimming in the ocean earlier that morning

3 When ready to cook, brush and oil the grill grate. Arrange the swordfish steaks on the hot grate, placing them on a diagonal to the bars. Grill the steaks for 2 minutes, then rotate them a quarter turn to create an attractive crosshatch of grill marks. Continue grilling the swordfish until the undersides are nicely browned, about 2 minutes longer. Repeat on the second side. To test for doneness, press one of the swordfish steaks with your finger; it will break into clean flakes when fully cooked. Another test is to insert a metal skewer through the side of one of the steaks for 20 seconds: It should come out very hot to the touch.

4 Transfer the grilled swordfish to a platter or plates. Spoon the salsa over the swordfish, garnish with the tarragon sprigs, and serve at once.

YIELD:

Serves 4

*Corn on the cob—
great for grilling,
great for salsas.*

Summer Salsa

Featuring ripe, ruby red tomatoes and the spontaneous crunch of raw sweet corn—this salsa is summer in a bowl. For an added dimension of flavor, brush the corn with olive oil and grill it (you'll find instructions for doing this on page 145). The salsa would be terrific with any sort of grilled seafood, not to mention grilled chicken or pork.

INGREDIENTS:

2 ears sweet corn, shucked
1 clove garlic, minced
Coarse salt (kosher or sea)
2 medium-size luscious, ripe red tomatoes, finely diced, with their juices
1 scallion, both white and green parts, trimmed and finely chopped
2 tablespoons chopped fresh tarragon, or other fresh herb
1 tablespoon fresh lemon juice, or more to taste
3 tablespoons diced pitted oil-marinated black olives (optional)
3 tablespoons extra-virgin olive oil
Freshly ground black pepper

1 Cut the kernels off the cobs, using lengthwise strokes of a chef's knife.

2 Place the garlic and ½ teaspoon of salt in the bottom of a nonreactive mixing bowl. Mash to a paste with the back of a wooden spoon. Add the corn kernels and the tomatoes, scallion, tarragon, lemon juice, olives, if using, olive oil, and a few twists of black pepper but do not toss the salsa.

3 When ready to serve, toss the salsa, then taste for seasoning, adding more salt and/or lemon juice as necessary.

YIELD:
Makes 1½ to 2 cups

Scottsdale, Ariz.

GRILLED SWORDFISH With Orange and Caper Sauce

Like many people who now live in Scottsdale, Arizona, Lenard Rubin came for a brief visit and wound up settling down. He fell in love with the big sky and wide open spaces, not to mention the local obsession with chiles and spices. So he opened a restaurant quite unlike any other in the area—Medizona, which specializes in a fusion of Mediterranean and Southwestern flavors. Now, I'm not a big fan of fusion food—all too often it short changes the cuisines being fused. But Rubin has worked in cities as far-flung as St. Petersburg, Moscow, and Boston, plus several of the top resorts in Arizona. He understands Southwestern and Mediterranean flavors well enough to merge them without muddying the waters. If you like the sweet-sour tang of orange juice and the tart, salty bite of capers, you'll love his simple but elegant grilled swordfish.

METHOD:
Direct grilling

FOR THE ORANGE AND CAPER SAUCE:
1 clove garlic, minced
¼ cup dry white wine
**½ cup thawed frozen orange juice
    concentrate**
1½ cups heavy (whipping) cream
1 tablespoon drained capers
1 tablespoon unsalted butter
**1 tablespoon finely chopped
    fresh flat-leaf parsley**
**Coarse salt (kosher or sea) and
    freshly ground black pepper**

FOR THE SWORDFISH:
**4 swordfish steaks (each about
    ¾ inch thick and 6 to 8 ounces)**
**Coarse salt (kosher or sea) and
    freshly ground black pepper**
1 to 2 tablespoons extra-virgin olive oil
1 juicy lemon, cut in half and seeded
4 sprigs fresh flat-leaf parsley for garnish

1 MAKE THE ORANGE AND CAPER SAUCE: Combine the garlic and wine in a heavy nonreactive saucepan over high heat, bring to a boil, and let boil until reduced by half, about 2 minutes. Add the orange juice concentrate and cream and let boil until reduced by half, 6 to 8 minutes. Whisk in the capers, butter, and chopped parsley, reduce the heat to medium, and let simmer for 2 minutes. Season with salt and pepper to taste; the sauce should be highly

TIPS

■ Lenard Rubin prepares this dish with swordfish, but the piquant sauce would go well with almost any type of grilled seafood, from salmon to shrimp or lobster. For that matter, it would pair nicely with a grilled chicken breast.

■ Remember to thaw the orange juice concentrate ahead of time so you can measure a half cup.

Chef Lenard Rubin, of Medizona in Scottsdale, has found inspiration under the desert sun.

for 2 minutes, then rotate them a quarter turn to create an attractive crosshatch of grill marks. Continue grilling the swordfish until the undersides are nicely browned, about 2 minutes longer. Turn the swordfish steaks over, squeeze lemon juice over them, and grill and rotate as you did on the first side. To test for doneness, press one of the swordfish steaks with your finger; it will break into clean flakes when fully cooked. Another test is to insert a metal skewer through the side of one of the steaks for 20 seconds: It should come out very hot to the touch.

5 Transfer the grilled swordfish to a platter or plates. Spoon the warm sauce over the fish, then garnish each steak with a sprig of parsley. Serve at once.

YIELD:
Serves 4

seasoned. Keep the sauce in warm spot (but not directly over the heat) while you light the grill and cook the fish. The sauce can be prepared several hours ahead and reheated over low heat, whisking steadily.

2 Rinse the swordfish steaks under cold running water, then blot them dry with paper towels. Generously season the swordfish steaks with salt and pepper. Drizzle olive oil over them, gently rubbing it onto the fish with your fingertips.

3 Set up the grill for direct grilling (see page 21 for charcoal or gas) and preheat to high.

4 When ready to cook, brush and oil the grill grate. Arrange the swordfish steaks on the hot grate, placing them on a diagonal to the bars. Grill the steaks

Chicago, Ill.

GRILLED TUNA
With Niçoise "Salsa"

I first tasted *salade niçoise* in its birthplace, Nice, on the Côte d'Azur. It wasn't what you'd call love at first bite (I didn't travel five thousand miles to eat a canned tuna and hard-boiled

egg salad). As far as I'm concerned, the salad didn't reach its full potential until progressive American chefs began preparing it with grilled fresh tuna. The recipe here was inspired by a dish served at an ultra-hip Chicago restaurant called Naha. Tuna is the focal point, while the salad is more of an intensely flavored salsa.

METHOD:
Direct grilling

FOR THE NIÇOISE "SALSA":
Coarse salt (kosher or sea)
½ pound haricots verts or green beans,
    stemmed and cut into 1-inch pieces
1 pound fingerling potatoes with their skins
8 quail eggs, or 2 large hen's eggs
12 cherry tomatoes
½ cup niçoise, kalamata, or other
    black olives
¼ cup caper berries with their stems,
    or 2 tablespoons drained capers
8 fresh basil leaves, thinly slivered
    (see Note)
2 to 3 tablespoons extra-virgin olive oil
1 tablespoon red wine vinegar,
    or more to taste
Cracked black peppercorns

FOR THE TUNA:
4 sushi-quality tuna steaks (each about
    1 inch thick and 6 ounces)
1 to 2 tablespoons extra-virgin olive oil
Coarse salt (kosher or sea) and
    cracked black peppercorns
½ lemon, seeded
4 whole basil leaves, for garnish

1 MAKE THE NIÇOISE "SALSA": Bring 3 quarts of salted water to a boil in a large saucepan over high heat. Add the haricots verts and cook until crisp-tender, about 2 minutes. Using a slotted spoon, transfer the boiled *haricots verts* to a strainer (let the water continue to boil). Rinse the *haricots verts* under cold running water until cold. Drain the *haricots verts* well and place in a large non-reactive mixing bowl.

2 Add the potatoes to the boiling water and cook until just tender, 5 to 8 minutes. Transfer the boiled potatoes to the strainer (let the water continue to boil). Rinse the potatoes under cold running water until cold. Drain well, cut each potato in half crosswise on the diagonal, and add to the bowl with the *haricots verts.*

3 Add the quail eggs to the boiling water and cook for 4 minutes (hen's eggs will need to boil for 11 minutes). Transfer the boiled eggs to the strainer and rinse under cold running water until cold. Shell the quail eggs and cut them in half crosswise (cut hen's eggs in quarters). Add the eggs to the bowl with the *haricots verts* and the potatoes.

4 Cut the cherry tomatoes in half and add them to the bowl with the *haricots verts* along with the olives, caper berries, sliced basil, olive oil, and vinegar but do not toss. Set the "salsa" aside; you'll season it with salt and cracked peppercorns when you toss it. The "salsa" will keep for 2 hours, untossed.

5 Trim any skin or dark or bloody spots off the tuna steaks. Rinse the tuna under cold running water, then blot it dry with paper towels. Place the

TIPS

A few ingredients here may need clarification.

Haricots verts are skinny French green beans. Look for them in upscale supermarkets or gourmet shops or use the slenderest green beans you can find.

Fingerling potatoes are baby spuds— you could certainly use diced larger potatoes.

Quail eggs are a little precious, but they have sufficiently wide acceptance to be sold at my local supermarket. You can substitute diced hard-cooked eggs.

Caper berries are the fruit of the caper bush; they're picked with the stem attached and sold in jars at most gourmet shops.

tuna steaks in a baking dish and brush on both sides with olive oil. Generously season the tuna with salt and pepper. Let the tuna marinate while you set up the grill.

KNOW YOUR TUNA

Yellowfin, bluefin, albacore, ahi (also known as bigeye)—any of these varieties of tuna will work in the recipes you'll find on pages 464 through 480. What's crucial is that the tuna be impeccably fresh—of sushi quality—since you are most likely going to be serving it charred on the outside and rare inside. The cut that's most readily available to you will depend upon where you live. Tuna loins (cylindrical pieces of tuna that are about six inches long and look something like pork tenderloins) are common on the West Coast and in Hawaii. These can be sliced into nifty little medallions. On the East Coast you're more likely to find tuna steaks, but loins can sometimes be specially ordered from your fishmonger.

Landing a big-boy tuna: Size does matter.

6 Set up the grill for direct grilling (see page 21 for charcoal or gas) and preheat to high.

7 When ready to cook, brush and oil the grill grate. Arrange the tuna steaks on the hot grate, placing them on a diagonal to the bars. Grill the steaks for 1½ minutes, then rotate them a quarter turn to create an attractive crosshatch of grill marks. Continue grilling until the undersides are nicely browned, 1½ to 3 minutes longer. Turn the tuna steaks over, squeeze lemon juice over them, and grill until cooked to taste, 3 to 5 minutes longer for medium-rare. Again, rotate the steaks a quarter turn after 1½ minutes to create a crosshatch of grill marks. Test for doneness using the poke method: A rare tuna steak will be quite soft, with just a little resistance at the surface; a medium-rare steak will be gently yielding; and a medium steak will be firm.

8 Transfer the grilled tuna to a platter or plates. Toss the "salsa" and season to taste with salt and cracked peppercorns. Spoon the "salsa" over the tuna, garnishing each steak with a basil leaf. Serve at once.

YIELD:
Serves 4

NOTE: The easiest way to slice basil or other leafy herbs into thin slivers is to stack several of the leaves in a single pile, roll them up crosswise into a tight tube, then thinly slice the tube crosswise with a sharp knife. Fluff the resulting slices with your fingers.

The Southwest

ACHIOTE-GRILLED TUNA

Most Americans are just discovering achiote, also known as annatto—a rust-colored spice with a tangy, earthy flavor that may remind you of iodine . . . in a good way, the way a fresh, briny oyster does. But achiote has been part of the American barbecue experience for hundreds, probably thousands, of years. Native to the Yucatan, the reddish brown seeds are used in the marinades for Mexico's famous *pescado tikin xik* (achiote-marinated grilled fish) and *pibil* (pork or chicken seasoned with achiote paste, wrapped in banana leaves, and barbecued in a pit). Achiote is gaining a following among American barbecue buffs and chefs. The following recipe combines the haunting flavors of achiote, cilantro, and garlic with America's favorite steak fish, tuna.

METHOD:
Direct grilling

ADVANCE PREPARATION:
4 to 12 hours for marinating the tuna

INGREDIENTS:
2 tablespoons achiote seeds or paste
1/2 cup fresh cilantro leaves
(from 1/2 bunch)
8 cloves garlic, coarsely chopped

1 serrano pepper, trimmed, seeded, and coarsely chopped
2 scallions, both white and green parts, trimmed and coarsely chopped
1 teaspoon coarse salt (kosher or sea)
1 teaspoon freshly ground black pepper
1/2 cup vegetable oil
4 sushi quality tuna steaks (each about 3/4 inch thick and 6 to 8 ounces)
Tomatillo Salsa (optional; recipe follows)

1 If using achiote seeds, grind them to a fine powder in a spice mill or coffee grinder. If using the paste, break it into pieces. Place the achiote, cilantro, garlic, serrano, scallions, salt, and black pepper in a food processor fitted with the metal blade. Process to finely chop. Gradually add the oil to obtain a thick fragrant paste.

2 Trim any skin or dark or bloody spots off the tuna steaks. Rinse the tuna steaks under cold running water and blot them dry with paper towels. Place the tuna steaks in a baking dish just large enough to hold them. Spread the achiote mixture on both sides of the tuna and let it marinate in the refrigerator, covered, for at least 4 hours or as long as overnight.

3 Set up the grill for direct grilling (see page 21 for charcoal and gas) and preheat to high.

4 When ready to cook, brush and oil the grill grate. Scrape most of the achiote mixture off of the tuna with a rubber spatula. Arrange the tuna on the hot grate, placing it on a diagonal to the bars. Grill the fish until cooked to taste, 3 to 5 minutes per side for medium-rare,

Achiote (as it's called by Mexican Americans; Cubans and Puerto Ricans call it annatto) comes in two forms: seeds and paste. Seeds are favored by Americans of Spanish Caribbean descent; Mexicans prefer the paste. If you live in a city with a large Hispanic population, you'll probably be able to find some form of achiote at your local supermarket. Otherwise, you can order it by mail from one of the sources on page 742. There's no real substitute for achiote, but a tasty marinade can be made by substituting one teaspoon of saffron threads for the achiote in the recipe here.

4 to 6 minutes per side for medium. Test for doneness using the poke method: A medium-rare tuna steak will be gently yielding; a medium steak will be firm. Serve with the Tomatillo Salsa, if desired.

YIELD:

Serves 4

VARIATION: I call for tuna in this recipe, but the achiote paste is fabulous on any type of seafood, from sea bass to swordfish, not to mention on chicken and pork.

Tomatillo Salsa

The tomatillo is a mainstay of Mexican and Southwestern cooking, and it's sufficiently popular in the United States to be available at many supermarkets. Once the papery covering is removed, a tomatillo looks like a green cherry tomato, and its fruity tartness is ideal for pairing with fish. As for jicama, it's a light brown tuber with white flesh that's often described as a cross between a potato and an apple. Its audibly crisp texture and earthy flavor make for an unconventional but irresistible salsa.

INGREDIENTS:

2 cups (8 to 10 ounces) tomatillos
1 cup finely diced peeled jicama
½ cup finely diced red bell pepper
(¼ to ½ bell pepper)
¼ cup chopped fresh cilantro

3 tablespoons chopped white onion
2 tablespoons fresh lime juice,
or more to taste
Coarse salt (kosher or sea)

Peel off and discard the papery husks of the tomatillos then rinse them under cold running water and blot them dry with paper towels. Cut the tomatillos into ¼-inch dice. Place them in a nonreactive mixing bowl and stir in the jicama, bell pepper, cilantro, onion, and lime juice. Taste for seasoning, adding more lime juice as necessary and seasoning with salt to taste; the salsa should be highly seasoned.

YIELD:

Makes about 3 cups

San Francisco, Calif.

SPICE-CRUSTED TUNA

San Francisco chef Gary Danko is one of the lions of haute Franco-Californian cuisine—not the sort of guy you'd expect to find messing around with barbecue. But at his eponymous restaurant, I enjoyed a spice-crusted tuna that positively begged for the grill. As in so much Bay

Area cooking, the seasonings were those used in the Mediterranean but from all different corners of the Mediterranean at once: coarse sea salt from France, dried rosemary from Italy, even cracked coriander seeds and white peppercorns from Morocco. Uncomplicated-sounding ingredients, but when you put them together (a process that will take you maybe five minutes) you get a tuna that explodes with flavor. The sauce is my own invention: a reduction of cream and *harissa* (a North African hot sauce).

METHOD:
Direct grilling

ADVANCE PREPARATION:
15 to 30 minutes for marinating the tuna

FOR THE TUNA:
1½ pounds tuna loin, or 4 tuna steaks
   (each about 1 inch thick and
   6 ounces)
¼ cup extra-virgin olive oil

FOR THE RUB:
1 tablespoon coriander seeds
1 tablespoon white peppercorns
1 tablespoon dried rosemary
1 tablespoon coarse salt
   (kosher or sea)

FOR SERVING:
Harissa Cream Sauce (recipe follows)
4 sprigs fresh cilantro, for garnish

1 Trim any skin or dark or bloody spots off the tuna. Rinse the tuna under cold running water, then blot dry with paper towels. If using tuna loins, cut them into 1-inch-thick medallions.

Place the tuna in a baking dish and pour the olive oil over them. Let the tuna marinate in the refrigerator, covered, for 15 to 30 minutes, turning the medallions a couple of times to coat thoroughly with oil.

2 MAKE THE RUB: Coarsely grind or crack the coriander seeds and peppercorns, using a spice mill or mortar and pestle. You want small pieces, but not a fine powder. Crumble the rosemary needles into a bowl with your fingers. Stir in the ground coriander and peppercorns and the salt.

3 Set up the grill for direct grilling (see page 21 for charcoal or gas) and preheat to high.

4 When ready to cook, drain and discard the olive oil from the tuna. Sprinkle each piece on all sides with the rub, patting it onto the tuna with your fingertips. Brush and oil the grill grate. Place the tuna on the hot grate and grill until seared on the outside and cooked to taste inside, 1 to 2 minutes per side for medium-rare medallions; 3 to 5 minutes per side for medium-rare tuna steaks. Test for doneness using the poke method: A medium-rare tuna steak will be gently yielding.

5 Spoon the Harissa Cream Sauce on a platter or plates and place the grilled tuna on top (alternatively, place the tuna on a platter or plates and spoon the sauce over it). Garnish with the cilantro sprigs and serve at once.

YIELD:
Serves 4

Gary Danko serves the tuna in medallions cut from the small, cylinder-shaped tuna roasts called loins. When serving tuna steaks, cut them crosswise into slices that are a quarter inch thick and fan these out on the plate.

Harissa Cream Sauce

The intriguing color and heat of this sauce comes from *harissa,* a North African condiment made with red chiles, coriander, garlic, and cumin, among other things. You can find *harissa* at North African markets and gourmet shops (see Mail-Order Sources, page 742, for other sources). Alternatively, substitute a teaspoon of hot paprika or *chinata*—Spanish smoked paprika—in addition to the sweet paprika.

INGREDIENTS:

1 cup bottled clam broth
2 cloves garlic, peeled and gently crushed with the side of a cleaver
1¾ cups heavy (whipping) cream
1 to 2 tablespoons harissa
1 teaspoon sweet or smoked paprika
2 tablespoons (¼ stick) unsalted butter
Coarse salt (kosher or sea) and freshly ground black pepper

1 Place the clam broth and garlic in a heavy saucepan and bring to a boil over medium-high heat. Let boil until reduced to ¼ cup, 5 to 8 minutes. Add the cream, harissa, and paprika and let boil until only 1 cup of sauce remains, 5 to 8 minutes. Whisk the sauce from time to time as it boils to keep it from scorching. The sauce can be prepared up to this stage a day ahead. Let cool to room temperature, then refrigerate it, covered. Reheat the sauce over medium-low heat before continuing with Step 2.

2 Just before serving, whisk the butter into the cream sauce and season with salt and pepper to taste.

YIELD:
Makes 1¼ cups

The Southwest

MESQUITE-GRILLED TUNA With Fire-Charred Tomato Chipotle Salsa

If you like smoke and fire, you'll love this Southwestern grilled tuna. The high heat of the mesquite sears the fish like nobody's business, imparting a sharp, rich flavor of wood smoke. The salsa reinforces the smoke taste, made as it is with fire-charred tomatoes, onion, and garlic. The chipotle peppers notch up the heat, adding yet another layer of smoke flavor. As for the tuna, it's marinated in an aromatic paste of garlic, cilantro, and lime juice.

METHOD:
Direct grilling

ADVANCE PREPARATION:
30 minutes for marinating the tuna

INGREDIENTS:
2 cloves garlic, minced
1 teaspoon coarse salt (kosher or sea)
1/2 teaspoon freshly ground black pepper
3 tablespoons chopped fresh cilantro
2 tablespoons fresh lime juice
2 tablespoons extra-virgin olive oil,
    plus 1 to 2 tablespoons for brushing
    the tuna
4 sushi quality tuna steaks (each about
    3/4 inch thick and 6 ounces)
4 flour tortillas (8 inches each)
Fire-Charred Tomato Chipotle Salsa
    (recipe follows)
Cilantro sprigs for garnish

YOU'LL ALSO NEED:
1 cup wood chips or chunks
    (preferably mesquite), unsoaked

1 In a mortar using a pestle or in a small nonreactive bowl using the back of a spoon, mash together the garlic, salt, black pepper, and cilantro. Stir in the lime juice and 2 tablespoons of the olive oil.

2 Trim any skin or dark or bloody spots off the tuna steaks. Rinse the tuna under cold running water, then blot it dry with paper towels. Place the tuna steaks in a nonreactive baking dish just large enough to hold them and pour the marinade over the fish. Let the tuna marinate in the refrigerator, covered, for 30 minutes, turning once or twice so that it marinates evenly.

3 Set up the grill for direct grilling (see page 21 for gas or charcoal) and preheat to high. If using a gas grill, place all of the wood chips or chunks in the smoker box or in a smoker pouch (see page 24) and run the grill on high until you see smoke. If using a charcoal grill, preheat it to high, then toss all of the wood chips or chunks on the coals.

4 When ready to cook, drain the marinade from the tuna steaks and discard the marinade. Lightly brush both sides of the tuna with olive oil. Brush and oil the grill grate. Arrange the tuna on the hot grate, placing it on a diagonal to the bars. Grill the fish until cooked to taste, 3 to 5 minutes per side for medium-rare, 4 to 6 minutes per side for medium, rotating each steak a quarter turn after 1 1/2 minutes or so on each side to create an attractive crosshatch of grill marks. Test for doneness using the poke method: A medium-rare tuna steak will be gently yielding; a medium steak will be firm.

5 Meanwhile, warm the tortillas on the grill; it will take 10 to 20 seconds per side. Wrap the tortillas in a cloth napkin and place in a basket.

6 There are two ways to serve the tuna. Place the tortillas on a platter or plates, arrange the grilled tuna steaks on top, and spoon the salsa over them. Or you can cut the fish into thin slices and pile

In the best of all possible worlds, you'd grill the tuna and the salsa ingredients over a mesquite wood fire. Mesquite chunks are available from W.W. Wood of Texas (see Mail-Order Sources, page 742). See page 20 for instructions on grilling over a wood fire. Another choice is to toss a handful of mesquite chips on the fire before grilling, or if you have a charcoal grill, stoke it with mesquite charcoal.

Tuna loins ready for slicing into steaks or medallions.

them on the tortillas, spooning the salsa on top. Garnish with the cilantro sprigs.

YIELD:
Serves 4

Fire-Charred Tomato Chipotle Salsa

You can certainly grill the vegetables for the tomato chipotle salsa and then cook the mesquite-grilled tuna over the same fire, adding fresh coals and mesquite chips as necessary. Or you can grill the salsa ingredients a day or two ahead of time when you've got the grill fired up for something else. Either way, grilling gives this salsa a heady smoke flavor that reinforces the heat of the chipotles.

INGREDIENTS:

2 large ripe red tomatoes

1 small white onion, peeled and quartered

3 cloves garlic, peeled and skewered on a wooden toothpick

1 to 2 chipotle peppers (see Note)

3 tablespoons coarsely chopped fresh cilantro

1 tablespoon fresh lime juice, or more to taste

Coarse salt (kosher or sea) and freshly ground black pepper

YOU'LL ALSO NEED:

1 cup wood chips or chunks (preferably mesquite), unsoaked

1 Set up the grill for direct grilling (see page 21 for gas or charcoal) and preheat to high. If using a gas grill, place all of the wood chips or chunks in the smoker box or in a smoker pouch (see page 24) and run the grill on high until you see smoke. If using a charcoal grill, preheat it to high, then toss all of the wood chips or chunks on the coals.

2 When ready to cook, place the tomatoes, onion, and garlic on the hot grate. Grill the tomatoes and onion until the skins are dark and blistered; grill the garlic until lightly browned. This will take 2 to 3 minutes per side (8 to 12 minutes in all) for the tomatoes and onion and 2 to 3 minutes per side (4 to 6 minutes in all) for the garlic. Transfer the grilled tomatoes, onion and garlic to a plate and let cool. Remove the toothpick from the garlic. The grilled vegetables can be refrigerated, covered, for up to 2 days.

3 Mince the chipotle(s). Scrape any really burnt bits off the tomatoes. Combine the minced chipotles, cilantro, and lime juice with the grilled tomatoes, onion, and garlic in a food processor and process to a coarse purée. Taste for seasoning, adding salt and pepper to taste and more lime juice as necessary; the salsa should be highly seasoned. The salsa is best served within 3 to 4 hours of being made.

YIELD:
Makes 1 to 1½ cups

NOTE: Chipotle peppers (smoked jalapeños) are available both canned and dried. I prefer the ones in cans, which come in a flavorful sauce called adobo. If your chipotles are dried, soak them in warm water for 30 minutes before using, then drain them and tear them into 1-inch pieces. For a milder salsa, discard the seeds.

Baton Rouge, La.

CAJUN TUNA PIPERADE

Jan Birnbaum may run the popular Catahoula Restaurant & Saloon in Calistoga, California, and Sazerac in Seattle, but the Louisiana roots of this Baton Rouge–born chef are immediately apparent. The first thing you smell when you enter one of his restaurants is the "Holy Trinity" of Creole cuisine—the sweet scent of sautéed onion, celery, and bell pepper. The produce and seafood may be West Coast, but the soul of the food is pure Creole. One of the specialties of Jan's Seattle restaurant is grilled tuna served with *pipérade,* a colorful sauté of bell peppers and tomato. I love the way it rounds out the tuna, especially when "Cajunized" with smoky tasso.

METHOD:
Direct grilling

ADVANCE PREPARATION:
30 minutes for marinating the tuna

FOR THE PIPERADE:
3 tablespoons extra-virgin olive oil
1 medium-size onion, cut into thin wedges
1 small red bell pepper, cored, seeded, and cut lengthwise into thin slices
1 small yellow bell pepper, cored, seeded, and cut lengthwise into thin slices
1 small green bell pepper, cored, seeded, and cut lengthwise into thin slices
1 to 2 jalapeño peppers, seeded and thinly sliced (for a hotter pipérade, leave the seeds in)
2 ounces tasso or andouille sausage (see Note), cut into matchstick slivers
2 cloves garlic, thinly sliced
1 tablespoon sweet, hot, or smoked paprika
1 large luscious, ripe red tomato, peeled, seeded, and cut into ½-inch dice
Coarse salt (kosher or sea) and freshly ground black pepper

FOR THE TUNA:
4 sushi quality tuna steaks (each about 1 inch thick and 6 ounces)
2 tablespoons extra-virgin olive oil
2 tablespoons Cajun Rub (page 420) or your favorite commercial rub
2 cloves garlic, minced
4 sprigs flat-leaf parsley, or 2 tablespoons finely chopped flat-leaf parsley (optional)

YOU'LL ALSO NEED:
2 cups wood chips or chunks (optional; preferably oak), unsoaked

TIPS

■ Don't be intimidated by the seemingly large number of ingredients here. The recipe is a series of simple steps, and the *pipérade* can be made a day ahead. Smok-a-holics would grill the onion and peppers for the *pipérade* prior to sautéing (do this when you've got the grill lit for something else). This will make the sauce taste even smokier. Sauté the grilled veggies for two to three minutes to blend the flavors before adding the tasso and other ingredients as described in Step 1.

■ I like to give the fish a light wood smoke flavor, so I often toss unsoaked wood chips on the coals.

1 MAKE THE *PIPERADE:* Heat the olive oil in a large deep skillet over high heat. Add the onion, bell peppers, jalapeño(s), and tasso and sauté until the onions and peppers are lightly browned, 4 minutes, tossing or stirring the ingredients to ensure even browning. Add the sliced garlic and paprika after 2 minutes. Add the tomato after 2 more minutes and cook over high heat until most of the tomato juices have evaporated, about 2 minutes longer. Season with salt and black pepper to taste; the *pipérade* should be highly seasoned. The *pipérade* can be prepared up to 48 hours ahead and kept refrigerated, covered.

2 Trim any skin or dark or bloody spots off the tuna steaks. Rinse the tuna under cold running water, then blot it dry with paper towels. Lightly brush the tuna steaks on both sides with about 1 tablespoon of the olive oil. Sprinkle the tuna on both sides with the Cajun Rub and minced garlic, patting the seasonings onto the fish with your fingertips. Let the tuna marinate for 30 minutes.

3 Set up the grill for direct grilling (see page 21 for gas or charcoal) and preheat to high. If using a gas grill, place all of the wood chips or chunks, if desired, in the smoker box or in a smoker pouch (see page 24) and run the grill on high until you see smoke. If using a charcoal grill, preheat it to high, then toss all of the wood chips or chunks, if desired, on the coals.

4 When ready to cook, brush and oil the grill grate. Brush the tuna steaks with the remaining 1 tablespoon of olive oil. Arrange the tuna on the hot grate, placing it on a diagonal to the bars. Grill the fish until cooked to taste, 3 to 5 minutes per side for medium-rare, 4 to 6 minutes per side for medium, rotating each steak a quarter turn after 1½ minutes on each side to create an attractive crosshatch of grill marks. Test for doneness using the poke method: A medium-rare tuna steak will be gently yielding; a medium steak will be firm. Reheat the *pipérade* on the side burner or on an empty area of the grill.

5 Transfer the grilled tuna steaks to a platter or plates and spoon the *pipérade* over them. Garnish or sprinkle with parsley, if using, and serve at once.

YIELD:
Serves 4

NOTE: Tasso, cured pork shoulder, is a spicy, smoky Cajun specialty. As an alternative, you could use the smoky Cajun sausage called andouille. Both are available at gourmet shops, or you can order them by mail (see Mail-Order Sources, page 742).

Jan Birnbaum with some of his Louisiana-inspired specialties.

Hawaii

HIBACHI-STYLE TUNA
With Radish Sprout Slaw

Roy Yamaguchi is one of Hawaii's most celebrated chefs, and also one of its most prolific, with restaurants on the Hawaiian islands and coast to coast on the mainland, not to mention at overseas locations as far flung as Hong Kong, Tokyo, and Guam. Yamaguchi blends elements from his Japanese ancestry with the best of contemporary American cuisine. Case in point, the Yamaguchi-inspired recipe here. The sauce is a Hawaiian take on *ponzu*, a Japanese dipping sauce that plays the acidic tang of lemon juice (or more traditionally, *yuzo* juice) against the sweet-salty yin and yang of mirin and soy sauce. Put it all together and you get a grilled fish dish that bursts with Hawaiian flavor.

METHOD:
Direct grilling

ADVANCE PREPARATION:
1 hour for marinating the tuna

FOR THE TUNA AND MARINADE:
**4 sushi-quality tuna steaks (each about
    1 inch thick and 6 ounces)**

¹⁄₂ cup soy sauce
¹⁄₄ cup sugar
**4 scallions, both white and greens parts,
    trimmed and thinly sliced**
**1 tablespoon minced peeled fresh
    ginger**
1¹⁄₂ teaspoons minced garlic

FOR THE PONZU SAUCE:
1 cup mirin (see Notes)
¹⁄₄ cup soy sauce
¹⁄₄ cup fresh lemon juice
¹⁄₂ teaspoon grated lemon zest
**¹⁄₂ to 1 teaspoon hot red pepper
    flakes**

FOR THE SLAW:
**¹⁄₂ Maui onion or other sweet onion,
    thinly sliced**
**1 cucumber, peeled, seeded, and
    cut into matchstick slivers**
**1 package (2 ounces) radish sprouts
    (see Notes)**

1 Trim any skin or dark or bloody spots off the tuna steaks. Rinse the tuna under cold running water, then blot it dry with paper towels. Place the tuna steaks in a baking dish just large enough to hold them.

2 MAKE THE MARINADE: Combine the soy sauce, sugar, scallions, ginger, and garlic in a mixing bowl and whisk until the sugar dissolves. Pour this mixture over the tuna and let it marinate for 1 hour in the refrigerator, covered, turning the fish several times so that it marinates evenly.

3 MAKE THE *PONZU* SAUCE: Place the mirin in a heavy nonreactive saucepan over medium-high heat, bring

TIPS

■ A number of kinds of tuna will work here, including yellowfin, bluefin, or bigeye. You're going to be serving the fish very rare, so what's important is that it be impeccably fresh.

■ Small is beautiful. For this recipe a hibachi is perfect for grilling the tuna steaks.

American chefs today are as likely to grill fish as meat.

to a boil, and let boil until reduced to ⅓ cup, about 5 minutes. Remove the saucepan from the heat and whisk in the soy sauce, lemon juice, lemon zest, and hot red pepper flakes. Set the *ponzu* sauce aside.

4 MAKE THE SLAW: Combine the onion, cucumber, and sprouts in a mixing bowl and toss to mix. Set the slaw aside.

5 Set up the grill for direct grilling (see page 21 for charcoal or gas) and preheat to high.

6 When ready to cook, brush and oil the grill grate. Drain the marinade from the tuna steaks and discard the marinade. Place the tuna on the hot grate and grill until charred on the outside, but still quite rare inside, 1 to 2 minutes per side. Test for doneness using the poke method: A rare tuna steak will be quite soft, with just a little resistance at the surface.

7 To serve, place the slaw on a platter or plates. Place the grilled tuna on top. Spoon the *ponzu* sauce over the fish and vegetables and serve at once.

YIELD:
Serves 4

NOTES:

■ Mirin is a sweet rice wine from Japan. Depending upon where you live, it's available at Asian markets, natural foods markets, and an increasing number of supermarkets. White wine sweetened with a little sugar is a substitute.

■ Radish sprouts are available at most major supermarkets. If you can't find them, you can substitute an equal amount of alfalfa or sunflower seed sprouts.

New York, N.Y.

TUNA WITH GINGER AND SHERRY (Barbecutioner's Tuna)

Eric Campbell is a third-generation bridge painter (his family has the contract to paint New York City's George Washington Bridge), but his true passion in life is obvious in his nickname. I met him at the Food & Wine Aspen Classic, where I was teaching a grilling class. When he asked me to sign his book for "The Barbecutioner," I knew I'd met a kindred spirit. Eric's tuna sounds an East-West theme: a ginger-soy marinade paired with a smoky swaddling of bacon.

METHOD:
Direct grilling

ADVANCE PREPARATION:
2 to 3 hours for marinating the tuna

INGREDIENTS:

4 sushi quality tuna steaks
   (each about 1 inch thick and
   6 ounces)
1 piece (2 inches) fresh ginger,
   peeled and finely grated
   (see Note)
½ cup soy sauce
½ cup cream sherry
3 tablespoons Asian (dark) sesame oil
   or canola oil
3 tablespoons brown sugar
2 scallions, trimmed, white part
   cut into 3 pieces and
   gently crushed with the
   side of a cleaver, green
   part finely chopped
3 cloves garlic, peeled and
   gently crushed with the side
   of a cleaver
1 pound sliced bacon

YOU'LL ALSO NEED:
Wooden toothpicks

1 Trim any skin or dark or bloody spots off the tuna. Rinse the tuna under cold running water, then blot it dry with paper towels. Cut each tuna steak lengthwise into strips that are 1 inch wide and 3 to 4 inches long. Place the tuna in a nonreactive baking dish.

2 Put the ginger, soy sauce, sherry, sesame oil, brown sugar, scallion whites, and garlic in a nonreactive mixing bowl and stir until the brown sugar dissolves. Pour this marinade over the tuna and let it marinate for 2 to 3 hours in the refrigerator, covered, turning the tuna several times so that it marinates evenly.

TIPS

Whenever you grill bacon, be prepared for flare-ups. I like to have an aluminum foil shield at the ready to slide under the fish when this happens. Or, as I've suggested here, you can build a two-zone fire, leaving a portion of the grill unlit so that you can move the tuna there temporarily to take refuge from the flames.

3 Drain the marinade from the tuna, transferring the marinade to a small saucepan. Bring the marinade to a boil over high heat and let boil until it becomes a syrupy glaze, 4 to 6 minutes. Wrap a slice of bacon, around the edge of each piece of tuna, leaving the top and bottom bare. Use a toothpick to secure the bacon to the fish.

4 Set up the grill for direct grilling using a two-zone fire (see page 22 for charcoal or gas); preheat one zone to high and leave the other zone unlit.

5 When ready to cook, brush and oil the grill grate. Place the tuna on the hot grate with one of the bacon wrapped edges down. Grill the tuna until the bacon is crisp and the fish is cooked to taste, 1 to 2 minutes per side (6 to 8 minutes in all) for medium-rare tuna. If the dripping bacon fat starts a flare-up, move the fish to the unlit zone of the grill. Baste the tuna with some of the boiled marinade as it grills.

6 Transfer the grilled tuna to a platter or plates and remove the toothpicks. Drizzle any remaining glaze over the fish, sprinkle the chopped scallion greens over it, and serve at once. And think of the Barbecutioner the next time you drive over the George Washington Bridge.

YIELD:

Serves 4

NOTE: Use a Microplane, the fine side of a box grater, or a Japanese ginger grater to grate the ginger.

Hawaii

TUNA "LONDON BROIL" With Wasabi Cream Sauce

Seared tuna, served charred on the outside, and rare—make that raw—inside, began turning up on menus in the United States during the late 1980s. It was love at first sight and bite. We adored the way the charred black crust set off the velvety crimson interior. And tuna was enough like beef that even meat-and-potatoes guys could enjoy it. Seared tuna was easier for squeamish eaters to handle than sushi because the outside of the fish was cooked. It quickly became an American classic and no one does it better than the chefs of Hawaii, who have some of the world's best tuna to choose from. I think you'll find the sesame-pepper-wasabi crust delectably different.

METHOD:
Direct grilling

ADVANCE PREPARATION:
30 minutes to 1 hour for marinating the tuna

FOR THE TUNA AND THE RUB:
2 teaspoons untoasted sesame seeds
2 teaspoons wasabi powder
2 teaspoons cracked black peppercorns
2 teaspoons garlic salt
1½ pounds tuna loin, or 4 tuna steaks (each about 1 to 1½ inches thick and 6 to 8 ounces)
2 teaspoons Asian (dark) sesame oil

FOR SERVING:
Wasabi Cream Sauce (recipe follows)
2 tablespoons thinly sliced scallion greens or chives
2 tablespoons toasted or black sesame seeds (see Note)

1 MAKE THE RUB: Place the untoasted sesame seeds, wasabi powder, peppercorns, and garlic salt in a spice mill or coffee grinder and grind to a fine powder. Or place them in a mortar and, using a pestle, grind them to a fine powder.

2 Trim any skin or dark or bloody spots off the tuna. Rinse the tuna under cold running water, then blot it dry with paper towels. Place the tuna in a baking dish. Sprinkle the rub all over the tuna on both sides, patting it onto the fish with your fingertips. Drizzle the sesame oil over the tuna and rub it on with your fingertips. Let the tuna marinate in the refrigerator, covered, for 30 minutes to 1 hour.

3 Set up the grill for direct grilling (see page 21 for charcoal or gas) and preheat to high.

4 When ready to cook, brush and oil the grill grate. Place the tuna on the hot grate and grill until cooked to taste. Grill tuna loin until the outside is nicely seared, 1 to 2 minutes per side (4 to 8 minutes in all) turning the loin with tongs. Grill tuna steaks for about 2 minutes per side for rare; 3 to 5 minutes per side for medium-rare; 4 to 6 minutes per side for medium, rotating each steak a quarter turn halfway through grilling on each side to create an attractive crosshatch of grill marks. Test for doneness using the poke method: Rare tuna will be quite soft, with just a little resistance at the surface; medium-rare tuna will be gently yielding; and medium tuna will be firm.

5 Transfer the grilled tuna to a cutting board and let it rest for 2 minutes. Carve tuna steaks into broad, thin slices, holding the knife at a 45 degree angle to the top of the fish. Carve tuna loin crosswise into ¼-inch-thick medallions. Fan out the tuna slices on a platter or plates. Squirt zigzags of

TIPS

A sesame-crusted beef London broil is delicious made in a similar fashion. Use an inch-thick slab of sirloin, top or bottom round, or even a flank steak.

Wasabi Cream Sauce over the tuna, top with the scallions and toasted or black sesame seeds, and serve at once. Serve the remaining Wasabi Cream Sauce on the side.

YIELD:

**Serves 8 as an appetizer,
    4 as a main course**

NOTE: To toast sesame seeds, place them in a dry skillet over medium heat (do not use a nonstick skillet for this). Cook until the seeds are lightly toasted, 2 to 3 minutes, shaking the pan to ensure even toasting. Transfer the seeds to a heatproof bowl to cool.

Wasabi Cream Sauce

Wasabi is frequently described as Japanese horseradish. Actually, the root belongs to a different plant family, but there's certainly something horseradishy about its bite. Wasabi is most commonly sold in powdered form—simply mix the powder with enough water to form a thick spicy paste. Not only is the wasabi cream delicious with tuna, it's great served with grilled beef or chicken.

INGREDIENTS:

1 to 2 tablespoons wasabi powder

1/2 cup mayonnaise (preferably Hellmann's)

1/2 cup sour cream

1 tablespoon fresh lemon juice

1 tablespoon soy sauce

1 Place the wasabi in a nonreactive mixing bowl. Add 1 tablespoon of cold water and stir to form a thick paste. Let sit for 5 minutes.

2 Add the mayonnaise, sour cream, lemon juice, and soy sauce and whisk to mix. The mixture should be thick but pourable. If necessary, thin with a little more water. Although the wasabi cream tastes best served within a few hours of making, it can be refrigerated, covered, for several days.

YIELD:

Makes about 1 cup

Maui, Hawaii

RICE-CHARRED TUNA With Grilled Pineapple Relish

Rice powder (pan-roasted ground rice) isn't a particularly common seasoning in mainland North America, but grill jockeys in Asia use it on everything from grilled seafood to salads and beef. I got the idea for this tuna recipe in Maui, where Asian grill parlors are as commonplace as rib emporiums are in Memphis. Of course, the Asian seasonings are only part of what makes this recipe Hawaiian—there's also the grilled pineapple relish, made with Hawaii's best-known fruit.

METHOD:
Direct grilling

ADVANCE PREPARATION:
30 minutes for marinating the tuna

FOR THE ROASTED-RICE RUB:
**3 tablespoons uncooked
     jasmine rice**
**1 tablespoon coarse salt
     (kosher or sea)**
**1 teaspoon freshly ground
     white pepper**
**1 teaspoon Chinese five-spice
     powder**

FOR THE TUNA:
**1½ pounds sushi quality tuna loin,
     or 4 sushi quality tuna steaks
     (each about 1 inch thick and
     6 ounces)**
**1 tablespoon Asian (dark)
     sesame oil**
**Grilled Pineapple Relish
     (recipe follows)**

1 MAKE THE ROASTED-RICE RUB: Place a small skillet over a medium heat (do not use a nonstick skillet for this). Add the rice and toast it, shaking the skillet, until lightly browned and very fragrant, 3 to 5 minutes. Transfer the toasted rice to a bowl and let cool.

2 Place the toasted rice in a spice mill or coffee grinder and grind to a fine powder. Add the salt, pepper, and five-spice powder and pulse just to mix.

3 Trim any skin or dark or bloody spots off the tuna. Rinse the tuna under cold running water, then blot it dry with paper towels. Place the tuna in a baking dish. Sprinkle the rub over the tuna on both sides, patting it onto the fish with your fingertips. Drizzle the sesame oil over the tuna and rub it on with your fingertips. Let the fish marinate in the refrigerator, covered, for 30 minutes.

4 Set up the grill for direct grilling (see page 21 for charcoal or gas) and preheat to high.

5 When ready to cook, brush and oil the grill grate. Place the tuna on the hot grate and grill until the outside is nicely charred, leaving the inside quite rare, 1 to 1½ minutes per side (4 to 6 minutes in all) for tuna loin; about 2 minutes per side (4 minutes in all) for tuna steaks. Test for doneness using the poke method: Rare tuna will be quite soft with just a little resistance at the surface.

6 Transfer the grilled tuna to a cutting board and let it rest for 1 minute. To serve, cut the tuna loin or steaks crosswise into ¼-inch-thick slices. Fan these out on a platter or plates, overlapping the slices. Spoon the pineapple relish alongside.

YIELD:
Serves 4

TIPS

Rice-Charred Tuna is quick and easy, but it does contain a few distinctive ingredients. The first is rice powder, made by toasting rice in a dry skillet, then grinding it in a spice mill (see Steps 1 and 2). The second is five-spice powder, a Chinese seasoning made from star anise, fennel seeds, cinnamon, Szechuan peppercorns, and white pepper. Look for it at gourmet shops and most supermarkets.

■ A melon baller makes a good tool for coring pineapples.

■ While it's not absolutely essential to grill the pineapple for the relish, you'll get a more interesting relish if you do. You can certainly grill the pineapple a day or two ahead of time, when grilling something else.

Hollowed-out pineapple shells would make novel bowls for serving the salsa.

Grilled Pineapple Relish

Pineapple is native to South America, but most of the fruit sold in North America historically has come from Hawaii. When buying this tropical fruit, look for a golden pineapple—bronze-colored and exceptionally sweet and fragrant. Note: This recipe makes just the amount of relish you'd need to serve with a pound and a half of tuna. I'd probably prepare a triple batch, using a whole pineapple—this relish is super with just about everything.

METHOD:
Direct grilling

INGREDIENTS:

8 thin (¼-inch) slices pineapple, rind and core removed

½ red bell pepper

2 scallions, trimmed

1 to 2 jalapeño peppers

3 tablespoons chopped fresh cilantro

1 tablespoon soy sauce

1 tablespoon fresh lime juice, or more to taste

1 tablespoon brown sugar, or more to taste

2 teaspoons finely grated peeled fresh ginger (see Note)

1 Set up the grill for direct grilling (see page 21 for charcoal or gas) and preheat to high.

2 When ready to cook, brush and oil the grill grate. Place the pineapple, bell pepper, scallions, and jalapeño(s) on the hot grate and grill until darkly browned, 3 to 5 minutes per side. Transfer the grilled fruit and vegetables to a cutting board and let cool. Cut the pineapple, bell pepper, and jalapeño(s) into ¼-inch dice. For a milder relish, seed the jalapeño(s) before dicing. Cut the scallions into ¼-inch slices.

3 Combine the diced pineapple and vegetables in a nonreactive mixing bowl. Add the cilantro, soy sauce, lime juice, brown sugar, and ginger and toss to mix. Taste for seasoning, adding more brown sugar and/or lime juice as necessary. Although the relish tastes best served within a few hours of making it, it can be refrigerated, covered, for several days. Bring to room temperature before serving.

YIELD:
Serves 4

NOTE: Use a Microplane, the fine side of a box grater, or a Japanese ginger grater to grate the ginger.

San Francisco, Calif.

GRILLED PETRALE SOLE
With Made-from-Scratch Tartar Sauce

P etrale sole is a fish that tests the mettle of grill masters (it also tries their souls). This delicate, tender, mild-flavored white fish is a San Francisco Bay delicacy—not to mention the house specialty at one of San Francisco's oldest restaurants, the Tadich Grill, founded in 1849. Problem is, most fish has a tendency to stick to the grill grate, and the soft-textured petrale sole is one of the worst offenders.

Tadich grill master Bill Counts uses three ingenious techniques for keeping the fish from sticking. First, he rolls it in a pan with a little squirt of oil (*little* is the key word here) prior to placing it on a superhot, superclean, and super well oiled grill grate. When he places the fish on the grate, he does so by hand, gently sliding the fish forward to make sure it doesn't stick. Finally, when he turns the fish over, he moves it to a virgin section of the grate—that is, a section that the fish hasn't touched, so the oil is still on the metal. This recipe, inspired by the Tadich's

petrale sole, may seem straightforward, but few things taste better than a perfectly grilled fish fillet served with homemade tartar sauce. And once you master petrale sole, you'll be able to grill any fish that swims.

METHOD:
Direct grilling

FOR THE TARTAR SAUCE:
¾ cup mayonnaise (preferably Hellmann's)
3 tablespoons Dijon mustard
1 shallot, minced
1 tablespoon capers, drained and minced
1 tablespoon minced cornichons or dill pickles
1 tablespoon chopped fresh tarragon
1 tablespoon tarragon vinegar or distilled white vinegar, or more to taste
Coarse salt (kosher or sea) and freshly ground black pepper

FOR THE SOLE:
1½ pounds petrale sole or other thin fish fillets, or broad, thin slices of thicker fish fillets
1 tablespoon vegetable oil
Coarse salt (kosher or sea) and freshly ground black pepper
Lemon wedges, for serving

1 MAKE THE TARTAR SAUCE: Place the mayonnaise, mustard, shallot, capers, cornichons, tarragon, and vinegar in a nonreactive mixing bowl and whisk to mix. Season with salt and pepper to taste. Place the sauce in 4 small, attractive nonreactive bowls for serving.

■ If you live in the Bay Area, you'll probably be able to find petrale sole at your local fishmonger or supermarket. If it's unavailable, you could substitute fillets of snapper, black bass, or if you're feeling ambitious, flounder (which is as prone to sticking to the grill as petrale sole is). When using larger fillets, such as striped bass or sea bass, cut them sharply on the diagonal into ½-inch-thick slices to maximize the surface area that will be exposed to the fire. This is also a good way to fix another Bay Area fish, sand dab.

■ For more techniques for preventing fish from sticking to the grill, see the box on page 438.

2 Rinse fish fillets under cold running water and then blot dry with paper towels.

3 Set up the grill for direct grilling (see page 21 for charcoal or gas) and preheat to high.

4 When ready to cook, brush and oil the grill grate. Lightly brush the fish fillets on each side with the oil and season generously with salt and pepper. Arrange the fillets on the hot grate, placing them on a diagonal to the bars. As you lay each piece on the grill, gently slide it forward about a half inch to keep it from sticking. Grill until the undersides of the fillets are nicely browned and the edges of the tops start to turn white, 3 to 5 minutes.

5 Using a spatula, turn the fillets over onto a part of the grate that has not yet been used for grilling, placing them on a diagonal to the bars. Again, as you lay them on the grill, gently slide each piece of fish forward about a half inch. Continue grilling the fish until it is cooked through, 3 to 5 minutes more. To test for doneness, press the fish with your finger; it should break into clean flakes. Transfer the grilled fish to a platter or plates and serve with lemon wedges and the tartar sauce on the side.

YIELD:
Serves 4

TADICH GRILL

TADICH GRILL

**240 California Street
San Francisco, California
(415) 391-1849**

No one grills fish better than the grill jockeys at the Tadich Grill in San Francisco, who perform the nearly impossible feat of grilling a soft flimsy fish like petrale sole. With roots that go back to 1849, the restaurant has become a city landmark. Its long, narrow, bare-bones dining room, with its equally long bar and private alcove booths, plays to standing-room-only crowds. Located in the heart of the business district, the Tadich Grill is as popular with locals as it is with tourists. A temple of high gastronomy it isn't, but the way they grill fish—petrale sole, sand dabs, Pacific red snapper, and other Bay Area specialties—is perfection itself.

Grilled fish and Pacific seafood are the specialties of the Tadich Grill, a San Francisco institution since 1849.

By an archaic twist of linguistic fancy, "grilled" actually means griddled or sautéed in Tadich speak, while "broiled" is the term to use if you want something grilled over charcoal (failure to keep these terms straight will get you into trouble). The "broiler," as the grill is called here, is a magnificent old charcoal-burning Montague constructed of black cast iron and stainless steel and stoked with a lava-red bed of burning mesquite that can get as hot as 600° to 800°F by my estimate. Come for an early lunch or expect to wait. And be sure to make your way back to the open kitchen to watch the grill men ply their trade.

TIPS

I first tasted this dish made kebab style with chunks of cod. I call for cod steaks or fillets here since they are less likely to fall apart on the grill (if you're worried about the fish sticking, use a fish basket). In the event you can't find fresh cod, the marinade works well with many types of fish, including salmon steaks, swordfish, and mahimahi.

New York, N.Y.

BIG APPLE COD With Afghan Spices

New York City is home to every imaginable kind of ethnic restaurant; you can literally trace the world's barbecue trail without stepping outside the five boroughs. The Silk Route is represented here with a recipe inspired by a chain of Afghan eateries in the Big Apple called the Afghan Kebab House. Its spicing—made with commonplace North American ingredients but reminiscent of those used in central Asia—is assertive without being overpowering, exactly what you want for a delicate fish like cod.

METHOD:
Direct grilling

ADVANCE PREPARATION:
2 to 12 hours for marinating the cod

FOR THE COD AND MARINADE:
**4 fresh cod steaks (each about 1 inch
    thick and 8 ounces), or 4 pieces
    cod fillet (each about 6 ounces)**
1 small onion, coarsely chopped
3 cloves garlic, coarsely chopped
**1 piece (1 inch) fresh ginger, peeled
    and coarsely chopped**
**1 to 2 serrano or jalapeño peppers, seeded
    and coarsely chopped (for a hotter fish,
    leave the seeds in)**
3 tablespoons fresh lemon juice
3 tablespoons vegetable oil

**1½ teaspoons coarse salt
    (kosher or sea)**
1 teaspoon ground coriander
½ teaspoon freshly ground black pepper

FOR THE BASTING MIXTURE:
½ teaspoon coarse salt (kosher or sea)
½ teaspoon freshly ground black pepper
½ teaspoon hot red pepper flakes
3 tablespoons vegetable oil

FOR SERVING:
Lemon wedges
Cilantro Sauce (optional; recipe follows)

YOU'LL ALSO NEED:
**Fish basket (optional); cooking oil spray
    (optional)**

1 Rinse the cod under cold running water, blot it dry with paper towels, then place it in a nonreactive baking dish.

2 MAKE THE MARINADE: Combine the onion, garlic, ginger, pepper(s), lemon juice, oil, salt, coriander, and black pepper in a blender, add 2 tablespoons of water, and purée until smooth, adding more water as necessary to obtain a thick but pourable marinade. Pour the marinade over the cod, turning the fish once or twice to coat it evenly. Let the cod marinate in the refrigerator, covered, for at least 2 hours or as long as overnight, turning it once or twice so that it marinates evenly.

3 MAKE THE BASTING MIXTURE: Put the salt, black pepper, hot pepper flakes, and oil in a small bowl and stir with a fork to mix. Set the basting mixture aside.

4 Set up the grill for direct grilling (see page 21 for charcoal or gas) and preheat to high (Afghans would use a charcoal grill).

5 When ready to cook, brush and very generously oil the grill grate. Drain the marinade from the cod and discard the marinade. Generously brush each piece of fish on both sides with the basting mixture. If using a fish basket, spray or brush it with oil and fasten the marinated cod inside. Place the fish or the fish basket on the hot grate and grill until the cod is cooked through, 4 to 6 minutes per side. If grilling the fillets directly on the grate, arrange them on a diagonal to the bars, then rotate them a quarter turn after 2 minutes on each side to create an attractive crosshatch of grill marks. Turn the cod over when the bottom is golden brown. To test for doneness, press the fish with your finger; it should break into clean flakes. Brush the fish with any remaining basting mixture as it cooks. Transfer the grilled cod to a platter or plates and serve with lemon wedges and Cilantro Sauce, if desired.

YIELD:
Serves 4

Cilantro Sauce

Here's the Afghan version of barbecue sauce—a garlicky, tart purée of cilantro, peppers, and walnuts that is served with every imaginable kebab,

A taste of Kabul in Midtown Manhattan.

grilled meat, or seafood. While the combination may sound exotic, you'll find variations of the sauce in New York City's hundreds of Afghan, Indian, Pakistani, and Persian restaurants.

INGREDIENTS:
1 bunch cilantro, stemmed, washed, and coarsely chopped (for 1 cup)
¼ cup chopped walnuts
2 cloves garlic, coarsely chopped
1 to 2 serrano or jalapeño peppers, seeded and coarsely chopped (for a hotter sauce, leave the seeds in)
¼ cup distilled white vinegar, or more to taste
2 tablespoons vegetable oil
1 teaspoon coarse salt (kosher or sea), or more to taste
½ teaspoon freshly ground black pepper, or more to taste

Place the cilantro, walnuts, garlic, pepper(s), vinegar, oil, salt, and black pepper in a blender, add 3 tablespoons cold water, and purée to a smooth paste, scraping down the sides of the blender with a spatula a few times. Add more cold water as needed to obtain a pourable sauce. Taste for seasoning, adding more vinegar, salt, and/or black pepper as necessary; the sauce should be highly seasoned. Although the sauce tastes best served within a few hours of making it, it will keep for several days in the refrigerator, covered. Bring to room temperature before serving.

YIELD:
Makes about 1 cup

Key Largo, Fla.

GROUPER MATECUMBE With Tomato "Hash"

The Fish House in Key Largo is one of those anonymous storefronts you whiz by as you drive north from Key West to Miami, but behind it is a lively and wildly popular seafood restaurant built around a fish market supplied by a fleet of local fisher folk. Grouper, snapper, yellowfin tuna, and other impeccably fresh local fish are available a dozen different ways. My favorite is Matecumbe style (named for one of the islands in the Florida

Keys)—topped with a summery "hash" of shallots, capers, basil, and fresh tomatoes. I took this dish as a jumping-off point for the recipe you'll find here. By the way, the Fish House is a fun place to have a birthday; instead of a cake, they bring you a giant fish with a candle on top.

METHOD:
Direct grilling

ADVANCE PREPARATION:
30 minutes for marinating the grouper

FOR THE GROUPER:
4 pieces grouper fillet
(about 6 ounces each)
2 tablespoons extra-virgin olive oil
Coarse salt (kosher or sea) and
freshly ground black pepper
2 cloves garlic, minced
8 fresh basil leaves, thinly slivered
(see Note)
2 tablespoons fresh lemon juice

FOR THE TOMATO, SHALLOT, AND
BASIL "HASH":
4 tablespoons extra-virgin olive oil
2 large shallots, thinly sliced
(about 1/2 cup)
1 large or 2 medium-size ripe tomatoes,
seeded and cut into 1/2-inch dice
1 1/2 tablespoons drained capers
8 basil leaves, thinly slivered (see Note)
2 tablespoons fresh lemon juice
Coarse salt (kosher or sea) and
freshly ground black pepper
Lemon wedges, for serving

1 Rinse the grouper under cold running water, then blot it dry with paper towels. Place the grouper pieces

TIPS

I've called for grouper here, a mild, bone-white fish found off the coast of Florida and in the Gulf of Mexico. The dish is equally good made swordfish, tuna, bluefish, or mahimahi.

in a nonreactive baking dish just large enough to hold them. Drizzle the olive oil over the fish, rubbing it onto both sides with your fingertips. Generously season the fish on both sides with salt and pepper and sprinkle with the garlic and basil. Pour the lemon juice over the fish, turning the fillets to coat both sides. Let the fish marinate for 30 minutes in the refrigerator, covered, turning it once so that it marinates evenly.

2 MAKE THE TOMATO, SHALLOT, AND BASIL "HASH": Heat 2 tablespoons of the olive oil in a nonstick skillet over medium-high heat. Add the shallots and cook until they've lost their rawness, about 2 minutes. Don't overcook; the shallots should retain their crispness. Add the tomatoes and capers and cook for 1 minute. Remove the skillet from the heat and stir in the basil and lemon juice and the remaining 2 tablespoons of olive oil. Season with salt and pepper to taste; the mixture should be highly seasoned. Set the hash aside. It can be kept at room temperature for several hours.

3 Set up the grill for direct grilling (see page 21 for charcoal or gas) and preheat to high.

4 When ready to grill, brush and oil the grill grate. Arrange the grouper fillets on the hot grate, placing them on a diagonal to the bars. Grill the grouper until cooked through, 3 to 5 minutes per side, rotating each fillet a quarter turn after 1½ minutes on each side to create an attractive crosshatch of grill marks (use a broad spatula to turn the fillets over). To test for doneness, press the fish with your finger; it should break into clean flakes. Transfer the grilled grouper to a platter or plates. Spoon the hash over the fish and serve at once, with lemon wedges.

YIELD:
Serves 4

NOTE: The easiest way to slice basil or other leafy herbs into thin slivers is to stack several of the leaves in a single pile, roll them up crosswise into a tight tube, then thinly slice the tube crosswise with a sharp knife. Fluff the resulting slices with your fingers.

The boisterous Fish House serves some of the freshest grilled fish in the Florida Keys.

TIPS

Bluefish is exquisite when it's very fresh and downright offensive when it's not. If you can't catch your own, buy it from your local fishmonger and ask to smell it first.

Long Island "blues"—exquisite when just out of the water.

Long Island, N.Y.

LONG ISLAND BLUEFISH
Grilled in Bacon with Scallions

A whole grilled fish makes a spectacular centerpiece for a beach house cookout, especially when it's stuffed with lemon and herbs and grilled wrapped in smoky bacon. If you happen to be vacationing on the East Coast, you can make this recipe with one of the best summer fishes of all: fresh bluefish. Bluefish has a soft, sweet, light-gray meat that readily takes on smoke and herb flavors— without surrendering any of its own. Elsewhere in the country, you could use whole striped bass or salmon; if you'd like to grill bluefish fillets, you'll find a recipe on the facing page.

METHOD:
Indirect grilling

INGREDIENTS:
1 whole bluefish, cleaned, with head on (6 to 8 pounds)
Coarse salt (kosher or sea) and freshly ground black pepper
3 thin slices lemon, plus lemon wedges for serving
2 scallions, trimmed
2 cloves garlic, peeled and gently crushed with the side of a cleaver
6 sprigs fresh dill or flat-leaf parsley
12 slices bacon (see Note)

YOU'LL ALSO NEED:
A piece of cardboard as large as the bluefish

1 Cut out a cardboard rectangle about the length and width of the fish. Wrap the cardboard in a triple layer of aluminum foil (shiny side out) and set aside. (Placing the fish on this will help get it on and off the grill.)

2 Rinse the bluefish, inside and out, under cold running water, then blot it dry, inside and out, with paper towels. Generously season the fish, inside and out, with salt and pepper. Stuff the cavity with the lemon slices, scallions, garlic, and dill.

3 Place 4 slices of the bacon on the aluminum foil–wrapped cardboard (the slices should run lengthwise). Place

the fish on top of the bacon. Drape the remaining slices of bacon over the fish, placing them on a diagonal to the fish to cover the maximum surface area.

4 Set up the grill for indirect grilling (see page 22 for charcoal or page 23 for gas) and preheat to medium-high.

5 When ready to cook, place the bluefish on its cardboard in the center of the hot grate, away from the heat. Cover the grill and cook the fish until the bacon is nicely browned and the fish is cooked through, 40 minutes to 1 hour. To test for doneness, insert a slender metal skewer into the thickest part of the fish for 20 seconds: It should come out very hot to the touch.

6 Remove the cardboard from the grill with the grilled fish on top. Using 2 spatulas, carefully transfer the fish to a platter. To carve, run the edge of a serving spoon or a knife the length of the fish just above the backbone and across the bottom of the head. Loosen the flesh on top from the backbone and cut it crosswise into 4 to 6 portions, lifting each off the bones. Lift off the head and bones and discard them. Cut the bottom half of the fish crosswise into 4 to 5 portions. Serve at once, with lemon wedges, including a few pieces of bacon with each portion of fish.

YIELD:
Serves 8 to 10

NOTE: For the best results, use an artisanal smokehouse bacon (see Mail-Order Sources, page 742).

Long Island, N.Y.

FLAME-SEARED BLUEFISH FILLETS

Use this recipe when whole bluefish are unavailable or when you'd prefer to cook and serve fillets. The fish bundles, wrapped with bacon and tied with string, look cool as all get out, and the recipe has an added advantage: You can grill it using the direct method. You can use this technique for grilling just about any kind of fish fillet, from salmon to mahimahi.

METHOD:
Direct grilling

INGREDIENTS:
4 pieces bluefish fillet, skin on
    (6 to 8 ounces each)
Coarse salt (kosher or sea) and
    freshly ground black pepper
8 slices bacon, cut in half crosswise
8 thin slices onion
8 thin slices lemon (seeds removed),
    plus lemon wedges for serving
8 sprigs fresh dill or flat-leaf parsley

YOU'LL ALSO NEED:
Butcher's string

1 Rinse the bluefish under cold running water, then blot it dry with

TIPS

Grilling bluefish fillets directly over a medium fire has two advantages: The fish cooks more quickly and the bacon will be more crisp than if you use the indirect method. However, you will need to watch for flare-ups from the dripping bacon fat. Build a two-zone fire (see page 22) so that you have a safety zone where you can move the fish to keep it from burning.

paper towels. Season the fish on both sides with salt and pepper.

2 ASSEMBLE THE FISH BUNDLES: Cut eight 12-inch pieces of butcher's string. Lay out a piece of string on your work surface. Place 2 of the half slices of bacon side by side in the center of the string so that they are perpendicular to it. Place an onion slice on top of the pieces of bacon. Stack a lemon slice on top of the onion, followed by a dill sprig. Place a bluefish fillet on top of the dill so that the long side of the fillet is perpendicular to the string. Stack another dill sprig, lemon slice, and onion slice on top of the fillet. Arrange 2 more of the half slices of bacon on top of the onion. Draw the ends of the string up and tie them together to form a bundle. Tie a second string around the fish bundle so that it is perpendicular to the first string. Assemble 3 more fish bundles the same way. The fish bundles can be prepared to this stage up to several hours ahead and refrigerated, covered.

3 Set up the grill for direct grilling using a two-zone fire (see page 22 for charcoal or gas); preheat one zone to medium and leave the other zone unlit.

4 When ready to cook, place the bluefish bundles on the hot grate, skin side down. Grill until the bacon is golden brown and the fish is cooked through, 6 to 8 minutes per side. Turn the fish bundles over when the bottoms are browned. If the dripping bacon fat causes flare-ups, move the fish to the unlit zone of the grill. To test for doneness, insert a slender metal skewer into the side of a fish fillet for 20 seconds: It should come out very hot to the touch.

5 Transfer the grilled fish bundles to a platter or plates and place the lemon wedges alongside. Present the fish bundles in all their glory to your diners and then cut the strings with scissors as you serve.

YIELD:
Serves 4

The Eastern Seaboard

GRILLED BLUEFISH With Heirloom Tomato Corn Relish

Bluefish is either revered or reviled and the reason is simple. When fresh out of the water, nothing can beat the rich, sweet taste of this delicate, dark, oily fish. When less than impeccably fresh, bluefish tastes strongly fishy—a turnoff to anyone. New Englanders and mid-Atlantic Coasters are at an advantage, as these are the bluefish's waters. Pair the bad

... the bad boy of the ocean ...

boy of the ocean with the very finest olive oil and salt money can buy and a soulful relish of grilled corn and local heirloom tomatoes, and you'll be happily singing the blues.

METHOD:
Direct grilling

FOR THE RELISH:
4 ears sweet corn, shucked
1 to 2 tablespoons extra-virgin olive oil
Coarse sea salt (preferably fleur de sel)
    and coarsely ground black pepper
3 tablespoons finely diced red bell pepper
3 tablespoons finely diced green
    bell pepper
1 shallot, minced (about 3 tablespoons)
1 clove garlic, minced
1 tablespoon chopped fresh tarragon
2 tablespoons white wine vinegar,
    or more to taste
1 pound heirloom tomatoes, cut into
    ½-inch dice, with their juices

FOR THE BLUEFISH:
4 pieces bluefish fillet (skin on or off;
    each 6 to 8 ounces; see Note)
Coarse sea salt (preferably fleur de sel)
    and coarsely ground black pepper
1½ tablespoons extra-virgin olive oil

YOU'LL ALSO NEED:
Fish basket (optional); cooking oil
    spray (optional)

1 Set up the grill for direct grilling (see page 21 for charcoal or gas) and preheat to high.

2 MAKE THE RELISH: When ready to cook, brush the corn with olive oil and season generously with salt and pepper. Place the corn on the hot grate and grill the until the kernels are golden brown, 2 to 3 minutes per side (8 to 12 minutes in all). Transfer the grilled corn to a cutting board and let it cool (let the fire continue to burn in the grill).

3 Cut the kernels off the corn cob using lengthwise strokes of a chef's knife. Place the corn kernels and the red and green bell peppers, shallot, garlic, tarragon, vinegar, and tomatoes in a nonreactive mixing bowl but do not toss.

4 Place the bluefish fillets in a baking dish just large enough to hold them. Generously season the fillets with salt and pepper. Drizzle the olive oil over the fillets, patting it onto them with your fingertips. Let the fish marinate for 5 minutes.

5 When ready to cook, brush and oil the grill grate. If using a fish basket, spray or brush it with oil and fasten the bluefish inside. Place the fish or the fish basket on the hot grate and grill until just cooked through, 4 to 6 minutes per side. The skin side of the fillets, if any, should be down. If grilling the fillets directly on the grate, arrange them on a diagonal to the bars, then rotate them a quarter turn after 2 minutes on each side to create an attractive crosshatch of grill marks. To test for doneness, press the fish with your finger; it will

TIPS

■ I spent forty years on this planet without tasting an heirloom tomato. Now these green, yellow, or almost purple, sometimes striped or spotted, fruits—frequently misshapen or in odd sizes—are turning up at restaurants, farmers' markets, and even my local supermarket. Their intriguing flavor beats conventional tomatoes hollow. Try to buy tomatoes that have never been refrigerated, and if they aren't ready to use, let them ripen at room temperature.

■ A word on salt: Look for the French *fleur de sel*, literally flower of salt, a coarse, moist, grayish sea salt that fairly explodes with briny flavor.

break into clean flakes when fully cooked. Another test is to insert a slender metal skewer into the side of the fish for 20 seconds: It should come out very hot to the touch.

6 Place the grilled fish, skin side down if there is one, on a platter or plates. Toss the relish, then taste for seasoning, adding salt and pepper to taste and perhaps a few more drops of vinegar as necessary. Spoon the relish over the fish and serve at once.

YIELD:
Serves 4

NOTE: If you can't get impeccably fresh bluefish, try the recipe with pompano, mahimahi, or even salmon.

New Orleans, La.

GRILL-BLACKENED REDFISH

Ubiquitous blackened fish has become such a culinary icon that it's hard to believe just how revolutionary it seemed when Paul Prudhomme first served it. Here was this burly guy in New Orleans, burning up an old cast-iron skillet (not even a sauté pan, for gosh sake),

Louisiana's legendary Paul Prudhomme launched the Cajun cooking revolution.

which filled the kitchen with clouds of acrid smoke that scorched nasal passages and made eyes water. And what came out of the pan was even more shocking—a virtual trash fish called redfish that arrived at the table so burnt looking and dark, you didn't know whether to taste it or send it back. Then you tried it and knew—it was heaven. Because of all the smoke, chef Prudhomme urged people to blacken their fish outdoors on the grill. So that set me thinking—why not do away with the frying pan altogether and simply blacken the fish directly on the grate? You might even get some additional flavor from the fire.

METHOD:
Direct grilling

FOR THE BLACKENING MIXTURE:
**1 tablespoon coarse salt
    (kosher or sea)**
1 tablespoon garlic powder
1 tablespoon onion powder
1 tablespoon dried oregano
1 tablespoon sweet paprika
**2 teaspoons freshly ground
    black pepper**
**2 teaspoons freshly ground
    white pepper**
2 teaspoons dried thyme
1 teaspoon cayenne pepper

FOR THE REDFISH:
**4 chilled redfish fillets
    (each 6 to 8 ounces)**
**2 to 3 tablespoons butter,
    melted**
Lemon wedges, for serving

1 MAKE THE BLACKENING MIXTURE: Combine the salt, garlic and onion powders, oregano, paprika, black and white peppers, thyme, and cayenne in a bowl and stir to mix. (Actually, if you don't have sensitive skin, your fingers work better for mixing a rub than a spoon or a whisk does.)

2 Rinse the redfish fillets under cold running water, then blot dry with paper towels. Using a pastry brush, generously brush the fish on both sides with melted butter. Thickly sprinkle each fish fillet with the blackening mixture, patting it onto the fish with your fingertips. Refrigerate the fillets, covered, until ready to grill. The fillets should be cold—straight out of the refrigerator—when you put them on the grill.

3 Set up the grill for direct grilling (see page 21 for charcoal or gas) and preheat to high.

4 When ready to cook, brush and oil the grill grate. Arrange the fish fillets on the hot grate, placing them on a diagonal to the bars, and grill until blackened on the outside and cooked through, 4 to 6 minutes per side. To test for doneness, press the fish with your finger; it should break into clean flakes. Transfer the grilled fish to a platter or plates and serve with lemon wedges.

YIELD:
Serves 4

TIPS

Chef Paul Prudhomme pioneered this dish with redfish, a once cheap fish from the Gulf of Mexico. Such was its astonishing popularity that redfish prices tripled within a decade; there were even reports that it was on the verge of becoming extinct. You can certainly make this dish with redfish; I hope you do. But any fish fillet or steak can be blackened, from cod to swordfish.

■ Striped bass was overfished almost to extinction by the 1980s. Happily, it has made a comeback in the last decade, and you can now find it at fish markets up and down the East Coast (it's also being raised on fish farms). On the West Coast, you could use halibut or mahimahi.

■ I like a light wood smoke flavor with this grilled fish, so I use unsoaked wood chips in the fire, but wood is optional.

■ For instructions on how to prevent fish from sticking to the grate when grilling, see page 438. To make grilling really easy, you could use a fish grate or hinged fish basket. Barring that, brush and oil the grill grate exceptionally well before putting on the fish.

Cape Cod, Mass.

CHILE-RUBBED STRIPED BASS With Grilled Corn Salsa

You'll find the influence of both New England and the Southwest in this recipe inspired by Pat and Nitzi Rabin, owners of the Chillingsworth and Bistro restaurants in Brewster on Cape Cod. Nitzi received classical culinary training in France, but his menu is broad-minded enough to blast taste buds with Southwestern chiles. Consider this spice-rubbed striped bass served with grilled corn salsa— the salsa made with the supersweet, superfresh corn for which Cape Cod is famous. Striped bass is a sweet-fleshed, full-flavored but delicate fish that's in its prime in the summer, a perfect partner for the corn.

METHOD:
Direct grilling

ADVANCE PREPARATION:
30 minutes for marinating the fish

FOR THE RUB:
2 teaspoons pure chile powder
1 teaspoon coarse salt (kosher or sea)
1/2 teaspoon freshly ground black pepper
1/2 teaspoon dried oregano

1/2 teaspoon ground cumin
1/4 teaspoon ground cinnamon

FOR THE BASS:
4 skinless striped bass fillets (each about 6 ounces)
1 to 2 tablespoons extra-virgin olive oil
Grilled Corn Salsa (recipe follows)
Lime wedges, for serving

YOU'LL ALSO NEED:
2 cups wood chips or chunks (optional; preferably oak), unsoaked; fish basket (optional); cooking oil spray (optional)

1 MAKE THE RUB: Place the chile powder, salt, pepper, oregano, cumin, and cinnamon in a small bowl and stir to mix. (Actually, if you don't have sensitive skin, your fingers work better for mixing a rub than a spoon or a whisk does.)

2 Rinse the fish fillets under cold running water, then blot them dry with paper towels. Sprinkle the rub all over the fillets on both sides, patting it onto the fish with your fingertips. Lightly brush the fish on both sides with olive oil. Let the fish marinate in the refrigerator, covered, for 30 minutes.

3 Set up the grill for direct grilling (see page 21 for gas or charcoal) and preheat to high. If using a gas grill, place all of the wood chips or chunks, if desired, in the smoker box or in a smoker pouch (see page 24) and run the grill on high until you see smoke. If using a charcoal grill, preheat it to high, then toss all of the wood chips or chunks, if desired, on the coals.

4 When ready to cook, brush and very generously oil the grill grate. If using a fish basket, spray or brush it with oil and fasten the marinated fillets inside. Place the fish or the fish basket on the hot grate and grill until the fillets are nicely browned and cooked through, 4 to 6 minutes per side. To test for doneness, press the fish with your finger; it should break into clean flakes.

5 Transfer the grilled fillets to a platter or plates. Spoon the Grilled Corn Salsa over it and serve with lime wedges.

YIELD:
Serves 4

Grilled Corn Salsa

Grilling lends a smoky flavor to this summery salsa, mellowing the bite of the jalapeños and reinforcing the sweetness of the bell pepper and corn. Serve it with the grilled striped bass, of course, but the salsa also goes exceedingly well with other types of seafood or even grilled chicken or pork.

INGREDIENTS:

4 ears sweet corn, shucked
2 tablespoons butter, melted
Coarse salt (kosher or sea) and
      freshly ground black pepper
1 red bell pepper

2 jalapeño peppers
1 medium-size red onion, peeled and
      cut lengthwise into quarters
¼ cup chopped fresh cilantro
3 tablespoons fresh lime juice,
      or more to taste
1 teaspoon light brown sugar,
      or more to taste

1 Set up the grill for direct grilling (see page 21 for charcoal or gas) and preheat to high.

2 When ready to cook, lightly brush the corn with some of the melted butter and season with salt and black pepper. Brush and oil the grill grate. Place the corn, bell pepper, jalapeños, and onion on the hot grate. Grill the corn until nicely browned on all sides,

Don't let Nitzi Rabin's chef's coat and starched apron fool you. The classically trained chef can smoke and grill with the best of them.

the bell pepper and jalapeños until charred on all sides, and the onion until lightly charred on the outside and soft in the center. This will take 2 to 3 minutes per side (8 to 12 minutes in all) for the corn, 3 to 4 minutes per side (12 to 16 minutes in all) for the bell pepper, 2 to 3 minutes per side (4 to 6 minutes in all) for the jalapeños, and 3 to 4 minutes per side (9 to 12 minutes in all) for the onion wedges. Transfer the grilled vegetables to a cutting board and let cool.

3 Cut the kernels off the corn cobs, using lengthwise strokes of a chef's knife. Scrape any really burnt skin off the bell pepper, jalapeños, and onion (leave a few burnt bits for color and flavor). Core and seed the bell pepper and jalapeños and cut all of the vegetables into ¼-inch dice. Place the corn kernels, diced bell pepper, jalapeños, and onion, along with the cilantro, lime juice, and brown sugar in a nonreactive mixing bowl and stir to mix. Taste for seasoning, adding more lime juice and/or brown sugar as necessary. The salsa can be refrigerated, covered, for 6 hours. Bring to room temperature before serving.

YIELD:
Makes 3 to 4 cups

Grilling fever is so contagious it has even infected this landmark French restaurant on Cape Cod.

New York, N.Y.

HERB-GRILLED BLACK SEA BASS
With Garlic Mint Vinaigrette

If you like grilled fish and fresh herbs, you'll flip for this simple, spectacular grilled black sea bass. After being stuffed with fresh mint, the fish finishes grilling atop more mint. As the herb is heated by the fire, it gives off a wonderful perfume. And you can throw the dish together in about fifteen minutes. The idea was inspired by Frank De Carlo, owner-chef of New York's SoHo restaurant, Peasant, where all the cooking is done over charcoal and wood.

METHOD:
Direct grilling

FOR THE FISH:
**4 whole black sea bass
    (each about 1½ pounds),
    cleaned and trimmed**
3 to 4 tablespoons extra-virgin olive oil
**Coarse salt (kosher or sea) and
    freshly ground black pepper**
1 lemon, thinly sliced
3 bunches fresh mint, rinsed

FOR THE GARLIC MINT VINAIGRETTE:

3 tablespoons red wine vinegar

¹/₂ teaspoon coarse salt (kosher or sea)

¹/₂ teaspoon freshly ground black pepper

³/₄ cup extra-virgin olive oil

**2 cloves garlic, peeled and gently crushed
    with the side of a cleaver**

¹/₄ cup chopped fresh mint leaves

1 Rinse the fish, inside and out, under cold running water, then blot them dry, inside and out, with paper towels. Make 3 parallel cuts all the way to the bone on both sides of each fish (this helps ensure even cooking). Rub the fish inside and out with the olive oil and season generously with salt and pepper. Place an equal number of lemon slices in the cavity of each of the 4 fish. Place a few mint sprigs in each cavity. Set the remaining mint aside for grilling. Place the fish in a baking dish and set aside while you set up the grill and make the vinaigrette.

2 Set up the grill for direct grilling (see page 21 for charcoal or gas) and preheat to medium-high.

3 MAKE THE GARLIC MINT VINAI-GRETTE: Not more than 30 minutes before serving, place the vinegar in a nonreactive mixing bowl and add the salt and pepper. Whisk until the salt dissolves. Whisk in the olive oil in a thin steam, then add the garlic and chopped mint.

4 When ready to cook, brush and oil the grill grate. Place the fish on the hot grate and grill until just cooked through, 6 to 10 minutes per side. To check for doneness, use a slender

paring knife to cut into the fish at the backbone: The flesh should come away from the bones easily. Using a long spatula, move the fish to the side of the grill. Lay the remaining mint on the grill over the hottest part of the fire, arranging the stems so that they are perpendicular to the bars of the grate. Place the fish on top and let it cook for a couple minutes longer to absorb the grilled mint flavor.

5 Transfer the grilled fish to a platter. Remove the mint from the grill and discard it. Remove and discard the garlic cloves from the vinaigrette then stir it with a fork to recombine. Serve the fish with the vinaigrette spooned over it.

YIELD:
Serves 4

Florida

JERK SNAPPER

Jerk can be found all over the United States, of course, but the most authentic I've ever tasted was in South Florida, which is home to a flourishing Jamaican community. Of course, we Americans have adopted jerk as our own, adapting this fiery way of fixing pork to foods most Jamaicans would probably never think of jerking—from

T I P S

Frank De Carlo uses a fish imported from Italy called *orata*. The closest equivalent in the United States is black sea bass, a handsome black fish in the porgy family that is widely available in the mid-Atlantic. (Don't confuse black sea bass with sea bass—the latter is a large, gelatinous-textured fish from South America.) If black sea bass is unavailable, you could use porgie, pompano, snapper, or any other single-portion whole fish.

lobster to tofu to pasta (that last has appeared on the menu of the East Coast Grill in Cambridge, Massachusetts). The essence of jerk is its marinade: a heated paste of Scotch bonnet chiles, aromatic root vegetables, and herbs and spices. Equally important is the smoke from fragrant allspice wood in Jamaica or a more pedestrian, but no less tasty, hickory or oak when made in the United States.

METHOD:
Direct grilling

ADVANCE PREPARATION:
1 to 2 hours for marinating the snapper

INGREDIENTS:
4 small snappers or other small whole fish (each 1 to 1½ pounds), cleaned
1 to 3 Scotch bonnet chiles, stemmed and seeded (for a hotter jerk, leave the seeds in)
4 large scallions, both white and green parts, trimmed and coarsely chopped
3 cloves garlic, peeled
1 small shallot, coarsely chopped
1 piece (½ inch) fresh ginger, peeled and coarsely chopped
3 tablespoons chopped fresh cilantro
1 teaspoon fresh or dried thyme
1½ teaspoons coarse salt (kosher or sea), or more to taste
1 teaspoon brown sugar, or more to taste
½ teaspoon ground allspice
½ teaspoon freshly ground black pepper
¼ teaspoon ground cinnamon
2 tablespoons vegetable oil
1 tablespoon dark rum
1 tablespoon fresh lime juice, or more to taste, plus lime wedges for serving
2 teaspoons soy sauce

YOU'LL ALSO NEED:
2 cups wood chips or chunks (preferably hickory or oak), soaked for 1 hour in water to cover, then drained; fish basket (optional); cooking oil spray (optional)

1 Trim the fins off the fish using kitchen shears. Rinse the fish, inside and out, under cold running water, then blot them dry, inside and out, with paper towels. Make 3 or 4 deep diagonal slashes in the side of each fish. Place the fish in a nonreactive baking dish just large enough to hold them.

2 Place the Scotch bonnet(s), scallions, garlic, shallot, ginger, cilantro, thyme, salt, brown sugar, allspice, pepper, and cinnamon in a food processor and finely chop. Add the oil, rum, lime juice, and soy sauce and 1 tablespoon of water and process to a coarse paste. Taste for seasoning, adding more salt, brown sugar, and/or lime juice as necessary; the jerk seasoning should be highly seasoned.

3 Stuff some of the jerk seasoning into the fish cavities and some into the slits in the sides of the fish. Spread the remaining jerk seasoning over the fish and let marinate in the refrigerator, covered, for 1 hour, turning once or twice so that they marinate evenly.

4 Set up the grill for direct grilling (see page 21 for gas or charcoal) and preheat to medium-high. If using a gas grill, place all of the wood chips or chunks in the smoker box or in a smoker pouch (see page 24) and run the grill on high until you see smoke, then reduce the heat to medium-high. If using a charcoal grill, preheat to medium-high, then toss all of the wood chips or chunks on the coals.

5 When ready to cook, brush and oil the grill grate. If using a fish basket, spray or brush it with oil and fasten the fish inside. Place the fish or the fish basket on the hot grate and grill the fish until cooked through, 6 to 10 minutes per side (depending on the size of the fish), turning gently with a spatula or by inverting the fish basket. To test for doneness, press the flesh with your finger: It will break into clean flakes when fully cooked. The flesh will come cleanly away from the bones when pried loose with the tip of a paring knife and a slender metal skewer inserted into the thickest part of a fish for 20 seconds should come out very hot to the touch. Transfer the grilled fish to a platter or plates and serve at once with the lime wedges.

YIELD:
Serves 4

Los Angeles, Calif.

SARDINES GRILLED IN GRAPE LEAVES

The flavors may be Mediterranean, but the setting and chef are pure Californian. I'm talking about Los Angeles's celebrated restaurant Campanile, where sardines grilled in grape leaves are a specialty. This handsome edifice, with its *campanile* (bell tower), was built in 1929 to house Charlie Chaplin's business offices (he lost the building in a divorce settlement). In 1989, chef Mark Peel and pastry diva Nancy Silverton converted the historic building into a restaurant and the La Brea Bakery. Peel cut his teeth as a chef in California, peeling vegetables at Ma Maison for a young Wolfgang Puck. His cooking is firmly rooted in the California-Mediterranean tradition, applying the bold, simple flavors of France and Italy to California's superlative seafood and produce. Witness these sardines stuffed with currants and pine nuts, which are grilled swaddled in grape leaves.

TIPS

This recipe calls for pickled grape leaves from a jar. If you're lucky enough to have your own vines, you can use fresh leaves—provided they haven't been treated with chemical pesticides.

Snapper so fresh it talks back to you.

METHOD:
Direct grilling

ADVANCE PREPARATION:
1 hour for soaking the grape leaves

FOR THE STUFFING:
2 tablespoons extra-virgin olive oil
2 scallions, both white and green parts
trimmed and finely chopped
¼ cup currants
¼ cup pine nuts
¼ cup coarsely chopped fresh flat-leaf
parsley or mint
½ teaspoon grated lemon zest
Coarse salt (kosher or sea) and
freshly ground black pepper

FOR THE SARDINES:
12 whole fresh sardines, cleaned
2 tablespoons extra-virgin olive oil
Coarse salt (kosher or sea) and
freshly ground black pepper
12 grape leaves, soaked (see Note)
Lemon wedges, for serving

YOU'LL ALSO NEED:
Butcher's string

TIPS

Fresh sardines can be found at the fishmongers or in Spanish or Portuguese markets. If they're unavailable, you can cut salmon fillets into long thin strips (say, four inches long and two inches wide), cut a pocket in one side, and stuff and wrap these as you would the sardines. Salmon and sardines may sound dissimilar, but both are rich, oily fish.

1 MAKE THE STUFFING: Heat the olive oil in a sauté pan over medium heat. Add the scallions, currants, and pine nuts and cook until the scallions are softened and have lost their rawness and the pine nuts are fragrant and just beginning to brown, 3 to 4 minutes. Remove the pan from the heat and stir in the parsley and lemon zest. Season with salt and pepper to taste and let cool to room temperature.

2 Rinse the sardines, inside and out, under cold running water, then blot them dry, inside and out, with paper towels. You can stuff and grill the sardines as is or, if you're feeling ambitious, you can bone them: Open up the cavity of a fish and, using kitchen shears, cut through the backbone at the head and tail. Gently pull out the backbone, using needle-nose pliers or tweezers. Pull out and discard any remaining bones. Repeat with the remaining sardines.

3 Spoon the stuffing into the cavity of each sardine, dividing it evenly among them. Brush the outsides of the fish with the olive oil and season with salt and pepper.

4 Drain the grape leaves, rinse, and blot them dry with paper towels. Wrap each fish in a grape leaf: Place a grape leaf on your work surface, stem end toward you. Place a sardine at the left edge of the leaf, then roll up the sardine in the leaf and tie the bundle with butcher's string. Repeat with the remaining sardines. They can be prepared to this stage several hours ahead and kept, covered, in the refrigerator.

5 Set up the grill for direct grilling (see page 21 for charcoal or gas) and preheat to high.

6 When ready to cook, brush the grill grate. Place the grape leaf–wrapped sardines on the hot grate and grill until the grape leaves are golden brown and the fish is cooked through, 3 to 5 minutes per side. To test for doneness, insert a slender metal skewer into the thickest part of a sardine for 20 seconds: When it is done, the skewer should come out very hot to the touch.

7 Transfer the grilled sardines to a platter or plates. Serve at once with the lemon wedges. Instruct everyone to unwrap the sardines—you don't eat the grape leaves—and watch out for the fish bones.

YIELD:
Serves 4

NOTE: Grape leaves are available in jars in most supermarkets or at Greek or Middle Eastern grocery stores. To remove the excess salt, soak the leaves for 1 hour in a large bowl with enough cold water to cover them by several inches, changing the water two or three times.

New York, N.Y.

GRILLED SARDINES
With Fennel Orange Salad

"We try to keep the food simple, letting the flavor come from the fire and wood smoke," observes Tom Colicchio, chef and co-owner of New York's Gramercy Tavern (you'll find a description of the restaurant on page 504). Colicchio presides over one of the few wood-burning grills in Manhattan, and his food is remarkable for its intense flavor and restraint. Here's my rendition of Tom's grilled sardines, which are served over a simple fennel and orange salad.

METHOD:
Direct grilling

INGREDIENTS:
2 large oranges
1 small fennel bulb
¼ medium-size red onion,
    very thinly sliced
3 tablespoons coarsely chopped
    fresh flat-leaf parsley
2 tablespoons extra-virgin olive oil,
    plus oil for brushing the fish
1 tablespoon red wine vinegar,
    or more to taste
12 whole fresh sardines, cleaned
Coarse salt (kosher or sea) and
    freshly ground black pepper
Lemon wedges, for serving

YOU'LL ALSO NEED:
2 cups wood chips or chunks
    (optional; preferably oak),
    unsoaked

1 Using a very sharp knife, cut the rind and white pith off the oranges, exposing the bright orange flesh. Working over a large nonreactive bowl to catch the juice and making V-shape cuts between the membranes, cut out the orange segments and place them in the bowl. Using a fork, remove any seeds. Squeeze any orange juice remaining in the membranes into the bowl, and then discard the membranes.

TIPS

Gramercy Tavern serves its sardines boned. I'm more inclined to grill and serve the fish whole. For the full effect of this simple salad, grill the sardines over an oak fire (see page 20). If not, use wood chips; you want a light wood—not a heavy smoke—flavor, so don't bother to soak the chips.

GRAMERCY TAVERN

GRAMERCY TAVERN

42 East 20th Street
New York, New York
(212) 477-0777

Say the word *tavern* and what do you think of? Do you picture a hospitable taproom? One with a blazing hearth—the sort of place where you can warm up with a steaming grog or slake your thirst with a cold ale; a spot where you seek shelter from the elements and companionship from your fellow man.

Well, it turns out that New York restaurateur Danny Meyer and chef Tom Colicchio had a similar vision when they opened the Gramercy Tavern in New York's Flatiron district. And while you'd never mistake the restaurant's understated elegance for the sort of dark smoky saloons where Peter Stuyvesant or Washington Irving would have tippled, comfort and warmth infuse Gramercy Tavern's atmosphere.

The critics may wax grandiloquent about the wood-beamed, antique-filled dining room. For me the heart of the restaurant is the wood-burning grill, one of the few in Manhattan. It's a brick-lined, black steel Wood Shaw "Broiler" built by J & R Manufacturing, a company appropriately located in Mesquite, Texas. Gramercy Tavern chefs burn something on the order of fifteen cords of Pennsylvania oak a week to prepare the simply grilled meats, poultry, seafood, and vegetables served in the restaurant.

"We don't go in for a lot of rubs or marinades," explains Colicchio, who largely limits seasonings to olive oil, salt, and pepper. "We want our fish and meat to taste exactly like it tastes." That's not to say dull. Grilled sardines may be served over a zesty salad of oranges and fennel, for example, while grilled baby octopus might be paired with roasted peppers and chickpeas. "We don't really have a house specialty per se," Colicchio explains, "but if I ever took the grilled filet mignon with balsamic onion jam off the menu, we'd have a revolution."

Colicchio had never cooked on a wood-burning grill prior to opening Gramercy Tavern, and he concedes it was a challenge. "You can't turn it up and down like a stove—you have to regulate the heat by moving the food from hot spots to cool spots." Today, Colicchio swears by the forthright flavors of wood grilling, and it's easy to see why Gramercy Tavern has such a loyal local following.

The focal point of the Gramercy Tavern is the wood-burning grill, seen here in the background.

2 Cut the stalks and outside leaves off the fennel bulb, setting aside 4 fronds for a garnish, if desired. Cut the fennel bulb in half lengthwise. Cut out and discard the core. Cut each half crosswise into paper-thin slices, using a mandoline, food processor fitted with the slicing disc, or a sharp knife. Add the sliced fennel to the orange segments, along with the onion, parsley, 2 tablespoons of the olive oil, and the vinegar, but don't toss the salad.

3 Rinse the sardines, inside and out, under cold running water, then pat them dry, inside and out, with paper towels. You can grill the sardines as is or, if you're feeling ambitious, you can bone them: Open up the cavity of a fish and, using kitchen shears, cut through the backbone at the head and tail. Gently pull out the backbone, using needle-nose pliers or tweezers. Pull out and discard any remaining bones. Repeat with the remaining sardines.

4 Set up the grill for direct grilling (see page 21 for gas or charcoal) and preheat to high. If using a gas grill, place all of the wood chips or chunks, if desired, in the smoker box or in a smoker pouch (see page 24) and run the grill on high until you see smoke. If using a charcoal grill, preheat the grill to high, then toss all of the wood chips or chunks, if desired, on the coals.

5 When ready to cook, brush and oil the grill grate. Lightly brush each sardine with olive oil and season with salt and pepper. Place the sardines on the hot grate and grill until handsomely browned on the outside and just cooked through, 2 to 4 minutes per side. To test for doneness, press a sardine with your finger: It will break into clean flakes when fully cooked.

6 Toss the orange and fennel salad, seasoning it with salt and pepper to taste. Taste for seasoning, adding more vinegar as necessary. Place the salad on a platter or plates. Place the grilled sardines on top, 3 to a serving. Garnish with the fennel fronds, if using, then serve at once with the lemon wedges.

YIELD:
Serves 4

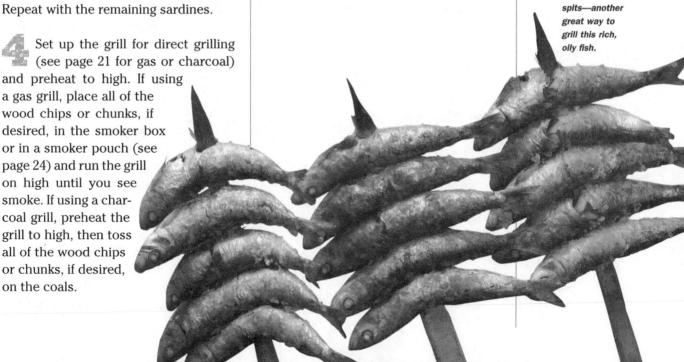

Sardines on spits—another great way to grill this rich, oily fish.

Using a fish basket reduces the risk of the trout sticking to the grill and facilitates turning (see Mail-Order Sources on page 742).

Montana

BACON-GRILLED TROUT

If you want to know something about the Montanan's passion—no, obsession—for fly fishing, read *A River Runs Through It* by Norman MacLean (or rent the movie). The melting snow–swollen river, the solitary angler, the floating gossamer zig zig of a perfect cast—these are the stuff of dreams, and their singular beauty almost makes landing a fish superfluous. Almost, for few dishes are more exquisite than freshly caught trout grilled on the end of a stick over a campfire by the side of a river (see the box on page 508). And if you can't enjoy trout in that bucolic setting, it's very nearly as good cooked on the grill, as you will discover when you try this recipe.

METHOD:
Direct grilling

INGREDIENTS:
4 whole trout (each 12 to 16 ounces; see Note), cleaned
Coarse salt (kosher or sea) and freshly ground black pepper
2 tablespoons salted butter, at room temperature
4 whole scallions, trimmed
8 slices bacon
Lemon wedges, for serving

YOU'LL ALSO NEED:
Wood chunks for building a fire, or 2 cups wood chips or chunks (preferably apple or cherry), unsoaked; butcher's string; fish basket (optional); cooking oil spray (optional)

1 Rinse the trout, inside and out, under cold running water, then blot them dry, inside and out, with paper towels. Make a couple of diagonal slashes to the bone in each side of each fish (this speeds up the cooking and allows for more absorption of the smoke flavor). Generously season the trout, inside and out, with salt and pepper. Smear a little butter inside each trout and place a scallion in the cavity of each. Smear a little butter on the outside of each fish. Place a slice of bacon lengthwise on each side of each trout. Tie the bacon in place with butcher's string.

2 Set up the grill for direct grilling (see page 21 for gas or charcoal) and preheat to medium-high. If using a gas grill, place all of the wood chips or chunks in the smoker box or in a smoker pouch (see page 24) and run the grill on high until you see smoke, then reduce the heat to medium-high. If using a charcoal grill, preheat it to medium-high, then toss all of the wood chips or chunks on the coals.

3 When ready to cook, brush and oil the grill grate. If using a fish basket, spray or brush it with oil or bacon fat and fasten the trout inside. Place the fish or the fish basket on the hot grate. Grill the trout until nicely browned on the outside and cooked through, 6 to 10 minutes per side. Turn the fish as gently as possible, using a long spatula, or inverting the fish basket. Leave plenty of open space on the grill, so you can move the trout in the event of flare-ups. To test for doneness, insert a slender metal skewer into a trout for 20 seconds: It should come out very hot to the touch.

4 Transfer the grilled trout to a platter or plates. Snip the strings and serve the trout with the bacon and lemon wedges.

YIELD:
Serves 4

NOTE: In case you are wondering why the trout here weigh less than those in the recipes that follow, trout you catch may be smaller than trout you purchase. Smaller trout cook faster.

The Southwest

GRILLED TROUT
With Poblano and Corn Relish

Asked to describe the essential flavors of the American Southwest, I'd focus on two native ingredients: chile peppers and corn. Peppers come in a staggering variety of kinds, from the small fiery serrano to the large aromatic poblano. As for corn, it possesses an earthy sweetness that counters the heat of a chile. Put them together in a relish and you get one of the great balances of yin and yang in

TIPS

■ You could prepare the trout and the corn relish at a single grilling session, but I find it more convenient to grill the peppers and corn a day or so ahead (when I'm grilling something else) and to concentrate just on the trout the day I plan to serve it.

■ The one drawback to cooking a delicate whole fish like trout is its tendency to stick to the grill grate. To minimize the risk of this happening, after preheating, brush and oil your grill grate well. Safer still, grill the fish in a hinged fish basket (see page 438). If you do use a basket, the easiest way to oil it is with spray oil.

A good grilling will get him to talk.

TROUT ON A STICK

To grill trout on a stick, you'll need to build a campfire and let it die down to glowing embers. Prepare the trout as described in Step 1 on page 506, then impale each trout on a stick. Forked sticks that are 2½ to 3 feet long will work best for this; insert the ends of each fork into the cavity of a trout. Holding the trout about ten inches above the coals, grill it until the bacon and/or skin are nicely browned and the fish is cooked through, six to ten minutes per side. Move the trout as needed to dodge any bacon fat fires.

American cuisine. A sprinkling of cornmeal gives the trout a delicious crust.

METHOD:
Direct grilling

INGREDIENTS:
4 large whole trout (each about
    1¼ pounds; see Note), cleaned
Coarse salt (kosher or sea) and
    freshly ground black pepper
Poblano and Corn Relish
    (recipe follows)
2 tablespoons olive oil, melted
    butter, or bacon fat
About ¼ cup cornmeal
Lime wedges, for serving

YOU'LL ALSO NEED:
2 cups wood chips or chunks
    (preferably hickory or pecan)
    or pecan shells, unsoaked;
    8 wooden toothpicks; fish basket
    (optional); cooking oil spray
    (optional)

1 Rinse the trout, inside and out, under cold running water, then blot dry, inside and out, with paper towels. Season the cavity of each fish with salt and black pepper. Spoon a little of the Poblano and Corn Relish into the cavity of each fish (save the remaining relish for serving). Secure the cavity of each trout closed with 2 toothpicks. Brush the trout on the outside with olive oil, season with salt and pepper, and lightly sprinkle both sides with cornmeal.

2 Set up the grill for direct grilling (see page 21 for gas or charcoal) and preheat to medium-high. If using a gas grill, place all of the wood chips or chunks or the pecan shells in the smoker box or in a smoker pouch (see page 24) and run the grill on high until you see smoke, then reduce the heat to medium-high. If using a charcoal grill, preheat it to medium-high, then toss all of the wood chips or chunks or the pecan shells on the coals.

3 When ready to cook, brush and oil the grill grate. If using a fish basket, spray or brush it with oil and fasten the trout inside. Place the fish or the fish basket on the hot grate. Grill the trout until nicely browned on the outside and cooked through, 6 to 10 minutes per side. Turn the fish as gently as possible, using a long spatula, or inverting the fish basket. To test for doneness, insert a slender metal skewer into a trout for 20 seconds: It should come out very hot to the touch.

4 Transfer the grilled trout to a platter or plates and spoon the remaining relish over them. Serve with lime wedges.

YIELD:
Serves 4

NOTE: If you can't find trout at your fish market, they're available by mail (see page 742).

Poblano and Corn Relish

The poblano pepper is the work-horse of Southwestern chiles. It's used for stuffing, roasting, and grilling, not to mention flavoring salsas and relishes. Piquant without being too fiery, and herbaceous, almost grassy, the poblano has the popular

appeal of a green bell pepper but with infinitely more finesse. It's right at home in a relish that fairly explodes with the flavors of chiles, corn, and pine nuts.

INGREDIENTS:
2 ears sweet corn, shucked
2 tablespoons olive oil
Coarse salt (kosher or sea) and
freshly ground black pepper
2 large or 3 or 4 small poblano peppers
1 bunch scallions
1 clove garlic, minced
3 tablespoons pine nuts
2 tablespoons chopped fresh cilantro
1 tablespoon fresh lime juice,
or more to taste

1 Set up the grill for direct grilling (see page 21 for charcoal or gas) and preheat to high.

2 When ready to cook, brush the corn with 1 tablespoon of the olive oil and season it generously with salt and black pepper. Brush and oil the grill grate. Place the poblanos, scallions, and corn on the hot grate. Grill the poblanos until blackened and blistered on all sides, the scallions until nicely browned on all sides, and the corn until darkly browned. This will take 3 to 4 minutes per side (9 to 12 minutes in all) for the poblanos, 3 to 5 minutes per side (6 to 10 minutes in all) for the scallions, and 2 to 3 minutes per side (8 to 12 minutes in all) for the corn.

Poblano peppers soak up the smoky flavor of the fire, imparting a gentle heat of their own.

T I P S

Grill klutzes take note: Poblano peppers not only can, but should, be burned. The charring imparts an irresistible smoke flavor. Wrap the charred peppers in wet paper towels or place them in a bowl covered with plastic wrap to steam off the skins.

Wrap the grilled poblanos in wet paper towels or place them in a bowl, cover with plastic wrap, and let cool to room temperature (the steam helps to loosen the skin from the peppers). Transfer the grilled scallions and corn to a plate and let cool.

3 Scrape the burnt skin off the poblanos, cut each in half, and remove all the seeds. Cut the poblanos into ½-inch dice. Cut the scallions crosswise into ¼-inch slices, discarding the roots. Cut the corn kernels off the cobs, using lengthwise strokes of a chef's knife.

4 Heat the remaining 1 tablespoon of olive oil in a saucepan over medium heat. Add the garlic and pine nuts and cook until lightly browned, 2 to 3 minutes. Stir in the grilled poblanos, scallions, and corn, and the cilantro and lime juice and cook until the flavors blend, about 4 minutes. Remove the saucepan from the heat, season the relish with salt and black pepper to taste, and let it cool. The relish can be prepared several days ahead and refrigerated, covered. If you do make it in advance, bring it to room temperature, then taste for seasoning before serving, adding more salt and/or lime juice as necessary.

YIELD:

Makes about 1½ cups

Georgia pecans and country smoked bacon make the perfect stuffing for Idaho's trout.

Idaho

GRILLED TROUT
With Pecan "Hash"

I daho meets the South in this soulful recipe, featuring fresh brook trout stuffed with a smoky "hash" of bacon, onion, and pecans. The trout, for which Idaho is so justly famed, is a great fish for grilling: It's small enough to be easy to cook and turn whole but large enough that a single fish will satisfy a healthy appetite. (I wish I could tell you I catch the trout myself. But my limited adventures with fly-fishing landed more leaves from overhanging

trees than actual fish.) The Southern roots of the pecan stuffing will be immediately apparent.

METHOD:
Direct grilling

FOR THE PECAN "HASH":
1 tablespoon butter
3 slices bacon, cut crosswise into
    ¼-inch slivers
1 medium-size onion, finely chopped
3 ribs celery, finely chopped
½ red or yellow red bell pepper,
    finely chopped
1 cup coarsely chopped pecans
    or pecan pieces
4 large fresh sage leaves, finely chopped
    (for 2 teaspoons), or ½ teaspoon
    dried sage
½ teaspoon finely grated lemon zest
Coarse salt (kosher or sea) and
    freshly ground black pepper

FOR THE TROUT:
4 large whole trout (each about
    1¼ pounds; see Note), cleaned
Coarse salt (kosher or sea) and
    freshly ground black pepper
Lemon wedges, for serving

YOU'LL ALSO NEED:
Wooden toothpicks; hickory chunks for
    building a fire, or 2 cups wood chips
    or chunks (preferably hickory or pecan)
    or pecan shells, unsoaked; fish basket
    (optional); cooking oil spray (optional)

1 MAKE THE PECAN "HASH": Melt the butter in a large heavy skillet over medium-high heat. Add the bacon and cook until just beginning to brown, about 3 minutes. Pour off 2 tablespoons of the fat and set aside. Add the onion, celery, bell pepper, pecans, sage, and lemon zest and sauté until the onion is golden brown, 3 to 5 minutes. Season with salt and pepper to taste. The hash can be prepared to this stage up to 1 day ahead and kept refrigerated, covered.

2 Rinse the trout, inside and out, under cold running water, then blot them dry, inside and out, with paper towels. Generously season the cavity of each fish with salt and black pepper. Spoon a little hash into the cavity of each fish; save the remaining hash for serving. Secure the cavities of each trout closed with 2 toothpicks. Brush the trout on the outside with the reserved bacon fat and season generously with salt and pepper.

3 If necessary, reheat the pecan hash over medium heat.

Trout has a natural affinity for wood smoke—a fact that is appreciated by anyone who has cooked one over a campfire or enjoyed smoked trout with horseradish sauce. In the best of all possible worlds, you'd grill the fish over wood (see **Grilling over a Wood Fire**, page 20). If this is impractical, at the very least add some wood chips to the fire. To reinforce the pecan theme, you could use pecan wood or shells for your smoke—see **Mail-Order Sources** on page 742.

4 Set up the grill for direct grilling (see page 21 for gas or charcoal) and preheat to medium-high. If using a gas grill, place all of the wood chips or chunks or pecan shells in the smoker box or in a smoker pouch (see page 24) and run the grill on high until you see smoke, then reduce the heat to medium-high. If using a charcoal grill, preheat it to medium-high, then toss all of the wood chips or chunks or pecan shells on the coals.

5 When ready to cook, brush and oil the grill grate. If using a fish basket, spray or brush it with oil and fasten the trout inside. Place the fish or the fish basket on the hot grate on a diagonal to the bars. Grill the trout until nicely browned on the outside and cooked through, 6 to 10 minutes per side. Turn the fish as gently as possible, using a long spatula, or invert the fish basket. To test for doneness, insert a slender metal skewer into a trout for 20 seconds: It should come out very hot to the touch.

6 Transfer the grilled trout to a platter or plates and spoon the remaining pecan hash over it. Serve with lemon wedges on the side.

YIELD:
Serves 4

NOTE: If your local fishmonger doesn't stock fresh trout, you can buy it by mail order; see page 742.

Idaho

TROUT NAILED TO A BOARD

A real eyepopper, this dish was inspired by one of the best books ever written on seafood, *The Encyclopedia of Fish Cookery* by A. J. McClane. The original recipe was Finnish, but roasting a fish in front of a blazing fire has deep roots in America—consider the planked shad of Connecticut (page 518) or the planked salmon of the Pacific Northwest (page 454). As a mental warm-up, I imagine I'm on the banks of Lake Pend Oreille in northern Idaho. I've just landed a "shaker," as oversize rainbow trout are called in these parts. My buddy builds a blazing oak fire, while I split the fish, paint it with melted butter, crust it with herbs and spices, and stand it in front of the fire. Barbecue at its best, and it doesn't even require a grill!

METHOD:
Grilling on a plank in front of a fire

INGREDIENTS:
1 whole trout (about 2 pounds, if you're a really good fisherman; see Notes), cleaned, head and gills removed
4 tablespoons (1/2 stick) butter, melted
Coarse salt (kosher or sea) and cracked black peppercorns
1 tablespoon brown sugar
1 tablespoon dry mustard

1 tablespoon sweet paprika
2 tablespoons chopped fresh dill
Lemon wedges, for serving

YOU'LL ALSO NEED:
A clean untreated oak or cedar plank
(see Notes), 8 inches longer than
the fish (if using a charcoal grill)
or a clean oak or cedar plank,
about 10 inches wide, 3 feet tall,
and 1 inch thick (if grilling in front
of a campfire); about 6 small flattop
nails; hammer; 2 or 3 wood chunks
or 2 cups wood chips (preferably
oak), soaked for 1 hour in water
to cover, then drained (if using a
charcoal grill), or enough oak or
hardwood logs to build a campfire

1 If you've caught the trout yourself, split it through the back to, but not through, the belly. Remove the backbone and viscera, and butterfly the trout so you can spread it open like a book. If your trout has already been dressed, just remove the backbone and butterfly the fish. Rinse the trout, inside and out, under cold running water, then blot it dry, inside and out, with paper towels.

2 Brush the skin side of the trout with some of the melted butter, season it with salt and peppercorns. Nail the trout, skin side down, to the cedar plank, positioning the head end about 8 inches from one of the short ends of the plank. Do not pound the nails in all the way; leave the heads sticking out to facilitate removing them.

3 Place the brown sugar, mustard, paprika, and dill in a small bowl and stir to mix. (Actually, your fingers work better for mixing a rub than a spoon or whisk does.) Brush the top of the trout all over with some of the

TIPS

Traditionally, trout on a board is cooked in front of a campfire. You can achieve a similar effect with a charcoal grill. With a gas grill, you'll have to use the indirect method to grill the fish on a plank (for that matter, you could also grill it using the indirect method on a charcoal grill). You'll find instructions for grilling the trout indirectly in the Variation on page 514.

Eleven great reasons to fire up the grill.

melted butter, then sprinkle the rub all over it, patting the seasonings onto the fish with your fingertips.

4 If using a charcoal grill: Light the coals in a large chimney starter. When they burn red, dump them into a pile on one side of the grill, leaving the other side bare (you don't use a grate for this method). Toss all of the wood chunks or chips on the coals.

If grilling in front of a campfire: Build the fire with the hardwood logs. Let it burn until all the logs are lit, glowing orange, lightly ashed over at the edges, and the flames have subsided.

5 If using a charcoal grill: Lean the plank against the inside wall of the grill, on the side opposite the fire. The trout should be facing the fire, head end down. The plank should be 10 to 12 inches away from the coals.

If grilling in front of a campfire: Stand the board with the trout in front of the fire, with the head end at the bottom, propping it upright with a stick or two. The trout should be 12 to 18 inches away from and facing the fire.

6 Grill the trout until golden brown and cooked through, 15 to 20 minutes. To test for doneness, press the fish with your finger: It will break into clean flakes when fully cooked.

7 Transfer the plank with the grilled fish to a heatproof surface. Carefully remove the nails from the plank and place the trout on a platter. Drizzle any remaining butter over the trout and serve at once with the lemon wedges.

YIELD:

Serves 2 and can be multiplied as desired

NOTES:

■ If the trout in your stream are small, grill two 1-pound fish; you'll need two wood planks.

■ Cedar planks are available at grill and cookware shops or see Mail-Order Sources on page 742. Soak the plank in water to cover for 2 hours before grilling; this will prevent it from burning, or at least delay this.

VARIATION: To cook the trout using the indirect method, you'll need a clean oak or cedar plank 6 by 12 inches and 2 cups of wood chips or chunks (preferably oak), soaked for 1 hour in water to cover, then drained. Prepare the trout as described in Steps 1 through 3 above but place the trout on the plank without nailing it to it.

Set up the grill for indirect grilling (see page 23 for gas or page 22 for charcoal) and preheat to medium-high. If using a gas grill, place all of the wood chips or chunks in the smoker box or in a smoker pouch (see page 24) and run the grill on high until you see smoke, then reduce the heat to medium-high. If using a charcoal grill, preheat it to medium-high, then toss all of the wood chips or chunks on the coals. When ready to cook, place the plank in the center of the hot grate, away from the heat, and cover the grill. Grill the fish until cooked through, 20 to 30 minutes. When cooked the fish will break into clean flakes when pressed with your finger. Transfer the grilled trout to a platter and serve with the lemon wedges.

Connecticut

PLANKED SHAD

In this age of bioengineered food and fading ethnic culinary boundaries, it's reassuring to know that there are still a few dishes that remain truly regional and can only be enjoyed in their season. Consider Connecticut's planked shad (or shad bake, in local parlance). Prepared by a handful of fraternal organizations, it's available only on select weekends in May, and you must go to a community shad bake to enjoy it. Or must you? Here's an authentic version you can make at home in a charcoal grill, and a tasty if somewhat modified version you can cook on a gas grill. You *will* have to find boned shad fillets. Look for them at a specialty fishmonger; just remember, you will only find them in the spring.

METHOD:
Grilling on a plank in front of a fire

INGREDIENTS:
1½ to 2 pounds boneless shad fillets or whole sides of fish
Coarse salt (kosher or sea) and freshly ground black pepper (see Notes)
Sweet paprika
About 8 long thin strips (8 inches long, 1 inch wide, ⅛ inch thick) salt pork or fatty bacon (see Notes)
Lemon wedges, for serving

YOU'LL ALSO NEED:
A clean untreated oak or cedar plank (see Notes), 8 inches longer than the fish (if using a charcoal grill) or a clean oak or cedar plank, about 10 inches wide, 3 feet tall, and 1 inch thick (if grilling in front of a campfire); about 6 small flattop nails; hammer; 2 or 3 wood chunks or 2 cups wood chips (preferably oak), soaked for 1 hour in water to cover, then drained (if using a charcoal grill), or enough oak or hardwood logs to build a campfire

1 Rinse the shad under cold running water and blot it dry with paper towels. Generously season it on both sides with salt and pepper and sprinkle paprika over it.

2 Lay the pieces of shad lengthwise on the plank. Place a strip of salt pork or bacon crosswise across the top and bottom of each piece of shad. Nail the ends of the salt pork to the board. Do not pound the nails in all the way; leave the heads sticking out to facilitate removing them.

TIPS

The traditional way to roast planked shad is in front of a campfire. You can achieve a similar effect with a charcoal grill by raking the coals into a mound on one side of the grill and standing the plank upright in front of the fire on the opposite side. If you are using a gas grill, you'll have to use the indirect method, but you'll still get a great flavor (you'll find instructions in the Variation on page 516).

Shad boned and ready for planking.

3 If using a charcoal grill: Light the coals in a large chimney starter. When they burn red, dump them into a pile on one side of the grill, leaving the other side bare (you don't use a grate for this method). Toss all of the wood chunks or chips on the coals.

If grilling in front of a campfire: Build the fire with the hardwood logs. Let it burn until all the logs are lit, glowing orange, lightly ashed over at the edges, and the leaping flames have subsided.

4 If using a charcoal grill: Lean the plank with the shad against the inside wall of grill, on the side opposite the fire. The shad should be facing the fire. The plank should be 10 to 12 inches away from the coals.

If grilling in front of a campfire: Stand the board with the shad in front of the fire, propping it upright with a stick or two. The shad should be 12 to 18 inches away from and facing the fire.

5 Grill the shad until golden brown and cooked through, 15 to 20 minutes. To test for doneness, press the fish with your finger: It will break into clean flakes when fully cooked.

6 Transfer the plank with the grilled fish to a heatproof surface. Discard the salt pork. Loosen the fish from the nails, place it on a platter, and serve at once with the lemon wedges.

YIELD:
Serves 4

NOTES:
■ Salt pork is salt-cured fat streaked with a little meat. It comes from a pig's belly or sides. Be sure to look for streaks of red in the fat. If you cannot find it at the supermarket, try a butcher shop or an ethnic market. In a pinch you can use slices of fatty bacon.

■ Cedar planks are available at grill and cookware shops (see Mail-Order Sources, page 742). Soak the plank in water to cover for 2 hours before grilling; this will prevent it from burning, or at least delay this.

VARIATION: To cook the shad using the indirect method, you'll need a clean oak or cedar plank 6 by 12 inches and 2 cups of wood chips or chunks (preferably oak), soaked in water to cover for 1 hour, then drained. Prepare the shad as described in Steps 1 and 2 above but place the shad and salt pork on the plank without nailing them to it.

Set up the grill for indirect grilling (see page 23 for gas or page 22 for charcoal) and preheat to medium-high. If using a gas grill, place all of the wood chips or chunks in the smoker box or in a smoker pouch (see page 24) and run the grill on high until you see smoke, then reduce the heat to medium-high. If using a charcoal grill, preheat it to medium-high, then toss all of the wood chips or chunks on the coals. When ready to cook, place the plank with the shad and salt pork in the center of the hot grate, away from the heat, and cover the grill. Grill the fish until cooked through, 20 to 30 minutes. When cooked, the fish will break into clean flakes when pressed with your finger. Discard the salt pork, then transfer the grilled shad to a platter or plates and serve with the lemon wedges.

The Eastern Seaboard

BACON-GRILLED SHAD ROE

Shad roe is like *Cats* or Stravinsky: You either love it or hate it. There's no middle ground for this East Coast springtime delicacy. For devotees (of which I'm one), shad roe is the sort of fare you savor in reverential silence—perhaps kneeling, with your head bared. The taste of shad roe defies easy description. To get an idea, imagine combining the earthy richness of sweetbreads, the buttery flavor of foie gras, and the sensuous crunch of fine caviar. If I have failed to convince you of its merits, please pass me your plate; I'll be happy to eat it for you!

METHOD:
Direct grilling

INGREDIENTS:

2 large or 4 small pairs shad roe
   (about 1½ pounds total)
Coarse salt (kosher or sea) and
   freshly ground black pepper
8 slices bacon
2 tablespoons capers, drained
Lemon wedges, for serving

YOU'LL ALSO NEED:
Butcher's string

1 Place the shad roe in a large bowl and add cold water to cover by 3 inches. Let soak for 5 minutes, then change the water. Repeat this rinsing process 3 times. Transfer the roe to paper towels to drain and blot them dry with paper towels.

2 Season the roe with salt and pepper. Starting at one end, wrap each lobe of roe in bacon, winding it around the roe like the stripe on a candy cane. Tie the bacon in place at each end of the roe with butcher's string.

3 Set up the grill for direct grilling using a three-zone fire (see page 21 for charcoal or gas) and preheat one zone to medium-high and one zone to medium; leave the third zone unlit.

4 When ready to cook, brush and oil the grill grate. Place the shad roe over the medium-high zone and grill until the bacon is browned and crisp and the roe is cooked through, 8 to 10 minutes per side, depending on the size of the roe. Turn the roe over when the bacon is sizzling and golden brown. If the bacon begins to get too brown, move the roe to the medium or cool zone. Transfer the grilled roe to a platter or plates and remove and discard the strings. Sprinkle the capers over the roe and serve at once, with the lemon wedges.

YIELD:
Serves 4

TIPS

■ Shad roe is available in the spring in fine fish markets in New England and the mid-Atlantic.

■ Traditionally, shad roe is poached or panfried, but I like to wrap it in bacon and grill it. You'll need a fairly delicate heat here, so I like to build a three-zone fire so there's a medium-high zone, a medium zone, and an unlit zone. This lets you cook the roe through without burning the bacon.

A Connecticut
SHAD BAKE

Every May thousands of shad, shiny and fat from a winter in the icy Atlantic, swim up the Connecticut River to their traditional spawning grounds. And every year, Earl Endrich will be waiting for them. Retired insurance agent, former state representative, Masonic lodge member in good standing, and above all avid fisherman, Earl is one of the organizers of the traditional shad bake held every year, the second Sunday in May, in Fireman's Field in Old Saybrook, Connecticut. It's a tradition that dates back half a century among lodge members there, although there were shad roasts in these parts long before the arrival of the first Europeans.

Shad is problematic. A member of the herring family, shad possesses more bones than virtually any other fish on the planet (about three hundred according to marine biologists). The rich, oily flesh smells up your kitchen when you attempt to cook it indoors. But properly filleted (and only a handful of highly trained fishmongers know how to do that) and roasted in front of a blazing bonfire, the rich flavor of shad is a taste the people of Connecticut eagerly look forward to each year.

At one time there were throngs of shad in East Coast rivers from the Chesapeake Bay to Maine. Shad bakes have changed little since Mary Randolph described one in an early American cookbook, *The Virginia Housewife,* published in 1824:

> **To Roast a Shad, Fill the cavity with good forcemeat, sew it up, and tie it on a board of proper size, cover it with bread crumbs, with some salt and pepper, set it before the fire to roast; when done on one side, turn it, tie it again, and when sufficiently done, pull out the thread, and serve it up with butter and parsley poured over it.**

SHAD BAKES

Shad bakes take place along the Connecticut coast each May. For information on the Old Saybrook shad bake, call (860) 388-9362

The Haddam Shad Museum at 212 Saybrook Road in Higganum is open every Sunday from mid-April through June; (860) 267-0388

You'll find more about shad at: www.mycoast.com; www.ctseafood.org/shad_museum.htm; www.ctseafood.org/recipes.htm

PLANKING THE SHAD

The Masonic Lodge shad bake begins at 10 A.M. on Sunday morning at Fireman's Field, but preparations have been in full swing since the week before. There are potato salads and other side dishes to be made, and cakes and pies to bake from scratch. Once caught, the fish must be cleaned and filleted. Logs are hauled and split, then fires are built. There must be enough to serve a crowd of twelve hundred.

Early Sunday morning, Earl and his co-workers start readying the planks—massive oak boards, each about two feet tall, eighteen inches wide, and two inches thick, and dotted with nail holes from previous shad bakes. Stored in a local barn, some planks have been in service for half a century. They are scraped clean with paint scrapers before and after use, but are never touched with soap and water. "Washing would do them in," says Earl.

Seasoning is kept to a minimum: salt, pepper, a sprinkle of paprika. The shad fillets are placed on the planks and strapped down with thin strips of salt pork laid crosswise. Salt pork was a staple in Colonial New

Connecticut shad by the net-full. Fire up the pit.

England, but it's gotten harder to find these days. The lodge has the strips specially cut at a local meat market called Walt's. The prep area resounds with the pounding of hammers, as the ends of the salt pork are nailed in place with sixpenny nails.

The fires are left to burn down to glowing embers. "People can't seem to understand you need a quiet fire," Earl says, and then explains that flames and smoke would make the fish sooty. Supported by wooden braces, the planks are stood in front of the fire. The salt pork sizzles and melts, basting the fish as it roasts. Twenty minutes is all it takes to turn the humble shad into an unforgettably buttery, crusty, oak smoke–scented masterpiece.

Portioning shad is done by hand.

Sizzling

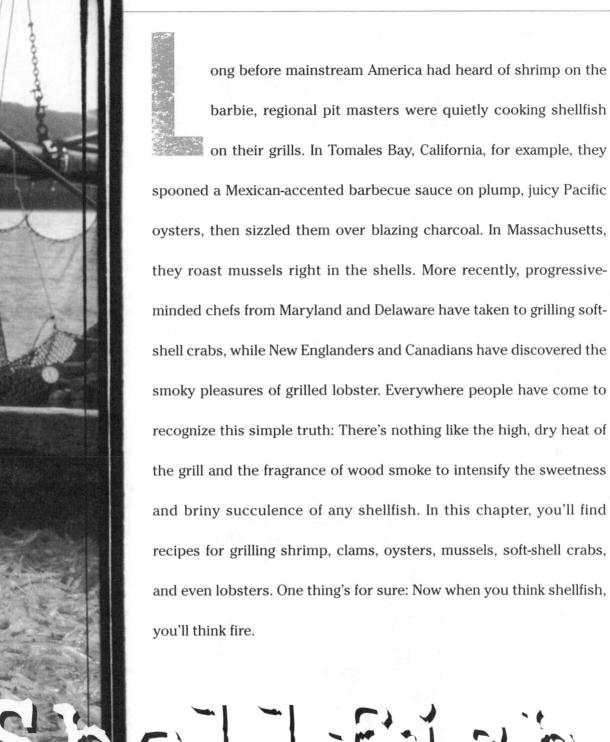

Long before mainstream America had heard of shrimp on the barbie, regional pit masters were quietly cooking shellfish on their grills. In Tomales Bay, California, for example, they spooned a Mexican-accented barbecue sauce on plump, juicy Pacific oysters, then sizzled them over blazing charcoal. In Massachusetts, they roast mussels right in the shells. More recently, progressive-minded chefs from Maryland and Delaware have taken to grilling soft-shell crabs, while New Englanders and Canadians have discovered the smoky pleasures of grilled lobster. Everywhere people have come to recognize this simple truth: There's nothing like the high, dry heat of the grill and the fragrance of wood smoke to intensify the sweetness and briny succulence of any shellfish. In this chapter, you'll find recipes for grilling shrimp, clams, oysters, mussels, soft-shell crabs, and even lobsters. One thing's for sure: Now when you think shellfish, you'll think fire.

Shellfish

How to Peel and Devein
SHRIMP

If you like shrimp hot off the grill as much as I do, you'll want to know how to peel and devein them quickly and easily. It's really not hard at all. Here are a few reliable methods.

TO PEEL USING A SHRIMP PEELER: This device looks like a long, slender plastic knife with a blade that tapers to a knitting needle–thin point. Straighten out a shrimp with one hand. Insert the pointed end of the peeler in the large end of the shrimp where the black dot of the vein appears. Push the peeler through to the other end, continuing to hold the shrimp straight. The serrations on top of the peeler blade will cut through the top shell, while the pointed end will remove the vein. Simply pull off the loose shell.

BY HAND: Grab the shrimp legs between the thumb and curled forefinger of one hand and gently lift one side in a tearing motion, as though you were peeling a tangerine. This will remove the top two-thirds of the shell. Now gently pinch the tail section to force the shrimp out of the tail shell.

TO DEVEIN USING A BUTTERFLY CUT: Lay a peeled shrimp on a cutting board. Using a sharp paring knife, make a diagonal cut a quarter inch deep running the length of the shrimp just above the vein. Turn the shrimp over and do the same thing on the other side. This enables you to remove a slender V-shaped strip of shrimp from the back that will contain the vein. This method is a little more time consuming than the next one, but the shrimp pops open in a handsome way when you grill it.

USING A FORK OR SKEWER: This is the lazy man's method for deveining. Hold a peeled shrimp in one hand so that the rounded back faces up. Insert one tine of a fork or skewer in the center of the back under the vein (about a quarter inch from the surface). Gently pull the fork away from the shrimp—the vein should come out with it. This method works best where there is a large vein. It may not work for all shrimp.

WITH THE SHELL ON: I'm a great fan of grilling shrimp in the shells. The shells hold in the juices and impart a distinctive flavor (besides, eating shrimp with the shells on is messy fun). First, using kitchen shears, make a lengthwise cut in the top of the shell from the head end to the tail. Then, reach into the slit with the tine of a fork or tip of a paring knife or metal skewer and scrape out the vein.

Shrimp by the pound; grill them whole or peeled.

Louisiana

COUSIN DAVE'S GRILL-TOP SHRIMP "BOIL"

Necessity is the mother of invention, goes the saying. My cousin David Raichlen is the grill master of the Gen Xers in our family, and when his graduate school buddies need someone to barbecue a brisket or roast a whole pig, Dave always steps up to the fire. One time Dave was charged with whipping up a Louisiana-style shrimp boil for fifty. He didn't let the lack of a large pot stop him, no. He cooked the shrimp on the grill. There are three advantages to this method: First, it adds the gutsy flavors of fire and wood smoke to this classic Louisianan party dish. Second, it moves the mess outside—always a plus in my book. Finally, I'd much rather have guests gather around a flaming grill than around some big, old, steamy stockpot.

METHOD:
Direct grilling

ADVANCE PREPARATION:
1 hour for marinating the shrimp

INGREDIENTS:
3 pounds extra-large or jumbo shrimp
   in the shell
3 tablespoons Old Bay seasoning

3 tablespoons Cajun Rub (page 420)
   or your favorite commercial rub
1 tablespoon ground coriander
1 tablespoon cracked black peppercorns
1 to 3 teaspoons cayenne pepper
¼ cup olive oil
6 tablespoons fresh lemon juice
1 bottle or can (12 ounces) beer
1½ cups heavy (whipping) cream
¾ cup dark corn syrup
6 tablespoons Worcestershire sauce
2 thin slices lemon (with rind),
   seeds removed
3 to 4 tablespoons hot sauce
   (such as Crystal, Louisiana,
   or Tabasco)
2 tablespoons brown sugar
4 cloves garlic, peeled and gently crushed
   with the side of a cleaver
¾ cup (1½ sticks) unsalted butter,
   cut into 1-inch pieces
Coarse salt (kosher or sea) and
   freshly ground black pepper
Crusty bread or Grilled Garlic Bread #5
   (page 134), for serving
Grilled corn (optional; pages 600 to 605)

YOU'LL ALSO NEED:
Kitchen shears; 3 cups wood chips
   or chunks (preferably hickory
   or pecan), soaked for 1 hour in
   water to cover, then drained;
   2 aluminum foil pans
   (8 by 12 inches)

1 Rinse the shrimp under cold running water, then drain and blot them dry with paper towels. Using kitchen shears, make a lengthwise cut through the shell, down the back of each shrimp. Use the tine of a fork or the tip of a bamboo skewer to pull out the vein if you see one. Remember, not every shrimp

Traditionally shrimp for a shrimp boil are cooked in the shell, which gives you more flavor and keeps the shellfish moist. However, they're somewhat messy to eat this way. My compromise is to slit the shrimp down the back, cutting through the top of the shell with kitchen shears. This enables you to devein the shrimp and facilitates eating. However, if you prefer the convenience of peeled, deveined shrimp, by all means use them instead.

My cousin Dave hard at work on his Grill "Master's" degree.

has a visible vein. Place the shrimp in a large bowl.

2 Place the Old Bay seasoning, Cajun Rub, coriander, black peppercorns, and cayenne in a small bowl and stir to mix. (Actually, your fingers work better for mixing a rub than a spoon or whisk does.) Set 1½ tablespoons of this rub aside for the sauce. Sprinkle the remaining rub over the shrimp and toss to mix. Stir in the olive oil and 3 tablespoons of lemon juice and stir to mix. Let the shrimp marinate in the refrigerator, covered, for 1 hour.

3 Place the beer in a heavy nonreactive saucepan and bring to a boil over high heat. Let boil until only about ⅓ of a cup remains, 6 to 10 minutes. Add the cream and let boil until the mixture is reduced by half, 7 to 10 minutes more. Add the corn syrup, Worcestershire sauce, lemon slices, hot sauce, brown sugar, and garlic, and the remaining 3 tablespoons of lemon juice and 1½ tablespoons of reserved rub. Let boil until thick and syrupy, 3 to 6 minutes. Whisk in the

butter, piece by piece, and let the sauce boil until heated through and well combined, about 1 minute. Season with salt and pepper to taste; the sauce should be highly seasoned. Keep the sauce warm, at the edge of the grill; do not let it return to a boil.

4 Set up the grill for direct grilling (see page 21 for gas or charcoal) and preheat to high. If using a gas grill,

The shrimp master and his buddy go whole hog.

. . . adds the gutsy flavors of fire and

place all of the wood chips or chunks in the smoker box or in a smoker pouch (see page 24) and run the grill on high until you see smoke. If using a charcoal grill, preheat it to high, then toss all of the wood chips or chunks on the coals.

5 When ready to cook, brush and oil the grill grate. Place the marinated shrimp on the hot grate and grill until just cooked through, 1 to 3 minutes per side. When done, the shrimp will turn a pinkish white and feel firm to the touch (see Note).

6 Transfer the grilled shrimp to aluminum foil pans and place the pans on the grill. Pour the sauce over them and cook for a minute or so to warm the shrimp in the sauce. Serve the shrimp at once with the sauce slathered over them and the bread and grilled corn on the side, if desired.

YIELD:
Serves 8

NOTE: To speed up the grilling process here, skewer the shrimp on bamboo skewers. You'll need about 8. Use skewers that are 10 to 12 inches long and place about 6 shrimp on each. When you thread the shrimp on a skewer, insert it near the head and tail ends so that the shrimp looks like the letter C. It's a lot faster turning 8 kebabs than all those individual shrimp.

The Gulf Coast

A NEW SHRIMP AND SMOKIES

The shrimp boils popular in Louisiana and Mississippi—in fact, all along the Gulf Coast—were the inspiration for these sizzling kebabs. The basic procedure is simple enough: You boil a mess of shrimp in beer with spices and some sort of sausage. If you're scratching your head to figure out why boiled shrimp should appear in a barbecue book, just remember Raichlen's rule: If it tastes good boiled, broiled, baked, sautéed, or deep-fried, there's probably a way to make it taste even better grilled. Here briny Gulf shrimp are sandwiched between smoky, garlicky chunks of andouille sausage. The basting and barbecue sauces feature the beer, butter, shrimp boil, and other seasonings you'd use to cook up a traditional pot of shrimp and smokies. (If you're in a hurry, you can skip the sauce, and the shrimp will still be tasty.) Call it blasphemy or call it brilliance, here are shrimp and smokies you can enjoy hot off the grill.

TIPS

Andouille is a spicy, garlicky Cajun sausage. It's sold at many supermarkets and meat markets, or can be ordered by mail (see Mail-Order Sources, page 742). For a taste of Chicago, you could use kielbasa instead. For a Wisconsin flavor, use bratwurst. Bay Staters would use *linguica* (a Portuguese American sausage). Or for a Floridian or Tex-Mex touch, substitute the spicy Spanish chorizo. No matter what kind of sausage you use, be sure it's precooked.

wood smoke to this classic party dish.

METHOD:
Direct grilling

INGREDIENTS:

16 jumbo shrimp (about 1¼ pounds),
    peeled and deveined
10 to 12 ounces andouille sausage,
    cut crosswise into ½-inch slices
2 red bell peppers, cut into 1-inch squares
2 tablespoons extra-virgin olive oil
Coarse salt (kosher or sea) and
    freshly ground black pepper
Beer Butter Baste and Barbecue Sauce
    (optional; recipe follows)
Lemon wedges, for serving

YOU'LL ALSO NEED:

4 long (10- to 12-inch) metal skewers
    or 8 bamboo skewers

1 Thread the shrimp, sausage, and bell pepper squares onto the skewers, alternating the ingredients to make attractive kebabs. Pierce the shrimp twice, at the head end and tail end, so that they curl like the letter C. Lightly brush the kebabs with the olive oil and season with salt and black pepper.

2 Set up the grill for direct grilling (see page 21 for charcoal or gas) and preheat to high.

3 When ready to cook, brush and oil the grill grate. Place the kebabs on the hot grate and grill until the shrimp are just cooked through and the sausage and peppers are browned and sizzling, 1 to 3 minutes per side. When done, the shrimp will turn a pinkish white and feel firm to the touch. Use half of the barbecue sauce, if desired, to baste the kebabs as they cook.

4 Transfer the skewers to a platter or plates and spoon the remaining sauce, if desired, over the kebabs before serving. If using metal skewers, unskewer the shrimp, sausage, and peppers before serving; there's nothing worse than burning your lips on a hot metal skewer.

YIELD:
Serves 4

Blues, brew, and barbecue—a Gulf tradition.

Beer Butter Baste and Barbecue Sauce

This versatile sauce is modeled on the spicy broth traditionally used to cook shrimp and smokies. Liquid shrimp or crab boil is a highly concentrated shellfish seasoning. One good brand is Zatarain's.

INGREDIENTS:

1 cup beer

2 cloves garlic, peeled and gently
    crushed with the side of a cleaver

1 strip lemon zest (2 by ½ inch; see Note)

2 tablespoons fresh lemon juice

2 tablespoons Worcestershire sauce

2 tablespoons dark corn syrup,
    or more to taste

1 tablespoon liquid shrimp or crab boil,
    or 1 tablespoon dry shrimp or
    crab boil

8 tablespoons (1 stick) cold unsalted
    butter, cut into 1-inch pieces

Coarse salt (kosher or sea) and
    freshly ground black pepper

1 Place the beer, garlic, and lemon zest in a heavy nonreactive saucepan and bring to a boil over high heat. Let boil until reduced to ½ cup, 5 to 8 minutes. Add the lemon juice, Worcestershire sauce, corn syrup, and shrimp boil, bring to a boil, and let boil until the mixture is reduced to ½ cup again, about 3 minutes. Using tongs, remove and discard the garlic cloves and lemon zest.

2 Reduce the heat to medium, then whisk in the butter, piece by piece, to create a smooth sauce. The sauce can boil while you're adding the butter, but it shouldn't come to a boil once all the butter is in. Taste for seasoning, adding more corn syrup as necessary and salt and pepper to taste. The sauce can be made up to 30 minutes ahead. Keep it warm until ready to use.

YIELD:
Makes about 1 cup

NOTE: You can use a vegetable peeler to remove the oil-rich, yellow outer rind of the lemon in strips of zest. Be careful to leave behind the bitter white pith.

Nevada

GREEN LIGHTNING SHRIMP

It takes only about ten minutes to prepare these colorful shrimp kebabs, but the flavor is electrifying. The first jolt comes from jalapeño peppers—lots of them—and it's followed by aromatic blasts of cilantro, scallion, and cumin, flavorings that are typical of grilling in the Southwest. You've probably noticed that shrimp have a tendency to dry out when grilled, even after they've been marinated. To remedy this problem, I baste the shrimp with garlic butter as they grill.

METHOD:
Direct grilling

ADVANCE PREPARATION:
30 minutes for marinating the shrimp

TIPS

■ To assemble the kebabs, I use a technique called double skewering. (Did you ever notice how shrimp slide around on a single skewer?) You can keep them from slipping by inserting two slender skewers through the shrimp so that they are parallel to each other.

■ For extra color, you could place a square of poblano pepper or green bell pepper between each of the shrimp on the skewers.

WALL OF FLAME

MEMPHIS CHAMPIONSHIP BARBECUE

Mike Mills, of Apple City Barbecue team fame (see page 294) brings his unique, spice-rubbed, dry-smoked barbecue to glittery Las Vegas. All three of his Vegas restaurants serve smoked chicken wings, barbecue salad, Memphis hot links, and the sort of suave smoky baby back ribs that have made Mills a barbecue legend.

4379 North Las Vegas
   Boulevard
Las Vegas, Nevada
(702) 644-0000
(and other locations)
www.memphis-bbq.com

INGREDIENTS:

2¹/₂ pounds jumbo shrimp

1 bunch cilantro, rinsed, stemmed, and
   coarsely chopped (about 1 cup)

4 to 8 jalapeño peppers, seeded and
   coarsely chopped (for hotter shrimp,
   leave the seeds in)

1 bunch scallions, both white and
   green parts, trimmed and coarsely
   chopped

5 cloves garlic, 3 cloves coarsely chopped,
   2 cloves minced

1¹/₂ teaspoons coarse salt
   (kosher or sea)

1 teaspoon freshly ground black pepper

1 teaspoon ground cumin

¹/₂ cup extra-virgin olive oil

¹/₂ cup fresh lime juice

8 tablespoons (1 stick) salted butter

Lime wedges, for serving

YOU'LL ALSO NEED:

About 12 long (10- to 12-inch)
   metal or bamboo skewers

1 Rinse the shrimp under cold running water and then drain and blot them dry with paper towels. Peel and devein the shrimp (see box, page 522). Thread the shrimp onto 2 parallel skewers, using 2 skewers for each kebab. Arrange the kebabs in a nonreactive baking dish.

2 Set aside 3 tablespoons of the cilantro for the garlic cilantro butter. Place the remaining cilantro, the jalapeños, scallions, chopped garlic, salt, black pepper, and cumin in a

food processor and finely chop. With the machine running, add the olive oil and lime juice through the feed tube and purée to a bright green paste. Pour this marinade over the shrimp and let them marinate in the refrigerator, covered, for 30 minutes, turning the kebabs several times so they marinate evenly.

3 Melt the butter in a saucepan over medium heat. Add the minced garlic and the 3 tablespoons of reserved cilantro and cook until the garlic is fragrant and sizzling, but not browned, about 2 minutes. Keep the garlic cilantro butter warm until ready to use.

4 Set up the grill for direct grilling (see page 21 for charcoal or gas) and preheat to high.

5 When ready to cook, brush and oil the grill grate. Drain the marinade from the shrimp kebabs and discard the marinade. Place the shrimp kebabs on the hot grate and grill until just cooked through, 1 to 3 minutes per side, basting with the garlic cilantro butter. When done, the shrimp will turn pinkish white and feel firm to the touch. Transfer the grilled shrimp to a platter or plates, pour any of the remaining butter sauce over them, and serve with the lime wedges.

YIELD:
Serves 6

THE HITCHING POST

THE HITCHING POST

3325 Point Sal Road
Casmalia, California
(805) 937-6151
www.hitchingpost1.com

"**M**y mom thought my father was nuts," recalls Terri Ostini Stricklin. The year was 1952, and the former cabinetmaker proudly announced the purchase of a rustic restaurant called The Hitching Post. Never mind that it was located in the one-street town of Casmalia, surrounded by the stark rolling hills of central California ranch country.

But Frank Ostini saw potential in the hundred-year-old red clapboard building. After all, Camp Cooke army base was located nearby. (Cooke closed shortly afterward, reopening in 1957 as the United States' first space and ballistic missile training base. In 1958, it was renamed Vandenberg.) So he filled the ninety-seat restaurant with antique farm equipment and tables draped with bordello red tablecloths. He taught himself how to fire up the rectangular brick pit with local red oak and grill the beef for which the local ranches were famous.

A half century later, the Hitching Post is still in the middle of nowhere. And still going strong. Five of the Ostinis' six children work in the business, including daughter Terri, who runs the front of the house, and youngest son Bob, who mans the pit. The once relentlessly carnivorous menu has been broadened to include grilled halibut, shrimp kebabs, and quail grilled with butter and garlic. Even vegetarians will find something to rejoice in: a remarkable grilled artichoke bursting with smoky oak flavors and served with a fiery dipping sauce concocted from mayonnaise and salsa. As befits an American barbecue joint, you can get baby back pork ribs here, but in the central California tradition they come grilled, not smoked.

Most of the customers order beef: baseball-thick filets mignons seasoned with garlic, salt, and pepper and basted with oil and wine vinegar as they grill. Or meaty slabs of top sirloin—the traditional central California cut comes sanguine, smoky, tender, flavorful, and reasonably priced at $27.95 for two. The best seats in the house are in the barbecue room, where a handful of lucky diners get to sit at tables directly facing the pit.

While in the area, you can visit the Guadalupe-Nipomo Dunes Preserve, where Cecil B. DeMille filmed the 1923 film classic, *The Ten Commandments*.

Dayton, Ohio

FENNEL-GRILLED SHRIMP
With Grilled Fennel

TIPS

■ This recipe calls for two forms of fennel: fennel seeds, which are available on supermarket spice shelves, and fresh fennel, which comes in large, greenish-white bulbs and tastes like licorice-flavored celery. It, too, is available at most supermarkets or, if not, at greengrocers or Italian markets.

■ When peeling and deveining shrimp, I like to leave the tail shells on. This looks cool, and when the shells crisp up over the fire, you can munch on the tails like popcorn.

Dayton, Ohio, is a popular stop on the book tour circuit, thanks to a terrific independent bookstore called Books & Co. Whenever I'm there, I look forward to visiting the Oregon district—a historic neighborhood of lovingly restored early-nineteenth-century brick houses and home of an edgy contemporary American bistro called the Blue Moon. These shrimp—inspired by the Blue Moon—are more Mediterranean than Midwestern in their mood, but I never met anyone who tasted them who didn't love them. The grilled fennel slices play off the licorice tones of the fennel seeds in the shrimp rub.

METHOD:
Direct grilling

ADVANCE PREPARATION:
30 minutes for marinating the shrimp and fennel

INGREDIENTS:
1½ pounds jumbo shrimp
1 large or 2 small bulbs fennel, stalks trimmed off (see Note)

2 teaspoons fennel seeds
2 teaspoons hot red pepper flakes, or more to taste
2 teaspoons cracked black peppercorns
2 teaspoons coarse salt (kosher or sea)
¼ cup extra-virgin olive oil
¼ cup fresh orange juice
¼ cup fresh lemon juice

YOU'LL ALSO NEED:
About 12 long (10- to 12-inch) bamboo skewers; 2 cups oak chips or chunks or grape vine trimmings (optional), unsoaked

1 Rinse the shrimp under cold running water, then blot them dry with paper towels. Peel and devein the shrimp (see page 522). Cut the fennel bulbs lengthwise into ¼-inch slices, cutting to form the broadest slices possible. Place the shrimp in a nonreactive mixing bowl and arrange the fennel slices in a single layer in a nonreactive baking dish.

2 Combine the fennel seeds, hot red pepper flakes, peppercorns, and salt in a small bowl and stir to mix. (Actually, your fingers work better for mixing a rub than a spoon or whisk does.) Sprinkle half of this rub over the shrimp and stir to mix. Add 2 tablespoons each of the olive oil, orange juice, and lemon juice to the shrimp and stir to mix. Drizzle the remaining 2 tablespoons of olive oil, 2 tablespoons of orange juice, and 2 tablespoons of lemon juice over both sides of the fennel slices. Sprinkle the remaining rub over both sides of the fennel slices, patting it on with your fingertips. Let the shrimp and fennel marinate for 30 minutes.

3 Drain the marinade off the shrimp and fennel into a small saucepan and bring it to a boil over high heat, then set the marinade aside. Thread the shrimp onto skewers, inserting them near the head and tail ends so that the shrimp will look like the letter C.

4 Set up the grill for direct grilling (see page 21 for charcoal or gas) and preheat to high. If using a gas grill, place all of the wood chips, if desired, in the smoker box or in a smoker pouch (see page 24) and preheat on high until you see smoke. If using a charcoal grill, preheat it to high, then toss all of the wood chips or chunks, if desired, on the coals.

5 When ready to cook, brush and oil the grill grate. Place the fennel and shrimp on the hot grate. Grill the fennel slices until nicely browned and tender, 3 to 6 minutes per side. Grill the shrimp until just cooked through 1 to 3 minutes per side, pouring the boiled marinade over them. When done, the shrimp will turn pinkish white and be firm to the touch. To serve, arrange the grilled fennel on a platter or plates and top with the grilled shrimp.

YIELD:
Serves 4

NOTE: If you have fennel stalks and fronds, you can substitute them for the wood chips or chunks to give the smoke a fennel flavor.

Shrimp for the barbie in a big way.

Quebec, Canada

PIERRE'S PERNOD AND DILL GRILLED LOBSTER

When it comes to lobster, it's hard to beat the crustaceans fished from the icy waters off Nova Scotia and Newfoundland. This dish was inspired by my Montreal colleague, Pierre Bourdin, publisher of the French edition of *How to Grill* and a grilling fanatic despite his country's short barbecue season. (Like all true barbecue buffs, Pierre fires up his grill even in winter.) It's the essence of the Quebec food experience—a fusion of pristine Canadian ingredients and Gallic savoir faire.

METHOD:
Direct grilling

INGREDIENTS:
12 tablespoons (1½ sticks)
   salted butter
3 shallots, finely chopped
   (for ½ cup)
¼ cup chopped fresh dill
3 tablespoons Pernod or other anise-
   flavored aperitif (see Note)
2 tablespoons fresh lemon juice
½ teaspoon freshly ground
   black pepper
Coarse salt (kosher or sea)
4 lobsters (each 1¼ to 1½ pounds)
8 fresh dill sprigs, for garnish

1 Melt 4 tablespoons of the butter in a heavy nonreactive saucepan over medium heat. Add the shallots and cook until fragrant and soft but not brown, about 3 minutes. Add the remaining 8 tablespoons of butter, and the chopped dill, Pernod, lemon juice, and pepper and cook until the butter is melted and the sauce is simmering, about 1 minute. Keep the sauce warm until ready to use.

2 Place 1 gallon of water and ¼ cup of salt in a large pot and bring to a boil over high heat. Add the lobsters and let boil for 2 minutes. Drain the lobsters in a colander and rinse with cold water until cool. Drain well, then transfer the lobsters to a cutting board—ideally, a grooved one, so you

can collect the juices. Using a large chef's knife or cleaver, break off the claws, then crack their shells in one or two spots using a nutcracker or a knife. Cut each lobster in half lengthwise. Remove the papery sacs behind the eyes and discard them. Remove the vein that runs the length of the tail and discard it.

3 Add any lobster juices (from the bodies as well as from the cutting board) to the sauce. Let the mixture simmer for 1 minute to cook the lobster juices.

4 Set up the grill for direct grilling (see page 21 for charcoal or gas) and preheat to high.

5 When ready to cook, brush and oil the grill grate. Brush the cut side of each lobster half with some of the sauce. Drizzle a little sauce into the cracks in each claw. Place the claws on the hot grate. Place the lobster halves on the grate, cut side down. Grill the claws for 4 to 6 minutes per side (8 to 12 minutes in all), dabbing some of the sauce into the cracks in the shells with a pastry brush. Grill the lobster halves for about 3 minutes, then turn and grill them cut side up until the meat is cooked through (it will be firm and white), 6 to 8 minutes longer, basting with some of the sauce.

6 Transfer the grilled lobsters with their claws to a platter or plates and garnish with the dill sprigs. Pour the remaining sauce into 4 ramekins to serve with the lobsters for dipping.

TIPS

When I grill lobsters, I like to use females, which have more meat in the tails and in the summer can contain roe (lobster caviar). To determine the sex of a lobster you look at the first pair of swimmerets (the tiny legs on the underside of the tail). Female lobsters have soft, feathery swimmerets, while males have hard ones. Ask your fishmonger to select females for you, if possible.

Serve at once. Be sure to provide nutcrackers, finger bowls, and a dish for the empty shells.

YIELD:
Serves 4

NOTE: Pernod is a French anise-flavored aperitif that is widely available in liquor stores. Substitutes include the French Ricard, Greek ouzo, or Turkish raki.

Menemsha, Mass.

GRILLED LOBSTER
With Caviar Cream

Sweet New England lobster, smokily grilled, served with a silky Cognac cream sauce that's dotted with salty red beads of lobster caviar—if such is your vision of paradise, head for the fishing village of Menemsha in Martha's Vineyard. I had this dish, or one very much like it, more than a decade ago, but the memory of the vibrant flavors has stayed with me. Here's my version, which naturally, is cooked on the grill. The sauce owes its color and flavor to the lobster roe (a.k.a. lobster caviar), which can

be found in female lobsters in the summertime. (I also add the tomalley, the lobster's liver.) If you can't find egg-bearing females, you can substitute *tobiko* (flying fish roe) or salmon caviar. Follow the instructions in the Note on page 535.

METHOD:
Direct grilling

INGREDIENTS:
Coarse salt (kosher or sea)
4 lobsters (each 1¼ to 1½ pounds;
    preferably female; see Tips,
    opposite page)
5 tablespoons unsalted butter
2 to 3 shallots, minced
    (about ½ cup)
¾ cup dry white wine
1 cup heavy (whipping) cream
2 tablespoons Cognac or brandy
1 pinch cayenne pepper
Freshly ground black pepper

1 Place 1 gallon of water and ¼ cup of salt in a large pot and bring to a boil over high heat. Add the lobsters and let boil for 2 minutes. Drain the lobsters in a colander and rinse with cold water until cool. Drain well, then transfer the lobsters to a cutting board—ideally a grooved one, so you can collect the juices.

2 Using a large chef's knife or cleaver, break off the claws, then crack their shells in one or two spots using a nutcracker or

TIPS

How to prepare a lobster for grilling can pose a moral dilemma. Do you cut the live lobster in half (as a professional chef would do) or parboil it and then do the cutting? Parboiling adds a step and a pot, but many cooks find it the less traumatic way to go. It's what I've called for here.

Don't bother grilling crustaceans unless they're live and kicking.

Menemsha on Martha's Vineyard—a quintessential fishing village, and the place where I buy my lobster.

a knife. Cut each lobster in half lengthwise. Remove the papery sacs behind the eyes and discard them. Remove the roe (the pinkish or reddish black mass located in the tail of the lobster right where it meets the body), if any. Set the roe aside. Remove the tomalley (the pale green liver) and set it aside with the roe. Remove the vein that runs the length of the tail and discard it.

3 Melt the butter in a heavy saucepan over medium heat. Spoon out 2 tablespoons of the butter to a small bowl and set aside. Add the shallots to the butter remaining in the saucepan and cook over medium heat until soft but not brown, 2 to 3 minutes. Increase the heat to high, add the wine, and let boil until reduced by three quarters, about 5 minutes.

Whisk in the cream, Cognac, lobster roe, if any, tomalleys, and any lobster juices. Reduce the heat to medium-high and let the sauce simmer briskly until thick, creamy, and reduced to about 1 cup, 5 to 8 minutes, whisking occasionally. Stir in the cayenne and season with salt and black pepper to taste; the sauce should be highly seasoned. Keep the sauce warm until ready to use.

4 Set up the grill for direct grilling (see page 21 for charcoal or gas) and preheat to high.

5 When ready to cook, brush and oil the grill grate. Brush the cut side of each lobster half with some of the reserved melted butter and season generously with salt and pepper. Drizzle a little butter into the cracks in each claw. Place the claws on the hot grate. Place the lobster halves on the grate, cut side down. Grill the claws for 4 to 6 minutes per side (8 to 12 minutes in all), dabbing some of the melted butter into the cracks in the shells with a pastry brush. Grill the lobster halves for about 3 minutes, then turn and grill them cut side up until the meat is cooked through (it will be firm and white), 6 to 8 minutes longer, basting with more melted butter.

6 Transfer the grilled lobsters with their claws to a platter or plates and spoon the sauce over them. Serve at once. Be sure to provide nut crackers, finger bowls, and a dish for the empty shells.

YIELD:
Serves 4

NOTE: If your lobsters do not have roe, you can substitute *tobiko,* flying fish roe, a small, crunchy red "caviar" commonly served at sushi bars. (Its mild flavor and snappy crunch have endeared it to chefs of all ethnic backgrounds.) *Tobiko* is available at Japanese markets and natural foods stores. Or use salmon roe, sometimes known as salmon caviar, which is available at Japanese markets and gourmet shops. You'll need about 4 tablespoons of *tobiko* or salmon caviar. Add it in Step 3 once the sauce has thickened; remove the saucepan from the heat first.

Baltimore, Md.

GRILLED SOFT-SHELL CRABS
With Old Bay Tartar Sauce

When you grow up in Baltimore, as I did, soft-shell crab becomes part of your culinary calendar—as much summer's calling card as the crack of a baseball bat at Camden Yards. The reason is simple: June is the time when blue crabs from the Chesapeake Bay begin to molt (shed their shells). A soft-shell is nothing more than a recently molted crab. At this stage it's exceptionally sweet, and you can eat the crab shell and all. This

I've called for the soft-shell crabs to be served as open-faced sandwiches, but you could also serve them without bread as an appetizer or main course.

Old Bay is the classic Baltimore seafood seasoning.

TIPS

Soft-shell crabs could once only be found in the towns where crabs are fished, but thanks to their skyrocketing popularity (think of the "spider rolls" served at sushi bars), you can now buy them at fish markets across the United States, especially in the coastal states of the mid-Atlantic, Southeast, Gulf Coast, and Texas. One good source is Legal Sea Foods (see Mail-Order Sources, page 742). For the sake of the squeamish, I'm going to assume you'll buy your crabs dressed (cleaned). If you're interested in learning how to do this yourself, see my book *How to Grill*.

gives you the sweet briny flavor of fresh crabmeat combined with a buttery crisp shell. The following soft-shells aren't exactly like the ones I grew up on (those were panfried or deep-fried), but grilling has a way of bringing out the crabs' sweetness without deep-frying.

METHOD:
Direct grilling

INGREDIENTS:
12 tablespoons (1½ sticks) unsalted butter
2 cloves garlic, minced
1 shallot, minced
2 teaspoons Old Bay seasoning
12 soft-shell crabs, cleaned
6 slices white bread
Old Bay Tartar Sauce (recipe follows)
6 Boston or Bibb lettuce leaves
1 ripe tomato, thinly sliced

1 Melt the butter in a small saucepan over medium-high heat. Add the garlic, shallot, and Old Bay seasoning and cook until the garlic and shallot have lost their rawness, about 2 minutes. They should be soft and translucent; do not let them brown. Set the flavored butter aside; you'll use it for basting.

2 Set up the grill for direct grilling (see page 21 for charcoal or gas) and preheat to high.

3 When ready to cook, brush and oil the grill grate. Brush the crabs on both sides with some of the flavored butter. Place the soft-shell crabs on the hot grate and grill until cooked through, 2 to 4 minutes per side, basting with

some of the flavored butter. When done the shells will turn bright red. Brush the bread slices with the remaining flavored butter and grill them as well, about 1 minute per side.

4 To serve, slather the toast with some of the Old Bay Tartar Sauce. Place a lettuce leaf, a few tomato slices, and 2 soft-shell crabs on top. Serve the remaining tartar sauce on the side.

YIELD:
Serves 6

Old Bay Tartar Sauce

Tartar sauce used to be a minor miracle—especially when homemade. Sugary commercial tartar sauce is about all you find these days, but if you're willing to spend a little time chopping, you can restore this rich, piquant sauce to its former glory. The one here is flavored with Old Bay seasoning, the traditional spice mix used by Marylanders to cook crab. Redolent with ginger, mace, and celery seed, Old Bay seasoning was invented in Baltimore by Gustav Brunn, a German Jewish spice merchant.

INGREDIENTS:
1 cup mayonnaise (preferably Hellmann's)
1 to 2 pickled jalapeño peppers, finely chopped
1 tablespoon drained capers
1 tablespoon chopped pickles (preferably cornichons)

1 tablespoon fresh lemon juice

1 tablespoon finely chopped fresh chives
	or scallion greens

1 tablespoon finely chopped fresh
	tarragon or basil

1 tablespoon Dijon mustard

1½ teaspoons Old Bay seasoning

Freshly ground black pepper

Place the mayonnaise, jalapeño(s), capers, pickles, lemon juice, chives, tarragon, mustard, and Old Bay seasoning in a nonreactive bowl and whisk to mix. Season with black pepper to taste. The sauce can be refrigerated, covered, for at least a week. Bring to room temperature before serving.

YIELD:

Makes about 1 cup

Wilmington, Del.

GRILLED SOFT-SHELL CRABS
With Mushrooms and Corn

Tobias Lawry likes to say his cooking career began at a wood pile. The place was a pizzeria with a wood-burning oven. Fourteen-year-old Lawry was charged with transporting the wood for the fire. Thus, the chef of Wilmington's acclaimed Restaurant 821 learned at an early age the potent power of live fire cooking over wood. So when Lawry, the youngest chef ever to be named a Rising Star by the *Wine Spectator,* teamed up with Obadiah Ostergard to open his restaurant, he made a wood-burning oven and a grill the restaurant's focal points. Lawry's passion for local ingredients borders on an obsession; when the first Delaware soft-shell crabs come in season, he fires up the grill to

T I P S

You can certainly grill the corn and mushrooms for the vinaigrette a few hours ahead, or even the day before.

greet them. His sauce is a ragout with grilled corn and exotic mushrooms. In the original version of this recipe, Lawry sautéed the mushrooms, but I like the smoke flavor grilling adds. This is my take on a Restaurant 821 summer classic.

METHOD:
Direct grilling

INGREDIENTS:
1 clove garlic, minced
Coarse salt (kosher or sea) and
      freshly ground black pepper
¼ cup balsamic vinegar
1 shallot, minced
3 tablespoons finely chopped
      fresh flat-leaf parsley
1 teaspoon fresh or dried thyme
1 cup extra-virgin olive oil
8 soft-shell crabs, cleaned
8 ounces exotic or button
      mushrooms
2 ears sweet corn, shucked

YOU'LL ALSO NEED:
4 short (6- to 8-inch) bamboo skewers

1 Place the garlic and ½ teaspoon each of salt and pepper in a nonreactive mixing bowl and mash to a paste with the back of a spoon. Add the vinegar and whisk until the salt dissolves. Whisk in the shallot, parsley, thyme, and olive oil. Brush the soft-shell crabs with 4 tablespoons of this vinaigrette. Set the remaining vinaigrette and the soft-shell crabs aside.

2 Trim the stems off the mushrooms and wipe the caps clean with a damp paper towel. Thread the mushrooms onto the skewers.

3 Set up the grill for direct grilling (see page 21 for charcoal or gas) and preheat to high.

4 When ready to grill, brush and oil the grill grate. Lightly brush the corn and mushrooms with some of the vinaigrette. Place the corn and mushrooms on the hot grate and grill until nicely browned on all sides. This will take 2 to 3 minutes per side (8 to 12 minutes in all) for the corn and 3 to 5 minutes per side (6 to 10 minutes in all) for the mushrooms. Transfer the grilled vegetables to a cutting board and let cool slightly. Let the fire continue to burn in the grill.

5 Cut the kernels off the corn cobs, using lengthwise strokes of a chef's knife. Add the corn kernels to the vinaigrette. Unskewer the grilled mushrooms, thinly slice them, and add them to the vinaigrette. Season with salt and pepper to taste.

6 Brush and oil the grill grate again. Generously season the soft-shell crabs on both sides with salt and pepper. Place the soft-shell crabs on the hot grate and grill until cooked through, 2 to 4 minutes per side. When done, the shells will turn bright red. Transfer the grilled crabs to a platter or plates. Spoon the mushroom and corn mixture over them and serve at once.

YIELD:
Serves 4

TIPS

You can use any kind of mushrooms for this: hen of the woods or porcini, or a mixture, or even commonplace button mushrooms (which definitely become more interesting when you grill them).

Stonington, Maine

PANCETTA-GRILLED DIVER SCALLOPS

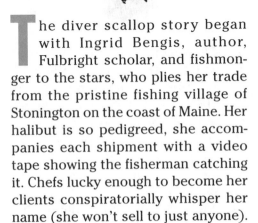

The diver scallop story began with Ingrid Bengis, author, Fulbright scholar, and fishmonger to the stars, who plies her trade from the pristine fishing village of Stonington on the coast of Maine. Her halibut is so pedigreed, she accompanies each shipment with a video tape showing the fisherman catching it. Chefs lucky enough to become her clients conspiratorially whisper her name (she won't sell to just anyone).

Fifteen years ago, Ingrid began supplying an elite coterie of chefs with sea scallops that were almost the size of hockey pucks. She pioneered these diver scallops, large, sweet, briny sea scallops that are harvested by hand by fishermen in scuba gear. I'm not sure all scallops sold as "diver scallops" these days are actually fished in this manner, but the term has come to mean a scallop of exceptional size and superior flavor. All of which is a lengthy prologue to a dish you can make in a matter of minutes and shows off the scallop in all its briny splendor.

METHOD:
Direct grilling

INGREDIENTS:

16 diver scallops or large sea scallops (about 1½ pounds total)

16 fresh sage leaves

16 thin slices pancetta (each 7 inches long; 10 to 12 ounces total; see Note)

2 tablespoons fresh lemon juice

2 tablespoons extra-virgin olive oil

Coarse salt (kosher or sea) and freshly ground black pepper

YOU'LL ALSO NEED:
Wooden toothpicks

1 Remove the small crescent-shaped muscle from the side of any scallop that has one. Rinse the scallops under cold running water, then drain and blot them dry with paper towels. Place a scallop flat on your work surface. Wrap a sage leaf around the side of the scallop, then wrap a slice of pancetta around the scallop. Run a toothpick through the scallop to hold the pancetta and sage in place. Wrap the remaining scallops the same way. Place the scallops in a nonreactive baking dish. Place the lemon juice, olive oil, and a little salt and pepper in a nonreactive bowl and beat with a fork to mix. Brush some of this mixture on the exposed part of the scallops.

TIPS

Pancetta is a sort of Italian bacon, made by curing pork belly like prosciutto (unlike bacon, however, it is rolled and not smoked). Look for it at Italian markets, gourmet shops, and many supermarkets. In a pinch, you could substitute regular bacon.

TRIMMING SCALLOPS

Scallops frequently have a small, crescent-shaped muscle on the side that's noticeably tougher than the rest of the shellfish. I recommend removing this muscle—it pulls off easily with your fingers. Not every scallop will have one: It may have fallen off or been removed by the fishmonger.

2 Set up the grill for direct grilling (see page 21 for charcoal or gas) and preheat to high.

3 When ready to cook, brush and oil the grill grate. Place the scallops on the hot grate and grill until the pancetta is browned and the scallops are cooked through, 3 to 4 minutes per side. When done, the scallops will be firm and opaque; don't overcook them or they'll become rubbery. Brush the scallops with the remaining lemon juice and oil, but do not baste them during the last minute. Turn the scallops on their sides with tongs to brown the pancetta. Transfer the grilled scallops to a platter or plates, then remove and discard the toothpicks and serve.

YIELD:

**Serves 6 to 8 as an appetizer,
    4 as a light main course**

NOTE: To get 7-inch-long slices of pancetta, it will be necessary to unroll it first.

TIPS

Diver scallops may be available at a good fishmonger or you can order them by mail (see Mail-Order Sources, page 742). You can also use regular sea scallops or Nantucket bay scallops. When grilling the smaller bay scallops however, thread them kebab style onto bamboo skewers to facilitate turning.

Maine

SESAME DIVER SCALLOPS
With Miso Barbecue Sauce

Miso entered the culinary vernacular of the United States with the health food movement of the 1960s. This nutritious paste of fermented soybeans (it tastes a lot better than it sounds) has become a staple in progressive American cooking. Originally from Japan, where it's a key ingredient in barbecue sauces, miso has a sweet, salty, nutty flavor that pairs perfectly with grilled seafood—

To find the choicest scallops, fishermen in Maine don wet suits to harvest by hand.

especially with the sweetest shellfish of all: grilled scallops. So it's not surprising that variations on this dish turn up at sushi bars from Maine to Malibu. The best sea scallops come from the icy waters of Maine, and the best of those are diver scallops.

METHOD:
Direct grilling

FOR THE MISO BARBECUE SAUCE:
**3 tablespoons white miso,
    at room temperature
1 teaspoon sugar, or more to taste
1/2 teaspoon finely grated lemon zest
3/4 cup mayonnaise (preferably Hellmann's)
1 tablespoon sake, mirin, or sherry,
    or more to taste**

FOR THE SCALLOPS:
**1 1/2 pounds diver scallops or
    large sea scallops (see Note)
2 tablespoons Asian (dark)
    sesame oil
Coarse salt (kosher or sea) and
    freshly ground black pepper
1 tablespoon black sesame seeds
    or toasted sesame seeds
    (see page 584)**

1 MAKE THE MISO BARBECUE SAUCE: Place the miso, sugar, and lemon zest in a nonreactive mixing bowl and mash to a paste with the back of a spoon. Whisk in the mayonnaise and sake. Taste for sweetness, adding more sugar and/or sake as necessary; the sauce should be salty and sweet, with just a little hint of lemon.

2 PREPARE THE SCALLOPS: Remove the small crescent-shaped muscle from the side of any scallop that has one. Rinse the scallops under cold running water, then drain and blot them dry with paper towels. Brush the scallops on both sides with the sesame oil and season generously with salt and pepper. Let the scallops marinate for 15 minutes.

3 Set up the grill for direct grilling (see page 21 for charcoal or gas) and preheat to high.

4 When ready to cook, brush and oil the grill grate. Place the scallops on the hot grate and grill until just cooked through, 2 to 3 minutes per side. When done, the scallops will be firm and opaque; don't overcook them or they'll become rubbery. If you're working with really huge scallops, you can create an attractive crosshatch of grill marks; simply rotate each scallop a quarter turn halfway through grilling on each side.

5 Transfer the grilled scallops to a platter or plates. Spoon the miso barbecue sauce over them and sprinkle the sesame seeds on top. Serve at once.

YIELD:
**Serves 6 to 8 as an appetizer,
    4 as a light main course**

NOTE: Scallops are about the smallest seafood you can put on a grill grate without their falling through the bars. Some people like to grill scallops on a fish grate, a perforated metal plate that holds them steady above the fire but allows the flavor of the fire to come through the holes in the plate. Preheat the grate when you set up the grill.

TIPS

■ If you've never tasted miso, this is a great introduction. Miso is now manufactured in the United States, and you can probably find it in the produce section of your local supermarket (if not, look for it at a Japanese market or natural foods store).

■ Black sesame seeds, which look very smart against the ivory-colored scallops, are also available at Japanese markets and natural foods stores. Or you can use toasted regular ones.

■ Sake and mirin are both Japanese rice wines, but while sake is dry, mirin is sweet. Depending upon where you live, they, too, may be available at natural foods stores and Japanese markets— or else in liquor stores. Sherry makes an acceptable substitute.

TIPS

■ True bay scallops are in season from late fall to the onset of spring. You'll be able to find them if you live in coastal New England or in New York or another major city. One good source is Legal Sea Foods (see Mail-Order Sources, page 742). Beware of bargain "bay scallops." If they're cheap, they lack the briny sweetness of New England bay scallops.

■ Look for an old-fashioned smokehouse bacon. One good manufacturer is Nueske's Hillcrest Farm (see Mail-Order Sources, page 742).

Nantucket, Mass.

BAY SCALLOPS
With Bacon and Lemon

If diver scallops are esteemed for their size and meatiness, bay scallops are prized for just the opposite—their diminutive dimensions and delicacy. Native to Massachusetts, bay scallops are about the sweetest nuggets of seafood ever to emerge from the ocean. I like to wrap them in bacon and serve them grilled on skewers.

METHOD:
Direct grilling

INGREDIENTS:
1½ pounds bay scallops (about 32)
1 lemon
1 pound thinly sliced bacon,
    each slice cut in half crosswise
Freshly ground black pepper

YOU'LL ALSO NEED:
About 16 small (6- to 8-inch)
    bamboo skewers; a 18- by 12-inch
    sheet of aluminum foil folded in thirds
    to form a 12- by 6-inch shield

1 Remove the small crescent-shaped muscle from the side of any scallop that has one. Remove and discard the lemon rind. Cut the lemon crosswise into paper-thin slices. Cut each slice into tiny (½-inch) wedges, removing any seeds with a fork. You'll need as many lemon wedges as you have scallops.

2 Hold a lemon wedge against a scallop, then wrap a piece of bacon around the lemon and scallop. Prepare another scallop the same way and push a skewer through the bacon wrapping of both scallops to secure them. Repeat with the remaining scallops and lemon wedges, securing 2 per skewer. Season the scallop kebabs with pepper.

3 Set up the grill for direct grilling (see page 21 for charcoal or gas) and preheat to high.

4 When ready to cook, brush and oil the grill grate. Place the scallop kebabs on the hot grate and grill until the bacon is browned and the scallops are cooked through, 2 to 3 minutes per side (4 to 6 minutes in all). When cooked, the scallops will be firm and opaque; don't overcook them or they'll become rubbery. Place a folded sheet of aluminum foil under the skewers to prevent them from burning. If the dripping bacon fat causes flare-ups, you may need to move the scallops themselves onto the aluminum foil to finish cooking. Transfer the grilled scallops to a platter or plates and serve at once.

YIELD:
Serves 6 to 8 as an appetizer,
    4 as a light main course

The Barbecued Oysters of
TOMALES BAY

"Barbecue Today" read the sign outside a white clapboard farmhouse turned restaurant in Olema, California. Although I was still dressed up after attending my cousin Martha's wedding, and although I had a hundred miles to drive to reach my hotel, I screeched my car to a halt.

Olema is the beginning of barbecued oyster country, you see, and I couldn't resist trying a dish for which California's central coast is famous. I made my way through The Olema Farm House's warren of cozy dining rooms to find a charcoal-fired grill on a deck. Their pit master had shucked so many oysters, he could probably do it in his sleep, and he knew to the second just how long to grill oysters so that the juices and barbecue sauce bubble but the bivalve itself didn't overcook.

The farmhouse served two types of barbecued oysters—one topped with garlic parsley butter, the other with a traditional sweet tomato-based sauce. As to which was superior, well, I would have had to eat several dozen oysters with each to make such a serious determination, and alas, I still had several more restaurants to try before nightfall.

A BAY AND ITS OYSTERS

In most parts of the United States, what people barbecue is beef or pork or chicken or even mutton, but in west Marin County it's oysters. Not just any oyster, but the *Crassostrea gigas;* the large, fleshy, succulent Pacific oyster, which ranges in size from that of a half-dollar to that of the sole of your shoe. These oysters are found from the bucolic town of Olema north to Point Reyes and Marshall. The oyster epicenter is on a long slender inlet called Tomales Bay. Travel the region's narrow roads on a weekend in the summer and you'll find dozens of restaurants, markets, seaside shacks, and oyster farm picnic areas where barbecued oysters are served.

Tomales Bay oysters sizzling away on the grill.

A lot of people claim to have invented or at least perfected barbecued oysters, but as I talked to folks in these parts, one name kept coming up: Anastacio Gonzalez. Gonzalez hails from the bayside village of Point Reyes Station, where he enjoys semiretirement—from barbecue at least—after a lifetime of grilled bivalve fame. According to him, the barbecued oyster was born after a shark and stingray fishing tournament in 1972. Gonzalez, a landfill worker at the time, and his buddies gathered at a restaurant called Nick's Cove to cook up the spoils of the derby. Gonzalez was busy grilling shark and stingray fillets when someone tossed him a burlap bag of the local oysters. "What do you want me to do with these?" he asked. "Why don't you grill them?" someone jokingly shouted. So a very dubious Gonzalez tossed the oysters, shells and all, on the grill.

While the oysters grilled, Gonzalez tried to reconstruct a cocktail sauce for shrimp that his mother made in his native Jalisco, Mexico. He rummaged through the restaurant's kitchen, found ketchup, white wine, soy sauce, Tabasco sauce, sugar, pepper, garlic powder, and the secret ingredient—Coca-Cola—and dumped them into a pot. Then he slathered the mixture on the grilled oysters.

A STAR IS BORN

I like to imagine the scene: A drunken carousal after two days of fishing and drinking, then suddenly, a hush falling over the crowd as the first barbecued oyster is tasted. Gradually, voices rise in approval, until the whole town is abuzz about barbecued oysters. Anyone who follows international espionage or the machinations of multinational corporations can guess what happened next. The owner of Nick's Cove offered to pay Gonzalez if he would return the following weekend to make barbecued oysters. Soon, dozens, hundreds, thousands of people began converging on this seaside fish house to sample the new creation. Subsequent grill sessions brought refinements to the original recipe. Gonzalez quickly discovered that the oysters were juicier and easier to eat if they were shucked first and barbecued on the half shell. He also added a second step to the grilling process, basting the oysters with garlic butter before slathering on the barbecue sauce.

Eventually, a neighboring restaurant, Tony's Seafood, hired Gonzalez away with the lure of a percentage of the business, not just an hourly wage. A few years after that, another restaurant, the Marshall Tavern, made an even better offer:

Barbecued oysters with all the fixin's— and the appropriate accompaniment, wine.

the HOG ISLAND OYSTER COMPANY

The Hog Island Oyster Company, where the oysters are always fresh and the grills are ready for charcoal.

Gonzalez could keep the entire take on the barbecued oysters; the increased bar business alone would make the transaction worthwhile for the tavern. By then, Gonzalez was cooking 4,500 oysters on a typical weekend.

Today, Gonzalez occasionally stages oyster roasts at weddings and parties for friends. Meanwhile, barbecued oysters have become big business for restaurants like Tony's Seafood, The Marshall Store, and The Olema Farm House. And local oyster farms frequently provide picnic tables and barbecue grills for do-it-yourselfers. Many San Franciscans take the weekend drive up the coast to sit by the shore and enjoy barbecued oysters.

Gonzalez's original recipe has inspired dozens of imitations. There are establishments that offer garlic butter oysters and red barbecue sauce oysters separately. Others adhere to Gonzalez's original practice of adding both to a single oyster. Chipotle peppers and horseradish have crept into some sauces, while you also find ones made with fresh herbs.

As for Gonzalez, he seems slightly bemused that an offhand challenge at a fishing tournament should have become a California barbecue tradition. He doesn't miss the oyster business, but he's not taking any chances. The recipe for his legendary barbecue sauce remains a secret for now.

WHERE TO SAMPLE TOMALES BAY BARBECUED OYSTERS

RESTAURANTS

THE MARSHALL STORE
19225 State Route 1
Marshall, California
(415) 663-1339

THE OLEMA FARM HOUSE
10005 State Highway 1
Olema, California
(415) 663-1264

TONY'S SEAFOOD
18863 Highway 1
Marshall, California
(415) 663-1107

OYSTER FARMS
These have picnic tables and grills so you can barbecue your own oysters.

THE HOG ISLAND OYSTER COMPANY
20215 Highway 1
Marshall, California
(415) 663-9218

TOMALES BAY OYSTER COMPANY
15479 Highway 1
Marshall, California
(415) 663-1242

TIPS

A true oyster lover may raise an eyebrow at the molasses and honey in The Olema Farm House's barbecue sauce. I did. Rest assured—it adds a pleasing roundness without being quite sweet. In fact, the sauce is no sweeter, and possibly even less so, than a traditional cocktail sauce.

Grilled oysters are a speciality of the Tomales Bay region in west Marin County.

Tomales Bay, Calif.

THE OLEMA FARM HOUSE BARBECUED OYSTERS

"**W**et or dry?" ask the pit masters of Memphis. "Red or white?" query the grill mavens in west Marin, California. Red refers to barbecued oysters slathered with a tomato-based barbecue sauce made sweet with molasses and honey and pungent with garlic and onion. White refers to a simple topping of garlic, parsley, and butter. For the ultimate barbecued oysters, baste the sizzling shellfish with both. The recipe here comes from The Olema Farm House, a rambling restaurant housed in an 1845 white clapboard farmhouse. Although many barbecued oyster joints in California now use gas grills, the farmhouse still roasts the shellfish the old-fashioned way, over crackling mesquite charcoal. Mesquite burns the hottest of all charcoals, and it has a disconcerting habit of popping and sparking. If you're grilling with it on a wood deck, take care to protect the deck.

METHOD:
Direct grilling

INGREDIENTS:

2 tablespoons salted butter

1 medium-size onion, finely chopped (for ½ cup)

2 cloves garlic, minced

1 teaspoon fresh or dried thyme leaves

1 cup canned tomato sauce

1 cup bottled chili sauce, such as Heinz

2 tablespoons cider vinegar, or more to taste

2 tablespoons molasses

1 tablespoon honey

1 teaspoon liquid smoke

½ teaspoon freshly ground white pepper

Coarse salt (kosher or sea)

24 large oysters

Crusty bread, for serving

1 Melt the butter in a heavy nonreactive saucepan over medium heat. Add the onion, garlic, and thyme and cook until the onion and garlic are soft and fragrant but not brown, about 3 minutes. Add the tomato sauce, chili sauce, vinegar, molasses, honey, liquid smoke, and pepper and gradually bring to a simmer. Let the sauce simmer gently (reduce the heat if necessary) until thick and flavorful, 10 to 15 minutes, stirring from time to time with a wooden spoon. Taste for seasoning, adding more vinegar as necessary and salt to taste. The sauce can be prepared several hours or even days ahead. Refrigerate, covered, until ready to use.

2 Scrub the oyster shells with a stiff brush to remove any grit or mud. Discard any oysters that fail to close when tapped. Shuck the oysters as described on page 550. Place the oysters flat on baking sheets, taking care not to spill the juices.

3 Set up the grill for direct grilling (see page 21 for charcoal or gas) and preheat to high.

4 When ready to cook, spoon 1 tablespoon of the barbecue sauce over each oyster. Place the oysters on the hot grate and grill until the sauce and oyster juices are bubbling and the oysters are cooked through, 4 to 6 minutes. Work in as many batches as necessary to avoid overcrowding the grill. Serve the oysters hot off the grill, with crusty bread for soaking up the juices.

YIELD:
Makes 24 oysters

Tomales Bay, Calif.

BARBECUED OYSTERS With Garlic Parsley Butter

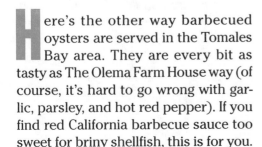

Here's the other way barbecued oysters are served in the Tomales Bay area. They are every bit as tasty as The Olema Farm House way (of course, it's hard to go wrong with garlic, parsley, and hot red pepper). If you find red California barbecue sauce too sweet for briny shellfish, this is for you.

METHOD:
Direct grilling

INGREDIENTS:
2 sticks (½ pound) salted butter
4 cloves fresh garlic, minced
¼ cup finely chopped fresh flat-leaf parsley
½ tablespoon hot red pepper flakes
½ tablespoon cracked or freshly ground black peppercorns
½ cup dry white wine (optional)
24 large oysters
Crusty bread, for serving

1 Melt the butter in a saucepan over medium heat. Add the garlic, parsley, hot red pepper flakes, and peppercorns and cook until the garlic is fragrant, 2 to 4 minutes. Do not let the garlic brown. Add the wine, if using (some people like the hint of acidity it adds, some don't), let come to a boil, and boil for 3 minutes.

2 Scrub the oyster shells with a stiff brush to remove any grit or mud. Discard any oysters that fail to close when tapped. Shuck the oysters as described on page 550. Place the oysters flat on baking sheets, taking care not to spill the juices.

3 Set up the grill for direct grilling (see page 21 for charcoal or gas) and preheat to high.

4 When ready to cook, spoon 1 tablespoon of the garlic parsley butter over each oyster. Place the oysters on the hot grate and grill until the sauce and oyster juices are bubbling and the oysters are cooked through, 4 to 6 minutes.

T I P S

For the best results—for the only truly acceptable results—start with whole garlic cloves and mince them when you need to use them. The prechopped garlic sold in oil in jars has a lingering flavor that I find very off-putting. You can chop larger quantities of garlic, like the four cloves called for here, in a food processor fitted with the metal blade; run the processor in bursts.

Work in as many batches as necessary to avoid overcrowding the grill. Serve the oysters hot off the grill, with crusty bread for soaking up the juices.

YIELD:
Makes 24 oysters

Tomales Bay, Calif.

BARBECUED OYSTERS With Hog Wash

Christine Johnson's family have been Tomales Bay oyster farmers for three generations. Their business, Johnson's Oyster Company, provides Marin County barbecue buffs with their favorite bivalves. When asked about the origin of barbecued oysters, Christine had a highly plausible response: "Someone probably lost his oyster knife." Since prehistoric times, coastal peoples have opened oysters by roasting them in campfires; here, however, we'll resort to a knife.

METHOD:
Direct grilling

INGREDIENTS:
2 to 3 shallots, minced (for ½ cup)
2 cloves garlic, minced

TIPS

This is the simplest way of all to prepare barbecued oysters. You don't even need a barbecue sauce, just Hog Wash, a simple garlic and shallot vinaigrette that may remind you of a *mignonette* sauce. The easiest way to make Hog Wash is to combine the ingredients in a jar with a tight lid and shake it.

1 tablespoon cracked black peppercorns
1 teaspoon coarse salt (kosher or sea), or more to taste
½ cup white wine vinegar or tarragon vinegar
1 cup extra-virgin olive oil
24 large oysters
Crusty bread, for serving

1 Combine the shallots, garlic, peppercorns, salt, vinegar, and olive oil in a large jar with a tight-fitting lid. Shake vigorously until the salt dissolves. Taste the Hog Wash for seasoning, adding more salt as necessary.

2 Scrub the oyster shells with a stiff brush to remove any grit or mud. Discard any oysters that fail to close when tapped. Shuck the oysters as described on page 550. Place the oysters flat on baking sheets, taking care not to spill the juices.

3 Set up the grill for direct grilling (see page 21 for charcoal or gas) and preheat to high.

4 When ready to cook, spoon 1 tablespoon of the Hog Wash over each oyster, shaking or stirring the jar from time to time to keep the ingredients mixed. Place the oysters on the hot grate and grill until the sauce and oyster juices are bubbling and the oysters are cooked through, 4 to 6 minutes. Work in as many batches as necessary to avoid overcrowding the grill. Serve the oysters hot off the grill, with crusty bread for soaking up the juices.

YIELD:
Makes 24 oysters

Tomales Bay, Calif.

HOG ISLAND OYSTERS
With Chipotle Horseradish Barbecue Sauce

Few settings are more conducive to an oyster barbecue than Hog Island, one of the oldest, most picturesque oyster farms on Tomales Bay. And they sure make it easy. Obviously, you can buy your oysters here, whole or shucked, and you'll also find barbecue sauce, picnic tables, charcoal, and even a bevy of kettle grills. The only thing you need to bring is an appetite—and the wine.

METHOD:
Direct grilling

INGREDIENTS:

1 cup canned tomato sauce
5 tablespoons cider vinegar
¼ cup honey
1 tablespoon Worcestershire sauce
2 tablespoons soy sauce
1 small onion, minced
2 cloves garlic, minced
1 to 2 canned chipotle peppers, minced
1 piece (about 2 inches) fresh horseradish, peeled and grated
Coarse salt (kosher or sea) and freshly ground black pepper
24 large oysters
Crusty bread, for serving

1 Place the tomato sauce, vinegar, honey, Worcestershire sauce, soy sauce, onion, garlic, and chipotle(s) in a heavy nonreactive saucepan over medium heat and bring to a simmer. Let the sauce simmer gently until thickened and richly flavored, 5 to 10

The smoky heat of the Hog Island barbecue sauce comes from chipotle peppers and horseradish. For optimal flavor the chipotles (smoked jalapeños) should be canned (they have more flavor than dried) and the horseradish, freshly grated. In a pinch, you could substitute two tablespoons of prepared horseradish for fresh.

At Hog Island, the oysters are grilled and eaten as fast as you can shuck them.

HOW TO SHUCK OYSTERS

Get yourself a good oyster knife—they have a short stubby blade with a bent tip. Set the oyster, flat shell side up, on a pot holder or dishcloth (this gives you better traction) on your work surface. Wiggle the tip of the knife into the "hinge," where the top and bottom shells are attached. Gently push the handle down: The hooked blade will give you the leverage to pop off the shell. Slide the knife blade under the top shell to cut the adductor muscle and discard the top shell. Take care not to spill the oyster juices.

minutes, stirring occasionally with a wooden spoon.

2 Remove the saucepan from the heat, let cool slightly and stir in the horseradish. Season with salt and pepper to taste; the sauce should be highly seasoned. The sauce can be made several hours or days ahead. Refrigerate, covered, until ready to use.

3 Scrub the oyster shells with a stiff brush to remove any grit or mud. Discard any oysters that fail to close when tapped. Shuck the oysters as described above. Place the oysters flat on baking sheets, taking care not to spill the juices.

4 Set up the grill for direct grilling (see page 21 for charcoal or gas) and preheat to high.

5 When ready to cook, spoon 1 tablespoon of the sauce over each oyster. Place the oysters on the hot grate and grill until the sauce and oyster juices are bubbling and the oysters are

cooked through, 4 to 6 minutes. Work in as many batches as necessary to avoid overcrowding the grill. Serve the oysters hot off the grill, with crusty bread for soaking up the juices.

YIELD:

Makes 24 oysters

Tomales Bay, Calif.

"DRUNKEN SAILORS" (Oysters with Cilantro, Tequila, and Asiago Cheese)

When I met Mike Sanders he was one of the happiest guys on the planet. As the manager of the Tomales Bay Oyster Company, he worked with a quality product in a spectacular bayfront setting, and he got to share both of these with hundreds of oyster lovers each weekend for do-it-yourself barbecues. Sanders can grill oysters with the best of them, and his contribution to this singular genre is a cilantro, cheese, and tequila topped barbecued oyster he aptly calls a "drunken sailor."

METHOD:
Direct grilling

INGREDIENTS:
24 large oysters
About 1 cup red California-style
barbecue sauce (see Notes)
About ¾ cup chopped fresh cilantro
About ¾ cup freshly grated Asiago cheese
A couple tablespoons of really
good tequila (see Notes)
Crusty bread, for serving

1 Scrub the oyster shells with a stiff brush to remove any grit or mud. Discard any oysters that fail to close when tapped. Shuck the oysters as described on the facing page. Place the oysters flat on baking sheets, taking care not to spill the juices.

2 Spoon about 2 teaspoons of the barbecue sauce over each oyster. Top each oyster with about 1½ teaspoons of the cilantro and 1½ teaspoons of cheese. Sprinkle a few drops of tequila over each oyster.

3 Set up the grill for direct grilling (see page 21 for charcoal or gas) and preheat to high.

4 When ready to cook, place the oysters on the hot grate and grill until the sauce and oyster juices are bubbling and the oysters are cooked through, 4 to 6 minutes. Work in as many batches as necessary to avoid overcrowding the grill. Serve the oysters hot off the grill, with crusty bread for soaking up the juices.

YIELD:
Makes 24 oysters

NOTES:

■ For barbecue sauce, use the one in The Olema Farm House Barbecued Oysters recipe on page 546 or your favorite commercial brand (Sanders swears by Leon's Bar-B-Q).

■ For tequila, the oyster man recommends Chinaco.

TIPS

For a twist on "Drunken Sailors," use aged dry Jack cheese instead of Asiago. Aged Jack is a rich-flavored California grating cheese; one good brand is Vella.

Barbecue with a bayfront view. It doesn't get much better than this.

TIPS

One way—used throughout this book—to keep the exposed ends of bamboo skewers from burning is to place them over an aluminum foil shield (a folded-up piece of foil). Another way is simply to load the skewers so completely with clam and peppers that there is no exposed bamboo.

The largest edible clam in North America, the geoduck is great for grilling.

Venice, Calif.

GRILLED CLAM AND PEPPER KEBABS

In a world of lightning change, it's reassuring to know that some things remain as good as you remember them. For example, the Hama sushi restaurant in Venice, California. More than two decades ago, some friends took me to this sizzling sushi bar in the heart of Los Angeles's outrageous beachfront community, and it's hard to say which impressed me more—the cutting-edge sushi or the archly hip crowd (many of whom arrived on roller skates). I recently returned to Hama, and much to my delight, the sushi was as innovative and fresh as I recalled. What I didn't remember was

the selection of grilled fare, including these simple but vibrant clam and pepper kebabs.

METHOD:
Direct grilling

INGREDIENTS:
1 pound geoduck clam meat
12 to 16 ounces shishito peppers,
    3 to 4 cubanelle peppers, or
    2 green bell peppers
2 tablespoons Asian (dark) sesame oil
Coarse salt (kosher or sea)
2 tablespoons shichimi or Pepper Poppy
    Sesame Blend (recipe follows)
Lemon wedges, for serving
Crusty bread, for serving

YOU'LL ALSO NEED:
About 8 short (6- to 8-inch) bamboo skewers

1 Cut the clam meat into 1-by-½-by-¼-inch pieces. If using shishito peppers, stem them (if using cubanelle peppers or green bell peppers, cut them into 1-by-½-inch pieces). Thread the clams and peppers onto skewers, alternating pieces of each. Lightly brush each kebab with sesame oil and sprinkle with salt.

2 Set up the grill for direct grilling (see page 21 for charcoal or gas) and preheat to high.

3 When ready to cook, place the kebabs on the hot grate. Grill the kebabs until the peppers are lightly browned and the pieces of clam are just cooked through, 3 to 4 minutes per side, turning with tongs. When done the clam pieces will be lightly browned at the edges and firm to the touch. Transfer the kebabs to plates or a platter, sprinkle with the *shichimi,* and serve at once, with lemon wedges and crusty bread.

YIELD:
Makes 8 kebabs

Pepper Poppy Sesame Blend

This simple spice blend is loosely modeled on a Japanese seasoning called *shichimi.* To make it more authentic, you'd add two teaspoons of finely chopped nori (seaweed) and a teaspoon of chopped dried orange peel. But the spice mix still has plenty of flavor without them. The recipe makes more than you need for the kebabs, but what's left over will keep well. It's tasty sprinkled over grilled chicken, seafood, and vegetables.

INGREDIENTS:

1 tablespoon sweet paprika
2 teaspoons hot red pepper flakes
2 teaspoons black or toasted white
    sesame seeds (see Notes)
2 teaspoons poppy seeds
1 teaspoon freshly ground black pepper

Combine the paprika, hot red pepper flakes, sesame seeds, poppy seeds, and black pepper in a small bowl and stir to mix. Stored in a sealed jar away from heat and light, the spice mix will keep for at least 6 months.

YIELD:
Makes about ¼ cup

NOTES:
■ Black sesame seeds are available at Japanese markets and natural foods stores.

■ To toast white sesame seeds, place them in a small dry skillet (don't use a nonstick skillet for this) over medium heat. Cook until the seeds are fragrant and lightly browned, 2 to 3 minutes, shaking the pan to ensure even toasting. Transfer the toasted sesame seeds to a heatproof bowl to cool.

GEODUCKS, SHISHITO PEPPERS, AND SHICHIMI

The clam kebabs are easy to make, but the recipe does have a few unusual ingredients (and in the event that you can't find them, I've suggested common substitutes). First the clams: Hama's chef uses geoducks (pronounced gooey-duck)—giant clams from the Puget Sound. These meaty clams are almost pure muscle, so they're easy to cut into bite-size pieces and thread onto skewers. If you live on the West Coast, particularly in the Pacific Northwest, you can probably find geoducks at your local fishmonger. If not, highly tasty kebabs can be made with shrimp or scallops. You'll need a pound.

Shishito peppers are elongated green peppers about the size of your baby finger. They've got some heat, although not as much as jalapeños. Look for them at Japanese markets or substitute horn or cubanelle peppers or even strips of green bell pepper or poblano pepper.

Shichimi—sometimes sold as "seven-spice powder"—is a Japanese spice blend that contains hot red pepper flakes, black hemp seeds, poppy seeds, sesame seeds, mandarin orange rind, bits of nori, and aromatic sansho pepper. *Shichimi* is available at Japanese markets and some natural foods stores. At left is a recipe for a quick homemade version, Pepper Poppy Sesame Blend, that uses easily available ingredients.

TIPS

■ Yes, it's possible to cook mussels on the grill. But why do this? The truth is that the intense heat of the grill sears in flavor, and nothing brings out a mussel's sweetness like the scent of wood smoke. Smoke is crucial here. Use plenty of oak chips or chunks.

■ You'll want to use a rugged cast-iron skillet for this recipe (not a brand-new nonstick frying pan), as it will get black on the grill. It looks great if you serve the mussels straight from the skillet. Set the skillet, which will be excruciatingly hot, on a trivet and serve the mussels using a large, long-handled spoon.

San Francisco, Calif.

FINGER-BURNER MUSSELS

Reed Hearon is the epitome of the new wave San Francisco restaurateur-chef. His edgy restaurants range from Mediterranean to Mexican, but they're always noisy, energetic, and packed with young people who love in-your-face flavors and cutting-edge food. Consider the *moules brûle doigts* (finger-burner mussels, literally) at his popular South of Market district restaurant, LuLu. The mussels are roasted in a wood-burning oven and served scalding hot in their shells. Whenever you combine garlic butter and wood smoke, you have a winner in my book—especially when paired with the fresh juicy mussels.

METHOD:
Direct grilling

INGREDIENTS:
4 pounds mussels
10 tablespoons (1¼ sticks) salted butter,
    at room temperature
3 cloves garlic, minced
¼ cup finely chopped fresh flat-leaf parsley
1 teaspoon finely grated lemon zest
    (see Note)
2 tablespoons fresh lemon juice
1 teaspoon cracked or coarsely ground
    black peppercorns
Crusty bread, for serving

YOU'LL ALSO NEED:
1 large or 2 medium-size cast-iron skillets;
    2 cups wood chips or chunks
    (preferably oak), soaked for 1 hour
    in water to cover, then drained

1 Pick through the mussels, discarding any with cracked shells or open shells that fail to close when the mussel is tapped. Debeard the mussels: Remove any clumps of black or brown threads on the sides of the shells by pinching them between your thumb and forefinger and pulling hard or use needle-nose pliers to do this. Scrub the mussels with a stiff brush under cold running water to remove any grit. Drain the scrubbed mussels in a colander, then blot them dry with paper towels.

2 Place the butter in a nonreactive bowl and beat with a wooden spoon or whisk until light and creamy. Beat in the garlic, parsley, lemon zest and juice, and pepper.

3 Set up the grill for direct grilling (see page 21 for gas or charcoal) and preheat to high. Place the cast-iron skillet(s) on the grill while it preheats. If using a gas grill, place all of the wood chips or chunks in the smoker box or in a smoker pouch (see page 24) and run the grill on high until you see smoke. If using a charcoal grill, preheat it to high, then toss all of the wood chips or chunks on the coals.

4 When ready to cook, add the garlic butter to the hot skillet(s). When the garlic butter is melted and sizzling, stir in the cleaned mussels and cover the grill. Cook the mussels until the shells open, 6 to 10 minutes, stirring from time to time with a long-handled spoon to give the shellfish on the bottom room to open. Keep the grill covered as much as possible to hold in the smoke. Transfer the cooked mussels and their juices to bowls and serve at once with crusty bread for soaking up the juices and a large empty bowl for the shells.

YIELD:

Serves 6 to 8 as an appetizer,
    4 as a light main course

NOTE: Use a vegetable peeler to remove the oil-rich, yellow outer rind of the lemon in strips of zest. Be careful to leave behind the bitter white pith.

Chicago, Ill.

BARBECUED MUSSELS FIRE AND SPICE

I encountered these mussels at a Moroccan-Mediterranean restaurant in Chicago called Tizi Melloul. It was love—no, lust—at first bite. I loved the gustatory pyrotechnics— the fierce intermingling of spice and smoke flavors with the briny juices of the shellfish. You'll be amazed at how

Stalking the wild mussel at low tide.

*Chicago's
Tizi Melloul is home to
Mussels Fire and Spice.*

TIPS

To be strictly
authentic, you'll
need one unusual
ingredient for the fire
and spice mussels:
smoked paprika, sold
by its Spanish name,
chinata. Look for it
in Spanish grocery
stores or order from
one of the spice
companies listed
in the Mail-Order
Sources on page
742. If you prefer,
you can use a
Spanish or Hungarian
sweet paprika. The
results will still be
spectacular.

roasting mussels in a superhot skillet
on the grill intensifies their taste.

METHOD:
Direct grilling

INGREDIENTS:
4 pounds mussels
3 tablespoons chopped fresh
    flat-leaf parsley
1 tablespoon chopped fresh marjoram,
    or 1 teaspoon dried marjoram
1 teaspoon fresh or dried thyme
2 cloves garlic, minced
2 teaspoons coarse salt
    (kosher or sea)
2 teaspoons smoked or sweet
    paprika
2 teaspoons ground cumin
1 to 2 teaspoons cayenne pepper
3 tablespoons extra-virgin olive oil,
    or 3 tablespoons melted butter
Crusty bread, for serving

YOU'LL ALSO NEED:
1 large or 2 medium-size cast-iron skillets;
    2 cups wood chips or chunks (optional;
    preferably oak), soaked for 1 hour in
    water to cover, then drained

1 Pick through the mussels, discarding
any with cracked shells or open
shells that fail to close when the mussel
is tapped. Debeard the mussels:
Remove any clumps of black or brown
threads on the sides of the shells by
pinching them between your thumb
and forefinger and pulling hard or use
needle-nose pliers to do this. Scrub the
mussels with a stiff brush under cold
running water to remove any grit. Drain
the scrubbed mussels in a colander,
then blot them dry with paper towels.

2 Place the cleaned mussels in a
large bowl and toss them with the
parsley, marjoram, thyme, garlic, salt,
paprika, cumin, and cayenne. Add the
olive oil and toss well.

3 Set up the grill for direct grilling
(see page 21 for gas or charcoal)
and preheat to high. Place the cast-iron
skillet(s) on the grill while it preheats. If
using a gas grill, place all of the wood
chips or chunks, if desired, in the
smoker box or in a smoker pouch (see
page 24) and run the grill on high until
you see smoke. If using a charcoal grill,
preheat it to high, then toss all of the
wood chips or chunks, if desired, on the
coals.

4 When ready to cook, add the
mussels to the hot skillet(s) and
cover the grill. Cook the mussels until
the shells open, 6 to 10 minutes, stirring

from time to time with a long-handled spoon to give the shellfish on the bottom room to open. Transfer the cooked mussels and their juices to bowls and serve at once with crusty bread for soaking up the juices and a large empty bowl for the shells.

YIELD:

Serves 6 to 8 as an appetizer,
4 as a light main course

Marshall, Calif.

GRILLED MUSSELS
With Thai Curry Sauce

Explosively flavorful, these grilled mussels come from the heart of California shellfish country—specifically, from The Marshall Store in the town of Marshall on Tomales Bay in west Marin County. While the shellfish are cultivated locally, the sauce is a sort of California remake of a classic Thai curry sauce, the interpretation of Marshall Store proprietor Kathryn Krohn. Nothing seems to bring out the sweetness in mussels like grilling, and if you haven't had them prepared this way, you're in for a revelation.

METHOD:
Direct grilling

INGREDIENTS:

1 tablespoon coriander seeds
1 tablespoon fennel seeds
1 tablespoon black peppercorns
1½ teaspoons curry powder
4 jalapeño peppers, seeded and chopped
    (for a hotter curry, leave the seeds in)
4 scallions, both white and green parts,
    trimmed and chopped
3 to 4 stalks lemongrass, trimmed
    and chopped
2 inches fresh ginger, peeled
    and chopped
2 cloves garlic, chopped
1 bunch cilantro, stemmed
    and chopped (for ¾ cup)
⅓ cup rice vinegar, or more to taste
5 tablespoons Asian fish sauce or soy
    sauce, or more to taste
1 can (15 ounces) unsweetened
    coconut milk
4 tablespoons (½ stick) unsalted butter
4 pounds mussels

1 Toast the spices: Place the coriander seeds, fennel seeds, and peppercorns in a small dry skillet over medium heat (do not use a nonstick skillet for this). Toast until fragrant, about 3 minutes. Stir in the curry powder and cook for 20 seconds. Transfer the spices to a heatproof bowl and let cool. Once cool, grind the toasted spices in a spice mill or coffee grinder. If you're in a hurry, toast already ground spices or skip the toasting all together.

2 Place the ground spices, jalapeños, scallions, lemongrass, ginger, garlic, cilantro, vinegar, fish sauce, and

Kathryn shucks her mussels in a microwave, zapping them just long enough to cause the shells to gap (in the old days, she would shuck them one by one with an oyster knife). Then she spoons in the sauce and grills them in the half shell. You can certainly try this time-consuming but delectable method if you like. I've opted for an easier version—grilling the mussels whole until they open, then tossing them in the sauce. They're a bit messier to eat this way but still off the charts in flavor.

coconut milk in a blender. Blend until smooth (this may take a few minutes).

3 Melt the butter in a large non-reactive saucepan over medium-high heat. Add the coconut milk mixture and bring to a boil. Reduce the heat to medium and let the mixture simmer gently for 5 minutes. Taste for seasoning, adding more vinegar and/or fish sauce as necessary; the mixture should be highly seasoned. The sauce can be prepared up to 1 day ahead to this stage, but should be reheated slowly just before serving.

4 Pick through the mussels, discarding any with cracked shells or open shells that fail to close when the mussel is tapped. Debeard the mussels: Remove any clumps of black or brown threads on the sides of the shells by pinching them between your thumb and forefinger and pulling hard or use needle-nose pliers to do this. Scrub the mussels with a stiff brush under cold running water to remove any grit. Drain the scrubbed mussels in a colander, then blot them dry with paper towels.

5 Set up the grill for direct grilling (see page 21 for charcoal or gas) and preheat to high. Have 4 large heat-proof bowls ready. Fill each with about one quarter of the curry sauce.

6 When ready to cook, place the mussels on the hot grate, rounded sides down, working in as many batches as necessary to not overcrowd the grill.

Grill the mussels just until the shells open, 2 to 6 minutes, then place them in one of the bowls of sauce, dividing them equally. Stir to mix and serve at once. This is deliciously messy, so provide extra bowls for the empty shells and fingerbowls or wet hand towels for hand washing.

YIELD:

**Serves 6 to 8 as an appetizer,
4 as a light main course**

Cambridge, Mass.

GRILLED MUSSELS
With Garlic, Wine, and Linguica

My enthusiasm for grilled shellfish knows no limit. There's something about a live fire that heightens their briny succulence. In this recipe, you cook the sauce right on the grill and add the grilled mussels to it as they open. This eliminates the need to transport a large number of mussels from the grill to the table without spilling the juices. It's a highly commonsensical approach to grilling, of course, so it's not surprising to learn that the recipe

TIPS

When buying mussels, look for ones with closed shells. They should smell like the seashore, not fishy.

. . . the briny succulence of mussels . . .

was inspired by my grilling buddy Chris Schlesinger, owner of the celebrated East Coast Grill in Cambridge, Massachusetts. The *linguica* (spicy sausage) pays homage to the Bay State's Portuguese community, which includes many descendants of whalers.

METHOD:
Direct grilling

INGREDIENTS:
4 pounds mussels

3 tablespoons butter

3 cloves garlic, minced

1/2 pound cooked linguica or
    chorizo sausage, finely diced

1 large ripe red tomato, peeled,
    seeded, and finely diced

2 cups dry white wine

1/2 cup chopped fresh flat-leaf parsley

Juice of 1 lemon (for 3 tablespoons)

Coarse salt (kosher or sea) and
    freshly ground black pepper

Crusty bread or Grilled Garlic Bread #5
    (page 134), for serving

YOU'LL ALSO NEED:
1 large aluminum foil drip pan

1 Pick through the mussels, discarding any with cracked shells or open shells that fail to close when the mussel is tapped. Debeard the mussels: Remove any clumps of black or brown threads on the sides of the shells by pinching them between your thumb and forefinger and pulling hard or use needle-nose pliers to do this. Scrub the mussels with a stiff brush under cold running water to remove any grit. Drain the scrubbed mussels in a colander, then blot them dry with paper towels.

2 Set up the grill for direct grilling using a three-zone fire (see page 21 for charcoal or gas) and preheat one zone to high, one zone to medium, and one zone to low.

3 When ready to cook, place the butter in the large aluminum foil drip pan and melt it over the hot zone of the fire. Add the garlic and *linguica* and cook until fragrant, about 2 minutes. Add the tomato and cook for 2 minutes. Add the wine and let it come to a boil, then move the pan so that it sits between the medium and low zones of the grill.

4 Arrange the mussels on the grill over the hot zone of the fire, rounded sides down. Cook a half dozen or so at a time. As soon as the shells pop wide open—this will take 2 to 6 minutes—add the grilled mussels to the aluminum foil pan with the sausage mixture. When all of the mussels are done, toss well, adding the parsley and lemon juice. Season with salt and pepper to taste. Transfer the mussels and sauce to bowls and serve at once with crusty bread and a large empty bowl for the shells.

YIELD:
Serves 6 to 8 as an
    appetizer, 4 as a light
    main course

Linguica is a spicy Portuguese sausage. If it's not available, you can substitute chorizo or another spicy sausage.

Empty shells mean the grill-roasted mussels were heartily enjoyed.

BARBECUE CONTESTS

Competition barbecue is a phenomenon unique to the United States, and its popularity is soaring. The Kansas City Barbecue Society boasts 2,800 members, who belong to teams with names like the Swine Flew, Smoking in the Boys Room, and Oink, Cackle, and Moo. Winning a regional or state championship entitles teams to compete at one of the Big Three invitational competitions for prizes worth up to $20,000. Each of the competitions has its own special character—the Mardi Gras boisterousness of Memphis in May; the World Series bonhomie of the American Royal in Kansas City; or the Wimbleton Cup seriousness of the Jack Daniel's World Championship Invitational Barbecue in Lynchburg, Tennessee.

Judging ballot for the Kansas City Barbecue Society (far left); sausages and meat loaf lined up for judging (left); barbecue flyboys with their airplane smoker (below); and the Lipton Tea Brewers and Bar-B-Quers—this kettle spouts smoke (right).

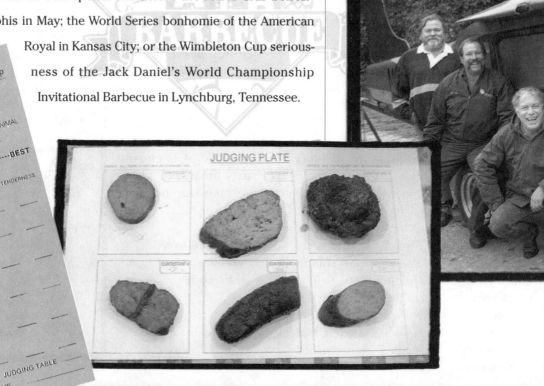

KCBS
KCBS JUDGING SLIP

CIRCLE CATEGORY:
CHICKEN, RIBS, PORK, BRISKET, SAUSAGE, BEEF, MISC., LAMB, WH. ANIMAL OTHER

POINTS
1 2 3 4 5 6 7 8 9------BEST

CONTESTANT TEAM NUMBER   APPEARANCE   TASTE   TENDERNESS

JUDGING TABLE

JUDGES NAME

JUDGING PLATE

CONTESTANT

Founded in May, 1978, the Memphis in May World Championship Barbecue Cooking Contest is the nation's oldest. According to the *Guinness Book of World Records,* it's also the largest, attracting more than 80,000 spectators to Tom Lee Park on the banks of the Mississippi River. Last year, more than 280 teams competed for $55,000 in cash prizes, with the grand champion taking home a five-foot-high trophy crowned with a silver meat cleaver. Pork is king here (despite frequent Elvis sightings), as demonstrated by a towering metal pig that bursts into flames every hour. Contestants

A big oink for the smoker that thinks it's a pig.

turing half-naked fat men in porcine drag.

The American Royal Barbecue Contest is more ecumenical, honoring brisket, chicken, and sausage, as well as pork. Appropriately, the event takes place at the American Royal Complex in Kansas City, a former livestock transit area and site of the oldest agricultural celebration in the Midwest. The pros compete in an international invitational, while amateur barbecuers strut their stuff at the American Royal Open. Wander the grounds and you'll see smokers ranging from conventional rigs to a giant smoking teapot (courtesy of the Lipton Tea Brewers and Bar-B-Quers) and even a Cessna airplane converted into a smoker (used by a team of sky divers). The contestants are judged in a blind tasting by more than four hundred judges. There's also a sauce competition called the Diddy-Wa-Diddy, presided over by barbecue authority Remus Powers.

compete in whole hog, pork shoulder, and pork rib categories, not to mention in a hog calling contest and a "Miss Piggy" competition fea-

A fife and drum corps, barbecue style (left); night falls on the American Royal Barbecue Contest in Kansas City (above); and dessert from the smoker (right).

GENTLEMAN JACK'S CONTEST

The Jack Daniel's World Championship Invitational Barbecue is the most serene of contests—perhaps because it's the smallest (only thirty teams are invited to compete). Or perhaps because it's held in a dry town, the village of Lynchburg, Tennessee, paradoxically the home of the Jack Daniel's Distillery. The absence of booze (at least booze you can buy) does not in any way diminish the festivity; in addition to world class barbecue prepared by some of the top smoke meisters in the world, there's lots of old-fashioned fun in the form of clog dancing, baton twirling, and greased pole climbing. Round out your eating pleasure with grilled corn prepared by the Lynchburg fire department (see page 602 for the recipe) and a Tennessee dessert specialty, fried pie.

All three barbecue festivals

It takes a happy pit master to turn out tender ribs.

WHERE TO FIND BARBECUE FESTIVALS

Here are some of the major barbecue festivals, along with phone numbers for further information.

AMERICAN ROYAL BARBECUE

American Royal Complex near Kansas City, Missouri. Takes place the first weekend in October. For information call (816) 221-9800. web site: www.americanroyal.com

JACK DANIEL'S WORLD CHAMPIONSHIP INVITATIONAL BARBECUE

Lynchburg, Tennessee. Takes place in October. For information call (615) 340-1065.

MEMPHIS IN MAY WORLD CHAMPIONSHIP BARBECUE COOKING CONTEST

Tom Lee Park in downtown Memphis, Tennessee. Takes place the third weekend in May. For information call (901) 525-4611. web site: www.memphisinmay.org

are open to the public, although you won't be allowed to sample the contestants' cooking unless you manage to wangle an invitation into one of the booths. (One of the best ways to experience a barbecue contest is as a judge. Both Memphis in May and the Kansas City Barbecue Society offer crash courses that cover the various cuts of meat, cooking techniques, and judging criteria.)

You won't go hungry, as concessionaires—many of them former contest winners—have championship barbecue for sale. What you must do is book a room early: Visitors to the Jack Daniel's, for example, routinely lodge twenty miles away.

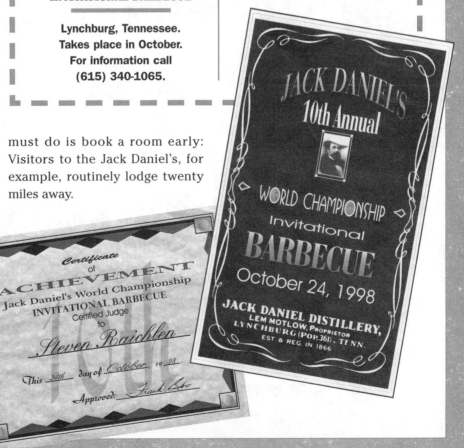

In order to become a barbecue judge, you must attend a day-long seminar—talk about a gut course (near right).

There once was a time when vegetarians lived in dread of being invited to a barbecue. Understandably, since their meal was likely to be nothing but a plate filled with potato salad and coleslaw, with nary a main dish, and certainly not a grilled one, in sight. But these days more and more Americans are embracing a diet that is at least partially vegetarian, and grill masters stand ready to serve meatless meals that are barbecue masterpieces in their own right: Grilled *chiles rellenos*. Hickory-smoked squash stuffed with baked beans. Portobello mushroom "steaks." Three kinds of flame-charred bean quesadillas. Tofu with lemon teriyaki sauce. When it comes to meatless grill, it's a whole new ball-game. Here's a score card to track a new team of players. Eat your vegetables? You bet.

ian Grill

TIPS

The traditional pepper for making *chiles rellenos* is the poblano, an elongated, dark green, mildly spicy pepper available at Mexican markets and most supermarkets. If you're using poblano peppers, choose large, rounded ones. Green bell peppers make for a more picturesque presentation. If you like this option, select peppers with flat bottoms, so they can stand upright.

The Southwest

BARBECUED BEAN & CHEESE CHILES RELLENOS

"If it tastes good baked or fried, it probably tastes better grilled." If barbecue is a religion, this is one of my catechisms and it's led me to some pretty offbeat dishes over the years, like the following *chiles rellenos.* In the traditional Mexican dish, poblano peppers are stuffed with cheese, dipped in egg batter, and deep-fried. Why not slash the fat and add the fragrance of wood smoke, I reasoned, by smoke roasting the peppers on the grill? To make this a more substantial dish, I add pinto beans or black beans to the cheese filling. The results are exceedingly cool-looking *chiles rellenos* that double as a vegetarian main dish.

METHOD:
Indirect grilling

INGREDIENTS:
6 large poblano peppers or green bell peppers
2 cans (16 ounces each) low-sodium pinto beans or black beans
3 tablespoons extra-virgin olive oil, plus 1 tablespoon for drizzling
1 medium-size onion, finely chopped
2 cloves garlic, finely chopped
2 jalapeño peppers, seeded and finely chopped (for a hotter filling leave the seeds in)
½ red bell pepper, finely chopped
¼ cup chopped fresh cilantro
¼ cup hulled pumpkin seeds (optional; see Note)
1 teaspoon ground cumin
1 to 3 teaspoons of your favorite hot sauce, or more to taste
3 cups (about 12 ounces) pepper Jack, Monterey Jack, or white Cheddar cheese, coarsely grated
Coarse salt (kosher or sea) and freshly ground black pepper

YOU'LL ALSO NEED:
1 cup wood chips or chunks (preferably mesquite), soaked for 1 hour in water to cover, then drained

Hot peppers by the pound.

When fresh in the pod, pinto beans display a gorgeous mosaic.

1 If using poblano peppers, cut them in half lengthwise and scrape out the seeds. If using bell peppers, cut off the tops about ½ inch below the stems. Scrape out the veins and seeds, taking care not to puncture the bottoms.

2 Drain the beans, place them in a colander, rinse under cold running water, then drain again.

3 Heat 2 tablespoons of the olive oil in a nonstick skillet over medium heat. Add the onion, garlic, jalapeños, red bell pepper, cilantro, pumpkin seeds, if using, and cumin and cook until golden brown, about 4 minutes. Stir in the beans, hot sauce, and 2 cups of the cheese. Taste for seasoning, adding salt, pepper,

and/or more hot sauce as necessary. Spoon the bean mixture into the hollowed-out peppers. Sprinkle the remaining cheese on top, dividing it evenly among the peppers. Drizzle the remaining 1 tablespoon of olive oil over the cheese.

4 Set up the grill for indirect grilling (see page 23 for gas or page 22 for charcoal) and preheat to medium. If using a gas grill, place all of the wood chips or chunks in the smoker box or in a smoker pouch (see page 24) and preheat on high until you see smoke, then reduce heat to medium. If using a charcoal grill, preheat it to medium, then toss all of the wood chips or chunks on the coals.

5 When ready to cook, place the peppers in the center of the hot grate, away from the heat. Cover the grill and cook the peppers until they are tender and the cheese is browned and bubbling, 30 to 40 minutes. Use a spatula to transfer the peppers to a platter or plates and serve at once.

YIELD:
Serves 6

NOTE: Hulled pumpkin seeds (*pepitas*) are available at natural foods stores and hispanic markets.

■ This is the first of three quesadilla combinations I'm suggesting (you'll find the other two on the facing page and page 570). Once you understand the principle behind making a quesadilla, the choice of fillings is limited only by your imagination.

■ A word of caution: Flour tortillas burn like paper. Preheat your grill to medium-high, but use a two-zone fire so you have a safety zone (a cool, unlit section of the grill) where you can move the quesadillas if they start to burn. When grilling quesadillas, never take your eyes off of them.

Miami, Fla.

BEAN QUESADILLAS
With Onions and Cheese

Who says vegetarians need to feel like second-class citizens at a barbecue? Whenever I have a cookout, I make sure to grill some quesadillas, those cheese "sandwiches" from Mexico. *Grill* is the operative word here, for while most quesadillas are cooked in the oven or on a griddle, you actually get a richer, smokier flavor when you grill them. The following recipe is inspired by a Salvadoran dish popular in Miami: *pupusa,* a sort of Central American quesadilla stuffed with beans, caramelized onions, and cheese.

METHOD:
Direct grilling

INGREDIENTS:
2 cans (14 ounces each) kidney beans
2 tablespoons olive oil, plus more for
    brushing the quesadillas
1 medium-size onion, finely chopped
2 cloves garlic, finely chopped
½ teaspoon ground cumin
Coarse salt (kosher or sea) and
    freshly ground black pepper
6 flour tortillas (10 inches each)
3 cups (about 12 ounces) coarsely grated
    Muenster or Jack cheese

1 Drain the beans, place them in a colander and rinse under cold running water, then drain again.

2 Heat the olive oil in a frying pan over medium heat. Add the onion, garlic, and cumin and cook until golden brown, 4 to 6 minutes, stirring occasionally to ensure even browning.

3 Remove the pan from the heat. Add the drained, rinsed beans and mash with a potato masher or the back of a wooden spoon. Alternatively, you can purée the beans and cooked onions and garlic in a food processor until they are thick but spreadable, like soft ice cream. Season with salt and pepper to taste (the beans are probably already quite salty, so you may not need to add any salt). The recipe can be prepared to this stage up to 48 hours ahead.

4 Set up the grill for direct grilling using a two-zone fire (see page 22 for charcoal or gas); preheat one zone to medium-high and leave the other zone unlit so you can move the quesadillas over it if they start to burn.

5 Lay the tortillas on a work surface. Lightly brush the tops with olive oil and turn the tortillas over. Spread the bean mixture over half of each of the tortillas, dividing it evenly among them. Sprinkle ½ cup of the cheese over the bean mixture on each tortilla. Fold the tortillas in half so the cheese is covered, making a sort of turnover.

6 When ready to cook, brush and oil the grill grate. Place the quesadillas on the hot grate and grill until they are nicely browned on the bottom, 1 to 2 minutes. Turn the tortillas over using tongs and a spatula and grill the other side the same way. When done, the cheese should be melted and the tortillas should be golden brown, not black; take care not to let them burn. If they start cooking too quickly, move the quesadillas to the unlit zone of the grill. Serve the quesadillas whole or cut into wedges.

YIELD:
Serves 6

Miami, Fla.

BLACK BEAN QUESADILLAS
With Queso Blanco

A Cuban influence, so pervasive in Miami, will be immediately apparent in the black beans and *queso blanco* in these quesadillas. *Queso blanco* is a firm, salty white cheese that's widely available in the supermarkets of Miami. If you can't find it, string cheese would make a good substitute.

METHOD:
Direct grilling

INGREDIENTS:
2 cans (14 ounces each) black beans
2 tablespoons olive oil, plus more
    for brushing the quesadillas
1 bunch scallions, both white
    and green parts, trimmed and
    thinly sliced
2 cloves garlic, finely chopped
1 cup grilled corn kernels
    (optional; page 145)
1 teaspoon dried mint or oregano
Coarse salt (kosher or sea) and
    freshly ground black pepper
6 flour tortillas (10 inches each)
3 cups (about 12 ounces)
    coarsely grated queso blanco
½ cup sour cream
¼ cup chopped fresh cilantro

1 Drain the beans, place them in a colander and rinse under cold running water, then drain again.

2 Heat the olive oil in a frying pan over medium heat. Add the scallions, garlic, corn, if using, and mint and cook until golden brown, 4 to 6 minutes, stirring occasionally to ensure even browning.

3 Remove the pan from the heat. Add the drained, rinsed beans and mash with a potato masher or the back of a wooden spoon. Alternatively, you can purée the beans and cooked vegetables in a food processor until they are thick but spreadable, like soft ice cream. Season with salt and pepper to taste (the beans are probably already quite salty, so you may not need to add any salt). The recipe can be prepared to this stage up to 48 hours ahead.

4 Set up the grill for direct grilling using a two-zone fire (see page 22 for charcoal or gas); preheat one zone to medium-high and leave the other zone unlit so you can move the quesadillas over it if they start to burn.

5 Lay the tortillas on a work surface. Lightly brush the tops with olive oil and turn the tortillas over. Spread the bean mixture over half of each of the tortillas, dividing it evenly among them. Sprinkle ½ cup of the cheese over the bean mixture on each tortilla. Top the cheese on each tortilla with 2 tablespoons of sour cream and 1 tablespoon of cilantro. Fold the tortillas in half so the cheese and sour cream are covered, making a sort of turnover.

6 When ready to cook, brush and oil the grill grate. Place the quesadillas on the hot grate and grill until the tortillas are nicely browned on the bottom, 1 to 2 minutes. Turn the tortillas over using tongs and a spatula and grill the other side the same way. When done the cheese should be melted and the tortillas should be golden brown, not black; take care not to let them burn. If they start cooking too quickly, move the quesadillas to the unlit zone of the grill. Serve the quesadillas whole or cut into wedges.

YIELD:

Serves 6

Nevada

PINTO BEAN QUESADILLAS
With Jalapeños and Cheese

The pinto is the preeminent bean of the Southwest, a mottled tan and brown legume with a rich, earthy flavor that makes it ideal for *frijoles refritos* (refried beans)—the inspiration for this recipe. Jalapeños and pepper Jack cheese add a welcome spark of heat. Best to warn diners to have a beer nearby—these are quesadillas you won't soon forget.

METHOD:

Direct grilling

INGREDIENTS:

2 cans (14 ounces each)
   pinto beans
6 flour tortillas (10 inches each)
2 tablespoons butter, melted
About 1 cup sour cream
3 cups (about 12 ounces) coarsely
   grated pepper Jack cheese
36 thin slices fresh or pickled
   jalapeño peppers (from 4 to 5
   jalapeños)
3 scallions, both white and green parts,
   trimmed and finely chopped
½ cup chopped fresh cilantro

1 Drain the beans, place them in a colander and rinse under cold running water, then drain again.

2 Set up the grill for direct grilling using a two-zone fire (see page 22 for charcoal or gas); preheat one zone to medium-high and leave the other zone unlit so you can move the quesadillas over it if they start to burn.

3 Lay the tortillas on a work surface. Lightly brush the tops with butter and turn the tortillas over. Spread 2 to 3 tablespoons of the sour cream on each tortilla. Spread the drained beans over half of each of the tortillas, dividing the beans evenly among them. Sprinkle ½ cup of the cheese over the beans on each tortilla. Put 6 jalapeño slices on the cheese on each tortilla. Sprinkle the scallions and cilantro over the cheese, dividing them evenly among the 6 tortillas. Fold the tortillas in half so the beans are covered, making a sort of turnover.

4 When ready to grill, brush and oil the grill grate. Place the quesadillas on the hot grate and grill until the tortillas are nicely browned on the bottom, 1 to 2 minutes. Turn the tortillas over using tongs and a spatula and grill the other side the same way. When done, the cheese should be melted and the tortillas should be golden brown, not black; take care not to let them burn. If they start cooking too quickly, move the quesadillas to the unlit zone of the grill. Serve the quesadillas whole or cut into wedges.

YIELD:
Serves 6

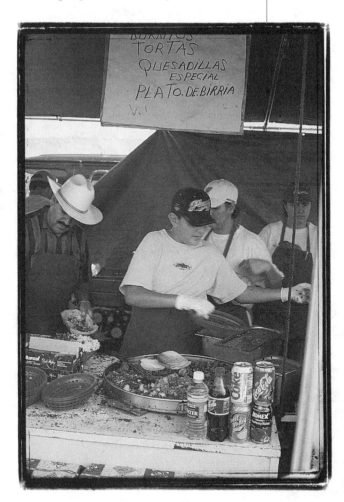

Quesadillas served without ceremony, but soulful to the last bite.

TIPS

For the sake of convenience, I call for stuffing the squash with canned vegetarian baked beans. However, if you want to use homemade, the squash will be even better.

Baked beans simmered over a log fire—the perfect stuffing for squash.

Maine

HICKORY-SMOKED BAKED BEAN SQUASH

Baked beans began as New England soul food—a veritable staple in Maine, where lumberjacks lived on them during wood-cutting expeditions and families traditionally supped on baked beans every Saturday night. Leftover beans reappeared the following morning at the breakfast table. Today baked beans are an integral part of American barbecue, but smoke

roasted in acorn squash, these beans are an unexpected take on an old favorite.

METHOD:
Indirect grilling

INGREDIENTS:
2 acorn squash (each about 28 ounces)
1 can (16 ounces) vegetarian baked beans, such as Bush's Best, drained
6 tablespoons of your favorite sweet smoky red barbecue sauce (like KC Masterpiece)
4 tablespoons maple syrup or honey
4 tablespoons dark brown sugar
4 tablespoons salted butter

YOU'LL ALSO NEED:
1 cup wood chips or chunks (optional; preferably hickory), soaked for 1 hour in water to cover, then drained

1 Cut each squash in half crosswise. Cut ¼ inch off the rounded end of each half so the squash sits level without wobbling. Scrape out the seeds with a spoon and discard.

2 Spoon one quarter of the beans into each squash half. Drizzle 1½ tablespoons of the barbecue sauce and 1 tablespoon of the maple syrup over the top of each bean-filled squash. Add 1 tablespoon brown sugar and place 1 tablespoon of butter on top. The squash can be prepared several hours ahead and refrigerated, covered.

3 Set up the grill for indirect grilling (see page 23 for gas or page 22 for charcoal) and preheat to medium.

If using a gas grill, place all of the wood chips or chunks, if desired, in the smoker box or in a smoker pouch (see page 24) and run the grill on high until you see smoke, then reduce the heat to medium. If using a charcoal grill, preheat it to medium, then toss all of the wood chips or chunks on the coals just prior to grilling.

4 When ready to cook, place the filled squash halves in the center of the hot grate, away from the heat. Cover the grill and cook the squash until tender and the filling is browned and bubbling, about 1 hour. When done, the sides of the squash will feel soft when squeezed. Use a spatula to transfer the grilled squash to a platter or plates and serve at once.

YIELD:
Serves 4

Pennsylvania

PORTOBELLO "CHEESE STEAKS"

When I was growing up, no one knew about portobellos. Today, we can't seem to live without these broad, fleshy mushrooms that taste like conventional white mushrooms, only more so. The portobello has been called the beef of the vegetable kingdom, and this jumbo fungus certainly cooks like a slab of beef on the grill. That set me thinking about a Philly "cheese steak" I could serve the vegetarians in the family.

METHOD:
Direct grilling

ADVANCE PREPARATION:
**30 minutes for marinating
    the mushrooms**

INGREDIENTS:
**4 large portobello mushrooms
    (each 5 to 6 inches across and
    8 to 10 ounces)
2 tablespoons Dijon mustard
2 tablespoons balsamic vinegar
2 cloves garlic, minced
½ cup extra-virgin olive oil,
    plus more for brushing the onion
Coarse salt (kosher or sea) and
    freshly ground black pepper
1 medium-size sweet onion,
    cut crosswise into slices
    (each about ½-inch thick)
2 green or red bell peppers
4 slices aged Provolone cheese
    (4 to 6 ounces total)
4 hoagie rolls
Mayonnaise (preferably Hellmann's),
    mustard, and/or ketchup or the
    condiment of your choice**

YOU'LL ALSO NEED:
4 small (6- to 8-inch) bamboo skewers

1 Using a paring knife, trim the stems off the portobellos. Wipe the caps clean with a damp paper towel (don't rinse them, or they'll become soggy).

TIPS

There's no need to rinse portobellos or other mushrooms; they quickly become waterlogged. Just wipe the caps clean with a damp paper towel.

2 Place the mustard, vinegar, and garlic in a nonreactive mixing bowl and whisk to mix. Gradually whisk in the ½ cup of olive oil, then season with salt and black pepper to taste; the mixture should be highly seasoned. Brush each mushroom on both sides with some of the mustard mixture, using about 1 tablespoon per mushroom cap. Let the mushrooms marinate for 30 minutes. Skewer each onion slice crosswise (this will keep them from falling apart while they grill).

3 Set up the grill for direct grilling using a two-zone fire (see page 22 for charcoal or gas); preheat one zone to high and the other to medium so you can move the mushrooms over it if they start to burn.

4 When ready to cook, brush and oil the grill grate. Place the bell peppers on the hot grate and grill until nicely browned on all sides, 3 to 4 minutes per side (12 to 16 minutes in all). Add the skewered onion slices and grill until golden brown, 3 to 6 minutes per side (6 to 12 minutes in all). Transfer the grilled bell peppers and onion slices to a cutting board and let cool. Let the grill continue to burn. Core, seed, and thinly slice the bell peppers. Unskewer the onion slices. Place the vegetables in a bowl, add 3 tablespoons of the mustard mixture, and toss to mix. Taste for seasoning, adding more salt and black pepper as necessary; the mixture should be highly seasoned.

5 Place the portobellos on the hot grate, gill side down, and grill for about 3 minutes. Turn the mushrooms over and brush the remaining mustard mixture into the caps. Continue grilling until the portobellos are browned and very tender, about 4 minutes longer. The mushrooms are done when they can be easily pierced with a skewer. If they start to brown too much before they become tender, move them over the medium zone of the grill. After the mushrooms have grilled for 2 minutes on the second side, place a slice of cheese on each and cover the grill to melt the cheese.

6 Place the portobellos and melted cheese on hoagie rolls generously slathered with mayonnaise or other condiment(s). Mound the vegetables with their juices on top of the cheese. Serve the "cheese steaks" at once.

YIELD:
Serves 4

Pennsylvania

PORTOBELLO "BURGERS"

The summer cookout used to be so easy. You fired up the grill and threw on some steaks or burgers. That was back in the days before your wife stopped eating beef, your daughter stopped eating meat altogether, and your doctor warned you to watch your cholesterol. Before anyone worried about the nitrates in hot dogs, the microbes in hamburgers, or the health risks of steaks. Which brings me in a roundabout way to the meatiest of mushrooms, the portobello. This thick round mushroom has the color, shape, and even something of the earthy richness of a burger. And to reinforce its meaty flavor, I marinate it in mustard, barbecue sauce, and A.1. steak sauce. Grill portobellos topped with cheese, and no one will miss the beef. So what's the connection to Pennsylvania? More mushrooms are grown there than anywhere else in the United States.

METHOD:
Direct grilling

ADVANCE PREPARATION:
**1 to 2 hours for marinating
the mushrooms**

INGREDIENTS:
**6 large portobello mushrooms
(each 5 to 6 inches across
and 8 to 10 ounces)**
**3 large cloves garlic, cut into
matchstick slivers**
3 tablespoons Dijon mustard
3 tablespoons A.1. steak sauce
3 tablespoons Worcestershire sauce
**3 tablespoons of your favorite
barbecue sauce (or see one of
the sauces on pages 661 to 681)**
3 tablespoons balsamic vinegar
½ teaspoon liquid smoke
**½ teaspoon coarse salt
(kosher or sea)**

½ teaspoon freshly ground black pepper
¾ cup extra-virgin olive oil
**12 fresh basil leaves, thinly slivered,
or 2 teaspoons dried basil**
**6 thin slices Cheddar or Jack cheese
(about 6 ounces total)**
**6 hamburger buns, lightly brushed
with a little olive oil or
melted butter**
**1 large ripe tomato, thinly sliced
(optional)**
1 sweet onion, thinly sliced (optional)
Boston lettuce leaves (optional)
**Mustard, ketchup, mayonnaise,
barbecue sauce, and/or relish
or Miso Mayonnaise (page 582)**

1 Using a paring knife, trim the stems off the portobellos. Wipe the caps clean with a damp paper towel (don't rinse them or they'll become soggy). Using a sharp object, such as the tip of a metal skewer, make a series of holes in the gill side of the mushrooms, about 1 inch apart. Insert the garlic slivers into these holes, dividing them evenly among the 6 mushrooms.

2 Combine the mustard, steak sauce Worcestershire sauce, barbecue sauce, vinegar, liquid smoke, salt, and pepper in a mixing bowl and whisk until the salt dissolves. Whisk in the olive oil and basil. Pour one third of the mixture in the bottom of a nonreactive baking dish and place the mushrooms in it, gill side up. Swish the mushrooms around to coat the bottoms with marinade. Spoon the remaining marinade over the

TIPS

I like to grill portobellos on both sides. This maximizes the flavor, but causes you to loose some of the juices. To keep the portobellos moist, I drain off the marinade *before* grilling the mushrooms, then spoon it back over them once the caps have been turned gill side up.

no one will miss the beef

TIPS

■ *Pico de gallo* is the Tex-Mex version of salsa; because this one contains only a handful of ingredients, it lives or dies by the ripeness of the tomatoes. You can chop the ingredients ahead of time, but don't mix them more than 30 minutes before serving.

■ For the sake of simplicity, I've made the toast optional, but it adds a nice contrast in texture to the grilled mushrooms.

mushrooms. Let them marinate for 1 to 2 hours.

3 Set up the grill for direct grilling using a two-zone fire (see page 22 for charcoal or gas); preheat one zone to high and the other zone to medium so you can move the mushrooms over it if they start to burn.

4 When ready to cook, drain the mushrooms over a small nonreactive bowl to reserve the remaining marinade. Place the portobellos on the hot grate, gill side down, and grill for about 3 minutes. Turn the mushrooms over and spoon 1 tablespoon of the reserved marinade into each cap. Continue grilling until the portobellos are browned and very tender, about 4 minutes more. The mushrooms are done when they can be easily pierced with a skewer. If they start to brown too much before they become tender, move them over the medium zone of the grill. After the mushrooms have grilled for 2 minutes on the second side, place a slice of cheese on each and cover the grill to melt the cheese. Lightly toast the hamburger buns on the grill, 1 to 2 minutes.

5 To serve, place each grilled portobello on a hamburger bun. Garnish with tomato and onion slices, and/or lettuce, if using, and the condiment of your choice.

YIELD:
Serves 6

Houston, Tex.

"CHURRASCO" OF PORTOBELLO MUSHROOMS

It's hard to be a vegetarian at a restaurant founded by a beef-loving Nicaraguan. Or so I thought until I dined at the cutting-edge *Nuevo Latino Américas* in Houston. *Churrasco* is Nicaragua's national beef dish, a thinly sliced grilled beef tenderloin, but for vegetarians, chef Michael Cordua serves up grilled portobellos with a garlicky *chimichurri* sauce. *Chimichurri* is traditionally made with parsley, but fresh mint makes it even more vibrant.

METHOD:
Direct grilling

ADVANCE PREPARATION:
**2 to 4 hours for marinating
    the mushrooms**

**FOR THE CHIMICHURRI AND
    MUSHROOMS:**
**4 medium-size portobello mushrooms
    (each about 4 inches across and
    6 to 8 ounces)**
**1 bunch fresh mint, rinsed and stemmed
    (for about ¾ cup)**
3 cloves garlic, coarsely chopped
½ cup extra-virgin olive oil
**2 tablespoons wine vinegar,
    or more to taste**

1 teaspoon coarse salt (kosher or sea),
    or more to taste

½ teaspoon hot red pepper flakes

½ teaspoon freshly ground black pepper,
    or more to taste

FOR THE PICO DE GALLO:

1 large ripe tomato, seeded and
    cut into ¼-inch dice (for about
    1 cup)

3 scallions, both white and green parts,
    trimmed and finely chopped

¼ cup finely chopped fresh mint

1 clove garlic, minced

1 to 2 jalapeño peppers, seeded and
    minced

2 tablespoons fresh lime juice,
    or more to taste

Coarse salt (kosher or sea) and
    freshly ground black pepper

4 thin (½-inch) slices French bread
    (optional)

1 Using a paring knife, trim the stems off the portobellos. Wipe the caps clean with a damp paper towel (don't rinse them, or they'll become soggy). Place the caps, gill side up, in a nonreactive baking dish just large enough to hold them.

2 MAKE THE *CHIMICHURRI:* Place the mint and garlic in a food processor fitted with the metal blade and finely chop them. Add the olive oil, vinegar, salt, hot pepper flakes, and black pepper and process to a coarse purée. Taste for seasoning, adding more vinegar, salt, and/or black pepper as necessary; the sauce should be highly seasoned. Pour the *chimichurri* over the mushroom caps. Let the mush-

rooms marinate in the refrigerator, covered, for 2 to 4 hours, turning them several times so that they marinate evenly.

3 MAKE THE *PICO DE GALLO:* Combine the tomato, scallions, mint, garlic, jalapeño(s), and lime juice in a nonreactive mixing bowl. Not more than 30 minutes before serving, toss to mix. Taste for seasoning, adding more lime juice if necessary. Season with salt and black pepper to taste; the *pico de gallo* should be tart and flavorful.

4 Set up the grill for direct grilling using a two-zone fire (see page 22 for charcoal or gas); preheat one zone to high and the other zone to medium so you can move the mushrooms over if they start to burn.

5 When ready to cook, brush and oil the grill grate. Drain the *chimichurri* from the mushrooms, reserving it for use as a sauce. Place the portobellos, on the hot grate, gill side down. Grill until lightly browned, about 3 minutes. Turn the mushrooms over and spoon a little *chimichurri* into the caps. Continue grilling until browned and very tender, about 4 minutes longer. The mushrooms are done when they can be easily pierced with a skewer. If they brown too much before

Michael Cordua, ardent carnivore with a soft spot for vegetarians.

they are done, move them over the medium zone of the grill.

6 Transfer the grilled mushrooms to a cutting board and cut them into ¼-inch slices. Brush the bread slices, if using, with a little of the *chimichurri* and grill until lightly toasted, about 1 minute per side. Transfer the toasts to a platter or plates and place the mushrooms on top. Spoon any remaining *chimichurri* over the mushrooms and top with a generous spoonful of *pico de gallo*.

YIELD:
Serves 4

Miami, Fla.

JAKE'S LOG CABINS (Grilled Asparagus and Portobellos)

Credit for this recipe goes to my stepson Jake—chef extraordinaire, barbecue buddy, and general partner in crime. Jake created this dish at a restaurant on Lincoln Road in Miami Beach, where at the age of twenty-four, he became chef. With a little imagination, these do look like log cabins, with asparagus "log" walls crowned with portobello mushroom "roofs."

METHOD:
Direct grilling

ADVANCE PREPARATION:
2 to 4 hours for marinating the mushrooms

FOR THE MUSHROOMS AND MARINADE:
6 small portobello mushrooms
    (each 4 to 5½ inches across
    and 4 to 5 ounces)
⅓ cup sherry vinegar
⅓ cup honey
⅓ cup Asian (dark) sesame oil
½ teaspoon coarse salt (kosher or sea)
½ teaspoon freshly ground black pepper

FOR THE MUSHROOM STUFFING:
1 tablespoon Asian (dark) sesame oil
1 shallot, minced
1 clove garlic, minced
3 tablespoons chopped fresh cilantro
    or flat-leaf parsley
1 cup grated white Cheddar, Jack,
    or Parmesan cheese
Coarse salt (kosher or sea) and
    freshly ground black pepper

FOR THE ASPARAGUS RAFTS:
24 thick asparagus stalks
1 to 2 tablespoons Asian (dark) sesame oil
Coarse salt (kosher or sea) and
    freshly ground black pepper

YOU'LL ALSO NEED:
Wooden toothpicks or small (6-inch)
    bamboo skewers

1 Wipe the mushrooms clean with a damp paper towel (don't rinse them or they'll become soggy). Cut the stems off the portobellos and trim off and discard the gritty end of each stem. Coarsely chop the stems and 2 of the mushroom caps. You should have about 1½ cups. Set the chopped mushrooms aside. Place the remaining whole mushroom caps in a nonreactive baking dish just large enough to hold them.

2 MAKE THE MARINADE: Combine the vinegar, honey, sesame oil, salt, and pepper in a nonreactive mixing bowl. Whisk to mix until the salt dissolves. Pour the marinade over the mushroom caps and let them marinate for 30 minutes, turning the mushrooms several times so they marinate evenly.

3 MAKE THE MUSHROOM STUFFING: Place the reserved chopped mushrooms in a food processor and pulse in short bursts to finely chop them. Don't overprocess or you'll reduce the mushrooms to mush. Heat the sesame oil in a skillet over medium heat. Add the shallot and garlic and cook until just beginning to brown, about 3 minutes. Add the finely chopped mushrooms and the cilantro, increase the heat to high, and cook until all the mushroom liquid has evaporated, 3 to 5 minutes. Remove the skillet from the heat and let cool slightly. Stir in the cheese and season with salt and pepper to taste. Set the stuffing aside.

4 MAKE THE ASPARAGUS RAFTS: Snap the fibrous ends off the asparagus stalks; the easiest way to do this is to grab a stalk by its base with one hand and bend the stalk with your other hand. The asparagus will snap where the woody part ends. The remaining piece should be about 4 inches long. Arrange 3 or 4 stalks side by side all facing the same way and skewer them crosswise in two places with toothpicks. Lightly brush the asparagus rafts with sesame oil and season with salt and pepper. The recipe can be prepared to this stage several hours ahead. Refrigerate the stuffing and asparagus rafts separately, covered.

5 Set up the grill for direct grilling (see page 21 for charcoal or gas) and preheat to high.

6 When ready to cook, drain the marinade from the mushroom caps, reserving the marinade. Place the mushroom caps on the hot grate, gill side down, and grill until golden brown, about 4 minutes. Turn the caps over, spoon 1 tablespoon of the reserved marinade into each, and continue grilling until the mushrooms are browned and tender, 3 to 4 minutes. The mushrooms are done when they can be easily pierced with a skewer. Transfer the grilled mushrooms to a plate.

7 Place the asparagus on the hot grate and grill until golden brown, 2 to 4 minutes per side. Transfer the grilled asparagus to a plate and remove the toothpicks.

8 In the center of each of 4 serving plates, stack the asparagus stalks as you would build a log cabin: 2 parallel to each other and about 2 inches apart; then 2 more on top, parallel to each

A lactovegetarian could add a cup of nuts to the mushroom stuffing of the log cabins in place of the cheese.

other and perpendicular to the first 2; then place 2 more on top, parallel to each other and to the first set of stalks. Spoon the mushroom stuffing in the center. Set a mushroom cap on top of each. Serve hot or at room temperature.

YIELD:

**Serves 4 as an appetizer,
2 as a light main course**

TIPS

Be sure to use extra-firm or firm tofu for this recipe.

Ayer, Mass.

LEMON TERIYAKI TOFU

Grilled tofu isn't exactly what you'd call mainstream, but it's not uncommon to find it at cookouts. The fact is there's a rich tradition of grilling tofu in Asia, and many American grill masters are taking advantage of tofu's unique ability to absorb marinade, fire, and smoke flavors without surrendering its own delicate nutty taste. Nasoya, one of the major brands of top quality tofu in the United States, is headquartered in Ayer, Massachusetts, of all places. They make true extra-firm tofu—the best type to grill.

METHOD:
Direct grilling

INGREDIENTS:
**2 blocks extra-firm or firm tofu
    (1 pound each)
2 tablespoons Asian (dark) sesame oil
Honey Lemon Teriyaki Sauce
    (recipe follows)
2 tablespoons very thinly sliced
    scallion greens
1 tablespoon toasted sesame seeds
    (see Note)**

1 Holding your knife parallel to the cutting board, cut each block of tofu in half through the side to form a total of 4 broad, thin slabs. Blot the tofu pieces dry with paper towels.

2 Set up the grill for direct grilling (see page 21 for charcoal or gas) and preheat to high.

3 When ready to cook, brush the tofu pieces with the sesame oil. Brush and oil the grill grate. Arrange the tofu slices on the hot grate, placing them on a diagonal to the bars. Grill until nicely browned and heated through, 4 to 6 minutes per side. Using a pastry brush, generously baste the tofu on both sides with some of the Honey Lemon Teriyaki Sauce as it grills.

4 Transfer the grilled tofu to a platter or plates and drizzle the remaining sauce over it. Sprinkle the scallion greens and sesame seeds over the tofu and serve at once.

YIELD:
Serves 4

Extra-firm tofu awaiting the grill.

NOTE: To toast sesame seeds, place them in a preheated dry skillet over medium heat (don't use a nonstick skillet for this). Cook the sesame seeds until fragrant and lightly browned, 2 to 3 minutes, shaking the skillet to ensure even toasting. Immediately transfer the toasted sesame seeds to a small heat-proof bowl to cool.

Honey Lemon Teriyaki Sauce

Teriyaki is one of the few barbecue sauces adored by Americans that *didn't* originate in the United States. The traditional version contains just four ingredients—soy sauce, sake (rice wine), mirin (sweetened rice wine), and sugar—but I like the edgy energy of lemon juice and zest and the mellowness that honey adds. For extra finesse use Meyer lemons, round fruits with a brassy lemon flavor but with less acidity than regular lemons.

INGREDIENTS:

½ **cup soy sauce**

½ **cup sake**

½ **cup mirin (sweet rice wine; see Notes)**

2 **tablespoons honey**

2 **teaspoons finely grated lemon zest**

1 **teaspoon cornstarch**

3 **tablespoons fresh lemon juice (preferably from 1 to 2 Meyer lemons; see Notes)**

1 Combine the soy sauce, sake, mirin, honey, and lemon zest in a nonreactive saucepan over high heat and bring to a boil. Reduce the heat to medium and let the sauce simmer until fragrant and syrupy, 8 to 12 minutes.

2 Dissolve the cornstarch in the lemon juice in a small nonreactive bowl. Whisk this mixture into the teriyaki mixture; the sauce should thicken slightly. Let cool to room temperature before using. The sauce can be refrigerated, covered, for 2 days. Bring to room temperature before using.

YIELD:

Makes about 1 cup

NOTES:

■ Depending upon where you live, mirin may be available at Japanese markets,

TIPS

Sure, you could use commercial teriyaki sauce for this recipe, adding a squeeze of lemon juice and a grating of lemon zest. But it's easy to make your own from scratch, as you'll see here.

natural foods stores, and some supermarkets. Cream sherry makes a good substitute, or you can sweeten regular wine by adding 1 tablespoon of sugar to ½ cup of dry white wine.

■ The Meyer lemon is thought to be a cross between a lemon and a mandarin orange that was developed in China. It was introduced to the United States by Frank Meyer, a Department of Agriculture plant expert, in 1908. Today, most of the nation's Meyer lemons are grown in the Central Valley of California. You may be able to find them at a gourmet shop or upscale supermarket. The peak season for them is November through January.

California

GINGER GRILLED TOFU "STEAKS" With Miso Mayo

Here's a North American take on a Japanese favorite: grilled tofu with miso. These salubrious soy foods have been gaining in popularity in North America—indeed world-class miso is manufactured in California. Perhaps the greatest tribute to this

particular dish is that I finally got my wife to eat it, and no one disliked tofu (or thought she disliked it) more than she did. But the singular seasoning method—studding the tofu with slivers of ginger—not to mention the creamy sweet miso sauce, is designed to make believers out of skeptics. And the tofu tastes great cold as well as hot, in the unlikely event you have leftovers.

METHOD:
Direct grilling

ADVANCE PREPARATION:
1 hour for marinating the tofu

FOR THE TOFU AND THE MARINADE:
**2 blocks extra-firm or firm tofu
    (1 pound each)
1 piece (1 inch) fresh ginger,
    peeled
⅓ cup soy sauce
⅓ cup mirin (sweet rice wine;
    see Note on page 581) or
    cream sherry
3 tablespoons Asian (dark) sesame oil
½ teaspoon coarsely ground
    black pepper**

FOR THE MISO MAYONNAISE:
**⅓ cup mayonnaise
⅓ cup white miso
1 tablespoon sugar, or more to taste
2 teaspoons grated or finely chopped
    peeled fresh ginger
1 clove garlic, minced
1 teaspoon grated lemon zest
½ teaspoon freshly ground white
    or black pepper
1 tablespoon vegetable oil
1 tablespoon fresh lemon juice
    or rice vinegar, or more to taste**

TIPS

Miso is a sweet-salty paste of cultured grains and soybeans. Look for it and tofu in the produce or refrigerated foods sections of your supermarket or natural foods store. Any extra miso mayonnaise will keep for a week in the refrigerator and makes a great dip for grilled vegetables.

1 Holding your knife parallel to the cutting board, cut each block of tofu in half through the side to form a total of 4 broad, thin "steaks." Blot the tofu steaks dry with paper towels. Cut the piece of ginger crosswise into 8 slices, each ⅛ of an inch thick. Cut each ginger slice into 5 slivers (you'll have 40 in all). Insert 5 slivers of ginger into the top and 5 slivers into the bottom of each piece of tofu; they should go right in, but if you need to, make starter holes with the tip of a skewer. Place the tofu steaks in a baking dish.

2 MAKE THE MARINADE: Combine the soy sauce, mirin, sesame oil, and black pepper in a small nonreactive bowl and whisk to mix. Pour this mixture over the tofu, turning the pieces to coat with marinade. Let marinate in the refrigerator, covered, for 1 hour.

3 MAKE THE MISO MAYONNAISE: Place the mayonnaise, miso, sugar, grated ginger, garlic, lemon zest, and pepper in a food processor and purée to a smooth paste, scraping down the side of the bowl once or twice with a rubber spatula. With the motor running, add the oil and lemon juice through the feed tube. Taste for seasoning, adding more sugar and/or lemon juice as necessary; the sauce should be sweet with just a hint of tartness.

4 Set up the grill for direct grilling (see page 21 for charcoal or gas) and preheat to high.

5 When ready to cook, brush and oil the grill grate. Place the marinated tofu on the hot grate and grill until nicely browned, 4 to 6 minutes per side. Pour any leftover marinade over the grilling tofu, dividing it evenly between the 2 sides. After turning each piece of tofu, spoon a little miso mayonnaise over it. Transfer the grilled tofu to a platter or plates. Serve the remaining miso mayonnaise on the side.

YIELD:
Serves 4

Tofu comes in two forms, regular and silken. Silken tofu has a smooth, custardlike texture that's great for soups but too fragile for grilling, even if it is labeled extra-firm. Regular tofu is usually sold in transparent tubs or plastic packages, while silken tofu comes in sealed cardboard cartons.

Soy products for grilling—not like the barbecue I grew up on.

Hyde Park, N.Y.

GRILLED TOFU
With Flame-Wilted Spinach

Fritz Sonnenschmidt is about the last guy you'd expect to grill tofu. First because of his birthplace, staunchly carnivorous Germany; then because of his position as dean of that bastion of classical cuisine, The Culinary Institute of America in Hyde Park, New York. But the European-trained chef is open-minded enough to accept bean curd into the barbecue pantheon, and he's venturesome enough to grill spinach. The port, orange, and balsamic vinegar marinade loads the tofu with flavor. Besides, how often do you get to grill spinach?

HOW TO TOAST NUTS AND SEEDS

To toast nuts and seeds, heat a dry cast-iron skillet over medium-high heat until hot, 3 to 5 minutes. (You must use a heavy skillet for this; do not use a nonstick one.) Add the nuts or seeds and cook over medium-high heat until fragrant and lightly browned, shaking the pan to ensure even toasting. Immediately pour the nuts or seeds into a shallow heatproof bowl and let cool.

- Walnuts will take 3 to 4 minutes to brown lightly.
- Celery seeds will take 1 to 2 minutes.
- Sesame seeds will take 2 to 3 minutes.

METHOD:
Direct grilling

ADVANCE PREPARATION:
2 to 12 hours for marinating the tofu

INGREDIENTS:
**2 blocks extra-firm or firm tofu
    (1 pound each)**
⅔ cup port
⅔ cup balsamic vinegar
⅔ cup fresh orange juice
¼ cup soy sauce
¼ cup honey
**6 to 8 tablespoons Asian (dark) sesame oil
    or olive oil**
24 ounces fresh spinach
**4 oranges, peeled, cut into segments,
    membranes and seeds removed**
**2 tablespoons toasted celery seed
    (see box below)**

1 Holding your knife parallel to the cutting board, cut each block of tofu in half through the side. Cut each of these pieces in half again to form a total of 8 broad, thin slabs. Blot the tofu pieces dry with paper towels, then place them in a nonreactive baking dish.

2 Combine the port, vinegar, orange juice, soy sauce, honey, and 4 tablespoons of the sesame oil in a nonreactive bowl and whisk to mix. Pour this mixture over the tofu and let marinate in the refrigerator, covered, for at least 2 hours or as long as overnight, turning the tofu pieces several times so they marinate evenly.

3 Stem the spinach, rinse it, and spin it dry in a salad spinner or shake it dry. Place the spinach in a large nonreactive bowl.

4 Set up the grill for direct grilling (see page 21 for charcoal or gas) and preheat to high.

5 Drain the marinade from the tofu into the spinach and toss to coat the spinach.

6 When ready to cook, brush and oil the grill grate. Lightly brush the tofu pieces on both sides with sesame oil. Arrange the marinated tofu pieces on the hot grate, placing them on a diagonal to the bars. Grill until lightly browned on both sides, 3 to 4 minutes per side. Transfer the grilled tofu to a platter or plates.

7 Place the spinach on the grate and cook until wilted (the edges will crisp), 2 to 4 minutes per side, turning the leaves with tongs. Place the grilled spinach on top of the tofu. Top with the orange segments, sprinkle the toasted celery seed over all, and serve at once.

YIELD:
Serves 4

VARIATION: This recipe works equally well with tempeh. Tempeh is another popular vegetarian grill item originally from Indonesia and made with cultured soybeans. Look for it at natural foods stores and in the produce section of many supermarkets. You'll need 2 pounds.

Flame-Roasted

Grilled vegetables burst upon the American dining scene in the 1980s. From flame-roasted peppers to barbecued squash and potatoes—it was love at first sight and bite. Of course, it didn't hurt that grilling is a remarkably healthy way to cook vegetables, boosting flavor while adding little or no fat. Or that the high dry heat of the grill caramelized the plant sugars, intensifying a vegetable's sweetness, without masking its primal taste. Today, a barbecue without some sort of grilled vegetable is as inconceivable as the cookouts of yesteryear would have been without steak. You'll find everything from artichokes (in the style of Walt's Wharf in Seal Harbor, California) to Cajun asparagus and grilled French fries in this chapter. Master the art of barbecuing whole vegetables, including bacon–stuffed Vidalia onions and an eye-popping, jaw-dropping Santa Fe cabbage. Plunge into the great grilled corn debate—husk on or husk off? You can even grill a corn pudding. Thinking vegetables? Fire up your grill!

vegetables

TIPS

■ Many people discard the artichoke stem, but it's almost as tasty as the heart. Cut the stem off flush with the base of the artichoke so the artichoke will sit flat on the grill grate. Cook the stems alongside.

■ If you want the very best flavor, grill the artichokes over a wood fire (see page 20).

Castroville, Calif.

GRILLED ARTICHOKES

"Selecting artichokes for grilling may run counter to your intuition: The best are older chokes whose leaves have started to spread open. Avoid hard, tightly closed globe artichokes, which may taste great boiled or steamed, but are difficult to grill." I wrote these words in my last book, *Beer-Can Chicken,* and they've always bothered me, because a jumbo globe artichoke is a magnificent vegetable—the pride of Californian produce. A visit to Castroville (California's artichoke capital) convinced me I would have to figure out how to grill this handsome vegetable in all its rotund glory. The secret is to spread the artichoke open like a flower as it cooks, much as Romans do when they fry artichokes to make *carciofi alla giudea.*

METHOD:
Direct grilling

INGREDIENTS:
4 large globe artichokes
1 lemon, cut in half
1 cup extra-virgin olive oil
3 cloves garlic, minced
Coarse salt (kosher or sea) and
**   freshly ground black pepper**
Dipping sauce, (see Note) for serving

1 Using a sharp knife, cut off and discard the top third of each artichoke. Using kitchen shears, cut off and discard the spiny tips on the remaining artichoke leaves. Trim ¼ inch off the end of each stem, then cut the stems off the artichokes so the bottoms of the chokes are flat. Reserve the stems. Rub all of the cut edges with lemon to prevent them from browning.

2 Using a grapefruit spoon or a melon baller, scrape out the purplish inside leaves and fibrous part in the center of each artichoke, creating a hollow cavity. Squeeze lemon juice into the cavities.

3 Combine the olive oil and garlic in a bowl and stir to mix. Generously brush the artichokes inside and out

ARTICHOKE FESTIVAL SEPT 16-17

CASTROVILLE
THE ARTICHOKE CENTER OF THE WORLD

this handsome vegetable in all its rotund glory

with some of the garlic oil and season with salt and pepper.

4 Set up the grill for direct grilling using a two-zone fire (see page 22 for charcoal or gas) and preheat one zone to medium and the other to low.

5 When ready to cook, brush the grill grate. Place the artichokes over the medium zone of the grill, stem end up, and grill until the cut sides are nicely browned, about 30 minutes. Rotate the artichokes from time to time or move them to the cooler zone of the grill if needed to keep them from burning.

6 Turn over the artichokes and generously brush them inside and out with some more garlic oil (really slop it into the cavity). Season the artichokes with salt and pepper. Brush the reserved artichoke stems with garlic oil and season them with salt and pepper. Place the stems on the grate next to the chokes. Cover the grill and continue grilling the artichokes, until almost tender, 30 to 45 minutes longer. Baste the chokes and stems with some of the garlic oil every 15 minutes. Turn the stems often to ensure even browning. If using a charcoal grill, after 1 hour you'll need to add 12 fresh coals to each side.

7 Check the stems to see if they are cooked through. Then, using tongs and starting in the center, spread the chokes open, like petals of a flower (you should wind up with something that looks like a sunflower). Brush the leaves with the remaining garlic oil. Grill until the leaves are crisp and golden-brown and the centers are tender (the leaves should pull out easily), 5 to 8 minutes more per side. Place the grilled chokes on a platter stem side down, place the stems alongside, and serve with your favorite dipping sauce. Provide bowls for the discarded leaves and wet napkins for greasy fingers.

YIELD:
Serves 4

NOTE: I like a simple mustard dipping sauce. You can make one by mixing equal parts of Dijon mustard and mayonnaise and adding a splash of Tabasco sauce or Worcestershire sauce to taste.

Seal Beach, Calif.

ARTICHOKES
In the Style of Walt's Wharf

I admit to being obsessed with grilled artichokes. I love the way hot dry heat sears artichokes without making them soggy or mushy. I love the way

When buying artichokes for this recipe, choose large, firm artichokes with tightly closed leaves.

the convoluted leaves absorb the heady scent of wood smoke. I'm not alone in my obsession, for grilled artichokes are the house specialty of a restaurant in Seal Beach, California, called Walt's Wharf. Walt's steams the artichokes just enough to soften them, then chars them over the dancing flames of an oak-burning grill. And they replace the hollandaise sauce served atop artichokes in days gone by with a tangy Worcestershire cream sauce.

METHOD:
Direct grilling

FOR THE ARTICHOKES:
6 large artichokes
1 lemon, cut in half
Coarse salt (kosher or sea; optional)

FOR THE GARLIC BUTTER:
1 cup (2 sticks) salted butter
4 cloves garlic, minced
¼ cup finely chopped flat-leaf parsley (optional)
¼ cup white wine or vermouth
½ teaspoon freshly ground black pepper

Worcestershire Cream Sauce (recipe follows)

YOU'LL ALSO NEED:
2 cups wood chips or chunks (preferably oak), soaked for 1 hour in water to cover, then drained

1 Using a sharp knife, cut off and discard the top third of each artichoke. Trim the bottom ¼ inch off the end of each stem. Using kitchen shears, cut off and discard the spiny tips on the remaining artichoke leaves. Cut each artichoke lengthwise in quarters, including the stem (see Notes). Rub all of the cut edges of the artichokes with lemon to prevent them from browning. Cut out the fibrous centers, then rub the cut edges with lemon.

2 Set up a steamer (using a pot and a steaming basket) and steam the artichokes over boiling water until just tender, 15 to 20 minutes. Alternatively, cook the artichokes in boiling salted water for 6 to 10 minutes. Drain the artichokes in a colander, rinse with cold water to chill, then drain well again.

3 MAKE THE GARLIC BUTTER: Melt the butter in a saucepan over medium heat. Add the garlic and parsley, if using, and cook until the garlic is fragrant but not brown, about

The artichoke is a flower you can actually cook on the grill.

3 minutes. Add the wine and bring to a boil. The recipe can be prepared up to 2 days ahead to this stage. Keep the garlic butter and the steamed artichokes refrigerated, covered, separately and reheat the butter to melt it before using.

4 Set up the grill for direct grilling (see page 21 for gas or charcoal) and preheat to high. If using a gas grill, place all of the wood chips or chunks in the smoker box or in a smoker pouch (see page 24) and run the grill on high until you see smoke. If using a charcoal grill, preheat it to high, then toss all of the wood chips or chunks on the coals.

5 When ready to cook, place the artichoke quarters on the hot grate and grill until nicely browned and sizzling hot, 3 to 6 minutes (6 to 12 minutes in all) per side, basting with garlic butter. Transfer the grilled artichokes to a platter or plates, pour any remaining garlic butter over them, and serve with Worcestershire Cream Sauce.

YIELD:
Serves 6

NOTES:
■ The stem (at least the couple of inches closest to the choke) of an artichoke is edible, offering the same anisy sweetness as the heart. So when I trim an artichoke, I always leave as much of the stem as possible.

■ Rubbing the cut edges of the artichoke with cut lemon prevents them from discoloring. Or, you can place the artichoke quarters in a bowl of water and lemon juice until you are ready to cook them.

VARIATION: The garlic butter and the cream sauce are an excellent accompaniment to just about any grilled vegetable, from asparagus to zucchini.

Worcestershire Cream Sauce

Walt's serves its grilled artichokes with a creamy sauce flavored with Lea & Perrins Worcestershire sauce. (John Lea and William Perrins were nineteenth-century British chemists who developed Worcestershire sauce.) I like a sauce with a bit less sweetness so I've upped the amount of lemon juice, added a little mustard, and made the honey optional.

INGREDIENTS:
1 cup mayonnaise (preferably Hellmann's)
**¼ cup Lea & Perrins Worcestershire sauce,
    or more to taste**
¼ cup olive oil
¼ cup Asian (dark) sesame oil
3 tablespoons honey (optional)
**2 tablespoons fresh lemon juice,
    or more to taste**
1 tablespoon Dijon mustard (optional)
**2 teaspoons Smelling Salts (page 707),
    or a commercial seasoned salt,
    such as Lawry's**

Walt's fuels its grill with native oak; if you want to do this, you'll find instructions for grilling over wood on page 20. A handful of oak chips will give you the requisite smoke flavor on a charcoal or gas grill.

ombine the mayonnaise, Worcestershire sauce, olive oil, sesame oil, honey, if using, lemon juice, mustard, if using, and seasoned salt in a nonreactive mixing bowl and whisk to mix. Taste for seasoning, adding more lemon juice and/or Worcestershire sauce as necessary. The sauce can be refrigerated, covered, for up to 4 days.

YIELD:
Makes about 2 cups

California

WOOD-GRILLED ASPARAGUS
With Lemon, Garlic, and Aged Jack Cheese

here's nothing like live fire to bring out a vegetable's sweetness, especially when it's grilled over wood, a practice Californians have enthusiastically adopted. Consider the asparagus here. In the best of circumstances it would be grilled over blazing oak. This is easy to do: Simply fill your chimney starter with oak chunks (available at grill shops and hardware stores), then light these the same way you would charcoal (for more on grilling

over wood, see page 20). If your fuel is gas or charcoal, you can use wood chips. I don't soak them, as I'm looking for a light wood flavor rather than a heavy smoke flavor.

METHOD:
Direct grilling

INGREDIENTS:
1 pound asparagus (choose thick stalks)
3 tablespoons extra-virgin olive oil
2 cloves garlic, minced
1 teaspoon grated lemon zest
**Coarse salt (kosher or sea) and
    freshly ground black pepper**
**2 ounces aged Jack cheese (see Note)
    or Parmesan cheese**

YOU'LL ALSO NEED:
**Wooden toothpicks or small bamboo
    skewers; 2 cups wood chips or chunks
    (preferably oak), unsoaked**

T I P S

For ease in skewering, not to mention maximum "Wow!" power, choose fat asparagus stalks—ones that are at least 3/8 of an inch thick.

1 MAKE THE ASPARAGUS RAFTS (see box, right): Snap the fibrous ends off the asparagus; the easiest way to do this is to grab a stalk by its base with one hand and bend the stalk with your other hand. The asparagus will snap where the woody part ends. Arrange 4 or 5 stalks side by side all facing the same direction and skewer them crosswise in two spots with toothpicks.

2 In a small bowl, combine the olive oil, garlic, and lemon zest and stir with a fork to mix. Brush some of this mixture on both sides of the asparagus rafts. Season the asparagus with plenty of salt and pepper.

3 Set up the grill for direct grilling (see page 21 for gas or charcoal) and preheat to high. If using a gas grill, place all of the wood chips or chunks in the smoker box or in a smoker pouch

ASPARAGUS RAFTS

Like all slender vegetables, grilled asparagus has a tendency to fall through the bars of the grate. To prevent this, I suggest a technique I call rafting—skewering several asparagus stalks together crosswise to make a sort of raft. This way you turn the raft, not the individual stalks.

(see page 24) and run the grill on high until you see smoke. If using a charcoal grill, preheat it to high, then toss all of the wood chips or chunks on the coals.

4 When ready to cook, brush and oil the grill grate. Place the asparagus rafts on the hot grate and grill until nicely browned on both sides, 2 to 4 minutes per side. Transfer the grilled asparagus to a platter or plates (you can serve them in raft form or unskewered). Drizzle any remaining lemon garlic oil over the asparagus and grate the cheese over top.

YIELD:
Serves 4

NOTE: Aged Jack is California's answer to Parmesan—a hard, dense, sweet, rich-flavored cheese that's perfect for grating. Look for it at gourmet shops or natural foods markets. If you can't find it, you can substitute Parmesan.

VARIATION: Other slender vegetables work well prepared this way, including okra, scallions, and even green beans.

Sorting and tying asparagus bundles is serious business.

TIPS

I call for a quick homemade Cajun seasoning here, but your favorite commercial brand will work fine, too.

Louisiana

CAJUN GRILLED ASPARAGUS

Although it's possible it's never actually been served there, this variation of grilled asparagus is certainly Louisianan in inspiration. After skewering the stalks together to make them easy to grill, you brush them with olive oil and sprinkle them with Cajun seasoning. The result may be more of a conversation piece than the main dish.

In spring, stalks of asparagus stand like soldiers, ready to be harvested.

METHOD:
Direct grilling

INGREDIENTS:

1 pound asparagus
(choose thick stalks)
1 tablespoon extra-virgin olive oil
1 to 2 tablespoons Cajun Rub
(page 420)

YOU'LL ALSO NEED:
Wooden toothpicks or small
bamboo skewers

1 MAKE THE ASPARAGUS RAFTS: (see page 593). Snap the fibrous ends off the asparagus; the easiest way to do this is to grab a stalk by its base with one hand and bend the stalk with your other hand. The asparagus will snap where the woody part ends. Arrange 4 or 5 stalks side by side all facing the same direction and skewer them crosswise in two spots with toothpicks. Lightly brush the stalks on both sides with the olive oil and sprinkle them with Cajun Rub.

2 Set up the grill for direct grilling (see page 21 for charcoal or gas) and preheat to high.

3 When ready to cook, brush and oil the grill grate. Place the asparagus rafts on the hot grate and grill until nicely browned on both sides, 2 to 4 minutes per side. Transfer the grilled asparagus to a platter or plates and serve at once.

YIELD:
Serves 4

Santa Fe, N.Mex.

BARBECUED CABBAGE SANTA FE

A freshly cut cabbage displays lavish foliage—not so humble after all.

Barbecued cabbage is one of the wackier dishes found on the American barbecue trail. It's amazing how smoke and fire can raise a lowbrow food like cabbage to the level of art. I've tried grilling it with bacon and with kielbasa; this recipe serves up the sizzle of a spicy Mexican sausage called chorizo. It was inspired by a dish I had in Santa Fe, New Mexico—the cabbage is perfumed by the Southwestern seasonings and sausage.

METHOD:
Indirect grilling

INGREDIENTS:

3 to 4 ounces fresh chorizo sausage,
    casings removed
1 small onion, finely chopped
1 clove garlic, minced
1 to 2 jalapeño peppers,
    seeded and minced
¼ cup grated Jack or Cheddar
    cheese
1 medium-size head green cabbage
    (about 2 pounds)
Coarse salt (kosher or sea) and
    freshly ground black pepper
1 tablespoon butter

YOU'LL ALSO NEED:

1½ cups wood chips or chunks
    (preferably mesquite), soaked for
    1 hour in water to cover,
    then drained

1 Heat a frying pan over medium-high heat. Add the chorizo and cook until the fat starts to render, breaking the meat up with a wooden spoon. Add the onion, garlic, and jalapeño(s) and cook until the chorizo and vegetables are lightly browned. Drain the sausage mixture in a strainer over a heatproof bowl, reserving the sausage fat. Transfer the sausage mixture to a bowl and stir in 2 tablespoons of the cheese.

TIPS

Ideally, when you stuff the cabbage you'll use fresh (uncooked) chorizo, which is available at Hispanic markets and at many supermarkets. If the chorizo you find is cooked, you'll need to chop it fine as dust and add a little oil to the pan when cooking the onions.

Cabbage trimmed and ready for barbecuing or slaw.

in the chorizo mixture. Top with the remaining 2 tablespoons of cheese and place the butter on top. Paint the sides of the cabbage with the reserved sausage fat and season with salt and pepper. The recipe can be prepared up to this stage several hours ahead: Keep the cabbage in the refrigerator, covered.

4 Set up the grill for indirect grilling (see page 23 for gas or page 22 for charcoal) and preheat to medium. If using a gas grill, place all of the wood chips or chunks in the smoker box or in a smoker pouch (see page 24) and run the grill on high until you see smoke, then reduce the heat to medium. If using a charcoal grill, place a large drip pan in the center, preheat the grill to medium, then toss all of the wood chips or chunks on the coals.

5 When ready to cook, place the cabbage on its aluminum foil ring in the center of the hot grate, over the drip pan and away from the heat. Cover the grill and cook the cabbage until very tender (when done it will be easy to pierce with a skewer), 1 to 1½ hours. If the cabbage or topping starts to brown too much, cover it loosely with aluminum foil. If using a charcoal grill, after 1 hour you'll need to add 12 fresh coals per side if the cabbage is not done.

6 Transfer the grilled cabbage on its ring to a round platter and present it to your guests. Peel off and discard any dried out or charred outside leaves, then cut the cabbage into wedges for serving.

YIELD:
Serves 6 to 8

2 Crumple a 12-inch-long piece of aluminum foil and shape it into a ring about 3 inches in diameter. Place the cabbage on the ring, stem side up. Using a sharp paring knife, cut out the core: Angle your knife about 3 inches down toward the center of the cabbage, then cut a circle that is about 3 inches in diameter. Pull out the cone-shaped core and discard it.

3 Season the cavity in the cabbage with salt and pepper, then spoon

Pontiac, Mich.

SMOKY STEWED CABBAGE

Sometimes I substitute smoked turkey wings for the ham hocks for my non–pork-eating friends.

While this dish doesn't ever touch the grill, it does make use of one of the tastiest morsels of meat ever to emerge from the smokehouse: ham hocks. The cabbage is almost embarrassingly simple to make, but I've never attended a barbecue where it wouldn't be welcome—indeed, in many parts of the country it's a barbecue tradition. The idea for the recipe comes from C & J Soul Food Carry Out, a barbecue joint and car wash in Pontiac, Michigan.

INGREDIENTS:

1 bay leaf
1 medium-size onion, peeled and
    quartered
1 whole clove
1 large or 2 small ham hocks
    (about 1 pound)
1 medium-size head green
    cabbage
    (about 2 pounds)
Coarse salt (kosher or sea) and
    freshly ground black pepper
2 tablespoons butter (optional)

1 Pin the bay leaf to one of the onion wedges with the clove. Place the onion and ham hock(s) in a large pot and add 2 quarts of water. Bring to a boil over high heat, reduce the heat to medium, and let simmer, uncovered, for 30 minutes.

2 Core the cabbage and cut it into 2-inch pieces. Add the cabbage to the pot and cook until tender but not too soft, about 20 minutes. Add salt (you won't need much; ham hocks are quite salty) and pepper to taste.

3 Using a slotted spoon, transfer the ham hock(s) to a cutting board. When cool, pull the meat off the bones and dice it, discarding the skin and fat. Transfer the cooked cabbage to a serving bowl, adding enough cooking liquid to keep it moist. Stir in the diced ham hock(s). Adding a pat or two of butter wouldn't hurt, either.

YIELD:

Serves 6 to 8

A cabbage patch on wheels.

THE GRILLED CORN DEBATE

The world of barbecue is rife with great debates. Charcoal versus gas. Dry ribs versus wet. Tomato-based sauce versus vinegar. And now there's a new dispute to consider: What's the best way to grill corn?

One side advocates grilling corn in the husk. These pit masters argue that corn tastes best roasted in its verdant sheathing. The husk keeps the corn moist, they maintain, preventing the delicate kernels from scorching.

"Balderdash!" cry the partisans of husk-off grilling. From their point of view, there's nothing like direct live fire for bringing out corn's sweetness. Exposing the kernels to the flames is the only way to get the rich taste of caramelized plant sugar. Grilling is all about smoke flavors, they argue, and you won't achieve the proper char unless nothing but the grill grate comes between the flames and the corn.

If it were up to the practices of international grill jockeys, the debate would be handily settled; outside the United States, most grill without the husk. From the corn vendors in Queen's Park Savannah in Port of Spain on the island of Trinidad to the street merchants at the 20 de Noviembre market in Oaxaca, Mexico, the world's pit masters grill their corn naked. Incidentally, the Mexicans have a singular technique for seasoning the smoky brown kernels: They slather the corn with mayonnaise, sprinkle

Winning big at the Jack Daniel's World Championship Invitational Barbecue Cook-Off.

Tensions mount as Jack Daniel's competitors wait to hear from the judges.

lively trade in corn dogs, funnel cakes, and other classic American street foods. But the longest lines form in front of the stall manned by the Metro Moore County volunteer firefolk in Lynchburg where the specialty is corn grilled in the husk.

"We start with sweet yellow corn," explains fire department treasurer Regina Qualls. "We soak it in huge tubs of salt water with plenty of ice to give it extra flavor and keep it from burning." The corn is charred over a hot fire until the husk is as burnt and black as a fireman's nightmare. When the burnt husk is scraped off, you get corn that's a paragon of moistness, sweetness, and smoke flavor. The only challenge in doing this at home is getting your grill hot enough to burn the husk. One trick I use with a charcoal grill is to lay the ears of corn directly on the glowing embers. In the Variation on page 603 you'll find instructions for doing this.

Without a doubt, there's one thing everyone can agree about: Husk on or husk off, corn always tastes best when you grill it.

it with sharp grated cheese and chile powder, and add a vivifying squeeze of fresh lime juice. It sounds weird, but the combination is irresistible (for a Mexican-influenced Chicago version, see page 604).

When grilling corn sans husk (the method I prefer), I like to shuck the ears, but leave the husk attached to the stem of the cob, which I tie together with string. This forms a nifty handle for holding the corn, making it easy to munch.

FANS OF THE HUSK

Husk-on grillers also have their partisans, including the fire department in Lynchburg, Tennessee. You might know Lynchburg as the home of the distillery that makes Jack Daniel's. But for 'que it's probably better known as the Pimlico or Churchill Downs of competition barbecue. Every fall thousands of barbecue buffs descend on the tiny town for one of America's great barbecue festivals: the Jack Daniel's World Championship Invitational Barbecue Cook-Off. To feed the multitudes, local vendors do a

The husk is as burnt and black as a fireman's nightmare.

TIPS

■ When buying corn for grilling, look for ears that feel heavy in your hand, with shiny, plump, sweet kernels. (It's OK to strip back a little of the husk to examine the corn inside. I'll even go so far as to jab a fingernail into one of the kernels to check its juiciness.) If the kernels look shriveled or dried out, choose another ear.

■ If you don't have butcher's string you can remove thin strips of the husk and use these instead to tie the husk handles.

Maryland

EASTERN SHORE GRILLED CORN
With Sweet Butter

H usk on or husk off? When it comes to grilling corn, that's the question and it's hotly debated on the barbecue circuit (for a full discussion of the controversy, see page 598). Partisans of the husk-off school (to which I belong) argue that corn can't pick up the flavor of fire and smoke with the husk on, and moreover, that the husk prevents caramelization (that tasty burning of the plant sugars).

Fire roasting corn is an American tradition that goes back centuries—make that millennia—long before the first Europeans tasted the distinctive New World grain. Of course, grilled corn is only as good as the raw materials you start with, and you can't beat the sweet shoe peg corn from Maryland's Eastern Shore—the sort you buy from roadside stands in the summer. This is the corn I grew

up on (although we boiled it instead of grilling it) and childhood loyalties run deep. The fact is you can't go wrong with summer fresh corn from anywhere in America—especially when you grill it the same day it was picked.

METHOD:
Direct grilling

INGREDIENTS:
8 ears sweet corn in the husk
6 to 8 tablespoons (¾ to 1 stick) unsalted butter, melted
Coarse salt (kosher or sea) and freshly ground black pepper

Sweet corn grilled husk-free.

YOU'LL ALSO NEED:

Butcher's string

1 Shuck the corn, stripping the husk back as though you were peeling a banana but leaving the husk attached at the stem end (leave the stem on). Holding an ear of corn in one hand, gather the husk together so that it covers the stem and then tie it with a piece of butcher's string. This forms a sort of handle. Remove the corn silk. Repeat with the remaining ears of corn.

2 Set up the grill for direct grilling (see page 21 for charcoal or gas) and preheat to high.

3 When ready to cook, lightly brush each ear of corn with some of the melted butter and season generously with salt and pepper. Arrange the corn on the hot grate so that the husks hang over the edge of the grill (this keeps them from burning) or place a folded sheet of aluminum foil under the husks to shield them. Grill the corn until nicely browned on all sides, 2 to 3 minutes per side (8 to 12 minutes in all), turning with tongs. As the corn grills, baste it with melted butter and season it again with salt and pepper. Transfer the grilled corn to a platter or plates and serve at once.

YIELD:

Makes 8 ears; serves 4 to 8

Midwest

GRILLED CORN
With Maytag Blue

Mention barbecue and I'm pretty sure Iowa won't be the first place that comes to mind, but corn is an entirely different matter. And the Hawkeye State also is home to one of America's most distinctive cheeses: piquant, creamy Maytag Blue. Bring them together on a blazing grill and you get some of the most delectable corn ever to grace a summer cookout. This recipe uses the husk-off method for grilling the corn (for more about the Grilled Corn Debate, see page 598).

METHOD:

Direct grilling

INGREDIENTS:

8 ears sweet corn in the husk

3 tablespoons Maytag Blue cheese, at room temperature

6 tablespoons (¾ stick) unsalted butter, at room temperature

3 tablespoons finely chopped fresh flat-leaf parsley

Coarse salt (kosher or sea; optional) and freshly ground black pepper

YOU'LL ALSO NEED:

Butcher's string

1 Shuck the corn, stripping the husk back as though you were peeling a

TIPS

Maytag Blue can be found at select gourmet food stores, cheese shops, and supermarkets, or see the Mail-Order Sources on page 742. For an interesting twist, try another blue cheese, like Roquefort or Cabrales.

banana, but leaving the husk attached at the stem end (leave the stem on). Holding an ear of the corn in one hand, gather the husk together so that it covers the stem and then tie it with a piece of butcher's string. This forms a sort of handle. Remove the corn silk. Repeat with the remaining ears of corn.

2 Place a small metal strainer over a mixing bowl. Push the cheese through it with the back of a spoon (this is a highly effective way of puréeing blue cheese). You can also mash the cheese in the bottom of a small mixing bowl with a fork. Add the butter and parsley, then beat until the cheese mixture is smooth and creamy. Taste for seasoning, adding salt if necessary and pepper to taste. Thanks to the salt in the cheese, the mixture may be salty enough already.

3 When ready to cook, lightly brush the corn with a little of the cheese mixture. Arrange the corn on the hot grate so that the husks hang over the edge of the grill (this keeps them from burning) or place a folded sheet of aluminum foil under the husks to shield them. Grill the corn until nicely browned on all sides, 2 to 3 minutes per side (8 to 12 minutes in all), turning with tongs and basting with the remaining cheese mixture. Transfer the grilled corn to a platter or plates and serve at once.

YIELD:
Makes 8 ears; serves 4 to 8

Lynchburg, Tenn.

FIREMEN'S CORN

It's obvious by now that when it comes to grilling corn, I'm a partisan of husk-off grilling. But if anyone were to cause me to rethink my position, it's the pit masters of the Metro Moore County Volunteer Fire Department in Lynchburg, Tennessee. These fire folk know a thing or two about grilling corn: They serve up to eight hundred ears a day at festivals like the Jack Daniel's World Championship Invitational Barbecue Cook-Off and Frontier Days at the beginning of July. The corn is soaked in salted, sugared water to add flavor and slow down combustion and then cooked on a grill that's hot as a blast furnace until the ears look like something that might be left in the wake of an arsonist. When you pull off the burnt husk, you get corn of incomparable moistness and sweetness.

METHOD:
Direct grilling

ADVANCE PREPARATION:
4 to 8 hours for soaking the corn

INGREDIENTS:
½ cup sugar
Coarse salt (kosher or sea)

8 ears sweet corn in the husk
8 tablespoons (1 stick) butter,
    melted
Freshly ground black pepper
Cayenne pepper (optional)

YOU'LL ALSO NEED:
Bags of ice (optional)

1 Combine the sugar with ½ cup of salt and 1 gallon of water in a large pot or clean bucket and stir until the salt and sugar dissolve. Cut off the stems and ¼ inch of the tip of each ear of corn and remove any protruding silk. Place the ears in the brine, stem end up. Let the corn soak for at least 4 hours or as long as 8 in the refrigerator. If the corn won't fit in the refrigerator, keep it cold with bags of ice.

2 Set up the grill for direct grilling (see page 21 for charcoal or gas) and preheat to as hot as possible.

3 When ready to cook, place the soaked corn on the hot grate and grill until the husks are charred and blackened, 5 to 8 minutes per side (20 to 32 minutes in all).

4 Wearing clean gloves or using a stiff bristled brush, strip the charred husks off the corn. Roll each ear of corn in the melted butter, season with salt, black pepper, and cayenne, if using, and serve at once.

YIELD:
Makes 8 ears; serves 4 to 8

VARIATION: One novel and extremely effective way to grill corn in the husk is directly on the embers. When the coals glow orange, rake them into an even layer and arrange the ears of corn on top. This method gives you fool-proof charring and a super smoky flavor. It will take 2 top 3 minutes per side (8 to 12 minutes in all).

The Lynchburg Volunteer Fire Department uses an industrial-strength grill that chars the husks right off the corn in a manner of minutes. It'd be difficult to achieve this intense heat on a home grill—especially when cooking with gas. If you're using a gas grill, preheat it to high, walk away for 15 minutes, and let it preheat to high some more. It's easier bringing a charcoal grill to the right temperature: Simply add 50 percent more charcoal than you'd normally use.

A mountain of corn. Gentlemen, fire up your grills.

The traditional cheese for Mexican-style grilled corn is Cotija—a hard, tangy, sourish cheese with a flavor similar to Greek feta. You can find it at Mexican grocery stores or specialty food shops, or perhaps at your local supermarket. Feta, Romano, or Parmesan cheese can all be used instead.

The NEW Maxwell STREET MARKET

Chicago, Ill.

WINDY CITY MEXICAN GRILLED CORN

This may be the most singular grilled corn you've ever eaten. I first tasted it at the central food market in Oaxaca, Mexico. Closer to home, it turns up at the Maxwell Street Market near the Mexican-American neighborhood of Pilsen in Chicago.

Mayonnaise, cheese, and corn may seem like strange bedfellows—you'll just have to trust me that the combination tastes better than it sounds. The dish is wonderfully interactive: You and your guests get to slather and season your corn however you please.

METHOD:
Direct grilling

INGREDIENTS:

8 ears sweet corn in the husk
1 cup mayonnaise (preferably Hellmann's)
1 cup (about 4 ounces) grated Cotijo, Romano, or Parmesan cheese
3 tablespoons pure chile powder (see Note)
Lime wedges

YOU'LL ALSO NEED:
Butcher's string

1 Shuck the corn, stripping the husk back as though you were peeling a banana, but leaving the husk attached at the stem end (leave the stem on). Holding an ear of the corn in one hand, gather the husk together so that it covers the stem and then tie it with a piece of butcher's string. This forms a sort of handle. Remove the corn silk. Repeat with the remaining ears of corn.

2 Place the mayonnaise, cheese, chile powder, and lime wedges in small attractive bowls. Have these ingredients ready on the table, along with butter knives for spreading the mayonnaise.

3 Set up the grill for direct grilling (see page 21 for charcoal or gas) and preheat to high.

4 When ready to cook, arrange the corn on the hot grate so that the husks hang over the edge of the grill (this keeps them from burning) or place a folded sheet of aluminum foil under the husks to shield them. Grill the corn until nicely browned on all sides, 2 to 3 minutes per side (8 to 12 minutes in all), turning with tongs.

5 Transfer the grilled corn to a platter. To serve, tell everyone to spread mayonnaise on the corn, then, working over a plate or the platter, sprinkle the ears with cheese and chile powder. Squeeze lime juice to taste over the corn and eat the kernels right off the cob.

YIELD:

Makes 8 ears; serves 4 to 8

NOTE: I like to use chile powder made with ancho chiles. If you can't find it in a store near you, you can order it by mail (see page 742).

Midwest

GRILLED CREAMED CORN

Creamed corn ranks high on the list of America's favorite comfort foods. Why not enrich its flavor by grilling the principal ingredients, onion and corn? This dish takes only a few minutes to make (especially if you have leftover grilled corn and onion), but the contrast of flavors and textures—sweet and smoky, creamy and crunchy—will take your breath away.

METHOD:
Direct grilling

INGREDIENTS:
4 ears sweet corn, shucked
(for 3 cups grilled corn kernels)
1 medium-size onion, peeled and
cut lengthwise in quarters
(leave the root end attached)
3 tablespoons butter, melted
Coarse salt (kosher or sea) and
freshly ground black pepper
2 teaspoons cornstarch
1½ cups half-and-half, light cream,
or heavy (whipping) cream
1 tablespoon brown sugar
or granulated sugar, or
more to taste
Freshly grated nutmeg

1 Set up the grill for direct grilling (see page 21 for charcoal or gas) and preheat to high.

2 Lightly brush the corn and onion quarters with some of the melted butter and season generously with salt and pepper.

3 When ready to cook, place the corn and onions on the hot grate and grill until golden brown on all sides, 2 to 3 minutes per side (8 to 12 minutes in all) for the corn and 3 to 4 minutes per side (9 to 12 minutes in all) for the onion quarters. Baste the vegetables with more melted butter as they cook. Transfer the grilled corn and onions to a platter and let cool. The grilled vegetables can be refrigerated, covered, for up to 48 hours.

TIPS

You could cream the corn directly after grilling it. Indeed, that's what the recipe calls for. But I'm most likely to make this dish when I have grilled corn and onions on hand from a previous grill session, so I don't have to cook both outdoors and inside. Of course, if your grill has a side burner, you can do all the work outside.

Corn is at its sweetest fresh off the stalk.

4 Cut the corn kernels off the cobs, using lengthwise strokes of a chef's knife. Trim off and discard the roots from the onion, then finely chop it. Transfer the corn kernels and chopped onion to a saucepan and stir in the cornstarch. Cook over medium heat for 1 minute.

5 Stir the half-and-half and sugar into the corn mixture and bring to a boil over high heat. Reduce the heat to medium and let simmer until thick and richly flavored, about 5 minutes. Add any butter left over from basting and a pinch of nutmeg to the creamed corn, then season it with salt and pepper to taste and more brown sugar, if necessary; the creamed corn should be highly seasoned. Transfer the creamed corn to a serving bowl and garnish with a whisper of grated nutmeg.

YIELD:
Serves 4

Corn Country, U.S.A.

GRILLED CORN PUDDING

Corn pudding in the United States goes way back, and the advent of grilled vegetables is about to make it taste even better. The smoky flavor of grilled corn kernels adds a whole new dimension to the pudding. Mark Twain once observed that the proper way to eat corn was to set up the pot for cooking it right in the field, and while this may not be entirely practical in the post-agrarian age, it does serve to remind us that corn is at its sweetest the moment it's harvested (the sweetness inexorably declines as the sugars in the kernels are converted to starch). For the best results, use farm-stand corn and make the pudding the same day you buy the corn.

METHOD:
Direct grilling and indirect grilling

INGREDIENTS:
6 ears sweet corn, shucked
Olive oil
Coarse salt (kosher or sea) and
   freshly ground black pepper
1 cup heavy (whipping) cream
3 large eggs, separated
¼ teaspoon freshly grated nutmeg,
   or more to taste
1 to 3 teaspoons sugar (optional)
½ teaspoon cream of tartar

YOU'LL ALSO NEED:

**1 cup wood chips or chunks
(optional; preferably hickory or oak),
soaked for 1 hour in water to
cover, then drained; one 12 inch
(6 cup) heat- or grill-proof oval
baking dish**

1 Set up the grill for direct grilling (see page 21 for charcoal or gas) and preheat to high.

2 Lightly brush each ear of corn with olive oil and season with salt and pepper.

3 When ready to cook, place the corn on the hot grate and grill until golden brown on all sides, 2 to 3 minutes per side (8 to 12 minutes in all), turning with tongs. Transfer the grilled corn to a cutting board and let cool.

4 Cut the corn kernels off the cobs, using lengthwise strokes of a chef's knife. Break 3 of the cobs in half and place them in a saucepan with the cream over medium heat and bring to a simmer. Let the cream simmer gently for 15 minutes to infuse it with corn flavor. Remove the pan from the heat and let the cream cool.

5 Place half of the corn kernels in a food processor and purée to a smooth paste. Add the egg yolks and process to mix. Strain in the cooled cream and pulse just to mix. Transfer the corn mixture to a large bowl and stir in the remaining whole corn kernels and the nutmeg. Season with salt and

pepper to taste. Taste for seasoning, adding sugar and/or more nutmeg as necessary; the corn mixture should be highly seasoned.

6 Set up the grill for indirect grilling (see page 23 for gas or page 22 for charcoal) and preheat to medium. If using a gas grill, place all of the wood chips or chunks, if desired, in the smoker box or in a smoker pouch (see page 24) and run the grill on high until you see smoke, then reduce the heat to medium. If using a charcoal grill, preheat it to medium, then toss all of the wood chips or chunks, if desired, on the coals.

7 Using a stand mixer or a clean metal bowl and a hand mixer, beat the egg whites with the cream of tartar until soft peaks form (they should be firm and glossy but not dry). Gently fold the egg whites into the puréed corn mixture with a rubber spatula. Lightly oil the baking dish, then spoon the corn mixture into it. Don't over fold, or you'll deflate the egg whites.

8 Place the filled baking dish in the center of the hot grate, away from the heat, and cover the grill. Grill the pudding until puffed, browned on top, and cooked through, 20 to 30 minutes To test for doneness, insert a toothpick or metal skewer in the center of the pudding; it should come out clean. Serve the pudding at once.

YIELD:
Serves 8

T I P S

The die-hard pit master will want to use the grill twice: first to grill the corn, then to grill the pudding. The advantage of this method is that you can toss some wood chips on the coals, imbuing the pudding with additional smoke flavor. However, you can also cook the pudding in an oven preheated to 350°F. It will take about 30 minutes. This will free up the grill for cooking steaks, fish, or some other main course.

The best place to find green garlic is at a farm stand in an area that grows garlic. Scallions, small green onions, and baby leeks can all be cooked the same way.

Grilled Green Garlic is a great match for fish, poultry, and pork.

The Redlands, Fla.

GRILLED GREEN GARLIC

An hour south of Miami is an agriculture district called the Redlands. Hailed as the Napa Valley of exotic fruit, the region produces most of the nation's mangoes, avocados, litchis, and star fruit, not to mention Caribbean vegetables such as yucca and boniato. My wife and I like to shop at the farm stands along Krome Avenue and generally immerse ourselves in the rural atmosphere of the place, which is so utterly unlike nearby Miami. A recent visit turned up some green garlic. The leafy shoots of young garlic plants, these look like green onions and have an irresistible flavor that mingles garlic, scallion, and leek. Now, I never met a vegetable I didn't try to grill and these were out of this world. A similar dish is found in Spain, where bunches of a type of green onion called *calçot* are charred over grape vine trimmings and served wrapped in newspaper.

METHOD:
Direct grilling

INGREDIENTS:
2 bunches green garlic, scallions, or baby leeks, trimmed
3 tablespoons extra-virgin olive oil
Coarse salt (kosher or sea) and freshly ground black pepper
1 ounce Parmesan or Pecorino Romano cheese (optional)

1 Set up the grill for direct grilling (see page 21 for charcoal or gas) and preheat to high.

2 Lightly brush the garlic on both sides with about 1½ tablespoons of olive oil and season generously with salt and pepper.

3 When ready to cook, place the garlic on the hot grate with the stalks running perpendicular to the bars. Grill until the leaves are crisp and brown and the base is soft, 2 to 4 minutes per side. Transfer the grilled garlic to a platter. Drizzle the remaining 1½ tablespoons of olive oil on top and season with more salt and pepper, if desired. Serve the garlic at once, with freshly grated Parmesan cheese, if using.

YIELD:

Serves 4 to 6

VARIATIONS: For a Pacific Rim touch, baste the garlic with sesame oil instead of olive oil; for an Oregonian touch, use hazelnut oil.

Mississippi

BARBECUED OKRA

L et's get one thing straight: Okra doesn't have to be slimy. The slender green vegetable has the reputation for being as viscous as primeval ooze. True, its mucilaginous starches can be off-putting to the uninitiated (this very property endears the vegetable to chefs in Mississippi and Louisiana, who use it as a thickener for stews and gumbo). But grill the whole pods over a hot fire and okra remains as snappily crisp as the most fashionable al dente green bean. The trick is to keep the okra whole. This means trimming off the last eighth inch or so of the stem end; take care not to cut into the pod. There's an added advantage to grilling okra: The high dry heat of the fire caramelizes its sugar, accentuating the vegetable's sweetness. If you've always been put off by okra's notorious sliminess, the following recipe will come as a revelation.

METHOD:

Direct grilling

INGREDIENTS:

**1 teaspoon coarse salt
   (kosher or sea)**
1 teaspoon sweet paprika
1 teaspoon sugar
1 teaspoon ground coriander
1/2 teaspoon freshly ground black pepper
1/2 teaspoon cayenne pepper
1/4 teaspoon celery seed
1 pound fresh okra
**1 tablespoon unsalted butter, melted,
   or olive oil**

1 Place the salt, paprika, sugar, coriander, black pepper, cayenne, and celery seed in a small bowl and stir to mix (see Notes).

2 Rinse the okra under cold running water and blot dry with paper towels. Trim the tips off the stem ends of the okra but do not cut into the pods (this would expose the insides to air, making the okra slimy). Place the okra in a large mixing bowl. Add the butter and toss to coat. Add the rub and toss to coat.

3 Set up the grill for direct grilling (see page 21 for charcoal or gas) and preheat to high.

4 When ready to cook, arrange the okra on the hot grate so that they are perpendicular to the bars (see Notes). Grill the okra until nicely browned on both sides, 2 to 4 minutes per side, turning with tongs as needed. Transfer the grilled okra to a platter or plates and serve at once.

TIPS

Choose bright, crisp, pods of okra that are 2 to 3 inches long. You don't want jumbo okra, which are tough and stringy, or pods that are wilted or streaked with black.

YIELD:

Serves 4

NOTES:

■ If you're in a hurry, use 4 teaspoons of your favorite commercial barbecue rub instead of making your own following the directions in Step 1.

■ When grilling lots of okra, you may wish to place four or five pods side by side and skewer them crosswise at the top and bottom with slender bamboo skewers. It keeps stray okra from falling through the bars of the grate into the fire.

Georgia

BARBECUED ONIONS

When I was growing up, an onion was an onion. How times have changed! What was once the best kept secret in Georgia is now big news across the United States— namely that southeast Georgia produces some of the mildest, sweetest onions on the planet—the Vidalia. I've always enjoyed onions grilled directly over the coals. One day, I decided to stuff whole ones with bacon and butter and smoke them. The already estimable Vidalia just got a whole lot better.

METHOD:

Indirect grilling

INGREDIENTS:

8 Vidalia or other sweet onions (each 14 to 18 ounces)

5 tablespoons unsalted butter

4 slices bacon (preferably artisanal), cut crosswise into ¼-inch slivers

½ cup sweet red barbecue sauce (see pages 666 to 669 or use your favorite commercial brand)

Freshly ground black pepper

YOU'LL ALSO NEED:

8 pieces of aluminum foil (each 2 by 6 inches), twisted into 2-inch rings; 1½ cups wood chips or chunks (preferably hickory), soaked for 1 hour in water to cover, then drained

1 Peel the onions. Using a sharp paring knife and working opposite the stem end, cut a cone-shaped cavity in each onion by angling your knife about 1 inch down toward the center and cutting in a circle that is about 2½ inches in diameter. Remove and finely chop the cores. Set each onion on an aluminum foil ring, with the cavity facing up; the rings will hold the onions steady.

2 Melt 1 tablespoon of the butter in a skillet over medium heat. Add the bacon and chopped onion and cook over medium heat until lightly browned, 3 to 5 minutes. Drain the bacon in a strainer over a bowl. Place a spoonful of the bacon mixture in the cavity of each onion. Cut the remaining 4 tablespoons of butter into 8 equal pieces. Spoon 1 tablespoon of the

TIPS

The traditional season for Vidalias is April and May. Thanks to improved storage techniques, the onion's availability has been extended up until New Year's. Other sweet onions you could use for this recipe include Maui onions, Walla Wallas, Imperial Sweets, or Texas 1015s, not to mention a growing number of sweet onions imported from Central and South America.

In Georgia, roadside stands offer Vidalias by the bag.

barbecue sauce into each onion and place a piece of butter on top. Sprinkle some pepper on top of each onion. The recipe can be prepared several hours ahead up to this stage.

3 Set up the grill for indirect grilling (see page 23 for gas or page 22 for charcoal) and preheat to medium. If using a gas grill, place all of the wood chips or chunks in the smoker box or a smoker pouch (see page 24) and run the grill on high until you see smoke, then reduce the heat to medium. If using a charcoal grill, place a large drip pan in the center and preheat the grill to medium, then toss all of the wood chips or chunks on the coals.

4 When ready to cook, place the onions on their aluminum foil rings in the center of the hot grate, over the drip pan and away from the heat, and cover the grill. Cook the onions until they are golden brown and tender, 40 to 60 minutes. To test for doneness, pinch the side of an onion; it should be squeezably soft. If the filling starts to brown too much before the onions are fully cooked, cover the onions loosely with aluminum foil. Transfer the grilled onions to a platter or plates and serve at once.

YIELD:
Serves 8

CURTIS'S ALL AMERICAN BAR B Q

Vermont isn't exactly the heart of barbecue country, but if you happen to be visiting the Green Mountain State and get an itch for chicken or ribs, Curtis Tuff can scratch it. Raised in the South and recognizable by his salt-and-pepper beard and three gold earrings, Tuff is the tall, lanky man fussing over a 275-gallon oil drum that serves as pit, stoking the fire with ash, beech, maple, and other local hardwoods, and mopping his chickens and ribs with a Southern-style barbecue sauce made from ketchup, vinegar, and hot sauce.

Putney was one of the magnets of the great sixties hippy migration to Vermont, so it shouldn't come as too much of a surprise that Curtis's

**CURTIS'S
ALL AMERICAN
BAR B Q**

**Exit 4, I-91, Route 5
Putney, Vermont
(802) 387-5474**

prep kitchen and office occupy a pair of ancient, bright blue school buses. Keeping him company is a seven-year-old black pig named Isabel, who doesn't seem to mind that the house specialty involves some of her less fortunate brethren—plate-burying oversize spareribs, that are smoke roasted over the coals until they're darn near tender enough to fall off the bone. (Tuff uses "five and down"—ribs that weigh 5 pounds per rack. "Baby backs are too small," he explains with a hint of disdain.) Tuff practices open pit cooking—that is the chicken and ribs roast over blazing logs—a process more akin to grilling than smoking. The end result may lack the complexity of Bible Belt barbecue, but it sure hits the spot when you're feeling hungry.

When you're hankering for barbecue in southern Vermont, turn in at the powder-blue school bus.

Georgia & New Eng.

BARBECUED ONIONS
With Baked Beans

Two of America's favorite barbecue side dishes, baked beans and grilled onions, come together in these unusual stuffed onions. The onions are grilled with plenty of wood smoke. The result is a mouthwatering side dish the likes of which most people haven't seen before.

Barbecued Onions—you'll weep with pleasure.

METHOD:
Indirect grilling

INGREDIENTS:
8 Vidalia or other sweet onions
    (each 14 to 18 ounces)
1½ cups baked beans (follow the recipe
    on page 636 or use your favorite
    commercial brand; you'll need a
    14-ounce can)
¼ cup firmly packed dark brown sugar
½ cup sweet red barbecue sauce
    (St. Louis Red, page 666,
    or use your favorite commercial
    brand)
4 tablespoons (½ stick) butter,
    cut into 8 even pieces
Freshly ground black pepper
2 slices of bacon, each cut
    into 4-inch-long pieces
    (8 pieces in all; optional)

YOU'LL ALSO NEED:
8 pieces of aluminum foil (each
    2 by 6 inches), twisted into 2-inch
    rings; 1½ cups wood chips or
    chunks (preferably hickory),
    soaked for 1 hour in water to
    cover, then drained

1 Peel the onions. Using a sharp paring knife and working opposite the stem end, cut a cone-shaped cavity in each onion by angling your knife about 1 inch down toward the center and cutting in a circle that is about 2½ inches in diameter. Remove and finely chop the cores. Mix the chopped onion with the baked beans.

an eye-popping, mouthwatering side dish

2 Set each onion on an aluminum foil ring, with the cavity facing up; the rings will hold the onions steady. Spoon the baked bean mixture into the cavities in the onions, dividing it evenly among them. Spoon ½ tablespoon of the brown sugar into each onion over the beans, followed by 1 tablespoon of the barbecue sauce and a piece of butter. Sprinkle some pepper over each onion, then place a piece of bacon, if using, on top.

3 Set up the grill for indirect grilling (see page 23 for gas or page 22 for charcoal) and preheat to medium. If using a gas grill, place all of the wood chips or chunks in the smoker box or a smoker pouch (see page 24) and run the grill on high until you see smoke, then reduce the heat to medium. If using a charcoal grill, place a large drip pan in the center, preheat the grill to medium, then toss all of the wood chips or chunks on the coals.

4 When ready to cook, place the onions on their aluminum foil rings in the center of the hot grate, over the drip pan and away from the heat and cover the grill. Cook the onions until they are golden brown and tender, 40 to 60 minutes. To test for doneness, pinch the side of an onion; it should be squeezably soft. If the filling starts to brown too much before the onions are fully cooked, cover the onions loosely with aluminum foil. Transfer the grilled onions to a platter or plates and serve at once.

YIELD:
Serves 8

New York, N.Y.

PICKLED GRILLED PEPPERS

These pickled peppers are, to paraphrase Mark Twain, "deliciousness itself." You might be surprised to learn where I got the idea for the recipe—a Jewish restaurant on New York's Lower East Side called Sammy's Roumanian. Which makes me suspect that the idea of grilling peppers for pickling comes from the Balkans. (Similar peppers are served at a delicatessen in North Miami Beach called the Rascal House.) Grilling imparts an unexpected smoke flavor that gives complexity to a seemingly simple dish.

METHOD:
Direct grilling

ADVANCE PREPARATION:
24 hours for pickling the peppers

INGREDIENTS:
4 green bell peppers
2 cups distilled white vinegar
½ cup sugar, or more to taste
2½ tablespoons coarse salt
   (kosher or sea), or more to taste
5 sprigs fresh dill
3 cloves garlic, peeled
2 dried cayenne peppers or other
   dried hot red chile peppers

YOU'LL ALSO NEED:

One 2-quart crock or jar, washed and dried

1 Set up the grill for direct grilling (see page 21 for charcoal or gas) and preheat to high.

2 When ready to cook, place the bell peppers on the hot grate and grill until the skins are nicely browned and blistered on all sides, 3 to 5 minutes per side (12 to 15 minutes in all). Don't forget to grill the tops and bottoms.

3 Transfer the grilled bell peppers to a cutting board and let cool. Cut each bell pepper in quarters, discarding the stem, veins, and seeds.

4 Place the vinegar, sugar, and salt in the crock with 2 cups of water and whisk until the sugar and salt dissolve (if using a jar, tightly cover it and shake until the sugar and salt dissolve). Taste for seasoning, adding more sugar and/or salt as necessary. Add the pepper quarters, dill, garlic, and chiles. Cover the crock with plastic wrap or close the jar placing a piece of plastic wrap between the top of jar and the lid to keep it from corroding.

5 Let the peppers pickle in the refrigerator for 24 hours. Store in the refrigerator until serving.

YIELD:
Serves 4

TIPS

I suppose you could grill and pickle red or yellow peppers in this fashion, but green ones seem to taste the best (they're the most traditional, at least). If you want to add some heat, you could prepare horn peppers in this fashion. You'd need about a pound.

Sammy's on New York's Lower East Side is part of the city's ethnic food past—and its future.

Miami, Fla.

MADUROS ON THE GRILL
(Grilled Plantains)

Fried ripe plantains are a staple of the Latin American diet, and there's nothing like a quick plunge

To achieve the maximum sweetness, grill very ripe plantains—the sort with skins that are so black they look like you should throw them out. If you live near a Hispanic market, you may be able to buy them this ripe. If your plantains come from the supermarket, they'll probably be green. Let them ripen at room temperature in a loosely closed paper bag until black—a process that can take up to a week or two. Don't rush the process—only a black skinned plantain will have the proper banana-like sweetness.

Fried plantains are good; grilled, they're even better.

1 Set up the grill for direct grilling (see page 21 for charcoal or gas) and preheat to high.

2 Peel the plantains and slice them sharply on the diagonal into 1½-inch slices.

3 When ready to grill, brush and oil the grill grate. Place the plantain slices on the hot grate and grill until they are a dark, candied golden brown, 4 to 6 minutes per side.

4 Transfer the grilled plantains to a platter or plates and spoon the Mojo on top.

YIELD:
Serves 10 to 12

in sizzling oil to turn these jumbo cooking bananas into sweet, crusty mouthfuls of what might well be described as banana candy. Nothing? You guessed it, how about grilling? The high, dry heat caramelizes plant sugar as effectively as deep-frying—with much less fat. So consider this the healthy version of *maduros* (literally "ripe one"), a Spanish Caribbean classic.

METHOD:
Direct grilling

INGREDIENTS:
**5 to 6 very ripe plantains,
    unpeeled
About 1½ cups Mojo (page 259),
    for serving**

Hawaii

GRILLED PLANTAINS With Macadamia Nut and Garlic Butter

Plantains are also grown in Hawaii where they are eaten at every degree of ripeness—green (at which stage they taste starchy, like potatoes), yellow (the point at which they begin to taste fruity), and ripe to the point of blackness, when they have the honeyed sweetness of cooked bananas. In this recipe, the plantains are cut in half and grilled in their skins.

METHOD:
Direct grilling

INGREDIENTS:
6 tablespoons (¾ stick) salted butter
2 cloves garlic, thinly sliced
3 tablespoons coarsely chopped
   macadamia nuts
3 tablespoons chopped fresh
   cilantro or flat-leaf parsley
4 very ripe plantains, unpeeled

1 Melt the butter in a saucepan over medium-high heat. Add the garlic, macadamia nuts, and cilantro and cook until fragrant and the garlic and nuts are just beginning to brown, 3 to 6 minutes. Transfer the butter to a heatproof bowl and set aside.

2 Cut the ends off the plantains, then cut each plantain in half lengthwise. Lightly brush the cut sides of each half with some of the flavored butter.

3 Set up the grill for direct grilling (see page 21 for charcoal or gas) and preheat to high.

4 When ready to cook, brush and oil the grill grate. Place the plantains on the hot grate cut side down and grill until golden brown. Turn with tongs and grill until the peels are charred and the

plantain is soft, 4 to 6 minutes per side. Baste the plantains with a little more macadamia nut and garlic butter as they cook.

5 Transfer the grilled plantains to a platter or plates and pour the remaining macadamia nut garlic butter over them. Serve at once, telling everyone to eat the plantains out of the peels.

YIELD:
Serves 4

Dayton, Ohio

GRILLED FRENCH FRIES

Grill jockeys are an ingenious lot and few foods escape their fiery attentions. Not even french fries, as I learned at a book signing at Books & Co. in Dayton, Ohio. Whenever possible, I try to grill at these events, and my cookout drew Mike Kohl, a local barbecue buff and creator of this singular side dish. I always ask the audience what's the strangest thing they've ever grilled and Mike duly obliged with these fries. It's one more example of Raichlen's rule: If something tastes good baked, fried, sautéed, or steamed, chances are it will be even better grilled.

TIPS

■ I like to parboil the potatoes for french fries first, as raw spuds can be tricky to grill without burning. It also shortens the cooking time, so you can focus your attention on grilling the main dish.

■ Cutting potatoes into slabs, rather than like conventional fries, makes them less likely to fall through the bars of the grate.

METHOD:
Direct grilling

INGREDIENTS:

1½ pounds jumbo baking potatoes
   (2 to 3 potatoes)
Coarse salt (kosher or sea)
3 tablespoons extra-virgin olive oil
2 cloves garlic, finely chopped
2 tablespoons chopped fresh dill,
   or 2 teaspoons dried dill
1 teaspoon cracked black peppercorns
   (or to taste)

YOU'LL ALSO NEED:

1 cup wood chips or chunks (optional;
   preferably hickory), soaked for 1 hour
   in water to cover, then drained

Hand-cut fries at
Arthur Bryant's
in Kansas City.

1 Scrub the potatoes. Cut each one lengthwise into ½-inch-thick slices. Place the potatoes in a pot with cold salted water to cover and bring to a boil over high heat. Cook the potatoes until just tender, 4 to 6 minutes. Do not overcook. Drain the potatoes in a colander, rinse under cold water, and drain again. The recipe can be prepared up to this stage several hours ahead.

2 Blot the potatoes dry with paper towels and place in a bowl. Toss the potatoes with the olive oil. Add the garlic, dill, and pepper. Taste for seasoning, adding more pepper and salt to taste (lots), then toss to coat.

3 Set up the grill for direct grilling (see page 21 for gas or charcoal) and preheat to high. If using a gas grill, place all of the wood chips or chunks, if desired, in the smoker box or a smoker pouch (see page 24) and run the grill on high until you see smoke. If using a charcoal grill, preheat it to high, then toss all of the wood chips or chunks, if desired, on the coals.

4 When ready to cook, brush and oil the grill grate. Lay the potato slices on the hot grate so that they are perpendicular to the bars. Grill the potatoes until nicely browned on both sides, crisp on the outside and tender inside, 4 to 6 minutes per side, turning with tongs. Transfer the fries to a serving platter, season with salt and pepper, if necessary, and serve at once.

YIELD:
Serves 4

Idaho

BARBECUED BAKED POTATOES

Meat and potatoes are a long-standing tradition in the United States. Many places—Texas, Nebraska, Colorado, among them—vie for the title of best beef producer, but no one I know would dispute Idaho's supremacy when it comes to spuds. The Idaho potato is the very exemplar of the species: huge, flavorful, and when properly cooked, light—dare I even say, fluffy? (This may seem like an odd thing for a barbecue guy to obsess over, but the proof is in the tasting.) Like most Americans, I used to bake potatoes until I discovered the incredible depth of flavor that results when you smoke roast them on the grill. As for the topping, if you haven't tried a mixture of sour cream, butter, and barbecue sauce, then you haven't fully lived!

METHOD:
Indirect grilling

INGREDIENTS:

2 slices bacon, cut into ¼-inch slivers

4 baking potatoes (preferably Idaho, each 12 to 14 ounces)

Coarse salt (kosher or sea) and freshly ground black pepper

1 cup sour cream

½ cup of your favorite sweet smoky barbecue sauce, warm or at room temperature

4 tablespoons (½ stick) butter, cut into 4 pieces, at room temperature

2 tablespoons chopped fresh chives or scallion greens

YOU'LL ALSO NEED:

2 cups wood chips or chunks (preferably hickory), soaked for 1 hour in water to cover, then drained

1 Place the bacon in a small skillet over medium heat and fry until the fat renders and the bacon is crisp and lightly browned, 4 to 5 minutes. Drain the bacon in a strainer over a heatproof bowl and reserve the fat for brushing on the outside of the potatoes, if desired.

2 Prick each potato a half dozen times with a fork. Brush or rub the potatoes all over with the bacon fat, if desired, and season generously with salt and pepper.

3 Set up the grill for indirect grilling (see page 23 for gas or page 22 for charcoal) and preheat to medium-high. If using a gas grill, place all of the wood chips or chunks in the smoker box or in a smoker pouch (see page 24) and run the grill on high until you see smoke, then reduce the heat to medium-high. If using a charcoal grill, preheat it to medium-high, then toss all of the wood chips or chunks on the coals.

TIPS

For a crackling crisp skin, brush the outside of the potatoes with bacon fat before roasting.

You'll need a really big pit for this potato.

4 When ready to cook, place the potatoes in the center of the grate, away from the heat, and cover the grill. Cook the potatoes until cooked through, 1 to 1¼ hours. When done, the skins will be crisp and the potatoes squeezably soft. You should be able to pierce a potato easily with a metal skewer. If using a charcoal grill, after 1 hour you'll need to add 12 fresh coals to each side, if the potatoes are not done.

5 Transfer the grilled potatoes to a platter. Without breaking the skin, gently squeeze the potatoes all over to soften the flesh (wear gloves if you have heat-sensitive fingers). Cut an X in the top of each potato and squeeze the sides to open it up. Place a generous dollop of sour cream in each potato. Place a spoonful of barbecue sauce in the center of each dollop of sour cream. Place a pat of butter in the center of the barbecue sauce. Sprinkle the potatoes with the chives and the reserved bacon pieces.

YIELD:
Serves 4

VARIATION: I first tasted these potatoes cooked in a pit (a low-heat smoker) in Kansas City. But I like the fluffy consistency that results when you roast potatoes at the higher temperature you get on a grill. You can certainly feel free to cook them at a lower temperature—275°F—in a smoker. It will take 2 to 2½ hours.

San Antonio, Tex.

GRILLED-CORN MASHED POTATOES

Bruce Auden's voice is the last thing you'd expect to hear when you dial his restaurant in San Antonio. Although the British-born chef has spent most of his years in Texas, his English accent remains as heavy as that of an honor guard for the Queen. Auden's restaurant, Biga on the Banks, is equally cosmopolitan, fusing the foods and flavors of Texas with modern European cooking. The sleekly contemporary dining room would be at home in Manhattan. Auden can lobster and foie gras with the best of them, but what really grabbed my attention was his unique twist on a down-home favorite—mashed potatoes laced with grilled corn. The corn lends a smoky sweetness to commonplace mashed spuds, not to mention a brilliant contrast of textures. Here's how I imagine he makes it.

METHOD:
Direct grilling

INGREDIENTS:
3 ears sweet corn, shucked
1½ tablespoons extra-virgin olive oil or butter, melted

Coarse salt (kosher or sea) and freshly ground black pepper
2 pounds potatoes (preferably Yukon Gold), peeled
4 to 6 tablespoons (½ to ¾ stick) butter
About 6 tablespoons heavy (whipping) cream

YOU'LL ALSO NEED:
2 cups wood chips or chunks (optional; preferably oak or hickory), soaked for 1 hour in water to cover, then drained

1 Set up the grill for direct grilling (see page 21 for gas or charcoal) and preheat to high. If using a gas grill, place all of the wood chips or chunks, if desired, in the smoker box or in a smoker pouch (see page 24) and run the grill on high until you see smoke. If using a charcoal grill, preheat it to high, then toss all of the wood chips or chunks, if desired, on the coals.

2 When ready to cook, brush the corn with the olive oil and generously

TIPS

■ I always keep some grilled corn in my refrigerator to add to salads, soups, and sauces. If you're organized, you can grill the corn for this recipe at an earlier cookout. Just add the kernels to the mashed potatoes at the last minute.

■ For an even richer flavor, grill the corn over a wood fire (see page 20).

Chef Bruce Auden and private events director Penny Shea of Biga on the Banks.

season with salt and pepper. Place the ears of corn on the hot grate and grill until golden brown on all sides, 2 to 3 minutes per side (8 to 12 minutes in all), turning with tongs.

3 Transfer the grilled corn to a cutting board and let cool slightly. Cut the kernels off the cobs, using lengthwise strokes of a chef's knife. Set aside the corn cobs. The grilled corn can be refrigerated, covered, for up to 48 hours. Let the corn return to room temperature before proceeding with the recipe.

4 Cut the potatoes into 1-inch pieces, place them in a large saucepan, and add cold water to cover by 2 inches. Add the corn cobs and 1 teaspoon salt and gradually bring to a boil over medium-high heat. Reduce the heat to medium and let the potatoes simmer gently until very tender, 8 to 12 minutes. Use a metal skewer to test for doneness; the potatoes should be easy to pierce. Drain the potatoes well in a colander and discard the corn cobs.

5 Return the potatoes to the pan and cook over medium heat for a minute or so to evaporate any excess water. Using a potato masher, mash the potatoes, adding enough butter and cream so that they become soft and fluffy. (Don't purée the potatoes in a food processor or they will become gummy.) Stir in the corn kernels and season with salt and pepper to taste.

YIELD:
Serves 6

Vermont

MADEIRA GRILLED ACORN SQUASH

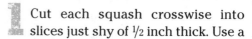

Autumn without squash is like, well, Thanksgiving without turkey. I created this recipe as an accompaniment for America's favorite holiday bird, and the handsome, golden, fluted squash rings look terrific nestled around it. But don't just make this recipe for Thanksgiving, because grilling is a delectable and highly novel way to prepare acorn squash. The Vermont inspiration for the recipe is obvious in the maple syrup. As for Madeira, it was a popular quaff in Colonial New England and its earthy sweetness makes a perfect foil for the squash.

METHOD:
Direct grilling

INGREDIENTS:
2 acorn squashes
4 tablespoons (1/2 stick) salted butter
1/4 cup maple syrup
1/4 cup Madeira
1/2 teaspoon ground cinnamon
Coarse salt (kosher or sea) and freshly ground black pepper, to taste

1 Cut each squash crosswise into slices just shy of 1/2 inch thick. Use a melon baller or paring knife to remove the seeds from the center of each ring. Place the squash rings on a baking sheet.

2 Melt the butter in a nonreactive saucepan over medium-high heat. Add the maple syrup, Madeira, and season with salt and cinnamon, pepper to taste, and let boil until syrupy, 3 to 6 minutes. Brush some of the maple butter mixture on the tops of the squash rings.

3 Set up the grill for direct grilling using a two-zone fire (see page 22 for gas or charcoal) and preheat one zone to high and the other to medium. If using a gas grill, place all of the wood chips or chunks in the smoker box or in a smoker pouch (see page 24) and run the grill on high until you see smoke, then lower one burner to medium. If using a charcoal grill, preheat one zone to high and the other to medium, then toss all of the wood chips or chunks on the coals.

4 When ready to cook, place the squash rings on the hot grate, brushed side down. Grill the squash until golden brown and tender, 4 to 6 minutes per side, basting both sides with some of the maple butter mixture. Transfer the grilled squash to a platter or plates and drizzle any remaining maple butter mixture on top.

YIELD:

Serves 6 to 8

TIPS

■ The secret to grilling a dense dry vegetable like squash is to work over a moderate fire. I usually build a medium-hot fire, but keep a second cooler safety zone, where I can move the squash if it starts to burn.

■ If you're feeling fancy, you can rotate the squash rings a quarter turn as they grill to create an attractive crosshatch of grill marks.

SONNY BRYAN'S SMOKEHOUSE

**THE ORIGINAL
SONNY BRYAN'S
SMOKEHOUSE**

2202 Inwood Road
Dallas, Texas
(214) 357-7120
www.sonnybryanbbq.com

First, the good news about Sonny Bryan's Smokehouse. If you land at Love Field airport in Dallas (a much easier airport to use than Dallas–Fort Worth), you can be at Sonny Bryan's in five minutes. That's enough time to chow down on some of the most justly famous barbecue in Texas before you catch your next flight.

Now the bad news. Unless, you arrive before 1:00 P.M., the restaurant will likely be closed. That's because this, the original Sonny Bryan's, stays open only as long as it takes to sell out of the thirty or so beef briskets they cook daily. And given the popularity of Bryan's brisket—the brisket is usually gone by 1:00 P.M.

In a state known for its barbecue, Sonny Bryan remains one of the most legendary pit masters, a man who served moguls and movie stars (but only when he felt like it), who once carved 250 briskets in a single day. (There were three things Sonny always insisted on doing himself: carving the brisket, cleaning the rest rooms, and carrying the money to the bank.) In the thirty-one years Sonny ran his barbecue stand on Inwood Road in Dallas, he acquired an international following for his brisket.

I never met Sonny, who retired in 1989 and died a few years later. But the staff speaks of him so vividly, I feel I practically know him. I see him as people did in the early 1960s when the black-and-white photograph in the restaurant was taken, a crisp white paper cap on his head, smile lines crinkling at the corners of his eyes, proudly holding a brisket.

That brisket is still awesome stuff—smoky as a fireplace, succulent as stew, and tender enough to pull apart with your fingers. The sauce comes in a beer bottle. It's tomatoey and tart with vinegar—not in the least bit sweet. That's real smoke flavor you taste: The sauce is actually cooked in the pit, as are the tangy baked beans.

Sonny Bryan with one of his legendary briskets.

IN HIS GENES

Sonny acquired his love and knowledge of barbecue from his grandfather Elijah, who opened a restaurant in the Oak Cliff district of Dallas in 1910 (the horseshoe that hung in Elijah's can now be seen in Sonny Bryan's). His father, Red Bryan, followed suit in 1935. In 1957, the community of Oak Cliff decided to ban the sale of alcohol. "I can't serve barbecue without beer," said Sonny, so he left Oak Cliff to open a barbecue joint on Inwood Road, in what was then a distant suburb of Dallas.

The original Sonny's wasn't much to look at (well, it still isn't): a rough-and-tumble, beige, one-story, cinder block building located next door to a Salvation Army thrift center. The location—a short hop from the Central Freight Lines Terminal—was a fortuitous one. At 7:00 A.M., freight handlers and truckers finishing the graveyard shift would crowd Sonny's parking lot for barbecued brisket. Business was good—so good, Sonny could afford to close by 2:00 P.M. Soon Mercedes were parked side by side the pickup trucks and 18-wheelers.

Somewhere along the line, Sonny installed a dining area with a row of windows and twenty ancient wooden school desks. Seating is very much a matter of first come, first served, as celebrities have learned to their consternation. A few years back, two stretch limos arrived at Sonny's and a man came in and said, "I have Sylvester Stallone in the car; I need twenty seats." Sonny looked over and said "You're welcome to wait for 'em or eat in a parking lot. I can't ask my regular customers to move." Stallone ate barbecue elsewhere.

THE RIGHT MAN FOR THE JOB

Sonny's current manager, Mike DeMaster, certainly has the right pedigree for a pit master. He was born in Tennessee and raised in Texas. And he looks the part, too, from his magisterial sideburns and handlebar mustache to the silver tips of his cowboy boots. Mike explains that the restaurant's pit, which Sonny designed himself, has burned every single day for the last forty years. Its doors are black with smoke. "I guess it's about seasoned," he observes.

Mike pulls one of the sliding metal grate drawers open and throws in a brisket. The restaurant uses whole ones with the "hump" (a layer of fat) and "deckel" (a fibrous, fatty portion) attached— 18 pounds of tough, fatty, exceptionally flavorful beef. For the next ten to twelve hours, the meat will smoke over smoldering Oklahoma hickory logs. "Here's our temperature control," quips Mike, pointing to a cup and a bucket of cold water. (The "fire suppression system" is an equally rudimentary rig consisting of a garden hose and a ladder.)

Briskets aren't the only thing Mike smokes in this remarkable pit: There are jalapeño sausages and St. Louis–style ribs (served with cloth napkins, no less). Even the baked beans and barbecue sauce come out of the pit. To round out the meal, there's another of Sonny's specialties: hand-cut, inch-thick onion rings.

When Sonny retired, selling his recipes and restaurant to a group of investors, the inevitable expansion followed. I've eaten at some of the new branches, but whenever I'm in Dallas, you'll find me at the original Sonny Bryan's for brisket made with forty years of smoke and dedication.

Sides from

Barbecue without baked beans is something like smoke without fire. But as with so much in American barbecue, baked beans are highly regional: What you get when you order them depends on where you are. In the Northeast and the South, baked beans come thick and sweet, loaded with brown sugar and molasses, while in Texas they come smoky and hot, with bacon and jalapeño peppers. If you live in southern California—especially the Santa Maria Valley— the bean in question is the small red pinquito bean from Mexico, stewed with the local version of salsa. This chapter focuses on beans and other side dishes that are almost meals in themselves—dirty rice, grilled grits, grilled polenta, flame-charred macaroni and cheese, and barbecue (yes, barbecue) spaghetti. For true barbecue junkies, side dishes aren't confined to the sidelines.

the Grill

TIPS

For an interesting variation on the glaze for the apples, substitute Coca-Cola or another soft drink for the apple cider.

New Hampshire

APPLE "STEAKS"

Baked and sautéed apples are the traditional accompaniment to pork in New Hampshire and throughout New England. And, as you well know, I'll try putting just about anything on the grill. So, figuring that apples were fair game I sliced up some Granny Smiths (admittedly not a traditional New England apple, but crisper and firmer and thus more likely to hold up to live fire) and tossed them on the grill grate. For a glaze, I boiled down apple cider, lemon juice, and honey. I call the results apple "steaks"—the griller's answer to an apple a day.

METHOD:
Direct grilling

INGREDIENTS:
- 1/2 cup apple cider
- 2 tablespoons honey
- 2 tablespoons fresh lemon juice
- 2 tablespoons salted butter
- 4 medium-size or 3 large Granny Smith apples
- 1/2 lemon

1 Place the cider, honey, lemon juice, and butter in a heavy nonreactive saucepan over high heat and bring to a boil. Let boil until thick, syrupy, and reduced by about one third, 6 to 10 minutes. Set the glaze aside.

2 Set up the grill for direct grilling (see page 21 for charcoal or gas) and preheat to high.

3 Cut the apples crosswise into 1/2-inch-thick round slices. Don't worry about the core—people will eat around it and the seeds add a rustic charm. Rub both sides of each apple slice with the cut side of the lemon to prevent discoloration.

4 When ready to cook, brush and oil the grill grate. Place the apple slices on the hot grate and grill until nicely browned and semisoft, 3 to 5 minutes per side. Rotate each slice a quarter turn after 1 1/2 minutes to create an attractive crosshatch of grill marks.

An apple for the grill master.

Baste both sides of the apple slices with some of the cider glaze as they grill.

5 Transfer the grilled apple slices to a platter or plates. Drizzle any remaining cider glaze over them and serve at once.

YIELD:
Serves 6 to 8

New England

A NEW BAKED APPLE
Stuffed with Sausage and Sage

Here's a dish with deep Yankee roots, but I'll wager no one has ever tasted its like before. The break with tradition is stuffing the apples with pork sausage and smoke roasting them on the grill. Like any true smoke-o-holic, I'm always looking for barbecue you can serve for breakfast, and this recipe fits the bill to a T. Of course, it's not half bad for lunch or supper or as a robust side dish with barbecued pork.

METHOD:
Indirect grilling

INGREDIENTS:

3 tablespoons butter

1 small onion, finely chopped

1 rib celery, finely chopped

12 ounces plain bulk pork sausage

1/2 teaspoon ground sage, or 4 fresh sage leaves, minced

Coarse salt (kosher or sea) and freshly ground black pepper

3 to 4 tablespoons maple syrup

8 large apples (see Note)

YOU'LL ALSO NEED:

1 cup wood chips (preferably apple or maple), soaked 1 hour in apple cider or water to cover, then drained

1 Melt 1 tablespoon of the butter in a large skillet over medium heat. Add the onion and celery and cook until golden brown, about 4 minutes. Add the sausage and sage, increase the heat to high, and cook, breaking up the meat with a wooden spoon, until the pork is lightly browned, 6 to 10 minutes. Season with salt and pepper to taste. Transfer the stuffing to a strainer set over a heatproof bowl to drain off the excess fat, reserving the fat for basting. If you want to assemble the apples ahead of time, let the stuffing cool to room temperature first.

2 Using a melon baller and starting at the stem end, remove the core from each apple to create a large cavity. Don't cut all the way through to the bottom. Spoon the stuffing into the apples, dividing it evenly among them and pressing it in firmly. Pour a

TIPS

The best tool for hollowing out an apple is a melon baller, which is available at cookware shops and many hardware stores.

WALL OF FLAME

OKLAHOMA JOE'S BARBECUE

Talk about satisfying the basic human needs! Oklahoma Joe's is a world-class barbecue joint located in a gas station. The all encompassing menu includes Missouri-style ribs, North Carolina–style pulled pork, and smoky Oklahoma-style brisket.

3002 West 47th Avenue
Kansas City, Kansas
(913) 722-3366

little of the maple syrup over the stuffing in each apple. Place a small piece of the remaining 2 tablespoons butter on top of each apple. Brush the sides of the apples with the reserved sausage fat. The apples can be prepared several hours ahead to this stage; cover them with plastic wrap and refrigerate.

3 Set up the grill for indirect grilling (see page 23 for gas or page 22 for charcoal) and preheat to medium. If using a gas grill, place all of the wood chips or chunks in the smoker box or in a smoker pouch (see page 24) and run the grill on high until you see smoke, then reduce the heat to medium. If using a charcoal grill, place a large drip pan in the center, preheat the grill to medium, then toss all of the wood chips or chunks on the coals.

4 When ready to cook, place the stuffed apples in the center of the hot grate, over the drip pan and away from the heat, and cover the grill. Cook the apples until soft, 40 to 60 minutes. Transfer the grilled apples to a platter or plates and serve at once.

YIELD:
Serves 4

NOTE: The traditional apple of New England is the McIntosh, but you can use anything here from a Cortland to a Granny Smith.

Oklahoma

BEST BARBECUED BEANS ON THE PLANET

Inventor, restaurateur, rub manufacturer, and winner of barbecue contests too numerous to mention, "Oklahoma" Joe Davidson isn't given to false modesty. So when the Oklahoma pit master proclaims these to be the "best barbecued beans on the planet," you'd best sit up and take notice. Joe's secret is to start with a mix of beans— baked, red, and black—then cook them in a smoker. Enriching the beans with a pound of chopped smoked brisket doesn't hurt either! I've tinkered with Joe's recipe a little, but I think you'll find that these live up to their name.

METHOD:
Indirect grilling

INGREDIENTS:
1 pound smoked brisket or bacon, cut into ¼-inch slivers
1 can (15 ounces) black beans
1 can (15 ounces) dark red kidney beans
3 cans (each 15 ounces) baked beans or pork and beans
1 large sweet onion, finely chopped
1 red bell pepper, cored, seeded, and finely chopped

1 poblano pepper or green bell pepper,
   seeded and finely chopped

4 cloves garlic, minced

3 to 6 jalapeño peppers, seeded and
   diced (for hotter beans,
   leave the seeds in)

2 cups sweet red barbecue sauce
   such as St. Louis Red (page 666),
   or your favorite commercial brand

1½ cups firmly packed light
   brown sugar, or more
   to taste

½ cup Dijon mustard, or more
   to taste

2 teaspoons liquid smoke
   (optional; see Note)

Coarse salt (kosher or sea) and
   freshly ground black pepper

YOU'LL ALSO NEED:

1 large (turkey-size) or 2 medium-size
   aluminum foil pans; 2 cups wood
   chips or chunks (preferably pecan
   or hickory) soaked for 1 hour
   in water to cover, then drained

1 If using bacon instead of brisket, place it in a large skillet over medium heat and fry until crisp and golden brown, about 5 minutes. Pour off all the bacon fat, saving a few tablespoons for the beans, if desired.

2 Empty the cans of black and kidney beans into a colander and drain. Rinse the beans under cold running water and drain again. Place all the beans in a large nonreactive mixing bowl and add the onion, bell and poblano peppers, garlic, and jalapeños and stir to mix. Add the barbecue sauce, brown sugar, mus-tard, liquid smoke, if using, and brisket or fried bacon and stir to mix. Taste for seasoning, adding more brown sugar and/or mustard as necessary, and salt and black pepper to taste; the beans should be very flavorful. Transfer the bean mixture to the aluminum foil pan or pans. (If you used bacon, you can drizzle a few tablespoons bacon fat over the beans for extra flavor.)

3 Set up the grill for indirect grilling (see page 23 for gas or page 22 for charcoal) and preheat to medium-low. If using a gas grill, place all of the wood chips or chunks in the smoker box or in a smoker pouch (see page 24) and run the grill on high until you see smoke, then reduce the heat to medium-low. If using a charcoal grill, preheat it to medium-low, then toss all of the wood chips or chunks on the coals.

4 When ready to cook, place the pan of beans in the center of the hot grate, away from the heat, and cover the grill. Cook the beans until they are thick and richly flavored, about 1 hour. If the beans start to dry out, cover them loosely with aluminum foil. Remove the beans from the grill and let them rest for 15 minutes, then serve.

YIELD:

Serves 12 to 16

NOTE: If you cook the beans in a gas grill, you probably won't be able to generate enough smoke for a strong wood flavor. Add the liquid smoke in this case.

TIPS

Guys like Joe Davidson always manage to have some extra smoked brisket on hand. I've made this recipe using crumbled fried bacon instead, with equally excellent results.

The Original
BAKED BEANS

You'll find beanhole festivals throughout New England, especially New Hampshire and Maine, and Quebec. Check with the local chamber of commerce. Civic organizations and churches are often likely sponsors for beanhole bean festivals.

There is one thing that had to be made clear before George Flanders would agree to talk to me: "We don't let the recipe out to nobody." The Epsom, New Hampshire, truck driver's beanhole beans are New England's answer to barbecue—beans slowly roasted in a log-fired hole in the ground that any barbecue buff would recognize as a pit. This is in keeping with a venerable New England tradition; beans have been pit roasted for many more years than they've been baked in crocks in the oven.

It goes back to the American Indians, who grew many varieties of beans and cooked them in stone-lined, fire-heated pits, adding maple sap for sweetness and bear fat to keep them moist. The Colonists added their own touches, substituting salt pork for the bear fat and molasses for the maple sap. Lumberjacks in New England and Quebec found pit-cooked beans ideally suited to their work schedules. They would bury pots on their way into the forest and feast on the baked beans several days later on their way back home.

Beans are in Flanders' blood: "When I was growing up, we'd have beans every Saturday night; one week pea beans, one week kidney beans." His family grew their own beans and dried them on the floor of the barn. "Lots of beans can be baked," Flanders explains, "navy beans, pea beans, soldier beans, Jacob's Cattle, and 'yeller eyes.'" (Those last take their name from their brown spots with yellowish centers.)

To make beanhole beans for a feast, Flanders picks through hundreds of beans one by one, discarding those that are shriveled, as well as bits of twig and pebbles. The beans soak in water overnight; this doubles their weight and bulk. The next ingredient is salt pork, and Flanders is mighty particular about what kind he uses. "The store-bought kind ain't worth heck," he warns. "We get bellies from old pigs and put the salt to 'em ourselves." (George uses two and a half pounds of coarse crystal salt for each pound of pork.) "I don't sell it, but if you ask me real nice, I just might give you a piece," he says.

THE BEAN HOLE

When he's ready to start cooking, Flanders inspects the bean hole. You have to plow back six

Baked beans—thick, sweet, and smoky—no barbecue is complete without them.

"The worse the sauce tastes, the better the beans will be."

inches of dirt and pull off a thick metal plate to find his pit, which is eight feet long, four feet wide, and four feet deep. It's lined with the sort of stones that New Hampshire farmers cleared from their fields and piled up to make fences. "You need weather-cured rocks for lining the pit," George explains. "Cinder blocks would just crumble with the intense heat."

Volunteers split and stack firewood. Most of the wood is put into the pit and ignited to create an enormous bonfire. What's left will stoke a fire to boil the beans before they're buried. It takes a full cord of wood to make a beanhole bean supper for the sizable crowd. Sizable is the operative word here. Flanders' beanhole bean feasts typically draw hundreds and hundreds of people.

The beans are parboiled in a 275-gallon oil tank. At the same time, Flanders makes the sauce, the main ingredients of which are mustard, molasses, and brown sugar. "The worse the sauce tastes, the better the beans will be," Flanders says. "If it don't make you pucker, it ain't worth a darn." An ocean of tears is shed over the fifty pounds of onions that go into each batch of beans.

THE BEAN POT

The traditional vessel for cooking the beans is a bean pot—fifty pounds of cast iron forged into a rotund vessel. Most bean pots in use today were made in the 1800s. Flanders lines his pots with salt pork and loads them with beans, sauce, and onions. A thick layer of salt pork goes on top. The salt pork will keep the beans from burning. Each batch of beans is "baptized" with a bottle of beer. Once the covers are snugly fit into place, the pots are lowered on chains onto the glowing embers of the pit. After the metal plate is slid back in place, dirt is shoveled over the hole. The beans will cook undisturbed for the next fifteen hours.

THE BEANS

At noon the next day, Flanders and his many friends clear away the dirt and haul the bean pots up from the pit. They put the pots on truck wheel rims that are set on top of tires. When the heavy lids are lifted off, the air fills with the fragrance of slow-cooked beans and salt pork, mustard and molasses, onions, and spices. You may not find barbecue in these northern parts, but I can't think of a better accompaniment for true 'que than traditional New England beanhole beans.

"If it don't make you pucker, it ain't worth a darn."

George Flanders

Maine & N.H.

BEANHOLE BEANS

Baked beans are an indispensable part of the barbecue tradition in the United States, yet they come from a part of the country that lies well outside the barbecue belt—indeed, from a place where barbecued ribs and brisket were virtually unknown until the middle of the twentieth century. Back around the time Virginians were roasting whole hogs over hickory-fired pits, New England and French Canadian lumberjacks would cook

Beanhole beans hot out of the pot.

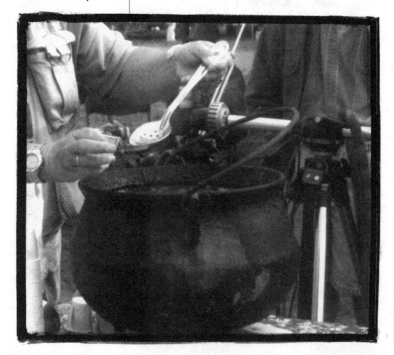

beans in huge cast-iron pots in wood-fired holes in the ground. Today, they're known as beanhole beans and, if you travel through the backwoods of New England in the summer, you may just be lucky enough to stumble on a beanhole bean feast. A lot of American pit masters make baked beans—and make good ones—usually starting with canned baked beans, which they doctor with sauces and sometimes smoke in the pit. If you're feeling ambitious, here's the granddaddy of all baked beans, made from scratch and cooked in a Dutch oven. The Hurried-Up Beanhole Beans that follow features the same molasses and mustard seasonings but are made with canned beans. Either way, you'll get highly superior beans.

METHOD:
Indirect grilling

ADVANCE PREPARATION:
4 to 12 hours for soaking the beans

INGREDIENTS:
1 pound dried yellow-eyed peas or other dried beans
10 slices thick-sliced bacon (about 10 ounces; see Notes), 4 slices cut into 1/4-inch slivers, 6 left whole
1 large onion, finely chopped
1 green bell pepper, finely chopped
2 cloves garlic, minced
1/2 cup molasses
1/2 cup ketchup
1/3 cup firmly packed brown sugar, or more to taste
6 tablespoons Dijon mustard, or more to taste

1 tablespoon Tabasco sauce
    (optional)
2 teaspoons liquid smoke
    (optional; see Notes)
Coarse salt (kosher or sea) and
    freshly ground black pepper
1/4 teaspoon ground cloves
1 cup beer

YOU'LL ALSO NEED:

A Dutch oven (10 to 12 inches across
    and 6 inches deep; see Notes)
    or heavy heatproof metal pot
    with a lid (like Le Creuset)
    or a ceramic bean pot;
    1 1/2 cups wood chips
    or chunks (preferably hickory),
    soaked for 1 hour in water
    to cover, then drained

1 Spread the beans out on a rimmed baking sheet and pick through them, discarding any foreign matter, such as pebbles or twigs. Place the beans in a colander and rinse them under cold running water; then place them in a large bowl and add water to cover by 4 inches. Let the beans soak in the refrigerator for at least 4 hours or as long as overnight.

2 Drain the soaked beans in a colander and place them in a large pot. Add water to cover by 4 inches and bring to a boil over high heat. Skim off any foam that rises to the surface, then reduce the heat to medium and cover the pot. Let the beans simmer until the beans are tender, 1 1/4 to 1 3/4 hours. When done, you should be able to crush a bean easily between your thumb and forefinger. Drain the beans well, reserving 2 cups of the bean-cooking liquid.

3 Place the drained beans in a large bowl. Stir in the bacon slivers, onion, bell pepper, garlic, molasses, ketchup, brown sugar, mustard, Tabasco sauce, liquid smoke, if using, and cloves. Taste for seasoning, adding more brown sugar and/or mustard as necessary and salt and pepper to taste; the beans should be highly seasoned. Add the beer and enough bean-cooking liquid to cover the beans by 1 inch. Place 3 of the whole bacon slices on the bottom of the Dutch oven. Spoon in the beans and arrange the remaining 3 bacon slices over the top. Cover the pot.

4 Set up the grill for indirect grilling (see page 22 for charcoal or page 23 for gas) and preheat to medium-low.

5 When ready to cook, place the Dutch oven in the center of the hot grate, away from the heat, and cover the grill. Cook the beans for 1 hour.

6 Uncover the pot and check to see that the beans are not starting to dry out. If they are, add some of the reserved bean-cooking liquid. Leave the beans uncovered. If using a charcoal grill, toss all of the wood chips or chunks on the coals and cover the grill. If using a gas grill, place all of the wood chips or chunks in the smoker box or in a smoker pouch and run the grill on high until you see smoke, then reduce the heat to medium and cover the grill. Continue cooking the beans until the juices are thick and the beans are very tender, 30 minutes to 1 hour longer. When the beans are done, they'll be soft, sweet, dark, rich and moist, but not soupy. If using a charcoal grill, after

TIPS

The first choice for a bean here is the yellow-eyed pea, a small bean with a brownish splotch on the side with a small yellowish center. One of a number of heirloom varieties from New England, the yellow-eye is thought to have been the original bean for baked beans. Soldier beans and Jacob's Cattle beans are also traditionally used to make beanhole beans, but you can use the more common-place navy beans or pea beans. (For a source for yellow-eyed peas, see Mail-Order Sources on page 742.)

1 hour you'll need to add 12 fresh coals to each side. You're probably planning to serve the beans within a few hours of making them, but leftovers also taste great. They can be refrigerated, covered, for up to 1 week. Reheat before serving.

YIELD:
Serves 6 to 8

NOTES:

■ New Englanders would use salt pork, but I like the added smoky richness of slab bacon.

■ Add the liquid smoke to the beans only if you are not using wood chips or chunks on your fire.

■ The traditional pot for beanhole beans, is a Dutch oven—a heavy cast-iron pot. Dutch ovens are available from cast-iron manufacturers such as Lodge Cast Iron in Tennessee (see Mail-Order Sources, page 742).

Hurried-Up Beanhole Beans

Don't have time to wait for dried beans to become tender? Here's a speeded-up version of beanhole beans for the pit master who has more taste than time.

METHOD:
Indirect grilling

INGREDIENTS:

2 cans (15 ounces each) yellow-eyed,
 navy, or great Northern beans
8 slices bacon (about 6 ounces),
 4 slices cut into 1/4-inch slivers,
 4 left whole
1 medium-size onion, chopped
1/3 cup molasses
1/3 cup ketchup
3 tablespoons honey
1 tablespoon Dijon mustard
2 teaspoons Tabasco sauce
 (optional)
1/2 teaspoon liquid smoke
 (optional; see Note)
1/4 teaspoon ground cloves
Coarse salt (kosher or sea) and
 freshly ground black pepper

YOU'LL ALSO NEED:

An 8-by-12-inch aluminum foil pan;
 2 cups wood chips or chunks
 (optional; preferably hickory),
 soaked for 1 hour in water to cover,
 then drained

1 Empty the cans of beans into a colander and drain. Rinse the beans under cold running water and drain again.

2 Place the bacon slivers and onion in a large skillet over medium heat and fry until both are golden brown, about 5 minutes. Pour off all but 2 tablespoons of the fat. If desired, set aside the bacon fat for another use.

3 Add the rinsed beans, molasses, ketchup, honey, mustard, Tabasco sauce and liquid smoke, if using, and cloves to the skillet and stir to mix. Season to taste with salt if needed and with pepper (canned beans are already quite salty, so you shouldn't need to add much salt). Place 2 slices of the bacon on the bottom of the aluminum foil pan. Spoon in the bean mixture and place 2 slices of bacon on top.

4 Set up the grill for indirect grilling (see page 23 for gas or page 22 for charcoal) and preheat to medium. If using a gas grill, place all of the wood chips or chunks, if desired, in the smoker box or in a smoker pouch (see page 24) and run the grill on high until you see smoke, then reduce the heat to medium. If using a charcoal grill, preheat it to medium, then toss all of the wood chips or chunks, if desired, on the coals.

5 When ready to cook, place the beans in the center of the hot grate, away from the heat, and cover the grill. Cook the beans until dark, thick, and rich, about 1 hour. If the beans start to dry out, cover them loosely with aluminum foil. Serve at once.

YIELD:
Serves 6 to 8

NOTE: Use the liquid smoke only if you are not using wood chips or chunks.

VARIATION: If you don't want to fire up your grill, you can also bake the beans in a 350°F oven for 30 to 40 minutes.

A Maine Logging Camp. The Cook at the "Bean-hole."

Maine logging camp—the cook at the bean hole.

West Virginia

ALLEGHENY MOUNTAIN BROWN BEANS
With Ham Hocks

Barbecue and baked beans go together like ham and eggs, but what kind of beans you're served, like barbecue itself, varies widely from region to region. The sweet molasses-y baked beans of New England and the American South give way to *charros* (Mexican-style stewed pinto beans) in Texas, for example, or pinquito beans in southern California. And a West Virginia pig pickin' just isn't complete without boiled brown beans made smoky with ham hocks.

T I P S

You get the best results if you cook dry pinto beans from scratch with ham hocks, which is what I've called for here. Soaking shortens the cooking time. For the quickest cooking time, cook dry beans in a pressure cooker for 30 to 40 minutes.

Barbecue and baked beans go together

ADVANCE PREPARATION:
4 to 12 hours for soaking the beans

INGREDIENTS:
1 pound dried pinto beans
1 whole clove
1 bay leaf
1 medium-size onion, peeled and quartered
1 large ham hock or 2 small ham hocks
Coarse salt (kosher or sea) and freshly ground black pepper

1 Spread the beans out on a rimmed baking sheet and pick through them, discarding any foreign matter, such as pebbles or twigs. Place the beans in a colander and rinse them under cold running water; then place them in a large bowl and add water to cover by 4 inches. Let the beans soak in the refrigerator for at least 4 hours or as long as overnight.

2 Drain the soaked beans in a colander and place them in a large pot. Use the clove to pin the bay leaf to one of the onion quarters. Add it to the pot along with the remaining onion quarters and the ham hock(s). Add water to cover by 4 inches and bring to a boil over high heat. Skim off any foam that rises to the surface. Reduce the heat to medium, cover the pot, and let the beans simmer gently until tender, about 1 hour. Check the beans after 45 minutes and add or ladle off water as needed; the beans should be moist, even wet, but not soupy.

3 Using a slotted spoon, fish out and discard the onion quarters and bay leaf. Lift out the ham hock(s), transfer to a cutting board, and let cool. When cool enough to handle, cut the meat off the bones, discarding the bones and skin. Finely chop the meat and add it to the beans. Season with salt and pepper to taste and serve hot.

YIELD:
Serves 6 to 8

Quick Brown Beans

Here's a quick version of Allegheny Mountain Brown Beans, made using canned pinto beans and bacon. It's best when made with low-sodium beans.

INGREDIENTS:
1 can (15 ounces) pinto beans
1 tablespoon vegetable oil or butter
3 slices bacon, cut into ¼-inch slivers
1 medium-size onion, finely chopped
Coarse salt (kosher or sea) and freshly ground black pepper

1 Empty the can of beans into a colander and drain. Rinse the beans under cold running water and drain again.

like ham and eggs.

2 Heat the oil in a large skillet over medium heat. Add the bacon and onion and cook, stirring occasionally with a wooden spoon, until lightly browned, 4 to 6 minutes. Pour off all but 2 tablespoons of the bacon fat. If desired, save the bacon fat for another use.

3 Stir in the beans and about ¾ cup of water. Let the beans simmer until they are moist but no longer soupy, about 10 minutes. Season to taste with salt if needed and with pepper.

YIELD:
Serves 4

Texas

CHARROS (Tex-Mex Beans)

Texas-style brisket without *charros* is a little like a cowboy without a Stetson hat or spurs. These soulful, spicy pinto beans turn up wherever briskets are roasted to smoky perfection or *cabritos* (baby goats) come off the turnspit crackling crisp. Native to northern Mexico, *charros* have become essential to Texas barbecue. But unlike the sweet baked beans served with Southern-style barbecue, *charros* contain not a grain of sugar—which makes them the perfect accompaniment for central Texas–style beef. The recipe here offers a tongue-tingling blast of bacon, garlic, tomato, and chiles (a quick version follows on page 641). Don't be surprised by the consistency of the beans: *Charros* are always served with lots of flavorful broth.

ADVANCE PREPARATION:
4 to 12 hours for soaking the beans

INGREDIENTS:
1 pound (2 cups) dried pinto beans
2 whole cloves
2 bay leaves
2 medium-size onions, 1 peeled and cut in half, the other finely chopped
Coarse salt (kosher or sea) and freshly ground black pepper
1 tablespoon vegetable oil or butter
3 slices bacon, cut into ¼-inch slivers
2 cloves garlic, finely chopped
1 medium-size tomato, seeded and finely chopped
2 to 4 jalapeño peppers, seeded and diced (for hotter charros, leave the seeds in)
¼ cup chopped fresh cilantro

1 Spread the beans out on a rimmed baking sheet and pick through them, discarding any foreign matter, such as pebbles or twigs. Place the beans in a colander and rinse them under cold running water; then place

TIPS

The purist will want to start with dry pinto beans and cook them from scratch. Not only does this give you the satisfaction of doing the job right, but you can also control the amount of sodium (most canned beans are off the chart in salt content) and you get a wonderful bean broth. But for those who don't have the time to cook dried beans, I also offer a highly tasty version of *charros* made with canned beans.

Pick through the beans to remove any pebbles or twigs.

WALL OF FLAME

SAM'S IN AUSTIN

Smoky chicken, two-fisted size ribs, and crusty briskets with shocking pink smoke rings—just about any time the barbecue itch strikes you, Sam's is open to scratch it, serving until 2:30 A.M. Sunday through Thursday and until 4 A.M. Friday and Saturday.

2000 East 12 Street
Austin, Texas
(512) 478-0378

them in a large bowl and add water to cover by 4 inches. Let the beans soak in the refrigerator for at least 4 hours or as long as overnight.

2 Drain the soaked beans in a colander, and place them in a large pot. Add water to cover by 4 inches. Use the cloves to pin the bay leaves to the onion halves and add these to the beans. Bring the beans to a boil over high heat. Skim off any foam that rises to the surface, then reduce the heat to medium and cover the pot. Let the beans simmer gently until tender, about 1 hour. When done, you should be able to crush a bean easily between your thumb and forefinger. Pour off some of the cooking liquid, if necessary, so that the beans are covered with 2 to 3 inches of liquid. Season with salt and pepper to taste.

3 Heat the oil in a skillet over medium heat. Add the bacon and cook until lightly browned, about 3 minutes. Add the chopped onion and garlic and cook until golden brown, 3 to 4 minutes. Add the tomato, jalapeños, and cilantro and cook until the tomato juices have evaporated, about 3 minutes. Remove the onion halves with the bay leaves and cloves from the beans and discard them, then stir the bacon mixture into the beans and let simmer for 10 minutes. Taste for seasoning, adding more salt and/or pepper as necessary; the beans should be highly seasoned. Serve the *charros* in small bowls to hold the broth.

YIELD:
Serves 6 to 8

30-Minute Charros

If you are making the charros with canned beans, it is best to use a low-sodium variety. Look for them at a natural foods store.

INGREDIENTS:

2 cans (15 ounces each) pinto beans
    (preferably low sodium)
2 cups chicken or veal stock
    (preferably homemade)
1 tablespoon vegetable oil or butter
3 slices bacon, cut into ¼-inch slivers
1 medium-size onion, finely chopped
2 cloves garlic, finely chopped
1 medium-size tomato, seeded and
    finely chopped
2 to 4 jalapeño peppers, seeded and
    finely chopped (for hotter charros,
    leave the seeds in)
¼ cup chopped fresh cilantro

1 Empty the cans of beans into a colander and drain. Rinse the beans under cold running water and drain again. Transfer the beans to a pot, add the stock, and bring to a simmer over medium heat. Let the beans simmer for 5 minutes.

2 Heat the oil in a skillet over medium heat. Add the bacon and cook until lightly browned, about 3 minutes. Add the onion and garlic and cook until golden brown, 3 to 4 minutes. Add the tomato, jalapeños, and cilantro and cook until the tomato juices have evaporated, about 3 minutes.

3 Stir bacon mixture into the beans and let simmer for 10 minutes. Taste for seasoning, adding more salt and/or pepper as necessary; the beans should be highly seasoned. Serve the *charros* in small bowls to hold the broth.

YIELD:
Serves 6 to 8

Santa Maria, Calif.

SANTA MARIA PINQUITO BEANS

The beans they cook in Santa Maria are a lot different from the baked beans that most Americans associate with barbecues. For starters, they're made with the unique small, pinkish red pinquito bean, which has a rich, earthy flavor (this bean may attest to the Mexican heritage of many of Santa Maria's first farm hands). And Santa Maria beans are a lot less sweet than the baked beans served in Kansas City or the South—the result of using tomato and chile sauce instead of ketchup and keeping the sugar to a minimum. If you don't live in the area, you'll have to order pinquito beans by mail (see page 742 for a source); they grow only in the Santa Maria Valley.

TIPS

To speed up the cooking process and produce beans that are always tender, you can use a pressure cooker to cook the tiny pinquitos. You'll need fifteen to twenty minutes.

WALL OF FLAME

SHORTY'S

At Shorty's, ribs and chicken are slow smoked over hickory, then flash grilled just before serving. There are two sauces: a thick, sweet molasses-based one and a sharp, gritty vinegar sauce. The baked beans are enriched with plenty of chopped smoked pork and the corn on the cob is soft, sweet, and buttery enough to give you a coronary. I should know: This is my home town hangout.

9200 South Dixie Hwy.
Miami, Florida
(305) 670-7732
And other locations

ADVANCE PREPARATION:
4 to 12 hours for soaking the beans

INGREDIENTS:
**1 pound dried pinquito beans or
    small kidney beans
1 tablespoon butter
2 slices bacon, cut into ¼-inch slivers
2 ounces cooked ham, finely chopped
1 small onion, finely chopped
2 cloves garlic, minced
3 tablespoons chopped fresh cilantro
¾ cup tomato purée
¼ cup red chile sauce (see Note)
1 tablespoon brown sugar
1 teaspoon dry mustard
½ teaspoon ground cumin
½ teaspoon dried oregano
Coarse salt (kosher or sea) and
    freshly ground black pepper**

1 Spread the beans out on a rimmed baking sheet and pick through them, discarding any foreign matter, such as pebbles or twigs. Place the beans in a colander and rinse them under cold running water; then place them in a large bowl and add water to cover by 4 inches. Let the beans soak in the refrigerator for at least 4 hours or as long as overnight.

2 Drain the soaked beans in a colander and place them in a large pot. Add water to cover by 4 inches and bring to a boil over high heat. Skim off any foam that rises to the surface, then reduce the heat to medium and cover the pot. Let the beans simmer until very tender, 1½ to 2 hours. When done you should be able to crush a bean between your thumb and forefinger. Pour off most of the cooking liquid, reserving 1½ cups.

3 Melt the butter in a nonreactive skillet over medium heat. Add the bacon and ham and cook until lightly browned, about 5 minutes. Add the onion, garlic, and cilantro and cook for 1 minute. Add the tomato purée, chile sauce, brown sugar, mustard, cumin, oregano, and about 1 teaspoon salt and ½ teaspoon pepper. Let the bacon and tomato mixture simmer until richly flavored, 8 to 12 minutes, stirring with a wooden spoon.

4 Stir the bacon and tomato mixture into the beans. Reduce the heat to low and let simmer until thick, rich, and flavorful, 10 to 15 minutes, stirring as needed to prevent scorching. Add enough bean cooking liquid to keep the beans moist but not quite soupy. Taste for seasoning, adding more salt and/or pepper as necessary.

YIELD:
Serves 6 to 8

NOTE: The preferred brand of red chile sauce in these parts is Las Palmas, but you can use any commercial taco sauce.

FAR WESTERN TAVERN

When the directors of the film *Sea Biscuit* sought the perfect Main Street in a quintessential ranch town, they chose Guadalupe, near the coast of central California. Or perhaps their selection stemmed from a baser motive: They simply wanted to eat—and eat often—at the Far Western Tavern. For the better part of a century, this ranch country restaurant has been dishing up thick, smoky steaks and Italian American side dishes to a clientele that has included cattle barons, ranch hands, and farmers.

The Far Western Tavern began as the Palace Hotel, which was built by Swiss Italian immigrants in 1912. The current restaurant dates from 1958, when the building was acquired by two cousins, Clarence Minetti and Dick Maretti. Beef raised on Minetti's Corralitos Ranch quickly became the house specialty, grilled the local way, over blazing red oak in an open brick pit. The side dishes—pinquito beans (the local

FAR WESTERN TAVERN

899 Guadalupe Street
Guadalupe, California
(805) 343-2211
www.farwesterntavern.com

version of baked beans; see page 641 for the recipe) and a thick cooked tomato salsa—came from the ranch house kitchen recipes of Dick's wife, Rosalie.

The dining room offers the unexpected elegance of vertiginously high ceilings with indolently spinning paddle fans, cowhide (yes, cowhide) curtains, blue wallpaper, mounted steer and deer heads, tables with white linens, and blue chairs on rollers (OK, the chairs aren't elegant, but they certainly have character). The wine list has a good selection of wines from central California and I, for one, was more than happy to wash my beef down with a local FoxTen vineyards syrah.

The star attraction here is clearly the beef—oak-grilled bull's eye (the Wild West's version of a rib eye); fork-tender filet mignon; meaty New York strip steak; and of course, "cowboy cut" top sirloin, a reasonably priced, intensely flavorful steak taken from the top block sirloin—a cut much prized in these parts. You'll also find exceptional grilled (not smoked) baby back ribs glazed with a bittersweet mixture of sherry, citrus fruit juice, and red currant jelly. The adventurous can try the crisply fried mountain oysters, which come from a part of the steer most guys would rather not think about and taste better than you might imagine.

Memphis, Tenn.

RED BEANS AND RICE

Most people think of Memphis as barbecue country, and with good reason. The dry rib was invented here, and smoked pork shoulder is accorded a respect—no, a reverence—you would normally associate with the Carolinas. But Memphis is also a Mississippi River town—the first great stop north after New Orleans, and a quick tour of the eateries on and around Beale Street reminds you that Louisiana-style gumbos and jambalayas are alive and well there. The red beans and rice here were inspired by the legendary Memphis rib emporium Charlie Vergos Rendezvous, and I can't think of a better accompaniment to Memphis-style ribs (see page 297) or pork shoulder.

INGREDIENTS:

4 tablespoons (½ stick) butter

6 ounces smoked sausage,
    cut into ¼-inch dice

1 medium-size onion, finely chopped

2 to 4 large jalapeño peppers, seeded
    and finely chopped (for hotter beans,
    leave the seeds in)

2 cloves garlic, minced

½ green bell pepper, finely chopped

4 ounces mushrooms, trimmed, wiped
    clean with damp paper towels,
    and thinly sliced

1 can (15 ounces) red beans with juices

1 can (28 ounces) peeled tomatoes with
    their juices, finely chopped

3 tablespoons Worcestershire sauce

2 tablespoons A.1. steak sauce

2 cups converted white rice
    (such as Uncle Ben's)

Coarse salt (kosher or sea) and
    freshly ground black pepper

1 Melt 3 tablespoons of the butter in a large saucepan over medium heat. Add the sausage, onion, jalapeños, garlic, and bell pepper. Cook until the vegetables are lightly browned, about 4 minutes. Increase the heat to high and add the mushrooms. Cook until the mushrooms are lightly browned and the juices are evaporated, about 3 minutes.

2 Add the beans, tomatoes, Worcestershire sauce, and steak sauce to the sausage mixture and stir to mix. Reduce the heat to medium-high and let the mixture come to a boil, stirring with a wooden spoon to prevent scorching.

3 Add the rice and season generously, and I mean generously, with salt and black pepper. Let the beans and rice come to a boil, stirring once or twice. Reduce the heat to low and cover the pan. Let the beans and rice simmer gently until the rice is just tender, about 20 minutes.

4 Add the remaining 1 tablespoon of butter and fluff the rice with a fork. Taste for seasoning, adding more salt and/or black pepper as necessary.

YIELD:
Serves 8 to 10

T I P S

The Rendezvous uses Hillshire Farm's smoked sausages. If this isn't available in your region, substitute kielbasa or for a Cajun touch, Louisianan andouille.

THELMA'S BAR-B-QUE

Located in a ramshackle white house in an out-of-the-way part of Houston, Thelma's is the sort of place every barbecue hound dreams of discovering—the food screams with authenticity. The Thelma in question, Thelma M. Williams, hails from Ville Platte, Louisiana, where she learned to stew exemplary okra and cook up extraordinary dirty rice (for the recipe, see page 646).

She moved to Houston thirty years ago and has been cooking there ever since. When most people think of Texas barbecue, they envision dry, Hill Country–style brisket, but Thelma marries Texas ways to the barbecue traditions of the Deep South. Like northern Texas pit masters, she slow roasts her briskets over smoldering oak. But she uses a traditional Southern wood—hickory—and in keeping with her Southern heritage, she also serves spareribs and chicken drenched in the typical thick, sweet barbecue sauce.

THELMA'S BAR-B-QUE

**1020 Live Oak Street
Houston, Texas
(713) 228-2262**

Her restaurant is only a couple of years old, but Thelma is already something of a neighborhood legend, and as her reputation grows, her proximity to the Houston convention center will find the dining room filling up with 'que heads.

Thelma Williams "babies" her barbecue.

TIPS

Thelma's dirty rice owes its richness to the addition of chicken livers and gizzards and chuck steak. To intensify the flavor she makes a broth with these ingredients and uses it to cook the rice. Depending on how impatient you are to try this recipe, you can either buy the livers and gizzards or freeze them each time you grill a chicken, then make the rice when you have enough.

Houston, Tex.

THELMA'S DIRTY RICE

Dirty rice is served at barbecues throughout Louisiana—and in much of the rest of the South. And no one makes it better than Thelma M. Williams, the petite and hair-netted Louisiana-born proprietor of Thelma's in Houston. Thelma's is the sort of barbecue joint you'd expect to find deep in the country, but instead, it's tucked in a forgotten neighborhood a stone's throw from the Houston convention center. Her brisket and ribs combine the intense smoke flavor of traditional Texas barbecue with the sweet, sticky, lemony barbecue sauce characteristic of Louisiana. But what really keeps me awake at night is dreaming about Thelma's peppery dirty rice.

INGREDIENTS:

6 ounces chicken livers
6 ounces chicken gizzards
6 ounces chuck steak,
    cut into 1-inch cubes
Coarse salt (kosher or sea)
3 tablespoons butter
1 medium-size onion, finely chopped
2 scallions, both white and green parts,
    trimmed and finely chopped
1 rib celery, finely chopped
1 clove garlic, minced
3 tablespoons chopped fresh
    flat-leaf parsley

2 cups converted white rice,
    such as Uncle Ben's
1 tablespoon Kitchen Bouquet
    (optional; see Note)
1/2 teaspoon Accent (optional; see Note)
Freshly ground black pepper

1 Place the chicken livers, gizzards, and chuck steak in a large pot, add 6 cups of water, and gradually bring to a boil over medium-high heat. Use a large spoon to skim off any foam that rises to the surface. Reduce the heat to medium-low, cover the pot, and let simmer gently until the beef is tender, about 1 hour. After the first 30 minutes, season with salt to taste. You'll need 4 cups of broth for the rice. Add more water if necessary.

2 Strain 4 cups of the broth into a large, heat proof measuring cup or bowl and set aside. Finely chop the chicken livers, gizzards, and chuck steak in a food processor or meat grinder and set aside.

3 Melt 2 tablespoons of the butter in a large heavy saucepan over medium heat. Add the onion, scallions, celery, garlic, and parsley and cook until lightly browned, about 4 minutes. Stir in the rice and cook until the grains are shiny, about 1 minute. Add the 4 cups of reserved broth, the chopped chicken livers, gizzards, and chuck steak, the Kitchen Bouquet and Accent, if using, and lots of pepper. Let the mixture come to a boil, then reduce the heat to medium-low (the idea is to cook the rice at the barest simmer). Cover the pot. Cook the rice until very tender, about 20 minutes. The rice should be moist but not soupy—uncover the pot for the last 5 minutes if necessary to let some of the water evaporate.

4 Add the remaining 1 tablespoon of butter and fluff the rice with a fork. Taste for seasoning, adding more salt and/or pepper as necessary; dirty rice should be highly seasoned. Try to make the rice as close to serving time as possible. If not serving the dirty rice right away, keep it warm on a warm corner of the stove, placing a clean dish towel under the pot lid to absorb the excess steam (which would make the rice soggy).

YIELD:
Serves 6 to 8

NOTE: Adding Kitchen Bouquet will result in a deeper brown color and increase the roasted flavor of the rice. Accent is a brand of MSG, a flavor enhancer. Both are optional.

West Virginia

GRILLED GRITS
With Virginia Ham

What would the South do without grits? But while most people think of them as breakfast food (the white mush that comes with eggs at eateries in the South), grits are sensational grilled. After all, Italians have been grilling polenta for centuries, and what are grits but polenta with a Southern accent? (Actually, grits are usually made with hulled white corn kernels, whereas polenta is made from ground yellow corn.) In this recipe, the grits are flavored with finely chopped Virginia ham, a trick I learned from my Greenbrier barbecue buddy Ethan Hileman. (Ethan also adds chopped ramps—wild leeks. You can substitute a mix of scallions and garlic.) For the best results, make the grits a day ahead, so they have plenty of time to firm up before grilling.

METHOD:
Direct grilling

ADVANCE PREPARATION:
4 hours for soaking the ham (optional), plus 6 to 12 hours for chilling the grits

INGREDIENTS:
3 ounces ham (preferably Smithfield; see Note)
3 ramps (wild leeks), or 3 scallions and 1 clove garlic, finely chopped
2 cups chicken stock (preferably homemade) or water
1 teaspoon coarse salt (kosher or sea), or more to taste
½ teaspoon freshly ground black pepper, or more to taste
1 cup quick-cooking (not instant) grits
3 tablespoons butter, melted, or extra-virgin olive oil (optional)

YOU'LL ALSO NEED:
A 12-by-17-inch baking sheet with a rim; a 2½- or 3-inch-round cookie cutter

WALL OF FLAME

VIRGIL'S

It's a long way from Times Square to Memphis, but the owners of Manhattan's popular Virgil's manage to smoke spare ribs, briskets, and pork shoulders the old-fashioned way—over seasoned fruit wood—until tender enough to cut with a fork. Shrimp comes smokily charred on the grill and barbecue sauce lurks in the tamales. Virgil's collard greens, dirty rice, melting hush puppies, and banana pudding are as good—if not better—as any side dish you'd get in the South. The photo-filled, wood-paneled dining rooms make a vintage setting for some of the most authentic 'que in Manhattan.

152 West 44th Street
New York, NY
(212) 921-9494
www.virgilsbbq.com

TIPS

There are three types of grits—regular, quick-cooking, and instant. I call for quick-cooking grits here, which are widely available, easy to use, and great for grilling. The purist will want to buy regular grits and increase the cooking time.

1 If using Smithfield ham, place it in a pot, cover it with warm water, and let soak for 4 hours, changing the water 2 or 3 times. This will remove the excess salt. Drain and coarsely chop the ham, then finely chop it in a food processor. If using another ham, just finely chop it in the food processor.

2 Place the chopped ham, ramps, stock, salt, and pepper in a large heavy saucepan and bring to a boil over high heat. Add the grits in a thin stream, stirring constantly. Reduce the heat to medium and let the grits simmer gently until thick, about 10 minutes, stirring from time to time to prevent sticking and scorching. Taste for seasoning, adding more salt and/or pepper as necessary.

3 Pour the grits onto the rimmed baking sheet and spread with a spatula into an even ¾-inch-thick layer; they will not cover the entire baking sheet. Let cool to room temperature, then cover with plastic wrap and refrigerate for at least 6 hours, preferably overnight, so the grits become firm.

4 Set up the grill for direct grilling (see page 21 for charcoal or gas) and preheat to high. Meanwhile, using the cookie cutter, cut the grits into half-moon crescents by working in rows and making each cut overlap the round before it (sort of like the links of a chain). You will have the least waste this way.

5 When ready to grill, brush and generously oil the grill grate. Place the half-moons of grits on the hot grate and grill until nicely browned and heated through, 2 to 4 minutes per side. For richer grits, lightly brush them with

Stone-ground grits are the first choice for grilling.

some of the melted butter after turning them over. Transfer the grilled grits to a platter or plates, brush the second side with butter, if desired, and serve at once.

YIELD:
Serves 6 to 8

NOTE: For the best flavor, use Smithfield ham, which is cured in a manner similar to Italian prosciutto. Smithfield ham can now be found at more and more supermarkets and at Asian markets (the Chinese love it), or see Mail-Order Sources on page 742. Alternatively, you could use chopped prosciutto, honey-baked ham, or any other ham you fancy.

South Florida

NUEVO LATINO GRILLED GRITS

If you know south Florida, you don't really think of it as part of the South. But northern Florida is very much the Deep South, which may explain why you find grits at so many Florida breakfast joints. That gave me the idea to combine this southern starch with the Latino flavors of Miami's Hispanic community. Bubba sure never saw grits the likes of these!

METHOD:
Direct grilling

ADVANCE PREPARATION:
6 to 12 hours for chilling the grits

INGREDIENTS:
2 tablespoons olive oil
2 cloves garlic, minced
1 small onion, finely chopped
½ red bell pepper, finely chopped
½ green bell pepper, finely chopped, or 2 to 4 seeded, finely chopped jalapeño peppers
2 cups chicken stock (preferably homemade) or water
3 tablespoons chopped fresh cilantro
1 teaspoon of your favorite hot sauce (optional)
1 teaspoon coarse salt (kosher or sea), or more to taste
½ teaspoon freshly ground black pepper, or more to taste
1 cup quick-cooking (not instant) grits
1 cup (about 4 ounces) grated Manchego or other cheese
3 tablespoons butter, melted, or extra-virgin olive oil (optional)

YOU'LL ALSO NEED:
A 12-by-17-inch baking sheet with a rim; a 2½- or 3-inch-round cookie cutter

1 Heat the olive oil in a large heavy saucepan over medium heat. Add the garlic, onion, and bell peppers and cook until soft and fragrant but not brown, about 3 minutes. Stir in the stock, cilantro, hot sauce, if using, salt, and black pepper and bring to a boil. Add the grits in a thin stream, stirring constantly. Reduce the heat to medium and let the grits simmer gently until

TIPS

There are lots of possibilities when picking a cheese. I like Manchego, a Spanish sheep's milk cheese. You could also use salty Central American *queso fresco,* or even a North American cheddar or Jack.

thick, about 10 minutes, stirring from time to time to prevent sticking and scorching. Stir in the cheese and taste for seasoning, adding more salt and/or black pepper as necessary.

2 Pour the grits onto the rimmed baking sheet and spread with a spatula into an even ¾-inch-thick layer; they will not cover the entire baking sheet. Let cool to room temperature, then cover with plastic wrap and refrigerate for at least 6 hours, preferably overnight, so the grits become firm.

3 Set up the grill for direct grilling (see page 21 for charcoal or gas) and preheat to high. Meanwhile, using the round cookie cutter, cut the grits into half-moon crescents by working in rows and making each cut overlap the round before it (sort of like the links of a chain). You will have the least waste this way.

4 When ready to grill, brush and generously oil the grill grate. Place the half-moons of grits on the hot grate and grill until nicely browned and heated through, 2 to 4 minutes per side. For richer grits, lightly brush them with some of the melted butter after turning them over. Transfer the grilled grits to a platter or plates, brush the second side with butter, if desired, and serve at once.

YIELD:
Serves 6 to 8

Philadelphia, Pa.

GRILLED POLENTA

Do you remember your first time? Mine was in Philadelphia's Little Italy in 1972. I'm not talking about sex, but about something almost as seductive: polenta. More specifically, I'm talking about realizing that something resembling mush could be cooked on the grill. This may be news for grill jockeys in the United States, but in northern Italy— particularly in the Veneto region— polenta is often chilled in thin slabs, cut into fanciful shapes, and grilled. Progressive American chefs have introduced the practice in this country. It's hard to say what gives grilled polenta more pizzazz, the handsome crosshatch of grill marks or the smoky taste of the fire. Grilled polenta makes a great accompaniment to all sorts of Italian American barbecue, from grilled peppers and other vegetables to flame-charred sausage. It would go nicely with Mario's Veal Chops with Lemon-Oregano Jam on page 222 or the BBQ Queens' Parmesan Pepper Rack of Lamb on page 319.

METHOD:
Direct grilling

INGREDIENTS:

1 package (1½ pounds) cooked polenta

2 to 3 tablespoons olive oil

1 clove garlic, minced

1 tablespoon chopped fresh rosemary or
    another herb (optional)

1 cup freshly grated Parmesan cheese

Freshly ground black pepper

1 Unwrap the polenta and cut it crosswise into ½-inch-thick slices. Combine the olive oil, garlic, and rosemary in a small bowl and stir with a fork to mix. Lightly brush the polenta slices on both sides with the flavored oil.

2 Set up the grill for direct grilling (see page 21 for charcoal or gas) and preheat to high.

3 When ready to cook, brush and generously oil the grill grate. Arrange the polenta slices on the hot grate and grill until lightly browned, 2 to 4 minutes per side, rotating each slice a

quarter turn after 1 minute, if desired, to create an attractive crosshatch of grill marks. Transfer the grilled polenta to a platter or plates and sprinkle the Parmesan and some pepper on top.

YIELD:
Serves 8

Memphis, Tenn.

BARBECUE SPAGHETTI

Leave it to the 'que heads of Memphis. So strong is their passion for barbecue, they even add it

TIPS

In the old days, you had to make polenta from scratch, a laborious process that required 45 elbow-torturing minutes of stirring. Today, you can buy ready-made polenta in plastic cylinders in the supermarket. I'm not sure it's quite as good as what your Italian grandmother used to make—if you were lucky enough to have one—but it's tasty enough and a heck of a lot easier. Polenta tends to stick to the grill grate, so you'll have to be extra conscientious about oiling it.

There's polenta aplenty in Philadelphia's Little Italy.

TIPS

You want a thick, smoky, red barbecue sauce for this spaghetti. Good candidates in this book include St. Louis Red (page 666), Skip's Apple Barbecue Sauce (page 673), Nashville Sweet (page 669), and The Doctor's Medicine (page 680). But it's certainly acceptable to use a good commercial sauce, like KC Masterpiece or Bull's-Eye.

to spaghetti. So, what happens when an Italian bolognese sauce is made by a Memphis pit master? The traditional beef and pork are replaced by chopped barbecued pork shoulder or brisket, and the tomato sauce is enriched with a shot of barbecue sauce. Barbecue spaghetti turns up in Memphis's barbecue joints, mom-and-pop Italian American eateries, and pizza parlors. Here's my version.

INGREDIENTS:

1 can (28 ounces) peeled plum tomatoes, with their juices
3 tablespoons olive oil
1 medium-size onion, finely chopped
1 medium-size carrot, peeled and finely chopped
1 rib celery, finely chopped
1 piece (2 by 3 inches) green bell pepper, finely chopped
2 cloves garlic, finely chopped
1 teaspoon dried oregano
1/2 to 1 teaspoon hot red pepper flakes
1/2 teaspoon freshly ground black pepper
2 tablespoons tomato paste

Cozy Corner's barbecue spaghetti up close.

4 fresh basil leaves, thinly slivered, plus 4 whole leaves or sprigs for garnish
1/3 cup smoky red barbecue sauce, or more to taste
1 to 2 cups finely chopped barbecued pork shoulder (page 241) or brisket (page 174)
Coarse salt (kosher or sea)
1/2 teaspoon sugar (optional)
12 ounces spaghetti
Freshly grated Parmesan cheese (see Note)

1 Coarsely purée the tomatoes with their juices in a food processor and set aside. Heat the olive oil in a large nonreactive saucepan over medium heat. Add the onion, carrot, celery, bell pepper, and garlic and cook until just beginning to brown, about 4 minutes. Add the oregano, hot red pepper flakes, and black pepper and cook for 30 seconds. Add the tomato paste and cook until fragrant, 1 to 2 minutes. Stir in the puréed tomatoes along with the slivered basil and the barbecue sauce. Add 1/4 cup of water and the diced meat and let simmer until the sauce is thick and richly flavored, 8 to 10 minutes, stirring occasionally with a wooden spoon to prevent sticking. Taste for seasoning, adding salt and/or more barbecue sauce as necessary. If the sauce tastes too acidic, add the sugar.

2 Meanwhile, bring 8 quarts of lightly salted water to a rapid boil in a large pot over high heat. Add the spaghetti and cook to taste, about 8 minutes for al dente. Drain the spaghetti in a colander.

3 To serve, divide the spaghetti among 4 large, shallow bowls. Spoon the sauce over the pasta and sprinkle Parmesan cheese on top. Garnish each serving with a basil leaf or sprig and serve at once.

YIELD:

Serves 4

NOTE: To be strictly authentic, you'd use the pregrated Parmesan that comes in a shiny green cardboard container—it's your call.

New Mexico

MACARONI AND CHEESE
With Grilled Onions, Chiles, and Corn

Barbecue spaghetti. Grilled grits. Is nothing sacred to the voracious Guru of Grilling? Perhaps not. How about barbecued macaroni and cheese? Anything that tastes half good baked in the oven is bound to taste even better smoke roasted on the grill. But smoke roasting is only part of what elevates the following mac and cheese from side dish to showstopper. This one electrifies your taste buds with flame-charred chiles, onion, and corn. Even the cheese—smoked cheese instead of the traditional cheddar—has a kick.

METHODS:
Direct grilling and indirect grilling

INGREDIENTS:

Coarse salt (kosher or sea)
2 cups (about 8 ounces) elbow macaroni
1 teaspoon vegetable oil
2 ears sweet corn, shucked
1 medium-size red onion,
    peeled and quartered
4 tablespoons (½ stick) unsalted butter,
    melted, plus 2 tablespoons butter
Freshly ground black pepper
6 to 8 New Mexican green chiles or
    Anaheim or California peppers,
    or 2 to 4 poblano peppers
1 yellow bell pepper
1 red bell pepper
2 cloves garlic, minced
1 shallot, minced
3 tablespoons flour
2 cups half-and-half, light cream, or milk
2 tablespoons Dijon mustard
2 cups (about 8 ounces) grated smoked
    cheese, preferably smoked cheddar
¼ cup dried bread crumbs (preferably
    homemade)

YOU'LL ALSO NEED:

An aluminum foil roasting pan or drip
    pan or grill-proof baking dish (about
    9 by 12 inches), sprayed or brushed
    with oil; 2 cups wood chips or chunks
    (optional; preferably hickory or oak),
    soaked for 1 hour in water to cover,
    then drained

TIPS

To experience this macaroni and cheese in all its smoky glory, you'll need to use your grill for both direct and indirect grilling. To get a leg up on the process, I would grill the peppers, onions, and corn a day ahead when you're grilling other things. On rainy days, you can bake the macaroni and cheese in the oven at 400°F for 15 to 20 minutes instead of grilling it.

1 Bring 8 quarts of lightly salted water to a rapid boil in a large pot over high heat. Add the macaroni and cook until al dente, about 8 minutes. Drain the macaroni in a large colander, rinse with cold water until cool, and drain again. Toss the macaroni with the oil to prevent sticking.

2 Set up the grill for direct grilling (see page 21 for charcoal or gas) and preheat to high.

3 When ready to cook, lightly brush the corn and onion with half of the melted butter and season with salt and pepper. Place the corn and onion on the hot grate and grill until nicely browned, 2 to 3 minutes per side (8 to 12 minutes in all) for the corn and 3 to 4 minutes per side (9 to 12 minutes in all) for the onion, turning with tongs as needed. Add the chiles and peppers to the hot grate and grill until the skins are charred, 3 to 5 minutes per side (6 to 10 minutes in all) for New Mexican chiles or 3 to 5 minutes per side (12 to 20 minutes in all) for poblano peppers, and 4 to 6 minutes per side (16 to 24 minutes in all) for the bell peppers. Transfer the corn and onion to a cutting board and let cool.

4 Transfer the grilled chiles and bell peppers to a baking dish and cover with plastic wrap. Let the peppers cool to room temperature, about 20 minutes (the steam trapped by the plastic wrap helps loosen the skin from the peppers). Scrape the skin off the cooled peppers, then core and seed them.

5 Cut the corn kernels off the cobs, using lengthwise strokes of a chef's knife. Thinly slice the onion quarters crosswise. Cut the chiles and peppers into 1/4-inch dice. The recipe can be prepared to this stage up to 2 days ahead.

6 Melt the 2 tablespoons butter in a large saucepan over medium heat. Add the garlic and shallot and cook until soft but not brown, 2 to 3 minutes. Stir in the corn kernels and grilled onion, chiles, and bell peppers. Stir in the flour and cook for 1 minute. Stir in the half-and-half and increase the heat to high. Let the mixture boil for 3 minutes, stirring well; it should thicken. Remove the pan from the heat and stir in the mustard and cooked macaroni, followed by the cheese. Season with salt and pepper to taste; the mixture should be highly seasoned. Spoon the macaroni and cheese into the oiled aluminum foil pan. Sprinkle the top of the macaroni with the bread crumbs and

Mac and cheese for the multitudes: You haven't fully experienced it until you've had it grilled.

drizzle the remaining 2 tablespoons melted butter over the bread crumbs. The recipe can be prepared to this stage up to 24 hours ahead.

7 Set up the grill for indirect grilling (see page 23 for gas or page 22 for charcoal) and preheat to medium-high. If using a gas grill, place all of the wood chips or chunks, if desired, in the smoker box or in a smoker pouch (see page 24) and run the grill on high until you see smoke, then reduce the heat to medium-high. If using a charcoal grill, preheat it to medium-high, then toss all of the wood chips or chunks, if desired, on the coals.

8 When ready to cook, place the macaroni and cheese in the center of the hot grate, away from the heat, and cover the grill. Cook the macaroni and cheese until the sauce is bubbly and the top is crusty and brown, 15 to 20 minutes. Serve at once.

YIELD:
Serves 4

Unbeatable

sk many folks what makes barbecue barbecue, and they're likely to say the sauce. But which sauce? There are dozens of regional styles to choose from. In Kansas City, barbecue sauce is a thick, sweet, smoky red condiment, while in South Carolina, mustard sauce is king. Travel farther along America's barbecue trail, and you'll find a sharp, tomato-based sauce in St. Louis, a chipotle-stung red sauce in Tomales Bay, California (served with barbecued oysters, no less), and an onion-soy-vinegar sauce called *finadene* in the American protectorate of Guam. Of course, in many parts of the country (especially southern California and the Southwest), the preferred accompaniment for barbecue is salsa. So, in this chapter you'll also find salsas ranging from flame-roasted tomato to strawberry. Offbeat enough for you? If not, how about other barbecue condiments like gooseberry or rhubarb chutney? The truth is, when it comes to barbecue sauce, the most important ingredient is imagination.

Sauces

THE DIDDY-WA-DIDDY

Barbecue Sauce Contest

Ardie Davis, a.k.a. Remus Powers, barbecue judge extraordinaire.

The contestants came in squirt bottles, shuttled to the battlefield in cardboard six-packs. They did combat on a red-and-white checkered tablecloth. When the last plate was cleaned and the last finger licked, hundreds of combatants had entered the fray and only one would emerge victorious. Welcome to the world's largest barbecue sauce contest, the Diddy-Wa-Diddy.

By the end of the morning, the judges were in sore need of mouthwash. I should know—I was one of the four hundred barbecue enthusiasts who paid $10 each to serve as a judge (the proceeds went to charity). I took my seat at a long table furnished with tasting forms, bottles of water and plates of bread for cleansing the palate, and platters of barbecued pork. The sauces were judged first on their own merits, then according to how well they went with meat. For the next two hours, I tasted not only barbecue sauces but also rubs and marinades until my tongue cried out for mercy.

There were mustard-based sauces the color of gold doubloons and tomato-based sauces as crimson as freshly spilled blood. Some sauces were as smooth as satin and others so chockablock full of herbs, spices, and vegetable chunks, you could eat them with a fork. Ranging from sweet as honey to as mouth-puckering as a swig of vinegar, there were sauces as mild as baby formula and as fiery as a bite of a high-voltage cable. Some were so good, I wanted to drink the whole bottle. Others were so ghastly, I wanted to see their makers jailed for inflicting cruel and unusual punishment.

The Diddy-Wa-Diddy is the brainchild of Ardie Davis, civil servant by day (he works for the Kansas Commission on Aging) but by calling a barbecue judge. If you've ever attended a major barbecue festival—Memphis in May, for example, or Kansas City's American Royal—you've surely seen him: a bearded man in a black bowler hat and tuxedo, a row of sparerib bones cascading down his chest where the tuxedo studs should be. Ardie's *nom de guerre* is Remus Powers, and he administers the judge's oath with a dignity worthy of a Supreme Court justice.

MUSIC TO HIS EARS

Ardie got the idea for a barbecue sauce contest while reading Michael and Jane Stern's *Roadfood*. He scoured Kansas City food markets and restaurant joints looking for barbecue sauces, turning up more than a hundred different bottles. The year was 1984, and Ardie was listening to Ry Cooder's new *Paradise and Lunch* album, so he decided to name the contest after his favorite song, "Diddy-Wa-Diddy."

Serving the sauces in Styrofoam cups, Ardie held the contest in his backyard, inviting dozens of friends to taste. It was such a rousing success that Mrs. Davis suggested that holding a second Diddy-Wa-Diddy at the family home might be grounds for divorce. So the next year, Ardie ran the contest as a fund-raiser for the Prairie Center, then for the Crown Center. Eventually, he teamed up with the nation's largest barbecue contest, the American Royal.

"I do solemnly swear to objectively and subjectively evaluate each barbecue sauce that is presented to my eyes, my nose, and my palate. I accept my duty to be a barbecue judge so that truth, justice, excellence in barbecue, and the American way of life may be strengthened and preserved forever," barbecue oath by Ardie Davis.

The contest has grown mightily over the years, with hundreds of sauces competing, not to mention dozens of rubs and marinades. The sauces are divided into two categories, mild or hot, and are grouped according to their main ingredient: tomato-based, vinegar-based, fruit-based, or soy-based. There is also a group of salsas. Winners have included such legendary elixirs as John Willingham's W'ham Sauce from Memphis (the first hot sauce to win the contest) and Gates's Extra Hot Sauce from Kansas.

What makes a great barbecue sauce? According to Ardie, character and balance. As for his favorite sauce, well, that would be like asking an oenophile to name his favorite wine. "Sometimes you want fruity, sometimes you want dry; sometimes tangy or sweet or fiery," he explains. "A fruit-based barbecue sauce goes great with chicken; a spicy vinegar or mustard sauce with pork. Beef generally tastes better without sauce," says Ardie—an opinion that no doubt will endear him to Texans.

As for how to use barbecue sauce, Ardie is unequivocal in his answer: "In moderation." Barbecue sauce should complement, not camouflage or overpower, the meat. Ardie always asks for sauce to be served on the side. Excessive use of barbecue sauce can signal a pit master who doesn't know how to cook meat. "If the meat is good enough without sauce, don't use it," says Ardie.

The only thing Ardie isn't moderate about is his sauce contest. He dreams of the day when there will be a thousand sauces to choose from.

I verily say, "Amen."

NINE RULES
for Great Barbecue Sauce

1 IT'S ONLY AS GOOD AS THE RAW MATERIALS. Some bubbas out there use the saucepan as a garbage can, adding leftover this and cut-rate that in the hopes that they'll add up to a decent barbecue sauce. It doesn't work; a sauce is only as good as its ingredients. Use the best ones you can buy, and never add a condiment, wine, spice, or fruit to a sauce that you wouldn't eat by itself.

2 KEEP IT BALANCED. Balance is the secret to great barbecue sauces. Play the sweetness of brown sugar or honey against the acidity of vinegar or lemon juice. Match the pungency of onion and garlic with the fruitiness of jam or apple cider. Use liquid smoke to pump up the smoke flavor and a fillip of hot sauce or cayenne to crank up the heat.

3 LESS IS MORE. Use strong seasonings sparingly. Cumin, curry powder, hot sauce, even garlic and whiskey work best in moderate quantities.

4 THINK OUTSIDE OF THE BOX. Any self-respecting barbecue sauce should have at least one oddball ingredient, from coffee to cola to cocoa. Remember, the stranger the ingredients, the more you can boast about your sauce.

5 WATER IS A LIFE BLOOD. One of the most important ingredients in many great barbecue sauces has no color, smell, or flavor—water. Water mellows the intensity of some stronger condiments, such as mustard or hot sauce. It helps to marry disparate flavor elements into a harmonious whole.

6 TIMING IS EVERYTHING. Barbecue sauces are like fine wines—most of them improve with age. In general, try to give your sauce two or three days, or even a week, in the refrigerator to "ripen," so the flavors blend and mature.

7 HANDLE WITH CARE. The beauty of a barbecue sauce is that you can't curdle it, scramble it, or break it. It will burn, however, particularly if it contains lots of sugar. If you are cooking a sauce, use a heavy pot and stir often with either a whisk or a wooden spoon to keep the sauce from scorching.

8 TRUST YOUR TASTE BUDS. The most important words in any sauce recipe are *season to taste*. Add any ingredient you feel you need to make the sauce taste good to you.

9 KNOW WHEN TO USE THE SAUCE. Barbecue sauces should be applied during the last five or ten minutes of cooking or served separately from the meat. Most American barbecue sauces contain sugar, so if you brush them on when you begin grilling they will burn before the meat is cooked through. If you've ever charred chicken on the grill, you'll appreciate this simple tip for avoiding a repeat mishap.

Santa Rita, Guam

FINADENE SAUCE (Guamanian Hot Sauce)

Whenever Guamanians gather, you find barbecue, and wherever you find Guamanian barbecue, you find *finadene*. The term refers to a family of hot sauces guaranteed to electrify your next barbecue. Here are three popular variations from grill jockey Rueben Olivas, who lives in Santa Rita, Guam.

Soy and Vinegar Finadene

A dark *finadene* is traditionally served with chicken and pork. I like the way the salty piquancy of the sauce counterpoints the richness of the meat.

INGREDIENTS:

1 small onion, sliced paper-thin

2 to 6 jalapeño peppers or other hot chiles, thinly sliced

½ cup soy sauce (preferably Kikkoman)

¼ cup distilled white vinegar

Balmy Guam, where the bananas are ripe for grilling and the barbecue sauce is always piquant.

Separate the onion slices into rings and place them in an attractive nonreactive serving bowl. Add the jalapeños, soy sauce, and vinegar and stir to mix. The sauce can refrigerated, covered, for several days.

YIELD:
Makes about 1 cup

Coconut Finadene

Light and creamy, this *finadene* is perfect for seafood and poultry. Coconut milk adds just the right degree of richness—ideal for foods that tend to dry out on the grill.

INGREDIENTS:

1 cup coconut milk (see Note)

4 cloves garlic, minced

1 tablespoon grated or minced peeled
   fresh ginger

3 to 4 tablespoons fresh lemon juice

Coarse salt (kosher or sea)

Freshly ground black pepper

1 small onion, thinly sliced crosswise
   and separated into rings

2 to 6 jalapeño peppers or other
   hot chiles, thinly sliced

Combine the coconut milk, garlic, ginger, and lemon juice in an attractive nonreactive serving bowl and stir to mix. Add the onion and jalapeños. Season to taste with salt and pepper. The sauce can be made several hours ahead.

YIELD:

Makes about 1½ cups

NOTE: Coconut milk is available in cans at most supermarkets as well as at Hispanic and Asian markets. Be sure to buy an unsweetened one. Shake the can well before opening.

Lemon Finadene

Traditionally served with grilled fish, this tangy *finadene* has an acidity that offsets the richness of a fish like salmon. Using salt instead of soy sauce keeps the fish from becoming discolored.

INGREDIENTS:

1 cup fresh lemon juice (from about
   6 lemons)

1 tablespoon coarse salt (kosher or sea),
   or more to taste

1 small onion, thinly sliced crosswise
   and separated into rings

4 cloves garlic, minced

2 to 6 jalapeño peppers or other
   hot chiles, thinly sliced

Combine the lemon juice, salt and ½ cup cold water in an attractive nonreactive mixing bowl and whisk until the salt dissolves. Stir in the onion, garlic, and jalapeños. Taste for seasoning, adding more salt as necessary. The sauce can be refrigerated, covered, for several days.

YIELD:

Makes about 1½ cups

Florida Keys

LIQUID FIRE (Scotch Bonnet Hot Sauce)

Although it contains only four ingredients, the blast-furnace heat of this sauce could wilt your whole neighborhood. Old-time Floridians may recognize it as a new and deadlier form of old sour, the traditional hot sauce of the Florida keys. Use Liquid Fire sparingly—a few drops are sufficient to send most people lunging for their beers.

INGREDIENTS:

**4 to 8 Scotch bonnet chiles,
    stemmed, seeded, and coarsely
    chopped**
4 cloves garlic, coarsely chopped
**1 cup fresh lime juice, key lime juice,
    or distilled white vinegar, or
    more to taste**
**1 tablespoon coarse salt (kosher or sea),
    or more to taste**

Combine the Scotch bonnets, garlic, lime juice, and salt in a blender and blend to a smooth purée. Taste for seasoning, adding more lime juice and/or salt as necessary. The sauce can be served immediately but will improve in flavor if you let it stand for a few hours or even a few days so that it mellows. If not serving the sauce immediately, transfer it to a clean glass jar, placing a piece of plastic wrap between the top of the jar and the lid to keep the lid from corroding. The sauce will keep for several weeks in the refrigerator.

YIELD:
Makes 1 cup

Santa Fe, N.Mex.

HABANERO MINT BARBECUE SAUCE

TIPS

Here in South Florida, we'd use Scotch bonnet chiles, or one of their Caribbean cousins to make Liquid Fire. If you live in the Southwest or California, you can substitute habañero peppers. For an even more tongue-blistering version, leave the seeds in the chiles. A popular variation on this sauce is to use distilled white vinegar instead of lime juice.

Here's a super-easy mint barbecue sauce that delivers a double wallop of flavor—a peppery blast of mint and an incendiary bite of habañero—the latter in the form of a hot sauce from

Scotch bonnets—the world's hottest chiles. Don't use more than you mean to.

T I P S

If you're feeling
ambitious when
you make the
Habañero Mint
Barbecue Sauce,
you can make your
own sweet and
smoky barbecue
sauce, following
the recipe for
St. Louis Red
on page 666.
Otherwise use a
good commercial
sauce, like KC
Masterpiece.

Santa Fe. This is a so-called doctor sauce—you start with commercial barbecue sauce and doctor it with other flavorings. It's particularly good with grilled lamb.

INGREDIENTS:

¾ cup barbecue sauce
3 tablespoons mint jelly
1 tablespoon habañero-based hot sauce,
    such as Coyote Café's Howling Hot
    Sauce or Melinda's
1 tablespoon fresh lime juice
Coarse salt (kosher or sea) and
    freshly ground black pepper

1 Combine the barbecue sauce, mint jelly, hot sauce, and lime juice in a nonreactive saucepan and gradually bring to a boil over medium heat, whisking to mix. Season with salt and pepper to taste.

2 If not serving the sauce immediately, transfer it to a clean glass jar, placing a piece of plastic wrap between the top of the jar and the lid to keep the lid from corroding. The sauce will keep for several weeks in the refrigerator.

YIELD:

Makes about 1 cup

VARIATION: For a West Indian version, substitute a Scotch bonnet–based hot sauce, such as Matouk's from Trinidad.

Sonoma, Calif.

ZINFANDEL BARBECUE SAUCE

What's the best wine to serve with barbecue? One often named by the pros is zinfandel. Born on California's sun-baked slopes, zinfandel is a strong, brawny wine with the vigor to stand up to spice and smoke flavors. It goes particularly well with beef and lamb—two of my favorite meats to cook on the grill—but it's also good with pork and poultry. I developed the following zinfandel barbecue sauce during a cooking class in the heart of the wine country, at Ramekins cooking school in Sonoma. The zinfandel cuts the sweetness of the brown sugar and honey, so if you don't like the cloying sweetness of many tomato-based barbecue sauces, this one's for you.

INGREDIENTS:

3 tablespoons butter
3 to 5 shallots, minced (for ¾ cup)
2 cloves garlic, minced
1½ cups zinfandel
¾ cup ketchup
2 tablespoons brown sugar, or more to taste
2 tablespoons honey
1 teaspoon liquid smoke
Coarse salt (kosher or sea) and
    freshly ground black pepper

Barbecue sauce on the vine.

1 Melt the butter in a heavy nonreactive saucepan over medium heat. Add the shallots and garlic and cook until just beginning to brown, 3 to 4 minutes, stirring with a wooden spoon.

2 Add all but 2 tablespoons of the wine and bring to a boil over high heat. Let the mixture boil until reduced to about ⅓ cup, 8 to 12 minutes.

3 Reduce the heat to medium and stir in the ketchup, brown sugar, honey, and liquid smoke. Season with salt and pepper to taste. Let the sauce simmer gently until thick and richly flavored, 6 to 10 minutes, adding the remaining 2 tablespoons of wine after 4 minutes. Taste for seasoning, adding more brown sugar, salt, and/or pepper as necessary. You can serve the sauce warm or at room temperature. It will keep in the refrigerator, covered, for several weeks. Bring to room temperature before serving.

YIELD:
Makes about 1¼ cups

California

ZINFANDEL BUTTER SAUCE

Most of us are now accustomed to sipping red wine with fish, but a decade or so ago the notion seemed revolutionary if not downright alarming. Ditto for accompanying grilled seafood with a barbecue sauce based on red wine. The truth is that the tannins in red wine go exceedingly well with the smoky flavor of grilled fish—especially rich fatty fish, like swordfish and salmon. French food buffs may recognize the following sauce as a variation on classic beurre blanc (a butter and shallot sauce), but there's nothing classic about it except the way it counterpoints fish. The purplish hue of the zinfandel certainly makes an eye-popping sauce.

TIPS

You needn't open a bottle from a prized vintage to make either Zinfandel sauce, but you should use a wine you wouldn't mind drinking.

The Zinfandel Butter Sauce is not difficult to make, but it will curdle if you're not careful. The secret is to let the sauce boil while you're adding the butter, but once it's made keep it warm, not hot, and certainly not boiling.

For some people, the sauce is the barbecue.

INGREDIENTS:

3 to 5 shallots, minced (for ¾ cup)
2 cloves garlic, minced
½ teaspoon liquid smoke
1½ cups zinfandel
10 tablespoons (1¼ sticks) cold
    unsalted butter, cut into
    ½-inch slices
Coarse salt (kosher or sea) and
    freshly ground or cracked
    peppercorns

1 Place the shallots, garlic, liquid smoke, and all but 2 tablespoons of the wine in a heavy nonreactive saucepan over high heat and bring to a boil. Let the mixture boil until reduced to ¼ cup, 9 to 12 minutes.

2 Working over high heat, whisk in the butter a piece at a time to create a smooth, silky sauce. Keep the sauce boiling while you're adding the butter. Whisk in the remaining 2 tablespoons of wine and let the sauce boil for 20 seconds. Remove the saucepan from the heat and whisk in salt and pepper to taste; the sauce should be highly seasoned.

3 Keep the sauce warm on top of your grill or on a back corner of the stove until you are ready to serve it but do not let it return to a boil or it will curdle.

YIELD:
Makes about 1 cup

St. Louis, Mo.

ST. LOUIS RED (Sweet Red Barbecue Sauce)

The thing I love best about barbecue (besides it being just plain good eating) is its powers of good will and friendship. When I was on book tour in St. Louis, a local barbecue team called Super Smokers brought samples of their award-winning 'que to the TV station where I was appearing. According to Super Smoker founders Terry Black and Skip Steele, the locals like their barbecue sauce mild and sweet. An advantage to their sauce is its convenience—you make it with ingredients you can grab off any grocery store shelf. Long on character and short on preparation time, St. Louis Red is a quintessential American barbecue sauce—equally appropriate for pork, chicken, and beef.

INGREDIENTS:

4 cups ketchup

1 bottle (10 ounces) A.1. steak sauce

1 bottle (10 ounces) Heinz 57 sauce

1½ cups apple juice or apple cider

⅓ cup Worcestershire sauce

⅓ cup dark Karo syrup

⅓ cup honey

¼ cup molasses

1½ teaspoons liquid smoke

2 teaspoons freshly ground black pepper

1 teaspoon granulated garlic (see Note)

1 Combine the ketchup, A.1. steak sauce, Heinz 57 sauce, apple juice, Worcestershire sauce, Karo syrup, honey, molasses, liquid smoke, pepper, and granulated garlic in a large heavy nonreactive saucepan and gradually bring to a simmer over medium-high heat, whisking to mix.

2 Reduce the heat to medium and let the sauce simmer to blend the flavors, 5 minutes. If not serving the sauce immediately, let cool to room temperature. Transfer to clean glass jars and refrigerate until serving; the sauce will keep for several months. Bring to room temperature before using.

YIELD:

Makes about 2 quarts

NOTE: Granulated garlic is a coarse garlic powder. You could also use an equal amount of garlic powder or dried garlic flakes.

Llano, Tex.

CENTRAL TEXAS BARBECUE SAUCE

For most Texans, the soul of barbecue is the meat, not the sauce. Often Texas barbecue sauces seem like an afterthought—meat drippings mixed with a little ketchup and vinegar, with spices and flavorings kept to a minimum. Pit masters in central Texas are suspicious of sugar in barbecue, and as a result their sauces tend to be more austere than those of Memphis or Kansas City. But when it comes to sauce for a brisket or a *cabrito* (roast goat), nothing tastes quite as good as a Texas-style sauce. This recipe is loosely modeled on the one served at the legendary Cooper's in Llano (see page 670 for more about Cooper's).

TIPS

When you cook a brisket, most likely you'll have plenty of meat drippings, the flavor-rich, fatty juices that collect in the drip pan or pan. Lacking these, you could use chicken stock. Or make the bacon and onion version on page 668.

INGREDIENTS:

1 cup meat drippings
   or chicken stock

1 cup ketchup

1/2 cup cider vinegar

2 tablespoons rendered bacon fat
   or lard

1 to 2 tablespoons of your favorite
   hot sauce

1 teaspoon liquid smoke
   (optional)

Coarse salt (kosher or sea) and
   freshly ground black pepper

1 Combine the meat drippings, ketchup, vinegar, bacon fat, hot sauce, and liquid smoke, if using, with 1/2 cup of water in a large heavy nonreactive pot. Slowly bring to a boil over medium heat. Reduce the heat to medium-low and let the sauce simmer gently until richly flavored and slightly reduced, about 30 minutes, stirring from time to time to prevent scorching. Taste for seasoning, adding salt and pepper to taste.

2 Let cool to room temperature, then refrigerate, covered, until serving. The sauce will keep for 3 days. Bring to room temperature or warm before using.

YIELD:
Makes about 2 cups

VARIATION: To approximate the flavor that comes from pit smoking, I've added a few drops of liquid smoke to the recipe here. If you're feeling ambitious, you can put the pot in your smoker and cook it for several hours in the presence of hickory smoke.

Llano, Tex.

BARBECUE SAUCE
If You Don't Have Meat Drippings

OK, so you're not a full-time pit master. And you don't have meat drippings on hand. Well, here's a central Texas–style barbecue sauce that even an East Coast city dweller can make, with bacon providing the meaty richness of drippings. The lack of a sweetener is characteristic of barbecue in this part of the United States.

INGREDIENTS:

2 slices bacon, finely chopped

1 small onion, finely chopped (for 1/2 cup)

1/2 cup cider vinegar

1 cup beef or chicken stock
   (preferably homemade)

1 cup ketchup

1 to 2 tablespoons of your favorite
   hot sauce

1/2 teaspoon liquid smoke

Coarse salt (kosher or sea) and
   freshly ground black pepper to taste

1 Heat a medium saucepan over medium heat. Add the bacon and cook until the fat starts to render, about 2 minutes. Add the onion and continue cooking until the onion and bacon are golden brown, about 2 minutes.

2 Stir in the vinegar and bring to a boil. Stir in the stock, ketchup, hot sauce, and liquid smoke and let return to a boil. Reduce the heat to medium-low and let the sauce simmer until richly flavored and slightly reduced, about 30 minutes, stirring from time to time to prevent scorching. Taste for seasoning, adding salt and pepper to taste.

3 Let cool to room temperature, then refrigerate, covered, until serving. The sauce will keep for 3 days. Bring to room temperature or warm before using.

YIELD:

Makes about 2 cups

Hot sauce—use it to electrify your barbecue sauce.

INGREDIENTS:

2 cups ketchup

½ cup firmly packed brown sugar

6 to 8 tablespoons fresh lemon juice (from 3 to 4 lemons)

1 teaspoon grated lemon zest

2 tablespoons molasses

1 tablespoon Worcestershire sauce

1½ teaspoons liquid smoke

2 teaspoons dry mustard

1 teaspoon onion powder

½ teaspoon freshly ground black pepper

Nashville, Tenn.

NASHVILLE SWEET

Gentry Hughes is a television cameraman in Nashville and a fellow barbecue buff. His barbecue sauce is the sort of anointment that chicken and ribs were born for. Sweeter than the vinegar sauces of eastern Tennessee (see page 680), it's properly balanced with a bit of lemon juice. In short, it's the sort of sauce you want to eat straight from the bowl with a spoon.

1 Combine the ketchup, brown sugar, lemon juice and zest, molasses, Worcestershire sauce, liquid smoke, mustard, onion powder, and pepper in a nonreactive saucepan and whisk to mix. Let the sauce gradually come to a simmer over medium heat and simmer until thick and flavorful, 8 to 10 minutes.

2 If not serving the sauce immediately, let cool to room temperature. Transfer to clean glass jars and refrigerate until serving; the sauce will keep for several weeks. Bring to room temperature before using.

YIELD:

Makes about 3 cups

COOPER'S OLD TIME

Pit Bar-B-Que

**COOPER'S OLD
TIME PIT
BAR-B-QUE**

**505 W. Dallas Street
Llano, Texas
(915) 247-5995**

For several years, I'd been hearing about Cooper's Old Time Pit in Llano, Texas—about smoky barbecued sirloins and briskets tender enough to cut with a fork. But what prompted me to rush to my rental car and drive the 70 miles between Austin and Llano—before even checking into my hotel—was the prospect of eating *cabrito*. *Cabrito* is young goat and Cooper's is one of the few remaining barbecue joints that still serve it. The meat of a young goat is moist and tender, tasting something like a cross between lamb and veal, and its ribs are about as slender as Popsicle sticks.

Cooper's began as a cinder block roadhouse on the route between Houston and west Texas. The low-lying farmland you find surrounding the Kreuz Market (see page 166) and Louie Mueller's (see page 678) has given way to rolling mesquite and scrub-covered hills. After its founder, Tommy Cooper, died in an auto accident in 1979, a former employee, Terry Wooten, bought the restaurant. It remains a family business to this day.

If you want to know how Texas barbecue is made, just visit Cooper's. Nothing about the process is secret. In fact, all the cooking is done outdoors in seven rectangular pits under a corrugated steel awning next to the parking lot. The first thing you see when you pull off the highway is a mountain of mesquite logs. The restaurant employs two men to do nothing but split and haul logs (on a busy Saturday or Sunday, Cooper's will burn three cords). The logs are burned to glowing embers in a man-high "burn barrel" that gets so hot, pit masters need a 12-foot-long shovel just to approach it.

MESQUITE MATTERS

This brings us to the first of two fundamental differences between Cooper's and the lowland barbecue joints: The meat owes its robust smoke flavor to mesquite, not oak, and it's cooked by a process more akin to direct grilling than barbecue. The pits are stoked with mesquite embers shoveled in every half hour or so from the burn barrel. The meat is positioned on a grate about 2 feet over the coals, so it sizzles directly over the fire. (Unlike the grilling you do at home, though, the distance between

. . . the battered pots simmering away at the back of the pit.

Tending the mesquite-wood–burning pit at Cooper's.

the food and the fire allows the meat to roast slowly without burning.) This unique configuration offers the best of both grilling and smoking, producing barbecue that's always crusty, succulent, and redolent with smoke.

There's something else that sets Cooper's apart, and it's visible in the battered pots simmering away at the back of the pit. Cooper's has a barbecue sauce that's actually used for cooking. By Kansas City standards, it would be pretty Spartan—a mixture of ketchup, vinegar, water, black pepper, Louisiana hot sauce, lard, and brisket drippings. What makes it so tasty is that the sauce is smoked on the pit for 48 hours, and much of the meat is actually dipped into it before serving. "Typically, we sear our briskets for a couple of hours over the coals, dip them in sauce, wrap them in foil, and finish cooking them over a low heat," explains manager Bruce Hatter. For the purist, Cooper's meat is also available dry, but 80 percent of the customers order it dipped.

Service at Cooper's is a pretty no-frills affair: You order at one of the pits, take your uncut meat inside, where it's weighed on a red plastic tray and sliced if you desire. The accompaniments include chopped onion, pickled jalapeño peppers, and simmering pots of barbecue sauce and pinto beans. The latter are flavored with bacon, garlic, and jalapeños, but not one grain of sugar. They are distant relations of the sweet baked beans served with most American barbecue, and their lack of sweetness makes them soulful companions for smoky brisket and goat.

Lining up at Cooper's for barbecue hot off the pit.

. . . barbecue that's always crusty, succulent, and redolent with smoke.

Louisville, Ky.

KENTUCKY BARBECUE SAUCE

I first met Jane Lee Rankin at a book signing. Her charming book, *Cookin' Up a Storm,* tells the story of Annie Johnson, a deeply religious black woman who came to work for the Rankins as a maid and wound up becoming a close friend and adopted family member. Annie Johnson excelled at the simple, soulful cooking for which her native Kentucky is famous, and just reading about her buttermilk biscuits, cheese grits, and chicken and dumplings makes my salivary glands ache. There's nothing really remarkable about her barbecue sauce— except that it's precisely the sort of sauce that legions of Southerners have slathered on their ribs for centuries: sweet, smooth, buttery, tangy with vinegar, and piqued with hot sauce. I've taken a few liberties with Annie Johnson's recipe, but remained faithful to the sauce's spirit. If ever there was a sauce for slow-smoked ribs, it's this one. It's also good on pork shoulder, barbecued chicken, and beef.

INGREDIENTS:

1 tablespoon vegetable oil
2 slices of bacon, cut into ¼-inch slivers
1 small onion, minced
2 cloves garlic, minced
1 piece (3 inches square) green bell pepper, minced
1 can (28 ounces) tomato purée
½ cup cider vinegar
¼ cup Worcestershire sauce
¾ cup firmly packed brown sugar
8 tablespoons (1 stick) unsalted butter
1 to 3 teaspoons hot sauce
1 teaspoon coarse salt (kosher or sea)
½ teaspoon freshly ground black pepper
½ teaspoon hot red pepper flakes

1 Heat the oil in a large heavy non-reactive saucepan over medium heat. Add the bacon and cook until the fat is rendered, about 3 minutes. Add the onion, garlic, and bell pepper and cook until the vegetables are soft and translucent and the bacon is crisp, about 3 minutes longer.

2 Whisk in the tomato purée, vinegar, Worcestershire sauce, brown sugar, butter, hot sauce, salt, black pepper, and hot red pepper flakes. Add ¾ cup of water and bring the sauce to a boil over medium heat. Reduce the heat to medium-low and let the sauce simmer,

Jane Lee Rankin and Annie Johnson: partners is sauce and Southern cooking.

uncovered, until thick and richly flavored, 20 to 30 minutes, stirring as
needed. The sauce can be served hot or
at room temperature.

3 If not serving the sauce immediately, let cool to room temperature. Transfer to clean glass jars and
refrigerate until serving; the sauce will
keep for several weeks. Bring to room
temperature before using.

YIELD:
Makes about 1 quart

St. Louis, Mo.

SKIP'S APPLE BARBECUE SAUCE

"**H**ere, taste this," said my St. Louis
barbecue buddy Skip Steele, placing a jar of reddish-brown barbecue sauce before me with an attitude of
defiant conspiracy. He seemed to be
suggesting that even though I was an
East Coaster I just might be able to
appreciate a St. Louis barbecue sauce
that owed its mellow fruity sweetness
to the addition of apple jelly—a sauce
that continues to be in the develop-
ment stage, although Skip has been

working on it for years. His defiance
seemed to challenge me to figure out
what else was in the sauce. Here's how
I would make Skip's sauce or something very nearly like it. I can't think of
a smoked pork, chicken, or rib that
wouldn't shine in its presence.

INGREDIENTS:
¾ **cup ketchup**
¾ **cup chili sauce, such as Heinz**
6 **tablespoons apple jelly**
3 **tablespoons cider vinegar**
2 **tablespoons brown sugar**
1 **tablespoon molasses**
1 **tablespoon Worcestershire sauce**
1 to 2 **teaspoons Tabasco sauce**
1 **teaspoon liquid smoke**
½ **teaspoon hot red pepper flakes**
½ **teaspoon freshly ground black pepper**

1 Combine the ketchup, chili sauce,
apple jelly, vinegar, brown sugar,
molasses, Worcestershire sauce, Tabasco
sauce, liquid smoke, hot red pepper
flakes, and black pepper with ½ cup
water in a large heavy nonreactive
saucepan and whisk to mix. Bring the
sauce to a simmer over medium-high
heat. Reduce the heat to medium-low
and let the sauce simmer gently until
thick and richly flavored, about 15 minutes, whisking occasionally.

2 If not serving the sauce immediately, let cool to room temperature. Transfer to a clean glass jar and
refrigerate until serving; the sauce
will keep for several weeks. Bring to
room temperature before using.

YIELD:
Makes about 2 cups

TIPS

Chili sauce comes
in twelve-ounce
bottles and can be
found next to the
ketchups and hot
sauces at most
supermarkets. One
well-known brand
is Heinz.

WALL OF FLAME

VINCE STATEN'S OLD TIME BARBECUE

The respect Vince Staten accords barbecue sauce will be apparent the moment you sit down—there are six at the ready to squirt onto hand-pulled shoulders, smoky briskets, and ribs tender enough to tug apart with your fingers. The timid of tongue can try the Texas sweet or the whisky-laced Jack sauce, while hot pepper fiends can test their capsaicin tolerance on Staten's Legal Limit. Save room for the homemade banana pudding.

9219 U.S. Highway 42
Prospect, Kentucky
(502) 228-7427

Lawrenceburg, Ky.

WILD TURKEY BARBECUE SAUCE

Booze and barbecue share traditions that go back to the founding of our country. The second time George Washington ran for public office he launched his campaign with a barbecue. (The first time he had neglected to do so, and lost the election—a mistake he never repeated.) The pairing remains part of the political process in the United States to this day.

This tangy sauce taps another venerable American tradition: spiking barbecue sauces with spirits, in this case Wild Turkey bourbon. The honey and brown sugar mellow the boozy bite of the alcohol. All manner of pork, from grilled chops to smoked ribs and shoulders, would be good with the sauce. Or serve it with any of the grilled or smoked turkeys on pages 411 through 425.

INGREDIENTS:

3 tablespoons unsalted butter
1 medium-size onion, finely chopped
2 cloves garlic, minced
1 piece (2 inches square) green bell pepper, minced
1 cup ketchup
1 cup chili sauce, such as Heinz
¹/₂ cup Wild Turkey bourbon
¹/₄ cup fresh lemon juice
¹/₄ cup cider vinegar
¹/₄ cup honey
¹/₄ cup firmly packed dark brown sugar
2 tablespoons Worcestershire sauce
2 tablespoons prepared mustard
2 to 4 teaspoons of your favorite hot sauce
1 teaspoon liquid smoke
¹/₂ teaspoon freshly ground black pepper

1 Melt the butter in a large heavy non-reactive saucepan over medium heat. Add the onion, garlic, and bell pepper and cook until the vegetables are soft but not brown, about 4 minutes.

2 Add the ketchup, chili sauce, bourbon, lemon juice, vinegar, honey, brown sugar, Worcestershire sauce, mustard, hot sauce, liquid smoke, and black pepper and stir to mix. Let come to a boil over medium heat, then reduce the heat to medium-low. Let the sauce simmer gently until thick and richly flavored, about 30 minutes, stirring often with a wooden spoon to prevent scorching.

3 If not serving the sauce immediately, let cool to room temperature. Transfer to clean glass jars and refrigerate until serving; the sauce will keep for several months. Bring to room temperature before serving.

YIELD:

Makes about 3 cups

Colorado

CHILE SAMBUCA BARBECUE SAUCE

Fraser Ellis is a Colorado-born barbecue buff and Broadway dancer turned chef. I met him in the kitchen of a fabulous Dallas cookware and tableware shop called Cookworks. His barbecue sauce executes an intricate ballet of sweetness and fire—the sweetness comes from brown sugar, molasses, and honey, the heat is supplied by Asian chile sauce and chipotle peppers. Then there's the unexpected shot of sambuca, and I think you'll find the hint of licorice it adds is as delectable as it is unexpected.

INGREDIENTS:

3 cups ketchup

1 cup molasses

6 tablespoons dark brown sugar

3 tablespoons liquid smoke

2 tablespoons Dijon mustard

2 tablespoons Worcestershire sauce

2 tablespoons tomato paste

2 tablespoons sambuca or other anise-flavored liqueur

1½ tablespoons honey

1 tablespoon chile garlic sauce

2 teaspoons soy sauce

2 canned chipotle peppers, minced, with 2 teaspoons can juices

1 Combine the ketchup, molasses, brown sugar, liquid smoke, mustard, Worcestershire sauce, tomato paste, sambuca, honey, chile garlic sauce, soy sauce, and the chipotles and their juices in a nonreactive saucepan. Bring to a simmer over medium heat. Let the sauce simmer until richly flavored, about 15 minutes, stirring occasionally with a wooden spoon.

2 If not serving the sauce immediately, let cool to room temperature. Transfer to clean glass jars and place a piece of plastic wrap between the jars and the lids to keep the lids from corroding. The sauce will keep, refrigerated, for several months. Bring to room temperature before using.

YIELD:

Makes about 5 cups

Kentucky

CHILI SAUCE BARBECUE SAUCE

As you travel the American barbecue trail, sauces made with chiles will be your constant companions. But just what the sauces are like

Chiles whole, pickled, or puréed add pizzazz to barbecue sauce.

varies widely from region to region. South of the border and in Texas and New Mexico, chili sauce describes a fairly incendiary condiment made from pickled fresh or ground dried chiles. In Asian neighborhoods on the West Coast, a request for chili sauce might bring you a sweet, sticky condiment that's only mildly hot. The barbecue sauce here is based on the mainstream American chili sauce—a variation on ketchup manufactured by Heinz and other companies. How it came to be labeled chili sauce has always perplexed me—it has no appreciable heat. Like many sauces from Kentucky this one emphasizes tomato rather than smoke.

INGREDIENTS:

¾ cup chili sauce, such as Heinz
⅓ cup tomato purée
3 tablespoons Worcestershire sauce
2 tablespoons cider vinegar, or more to taste
2 tablespoons canola oil
1 small onion, minced (for ½ cup)
1 clove garlic, minced
2 tablespoons brown sugar, or more to taste
1 teaspoon dry mustard
Coarse salt (kosher or sea) and freshly ground black pepper to taste

1 Combine the chili sauce, tomato purée, Worcestershire sauce, vinegar, oil, onion, garlic, brown sugar, and mustard with ¾ cup of water in a heavy nonreactive saucepan. Bring to a boil over medium-high heat. Reduce the heat to medium, loosely cover the pan, and let the sauce simmer gently until thick and richly flavored, 15 to 20 minutes, stirring as needed to keep it from scorching. If the sauce is too thick, add a little more water. Taste for seasoning, adding more vinegar and/or brown sugar as necessary and salt and pepper to taste; the sauce should be a little sweet, a little sour, and highly seasoned.

2 If not serving the sauce immediately, let cool to room temperature. Transfer to a clean glass jar and refrigerate until serving. It will keep for several weeks. Bring to room temperature before using.

YIELD:
Makes about 2 cups

Holmdel, N.J.

DONNA'S SWEET AND GARLICKY SLATHER SAUCE

A s publicist and trend watcher for the Hearth, Patio & Barbecue Association, Donna Myers probably knows more about the state of barbecuing and grilling in the United States than anyone else on the planet. But she's no mere theoretician. (Her deck in Holmdel, New Jersey, with its dozens of grills, would be the envy of pit masters everywhere.) And Donna's willing to put her proverbial money where her mouth is. Some years back, she created this kicky sauce for spareribs, and she liked it so much, she was soon slathering it on everything. The sauce has something for everyone: the sweetness of honey and corn syrup, the rich, salty tang of soy sauce, and vampire-defying doses of garlic. Best of all, you don't even have to cook it—ideal for layabouts who don't like to turn on the stove during the dog days of summer.

ADVANCE PREPARATION:
6 to 12 hours for refrigerating the sauce

INGREDIENTS:
6 scallions, both white and green parts, trimmed and cut into 2-inch pieces

6 cloves garlic, peeled and gently crushed with the side of a cleaver
1 piece (1 inch) fresh ginger, peeled, cut into ¼-inch slices, and gently crushed with the side of a cleaver
½ cup soy sauce (preferably Kikkoman)
¼ cup ketchup
¼ cup chili sauce
¼ cup dark corn syrup
¼ cup honey
½ teaspoon Wright's Liquid Hickory Smoke Seasoning

C ombine the scallions, garlic, ginger, soy sauce, ketchup, chili sauce, corn syrup, honey, and smoke seasoning with ¼ cup water in a nonreactive bowl, whisk to mix, and let stand, covered, in the refrigerator, for at least 6 hours, or better still, overnight. Strain the sauce into clean glass jars, discarding the scallions, garlic, and ginger. Refrigerate the sauce; it will keep for several weeks. Bring to room temperature before using.

YIELD:
Makes about 2 cups

TIPS

Donna makes a double batch of her sauce, then uses half as a baste for barbecued ribs (that's enough for four racks of baby backs) and serves the other half as a barbecue sauce at the table. The sauce goes exceedingly well with pork, chicken, shrimp, and even fish.

Pit mistress Donna Myers.

LOUIE MUELLER BARBEQUE

At Louie Mueller, each brisket is sliced by hand to order.

LOUIE MUELLER BARBEQUE

205 West Second
Taylor, Texas
(512) 352-6206
www.texasbbq.com
And other locations

Founded by a German American, Louie Mueller's began as a grocery store and meat market. Its menu and decor have remained pretty much the same since the 1940s. Located in the somnolent town of Taylor, Texas, Louie Mueller's is a time capsule: its mismatched wood tables lined up under bare florescent lights, its once green walls darkened by time to an indeterminate shade of brown. Decades worth of business cards flake off a bulletin board on one wall of the smoky dining room like paint off the side of an old barn.

If you want to know the secret ingredient at Louie Mueller's, just look up at a skylight. It's completely blackened with smoke. Just as his father did before him, the sexagenarian owner and pit master Bobby Mueller burns only native post oak in a pair of pits (one made of metal, the other of darkened white brick) that were built in 1959. There's nothing special about the seasonings, just salt and pepper. So why is the barbecue at Louie Mueller's so esteemed that customers start arriving at 10:00 A.M.?

For starters, there's the Mueller family work ethic. Louie himself worked until the age of 86. Bobby arrives at work on weekdays at 4:00 A.M. and on weekends at 1:30 A.M. to fire up the pits. All the sausages are made on the premises, although Bobby did recently break down and purchase a new electric sausage stuffer. He coddles the fifty briskets he cooks daily, swaddling each in red butcher paper the moment it's cooked to keep it from drying out.

SMOKE GETS IN YOUR EYES

Another key ingredient is time. Bobby smokes his briskets for seven hours; his dinosaur-size beef ribs for an hour and a half; and his peppery pork loins for an hour. Even his chicken breasts take a full forty-five minutes to smoke. After a lifetime in the business, he can tell if

Smoke from the pit leaves Louis Mueller in perpetual darkness.

a brisket is done by simply looking at it. Each and every order is sliced on the spot ("There are no steam tables here," observes Bobby). Then the brisket is rewrapped until the next customer places his order. "Every customer gets an end cut," Bobby says.

Mueller's smoky beef and pork are quintessential Texas barbecue, and the hot links (jalapeño sausages) all but burst under the weight of their own juices and squirt when you cut into them. Unlike the Kreuz Market in Lockhart, Texas (see page 166) Louie Mueller's deigns to serve barbecue sauce—a runny amalgam of ketchup, margarine, water, onion, salt, and pepper. "We keep it pretty simple," says Mueller. "We don't want to distract from the meat."

Patrons arrive in a trickle, then a stream; by lunchtime, there's a torrent. "How hungry are you?" the counter guy asks. "Hungry," said in a long, slow drawl, is the reply. So Bobby loads guests up with mountains of fresh sliced meat sold by the pound, delectable mustardy potato salad, and all the white bread they can eat. Nobody leaves Louie Mueller's hungry.

Patrons arrive in a trickle, then a stream and finally a torrent.

A sign you can't—and shouldn't—miss.

TIPS

Coca-Cola is a popular ingredient in Southern barbecue sauces—it's sweet, acidic, and highly aromatic—just what you want a barbecue sauce to be.

Franklin, Tenn.

THE DOCTOR'S MEDICINE

"So what's a Tennessee barbecue sauce?" I asked a roomful of students I was teaching at the Viking Culinary Arts Center in Franklin, Tennessee. I might just as well have queried a panel of medieval theologians on the number of angels that can dance on the head of a pin. After fifteen minutes of debate, I seemed to detect two distinguishing features emerging— the use of tomato sauce instead of ketchup as the base and the presence of a strong souring agent in the form of vinegar or fresh lemon juice. The very sort of sauce made by Tennessean Chris Gafford, physician when not captain of the General Porkitioners barbecue team. "What I like about medicine is that it pays for my barbecue habit," explains Chris, who formed his first barbecue team, the Flying Pigs, while still in med school. Now that's my kind of doctor, and this is definitely the kind of medicine I can swallow.

INGREDIENTS:

2 cups tomato sauce
¾ cup chili sauce, such as Heinz
¾ cup Coca-Cola
2 to 3 tablespoons fresh lemon juice
    (from 1 lemon; save the rind)
2 tablespoons Dijon mustard
1 tablespoon Worcestershire sauce
1½ teaspoons liquid smoke
1 teaspoon hot sauce, or more to taste
¼ cup firmly packed dark brown
    sugar
1 to 2 teaspoons freshly ground
    black pepper
½ teaspoon coarse salt (kosher or sea)
1 teaspoon garlic powder
1 teaspoon onion powder
1 teaspoon dry mustard

1 Combine the tomato sauce, chili sauce, cola, lemon juice and rind, prepared mustard, Worcestershire sauce, liquid smoke, hot sauce, brown sugar, pepper, salt, garlic powder, onion powder, and dry mustard in a large heavy nonreactive saucepan and whisk to mix. Gradually bring the sauce to a simmer over medium heat and let simmer until thick and flavorful, 20 to 30 minutes, stirring often to prevent scorching. Taste for seasoning, adding more hot sauce as necessary.

2 Remove and discard the lemon rind. If not serving the sauce immediately, let cool to room temperature. Transfer to clean glass jars and refrigerate until serving. It will keep for 1 month. Bring to room temperature before serving.

YIELD:
Makes about 1 quart

South Carolina

SMOKY HONEY MUSTARD BARBECUE SAUCE

Mustard sauces are one of the best kept barbecue secrets in the United States. They're primarily found in South Carolina and Georgia, although I've enjoyed them as far north as Boston. Barbecue buffs in Southern parts understand the small miracles that mustard can work on pork. A good mustard sauce is a study in equipoise: The bite of mustard and mouth-pucker of vinegar are offset by the sweetness of honey or brown sugar. I like to provide a smoke flavor by adding a strip of fried bacon. Coffee adds just the right touch of bitterness.

INGREDIENTS:

1 tablespoon salted butter

1 slice bacon, cut into ¼-inch slivers

1 medium-size onion, finely chopped

1 to 2 jalapeño peppers, seeded and
    finely chopped (for a hotter sauce leave
    the seeds in)

⅔ cup grainy mustard (preferably Meaux)

⅔ cup honey

½ cup cider vinegar

¼ cup brewed coffee

Coarse salt (kosher or sea) and
    freshly ground black pepper

1 Melt the butter in a heavy non-reactive saucepan over medium heat. Add the bacon and cook, stirring often, until the fat starts to render, about 3 minutes. Add the onion and jalapeño(s) and cook until the bacon is crisp and the onion is soft and translucent, 3 to 5 minutes.

2 Stir in the mustard, honey, vinegar, and coffee. Let the sauce simmer, uncovered, until thick and richly flavored, 6 to 10 minutes. Season with salt and pepper to taste. Let the sauce cool to room temperature before serving. If not serving the sauce immediately, transfer it to a clean glass jar. Place a piece of plastic wrap between the jar and the lid to keep the lid from corroding. The sauce will keep refrigerated, for at least a week. Bring to room temperature before using.

YIELD:
Makes 2 cups

Pittsburgh, Penn.

MADE-FROM-SCRATCH KETCHUP

Ketchup ranks among the world's most popular and widely used condiments, and although we

TIPS

Mustard sauces were originally designed for serving with pork, and this smoky honeyed sauce is great with everything from ribs to shoulders to chops. But that's just a start, because once you acquire a taste for mustard sauce, you'll want to slather it on chicken, turkey, beef, even rabbit and lamb.

TIPS

The first ketchups were more like chutneys than the smooth condiment we pour over hamburgers today. I call for this ketchup to be left chunky, but you could certainly purée it in a food processor if you prefer.

From this humble wagon, a global ketchup empire began.

Americans didn't invent the stuff (the first ketchups were made in England, inspired by a Malaysian pickled anchovy sauce called *ket-tsiap*), we've certainly made it a household staple. Ketchup's success is due in large part to Henry Heinz, the Pennsylvania entrepreneur who in the 1870s bottled what has become the world's best-known commercial ketchup. Given ketchup's universal availability, why would anyone bother to make it from scratch? Well, for starters, there's the pride of workmanship that comes from making your own sauce. And imagine the reaction at your next barbecue when you casually remark that the ketchup is homemade.

INGREDIENTS:

2 cans (35 ounces each) peeled tomatoes
3 tablespoons canola oil
1 large onion, finely chopped
   (for about 1½ cups)
2 cloves garlic, minced
½ cup firmly packed dark brown sugar,
   or more to taste
½ cup tarragon vinegar or distilled
   white vinegar, or more to taste
2 tablespoons pure chile powder
2 teaspoons Tabasco sauce
1 tablespoon yellow mustard
1 teaspoon coarse salt (kosher or sea),
   or more to taste
½ teaspoon freshly ground black pepper
½ teaspoon cayenne pepper
½ teaspoon celery seed
½ teaspoon ground coriander
¼ teaspoon ground allspice
¼ teaspoon ground cloves

1 Drain the tomatoes, reserving the juices. Cut each tomato in half and squeeze out the seeds. You should have about 4 cups of tomatoes.

2 Heat the oil in a large nonreactive saucepan over medium heat. Add the onion and garlic and cook, uncovered, until just beginning to brown, about 5 minutes. Increase the heat to high, add the tomato halves, brown sugar, vinegar, chile powder, Tabasco sauce, mustard, salt, black pepper, cayenne, celery seed, coriander, allspice, cloves, and 1 cup of the reserved tomato liquid and bring to a boil.

3 Reduce the heat to medium and let the ketchup simmer gently, uncovered, until the tomatoes have mostly disintegrated and the sauce is thick and rich, 30 to 40 minutes, adding tomato liquid as needed to keep the mixture wet. Taste for seasoning, adding more brown sugar, vinegar, and/or salt as necessary; the ketchup should be highly seasoned. Let cool to room temperature, then transfer to clean glass jars and place a piece of plastic wrap between the tops and the lids. The ketchup will keep, refrigerated, for several months.

YIELD:
Makes 3 to 4 cups

San Juan, P.R.

TROPICAL FRUIT KETCHUP

Go to a barbecue and you're sure to find ketchup. Oceans are consumed on hot dogs and burgers, and it's the primary ingredient in any number of barbecue sauces. So you may be surprised to learn that tomato ketchup is a relatively new invention (it dates from the nineteenth century) and that in the colonial period, pit masters had their choice of dozens of varieties of ketchup, made with everything from walnuts to anchovies. This tropical fruit ketchup has been simmering away in my mind ever since I toured the fruit markets and juice bars of San Juan, Puerto Rico, where locally grown pineapples, papayas, sapodillas, and soursops have an almost supernatural fragrance. Guava paste adds an unmistakable perfumed sweetness—a bright note to contrast the earthy aromatics of cardamom, coriander, and ginger. The most obvious destination for fruit ketchup is grilled pork or poultry, but you could certainly serve it with a rich grilled seafood, like salmon, mahimahi, or shrimp.

INGREDIENTS:
4 cups diced mixed fresh tropical fruits
    (including bananas, mangos, pineapple,
    papayas, and/or other exotic fruits)
1/4 cup dark raisins
1/2 cup pineapple juice
3 tablespoons dark rum
2 tablespoons unsalted butter
    or canola oil
1 small onion, finely chopped
1 tablespoon minced peeled fresh ginger
1 to 2 jalapeño peppers, seeded and
    minced (for a hotter ketchup,
    leave the seeds in)
1 teaspoon ground cardamom
1 teaspoon ground coriander
1 teaspoon ground cinnamon
1/2 teaspoon freshly ground black pepper
1/2 cup guava paste, cut into 1/2-inch dice
3 to 4 tablespoons brown sugar,
    or more to taste
3 tablespoons fresh lime juice
2 tablespoons cider vinegar,
    or more to taste
1/4 teaspoon coarse salt (kosher or sea),
    or more to taste

TIPS

■ When choosing fruits for this ketchup, let your nose, not your eyes, be your guide. Many tropical fruits smell and taste best when their skins are so shriveled and black they look like you should throw them out.

■ The best guava paste is the kind sold in flat cans. Look for it in the section of your local supermarket where preserves or ethnic foods are located.

Strawberries are even more perishable than tomatoes. You can have all the ingredients chopped ahead of time, but try to serve the salsa within fifteen minutes of mixing it.

1 Place the tropical fruit mix, raisins, pineapple juice, and rum in a nonreactive mixing bowl and toss to mix. Let the fruit sit for 15 minutes.

2 Meanwhile, melt the butter in a nonreactive saucepan. Add the onion, ginger, jalapeño(s), cardamom, coriander, cinnamon, and black pepper and cook over medium heat until the onion is just beginning to brown, about 4 minutes.

3 Stir in the fruit mixture, guava paste, brown sugar, lime juice, vinegar, and salt. Let the ketchup simmer, uncovered, until the guava paste is melted and the fruit is very soft, about 10 minutes. Transfer the ketchup to a blender or food processor and process or blend to a smooth purée. Taste for seasoning, adding more brown sugar, vinegar, and/or salt as necessary; the ketchup should be a little sweet, a little tart, and very flavorful. Let cool to room temperature, then transfer the ketchup to clean glass jars or squirt bottles. The ketchup will keep, refrigerated, for several weeks.

YIELD:
**Makes 2½ to
3 cups**

Santa Fe, N.Mex.

STRAWBERRY "SALSA"

S trawberry salsa? Sounds peculiar, but it tastes great, which is a paradox much prized by ambitious grill masters. At first glance the salsa looks like a conventional tomato one—a study of reds and whites (the onions), with vivid bits of green for accent. But one taste and you know you're not in Texas anymore. Actually, the strawberries, with their acidic sweetness, function in a way similar to that of the more traditional tomatoes. I first tasted this salsa in Santa Fe and I was struck by how intriguing it would be with grilled

Strawberry "Salsa"—who needs tomatoes?

chicken, duck, or salmon. Of course, you could also go the dessert route, adding a tablespoon or two of brown sugar and serving the salsa with grilled pineapple or pound cake.

INGREDIENTS:

- 1 pint ripe strawberries
- 1 to 4 serrano peppers, seeded and finely chopped (for a hotter salsa, leave the seeds in)
- 1/4 cup finely diced sweet white onion
- 1/4 cup finely chopped fresh mint
- 3 tablespoons fresh lime juice
- 1 to 2 teaspoons brown sugar (optional)

1 Rinse, hull, and blot the strawberries dry with paper towels. Trim any white or blemished spots off, then cut the berries into 1/4-inch dice.

2 Place the diced strawberries, the serranos, onion, mint, and lime juice in a nonreactive mixing bowl, but don't mix until right before serving (the virtue of this salsa is its freshness). Toss the ingredients gently to keep the berries from bruising. Taste for seasoning; if the strawberries are sweet, you won't need to add the brown sugar. Serve the salsa within 15 minutes of mixing.

YIELD:

Makes 1 1/2 cups

Baltimore, Md.

WATERMELON SALSA

When I was growing up, Baltimore was a pretty backwater town. We still had a "melon man," who drove a horse-drawn wagon piled high with enormous ripe watermelons. Occasionally, my grandfather would stop him to buy one (I was more interested in petting the horse). I swear those were the sweetest melons I ever

TIPS

■ There once was a time when there was only one type of watermelon: large, green, elongated, and bright red inside. Today, watermelons come in a stunning array of shapes and colors: large or small; round or oval; bright red, pale pink, or even yellow. Any of these will give you great salsa.

■ To make an uptown salsa, take the time to cut the watermelon into 3/4-inch balls, using a melon baller. Or you can cut it into 1/4-inch dice. If you're feeling really ambitious, you can cut off a quarter or a third of the watermelon and use the hollowed shell as a serving bowl.

Nothing beats the taste test for determining the sweetness of a watermelon.

tasted, especially when seasoned with years of nostalgia. Watermelon gets a twenty-first-century makeover in this recipe—a sizzling salsa made with watermelon and cucumber with just enough jalapeño for bite. Serve it whenever you need a colorful salsa with a succulence as refreshing as a swig of soda pop.

Serve this salsa with any of the smoked turkeys on pages 411 through 425. It would also be terrific with any sort of grilled wild game.

INGREDIENTS:

3 tablespoons fresh lime juice

2 tablespoons light brown sugar,
    or more to taste

4 cups watermelon balls or
    diced watermelon, seeds
    removed with a fork

1 cup cantaloupe or honeydew balls
    or diced cantaloupe or honeydew

1 medium-size cucumber, peeled, seeded,
    and cut into 1/2-inch dice

1/2 cup finely diced red onion

2 to 4 jalapeño peppers, seeded and
    finely chopped (for a hotter salsa,
    leave the seeds in)

2 tablespoons finely chopped
    candied ginger

1/4 cup chopped fresh mint

Combine the lime juice and brown sugar in a nonreactive bowl and whisk until the brown sugar dissolves. Add the watermelon, cantaloupe, cucumber, onion, jalapeños, ginger, and mint and gently toss to mix. Taste for sweetness, adding more brown sugar as necessary. You can cut up the ingredients ahead of time, but the salsa tastes best served within 1 hour of tossing.

YIELD:

Serves 6 to 8

Wisconsin

HELLFIRE CRANBERRY SALSA

Massachusetts is the best-known supplier of cranberries, but Wisconsin actually produces the most. If you've always found cranberry sauce to be too sweet, this brash salsa is for you. A modicum of brown sugar cuts the astringency of the cranberries, but because the berries are left raw, you'd never accuse this salsa of being overly saccharine.

INGREDIENTS:

1 bag (12 ounces) cranberries

1/3 cup toasted pecans (see page 728)

1/3 cup firmly packed brown sugar,
    or more to taste

3 scallions, both white and green parts,
    trimmed and coarsely chopped

1 clove garlic, finely chopped

2 jalapeño peppers, or more, seeded and
    coarsely chopped (for a hotter salsa,
    leave the seeds in)

1/3 cup coarsely chopped fresh cilantro

1/3 cup fresh lime juice, or more to taste

1 tablespoon olive oil

Coarse salt (kosher or sea) and freshly
    ground black pepper to taste

1 Spread the cranberries out on a rimmed baking sheet and pick through them, removing any stems.

2 Place the pecans and brown sugar in a food processor and coarsely chop. Add the cranberries, scallions, garlic, jalapeños, and cilantro to the food processor and pulse to coarsely chop the cranberries.

3 Add the lime juice and olive oil. Process just to mix. Taste for seasoning, adding more brown sugar and/or lime juice as necessary and season with salt and pepper to taste. The salsa can be refrigerated, covered, for 3 days, but tastes best served within 3 hours of being made. If refrigerated, bring to room temperature before using.

YIELD:

Makes about 2 cups

Georgia

HONEY BOURBON PEACH SALSA

Part sauce, part condiment, part salad, this salsa is 100 percent delicious. It's versatile enough to accompany barbecued chicken, smoked ham, and grilled salmon. (For that matter, it's pretty compelling eaten straight off the spoon.) Peaches are a Georgia specialty, of course, but serve this salsa with any sort of Southern-style barbecue or grilled food.

INGREDIENTS:

2 tablespoons honey, or more to taste

1 tablespoon bourbon

1 tablespoon sambal oelek (hot chile paste), or ½ to 1 Scotch bonnet chile or other hot chile, seeded and minced (for a hotter salsa, leave the seeds in)

3 tablespoons fresh lime juice, or more to taste

3 ripe peaches, peeled, pitted, and cut into ½-inch pieces (for a more rustic salsa, leave the skins on)

½ red bell pepper, cut into ¼-inch dice

1 poblano pepper, or ½ green bell pepper, cored, seeded, and cut into ¼-inch dice

¼ red onion, finely diced (for ¼ cup)

¼ cup chopped fresh mint

Combine the honey, bourbon, *sambal oelek,* and lime juice in a nonreactive mixing bowl and whisk until the honey is dissolved. Add the peaches, bell pepper, poblano, onion, and mint and gently toss to mix. Taste for seasoning, adding more lime juice and/or honey to taste; the salsa should be highly seasoned. Like most salsas, this one tastes best served within 30 minutes of mixing.

YIELD:

Makes about 3 cups

VARIATION: For an even more flavorful version of this recipe, grill the peaches and peppers over a hardwood fire.

TIPS

■ Use squeezably soft peaches so ripe and fragrant, you can smell them when you enter the room. If this is not the state of your peaches, let them ripen at room temperature until it is.

■ *Sambal oelek* is an Indonesian chile paste, but it's sufficiently popular among contemporary American chefs to be available at most gourmet shops and many supermarkets. If you can't find it, use a diced hot chile pepper.

TIPS

■ The root of a plant in the bean family, jicama was once found primarily in ethnic markets. It's now available in the produce section of most supermarkets. The easiest way to peel jicama is to use a sharp paring knife.

■ If a mango isn't available, you could certainly use a cantaloupe or even a peach in the Jicama Salsa.

New Mexico

JICAMA SALSA

Jicama is a crisp, turnip-shaped, tan-skinned, white-fleshed root vegetable that tastes like a cross between an apple and a potato. There's nothing like it for adding a refreshing crunch to a salsa or salad. Thus, jicama often turns up at barbecues on both sides of New Mexico's southern border (it's grown in Mexico). A salsa made from it may take people by surprise, but it goes great with any Southwestern-style grilled meat, poultry, or seafood.

INGREDIENTS:

1 medium jicama (about 1 pound),
   peeled and cut into 1/4-inch dice
1 ripe mango or small cantaloupe,
   cut into 1/4-inch dice
1/2 red bell pepper, cut into 1/4-inch dice
1/2 yellow bell pepper, or more
   red bell pepper, cut into 1/4-inch dice
2 scallions, both white and green parts,
   trimmed and finely chopped
2 to 4 jalapeño peppers,
   seeded and minced (for a hotter salsa,
   leave the seeds in)
1 tablespoon finely chopped candied or
   fresh ginger
1/3 cup chopped fresh mint or cilantro
3 tablespoons fresh lime juice,
   or more to taste
1 tablespoon extra-virgin olive oil
2 tablespoons brown sugar,
   or more to taste

Combine the jicama, mango, red and yellow bell peppers, scallions, jalapeños, ginger, mint, lime juice, olive oil, and brown sugar in a nonreactive mixing bowl and toss to mix. Taste for seasoning, adding more lime juice and/or brown sugar as necessary; the salsa should be a little sweet and a little sour. You can put the ingredients in the bowl up to 2 hours before serving but toss them at the last minute, ideally not more than 30 minutes before serving.

YIELD:
Makes 4 cups

El Paso, Tex.

EL PASO PICANTE

Picante is the name of a family of salsas enjoyed in Texas and in the American Southwest. Some are mildly *picante* (spicy); others are seriously hot. My advice is to add as many jalapeños as you dare. In southern Texas, it's customary to cook a *picante* after the ingredients are mixed together, but I like to grill the tomatoes, onions, peppers, and garlic before combining them to add an extra dimension of fire and wood smoke. Serve El Paso Picante with any sort of grilled meat, poultry, or seafood, especially beef. It also makes a righteous dip for chips.

METHOD:
Direct grilling

INGREDIENTS:

6 to 8 plum tomatoes (about 1½ pounds),
    cut in half lengthwise

1 medium-size onion, cut lengthwise into
    quarters (leave the skin and root end on)

2 to 4 jalapeño peppers

3 cloves garlic, skewered on a wooden
    toothpick (leave the skins on)

¼ cup chopped fresh cilantro

2 tablespoons fresh lime juice,
    or more to taste

Coarse salt (kosher or sea) and
    freshly ground black pepper

2 tablespoons lard or olive oil (optional)

YOU'LL ALSO NEED:

2 cups wood chips or chunks (preferably
    mesquite), soaked for 1 hour in water
    to cover, then drained

1 Set up the grill for direct grilling (see page 21 for gas or charcoal) and preheat to high. If using a gas grill, place all of the wood chips or chunks in the smoker box or in a smoker pouch (see page 24) and run the grill on high until you see smoke. If using a charcoal grill, preheat it to high, then toss all of the wood chips or chunks on the coals.

2 When ready to cook, brush the grill grate. Place the tomatoes, onion, garlic, and jalapeños on the hot grate and grill until darkly browned on all sides and tender. This will take 2 to 3 minutes per side (8 to 12 minutes in all) for the tomatoes, 3 to 4 minutes per side for the onion wedges, 3 to 4 minutes per side (9 to 12 minutes in all) for the jalapeños, and 2 to 4 minutes per side

(4 to 8 minutes in all) for the garlic. Transfer the grilled vegetables to a cutting board and let cool. Remove the toothpick from the garlic and cut the root end off the onion. Scrape any really burnt skin off the vegetables but leave most of it on; the dark spots will add color and character. For a milder salsa, seed the jalapeños.

3 Purée the grilled vegetables in a blender or food processor. Add the cilantro and lime juice. Taste for seasoning, adding more lime juice as necessary and salt and pepper to taste; the salsa should be highly seasoned.

4 The salsa can be served as is; it will be exquisite. For even more flavor, melt the lard or heat the olive oil in a deep saucepan over medium-high heat. Add the salsa and fry it until thick and fragrant, 4 to 6 minutes, stirring with a long-handled wooden spoon to prevent spattering. Let cool to room temperature, then refrigerate until serving. The salsa will keep in the refrigerator, covered, for

TIPS

■ The *picante* recipe calls for plum tomatoes. Their elongated shape maximizes the surface area exposed to the fire. Ripeness counts every bit as much, and should beefsteak or other tomatoes look better than plums, use them instead.

■ You don't need to set up the grill especially to make the *picante*. Grill the vegetables a day ahead when you are cooking other things.

TIPS

The peppers that are traditionally used to make *aji* in the Hispano-American United States are green jalapeños. You could also prepare *aji* with serrano peppers (you'd need about twice as many) or, for a particularly fiendish version, use northern Florida's fiery datil peppers, habañeros, or Scotch bonnets.

a day or two, but tastes best served within a few hours of being made. Bring to room temperature before using.

YIELD:

Makes 1½ cups

VARIATION: You can make a tasty *picante* even if you don't have time to grill the vegetables. Start the El Paso Picante recipe at Step 3, puréeing the raw vegetables. Heat the lard or olive oil in a saucepan and fry the sauce as described in Step 4. Let cool to room temperature before serving.

Fla. and Calif.

AJI
(Onion Jalapeño Sauce)

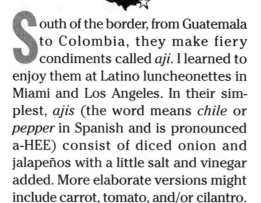

South of the border, from Guatemala to Colombia, they make fiery condiments called *aji*. I learned to enjoy them at Latino luncheonettes in Miami and Los Angeles. In their simplest, *ajis* (the word means *chile* or *pepper* in Spanish and is pronounced a-HEE) consist of diced onion and jalapeños with a little salt and vinegar added. More elaborate versions might include carrot, tomato, and/or cilantro.

Aji is meant to be served with grilled steak and other grilled meats. But it's not so overpowering that you couldn't serve it with grilled chicken, shrimp, or seafood. You can serve the *aji* right after making it, but it tastes best if you let it sit for a couple hours to allow the flavors to blend and mellow.

INGREDIENTS:

1 medium-size sweet white onion
3 to 6 jalapeño peppers
**¼ cup distilled white vinegar,
　　or more to taste**
¼ cup fresh lemon juice, or more vinegar
**1½ teaspoons coarse salt
　　(kosher or sea), or more to taste**
½ teaspoon freshly ground black pepper

1 Mince the onion and jalapeños by hand as finely as possible. (For a hotter *aji,* leave the seeds in the jalapeños; for a milder condiment, remove them.) Or if you prefer, mince them in a food processor fitted with the metal blade. To do this, cut the onion and chile into 1-inch pieces first, then pulse the machine to finely chop them. Take care not to over-process or you'll reduce the ingredients to mush.

2 Place the vinegar, lemon juice, salt, and black pepper in a nonreactive serving or mixing bowl and whisk until the salt dissolves. Stir in the minced onion and jalapeños. Taste for seasoning, adding more vinegar and/or salt as necessary; the *aji* should be highly seasoned. Let the sauce sit for 2 hours so the flavors can ripen. Serve at room temperature or chilled. Any leftover *aji* can be refrigerated, covered, for up to a week.

YIELD:

Makes about 1¼ cups

FLAME-ROASTED CHILES

Every barbecue region in America has its own distinctive aroma. The quintessential smell of New Mexico is the spicy scent of green chiles roasting in the fiery heat of a gas or charcoal burner. If you're lucky enough to visit a farmers' market in Santa Fe, Taos, or Dixon in the fall, it's a fragrance you'll never forget.

Like much barbecue, chile roasting began as a way to preserve perishable produce. "My grandmother would roast the green chiles over an apple wood fire, then dry them in the sun," recalls Don Bustos, president of the Santa Fe Farmers' Market and owner of Santa Cruz Farms in Espanola, which has been in his family for three hundred years. The roasted chiles lasted through winter, seasoning stews and spicing up tortillas.

Today, most growers use propane-fired chile roasters, like the one trucked around New Mexico by Matt Romero, owner of Romero Farms in Dixon. It consists of a horizontal heavy metal mesh drum that rotates over three jet-engine strength propane burners and looks something like an old-fashioned lottery drum.

"You need a blast furnace heat to properly blister the skins of the chiles," explains Romero, who roasts chiles at local farmers' markets five days a week during the season. Twenty pounds of New Mexican or Espanola chiles go in the hopper. For maximum control the roaster cranks the drum by hand. It takes seven to ten minutes to char the chiles.

They emerge from the roaster with an irresistible fragrance. Placed in plastic bags to "sweat," they are then peeled and seeded. "There's nothing better than a freshly roasted green chile on a corn tortilla with a sprinkle of garlic salt," says Bustos. Or you can use the chiles to top hamburgers, make a green chile relish or salsa, or freeze them for a later use. Some folks like to peel chiles before freezing; others maintain you get a better flavor if you freeze them whole. But one thing is for sure: These flame-roasted green chiles are essential for a New Mexican's happiness.

SANTA FE CHILE ROASTING

Chile roasting takes place at New Mexico's farmers' markets from the last week in August until the first freeze (usually the first week in October). Roasting reaches its peak at the Santa Fe Wine & Chile Fiesta, held annually toward the end of September; call (505) 438-8060 or visit www.santafewineandchile.org for information.

The quintessential smell of New Mexico...

TIPS

■ Dozens, perhaps hundreds, of different chile varieties are grown in New Mexico— most in such small quantities they never make it beyond the local farmers' markets. Outside New Mexico, look for an elongated, slender green chile like the New Mexico chile or the Anaheim.

■ Traditionally, chiles are roasted over a wood or charcoal fire. While more and more growers now use gas roasters, wood still gives you the best flavor (see Grilling over a Wood Fire on page 20.) But fine results can be obtained on a gas grill—just be sure to work over the highest possible heat.

Dixon, N.Mex.

NEW MEXICAN GREEN CHILE RELISH

The haunting smoke flavor of roasted green chiles is the very soul of New Mexican cooking. Here's a green chile relish from a man with a lot of roasting experience, chile grower Matt Romero of Romero Farms in Dixon. Use it to spice up everything from grilled steaks to seafood to burgers—or just scoop it up with tortilla chips.

METHOD:
Direct grilling

INGREDIENTS:
**1 pound fresh New Mexican or
    Anaheim green chiles
    (8 to 10 chiles)
1 tablespoon olive oil
1 to 2 cloves garlic, minced
Coarse salt (kosher or sea)**

1 Set up the grill for direct grilling (see page 21 for charcoal or gas) and preheat to high.

2 When ready to cook, brush the grill grate. Place the chiles on the hot grate and grill until darkened and blistered on all sides, 7 to 10 minutes in all, turning with tongs. Transfer the roasted chiles to a paper bag and fold over the top to seal or place the chiles in a bowl and cover it with plastic wrap. Let the chiles cool to room temperature; the resulting steam will loosen the skins.

3 Using a paring knife or your fingers, scrape or pull the skin off each chile. Cut off the stems. Cut the chiles in half lengthwise and scrape out the seeds. Cut the seeded chiles into ¼-inch dice.

4 Heat the olive oil in a skillet over medium heat. Add the garlic and cook until fragrant and translucent but not brown, 2 to 3 minutes. Remove the skillet from the heat and stir in the diced chiles. Season with salt to taste. Serve hot or at room temperature.

YIELD:
Makes about 2 cups

VARIATION: Roasted green chiles are sometimes turned into salsa. Prepare the recipe through Step 4. then purée the relish in a food processor or blender. Serve the salsa with grilled meats or as dip with chips.

Nova Scotia, Canada

RHUBARB CHUTNEY

Rhubarb by the armful.

One doesn't usually go to the coast of Nova Scotia for barbecue. Seafood, yes. But grilling? A few summers ago, I lunched at the Galley, a seaside fish house overlooking a sailboat-studded bay near the town of Chester. The Galley serves this rhubarb chutney with fish cakes, but I couldn't help thinking how delectable it would be with grilled chicken, pork chops, and seafood (especially a dark, oily, cold-water fish, like salmon, bluefish, or mackerel). Most Americans think of rhubarb as a dessert ingredient, but its fruity tartness makes it a perfect foil for barbecue.

INGREDIENTS:

2 pounds fresh or frozen rhubarb, trimmed and cut into 1-inch pieces

1½ cups firmly packed dark brown sugar, or more to taste

1 cup cider vinegar

⅓ cup dry red wine

1 medium-size onion, finely chopped

½ cup dark raisins

1 tablespoon finely chopped candied or fresh ginger

1 tablespoon fresh lemon juice

1 teaspoon grated lemon zest

1 teaspoon ground cinnamon

½ teaspoon ground allspice

½ teaspoon ground cloves

1 Combine the rhubarb, brown sugar, vinegar, wine, onion, raisins, ginger, lemon juice and zest, cinnamon, allspice, and cloves in a heavy nonreactive saucepan. Bring to a boil over medium-high heat. Reduce the heat to medium-low and let simmer, covered, until the rhubarb and onion are very soft and the chutney is thick and flavorful, 30 to 40 minutes.

2 Uncover the pan for the last 10 minutes of cooking, so that some of the liquid evaporates; the chutney should be the consistency of jam. Let cool to room temperature, transfer the chutney to clean glass jars. Place a piece of plastic wrap between the jars and the lids to keep the lids from corroding. The chutney can be refrigerated, covered, for several weeks.

YIELD:
Makes 4 cups

TIPS

Rhubarb is in season in spring and summer. Trim off the bottom half inch and any leafy tops before using.

THE SAUCE DOCTOR

KC MASTERPIECE BARBECUE & GRILL

4747 Wyandotte Street
(the Plaza)
Kansas City, Missouri
(816) 531-3332
and other locations
www.kcmrestaurants.com

Describe the perfect barbecue sauce. Rich? Red? Thick and sweet? With a tingle of spice, a pucker of vinegar, and a healthy whiff of wood smoke? If such is your vision of the perfect sauce—and it is for most Americans—you have one man to thank: the Sauce Doctor, Rich Davis.

Lots of us like to tinker with barbecue sauces, adding a splash of vinegar or an invigorating shot of hot sauce. Davis happens to be a real M.D. who doctored so well, he created the nation's best selling premium barbecue sauce: KC Masterpiece.

Davis came by his love of barbecue naturally. He grew up in one of the epicenters of barbecue in the United States—Missouri—in the town of Gotham. His father was an avid hunter and fisherman and he taught young Rich everything he knew about barbecuing and grilling. "Back in those days, you couldn't just go out and buy a barbecue grill," recalls Davis. "If you wanted a grill, you had to build one; if you wanted a barbecue sauce, you had to make it from scratch."

> "If you wanted a grill, you had to build one; if you wanted a barbecue sauce, you had to make it from scratch."

Davis carried his father's lessons with him as he pursued a career in medicine, first as a family and child psychiatrist, then as an educator and dean, and finally as a founder of a clinic and of the Eastern Virginia Medical School in Norfolk, Virginia. But he always kept his hand in barbecue, holding smoke fests on the weekends, constantly revising and improving his sauce. In 1984, Davis retired from medicine to pursue his lifelong passion. "People always loved my sauce," he says. "I decided to see if I could make it a commercial success."

THE BEST SAUCE TO CROSS ANY HOME PLATE

K.C. Masterpiece
The Barbecue Sauce

BARBECUE & BASEBALL!
Enjoy a delicious MASTERPIECE barbecued sandwich right here in the stadium. Look for our concession stands on PLAZA Level, Section 115 or 116 and in the General Admission concession areas.

Rich Davis mops sauce
on pit-roasted beef.

Davis studied what people liked in their barbecue sauces in other parts of the country: vinegar in the Carolinas, mustard in Georgia, chili powder and cumin in Texas. Given Kansas City's central location, it made sense to Davis to incorporate these regional elements into his sauce. The base would be tomato, of course, because Americans love tomato sauce (consider the popularity of ketchup). For sweeteners Davis chose molasses and corn syrup–molasses for the earthy, malty flavor; corn syrup for the velvety texture. Vinegar would balance the sweetness. Cumin and chili powder would kick up the heat.

But something was still missing, and Davis pondered this long and hard. Finally it occurred to him: "What people really like about barbecue is the smoke." So he added a shot of liquid smoke and uttered one of the great "eurekas!" in culinary history. KC Masterpiece was born.

To distinguish his sauce from the other bottles on the shelves, Davis put a simple black-and-white label on the bottle. To build the business, he brought in his two sons. Sales boomed in the Midwest, but Davis wanted to see his sauce go national. ("You need fifty million dollars to launch a food product nationwide," Davis explains.) So in 1986, he sold the sauce to the Clorox Company. Today, there are ten varieties of KC Masterpiece, and the company sells more than 42 million bottles a year.

The Davis family's latest venture is a chain of KC Masterpiece restaurants. At this writing, there are two in the Kansas City area (including one in the Plaza, one of the first shopping malls in the United States) and two in the St. Louis area, and they have plans for more. As for Davis, he maintains a travel schedule that would tire a man half his age. "I'm in my seventies, but I feel like I'm twenty-eight," he says. For centuries, people have searched for the fountain of youth. Dr. Davis found it in a bottle of barbecue sauce!

TIPS

The gooseberry is a tart, round, green fruit about the size of a grape. There's no mistaking its acidic musky flavor for anything else and there's certainly no substitute. However, if you can't find gooseberries, you could make an interesting chutney in the same spirit with pitted fresh cherries or diced pineapple.

Clayton, Mo.

GOOSEBERRY CHUTNEY

I arrived at the Kitchen Conservatory, a cooking school in Clayton, Missouri, outside St. Louis, just in time for gooseberry season. "These tart green berries are the closest we have to a regional delicacy," explained the conservatory owner, Anne Schlafly (daughter of the columnist Phyllis Schlafly). She remembers her grandmother gathering these handsome green berries and turning them into preserves. Anne had invited me to the conservatory to teach a grilling class, and I thought it only proper to create a chutney to serve with the grilled pork steaks so beloved by St. Louisans. (For a recipe, see Cider-Grilled Pork Porterhouse on page 274.) But don't stop there, because the perfumed acidity of gooseberry chutney is also perfect with grilled fish, chicken, or turkey.

INGREDIENTS:

1 pint fresh gooseberries, washed and drained
3 tablespoons diced red bell pepper
3 tablespoons diced green bell pepper
3 tablespoons diced onion
2 tablespoons finely chopped fresh mint or cilantro
1 tablespoon chopped candied ginger
1 teaspoon grated peeled fresh ginger
1/2 cup sugar, or more to taste
3 tablespoons cider vinegar, or more to taste
1/4 teaspoon cayenne pepper, or more to taste
1/4 teaspoon ground cinnamon
1/8 teaspoon ground cloves
1 pinch salt

1 Place the gooseberries, red and green bell peppers, onion, mint, candied and fresh ginger, sugar, vinegar, cayenne, cinnamon, cloves, and salt in a nonreactive saucepan and slowly bring to a simmer over medium heat, stirring with wooden spoon.

2 Let the chutney simmer gently, uncovered, until the berries are tender and the liquid has thickened, 5 to 8 minutes. Taste for seasoning, adding more sugar, vinegar, and/or cayenne as necessary; the chutney should be refreshingly tart but not sour. Let the chutney cool to room temperature, then chill until ready to serve. It will keep, covered, in the refrigerator, for several weeks. Bring to room temperature before using.

YIELD:

Makes 1 1/2 cups

Oregon

WASABI WHIPPED CREAM

Wasabi is a horseradish-like root from Japan—a traditional accompaniment to sushi. Most Americans are familiar with it in its reconstituted-powder form (the green stuff that looks like a dab of tooth-paste). What you may not know is that wasabi is grown in Oregon, and the fresh root is available at specialty greengrocers and high-end gourmet shops and by mail order (see page 742).

INGREDIENTS:

1 ounce fresh wasabi root, peeled,
    or 1 tablespoon wasabi powder

1 cup heavy (whipping) cream, chilled
1 teaspoon fresh lemon juice
1 tablespoon finely chopped perilla,
    fresh chives, or scallion greens
Coarse salt (kosher or sea) and
    freshly ground black pepper

1 If using fresh wasabi, finely grate it on a ginger grater or a box grater. If using wasabi powder, place it in a bowl with 1 tablespoon cool water; stir until a thick paste forms, then let sit for 5 minutes.

2 Place the cream in a chilled metal bowl (the cold helps stabilize the whipped cream). Using a handheld or stand mixer, beat the cream until soft peaks form. Using a spatula, gently fold in the wasabi, lemon juice, and perilla. Season with salt and pepper to taste; the sauce should be highly seasoned. Serve immediately or refrigerate, covered, for up to 3 hours.

YIELD:
Makes 1½ cups

TIPS

Just to be excruciatingly esoteric, you could flavor the whipped cream with perilla (often called shiso). This broad-leafed, green Japanese herb has a tart, tangy, basily, minty, almost metallic flavor. Look for it in Japanese markets and natural food stores or substitute chives or scallion greens.

Here's the

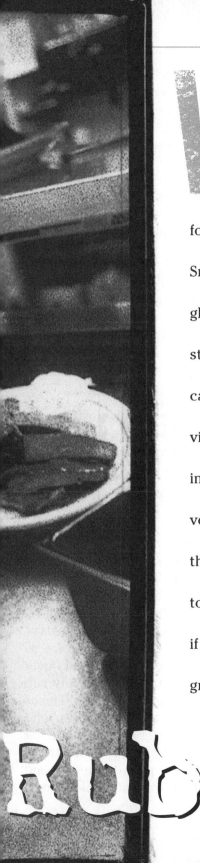

What makes good barbecue great and great barbecue the stuff of legends? Well, for a lot of pit masters, it's the rub. In the pages that follow, you'll find recipes for Cold Mountain Rub (the granddaddy of all barbecue rubs), Smelling Salts (my version of a seasoned salt), and a tongue-tingling mustard rub from Motown. But rubs are only part of the story, for a judicious use of marinades, mop sauces, and glazes can also add worlds of flavor to barbecue. Use the chile-laced vinegar marinade to spice up pork; the Tennessee mop sauce to invigorate pork shoulder; or the white-lightning glaze to add flavor and sheen to your next batch of ribs. What all the recipes in this chapter have in common is that they're meant to be applied to food prior to or during the grilling or smoking. Just remember, if it swims in the sea, flies in the air, or walks on or grows in the ground, chances are it will taste better with a rub or marinade.

Rub

TIPS

For optimal results, apply the rub to meat or poultry at least four hours before cooking so it has time to cure the meat.

White Sulphur Springs, W.Va.

BARBECUE UNIVERSITY RUB

I once gave a "final exam" at a rub and sauce seminar at my Barbecue University at The Greenbrier, and this rub aced the test. After learning the general principles for rub making from one of our distinguished guest instructors, KC Masterpiece Barbecue Sauce creator Dr. Rich Davis, each team of students was asked to create a rub. This one got the highest "grade" in the class. Mildly spicy and intensely aromatic, it's the perfect seasoning for beef, lamb, pork, and poultry. Use one to two tablespoons per pound of meat.

INGREDIENTS:

2 tablespoons ground coriander

2 tablespoons sweet paprika

2 tablespoons coarse salt
    (kosher or sea)

4 teaspoons ground cumin

4 teaspoons dried thyme

2 teaspoons dry mustard

2 teaspoons garlic powder

¼ teaspoon ground allspice

¼ teaspoon freshly ground
    white pepper

¼ teaspoon cayenne pepper

P lace the coriander, paprika, salt, cumin, thyme, mustard, garlic powder, allspice, white pepper, and cayenne in a small bowl and stir to mix. (Actually, if you don't have sensitive skin, your fingers work better for mixing a rub than a spoon or whisk does.) Store the rub in an airtight jar away from heat or light; it will keep for at least 6 months.

YIELD:
Makes about ½ cup

Detroit, Mich.

CAUCUS CLUB MUSTARD RUB

T he Caucus Club is the last of the Golden Age restaurants in downtown Detroit, a softly lit, clubby retreat located in the historic Penobscot Building, where generations of Detroit business folk have repaired for such stalwart fare as London broil, steak tartare, and Dover sole. The recipe for this lively rub comes to me from a longtime Caucus Club rib master, Marcus Yanes, who uses it as a base for his wildly popular mustard ribs. Use one to two tablespoons of it per pound of meat—and not just on ribs but also steaks, chops, and even burgers. The heat of the mustard and pepper will make you appreciate your beer.

INGREDIENTS:

⅓ **cup dry mustard**

⅓ **cup sweet paprika**

¼ **cup coarse salt (kosher or sea)**

1 **tablespoon garlic powder**

1 **tablespoon freshly ground black pepper**

Place the mustard, paprika, salt, garlic powder and pepper in a small bowl and stir to mix. (Actually, your fingers work better for mixing a rub than a spoon or whisk does.) Store the rub in an airtight jar away from heat or light; it will keep for at least 6 months.

YIELD:

Makes about 1 cup

Tennessee

COLD MOUNTAIN RUB

Here's the granddaddy of all American barbecue rubs. I found it not in an old cookbook but in Charles Frazier's magnificent Civil War period novel, *Cold Mountain*, which is set in Tennessee. (So vivid is Frazier's prose, just by reading about a dish, you can almost taste it.) The mix may seem straightforward, but like any great rub, it has the power to enhance the flavor of meat without camouflaging or overpowering it. I know of no other spice mixture that has quite such an ability to marry the flavors of food, smoke, and fire. And talk

204— PENOBSCOT BUILDING, DETROIT, MICH.

The Caucus Club is located in Detroit's historic Penobscot Building.

TIPS

The traditional mustard for the Caucus Club rub would be Colman's. To jazz it up, you could use Chinese mustard (or even a mixture of the two) and hot instead of sweet paprika.

about versatile—I've used the mixture with equal success on chicken, pork, beef, fish, and vegetables. (If it weren't for the salt, I'd probably even shake it over dessert!) Naturally, you can personalize the rub to suit your taste. For a milder pepper flavor, for example, use white pepper; for a sharper bite, freshly cracked black peppercorns. To turn up the heat, replace the sweet paprika with hot paprika or even chile powder.

The rub keeps well, but it's so quick and easy to make, I usually prepare it as I need it. Use one to two tablespoons per pound of meat. You can grill or smoke meat as soon as you have sprinkled the rub on, or you can let the seasoned meat cure in the refrigerator for four to twenty-four hours, which will give you a stronger flavor.

INGREDIENTS:

¹/₂ cup coarse salt (kosher or sea)
¹/₂ cup sugar
¹/₂ cup freshly ground black pepper
¹/₂ cup sweet paprika

Place the salt, sugar, pepper, and paprika in a bowl and stir to mix. (Actually, your fingers work better for mixing a rub than a spoon or whisk does.) Store the rub in an airtight jar away from heat or light; it will keep for at least 6 months.

YIELD:

Makes 2 cups

VARIATION: To make a barbecue butter for basting, melt a half a stick of unsalted butter and stir 1 tablespoon of the rub into it.

Originally designed for brisket, this rub goes exceedingly well with chicken, game hen, pork (especially shoulder and ribs), beef ribs, and salmon. To invigorate your favorite barbecue sauce or salad dressing, add a spoonful of the rub.

Kansas City, Mo.

K.C. PEPPER RUB

Hot enough for you? It will be after you've applied this tongue-tingling pepper rub, the creation of an all-woman barbecue team from Kansas City called the BBQ Queens. Mustard powder, chile powder, and black pepper produce a rub that can stand up to the most ornery brisket or spareribs. You'll need one to two tablespoons of rub per pound of meat. In more moderate quantities, you can use the rub to season chicken or a robust fish, like salmon or bluefish.

INGREDIENTS:

¹/₂ cup sweet paprika
¹/₃ cup onion salt
¹/₄ cup black pepper
3 tablespoons dry mustard
3 tablespoons pure chile powder
3 tablespoons celery seed

Place the paprika, onion salt, pepper, mustard, chile powder, and celery seed in a mixing bowl and stir to mix. (Actually, your fingers work better for mixing a rub than a spoon or whisk does.) Store the rub in an airtight jar away from heat or light; it will keep for at least 6 months.

YIELD:

Makes about 1¹/₂ cups

Tennessee

FOUR, THREE, TWO, ONE RUB

They're on to something in Tennessee, birthplace of this rub. It may be the easiest recipe there is to remember. Anyone who's had too much beer the night before will appreciate its numeric simplicity. But there's more to the rub than mnemonics, for the combination of paprika, salt, garlic, and pepper has just the right balance of earth and fire flavors. If you find most barbecue rubs too sweet, this one's for you: It contains not one whit of sugar. It goes great with just about everything: pork shoulder, ribs, brisket, chicken, even venison. Use about one tablespoon per pound of meat.

INGREDIENTS:

4 tablespoons sweet paprika
3 tablespoons salt
2 tablespoons garlic powder
1 tablespoon black pepper

Place the paprika, salt, garlic powder, and pepper in a bowl and stir to mix. (Actually, your fingers work better for mixing a rub than a spoon or whisk does.) Store the rub in an airtight jar away from heat or light; it will keep for at least 6 months.

YIELD:
Makes about ⅔ cup

Boston, Mass.

BONFIRE STEAK RUB

Bonfire is the sort of restaurant that makes grill fanatics drool, for chef-owner Todd English has filled the open kitchen of his Latin-themed steak house with oak-burning grills,

TIPS

■ Most of the recipes in this book call for freshly ground black pepper. Regular old supermarket pepper will work fine for Four, Three, Two, One: In fact, freshly ground would likely be too hot.

■ Other versions of this rub call for hot pepper (cayenne) in place of the black pepper, which will certainly kick up the heat.

just what the doctor ordered to spice it up

rotisseries, and smokers of his own invention. Take your seat at the oh-so-hip bar, and you'll be treated to the sight of cowboy steaks sizzling away over blazing oak, massive prime ribs rotating on vertical turnspits, and whole lambs roasting in a custom-built smoker. The sight alone is almost enough to sate you (almost), and the portions of thick-cut chops and steaks all but bury the plates. Todd seasons his steaks with an invigorating rub that contains salt, pepper, coriander, cloves, and espresso beans. The resulting combination of hot and pleasantly bitter flavors makes great meat taste even better. Use one to one and a half tablespoons per pound of meat.

INGREDIENTS:

1/4 cup coriander seeds

3 tablespoons black peppercorns

1 tablespoon whole cloves

3 tablespoons dark roast (French or Italian) coffee beans

1/4 cup coarse salt (kosher or sea)

1 Toast the coriander seeds, peppercorns, and cloves in a dry skillet over medium heat until roasted and fragrant, 3 minutes. Shake the pan so the spices cook evenly. Transfer the spices to a heatproof bowl and let cool to room temperature. (If you're in a hurry, you can use preground spices and coffee; the rub will still be good.)

2 Place the toasted coriander, peppercorns, and cloves and the coffee beans in a spice mill or coffee grinder and grind to a fine powder.

Transfer the powder to a jar and stir in the salt. Store the rub in a sealed jar away from heat or light; it will keep for several months.

YIELD:
Makes about 1 cup

VARIATION: This rub is designed for steak, but it's also terrific on pork, lamb, and poultry.

Boston, Mass.

MUSTARD HERB RUB

Fragrant with dried herbs and fiery with mustard seeds and black peppercorns, this rub is just what the doctor ordered to spice up red meats, like beef or lamb, or rich fish, like salmon and tuna. The brown sugar gives just the right touch of sweetness, without making the rub too sweet. The recipe comes from my spice master friend, John Darrick, president of the Dirigo Spice Corp. in Boston. Use one to two tablespoons for each pound of food. After sprinkling it on, let it cure for fifteen to thirty minutes, then grill the food over a hot fire.

WALL OF FLAME

TODD ENGLISH'S BONFIRE

Chef Todd English achieved international acclaim with the robust, refined Italo-Mediterranean fare at his flagship Charlestown, Massachusetts restaurant, Olives. But his pyromania reaches its apotheosis at his Latin-themed steak house, Bonfire.

50 Park Plaza
Boston, Massachusetts
(617) 262-3473

INGREDIENTS:

2 tablespoons yellow mustard seeds

¼ cup firmly packed light brown sugar

3 tablespoons dry mustard

**1 tablespoon coarse salt
(kosher or sea)**

1 tablespoon dried dill

1 teaspoon dried basil

1 teaspoon dried tarragon

**½ teaspoon cracked black
peppercorns**

½ teaspoon onion powder

1 Toast the mustard seeds in a dry skillet over medium heat. Shake the pan so they cook evenly, until fragrant and just beginning to brown, 2 to 3 minutes. Transfer the toasted mustard seeds to a heatproof bowl and let cool to room temperature. Coarsely crack the seeds under a rolling pin (place them in a heavy resealable plastic bag to keep them from scattering) or in a spice mill or blender, running the machine in short bursts.

2 Transfer the cracked mustard seeds to a mixing bowl and stir in the brown sugar, dry mustard, salt, dill, basil, tarragon, pepper, and onion powder. (Actually, your fingers work better for mixing a rub than a spoon or whisk does.) Store the rub in an airtight sealed jar away from heat or light; it will keep for at least 6 months.

YIELD:

Makes ¾ cup

Phoenix, Ariz.

MEGA HERB WET RUB

First, the bad news. RoxSand Scocos won't part with her barbecue sauce recipe. So if you want to taste that irresistible sauce—fruity with pineapple, salty with soy, and spicy with ginger— you'll just have to dine at her sleekly contemporary Southwestern restaurant, RoxSand, in Phoenix. The

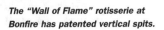
The "Wall of Flame" rotisserie at Bonfire has patented vertical spits.

TIPS

The Mustard Herb Rub can also be a starting point for other preparations. To make a spice paste, for example, stir three to four tablespoons of lemon juice or beer into the rub and spread this over duck, lamb, or seafood. To make a basting sauce, mix one part rub with two parts apple juice or fresh orange juice and stir in two parts olive oil. Brush this mixture on fish or chicken while it's grilling. To make a table sauce, you can combine the rub with cranberry or orange juice in a saucepan and let simmer for three minutes over medium-high heat; season with salt to taste.

TIPS

This fragrant rub goes great with everything, and I mean everything: seafood, poultry, meat, even vegetables, tofu, and tempeh. Marinate the food in the rub, turning occasionally, in the refrigerator. Small food, such as steaks or vegetables, will need to marinate four to six hours; large cuts will need eight hours or overnight. You'll wonder how you cooked without it.

The rubs come spicy and fragrant with herbs at RoxSand's in Phoenix.

good news is that this James Beard award–winning chef *will* share her recipe for her pungent herb wet rub. RoxSand is fairly broad-minded about the selection of herbs for the rub: You can use some or all of the ones listed below. Just be sure that the herbs are fresh and that you have one packed cup of leaves. As for the wine, use red wine and red wine vinegar when marinating dark meats, like beef or lamb, and white wine (or white vermouth) and white wine vinegar for poultry and seafood. You'll have enough for six steaks, one chicken or duck, two racks of baby back ribs, one rack of spare ribs, one leg of lamb, or about two and a half pounds of vegetables or tofu.

INGREDIENTS:

1 cup packed, rinsed, mixed fresh herb leaves, including basil, dill, fennel fronds (see Note), oregano, flat-leaf parsley, rosemary, and/or sage
2 cloves garlic, peeled
1½ teaspoons coarse salt (kosher or sea)
½ teaspoon freshly ground black pepper
½ cup red or white wine
½ cup red or white wine vinegar
1 cup extra-virgin olive oil

Finely chop the herbs and garlic by hand, or chop them in a food processor. Add the salt and pepper; then add the wine, vinegar, and olive

oil (through the feed tube with the motor running, if using a food processor) and stir or process to mix. The wet rub will keep in the refrigerator, covered, for several days but it tastes best used within a few hours of preparing.

YIELD:

Makes about 2¹⁄₂ cups

NOTE: Fennel fronds are the feathery green foliage on the stalks of fennel bulbs.

Los Angeles, Calif.

SMELLING SALTS

G rill masters and pit bosses everywhere use seasoned salt. The best-known commercial blend is Lawry's, created by Lawrence Frank in Los Angeles. Frank became restaurateur to the stars in the 1920s with the opening of the Tam O'Shanter, which is still in business in the same location today. In 1938, he solidified

his reputation with a Beverly Hills dining establishment specializing in a single dish, Lawry's The Prime Rib. Equally popular as the beef was a seasoned salt Frank developed to go with it. Indeed, shaker jars of the stuff disappeared into clients' pockets as fast as Frank could put them on the tables. According to the company Web site, Lawry's is the world's best selling seasoning today, and Americans spend more on seasoned salt than table salt. Forever the purist, I could not resist the temptation of developing a seasoned salt you could make from scratch.

INGREDIENTS:

1 cup coarse salt (kosher or sea)

2 tablespoons garlic flakes

2 tablespoons onion flakes

2 tablespoons dried parsley

**1 tablespoon cracked or coarsely
    ground black pepper**

2 teaspoons poppy seeds

1 teaspoon hot red pepper flakes

P lace the salt, garlic and onion flakes, parsley, black pepper, poppy seeds, and hot pepper flakes in a bowl and stir to mix. (Actually, your fingers work better for mixing a rub than a spoon or whisk does.) Store the rub in an airtight jar away from heat or light. Smelling salts will keep almost indefinitely.

YIELD:

Makes 1¹⁄₂ cups

TIPS

Use this fragrant spice mix in any recipe calling for commercial seasoned salt. You could jazz it up by adding toasted sesame seeds or sweet or hot paprika (I'd add two tablespoons of each).

MARINATING TIMES

How long should you marinate a chop or fish fillet before putting it on the grill? It's an easy question with a complicated answer, because the marinating time depends on the strength of the marinade, the particular food to be marinated, and the size and cut of the meat. For example, shrimp and chicken breasts obviously require less marinating than a whole chicken or whole fish; a light herb marinade takes longer to work than a strong marinade fiery with Scotch bonnet chiles and spices.

The following list will provide a rough guideline to marinating times. When in doubt, see the instructions in a particular recipe. Note: You can speed up the marinating time by making deep slashes in the sides of whole fish or chicken pieces.

■ Very large pieces of meat, such as brisket, prime rib, pork shoulder, leg of lamb, turkey, and capon: 12 to 24 hours.

■ Large pieces of meat, such as beef and pork tenderloins, pork loins, rack and butterflied leg of lamb, and whole chickens; large whole fish: 6 to 12 hours.

■ Medium-size pieces of meat, such as porterhouse steaks, double-cut pork chops, and chicken halves or quarters; small whole fish: 3 to 8 hours.

■ Medium-to-small pieces of meat, such as steaks, pork and lamb chops, and bone-in chicken breasts or legs; fish steaks, tofu, portobello mushrooms and other vegetables: 1 to 3 hours.

■ Small pieces of meat, such as boneless chicken breasts; fish fillets and shrimp: 15 minutes to 2 hours.

TIPS

The recipe makes enough mop sauce for eight to ten pounds of meat. Figure on one cup mop per two pounds of meat.

Tennessee

TENNESSEE MOP SAUCE

Mop sauces stand midway between a marinade and a barbecue sauce. They're too tart to lick off your fingers, but slather them on ribs or pork shoulders while they're smoking and you'll add layers of flavor you never dreamed possible. Besides, mopping gives you something to do during the four to eight hours it takes to make great barbecue. This will keep you out of trouble, especially the sort of trouble you get into when you try to baste meat with a sweet barbecue sauce, which will burn because of its high sugar content. Use this sauce as a mop for ribs, pork shoulders, briskets, and chickens. When making pulled pork you can use the mop as a sauce for the meat.

INGREDIENTS:

2 lemons

1 quart distilled white vinegar

⅓ cup ketchup

½ cup sweet paprika

3 tablespoons coarse salt (kosher or sea)

2 tablespoons freshly ground black pepper

1 to 2 tablespoons cayenne pepper

Squeeze the lemons through your fingers into a large nonreactive bowl or pot, catching the seeds in your fingers. Add the the lemon rinds and the vinegar, ketchup, paprika, salt, black pepper and cayenne and stir until the salt dissolves. The mop will keep for several days, covered, in the refrigerator, but remove the lemon rinds after about 4 hours or they'll make the mop bitter.

YIELD:

Makes about 5 cups

Kansas City, Kan.

POSSUM TROT MOP AND BARBECUE SAUCE

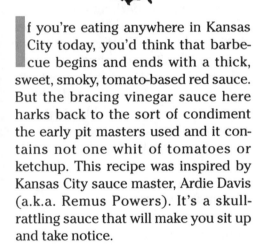

If you're eating anywhere in Kansas City today, you'd think that barbecue begins and ends with a thick, sweet, smoky, tomato-based red sauce. But the bracing vinegar sauce here harks back to the sort of condiment the early pit masters used and it contains not one whit of tomatoes or ketchup. This recipe was inspired by Kansas City sauce master, Ardie Davis (a.k.a. Remus Powers). It's a skull-rattling sauce that will make you sit up and take notice.

INGREDIENTS:

2 cups cider vinegar, or more
    to taste
1/4 cup honey, or more to taste
1/4 cup molasses
1/4 cup Worcestershire sauce
1 tablespoon of your favorite
    hot sauce
1 tablespoon coarse salt
    (kosher or sea), or more to taste
1 teaspoon freshly ground black
    pepper

Combine the vinegar, honey molasses, Worcestershire sauce, hot sauce, salt, and pepper with 1 cup of water in a nonreactive saucepan over medium heat. Bring the sauce to a simmer and let simmer gently until the flavors are blended, about 5 minutes (do not let the sauce come to a full boil). Remove the sauce from the heat and let cool to room temperature. Taste for seasoning, adding more vinegar, honey, and/or salt as necessary. This is a very intense sauce, so use it sparingly.

YIELD:

Makes about 3 cups

NOTE: The sauce will keep for several weeks in a glass jar stored away from heat and light. Place a piece of plastic wrap under the jar lid to keep it from corroding.

Ky. and Tenn.

WHITE LIGHTNING RIB GLAZE

Sweet and silky, this glaze owes its kick to a generous fillip of whiskey—preferably, a Tennessee

Like the vinegar sauces of the Carolinas, this one is designed to accompany pork-especially pulled pork shoulders and ribs.

No moonshine here—that's barbecue sauce in the jug.

layers of flavor you never dreamed possible

TIPS

Although White Lightning Glaze was designed for ribs, it also makes a great topping for grilled chicken, pork roasts and chops, ham steaks, and even dark rich fish, like salmon or bluefish. Brush it on during the last five or so minutes of cooking for a handsome sheen and potent blast of flavor.

or Kentucky sipping whiskey. Despite its name, you should use a whiskey you wouldn't mind sipping straight. Because of the high sugar content in the glaze, brush on ribs toward the end of grilling (otherwise, the sugar will burn). You'll have enough for six to eight pounds of ribs.

INGREDIENTS:

1 cup firmly packed dark brown sugar
1/2 cup whiskey
1/4 cup ketchup
4 tablespoons (1/2 stick) unsalted butter, cut into 1/2-inch pieces
2 tablespoons soy sauce
2 tablespoons fresh lemon juice
1 teaspoon grated fresh lemon zest
1 teaspoon garlic powder
1/2 teaspoon freshly ground black pepper

Place the brown sugar, whiskey, ketchup, butter, soy sauce, lemon juice, lemon zest, garlic powder, and pepper in a heavy nonreactive saucepan over high heat and bring to a boil. Reduce the heat to medium-high and let simmer briskly until the glaze is thick and flavorful, about 5 minutes. If not using the glaze right away, transfer it to an airtight jar and store it in the refrigerator for up to 2 weeks. You'll need to reheat it in a nonreactive saucepan to melt the butter before using.

YIELD:

Makes about 2 cups

Hornersville, Mo.

WICKER'S MARINADE

I can't name my source. I can't even say how it came into my possession. But here is one of the most coveted formulas on the barbecue trail—the alleged recipe for Wicker's Original Marinade. The Wicker family in Hornersville, Missouri, created a potent mixture of vinegar and spices in 1940, and since then, barbecue buffs have used it for marinating and basting. Use two cups marinade for each one and a half to two pounds of poultry or meat.

INGREDIENTS:

2 quarts distilled white vinegar
1/3 cup salt
1/3 cup chile powder
2 tablespoons plus 2 teaspoons sugar
2 tablespoons plus 2 teaspoons black pepper
2 tablespoons plus 2 teaspoons cayenne pepper
2 teaspoons vegetable oil

Place the vinegar, salt, chile powder, sugar, black pepper, cayenne, and oil in a large nonreactive bowl and stir until the salt and sugar dissolve. Store the marinade in jars, placing a sheet of plastic wrap under the lid of each to keep it from corroding.

YIELD:

Makes about 2 quarts

THE SALT LICK

THE SALT LICK BARBECUE RESTAURANT

18300 FM 1826
Driftwood, Texas
(516) 858-4959

'I've always been skeptical about restaurants that serve all you can eat, but the Salt Lick in Driftwood, Texas has made me a believer. If you don't have time to drive to Lockhart or Llano, this restaurant, located on 80 rolling acres 20 minutes outside Austin, is the perfect place to get you barbecue fix. The rambling dining room looks the way I imagine a ranch mess hall would, with swinging doors and big sunny windows looking out on twisted cedar trees and a pear orchard. It's a popular restaurant, attracting 5,000 people each weekend.

The Salt Lick was the brainchild of Thurman and Hisako Roberts, he a Texan, she a Hawaiian of Japanese descent. Thurman had been working as a bridge contractor—a job he hated because it meant spending extended time away from central Texas. One day he gave notice and sat down with his wife and a yellow legal pad and made a list of businesses they could run from Driftwood. A barbecue restaurant was number fourteen. In 1969, accompanied by his son, Scott, and a ranch hand, he strode to the center of a cedar grove, made a mark with his boot, and ordered the construction of a barbecue pit. He cut down just enough trees to make the site accessible from the road, and the Salt Lick was born.

The original pit, still very much in use and visible from the main dining room, looks like a circular brick well, it has a welded-steel grate on which meats slowly roast over an open oak fire. To satisfy the appetite of the hungry hordes, there are several mechanized industrial smokers in the kitchen, but all the meats are finished over the pit.

Like most Texas barbecue restaurants, the Salt Lick serves a fine brisket, but for my money, the must-tries here are the habañero chicken and the ribs. The chicken, served only on Sunday, owes its kick ass bite to a lengthy soak in habañero hot sauce. The ribs (spareribs during the week and baby backs on Sundays) feature a complex interplay of spice and smoke flavors and are just tender enough to pull apart with your fingers.

Then there's the golden mustardy, vinegary sauce that has been passed down from generation to generation. "The secret of our barbecue," says Salt Lick chef Carmen Gonzalez, "is the way the sauce bonds with the fire."

You can order each type of meat by itself, but most customers opt for a family-style, all-you-can-eat combo plate. For $9.95 at lunch or $13.95 at dinner, you stuff yourself silly on brisket, sausages, potato salad, coleslaw, and beans.

THE SALT LICK BAR B-Q
DRIFTWOOD, TEXAS

Great Grilled

Peanuts. Camembert. Bologna. Okra. What hasn't gone on the grill—yet? It's time for dessert: cakes, crisps, crumbles, pies, fruits, and even ice cream you cook over fire. Before you dismiss this as heresy, try the Grilled Banana Cream Pie or the Smoke-Roasted Apple Crisp. Or, how about flame-roasted sweet potatoes in a Tex-Mex spice-scented syrup, bananas Foster hot off the grill, or fresh peaches served shish kebab style on cinnamon sticks? Smoked roasted ice cream? When it comes to desserts that will keep people talking long after the fire is cold, you'll find grilled desserts are cool.

Desserts

TIPS

The McIntosh is the most common apple in New Hampshire, but any apple will do. Depending on where you live, you can use Galas, Cortlands, Macouns, or Red or Golden Delicious apples. Adjust the sugar as needed.

Glen, N.H.

SMOKE-ROASTED APPLE CRISP

I n the 1980s and '90s, I ran a cooking school in New Hampshire called A Taste of the Mountains. Each fall I would look forward to cooking with a fresh crop of apples. The locally grown McIntoshes, which tasted so ordinary when they came from a supermarket in Boston, acquired a preternatural fragrance when encountered at local orchards and fruit stands. One way of savoring this remarkable fruit was as

New England apples, from orchard to grill.

an apple crisp with a buttery, bubbling granola and brown sugar topping. Delectable, indeed, and that was *before* I became a smoke-o-holic. I now cook my crisps on the grill, adding a handful of wood chips to the fire. The smoke flavor seems to intensify the sweetness of the fruit.

METHOD:
Indirect grilling

INGREDIENTS:
8 sweet apples
½ teaspoon grated lemon zest
2 tablespoons fresh lemon juice
⅓ cup plus ½ granulated sugar, or more to taste
2 tablespoons arrowroot or cornstarch
2 teaspoons ground cinnamon
8 tablespoons (1 stick) cold unsalted butter, cut into 1-inch pieces
½ cup flour
½ cup granola
½ cup firmly packed brown sugar
1 pinch salt
Apple or cinnamon ice cream (optional), for serving

YOU'LL ALSO NEED:
One 10-inch cast-iron skillet;
    1 cup wood chips or chunks
    (preferably apple), soaked
    for 1 hour in water to cover,
    then drained

1 Peel and core the apples. Cut each in half crosswise, then cut the halves in quarters. Place the apples in a nonreactive bowl and toss with the lemon zest and juice. Add the ⅓ cup granulated sugar, the arrowroot, and 1 teaspoon of the cinnamon and toss to mix. Taste the apple mixture for sweetness, adding more granulated sugar as necessary. Spoon the apple mixture into the cast-iron skillet and set aside.

2 Combine the butter, flour, granola, remaining ½ cup granulated sugar, brown sugar, salt, and the remaining 1 teaspoon of cinnamon in a food processor fitted with the metal blade. Pulse until the mixture is coarse and crumbly. The butter should form pea-size pieces. Spoon the topping over the apple filling.

3 Set up the grill for indirect grilling (see page 23 for gas or page 22 for charcoal) and preheat to medium-high. If using a gas grill, place all of the wood chips or chunks in the smoker box or in a smoker pouch (see page 24) and run the grill on high until you see smoke, then reduce the heat to medium-high. If using a charcoal grill, preheat it to medium-high, then toss all of the wood chips or chunks on the coals.

4 When ready to cook, place the skillet in the center of the hot grate, away from the heat, and cover the grill. Cook the crisp until the apples are soft, the filling is bubbling, and the topping is nicely browned, 40 to 60 minutes. Let the crisp cool for a few minutes, then serve. I certainly wouldn't say no to a scoop of apple or cinnamon ice cream on top.

YIELD:
Serves 8

Maine

BLUEBERRY CRUMBLE

Each of us has his obsessions. My wife Barbara's are the tiny, sweet, incredibly fragrant low bush blueberries harvested in Maine at the end of July and the beginning of August. Mine, of course, is the grill. Now, marriage is a study in the art of compromise, so I created a blueberry crumble that would satisfy Barbara's passion for blueberries and mine for live fire cooking. A gentle whiff of wood smoke brings out the delicate flavor of the blueberries.

METHOD:
Indirect grilling

INGREDIENTS:
3 pints blueberries
¾ cup flour
½ cup granulated sugar
1 teaspoon grated lemon zest
2 tablespoons fresh lemon juice
2 ounces biscotti or gingersnaps,
    coarsely crumbled
    (½ cup crumbs)
½ cup firmly packed brown sugar
6 tablespoons (¾ stick)
    cold unsalted butter,
    cut into 1-inch pieces
1 pinch salt
Vanilla ice cream (optional),
    for serving

There are blueberries, and then there are blueberries. To enjoy this dish at its very best, you must use wild blueberries that have been combed from low bushes and sold at farm stands at the height of summer. You can make a perfectly tasty crumble with regular blueberries— just don't try serving it to Mrs. Raichlen.

YOU'LL ALSO NEED:

One 8-by-10-inch aluminum foil pan; cooking oil spray; 1 cup wood chips or chunks (preferably apple), soaked for 1 hour in water to cover, then drained

1 Pick through the blueberries, removing any stems, leaves, or bruised berries. Mrs. Raichlen would rinse and drain them—I don't bother. Place the berries in a large nonreactive mixing bowl. Add ¼ cup of the flour and the granulated sugar, lemon zest, and lemon juice and gently toss to mix.

Another thing to love about Maine — buckets of summer blueberries.

Spoon the blueberry mixture into the aluminum foil pan after lightly spraying it with cooking oil.

2 Place the biscotti, brown sugar, and the remaining ½ cup of flour in a food processor fitted with the metal blade and process until a coarse powder forms. Add the butter and salt, then pulse until the mixture is coarse and crumbly. Spoon the topping over the blueberry filling.

3 Set up the grill for indirect grilling (see page 23 for gas or page 22 for charcoal) and preheat to medium-high. If using a gas grill, place all of the wood chips or chunks in the smoker box or in a smoker pouch (see page 24) and run the grill on high until you see smoke, then reduce the heat to medium-high. If using a charcoal grill, preheat it to medium-high, then toss all of the wood chips or chunks on the coals.

4 When ready to cook, place the pan with the blueberries in the center of the hot grate, away from the heat, and cover the grill. Cook the crumble until the filling is bubbling and the topping is browned, about 40 minutes. Serve the crumble hot or warm, ideally with vanilla ice cream.

YIELD:
Serves 8

VARIATION: For an outrageously delicious twist on this crumble, replace half of the blueberries (3 cups) with diced ripe peaches.

BERN'S STEAK HOUSE

BERN'S STEAK HOUSE

1208 South Howard Avenue
Tampa, Florida
(813) 251-2421

To call Bern's a steak house is a little like calling Versailles a country cottage. The larger-than-life Tampa landmark was founded in the mid-1950s by Bernard Laxer, an advertising copywriter who decided to become a restaurateur. How many restaurants grow their own salad greens, grind their own wheat to make bread, roast their own coffee beans, keep live fish in 2,500-gallon tanks, and have a nearly 7,000-item wine list? (That's different wines, not bottles—those number in the half million.) How many restaurants test recipes as many as three hundred times and train their waiters for a full year (including a stint on the restaurant farm) before considering them qualified to take an order?

Bern's founder, Bernard Laxer.

Laxer reserved his greatest obsessiveness for the beef that made Bern's famous—U.S. Prime—aged for five to eight weeks at 34°F in a custom-designed meat locker. The list of Bern's meats reads more like a high-tech instruction manual than a menu, and the noble cuts (chateaubriand, porterhouse, Delmonico, filet mignon, strip steak, and so on) are available in every imaginable thickness, cooked to every possible degree of doneness.

If you've ever wondered about the precise meaning of rare or medium-well, listen up, for Bern's menu makes it crystal clear. A medium-thick (1¼- to 1¾-inch) rare steak will have a "small crust and warm red center," for example, while a medium-well-done steak will have a "thick crust and no color left" in the center.

Not surprisingly, the focal point of Bern's kitchen is the grill, which is only slightly smaller than the deck of an aircraft carrier. Presiding over it is Miss Essie, a veteran of more than twenty years at Bern's. The pit mistress stokes her grill with natural lump charcoal. Steaks are trimmed of all excess fat (unless you request otherwise), and once grilled, they're anointed with garlic butter just before serving.

As for the dining room, well, flocked red wallpaper, white statuary, and antique paintings give it the look of a Hollywood bordello. After dinner, you can ascend to the Harry Waugh dessert room, where several dozen homemade desserts will wreak further havoc on your waistline.

Perfect peaches—one of the best gifts of summer.

Georgia

GRILLED PEACH COBBLER

For a modern American it's almost inconceivable to imagine a kitchen without an oven. But for the two hundred years following the arrival of the first settlers at Plymouth, most people did their cooking in fireplaces. Desserts were baked by the heat of wood embers, in Dutch ovens, reflecting ovens, or beehive ovens built in the side of the hearth. What these lacked in convenience was surely made up for in the flavor imparted, for live fire and wood smoke do wondrous things for desserts. Smoke has a way of bringing out the caramel qualities of fruits and

fillings. Dry heat seems to make crusts and toppings extra crisp. So the idea of cooking a cobbler on the grill shouldn't seem quite so strange. The one here features those lasciviously fragrant, juicy peaches for which Georgia is so justly famous.

METHOD:
Indirect grilling

INGREDIENTS:
4 pounds very ripe peaches
(for about 8 cups diced)
¾ cup granulated sugar, or more
to taste
2 teaspoons ground cinnamon
2 tablespoons arrowroot or
cornstarch
½ teaspoon grated lemon zest
2 tablespoons fresh lemon juice,
or more to taste
8 tablespoons (1 stick) cold unsalted
butter, cut into 1-inch pieces
½ cup flour
½ cup quick-cooking (not instant)
oatmeal
½ cup firmly packed brown sugar
Vanilla ice cream (optional),
for serving

YOU'LL ALSO NEED:
One 10-inch cast-iron skillet; 1 cup wood
chips or chunks (preferably apple),
soaked for 1 hour in water to cover,
then drained

1 Rinse the peaches and blot them dry with paper towels. Cut each in half, remove and discard the pit, and cut the fruit into 1-inch chunks. Place ¼ cup of the granulated sugar, 1 teaspoon of the cinnamon, and the arrowroot in a large nonreactive mixing bowl and whisk to combine. Stir in the peaches, lemon zest, and lemon juice. Taste for sweetness, adding more sugar or lemon juice as necessary. Spoon the filling into the skillet.

2 Place the butter, flour, oatmeal, and brown sugar, and the remaining ½ cup of granulated sugar and 1 teaspoon of cinnamon in a food processor fitted with the metal blade. Pulse until the mixture is coarse and crumbly. The butter should form pea-size pieces. If you don't have a food processor, use a stand mixer fitted with a paddle, a pastry cutter, or two knives. Spoon the topping over the peach filling.

3 Set up the grill for indirect grilling (see page 23 for gas or page 22 for charcoal) and preheat to medium. If using a gas grill, place all of the wood chips or chunks in the smoker box or in a smoker pouch (see page 24) and run the grill on high until you see smoke, then reduce the heat to medium. If

Cobbler on the grill—a BBQ USA first!

using a charcoal grill, preheat it to medium, then toss all of the wood chips or chunks on the coals.

4 When ready to cook, place the skillet in the center of the hot grate, away from the heat, and cover the grill. Cook the cobbler until the filling is bubbling and the topping is nicely browned, 40 to 60 minutes. Let the cobbler cool for a few minutes, then serve with vanilla ice cream, if desired.

YIELD:
Serves 8

Georgia

CINNAMON-GRILLED PEACHES

O ne of my favorite ways to pump up a kebab's flavor is to use an herb or spice as a skewer. Lemongrass and rosemary are both very good for this. But Georgia's irresistible peaches led me to the spice rack. When peaches are in season, I use whole cinnamon sticks as skewers to grill the peaches and nectarines. Ripe peaches, fresh mint, and cinnamon—grilling doesn't get more fragrant than this.

TIPS

Peaches come in freestone and clingstone varieties, and you can tell them apart by how easy it is to remove the pit. Cut a peach in half along the crease, then twist the halves in opposite directions. In a freestone peach the halves will come apart easily. In a clingstone peach, they'll stick like crazy and you'll have to whittle the fruit off the pit. Freestone peach halves are ideal for grilling, while clingstones are perfect for cutting up to make cobblers.

TIPS

Much of what is called cinnamon is actually the smooth, hard, perfumed bark of the cassia tree. Cinnamon, which comes from the bark of a different tropical tree, is multilayered, fragile, even crumbly. Most of what's sold as cinnamon in the United States (and certainly in your supermarket spice rack) is cassia.

METHOD:
Direct grilling

INGREDIENTS:
4 large ripe freestone peaches
8 cinnamon sticks (each 3 inches long)
8 fresh mint leaves
4 tablespoons (1/2 stick) unsalted butter
1/4 cup firmly packed brown sugar
1/4 cup dark rum
1/2 teaspoon ground cinnamon
1 pinch salt
Peach or vanilla ice cream (optional),
    for serving

1 Rinse the peaches and blot them dry with paper towels. Cut each peach in half along the crease, running your knife in a circular motion around the peach and cutting to the pit. Twist the halves in opposite directions to separate them. Using a spoon, pry out and discard the pit. Cut each peach half in half. Using a pointed chopstick or metal skewer, make a starter hole in the center of each peach quarter, working from the pit side to the skin side. Skewer 2 peach quarters on each cinnamon stick, placing a mint leaf between the 2 quarters.

2 Combine the butter, brown sugar, rum, cinnamon, and salt in a saucepan and bring to a boil over high heat. Let the glaze boil until thick and syrupy, about 5 minutes.

3 Set up the grill for direct grilling (see page 21 for charcoal or gas) and preheat to high.

4 When ready to cook, brush and oil the grill grate. Place the skewered peaches on the hot grate and grill until nicely browned, 3 to 4 minutes per side, basting with the rum and butter glaze. Spoon any remaining glaze over the grilled peaches and serve at once. Peach or vanilla ice cream makes a great accompaniment.

YIELD:
Serves 4

San Antonio, Tex.

SPICE-SCENTED SWEET POTATOES

Grilled or roasted tubers served in an aromatic syrup are a popular dessert in Mexico. So it comes as no surprise that you would find them at the most famous Mexican restaurant in San Antonio, Mi Tierra. (The colorful restaurant was immortalized in the movie *Selena*.) The notion of a grilled sweet potato dessert may seem strange—until you taste it. To make a great offbeat dessert even better, serve the sweet potatoes over ice cream.

METHOD:
Direct grilling

INGREDIENTS:

2 pounds (2 very large or 3 to 4
    medium-size) sweet potatoes

About 12 ounces piloncillo (see Notes),
    or 1½ cups firmly packed dark
    brown sugar

2 strips orange zest (see Notes)

2 strips lemon zest (see Notes)

2 cinnamon sticks (each 2 inches long)

2 whole cloves

2 allspice berries

½ teaspoon anise seed

Whipped cream, for serving

1 Set up the grill for direct grilling (see page 21 for charcoal or gas) and preheat to medium-high.

2 When ready to cook, using a fork, poke a few shallow holes in the sweet potatoes. Place the sweet potatoes on the hot grate and grill until the skins are darkly browned and the flesh is tender, 30 to 40 minutes, turning with tongs. Use a slender skewer to test for doneness. You should be able to insert it easily. Transfer the grilled sweet potatoes to a cutting board and let cool until you can handle them.

3 Using a paring knife, scrape the burnt skin off the sweet potatoes. Cut the sweet potatoes crosswise into ½-inch slices and arrange these in an attractive heatproof serving dish.

4 Combine the *piloncillo,* orange and lemon zests, cinnamon sticks, cloves, allspice berries, and anise seed in a saucepan with 1½ cups of water and bring to a boil over high heat. You may need to break up the *piloncillo* with a spoon. Reduce the heat to medium and let the syrup simmer briskly until richly flavored and syrupy, 8 to 10 minutes. Remove the saucepan from the heat and let cool slightly. Strain the warm syrup over the sweet potatoes and let cool, turning the sweet potatoes several times to ensure even marinating.

5 Serve the sweet potatoes chilled or at room temperature with the syrup spooned over them. A dollop of whipped cream wouldn't hurt.

YIELD:

Serves 4

NOTES:

■ *Piloncillo* is a hard brown sugar from Mexico that comes in cone-shaped loaves. Its flavor is a little more caramel-like than American brown sugar, but brown sugar will work fine in this recipe. Look for *piloncillo* at Mexican markets, or see the Mail-Order Sources on page 742.

Mariachi music and Tex-Mex grilling at San Antonio's Mi Tierra.

TIPS

The easiest way to cook sweet potatoes is on the grate directly over the fire, the method you'll find here. But if you're feeling adventurous, you can roast the potatoes right in the embers—which is probably how tubers were cooked in pre-Columbian times. The potatoes will look black and inedible when you pull them out of the ashes, but when you scrape away the charred skin, you'll wind up with firm, dense sweet potatoes with an unbelievable smoke flavor. Instructions for doing this appear in the Variation on the next page. To ensure even cooking, choose sweet potatoes that are all the same size.

Boston's Quincy Market, where the exotic tropical fruit called the banana made its commercial debut.

■ You can use a vegetable peeler to remove the oil-rich outer rind of the fruit in strips of zest. Be careful to leave behind the bitter white pith.

VARIATION: To roast sweet potatoes in the embers, build a charcoal or wood fire and let it die down to glowing embers. Place the sweet potatoes on the coals and let them roast until they are charred on the outside and tender inside, 40 minutes to 1 hour, turning them with tongs. Transfer the charred sweet potatoes (they won't look very pretty—that's OK) to a heatproof plate or baking sheet and let cool until you can handle them, then proceed with Step 3. You'll need to cut off the burnt skin.

Boston, Mass.

GRILLED BANANAS With Spiced Butter and Rum

Round about the time that your grilling begins to feel predictable (not that barbecue is ever *truly* predictable), try grilling bananas. But why am I saying that this recipe has a link to Boston? In the eighteenth century, Boston was the world's rum capital, boasting as many as forty distilleries. (Rum not only flavors the bananas, it's used to flambé them.) And, grilled bananas are a specialty of the East Coast Grill in Cambridge, where they're charred in the skins over an oak-burning fire. Put all this together and you'll see bananas—not to mention dessert—in a whole new light.

METHOD:
Direct grilling

INGREDIENTS:
**4 tablespoons (½ stick)
    salted butter**
2 tablespoons brown sugar
**2 tablespoons dark rum, plus ¼ cup
    dark rum or 151-proof rum (optional)
    for flambéing the bananas**
½ teaspoon ground cinnamon

¼ teaspoon ground allspice

⅛ teaspoon ground cloves

4 large bananas (see box, at right)

YOU'LL ALSO NEED:

1 cup wood chips or chunks
(optional; preferably oak), unsoaked

1 Melt the butter in a saucepan over medium heat. Add the brown sugar, the 2 tablespoons of rum, and the cinnamon, allspice, and cloves and bring to a boil over high heat, stirring. Let the mixture boil until syrupy, 2 to 4 minutes. Remove the saucepan from the heat and set the spice butter aside.

2 Set up the grill for direct grilling (see page 21 for gas or charcoal) and preheat to high (you need a really hot grill to caramelize sugar; preheat the grill, then preheat it some more before adding the bananas). If using a gas grill, place all of the wood chips or chunks in the smoker box or in a smoker pouch (see page 24) and run the grill on high until you see smoke. If using a charcoal grill, preheat it to high, then toss all of the wood chips or chunks on the coals.

3 Meanwhile, cut each banana in half lengthwise (leave the skin on). Lightly brush the cut sides with some of the spice butter.

4 When ready to cook, brush and oil the grill grate. Place the bananas on the hot grate, cut side down, and grill them until caramelized (darkly browned), about 4 minutes, rotating the bananas a quarter turn after 2 minutes to create an attractive crosshatch of

HOW TO CHOOSE BANANAS FOR GRILLING

Grilling heightens a banana's sweetness, and wood smoke adds a whole new dimension to one of America's favorite fruits. But how do you know what's the best bunch?

When choosing bananas to grill, look for ones that are ripe (or very nearly ripe) but still firm, so they will hold up during grilling. The skin should be yellow, with tiny brown spots just beginning to form. In general, if you plan to grill bananas in their skins, they can be a little riper and softer than bananas you grill peeled.

I like to slice peeled bananas sharply on the diagonal into two or three pieces to maximize the amount of surface area exposed to the fire. When grilling bananas with their peels on, just cut them in half lengthwise. Grill them cut side down first, then turn them cut side up.

grill marks. Turn the bananas over and grill, skin side down, until the bananas are tender, 2 to 4 minutes more, basting the top sides (the cut sides) with more spice butter. Transfer the grilled bananas in their skins to a platter or plates and drizzle the remaining spice butter over them (when cooked, the bananas will pull away from their skins).

5 To flambé the bananas, warm the ¼ cup of rum in a small saucepan on the grill or over low heat on the stove. Do not let it boil. Remove the rum from the heat and, working away from anything flammable and making sure that your sleeves are rolled up and your hair is tied back, ignite the warm rum with a long kitchen match. Pour the flaming rum over the bananas and serve at once.

YIELD:

Serves 4

TIPS

You can grill the bananas over gas or charcoal, but the very best flavor comes if you grill over an oak fire (see page 20). I like a light smoke flavor, so if I'm using wood chips I don't bother to soak them.

■ The Sugar and Spice–Grilled Bananas recipe calls for salted butter. The salt brings out the sweetness of the glaze.

■ In the interest of speed, I don't add wood chips here. Feel free to use them, if a light smoke flavor is desired.

Grilling gives majesty to the humble banana.

Boston, Mass.

SUGAR AND SPICE–GRILLED BANANAS

Here's an even simpler version of grilled bananas, loaded with luscious burnt-sugar and spice flavors. The unabashedly tropical recipe would seem to come from the Caribbean or Florida, but its Massachusetts roots run deep. The Bay State was the home of the Boston Fruit Company—the nation's first banana importer (bananas began turning up at Quincy Market toward the end of the nineteenth century). You brush these bananas with melted butter and then dip them in cinnamon sugar before they're grilled. The sugar crust that forms may remind you of crème brûlée.

METHOD:
Direct grilling

INGREDIENTS:
- ½ cup granulated or light brown sugar
- 2 tablespoons ground cinnamon
- ½ teaspoon freshly grated nutmeg
- 4 large bananas (see box, page 723)
- 3 tablespoons salted butter, melted

1 Set up the grill for direct grilling (see page 21 for charcoal or gas) and preheat to high (you need a really hot grill to caramelize sugar; preheat the grill, then preheat it some more before adding the bananas).

2 Meanwhile, place the sugar in a bowl and stir in the cinnamon and nutmeg. Cut each banana in half lengthwise (leave the skin on). Generously brush the cut sides with melted butter. Sprinkle the sugar mixture on top to thickly crust the bananas, patting it onto the fruit with your fingertips.

3 When ready to cook, brush and oil the grill grate. Place the bananas on the hot grate, cut side down, and grill them until caramelized (darkly browned), 2 to 4 minutes. Using a spatula, turn the bananas and grill, skin side down, until tender, 2 to 4 minutes more (when cooked, the banana will pull away from their skins). Transfer the grilled

bananas in their skins to a platter or plates and serve at once. If you like, you can flambé the bananas as described in Step 5 on page 723.

YIELD:
Serves 4

New Mexico

BANANA SUNDAES
With New Mexican Chocolate Sauce

What's America's most decadent dessert? Strawberry shortcake? Coconut cream pie? My vote goes to the hot fudge sundae. Drowning in hot chocolate sauce and snowy with whipped cream, the sundae stands as a monument to the spirit of excess. It's about to get a lot more decadent with the addition of smokily grilled bananas and a cinnamon-scented New Mexican chocolate sauce spiked with chile powder. Don't be intimidated by the length of the recipe—it's really just a set of simple steps, many of which can be done ahead of time.

METHOD:
Direct grilling

FOR THE SPICED SUGAR:
½ cup granulated sugar
1 tablespoon unsweetened cocoa powder
2 teaspoons ground cinnamon
¼ teaspoon ground cloves

FOR THE WHIPPED CREAM:
1 cup heavy (whipping) cream
3 tablespoons confectioners' sugar
1 tablespoon dark rum
½ teaspoon vanilla extract

FOR THE CHOCOLATE SAUCE:
¾ cup heavy (whipping) cream
6 ounces semisweet chocolate, coarsely chopped
½ teaspoon ground cinnamon
½ teaspoon ancho or other pure chile powder
1 teaspoon vanilla extract

FOR SERVING:
2 pints vanilla ice cream
6 large bananas (see box, page 723)
⅓ cup toasted slivered almonds or pine nuts (see page 584)

1 MAKE THE SPICED SUGAR: Combine the granulated sugar, cocoa powder, cinnamon, and cloves in a small shallow bowl and stir to mix. Set the spiced sugar aside.

2 MAKE THE WHIPPED CREAM: Place the cream in a chilled mixer bowl or in a large metal bowl. Beat until soft peaks form, starting on the slow speed and gradually increasing the speed to high. The total beating time will be 5 to 8 minutes. When soft peaks have formed, add the confectioners' sugar, rum, and vanilla. Continue

TIPS

There are several options for bananas here, from the conventional Chiquitas to the newly fashionable apple bananas (often sold by their Spanish name, *platano manzano*). Apple bananas are short and stubby, with a pleasingly tart flavor reminiscent of apples. Look for them at Mexican and Hispanic markets (and at an increasing number of supermarkets).

TIPS

Chile powder may seem like an odd ingredient to include in a chocolate sauce, but that's how the Aztecs ate chocolate, and its spicy heat echos the smoke flavor of these grilled bananas.

beating the cream until stiff peaks form, about 2 minutes longer, but don't overbeat or it will start to turn to butter. Keep the whipped cream in the refrigerator, covered, until ready to use.

3 MAKE THE CHOCOLATE SAUCE: Combine the cream, chocolate, cinnamon, chile powder and vanilla, in the top of a double boiler or in a bowl set over barely simmering water. Stir frequently with a heatproof rubber spatula until the chocolate melts, about 5 minutes. Don't let the sauce boil or you will burn the chocolate. Remove from the heat and stir in the vanilla. Keep the chocolate sauce warm or reheat it just before serving.

4 Scoop balls of ice cream into 6 bowls and place them in the freezer. The recipe can be prepared to this stage several hours ahead.

5 Set up the grill for direct grilling (see page 21 for charcoal or gas) and preheat to high (you need a really hot grill to caramelize sugar; preheat the grill, then preheat it some more before adding the bananas).

6 Meanwhile, peel the bananas and slice each in half sharply on the diagonal. (This method of slicing maximizes the surface area exposed to the fire.) Dip each banana slice in the spiced sugar, shaking off the excess.

7 When ready to cook, brush and oil the grill grate. Place the banana slices on the hot grate and grill them until caramelized (darkly browned), on all sides, 2 to 4 minutes per side (6 to 12 minutes in all).

8 Lean the grilled banana slices upright on top of the ice cream in

... a monument to the spirit of excess

each bowl. Spoon the warm chocolate sauce over the top. Spoon or pipe the whipped cream on top and sprinkle with the almonds. Serve at once.

YIELD:

Serves 6

New Orleans, La.

GRILLED BANANAS FOSTER

To come to New Orleans without sampling bananas Foster at Brennan's is a bit like visiting London and missing Big Ben. Hyperbole, perhaps, but bananas sautéed with butter, brown sugar, banana liqueur, and rum is a New Orleans culinary tradition, and its popularity can be judged by the staggering quantity of bananas Foster served at Brennan's each year and the number of imitations it has spawned. Named for a local businessman (Richard Foster, owner of the Foster Awning Company in New Orleans), bananas Foster was created in the 1950s by Brennan's chef Paul Blangé. Chef Blangé would probably be scandalized by the notion of grilled bananas Foster, but the smoky char of the fire makes a great dessert even better. Brennan's serves its bananas over ice cream. Fire and ice—a combination I heartily recommend.

METHOD:

Direct grilling

INGREDIENTS:

4 tablespoons (½ stick) unsalted butter

1 cup firmly packed brown sugar

¼ cup banana liqueur

¼ cup dark rum

½ teaspoon ground cinnamon

1½ pints vanilla ice cream

4 large bananas (see box, page 723)

⅓ cup toasted chopped pecans (see Note)

YOU'LL ALSO NEED:

2 cups wood chips or chunks (preferably oak or mesquite), soaked for 1 hour in water to cover, then drained

1 Melt the butter in a deep frying pan over medium heat. Add the brown sugar, banana liqueur, rum, and cinnamon, increase the heat to high, and let the sauce boil until syrupy, 3 to 5 minutes. Remove the pan from the heat. The butter sauce can be made up to 2 hours before serving. It does not need to be refrigerated.

2 Scoop balls of ice cream into 4 bowls and place them in the freezer.

To maximize the taste of smoke, I like to grill the bananas over a wood fire (see page 20). Oak or mesquite are good choices. Wood chips or chunks will also add flavor.

The birthplace of traditional bananas Foster.

3 Set up the grill for direct grilling (see page 21 for gas or charcoal) and preheat to high (you need a really hot grill to caramelize sugar; preheat the grill, then preheat it some more before adding the bananas). If using a gas grill, place all of the wood chips or chunks in the smoker box or in a smoker pouch (see page 24) and run the grill on high until you see smoke. If using a charcoal grill, preheat it to high, then toss all of the wood chips or chunks on the coals.

4 Meanwhile, peel the bananas and slice each in half sharply on the diagonal. Reheat the butter sauce, if necessary. Lightly brush each piece of banana with a little of the butter sauce.

5 When ready to cook, brush and oil the grill grate. Place the banana halves on the hot grate and grill until caramelized (darkly browned) on all sides, 2 to 4 minutes per side (6 to 12 minutes in all), basting with some of the butter sauce. Be sure to reserve at least three quarters of the sauce for serving.

6 Place the grilled banana halves in the bowls on top of the ice cream. Pour the remaining butter sauce over them, sprinkle the pecans on top, and serve at once.

YIELD:
Serves 4

NOTE: There are at least three ways to toast pecans. You can place them in a dry skillet (don't use a nonstick one) over medium heat and cook until the nuts are fragrant and lightly browned, 3 to 6 minutes, shaking the pan to ensure even cooking. Or you can arrange the pecans in a single layer in an aluminum foil–lined roasting pan and bake them in a 400°F oven or toaster oven for 8 to 15 minutes, again shaking the pan from time to time to ensure even browning. Finally, a grill maniac would place the pecans in an aluminum foil pan and grill them using the indirect method (see page 22 for charcoal or page 23 for gas) for 8 to 15 minutes.

Mississippi

GRILLED BANANA CREAM PIE

How far would you go to achieve perfection? Would you make your own crust? Would you beat your own whipped cream? Would you lovingly coat bananas with cinnamon sugar and brown them on the grill until they are sweetly caramelized? I'm talking, of course, about the perfect banana cream pie, a classic dessert served at the classiest American barbecue restaurants, especially in Mississippi and other parts of the Deep South. And I'm about to make an extravagant claim: This one is hands down the best—first because it's made from scratch, but even more important, because you grill the bananas. (Remember Raichlen's rule: If it tastes good baked, boiled, stewed, or sautéed, it will probably taste even better grilled.) Don't let the length of the recipe put you off; it's a series of easy steps.

METHOD:
Indirect grilling (optional) and
    direct grilling

INGREDIENTS:
10 cinnamon graham crackers
    (for 1 cup crumbs)

¾ cup plus 3 tablespoons granulated
    sugar
8 tablespoons (1 stick) butter, melted
1 cup milk
Yolks of 3 eggs
2 tablespoons flour
2 tablespoons dark rum
1½ teaspoons vanilla extract
1 cup heavy (whipping) cream
¼ cup confectioners' sugar
1 tablespoon ground cinnamon,
    plus a little cinnamon for garnish
4 large bananas (see box,
    page 723)

YOU'LL ALSO NEED:
One 8-inch pie pan

1 Preheat the oven to 350°F. Die-hard grillers will set up the grill for indirect grilling (see page 22 for charcoal or page 23 for gas) and preheat to medium.

2 Break the graham crackers into pieces and, using a food processor fitted with the metal blade, pulse the cracker pieces until they are the consistency of granulated sugar. Add 3 tablespoons of the granulated sugar and the melted butter, and pulse to mix. Transfer this mixture to the pie pan. Using the back of a spoon, press it against the side and bottom of the pan. Bake the crust or grill it indirectly until lightly browned, 10 to 15 minutes. Transfer the crust to a wire rack and let it cool to room temperature.

3 Place the milk in a heavy saucepan over medium heat and heat, stirring occasionally, until it is steaming and small bubbles form around the edge of the pan. Do not let the milk boil.

TIPS

You'll find that one of the packages inside a box of graham crackers will give you enough graham crackers to make the crust for the banana cream pie.

Meanwhile, place the egg yolks, ¼ cup of the granulated sugar, and the flour in a mixing bowl and whisk just to mix. Whisk the hot milk into the yolk mixture in a thin stream. Return the egg mixture to the saucepan and place it over medium heat. Bring the pastry cream to a gentle boil and let boil, whisking constantly, until thickened, about 3 minutes. Return the pastry cream to the mixing bowl and whisk in 1 tablespoon of the rum and 1 teaspoon of the vanilla. Press a piece of plastic wrap on top of the pastry cream to prevent a skin from forming while it cools. Make a few small slits in the plastic wrap with the tip of a knife to allow the steam to escape. Let the pastry cream cool to room temperature.

4 Place the heavy cream in a chilled mixer bowl or in a large metal bowl. Beat until soft peaks form, starting on the slow speed and gradually increasing the speed to high. The total beating time will be 5 to 8 minutes. When soft peaks have formed, add the confectioners' sugar, the remaining 1 tablespoon of rum, and the remaining ½ teaspoon of vanilla. Continue beating the cream until stiff peaks form, about 2 minutes longer, but don't overbeat or it will start to turn into butter. Keep the whipped cream in the refrigerator, covered, until ready to use.

5 Place the remaining ½ cup of granulated sugar in a shallow bowl and stir in the tablespoon of cinnamon. Set the cinnamon sugar aside. The recipe can be prepared up to this stage several hours in advance.

6 Set up the grill for direct grilling (see page 21 for charcoal or gas) and preheat to high (you need a really hot grill to caramelize sugar; preheat the grill, then preheat it some more before adding the bananas).

7 Meanwhile, peel the bananas and slice each sharply on the diagonal into 2 or 3 pieces. Dip each piece of banana in the cinnamon sugar, shaking off the excess.

8 When ready to cook, brush and oil the grill grate. Place the pieces of banana on the hot grate and grill until caramelized (darkly browned) on all sides, 2 to 4 minutes per side (6 to 12 minutes in all). Transfer the grilled bananas to a plate and let them cool to room temperature, about 10 minutes.

9 To assemble the pie, spoon the pastry cream into the graham cracker crust. Arrange the grilled bananas on top of the pastry cream, pressing them into it. If you're feeling fancy, using a piping bag fitted with a large star tip, pipe the whipped cream in decorative swirls on top of the bananas. Or mound it atop the bananas, using a spoon. Lightly sprinkle the top of the pie with cinnamon. The pie can be refrigerated for several hours before serving. If this isn't the best banana cream pie you've ever tasted, let me know. (Better still, send me the recipe for the one you think is better: You can reach me at www.barbecuebible.com.)

YIELD:
Serves 8

Indianapolis, Ind.

POUND CAKE
With Grilled Lemon Curd and Fresh Berries

I know what you're thinking: There he goes again! Is nothing sacred to this barbecue-obsessed pyromaniac? If the Good Lord meant for us to grill pound cake, why did he give us ovens? And who else but a maniac would grill lemons to make that high tea favorite, lemon curd? I invented this dessert for a highfalutin barbecue I was asked to stage at the Grand Prix Formula One race in Indianapolis. Toasting the pound cake on the grill enhances its flavor and color, while grilling the lemons adds caramel overtones that utterly transform the fruit. You can make this colorful dessert ahead of time.

METHOD:
Direct grilling

INGREDIENTS:
4 to 5 lemons (for ¾ cup juice)
¾ cup sugar, placed
   in a shallow bowl
8 slices pound cake (each ½ inch thick)
8 tablespoons (1 stick) unsalted butter,
   cut into ½-inch pieces
4 large eggs
1 pint blueberries, raspberries,
   blackberries, or strawberries, or
   better still, a mix of berries,
   hulled, rinsed, and blotted dry
8 sprigs fresh mint, for garnish

1 Rinse the lemons and blot them dry with paper towels. Using a vegetable peeler, remove 3 strips of lemon zest, each 1 by ½ inch, taking only the yellow outer part, not the bitter white pith beneath it. Cut each lemon in half crosswise and remove any seeds with a fork. Set the lemon halves and zest aside.

2 Set up the grill for direct grilling (see page 21 for charcoal or gas) and preheat to high.

T I P S

You can grill pound cake in bite-size portions, using small squares of pound cake and small dollops or rosettes of lemon curd. For a more casual dessert, simply spoon the lemon curd over toasted slices of pound cake and sprinkle the berries on top.

Racing to taste pound cake on the grill in Indianapolis.

TIPS

I won't ask you to make your own pound cake (but I won't stop you either). And, for the sake of convenience, you can grill the pound cake several hours in advance. If you're feeling more ambitious, grill it to order.

3 When ready to cook, brush and oil the grill grate. Dip the cut side of each lemon half in the sugar to crust it. Set the sugar aside. Place the lemon halves, cut side down, on the hot grate and grill until the cut side is nicely caramelized (golden brown), 2 to 4 minutes. Transfer the grilled lemon halves to a plate and let them cool.

4 Brush and oil the grill grate again. Place the slices of pound cake on the hot grate and grill until nicely toasted, 1 to 3 minutes per side. Transfer the grilled cake slices to a wire rack to cool.

5 Juice the grilled lemons; you should have ¾ cup juice. Place the lemon juice, lemon zest, the remaining sugar from dipping the lemons, and the butter and eggs in a heavy nonreactive saucepan and whisk to mix. Place the pan over medium heat and let cook until the mixture is smooth and thick (the consistency of mayonnaise), 3 to 5 minutes, whisking steadily. Don't let the lemon curd boil or it will curdle.

6 Immediately transfer the lemon curd to a bowl. Remove and discard the 3 strips of lemon zest. Press a piece of plastic wrap on top of the lemon curd to prevent a skin from forming while it cools. Make a few small slits in the plastic wrap with the tip of a knife to allow the steam to escape. Let the lemon curd cool to room temperature, then refrigerate it until serving. It will keep for several days.

7 To serve, place the grilled pound cake slices on a platter or plates. Spoon the lemon curd over them, place the berries on top, garnish each slice with a mint sprig, and serve at once.

YIELD:
Serves 8

VARIATION: Grilled pound cake is delicious served hot. Grill the lemons and make the lemon curd ahead of time and then grill the pound cake just before serving.

Montreal, Canada

FRENCH TOAST ON THE GRILL

French toast on the grill? *Mais, oui!* Live fire imbues marshmallows, fruit, and cake with irresistible smoke flavors, so why not French toast? The one here was inspired by Montreal food celebrities Ricardo Larrivée and Brigitte Coutu, who like to dip slices of *quatre-quarts* (pound cake) in a light egg batter, then sizzle them on the grill. Naturally, the French toast is great for dessert, but it could also give you an excuse to fire up your grill for breakfast.

METHOD:
Direct grilling

FOR THE FRENCH TOAST:
2 large eggs
2 tablespoons maple syrup
1 cup milk
1 teaspoon pure vanilla extract
8 slices pound cake (each ½ inch
    thick)

FOR SERVING:
Confectioners' sugar
Fresh blueberries, raspberries, and/or
    other berries (optional)
Maple syrup (optional)

1 Place the eggs and maple syrup in a large, wide bowl and, using a whisk, beat just to mix. Whisk in the milk and vanilla.

2 Set up the grill for direct grilling (see page 21 for charcoal or gas) and preheat to medium-high.

3 When ready to cook, place the bowl with the egg mixture and a platter holding the pound cake slices by the grill. Brush and oil the grill grate. Dip each slice of pound cake in the egg mixture, letting it soak for 2 to 4 seconds per side. As they are coated, place the cake slices on the hot grate on the diagonal and grill until lightly browned, 2 to 4 minutes per side. If you're feeling fancy, you can give each slice a quarter turn to create a handsome crosshatch of grill marks.

4 Transfer the French toast slices to a platter or plates and sprinkle them with confectioners' sugar. Serve at once with fresh berries and/or more maple syrup, if desired.

YIELD:
Serves 4

Alaska

SMOKED ALASKA

Finding a way to grill ice cream is the barbecue buff's version of the quest for the Holy Grail. Every pit master aspires to conquer this improbable, contradictory dessert. Smoked Alaska was inspired by my barbecue buddy Rick Browne—photographer, smoke meister, and co-author of *Barbecue America: A Pilgrimage in Search of America's Best Barbecue.* Rick's approach to barbecue can be summed up by the "portrait" he took of me for his newspaper: Through the miracle of Photoshop, I wound up posing supine on a hot grill! When he heard I was writing this book, he volunteered a contribution—a baked Alaska you grill. It may sound complicated, but it's actually pretty easy to prepare, and it never

TIPS

The trick to making French toast on the grill is to soak the cake slices quickly—just long enough to moisten the exterior without making the cake soggy and fragile. A few seconds on each side should do it. As you can imagine, it's important to clean and oil the grate well before placing the cake slices on the grill.

TIPS

■ The recipe for Smoked Alaska uses the indirect method of grilling, but you need a high heat to brown the meringue before the ice cream melts. To do this on a charcoal grill, use about 50 percent more coals than normal, rake them into two large mounds, as usual, but don't cover the grill until the last minute and be sure that all the vent holes are wide open. On a gas grill, preheat all the burners with the grill covered and turn off the center burner right before you put on the Smoked Alaska.

■ I like to separate the egg whites in small bowls, one by one, inspecting each for any yolk before adding it to the mixer bowl. The least bit of yolk can prevent the whites from rising properly.

fails to draw gasps of admiration from the crowd. Of course, I've tinkered with the recipe (the wood chips are my idea, for example), but the basic procedure is Rick's. So, why is Alaska the place of origin? Any dessert that features a bedrock of ice cream, a glacier of fudge sauce, and snowy white mountains of meringue is the very embodiment of the last frontier state.

METHOD:
Indirect grilling

INGREDIENTS:
About 1½ cups of your favorite ice cream (I'm partial to Häagen Dazs vanilla), slightly softened
1 pound cake (16 ounces)
2 tablespoons white rum (optional)
½ cup cherry or apricot jam
About 2 cups chocolate fudge ice cream sauce
Whites of 6 large eggs (for ¾ cup)
1 teaspoon cream of tartar
1 cup plus 2 tablespoons superfine sugar or granulated sugar
¼ cup 151-proof rum (optional), for flambéing

YOU'LL ALSO NEED:
1 loaf pan about the same size as the pound cake; 1 wooden plank about 14 inches long, 8 inches wide, and 1 inch thick, soaked for 1 hour in water to cover, drained, then wrapped in aluminum foil; a pastry bag with a large star tip (optional); 1 cup wood chips or chunks (preferably oak or cherry), soaked for 1 hour in water to cover, then drained; an electric knife (optional)

1 Line the loaf pan with plastic wrap. Spoon the ice cream into the bottom of the pan in an even layer and freeze until solid.

2 Holding your knife parallel to the work surface, cut the pound cake in half. Place the bottom half of the cake on the aluminum foil–wrapped plank. Sprinkle this half with 1 tablespoon of the white rum, if using, and spread the jam over it in a thick layer. Pour about ½ cup of the chocolate fudge sauce over the cut side of the remaining piece of pound cake; the cake will absorb some, but not all, of the sauce. Unmold the ice cream in the loaf pan, peeling away the plastic wrap, and place it on top of the jam-covered pound cake. Place the second piece of pound cake, chocolate side down, on top of the ice cream. If using, sprinkle the top of the cake with the remaining 1 tablespoon of white rum. Place the cake, still on the plank, in the freezer while you make the meringue and set up the grill. Set the remaining chocolate fudge sauce aside for serving. The recipe can be prepared to this stage and frozen up to 2 days ahead. If you do this, cover the cake and ice cream with plastic wrap after they have frozen solid.

3 Place the egg whites and cream of tartar in the bowl of a stand mixer or in a metal bowl. Beat until soft peaks form (the mixture will look white and fluffy), starting on the slow speed and gradually increasing the speed to high. The total beating time will be about 8 minutes. Add ¼ cup of the sugar in a thin stream and continue beating until the whites are firm and glossy, 1 to 2 minutes longer. Using a rubber spatula, fold in the remaining sugar, working as gently as possible. Using the spatula, spread the meringue over the top and sides of the layered cake. If you're feeling fancy, you can pipe decorative swirls of meringue over the cake, using a pastry bag fitted with a large star tip. Either way, make sure the cake is completely covered with a thick layer of meringue. No leaks! The cake can be prepared to this stage and frozen for up to 2 months; cover the meringue with plastic wrap after it has frozen solid.

4 Set up the grill for indirect grilling (see page 23 for gas or page 22 for charcoal) and preheat to high. If using a gas grill, place all of the wood chips or chunks in the smoker box or in a smoker pouch (see page 24) and run the grill on high until you see smoke. If using a charcoal grill, preheat it to high, then toss all of the wood chips or chunks on the coals.

5 When ready to cook, place the cake, still on the foil-wrapped plank, in the center of the hot grate, away from the heat, and cover the grill. Cook the Smoked Alaska until the meringue is golden brown on all sides, 3 to 6 minutes. If using a charcoal grill, you can shine a flashlight into one of the vent holes to check on the browning. If using a gas grill that doesn't have a window, you'll need to quickly lift the lid to take a peek.

6 Transfer the grilled Smoked Alaska to a platter and bear it proudly to the table. For extra drama you can

serve it flambéed: Warm the 151-proof rum in a small saucepan on the grill or over low heat on the stove. Do not let it boil. Remove the rum from the heat and, working away from anything flammable and making sure that your sleeves are rolled up and your hair is tied back, ignite the warm rum with a long kitchen match. Pour the flaming rum over the Smoked Alaska. To slice the Smoked Alaska, use an electric knife or a long, slender knife you've heated in boiling water. Serve the remaining fudge sauce on the side.

YIELD:
Serves 8

*Did I hear a call
for egg whites?*

... the marshmallows should be homemade

T I P S

One fun way to toast these s'mores is outdoors over a charcoal-filled hibachi. Place the hibachi on a heatproof pad or inverted baking sheet, in the center of a table, making sure it can't slide or tip. Let your guests toast their marshmallows just as dark as they like (I like to catch mine on fire). Or you can rake coals in a charcoal grill into a mound and toast the marshmallows on the end of long skewers or sticks. You can even toast them in the flames of a side burner on a gas grill.

Aspen, Colo.

S'MORES FROM SCRATCH

Todd English achieved international acclaim with his sizzling Italo-Mediterranean restaurant Olives in Boston (or more precisely in Charlestown, Massachusetts). Today, he presides over an empire that includes restaurants in New York City, Aspen, and Las Vegas. The focal point of all his restaurants is a live-fire cooking complex that includes a wood-burning oven, grill, and rotisserie (indeed, Todd has patented several ingenious grilling devices).

It should come as no surprise that English has some very particular thoughts about that childhood favorite, the s'more. Namely, that the marshmallows should be homemade—ditto for the graham crackers—and that the candy bar of yesteryear should be replaced by a suave chocolate-hazelnut "smear." Todd pioneered his s'mores at the Aspen, Colorado, Olives, where they're served with a tiny, hand-forged charcoal brazier, so you can toast the marshmallows at your table.

METHOD:
Direct grilling

ADVANCE PREPARATION:
**4 to 12 hours for the marshmallows
to become firm enough to cut easily**

FOR THE MARSHMALLOWS:
**3 envelopes unflavored gelatin
(3 tablespoons)
Whites of 4 large eggs
1 teaspoon cream of tartar
2 cups granulated sugar
1 cup light corn syrup
2 teaspoons pure vanilla extract
2 teaspoons orange liqueur, such
as Cointreau (optional)**

FOR THE GRAHAM CRACKERS:
**1¾ cups all-purpose unbleached
white flour, plus more for
sprinkling
1½ cups whole wheat flour
¾ cup rye flour
1 tablespoon salt
2 teaspoons ground cinnamon
1 pound (4 sticks) cold unsalted butter,
cut into 1-inch pieces
⅔ cup honey
½ cup cold water**

FOR THE S'MORES:
**1 cup confectioners' sugar
2 jars (each 13 ounces) Nutella or
another chocolate-hazelnut spread**

YOU'LL ALSO NEED:
**Candy thermometer; one 8-by-12-inch
baking dish, lightly oiled with cooking
oil spray; 3-inch round cookie cutter;
long metal skewers or sticks for grilling
the marshmallows**

itto for the graham crackers . . .

1 MAKE THE MARSHMALLOWS: Sprinkle the gelatin over ½ cup of water and let stand until softened, about 5 minutes.

2 Meanwhile, place the egg whites and cream of tartar in the bowl of a stand mixer. Beat until soft peaks form, starting on the slow speed for about 2 minutes, then beating on medium for about 4 minutes, and finally on high for about 2 minutes; the total beating time will be about 8 minutes. If the whites begin to stiffen before the sugar syrup is ready, lower the beater speed to medium-low.

3 While the egg whites are beating, make a sugar syrup: Combine the sugar and corn syrup in a heavy saucepan over high heat and stir just to mix. Cover the pan and cook for 2 minutes. Remove the lid, attach a candy thermometer to the side of the saucepan, and let the sugar cook until it registers 240°F on the candy thermometer.

4 Once the sugar mixture has reached 240°F, remove it from the heat and quickly whisk in the softened gelatin, making sure that it fully dissolves. Pour the sugar mixture in a slow steady stream into the egg whites as they beat at high speed. Drizzle in the vanilla and orange liqueur, if using, and continue beating the marshmallow mixture until it is room temperature, 15 to 20 minutes. Spoon the mixture into the oiled baking dish, smoothing the top with a spatula. Let the marshmallow rest in a cool dry place at room temperature until firm, 4 hours or overnight.

5 MAKE THE GRAHAM CRACKERS: Place the white, whole wheat, and rye flours, salt, and cinnamon in a food processor fitted with the metal blade and process to mix. Add the butter and process until the mixture feels sandy, like cornmeal, 1 to 2 minutes. Add the honey and cold water and process in short bursts until the mixture comes together into a thick dough. Flour your hands and a work surface. Roll the dough into a ball, then flatten it. Wrap the dough in a large piece of plastic wrap and refrigerate it until firm, 3 to 4 hours.

6 Preheat the oven to 350°F. Lightly flour a work surface. Divide the graham cracker dough into several small batches (it's easier to work with this way), then roll each out to a thickness of ¼ inch. Using the 3-inch round cookie cutter, cut out circles of dough. Reroll out and cut the dough until all of it is used up. Place the dough circles on nonstick baking sheets and bake until golden brown, 15 to 20 minutes. When done, the graham crackers will be just starting to brown at the edges. Transfer the graham crackers to a wire rack and let them cool completely. Place the graham crackers on a serving dish or in a bowl or store them in an airtight container until you are ready

TIPS

■ This s'more recipe is a little involved—make that a lot involved. But just imagine how you'll feel when you nonchalantly announce that the marshmallows and even the graham crackers are homemade.

■ I've tinkered with Todd's original recipe a little, adding orange liqueur to the marshmallows and rye flour to the graham crackers. And while Todd makes his own chocolate-hazelnut spread, I've replaced that with Nutella.

Todd English, who makes his marshmallows and graham crackers from scratch.

to make the s'mores. They will keep for at least a week.

7 CUT OUT THE MARSHMALLOWS: Run the tip of a paring knife around the inside of the baking dish to loosen the marshmallow. Generously dust a work surface with confectioners' sugar. Turn the marshmallow out onto the dusted work surface, shaking the baking dish if necessary to release it. Using a long, slender knife, cut the marshmallow the short way into six 2-inch strips. Then make 7 cuts the long way at 1-inch intervals to create 48 rectangular marshmallows (see Note). Generously dust each of these with confectioners' sugar to keep them from sticking together. Place the marshmallows on a serving plate or in a bowl. The recipe can be prepared to this stage a day or two—even several weeks—ahead. If made ahead, store the marshmallows in an airtight cookie tin, placing sheets of plastic wrap between each layer. They can be refrigerated in the tin for several weeks.

8 Set up the grill for direct grilling (see page 21 for charcoal or gas). If using a gas grill, preheat the side burner or remove the grate and preheat the grill to high. If using a charcoal grill, when the embers glow orange and the flames have died down, rake the coals into a mound in the center. You don't need a grate.

9 To make the s'mores, have everyone spear a marshmallow at the end of a skewer and toast it over the fire until softened and browned to taste. Generously spread a graham cracker with some of the Nutella. Place the toasted marshmallow on top and top with another graham cracker. Squish it to make a gooey mess, then eat it.

YIELD:

Makes 24 s'mores;
    figure on 2 per person

NOTE: This makes about twice as many marshmallows as you need for the graham crackers. To use them all, make two batches of graham crackers.

VARIATION: Not wild about the flavor of hazelnuts? Substitute pieces of a premium American chocolate bar, such as one from Scharffen Berger.

Mississippi

DRUNKEN WATERMELON

Watermelon "is chief of this world's luxuries," observed Mississippi River pilot Mark Twain. "When one has tasted it, he knows what the angels eat." Amen! The only thing I'd add to Twain's observation is that a barbecue without watermelon is like a grill without fire, like a cookout without a crowd. My childhood buddy Nick Hall likes to fortify his watermelon with tequila or rum. True, this is one of the few recipes in this book that's not grilled, but if I omitted it from this book, I would be disloyal to the great American barbecue tradition. Just be sure to warn your guests that they are not eating innocent watermelon. This is one of the few desserts I know that can lead to a hangover!

ADVANCE PREPARATION:
2 to 4 hours for marinating the watermelon

INGREDIENTS:
1 large watermelon
2 to 4 cups tequila, rum, or vodka

Cut 2 or 3 cone-shaped 1-inch holes in the top of the watermelon by angling a paring knife about 2 inches down toward the center. Remove and set aside the "plugs." Pour in as much tequila, as the melon will absorb, then replace the plugs. Let the watermelon marinate for 2 to 4 hours in the refrigerator or at room temperature. Cut the watermelon into slices for serving.

YIELD:
Serves 12 to 14

How do you tell if an uncut watermelon is ripe? Connoisseurs insist you can "hear" it by rapping the melon with your knuckles. It should resound with a hollow *thunk*. The most reliable method is to taste another melon from the same batch. Many roadside farm stands will have one cut open for you to sample.

Wrap your lips around Drunken Watermelon.

Approximate Equivalents

1 STICK BUTTER = 8 tbs = 4 oz = 1/2 cup

1 CUP ALL-PURPOSE PRESIFTED FLOUR OR DRIED BREADCRUMBS = 5 oz

1 CUP GRANULATED SUGAR = 8 oz

1 CUP (PACKED) BROWN SUGAR = 6 oz

1 CUP CONFECTIONERS' SUGAR = 4 1/2 oz

1 CUP HONEY OR SYRUP = 12 oz

1 CUP GRATED CHEESE = 4 oz

1 CUP DRIED BEANS = 6 oz

1 LARGE EGG = about 2 oz = about 3 tbs

1 EGG YOLK = about 1 tbs

1 EGG WHITE = about 2 tbs

Please note that all conversions are approximate but close enough to be useful when converting from one system to another.

Weight Conversions

U.S.	METRIC	U.S.	METRIC
1/2 oz	15 g	7 oz	200 g
1 oz	30 g	8 oz	250 g
1 1/2 oz	45 g	9 oz	275 g
2 oz	60 g	10 oz	300 g
2 1/2 oz	75 g	11 oz	325 g
3 oz	90 g	12 oz	350 g
3 1/2 oz	100 g	13 oz	375 g
4 oz	125 g	14 oz	400 g
5 oz	150 g	15 oz	450 g
6 oz	175 g	1 lb	500 g

Liquid Conversions

U.S.	IMPERIAL	METRIC
2 tbs	1 fl oz	30 ml
3 tbs	1 1/2 fl oz	45 ml
1/4 cup	2 fl oz	60 ml
1/3 cup	2 1/2 fl oz	75 ml
1/3 cup + 1 tbs	3 fl oz	90 ml
1/3 cup + 2 tbs	3 1/2 fl oz	100 ml
1/2 cup	4 fl oz	125 ml
2/3 cup	5 fl oz	150 ml
3/4 cup	6 fl oz	175 ml
3/4 cup + 2 tbs	7 fl oz	200 ml
1 cup	8 fl oz	250 ml
1 cup + 2 tbs	9 fl oz	275 ml
1 1/4 cups	10 fl oz	300 ml
1 1/3 cups	11 fl oz	325 ml
1 1/2 cups	12 fl oz	350 ml
1 2/3 cups	13 fl oz	375 ml
1 3/4 cups	14 fl oz	400 ml
1 3/4 cups + 2 tbs	15 fl oz	450 ml
2 cups (1 pint)	16 fl oz	500 ml
2 1/2 cups	20 fl oz (1 pint)	600 ml
3 3/4 cups	1 1/2 pints	900 ml
4 cups	1 3/4 pints	1 liter

Oven Temperatures

°F	Gas	°C		°F	Gas	°C
250	1/2	120		400	6	200
275	1	140		425	7	220
300	2	150		450	8	230
325	3	160		475	9	240
350	4	180		500	10	260
375	5	190				

Note: Reduce the temperature by 20°C (68°F) for fan-assisted ovens.

Conversion Tables

Grilling Equipment and Accessories

CHICKCAN
(337) 478-8101
www.chickcan.com
Beer-can chicken device

CHEF REECE WILLIAMS CAJUN INJECTOR
9180 Highway 67 South
P.O. Box 97
Clinton, Louisiana 70722
(800) 221-8060
www.cajuninjector.com
Kitchen syringes

DIVERSITECH CORPORATION
2530 Lantrac Court
Decatur, Georgia 30035
(800) 397-4823
www.diversitech.com
Spark-resistant grill pads

GREATGRATE SWAMPER PRODUCTS
P.O. Box 663
Charlestown, Rhode Island 02813
(877) 768-5766
www.greatgrate.com
Shellfish grates

GRILL LOVER'S CATALOGUE
P.O. Box 1300
Columbus, Georgia 31902
(800) 241-8981
www.grilllovers.com
Accessories

GRILLA GEAR
P.O. Box 7369
Endicott, New York 13760
(800) 999-3436
www.worldkitchen.com
Barbecue utensils and other accessories

LODGE MANUFACTURING COMPANY
P.O. Box 380
South Pittsburg, Tennessee 37380
(423) 837-7181
www.lodgemfg.com
Cast-iron cookware

WEBER-STEPHEN PRODUCTS CO.
200 East Daniels Road
Palatine, Illinois 60067
(800) 446-1071
www.weber.com
Grills and grill accessories

Charcoal and Wood

BBQR'S DELIGHT
P.O. Box 8727
Pine Bluff, Arkansas 71661
(877) 275-9591
www.bbqrsdelight.com
Compressed wood pellets

CHINOOK PLANKS
P.O. Box 27469
Seattle, Washington 98125
(800) 765-4408
www.chinookplanks.com
Cedar and alder planks

NATURE'S OWN/PEOPLES WOODS
75 Mill Street
Cumberland, Rhode Island 02864
(800) 729-5800
www.peopleswoods.com
Chunk charwood

SMOKEY HOUSE CENTER
426 Danby Mountain Road
Danby, Vermont 05739
(802) 293-5121
Charcoal

Mail-Order Sources

W W WOOD, INC.
P.O. Box 398
1799 Corgey Road
Pleasanton, Texas 78064
(830) 569-2501
www.woodinc.com
Mesquite and hickory chunks,
smoking chips, lump charcoal

Ingredients

GENERAL

ALASKA SAUSAGE & SEAFOOD COMPANY
2914 Arctic Boulevard
Anchorage, Alaska 99503
(800) 798-3636
www.alaskasausage.com
Smoked salmon and sausages,
including reindeer sausage

AMERICAN SPOON FOODS
P.O. Box 566
Petoskey, Michigan 49770
(800) 222-5886
www.spoon.com
Assorted dried berries, preserves, compotes,
dressings, salsas, sauces, marinades

BOUDIN BAKERY
132 Hawthorne Street
San Francisco, California 94107
(800) 992-1849
www.boudinbakery.com
Sourdough and other specialty breads

BRUGGER BROTHERS
3868 N.E. 169th Street, Unit 401
North Miami Beach, Florida 33160
(800) 949-2264
www.talamoncapepper.com
Talamanca peppercorns

THE CHILE SHOP
109 East Water Street
Santa Fe, New Mexico 87501
(505) 983-6080
www.thechileshop.com
New Mexican chiles, sauces, salsas

D'ARTAGNAN
280 Wilson Avenue
Newark, New Jersey 07105
(800) 327-8246 ext. 0
www.dartagnan.com
Foie gras, andouille sausage

DEAN & DELUCA
560 Broadway
New York, New York 10012
(800) 999-0306
www.deandeluca.com
All kinds of foodstuffs, mandolines

EL PASO CHILE COMPANY
909 Texas Avenue
El Paso, Texas 79901
(800) 274-7468
www.elpasochile.com
Tex-Mex and Southwestern ingredients,
including jalapeño jelly

FOODALICIOUS
2035 N.E. 151st Street
North Miami, Florida 33162
(305) 945-0502
www.acoupleofbasketcases.com
Oils, vinegars, chiles, spices, Maytag blue
cheese, Asian ingredients, and so on

FRIEDA'S
4465 Corporate Center Drive
Los Alamitos, California 90720
(800) 241-1771
www.friedas.com
Specialty produce, including habañeros
and other chiles, fresh sugar cane,
tomatillos, and so on

HOLMQUIST HAZELNUT ORCHARDS
9821 Holmquist Road
Lynden, Washington 98264
(800) 720-0895
www.holmquisthazelnuts.com
Hazelnuts and hazelnut oil

HUDSON VALLEY FOIE GRAS
80 Brooks Road
Ferndale, New York 12734
(845) 292-2500
www.hudsonvalleyfoiegras.com
Foie gras

ISEAFOOD.COM
Grand Central Market
New York, NY 10017
(516) 764-5732
www.iseafood.com
Diver scallops, trout

JAMISON FARM
171 Jamison Lane
Latrobe, Pennsylvania 15650
(800) 237-5262
www.jamisonfarm.com
Artisanal lamb

KITCHEN MARKET
218 Eighth Avenue
New York, New York 10011
(888) 468-4433
www.kitchenmarket.com
Chiles, spices, including smoked paprika,
aji panca, and annato (achiote), hot
sauces, Mexican and Asian specialties

LEGAL SEA FOODS
33 Everett Street
Boston, Massachusetts 02134
(800) 328-3474
www.legalseafoods.com
Seafood

MARCHE AUX DELICES
P.O. Box 1164
New York, New York 10028
(888) 547-5471
www.auxdelices.com
Truffles and exotic mushrooms

MELISSA'S
P.O. Box 21127
Los Angeles, California 90021
(800) 588-0151
www.melissas.com
All sorts of chile peppers, fresh and dried
Latin American produce, *piloncillo*
(Mexican brown sugar)

MO HOTTA-MO BETTA
P.O. Box 1026
Savannah, Georgia 31402
(800) 462-3220
www.mohotta.com
Hot sauces, barbecue sauces, salsas, spices

NEBRASKA KNOLL SUGAR FARM
256 Falls Brook Lane
Stowe, Vermont 05672
(802) 253-4655
Maple sugar

THE NET RESULT
P.O. Box 1686
79 Beach Road
Vineyard Haven, Massachusetts 02568
(800) 394-6071
www.mvseafood.com
Martha's Vineyard bay scallops

NUESKE HILLCREST FARM
RR 2, P.O. Box D
Wittenberg, Wisconsin 54499
(800) 382-2266
www.nueske.com
Smokehouse bacon, ham,
and other meats

PACIFIC NORTHWEST GOURMET
800 Fifth Avenue, Suite 101-229
Seattle, Washington 98104
(888) 272-0171
www.pacificnw.us
Seafood

PENDERY'S
1221 Manufacturing Street
Dallas, Texas 75027
(800) 533-1870
www.penderys.com
Chiles and spices

PEPPERS
1815 Ocean Outlets, #3
Rehoboth, Delaware 19971
(800) 998-3473
www.peppers.com
Hot sauces

THE PERFECT PUREE OF NAPA VALLEY
2700 Napa Valley Corporate Drive, Suite L
Napa, California 94558
(800) 556-3707
www.perfectpuree.com
Cactus pear and other fruit purées

SANTA FE SEASONS
1590 San Mateo Lane
Santa Fe, New Mexico 87505
(800) 264-5535
www.santafeseasons.com
Salsas, jellies, spice blends, sauces

SMITHFIELD HAMS
The Smithfield Catalog Group
P.O. Box 250
Portsmouth, Virginia 23705
(800) 926-8448
www.smithfieldhams.com
Ham, sausages

THE SPICE HOUSE
1031 North Old World Third Street
Milwaukee, Wisconsin 53203
(414) 272-0977
www.thespicehouse.com
Dried bell pepper flakes, among other
    spices

SUSIE Q'S BRAND SPECIALTY FOODS
P.O. Box 2513
Santa Maria, California 93457
(800) 268-1041
www.susieqbrand.com
Pinquito beans

ETHNIC

HAJI BABA MIDDLE EASTERN FOOD & RESTAURANT
1513 East Apache
Tempe, Arizona 85281
(480) 894-1905
Middle eastern ingredients

HIROSHI'S ANZEN
736 Northeast Martin Luther King Boulevard
Portland, Oregon 97232
(503) 233-5111
Asian ingredients

INDIA SPICE & GIFT SHOP
3295 Fairfield Avenue
Bridgeport, Connecticut 06605
(203) 384-0666
Indian ingredients

JAMAICA GROCERIES & SPICES
Colonial Shopping Center
9587 S.W. 160th Street
Miami, Florida 33157
(305) 252-1197
Caribbean ingredients

THE ORIENTAL PANTRY AT JOYCE CHEN UNLIMITED
423 Great Road
Acton, Massachusetts 01720
(800) 828-0368
www.orientalpantry.com
Asian ingredients

ORIENTAL PASTRY AND GROCERY
170 Atlantic Avenue
Brooklyn, New York 11201
(718) 875-7687
Asian ingredients

PATEL BROTHERS
42-79C Main Street
Flushing, New York 11355
(718) 321-9847
www.patelbrothersusa.com
Indian ingredients

YEKTA SUPERMARKET
1488 Rockville Pike
Rockville, Maryland 20852
(301) 984-1190
Middle Eastern ingredients

Auchmuley, Jim, and Susan Puckett. *The Ultimate Barbecue Sauce Cookbook.* Atlanta: Longstreet Press, 1995.

Bayard, Ferdinand Marie. *Travels of a Frenchman in Maryland and Virginia with a description of Philadelphia and Baltimore in 1791.* Translated and edited by Ben C. McCary. Ann Arbor, Mich.: Edwards Brothers, 1950.

Bradley, Richard. *The Country Housewife, and lady's director for every month of the year . . . Containing the Whole Art of Cookery.* 1762. Reprint, Devon, Eng.: Prospect Books, 1981.

Brandau, Rosemary. "Early Fair Foods and Barbecuing." Williamsburg, Va.: Colonial Williamsburg Files, 1984.

Browne, Rick, and Jack Bettridge. *Barbecue America: A Pilgrimage in Search of America's Best Barbecue.* Alexandria, Va.: Time Life Books, 1999.

Bullock, Helen. *Williamsburg Art of Cookery.* 1930. Reprint, Williamsburg, Va.: Colonial Williamsburg Foundation, 1985.

Burnaby, Andrew. *Travels Throughout the Middle Settlements in North-America in the years 1759 and 1760: with observations upon the state of the colonies.* 1798. Reprint, Ithaca, N.Y.: Cornell University Press, 1968.

Carson, Jane. *Colonial Virginians at Play.* 1958. Reprint, Williamsburg, Va.: Colonial Williamsburg Foundation, 1989.

Child, Lydia Maria. *The American Frugal Housewife.* 1832. Reprint, Mineola, N.Y.: Dover Publications, Inc., 2000.

Craigie, William A., and James R. Hulbert. *A Dictionary of American English on historical principles.* Chicago: University of Chicago Press, 1938–44 (issued in 20 parts).

Dampier, William. *A New Voyage Round the World.* 1698. Reprint, Mineola, N.Y.: Dover Publications, 1968.

Davis, Ardie A., with Remus Powers. *The Great Barbecue Sauce Book: A Guide with Recipes.* Berkeley: Ten Speed Press, 1999.

Davis, Rich, and Shifra Stein. *Wild About Bar-B-Q Kansas City Style.* Kansas City: Pig Out Publications, 1997.

Duong, Bình, Bình Dng, and Marcia Kiesel. *Simple Art of Vietnamese Cooking.* New York: Simon & Schuster, 1991.

Elie, Lolis Eric. *Smokestack Lightning: Adventures in the Heart of Barbecue Country.* New York: Farrar, Straus & Giroux, 1996.

Fernández de Oviedo y Valdes, Gonzalo. Translated and edited by Sterling A. Stoudemire. *Natural History of the West Indies.* Chapel Hill: University of North Carolina Press, 1959.

Folkard, Claire, editor. *Guinness World Records 2003.* New York: Mint Publishers (Guinness Media, Inc.), 2002.

Bibliography

Foster, George H., and Petere C. Weiglin. *The Harvey House Cookbook: Memories of Dining Along the Santa Fe Railroad.* Marietta, Ga.: Longstreet Press, 1996.

Frazier, Charles. *Cold Mountain.* New York: Vintage Books, 1998.

Garner, Bob. *North Carolina Barbecue: Flavored by Time.* Winston-Salem, N.C.: John F. Blair, 1996.

Haber, Barbara. *From Hardtack to Homefries: An Uncommon History of American Cooks and Meals.* New York: Free Press, 2002.

Hariot, Thomas. *A Brief and True Report of the New Found Land of Virginia.* 1590. Reprint, Ann Arbor, Mich.: Edwards Brothers, 1931.

Im Thurn, Everard Ferdinand. *Among the Indians of Guiana: being sketches chiefly anthropologic from the interior of British Guiana.* 1883. Reprint, New York: Dover Publications, 1967.

Johnson, Greg, and Vince Staten. *Real Barbecue: The Only Barbecue Book You'll Ever Need: A Guide to the Best Joints, the Best Sauces, the Best Cookers—And Much More.* New York: HarperCollins, 1988.

Kirk, Paul. *Paul Kirk's Championship Barbecue Sauces.* Boston: Harvard Common Press, 1997.

Lanman, Charles. *Adventures in the Wilds of the United States and British American Province.* Philadelphia: J. W. Moore, 1856.

McClane, A. J. *The Encyclopedia of Fish Cookery.* Austin, Tex.: Holt Rinehart and Winston, 1977.

Molina, Martiniano. *Secretos de las Brasas: Cocina al aire libre.* Buenos Aires: Editorial Sudamericana, 2001.

Phelps, Carlene S., ed. *National Barbecue News,* monthly periodical published in Douglas, Georgia. Accessible online at www.barbecuenews.com.

Powers, Remus, and Ardie Davis. *Kansas City BBQ Pocket Guide.* Kansas City: Pig Out Publications, 1992.

Raichlen, Steven. *Barbecue! Bible Sauces, Rubs, and Marinades, Bastes, Butters, and Glazes.* New York: Workman Publishing, 2000.

——. *Beer-Can Chicken: And 74 Other Offbeat Recipes for the Grill.* New York: Workman Publishing, 2002.

——. *How to Grill: The Complete Illustrated Book of Barbecue Techniques.* New York: Workman Publishing, 2001.

——. *The Barbecue! Bible.* New York: Workman Publishing, 1998.

Ramsey, T. Upton. *George Washington Ate Here: A Frolic Through History with Food and Famous Folks.* Salt Lake City, Utah: Self-published (distributed by Origin Book Sales), 1997.

Randolph, Mary. *The Virginia Housewife: Methodical Cook: A Facsimile of an Authentic Early American Cookbook.* 1824. Reprint, Mineola, N.Y.: Dover Publications, 1993.

Rankin, Jane Lee, and Eugene Callender. *Cookin' Up a Storm: The Life & Recipes of Annie Johnson.* New York: Grace Publishers, 1998.

Reader, Ted and Kathleen Sloan. *Sticks & Stones: The Art of Grilling on Plank, Vine and Stone*. Minocqua, Wis.: Willow Creek Press, 1999.

Schlesinger, Chris, and John Willoughby. *The Thrill of the Grill*. San Francisco: Chronicle Books, 1997.

Simmons, Amelia. *The First American Cookbook*. A facsimile of *American Cookery, 1796*. Mineola, N.Y.: Dover Publications, 1984.

Smith, Philip Henry. *General History of Duchess County, from 1609 to 1876, inclusive*. Pawling, New York: Self-published, 1877.

Stedman, John Gabriel. *Narrative of a Five Year's Expedition against the Revolted Negroes of Surinam*. 1813. Edited by Richard Price and Sally Price. Baltimore: Johns Hopkins University Press, 1988.

Tannahill, Reay. *Food in History*. New York: Stein and Day, 1973.

Temple, Lou Jane. *Revenge of the Barbecue Queens*. New York: St. Martin's Press, 1997.

Tesene, R. H. *Santa Maria Style Barbecue*. Santa Maria, Calif.: Santa Maria Chamber of Commerce and Visitor & Convention Bureau, 1997.

Texas Monthly staff. "Barbecue! The 50 Best Barbecue Joints in Texas." *Texas Monthly*, May, 1997.

Trager, James. *The Food Book*. New York: Grossman Publishers, 1970.

Trillin, Calvin. *The Tummy Trilogy: American Fried; Alice, Let's Eat; Third Helpings*. New York: Noonday Press, 1994.

Trotter, Charlie, and Paul Elledge. *Charlie Trotter Cooks at Home*. Berkeley: Ten Speed Press, 2000.

Tylor, Edward Burnett. *Anahuac: or Mexico and the Mexicans, Ancient and Modern*. [1861]. In Stocking, George, ed. *Collected Works of E. B. Tylor*. New York: Routledge, 1994.

Venable, Bill, Rick Welch, and Bruce Daniel. *Kansas City Barbecue: From the Kansas City Barbecue Inner Circle*. New York: Hyperion, 1996.

Walsh, Robb. *Legends of Texas Barbecue Cookbook: Recipes and Recollections from the Pit Bosses*. San Francisco: Chronicle Books, 2002.

Washington, Martha. *Martha Washington's Booke of Cookery and Booke of Sweetmeats*. Edited by Karen Hess. New York: Columbia University Press, 1996.

Weld, Isaac. *Travels Through the States of North America and the provinces of Upper and Lower Canada, during the years 1765, 1796, and 1797*. London: J. Stockdale, 1799.

Wells, Carolyn. *Barbecue Greats Memphis Style*. Kansas City: Pig Out Publications, 1997.

Worgul, Doug. *The Grand Barbecue: A Celebration of the History, Places, Personalities and Techniques of Kansas City Barbecue*. Kansas City: Kansas City Star Books, 2001.

TITLE PAGE: Page iii: Portrait of author by Fernando Diez.

ACKNOWLEDGMENTS: Page iv: Steven Raichlen. Page v: (bottom center, bottom right, and center right) Steven Raichlen. Page v: (top right) Lisa Hollander. Page vi: Steven Raichlen. Page vii: (bottom right) Charles V. Tines/The Detroit News. Page vii (top left): David L. Moore. Page viii: Holly Moore of HollyEats.Com. Page ix: (bottom right) Courtesy of K.C. Masterpiece. Page ix: (top left) David L. Moore. Page x: Courtesy Johnsonville Sausage and Sheboygan Jaycees.

WHAT IS BARBECUE?: Page 1: Holly Moore of HollyEats.Com. Page 2: Holly Moore of HollyEats.Com. Page 3: John Dunham/The Messenger Inquirer.

Barbecue in America: Page 5: CORBIS. Page 6: The Mariners' Museum/CORBIS. Page 7: Culver Pictures. Page 8: CORBIS. Page 9: Bettmann/CORBIS. Page 10: Schomburg Center for Research in Black Culture (Creator: Taylor & Huntington). Page 11: Bettmann/CORBIS. Page 12: Weber-Stevens Products Co. Page 13: Holly Moore of HollyEats.Com. Page 14: (bottom right) Jefferson Steele Photography. Page 14: (center left) CORBIS. Page 14: (top right) Mike Maple/The Commercial Appeal. Page 15: (bottom left): Michael Stern: Roadfood.com. Page 15: (right) Courtesy of K.C. Masterpiece.

GETTING STARTED: Page 16: Barbara Raichlen. Pages 18, 20, 21, 22, 25, and 29: Frank Stewart.

OFF TO A FIERY START: Pages 32-33: Dietrich Gehring. Page 37: Special Collections, University of Memphis Libraries. Page 38: Billy Brown Photography, Inc. Page 40: Dietrich Gehring. Page 41: Marci Joy. Page 42: (bottom) Dietrich Gehring. Page 46: Courtesy Trader Vic's. Page 49: Steven Raichlen. Page 52: Gideon Lewin. Page 54: (all) Dianne Eastman. Page 56: Nik Wheeler/CORBIS. Page 58: Courtesy Zuni Grill. Page 61: Frank Stewart. Page 65: Robert Holmes/CORBIS. Page 67: Courtesy Lilly Library, Indiana University, Bloomington, IN. Page 70: Phillip Gould/CORBIS. Page 73: Dietrich Gehring. Page 74: Allison Dahlin/Keystone Film Prod., Inc. Page 78: Dave G. Houser/CORBIS. Page 79: Courtesy Four Seasons. Page 83: Courtesy of Wild Ginger.

Page 84: Dave Bartruff/CORBIS. Page 87: Courtesy of Wild Ginger. Page 90: Greg Smith/CORBIS. Page 92: Richard T. Nowitz/CORBIS. Page 95: Victoria Pearson/GETTY IMAGES. Page 97: Jeff Greenberg/AGE. Page 99: Joe Baraban/CORBIS. Page 100: Cynthia Hart Designer/CORBIS. Page 101: Tom Stewart/CORBIS. Page 103: Kit Warren. Page 107: Morton Beebe/CORBIS.

LIVE-FIRE SALADS: Pages 108-109: Stan Schnier. Page 110: Courtesy Walt's Wharf. Page 113: Owen Franken/CORBIS. Page 115: Courtesy Exploratorium/www.Exploratorium.edu. Page 118: Courtesy Charlie Trotter's. Page 120: Barry Winiker/IndexStock Imagery. Page 122: Catherine Karnow/CORBIS. Page 124: USDA. Page 128: Frank Stewart. Page 131: Courtesy Super Smokers BBQ.

BREADS AND PIZZAS: Pages 132-133: Dietrich Gehring. Page 135: Dietrich Gehring. Page 137: Owen Franken/CORBIS. Page 138: Horace Bristol/CORBIS. Page 141: Dietrich Gehring. Page 142: Stephen Cutri. Page 145: Courtesy The Greenbrier. Page 147: CORBIS. Page 148: Adam Woolfitt/CORBIS. Page 149: Pete Bond. Page 150: (bottom) Ken Ambrose. Page 151: (bottom) Courtesy Al Forno. Page 151: (top) Ken Ambrose. Pages 152, 155, 156, and 158: Dietrich Gehring. Page 160: Lake County Museum/CORBIS. Page 161: Pete Armato/The Kansas City Star.

GLORIOUSLY GRILLED BEEF: Pages 162-163: Danny Lehman/CORBIS. Page 165: Michael Stern: Roadfood.com. Page 166: (bottom) Wyatt McSpadden. Page 167: Wyatt McSpadden. Pages 169, 170, and 173: Jefferson Steele Photography. Page 174: Jeff Olson. Pages 177 and 178: Paula Willrath. Page 180: City Barbeque. Page 183: Santa Maria Valley Chamber of Commerce. Pages 187 and 188 (all): Santa Maria Historical Museum. Page 191: Courtesy Sammy's Roumanian Steak House. Page 193: Courtesy Lilly Library, Indiana University, Bloomington, IN. Page 196: Glen Bolivar/Adobe Press. Page 199: Mike McColl. Page 201: Frank Stewart. Page 203: CORBIS. Page 206: Courtesy St. Emo. Page 207: Courtesy Omaha Steaks. Page 210: Courtesy Geno's Steaks. Page 213: Jefferson Steele Photography. Pages 214-215 (all): Stan Schnier. Page 218: Jim Barcus/The Kansas City Star. Page 221: Robert Hall Photography. Page 226: Glen Bolivar/Adobe Press. Pages 229, 230, and 231: Courtesy Memphis in May.

Photography Credits

GOING WHOLE HOG: Pages 232-233: Special Collections, University of Memphis Libraries. Page 234: Jefferson Steele Photography. Page 235: Holly Moore of HollyEats.Com. Page 237: Will Byington. Pages 238, 240, 242, and 245: Holly Moore of HollyEats.Com. Page 247: Michael Stern: Roadfood.com. Page 248: Mike Maple/The Commercial Appeal. Page 249: Jefferson Steele Photography. Page 252: Michael S. Yamashita/CORBIS. Pages 255, 256, and 257: Cindy Karp. Page 261: Courtesy El Paso Chili Co. Page 264: Mary Nelson. Page 269: Frank Stewart. Page 270: Jeff Greenberg/AGE fotostock. Page 271: Dietrich Gehring. Pages 272 and 273: Michael Stern: Roadfood.com. Page 275: Amy Evans. Page 277: Joe York. Page 279: Courtesy Maytag Dairy Farms. Page 281: David Allison. Page 286: CORBIS. Page 287: (bottom right) Brian Cowen. Page 287: (top left) CORBIS. Page 288: Philip Gould/CORBIS. Page 290: Courtesy Super Smokers BBQ. Page 293: Peter Hvizdak/The Image Works. Page 295: Steve Odum. Page 297: Michael Stern: Roadfood.com. Page 300: Holly Moore of HollyEats.Com. Page 303: R. M. Wyatt. Page 305: Kevin Fleming/CORBIS. Page 306: Holly Moore of HollyEats.Com.

LAMB WITH SIZZLE: Pages 308-309: Frank Stewart. Page 311: John Dunham/The Messenger Inquirer. Page 312: Courtesy Rendezvous. Page 315 (both): Courtesy Dreamland. Page 317: Michael Stern: Roadfood.com. Page 319: Jim Barcus/Kansas City Star. Page 322: John Madere/CORBIS. Page 326: Ted Streshinsky/CORBIS. Page 330: Courtesy Moonlite Bar-B-Q.

BURGERS, DOGS & SAUSAGES: Pages 332-333: Frank Stewart. Page 336: Courtesy Louis Lunch. Page 339: Charles V. Tines/The Detroit News. Page 341: CORBIS. Page 342: Dietrich Gehring. Page 349: Robert Landau/CORBIS. Pages 350-351 (all): Courtesy Johnsonville Sausage and Sheboygan Jaycees. Page 353: Dan F. Martin Photography. Page 354: Courtesy Johnsonville Sausage and Sheboygan Jaycees. Page 356: Amy Evans. Pages 362-363: Holly Moore of HollyEats.Com.

BIRDS ON THE BARBECUE: Pages 364-365: Getty Images. Page 366: Courtesy Big Green Egg. Page 370: Lake County Museum/CORBIS. Page 375: Bettmann/CORBIS. Pages 376-377: (all) Courtesy of the Dr. Pepper Museum and Free Enterprise Institute. Pages 378-379: (all) Courtesy Big Bob Gibson. Page 382: John Pachal/Cornell University Photography. Page 383: AFP/CORBIS. Page 387: Richard T. Nowitz/CORBIS. Pages 389-390: David L. Moore. Page 394: Courtesy Powderpuff BBQ. Page 401: Courtesy National Cherry Festival. Pages 403-404: Courtesy Balthazar. Page 407: Wolfgang Kaehler/CORBIS. Page 411: Dietrich Gehring. Page 414: (bottom left) Bettmann/CORBIS. Page 414: (top right) Ted Horowitz/CORBIS. Page 415: Bettmann/CORBIS. Page 418: Getty Images. Page 419: CORBIS. Page 420: Owen Franken/CORBIS. Page 423: Deborah Jones. Page 425: Robert Maass/CORBIS. Page 427: Nik Wheeler/CORBIS. Page 430: (all) Michael Stern: Roadfood.com.

FLAME-SEARED FISH: Pages 432-433: Ibid Photo. Page 434: Reenie Raschke. Pages 436-437: (all) Fred Harvey Collection/Cline Library, Northern Arizona University. Page 438: Scott Eastman Photography. Page 439: Owen Franken/CORBIS. Page 441: Dave Bartruff/CORBIS. Page 443: Michael T. Sedam/CORBIS. Page 446: Ray Krantz/CORBIS. Page 447: Scott Eastman Photography. Page 448: Alex Steedman/CORBIS. Page 449: Paul A. Souders/CORBIS. Pages 450-451: Courtesy Holmquist Hazelnut Orchards. Page 453: Nik Wheeler/CORBIS. Page 454: Neil Rabinowitz/CORBIS. Page 455: Courtesy Tillicum Village. Page 456: Doug Scott/AGE fotostock. Page 457: Copyright 1991 Kevin Morris. Page 458: Courtesy Tillicum Village. Page 460: Hulton-Deutsch Collection/CORBIS. Page 462: Eric Berndt/MIDWESTOCK. Page 464: Courtesy Medizona. Page 466: Jeffrey L. Rotman/CORBIS. Page 471: Michael S. Yamashita/CORBIS. Page 474: Dave Bartruff/CORBIS. Page 476: Bob Krist/CORBIS. Page 478: Barry Winiker/Index Stock Imagery. Page 482: Ray F. Hillstrom, Jr. Page 484: Courtesy Tadich Grill. Page 485: (bottom) Robert Holmes/CORBIS. Page 485: (top) Kell-Mooney Photography/CORBIS. Page 487: Margaret Lanzoni. Page 489: (all) The Fish House. Page 490: Jeff Albertson/CORBIS. Page 494: Owen Franken/CORBIS. Pages 497-498: Barry Stott. Page 501: Kevin Fleming/CORBIS. Page 504: Stan Schnier. Page 505: Michael Busselle/CORBIS. Page 507: Layne Kennedy/CORBIS. Page 509: Dietrich Gehring. Pages 510-511: Nik Wheeler/CORBIS. Page 513: Bob Krist/CORBIS. Page 515: Dietrich Gehring. Page 519: (bottom) Dietrich Gehring. Page 519: (top) The Mariners' Museum/CORBIS.

SIZZLING SHELLFISH: Pages 520-521: Tim Thompson/CORBIS. Page 522: Bruce Hands/The Image Works. Page 524: (both) Damon Waters. Page 526: D. Boone/CORBIS. Page 529: (bottom) Michael Stern: Roadfood.com. Page 529: (top right) Michael Stern: Roadfood.com. Page 531: Cameramann/The Image Works. Page 533: James Marshall/CORBIS. Page 534: Charles E. Rotkin/CORBIS. Page 535: Robin Weiner/The Image Works. Page 537: Walter Bibikow/Danita Delimont, Agent. Page 540: Raymond Gehman/CORBIS. Page 543: Robert Holmes/CORBIS. Page 544: (both) Rory McNamara. Page 545:

(left) Courtesy The Marshall Store. Page 545: (right) Rory McNamara. Page 546: Courtesy Olema Farmhouse. Page 549: Rory McNamara. Page 551: Tom Zinn. Page 552: Michael T. Sedam/CORBIS. Page 555: Pitcairn-Knowles/The Image Works. Page 556: Courtesy Tizi Melloul. Page 559: Macduff Everton/CORBIS. Page 560: (top) Jason Cole/The Kansas City Star. Page 560: (left) Kansas City Barbeque Society. Page 560: (middle bottom) Talis Bergmanis/The Kansas City Star. Pages 560-561: Talis Bergmanis/The Kansas City Star. Page 561: (bottom) Talis Bergmanis/The Kansas City Star. Page 561: (top) Talis Bergmanis/The Kansas City Star. Page 562: (bottom left) Photos by Dane. Page 562: (bottom right) Photos by Dane. Page 562: (top left) Photos by Dane. Page 563: (top) Tim Janicke/The Kansas City Star. Page 563: (others) Steven Raichlen.

THE VEGETARIAN GRILL: Pages 564-565: Stan Schnier. Page 566: Peter Turnley/CORBIS. Page 567: CORBIS. Page 571: Ray F. Hillstrom. Page 572: Courtesy Lilly Library, Indiana University, Bloomington, IN. Page 577: Courtesy Americas. Page 581: Dietrich Gehring. Page 583: CORBIS.

FLAME-ROASTED VEGETABLES: Pages 586-587: Bettmann/CORBIS. Page 588: Joseph Sohm/CORBIS. Page 590: Gunter Marx Photography/CORBIS. Pages 592-593: Hulton-Deutsch Collection/CORBIS. Page 594: Hulton-Deutsch Collection/CORBIS. Page 595: Hulton-Deutsch Collection/CORBIS. Page 596: Holly Moore of HollyEats.Com. Page 597: Ludovic Maisant/CORBIS. Page 598: Courtesy Kansas City Barbeque Society. Page 599: Courtesy Kansas City Barbeque Society. Page 600: Karen Huntt Mason/CORBIS. Page 603: CORBIS. Page 604: Sandy Felsenthal/CORBIS. Page 606: USDA. Page 608: Dietrich Gehring. Page 611: Lee Snider/CORBIS. Page 612: (bottom) Michael Stern: Roadfood.com. Page 613: CORBIS. Page 615: Courtesy Sammy's Roumanian Steak House. Page 616: Carl & Ann Purcell/CORBIS. Page 618: Frank Stewart. Page 620: Kevin R. Morris/CORBIS. Page 621: Clem Spalding. Page 624: (bottom) Courtesy Sonny's. Page 625: Courtesy Sonny's.

SIDES FROM THE GRILL: Pages 626-627: Frank Stewart. Page 628: Dietrich Gehring. Page 632: (bottom) Dave Bartruff/CORBIS. Page 633:

Allen Crabtree. Page 634: Maine Folklife Center. University of Maine. Page 637: Maine Folklife Center. University of Maine. Page 640: Dietrich Gehring. Page 643: (bottom) Courtesy Far Western Tavern. Page 645: (bottom) Derron Neblet/Houston Press. Page 648: Michael Mercier. Page 651: Holly Moore of HollyEats.Com. Page 652: Michael Stern: Roadfood.com. Page 654: Stan Schnier.

UNBEATABLE SAUCES: Pages 656-657: Stan Schnier. Page 658: Frank Boyer. Page 659: Courtesy Kansas City Barbeque Society. Page 661: Michael S. Yamashita/CORBIS. Page 663: Lois Ellen Frank/CORBIS. Page 665: Morton Beebe/CORBIS. Page 666: Holly Moore of HollyEats.Com. Page 669: Stan Schnier. Page 670: Courtesy of Cooper's Old Time. Page 671: (top) Cooper's Old Time Pit Bar-B-Que. Page 672: John Lair. Page 677: Daryl Stone/Asbury Park Press. Page 678: Courtesy Louie Mueller Barbecue. Page 679: Michael Stern: Roadfood.com. Page 682: Bettmann/CORBIS. Page 684-685: USDA. Page 689: Richard Cummins/CORBIS. Page 693: David Turnley/CORBIS. Page 695: (both) Courtesy K.C. Masterpiece.

HERE'S THE RUB: Pages 698-699: Stan Schnier. Page 701: Lake Country Museum/CORBIS. Page 703: Chris Frothingham/Chris Ainsworth. Page 705: Chris Frothingham/Chris Ainsworth. Page 706: Courtesy Roxsand's. Page 709: Photo by trueart.net. Page 711: Courtesy The Salt Lick.

GREAT GRILLED DESSERTS: Pages 712-713: Tom Stewart/CORBIS. Page 714: Michael S. Yamashita/CORBIS. Page 716: Kevin Fleming/CORBIS. Page 717: (right) Courtesy Bern's Steak House. Page 718: Tony Arruza/CORBIS. Page 719: Holly Moore of HollyEats.Com. Page 721: Courtesy Mi Tierra. Page 722: Bettmann/CORBIS. Page 724: Aurora Photos. Page 726: Lake County Museum/CORBIS. Page 728: (bottom) Brennan's Restaurant. Page 728: (top) Neil Rabinowitz/CORBIS. Page 731: Hulton-Deutsch Collection/CORBIS. Page 735: Minnesota Historical Society/CORBIS. Page 738: The Olive Group. Page 739: CORBIS.

MAIL-ORDER SOURCES: Page 744: Jeff Greenberg/AGE. Page 745: Phillip Gould/CORBIS.

VW Bug used throughout: Photo by Dietrich Gehring.

Index